Fundamentals of Financial Accounting

(Theory and Practice)

(Second Edition)

Dr Naseem Ahmed
M.Com Ph.D. (Aligarh)
Associate Professor, Deptt. of Commerce,
Zakir Husain College (Delhi University)

Dr M. L. Gupta
M.Com (Alig.) Ph.D. (Meerut)
Associate Professor, Deptt. of Commerce,
Aurobindo College (Delhi University)

Dr Nawab Ali Khan
M.Com Ph.D. (Aligarh)
Professor, Deptt. of Commerce,
A.M.U., Aligarh

Ane Books Pvt. Ltd.

New Delhi ♦ Chennai

Fundamentals of Financial Accounting
Naseem Ahmed, M.L. Gupta and Nawab Ali Khan

Published by

Ane Books Pvt. Ltd.
4821, Parwana Bhawan, 1st Floor, 24 Ansari Road,
Darya Ganj, **New Delhi** - 110 002, India
Tel.: +91(011) 23276843-44, Fax: +91(011) 23276863
e-mail: kapoor@anebooks.com, Website: www.anebooks.com

Branch Office:

- Avantika Niwas, 1st Floor, 19 Doraiswamy Road, T. Nagar,
  Chennai - 600 017, Tel.: +91(044) 28141554, 28141209
  e-mail: rathinam@anebooks.com

ISBN : 978-81-8052-229-1

Printed at : Sagar Colorscan, New Delhi.

Fundamentals of
Financial Accounting
(Theory and Practice)

Preface to the Second Edition

We feel it great privilege to present before the esteemed readers, the second revised edition of the book "Fundamentals of Financial Accounting". We are highly grateful for their sincere patronage and warm response to the first edition.

In view of significant developments and issue of new accounting standards and guidance notes by Institute of Chartered Accountants of India (ICAI), the book has been updated and revised accordingly. The book has further been updated and restructured as per the revised syllabis of B.com (Programme) of Delhi University. The suggestions received from a wide cross sections of readers have been incorporated We express our gratitude to them and hope to enjoy their support & receive suggestions in future also.

We are sure that with changes and additions, the revised addition of the book will prove more useful and rewarding for the students. We hope that the revised edition will be welcomed by teachers & students alike with great warmth which the book deserves.

Lastly, we are thankful to Shri Sunil Saxena, Director, Ane Books Pvt. Ltd. Darya Ganj, New Delhi, and his team for their untiring zeal and efforts in bringing out this edition in time.

—Authors

Preface to the First Edition

The undersigned feel great pleasure to place before esteemed readers the first edition of the book "Fundamentals of Financial Accounting: Theory and Practice". The basic philosophy of the book is to provide conceptual clarity of the subject matter so as to develop thorough understanding of the basic fundamentals and reasoning required to solve the variety of problems of accounting in the shortest period of time. Further, the text provides a comprehensive coverage of each topic so as to make each chapter a self contained unit. A distinguishing feature of this book is the use of multidimensional illustrations of each chapter which permits substantial flexibility in sequencing the course material. The text is designed to provide theoretical exposition first, followed by the practical application thereof through graded illustrations. The explanatory working notes provide an insight into the basic techniques employed in solving the most intricate problems in a simple way. Thus the book will definitely replace memorisation with understanding and boost the self confidence among students appearing for various university and professional examinations.

In view of changes taking place in the field of accounting, the book has been updated in accordance with the latest changes in the various Accounting standards to facilitate "learning by doing" (solving) in consistent with the current accounting practices. Every effort has been made to present the subject matter in a very simple, lucid and systematic manner to help students achieve required level of proficiency and desired level of success.

Graded illustrations contain carefully selected problems from key professional and academic examinations that will help the students to maintain a meaningful focus on the examination standard while studying the subject exhaustively. The book is intended to serve as a standard text for the students pursuing B.Com. courses at various universities and colleges and other professional courses CA, CS, ICWA, CFA and BBA etc. We are sure that this work will endear students and teachers alike whose suggestions will always be welcomed to improve the overall quality of the present work.

We are highly grateful to the Directors of Studies, ICAI, ICWA and ICSI for granting permission to reproduce various questions set at their examinations.

We are also thankful to our colleagues, friends and family members who motivated and inspired us to work untiringly with zeal throughout the completion of this work. We shall always remain indebted to them.

Finally, thanks are due to Shri Sunil Saxena, Ane Books Pvt. Ltd., Daryaganj, New Delhi and his team for their matchless co-operation and efforts in bringing out this edition in record time.

—Authors

Contents

Unit-III

Unit-IV

Unit-V

Unit-VI

Unit-VII

Unit-I

1 INTRODUCTION

Accounting originated to serve the basic purpose of recording business transactions. Essentially, these were the credit transactions which necessitated to maintain accounting records. Generally, Accounting is said to be as old as the money itself. The present form of accounting has passed through various stages of evolution. It has developed to meet the emerging needs and requirements of growing society. Like any other discipline it has developed by adapting to changing environment. Book-keeping and accounting appeared not as a phenomenon, but directly in response to the world need.[1] With the changing forms of business organization starting from sole proprietorship, partnership, co-operative to company form of organization, the accounting has also brought about gradual change in its concepts, techniques, rules, procedures, methods of recording and presentation to suit social requirements. Thus the present form of accounting is the result of successive innovations, its adaptations and modifications to changing business environment. According to Welsch and Anthony the growth of business organization in size, particularly of publicly held companies, has brought pressure from stockholders, potential investors, creditors, government agencies and the public at large for increased financial disclosure. The public's right to know (Right to Information) more about organizations that directly or indirectly affect them (whether or not they are shareholders) is being increasingly recognized as essential. These characteristics make it essential that the member of that society be provided adequate, understandable and dependable financial information from the major institutions that comprise. Further there is a greater emphasis on disclosing more and more information through accounting statements. In many countries the Company Law Board through various legislations have made it mandatory for companies to disclose certain minimum information. In fact accounting as such has gone through many phases of changes due to changing socio-economic environment. Like any other discipline it has been adjusting itself to changing requirements and will continue to do so in future as well, to promote social welfare to enable its users to form rational and sound judgment and take appropriate decisions.[2]

Nature of Accounting

Accounting is often called the language of business. It is one of the means of communicating information regarding the affairs of business. As a language of business accounting conveys various information regarding business activities. A business organization makes numerous transactions with outsiders resulting in multiple implications, the most important being the financial or monetary effect of one person or organization in relation to other. In the process those who carry on business directly or those who help carry on business indirectly and those who have some interest and stake in business or those want to be interested in the result of day-to-day's affairs of business, expect systematic processing of all these transactions that meets the expectations of each one interested in the accounting (business) information. Therefore, the necessity of recording business transactions clearly and systematically is even more important. A clear and systematic record will serve the twin purpose.

(1) Measurement and ascertainment of result of business-transactions i.e. profits or loss made during any accounting period by preparing Profit & Loss A/c.

(2) The impact of these transactions on the net worth of the business unit i.e financial position of the business in terms of assets and liabilities of business as a whole by preparing a Balance sheet. Besides, accounting helps to keep permanent record of each transaction and its financial effect. This will satisfy the information needs of several interested parties such as shareholders, creditors, bankers, employees, researchers, potential investors, economists, financial analysts, Government and the management whose future decisions are based on historical (past) accounting. Since resources are limited it is wiser to account for regularly, of what has happened to our resources whether there has been any generation of income or squeezing or shrinking of resources. Even the nonprofit-making organizations are not free from use of accounting language. It is of profound importance and considered as an indispensable tool of measuring operating efficiency of any profit making or non-profit making entity. It is of great significance to all kinds of business and service concerns such as manufacturing, trading, finance and leasing, transportations, banking, insurance communication, storing, engineering and medicine. Thus, accounting can be treated as an effective information system.

Secondly, Accounting is a discipline which follows certain rules, principles and conventions on the basis of which accounting information is provided to various users and interested parties who use for decision-making purposes. However, accounting is a dynamic discipline in the sense that accounting rules, principles and standards are changing according to new business environment. There has been infact, global convergence of accounting standards into International Accounting Standards to suit the global accounting requirements.

Thirdly, of late, accounting has emerged as a profession because it is an organised and systematised body of knowledge which is practised by number of professional associations all over the world like Chartered Accountants & Certified Public Accountants etc. The Institute of Chartered Accountants of India has been entrusted with the task of issuing & revising accounting standards in India to bring accounting profession at par with the International Standards.

Fourthly, Accounting is both a science and art in the sense that science represents systematic body of knowledge based on certain principles. Accounting as such is based on principles which are known as GAAPs (Generally Acceptable Accounting Principles). The whole accounting system evolves around these GAAPs. Whereas recording of transactions their summarisation and interpretation is an art without which results cannot be attained.

Thus, the above arguments clearly reveal the nature of accounting. It is an effective "**information system**" based on organised and systematised body of knowledge which is practised as a "**profession**" worldwide and at the same time it is a perfect **discipline** which can well be treated as an "**art and science**" both.

DEFINITION OF ACCOUNTING

There is no unanimity of opinions regarding precise definition of accounting. Different authorities have given different definitions. However the central idea of all definitions has been the same almost except the fact that their emphasis has been shifting from one aspect to other. Each definition has its own merit except that boundaries are fuzzy. According to Vernon Kam a good definition, besides providing a description so that people have understanding of what the object is, should establish clear-cut boundaries. Any object that fall within the boundaries set is identified as a member of the set and any object that falls outside is then not a member of the set.[3]

Earlier, 'Accounting' and 'Book-keeping' were considered one and the same but later on a line of demarcation was drawn between these two. The first part of recording and posting was considered as 'Book-keeping' and the rest of process of analysis and interpretation as 'Accounting'. According to L.C. Copper, 'Book-keeping may be described as the science of recording transactions in money or money's worth in such a manner that, at any subsequent date, their nature and effect may be clearly understood and that, when required, a combined statement of their results may be prepared.[4] 'Book-keeping is an art of recording business transactions in a systematic manner' is the definition provided by A.H. Rosen Kempff.[5]

R.N. Carter stated 'Book-keeping is the science and art of correctly recording in books of accounts all those business transactions that result in transfer of money or money's worth.[6]

On the other hand American Institute of Certified Public Accountant (AICPA)[7] defined Accounting as under:

Accounting is an art of recording, classifying and summarizing in a significant manner and in terms of money, transactions and events which are, in part at least, of a financial character, and interpreting the results thereof.'

This definition was modified by Smith & Ashbume to throw light not only on the inherent functions or processes but the basic purpose or use for which the accounting stands. Accounting, therefore, is defined as "the science of recording and classifying business transactions and events, primarily of a financial character and the art of making significant summaries, analysis and interpretations of these transactions and events and communicating the results to persons who must make decisions or form judgments."

To emphasise the need and use of accounting for its users, 'the American Accounting Association (AAA)[8] quoted, "Accounting is the process of identifying, measuring and communicating economic information to permit informed judgments and decisions by users of the information."

However, AICPA further clarified in 1970 the concept of information with a modified version of this earlier (1941) notion of accounting. It regarded 'Accounting as a service activity. Its function is to provide quantitative information primarily financial in nature about economic activities that is intended to be useful in making economic decisions.'

From the above mentioned definitions the certain observations are drawn which can be interpreted as under :

Accounting is an art : in the sense that it is that part of knowledge that enables us to reach our goals. It shows the way as to how these goals can be attained in the best possible way. The computation of profits or loss in a systematic manner is a clear evidence of accounting being an art. Any deviations from prescribed form will not serve the purpose if transactions are not properly recorded results will be misleading. In fact this deals with the application of various accounting rules, principles, and concepts to achieve certain concrete results.

Accounting is a science : because like science, accounting is also based on established laws, principles or rules. Any knowledge based on certain principles, which have been developed as a result of study, observations, experiments, tests and experience, is a science. Science has been defined as body of knowledge based on certain principles, which have universal application. Accounting is a science because processing of business transactions is done on the basis of certain principles, which are generally acceptable and not universally applicable. Hence, accounting cannot be treated as pure science like physics, chemistry or life science, where cause and affect relationship is studied and perfect conclusions are drawn. It can be termed as Social Science, whose results depend upon social and economic factors and to a greater extent on human behaviour.

Recording : It is essentially a function of writing down the transaction as soon as it takes place in the books of original entry called journal or in subsidiary books such as Cash Book, Sales Book (Day Book), Purchases Book so as to maintain complete record of business activities or financial transactions taken place. The recording of these business transactions must be ensured chronologically in a systematic and orderly manner. The number of subsidiary books and means of recording will depend upon type, size and nature of business. The records may be kept in books, ledger, files and computer files etc. for further use.

Classification : It refers to thc arranging of recorded transactions under various appropriate groups, heads or accounts according to their nature. This makes the further process of analysis and interpretation easier. It also helps us to locate desired information as and when needed. This is done by opening different accounts in the books called ledgers. The process of classification is termed as posting.

Summarising : Once the process of classification of accounts for a given period is complete, such accounts are further processed in a manner so as to make these ledgers more understandable and useful. These ledgers are further regrouped to make data more precise. For example credit customers accounts are grouped under one single account named trade debtors and all suppliers who supply goods on credit basis, their accounts are converted into trade creditors account and so on. This leads to the preparation of Trial Balance, Trading or Manufacturing A/c, P & L A/c and Balance Sheet.

Interpretation and communicating : To make the results of business operations more meaningful and useful to the users of accounting information, it is the task of accountant to prepare and present statement and reports to explain the financial strength/financial position, progress of the enterprise, profitability trend and future economic viability with the help of ratios and analysis of trend, graphs, charts, diagram and flow statement taking past, present and future into consideration. This will form basis of decision-making by the various groups of the users of accounting information.

Financial transactions and events : Accounting recognizes and thus records only those transactions and events which have financial implications i.e. these should be expressed in terms of money e.g. purchase of a building consisting of ten rooms cannot find a place in accounting if the price of the building is not disclosed. Similarly, satisfied and dedicated labour force is of great use for the business but since it cannot be expressed in terms of money, it will not be recorded as a business transaction or event. Similarly an efficient, honest and healthy manager with proven initiative and imaginative skill can take the organisation on the path of success and prosperity, but the same fails to be recorded in accounting. On the other hand a sales promotion scheme, launching of new product are the events having financial implications and thus can be recorded in the accounting books.

Objectives of Accounting

With the evolution and development of accounting, its objectives have also been changing and adjusted to suit organisational, social and other requirements. The advent of Industrial Revolution, changing forms of business organisations, globalisation and worldwide competition, the emphasis has been shifted from self-centred (internal) objectives to serve owners and management to external objectives serving the interest of investors, creditors, consumers, bankers and government etc.

Initially accounting was supposed to :

1. Provide permanent record of each and every transaction.
2. Ascertain business profits and losses.
3. Protect business assets.
4. Know financial position of the business enterprise.
5. Determine amount to be collected from customers and to be paid to creditors.
6. To ascertain inflow and outflow of cash from operating, investing and financing activities.
7. Detect errors.
8. In view of changing business requirements and role of accounting with special emphasis on reporting, the American Accounting Association (AAA),[9] set the following objectives in the larger interest of the users of accounting information :
   (A) To provide information for making decisions concerning the use of limited resources.
   (B) To make information available for effectively directing and controlling the organisation's material and human resources.
   (C) To maintain systematic records and report on the custodianship of resources.
   (D) To provide factual and interpretive information about transactions and other events which is useful for predicting comparing and evaluating enterprise earning power.
   (E) To provide information useful to investors and creditors for predicting, comparing and evaluating potential cash flow.
9. To provide information that is useful to present and potential investors, creditors and other users in making rational investment, credit and similar decisions.[10]
10. To provide an accounting by management to both equity and debt investors in achieving the goal of producing a satisfactory economic performance by the enterprise and maintaining it in strong or healthy financial position.[11]
11. To help review various business policies such as price policy, sales and purchase policy, wage policy, credit policy etc., in the light of past accounting records.

USERS OF ACCOUNTING INFORMATION

As is clear from the aforesaid accounting objectives which have been recommended by the study groups committee of the American Institute of Certified Public Accountants, Financial Accounting Standard Board (FASB) USA and Canadian Chartered Accountants Institute (CCAI) that there is a shift on emphasis and priorities from traditional or narrow (internal) objectives to wider (external) objectives which highlight importance of external users of accounting information. These various groups of users analyse and interpret available accounting information for protecting and safeguarding their own interest while taking any crucial decision. These users are Owners, Management, Employees, Creditors, Investors, Government Agencies, Bankers, Research Scholars, Consumers and Others.

1. Owners i.e. Shareholders, Partners and Proprietors

They are the backbone of the business in the sense that they provide necessary funds for its smooth running, growth and development. There is always a keen desire on their part to see business is doing well in terms of profitability, increasing turnover, stable or rising dividend rate, sound financial position and constantly growing and expanding business volume and increasing Net Assets Value (NAV) for their shares along with future earning potential and growth prospects. Such information-needs of this group are satisfied through published accounts, annual report and other supplementary statements which helps them in the decision – making process.

2. Management

Management may consist of Board of Directors, (Top management) officers of the company or managers (Middle management) and Departmental heads or supervisors (Lower level management), who are entrusted with the task of policy formulation, policy execution or implementation and overall supervision. Through planning, organising, coordination, motivation and control, management tries to achieve/accomplish organisational goals. Accounting provides necessary information base for taking all managerial decisions. In the absence of accounting information neither the objectives of the enterprise can be laid down nor measurement and evaluation of performance is possible nor corrective measures can be taken. The managerial tool, such as Production Budget, Sales Budget and Cash Budget, Capital Budget and Master-Budget are the offsprings of accounting statements and reports. Similarly price policy, wage policy, credit policy, recruitment policy and other policy matters are decided after careful analysis of past accounting records.

3. Employees

Healthy industrial relations i.e. employer (management) and employee (trade union) relation is a must for enterprise prosperity and growth which is possible only through properly motivated, satisfied and satiated labour force. Accounting information helps settle industrial disputes, avert lockout and strike or likewise situation arising from demand for wage hike, bonus, higher compensation, more fringe benefits, better working conditions and so on. Trade union through accounting records knows the extent to which the management can yield to their tactics and concede their demands. Thus accounting information provides basis for collective bargaining and settlement. This develops sense of belongingness among the workers for they know that their interests are not being jeopardized.

4. Creditors

Trade creditors are those who supply goods on credit basis in anticipation that they will get their full payment on or before due date. Usually they extend credit for a very short period and hence keen to know whether or not the enterprise will be able to meet its financial commitments or obligations in time.

Accounting statements help to determine a company's short-term solvency and liquidity position on which creditors can rely upon and review their credit policy or supply decisions.

5. Investors

The investment decisions of the investors depend upon three factors viz. safety of investment (Principal), consistency in rate of return (dividend/interest) and regularity of return. Their analysis covers past, present and future profitability, dividend policy and yield. Their decisions are also guided by viability of present projects, future prospects, growth and expansion plans. In other words this group is very much keen not only on present overall health of the company but also its future fitness. The accounting statements and annual reports provide necessary information to substantiate their investment decisions. This group consists of banking, finance, mortgage, insurance companies and individuals.

6. Government Agencies

Government Agencies include taxation authorities and regulatory bodies such as Ministry of Trade and Commerce, Company Law Board, Registrar of Joint Stock Companies, Securities Exchange Board of India (SEBI). These agencies want to ensure that all the rules pertaining to preparation, presentation and disclosures have duly been complied with or not. Thus making accounting information available to various government agencies for different purposes. For example Income Tax department shall be interested in making proper assessment of tax-liability, the regulatory agencies are concerned with the task of protecting and safeguarding the interest of investors and public at large. Government departments seek information for framing business policies in the interest of the society as such and to provide necessary direction to the business activity in accordance with the national priorities and goals. The Central Statistical Organisation (CSO) uses this information for computing national income.

7. Others

This is the residuary class which includes the rest of the users of accounting information such as Researchers, consumers, stock exchange, brokers, underwriters, economists, press and public in general. Though their interests and goals altogether being different in nature, yet they require accounting information for serving their own ends i.e. Researchers may provide some startling facts and findings, which may be used by government to set its economic policy, by Regulatory agencies to take regulatory measures and by management to review its own policies. However, they are all interested in the general well-being and prosperity of the business enterprises and their impact on social, economic, financial and business environment. Thus we can say that the use of accounting information is so exhaustive that no one can be spared from its uses and benefits.

I. Functions of Accounting

1. *Maintaining systematic records* : It is a primary function of accounting to keep proper record of transactions and events taken place chronologically which provides a base for further processing and proof for checking and verification purposes. Had there been no recording, there would have been no accounting for human memory is too short to remember each and every transaction. It embraces writing in the original/subsidiary books of entry, posting to ledger, preparation of trial balance and final accounts.

2. *Meeting legal requirements* : Accounting helps to comply with the various legal requirements. It is mandatory for joint stock companies to prepare and present their accounts in a prescribed form. These shall further be audited as per the legal requirements. Various returns such as income tax returns, sales tax returns are prepared with the help of financial accounts.
3. *Protecting and safeguarding business assets* : Records serve as evidence in the event of any dispute regarding ownership title of any property or assets of the business. It also saves from unwarranted and unjustified use. Accounting has a well-designed system of inventory control, cash and human resource management to check pilferage, theft of goods, misappropriation or embezzlement of cash and manpower waste. This function is of paramount importance for it makes best use of available resources.
4. *Facilitates rational decision-making* : Accounting is a key to a success to a decision-making process. Managerial decisions taken on the basis of facts and figures take the organisation to the newer heights of success. An effective price policy, satisfied wage structure, collective bargaining decisions, competing with rivals, advertisement and sales promotion policy etc. owe to well set accounting structure. The management derives strength from accounting to make planning, organising, coordinating, controlling and motivating functions as a means of prosperity and growth and for realisation of enterprise goals. Accounting feeds back management on capital expenditure, cash flow, sales volume, purchase policy, credit worthiness, investment and cost structure. It also helps management to appraise its own performance and spot out the weak areas, if any. Thus accounting provides necessary database on which various set of alternative choices can be considered to make managerial decision-making process a rational one.
5. *Communicating and reporting* : The individual events and transactions so recorded and processed are given certain concrete form to convey some information to others. This economic information derived from financial statements and various reports is intended to be used by the different groups who are directly or indirectly interested or associated with the business enterprise. These groups include present and potential investors, managerial personnel, employees, bankers, financial institutions, lenders, creditors, consumers, government agencies, media and the public at large. If the Accountant fails to report or communicate the information required to satisfy the varied needs of different users, the very purpose of accounting shall be defeated. There are various legislations and laws requiring extensive financial information to be communicated or reported to the users for their decision-making purposes. Accounting does serve this function well by disclosing necessary economic information in the form of profitability, dividend, liquidity, solvency, net assets value (NAV) and overall financial position including turnover trend for its users.

Limitations

1. *Non-recording of non-financial transactions* : Financial Accounting fails to accommodate transactions and events of non-monetary nature howsoever important these may be for the organisation. For example quality of the product, farsightedness of management, satisfied, satiated and healthy labour force etc. are very crucial to enterprise success but these do not find a place in accounting.

2. *Estimates are not accurate* : Accountant not only takes the factual information into account but has to make estimates as well which are often not accurate. For example estimating the useful life of machine for depreciation purposes, estimating provision for doubtful debts or investment fluctuating fund etc. cannot be made with exactness.
3. *Price-level changes are ignored* : In accounting all transactions are recorded at historical cost i.e. cost actually incurred (due and paid) the payment of expenses or acquisition of assets is shown at cost/WDV and ignores totally the changes in the value of assets brought about by change in the value of money. Hence it fails to present true and correct value (worth) of business.
4. *Subjective approach of management* : Accounting information (profitability) cannot be taken as the only indicator of managerial performance. The profit figures, to the greater extent, are affected by managerial policy of charging depreciation, writing off fictitious assets, amortisation of intangible assets, allocation of advertisement cost, valuation of stock and application of FIFO, LIFO and other methods of recording inventories. Likewise the objectivity factor is lost while preparing Balance Sheet to depict the financial position of the concern.
5. *Conflicting principles* : According to principle of conservatism stock may be valued at cost or market price whichever is less. This implies that current assets are shown at cost in one year and at market price the other year, which shows clear violation of principle of consistency.Similarly the change of method of charging depreciation from straight-line method (SLM) to written down value (WDV) method and vice versa highlights contradiction in application of accounting principles.
6. *No suggestive approach but a past record only* : Financial account discloses information about the past (historical) activities of the enterprise i.e. what has happened? It does not give any reason why or how has it happened? If a company makes profits or incurs losses, the financial accounting will show only the amount of profits or losses made but fails to divulge any details as to why there is increase or decrease in profits or losses or any suggestion for future improvement or planning.
7. *Does not highlight the departmental efficiency or inefficiency* : Financial accounting shows the result of the organisation as a whole but fails to disclose the departmental contribution or profit and losses. Similarly if an enterprise producing and selling different products, it is difficult to ascertain as to which product is profitable and which one is unprofitable.
8. *Figures are not self-explaining* : How far the accounting information and records are useful to the users depends upon their ability to analyse and interpret accounting data for their decision-making purposes. Truly accounting is the language of business but accounting figures do not speak themselves, you need certain tools to make them speak. Every user is not supposed to be competent enough to draw desired conclusions from accounting records and data.

QUESTIONS

1. Define accounting and explain its objective in the light of modern business world.
2. 'Accounting is what accounting does. In the light of this statement explain the various functions of accounting.
3. Accounting is an art or science, explain. State the various limitations of accounting.
4. Define the terms accounting and discuss its functions. **[B.Com. (H) DU 1980]**
5. Define accounting? In what way accounting information is useful to (1) Owners (2) Managers (3) Creditors and (4) Employees of a business. **[B.Com. (H) DU 1985]**
6. Who are the users of accounting information and what are their information needs?
7. Explain the following terms with the help of suitable examples :
   (i) Sales (ii) Purchases (iii) Debtors
   (iv) Creditors (v) Revenue (vi) Expenses.
8. Distinguish between :
   (a) Sales and Turnover (b) Expenses and Expenditure (c) Stock and Inventories

REFERENCES

1. Maurice, M. and A.C.L. Hleton: Significant Accounting Essays. Prentice Hall, 1965 p. 12.
2. Clenn, A. Welsch and R.N. Anthony: Fundamentals of Financial Ace. Homewood: Richard D. Irwin, 1971 p. 19.
3. Vernon Kam: Accounting Theory. John Willey and Sons, 1990 p. 53.
4. L.C. Copper: Book-keeping and Accounts p. 1.
5. A.H. Rosen Kempff: Book-keeping, Theory and Practice p. 3.
6. R.N. Carter: Advanced Accounts p. 1.
7. AICPA: Committee on Terminology, Accounting Bulletin No. 1 (1941) Review and Resume p.
8. AAA: American Accounting Association, A Statement of Basic Accounting Theory 1966 p. 1.
9. The study group report: AICPA October 1973 satisfied and satiated labour force.
10. The Report of FASB November, 1978.
11. Financial Stamp Report CICA June, 1980.

❑❑❑

2 GENERALLY ACCEPTED ACCOUNTING PRINCIPLES (GAAPs) AND ACCOUNTING STANDARDS

Generally Accepted Accounting Principles (GAAPs) are the basic foundation of accounting structure. These broad guidelines are accounting standards in the form of rules, procedures, doctrines, tenets, assumptions, postulates, concepts and conventions which bring about uniformity in recording, classifying summarizing, interpreting, reporting and presentation of accounting information. Accounting principles have been defined by the Canadian Institute of Chartered Accountants 'as the body of doctrines commonly associated with the theory and procedure of accounting serving as an explanation of current practices and as a guide for the selection of conventions and procedure where alternatives exist. Rules governing the formation of accounting axioms and principles have arisen from the common experience, historical precedent, statements by individuals and professional bodies and regulation of government agencies.' In fact these principles have been developed over the years from experience, necessity, reason, custom, usage and individual and corporate practices, desirability of different Accounting Associations and the government regulations keeping in view the interest of users of accounting information.

AICPA (The American Institute of Certified Public Accountants) view accounting principles as 'a general law or rule adapted or professed as a guide to action, a settled ground or basis of conduct or practice.' To ensure confidence of various users of accounting information viz. owners, investors, lenders creditors, these principles are being constantly adapted, modified to bring about systematic processing of accounting information, transparency in reporting and to protect and safeguard the interest of all stakeholders. However, these principles so evolved or developed are not the result of any laboratory tests or experiments unlike the test of natural sciences but mere conventions, practices and regulatory pronouncements.

Therefore, it can be concluded that accounting principles are not eternal truths because they are not based on observations and experiments but based on conventions, reasons and experience and serve as guidelines to ensure uniformity and understandability and to enhance usefulness of accounting statements in fast changing business environment. However, these accounting principles must satisfy certain criteria that of relevance, objectivity and feasibility.

Relevance refers to usefulness i.e. application of such principles makes accounting information more meaningful and useful to the users. Any accounting guideline which does not enhance the utility of accounting records to its users cannot be accepted as an accounting principle.

Objectivity denotes free from personal bias. A principle must be objective in the sense that the accounting information is not affected or influenced by personal bias and whims but solidly supported by facts and figures. This in turn increases the reliability of accounting statements.

Feasibility relates to the operational aspect. Accounting principles must be applied easily and economically without any complexity or problem. The cost in terms of time, money, efforts should not out-weigh its benefits to the users of accounting data.

Therefore, it may be concluded that accounting principles should be recognized in the light of their usefulness to users of accounting information and their relevance to decision-making processes. Secondly, these principles ensure fairness, justice, impartiality in processing and reporting accounting information, which is free from undue influence. And thirdly, accounting principles should reflect economic reality and choice should depend upon economic consequences.

However, there is no consensus or uniformity of opinions of authorities regarding the common terminology for generally accepted accounting principles. What is referred to as concepts by some called postulates, principles or conventions by others? There is hardly any difference in their nature. However an attempt is made to define these terms.

Concepts : These are self-evident statements or truths and fundamental to accounting practice. Accounting concepts are so basic that people accept them as valid without questioning. Accounting concepts provide guidelines for processing accounting information viz., recording, classifying, summarizing, interpreting and reporting.

Conventions : Conventions connote customs, traditions or practices as a guide to preparation of accounting statements.

Postulates : Accounting postulates are basic assumptions concerning the business environment. Ahmed Balkaoui[1] defines accounting postulates as self-evident statements or axioms, generally accepted by virtue of their conformity to the objectives of financial statement., that portray the economic, political, sociological and legal environment in which accounting must operate.

Principles : Accounting principles are general decision rules derived from accounting concepts. According to AICPA,[2] Principles are a general law or rules adopted or professed as a guide to action, a settled ground or basis of conduct or practice. Principles are general approaches used in the recognition and measurement of accounting events.

The distinction between these terms is of mere academic importance. For the sake of clarity and understand ability these have been classified in three major groups viz. postulates, concepts and conventions.

(A) Postulates (assumptions)

1. Accounting Entity
2. Accounting period
3. Going concern
4. Money measurement/monetary unit

(B) Concepts

1. Cost concept
2. Dual aspect concept
3. Realisation concept (Revenue recognition)
4. Matching or accrual concept
5. Objectivity concept

(C) Conventions

1. Convention of disclosure
2. Convention of materiality
3. Convention of consistency
4. Convention of conservatism

(A) POSTUALTES (ASSUMTIONS)

1. Accounting Entity Postulate (assumption)

It assumes that business concern is separate and distinct from its owners irrespective of the nature or type of organization viz. sole-trade, partnership firm or joint stock company. This clearly draws the line of demarcation between business transaction and personal transaction, between business assets and personal assets, between business liabilities and personal liabilities, between business expenses and personal expenses and between operating incomes and non-operating incomes. The accounting equation, 'Capital + Liabilities = Assets' clearly expresses the application of entity assumption. Like other claimants (creditors, lenders, investors) the owner also owes money from business to the extent money invested as capital along with profit or loss made. That's why when a person starts business with some initial amount of capital, cash A/c is debited and capital A/c is credited. American Accounting Association (AAA) defines accounting entity is an area of economic interest of a particular individual or group. It implies that a business or accounting entity may be a sole proprietorship, partnership, company, government company, public undertaking, a club, a charitable institution, religious body or government itself or even a department.

However, the distinction between the business entity and outside interests is difficult to make in practice especially in case of small business (sole trade etc.) where owners control business affairs for financial and managerial accounting purposes. But in case of a company it is not so. A company has a distinct legal entity separate from its owners (shareholders). Distinction between owners and business exist for recording only. In law no such distinction is made except for a joint stock company. Thus accounting entity and legal entity do not necessarily co-exist.

2. Accounting Period Postulate (assumption)

Besides owners and management there are others who have stake in the business enterprises such as creditors, investors, lenders, employees and the government who are also interested in day-to-day performance of the company. However, perpetual succession (continuity) of the concern makes the measurement of performance a complicate process as the actual results (profits & losses) can be ascertained only on winding up. Obviously the net income of the concern can be measured by comparing net assets in the beginning and net assets at the time of winding up or dissolution. Since these groups cannot wait indefinitely or for very long period of time, the life of the business entity has been split into annual intervals known as accounting period. This will satisfy the curiosity of these claimants about the functioning of the organization

Besides owners and management there are others who have stake in the business enterprises such as creditors, investors, lenders, employees and the government who are also interested in day-to-day performance of the company. However, perpetual succession (continuity) of the concern makes the measurement of performance a complicate process as the actual results (profits & losses) can be ascertained only on winding up. Obviously the net income of the concern can be measured by comparing net assets in the beginning and net assets at the time of winding up or dissolution. Since these groups cannot wait indefinitely or for very long period of time, the life of the business entity has been split into annual intervals known as accounting period. This will satisfy the curiosity of these claimants about the functioning of the organization

Normally, accounting period adopted is one year. It helps to take any corrective measures by owners/management and appropriate decisions by the investors, lenders and others in the light of annual progress made. It also satisfies the legal requirements of Companies Act 1956 and makes compliance of legal provisions of Income Tax Act 1961 relating to filing of annual return.

Accounting period postulate not only helps to estimate profits or losses or exhibits true and fair view of state of affairs of business but also presents proper valuation of assets and liabilities at regular intervals. This assumption clearly makes distinction between expired and unexpired cost, outstanding and prepaid expenses, accrued and advance income revenue and deferred revenue expenditure. Even the allocation of capital expenditure over the effective life of the asset has been made possible because of accounting period assumption. Charging of annual depreciation to profit & loss A/c is a clear example of it. The current accounting practices now advocate of even an interim reporting by preparing final accounts of a six monthly or quarterly accounting period.

3. Going Concern Postulate

According to International `Accounting Standards (IAS). "The enterprise is normally viewed as a going concern, that is as continuing in operation for the foreseeable future. It is assumed that the enterprises has neither the intention nor the necessity of liquidation or of curtailing the scale of its operation." The simply implies that a business as an entity has a continuity of life and going to last indefinitely in the absence of evidence to the contrary. It will not be wound up in near future except those, which are intended to last for a short period of time (such as joint ventures). Continuity is applicable for all forms of accounting entities. Even a joint stock company is deemed to have perpetual succession. This does not mean that business entities will exist forever but for a sufficiently longer period of time. Accounting records or information is processed after due consideration to the continuity factor. The application of going concern assumption justifies accounting treatment of following transactions :

1. Making long-term investments in fixed assets.
2. Valuation of assets on (historical) cost basis rather than realisable value because business is not intended for sale or liquidation.
3. Charging of depreciation over the useful life of assets on written down value/cost basis and not on current market price.

4. Amortisation of intangible assets over their effective life.
5. Showing advance (prepaid) expenses, deferred revenue expenditure and unexpired cost as assets.
6. It facilitates to undertake long terms future contracts. However, this assumption does not apply if the business is to be dissolved. In the event of winding-up or liquidation the realisable value of the assets matters and not the cost.

4. Money Measurement Postulate

Accounting is language of business, which can be interpreted by a monetary unit. It is the only unit of measurement to account for the transactions of business enterprise. It implies that accounting records reports and interprets those business transactions and events, which can be expressed in terms of money. It measures material, labour, expenses, investment, sales, purchases, assets and liabilities in monetary unit, which provides a common denominator. The evets or transactions howsoever important these may be, if cannot be expressed in terms of money, do not find any place in the books of accounts. For example the quality of products, dedicated labour force, efficient and farsighted management, better working conditions, competitors strategy and price policy etc. all crucial for smooth running, expansion and growth of the enterprise but the same cannot be recorded in the books of accounts. Therefore, this assumption suffers from following limitations :

1. Financial accounting is limited to the information, events or happenings which can be expressed in monetary unit. Therefore, it does not give a complete account of happenings in business enterprise. Even the strike, lockouts, workers-management relations, impact of government policy on the business environment etc. cannot be recorded.
2. This postulate assumes that purchasing power of the monetary unit is stable. In other words the impact of price level changes are totally ignored. This leads to a distorted picture of state of affairs of business enterprise. For example if a building acquired for Rs. 2,00,000 in the year 1980 and another building of the same amount in the year 2000 arc rccorded at the same price although the building purchased in 1980 may be many times more than the value recorded due to rising prices.

(B) ACCOUNTING CONCEPTS

1. Cost Concept

Cost concept implies that all transactions relating to business such as purchase of goods and services, acquisition of assets, expenses etc. are recorded at historical cost i.e. money actually paid/payable. However, in case of fixed assets only unexpired portion of cost (cost-depreciation =WDV) is shown in the Balance Sheet in the subsequent years. Events, which do not cost any penny to the organization, are not recorded, although it may affect the valuation of enterprise. For example if some of the top reputed executives, who have taken to the business to new heights of success, desert the organization, the real value of the enterprise will change immediately which will be reflected in the market price of company's shares. This event, though of great importance, will not be recorded in the books of account. Similarly, the knowledge and skill that is built up as the business operate, the team work that grows up within the organization, a favorable location that becomes of increasing importance as time goes by a good reputation with its customers etc., none of these appear as an asset in accounts of the Company.[3]

Since valuation of fixed assets does not depend upon market valuation, this concept follows the objective approach, as the figures are not influenced by the personal bias. Had there been market value concept, it would have been a difficult job for accountant, which value to follow wholesale or retail. Which market value to follow and so on. Hence it is difficult and time consuming for an organization to determine market value. Cost approach is further justified from the fact that fixed assets are held for use in business and not for sale and there is verifiability in cost approach.

2. Dual Aspect Concept

This simply implies that each and every business transaction has two aspects. It may be either :

(i) Receiving the benefit and giving the benefit.

(ii) Source of benefit and use of benefit and so on.

These may involve acquisition of assets, purchase of goods for cash or on credit, sale of goods for cash or on credit and payment of salaries or other business expenses or raise loan or meeting any short- or long-term liability etc. In each of the above transactions it involves two aspects say purchase of goods for cash involves (i) receipt of goods (ii) payment of cash. If it is on credit basis it results (i) receipt of goods and (ii) acknowledgement of debt to the supplier. This recognition of two aspects relating to debit and credit known as dual aspect concept, which is essentially based on double entry system. Accordingly this system requires debit for what comes in and credit for what goes out, debit for the receiver and credit for the giver, debit for all the expenses and losses, credit for all the incomes and gains.

This can be put forth in the form of accounting equations.

1. 'X' starts business with initial capital of Rs. 5,00,000

   Capital = Cash

   Rs. 500,000 = Rs. 500,000

2. Deposited in a bank Rs. 4,50,000

   Capital = Cash + Bank

   Rs. 5,00,000 = Rs. 50,000 + 4,50,000

3. Purchased goods and paid by cheque Rs. 80,000

   Capital = Cash + Bank + Stock

   Rs. 5,00,000 = Rs. 50,000 + 3,70,000 + 80,000

4. Purchased goods on credit for Rs. 40,000

   Creditors + Capital = Cash + Bank + Stock

   Rs. 40,000 + 5,00,000 Rs. 50,000 + 3,70,000 + 1,20,000

5. Purchased machinery and paid by cheque Rs. 2,00,000

   Creditors + Capital = Cash + Bank + Stock + Machinery

   40,000 + 5,00,000 = 50,000 + 1,70,000 + 1,20,000 + 2,00,000

Thus dual aspect concept can be expressed as

Capital + Liabilities = Assets.

Capital = Assets – Liabilities

The accounting equation, therefore, states that there is a debit for every credit and vice versa.

3. Realisation Concept

This is also known as Revenue recognition concept. According to International Accounting Standards Committee, "Revenue is the gross inflow of cash, receivables or other consideration arising in the course of an enterprise from the *sale of goods,* from the *rendering of services* and *from holding the assets.* Revenue is measured by the charges made to customers or clients for goods supplied and services rendered to them and by the charges and rewards arising from the provisions of assets. It excludes amounts collected on behalf of third parties such as certain taxes."[4]

In other words this principle recognizes revenue when a transaction rendering services or for sale is effected. Whether it is a cash sale, a credit sale or an installment sale. This implies that revenue realization does not necessarily mean that revenue must realize in cash. 'Revenue are generally recognized in the accounting period in which goods are delivered to customers or the period in which services are rendered.[5] But in case of professionals such as Lawyers, doctors or other consultants who maintain their books of accounts on cash basis, revenue recognition and cash realization go together. However, where books of accounts are maintained on mercantile basis, revenue recognition takes place at the *point of sale*[6] – where property in goods is transferred immediately from seller to buyer.

However, there are four exceptions to this rule.

(i) *Goods sold on hire-purchase basis* : In this case revenues are not recognized on the date of sale but to the extent of amount realized and due during the accounting year because ownership of goods sold on hire purchase is transferred only when the last installment is paid.

(ii) *Long terms construction contract* : In case of contract accounts the profits are calculated on the basis of work certified and cash received and not on the date of signing of contract or completing contract e.g. if a contract for Rs. 5,00,000 has been signed and during the accounting year contractor incurs Rs. 2,50,000 and expects to incur another Rs. 1,50,000 for its completion. The contractee pays 75% of works approved or certified. The profits realized shall be calculated as under :

Estimate profits = contract price – (total expenditure incurred + estimated to be incurred)

Rs. 1,00,000 = 5,00,000 – (2,50,000 + 1,50,000)

Thus by applying the formula

We get $\frac{1,00,000 \times 4,00,000 \times 75}{5,00,000 \times 100}$

Revenue to be recognized Rs. 60,000

Some time profits so computed are recognized to the extent of 2 / 3rd, 1 / 3rd or, even nil depending upon the stage of completion of contract.

(iii) *Gold mining* : Revenue is recognized at the point of production and not when it is sold.

(iv) *Interest on fixed deposit* : Total interest payable on maturity is not recognized as revenue during the accounting period in which fixed deposit is made but only the proportionate interest that has accrued on the date of closing of books of accounts.

4. Matching Concept

Matching concept is based upon accounting period postulate which implies recognition of revenue and expenses on comparable basis to determine the profit and loss for a particular accounting period i.e. matching concept involves the process of relating expenses with revenue. However, matching concept is different under each system of accounting. Under cash system only actual receipts and actual payments are recognized as 'revenue' and 'expenses' for any accounting year. In other words revenues are recognized when realized in cash and expenses are recognized when actually paid in cash. This is irrespective of the goods supplied/services rendered or benefit received. The cheques received or cheque issued is treated at par with cash realized and cash paid. Whereas under accrual basis of accounting revenues are recognized when sale is made or service is rendered in any accounting period whether realized in cash or not. Expenses are recognized on due basis whether paid or not i.e. expenses related to the accounting period are accounted for. This process of recognizing and relating expenses with revenue is called matching concept. It should be remembered that expenses (costs) and revenues (income) that relate to the accounting period are considered. However, there are four major problems in the matching processes :

1. Writing off preliminary expenses, expenses on issue of shares and debentures and advertisement expenditure and thereby charging the same to profit and loss account cannot be done conveniently and accurately. It is very difficult to measure the actual benefit derived or revenue earned during each accounting year.
2. Charging of depreciation (expired cost) to profit and loss account for matching the revenue earned for any particular accounting year creates a serious problem of matching.
3. Recognising revenue (profit) in case of long-term contracts, where cash is not received in proportion to work completed point out towards drawbacks and limitations of matching concept.
4. Non-business receipts such as interest/dividend on investments and rent do not have any corresponding expenses to match.

However, despite these drawbacks and limitations matching concept does provide a sound basis for preparation of annual statements.

5. Verifiability and Objectivity Concept

Verifiability implies that each and every transaction recorded in the books of accounts must be supported by documentary evidence. Objectivity refers that accounting data must be free from personal bias. This will enhance reliability; trust worthiness and dependability of accounting statements among its users. To win the confidence of users of financial statements it is essential that necessary vouchers, receipts, invoices, cash memos, bank statement, ownership or title deeds and documents of disbursement are properly maintained. This will further minimize the chances of frauds and other malpractices. While estimating expected effective life of machine, provision of bad and doubtful debts the accountant should not be subjective or biased.

(C) CONVENTIONS

1. Convention of full Disclosure

One of the primary objectives of published corporate accounts is to provide such information and in such a form as to minimize uncertainty about the validity of information and to enable the users (creditors, shareholders, investors, bankers etc.) to make their own assessment of the risk associated with the enterprise. In other words this convention specifies that there should be complete and full disclosure of all significant information relating to the economic activity and financial affairs of the business enterprise. In fact the extent of disclosure should be determined in the light of need of users of financial statements. The mode or basis of valuation of certain assets (such as the market value of land and building, inventories, investment) change in the method of charging depreciation and even contingent liabilities are shown by means of footnote or as additional information. Companies Act 1956 also provides for forms and schedules of accounts, in which financial statements are to be prepared. In this way Companies Act also makes proper provisions for the disclosure of significant information relating to published accounts. However, disclosure also applies to the events occurring even after the date of closing of books of accounts. The impact of government regulation, exceptional contracts, natural calamities, acquisition, merger and exceptional losses be reported.

2. Convention of Materiality

According to American Accounting Association (AAA) an item should be regarded as material if there is reason to believe that knowledge of it would influence the decision of informed investors. As per IAS-1 materiality should govern the selection and application of accounting policies. IAS –5 states that all material information should be disclosed that is necessary to make the financial statements clear & understandable. Any information which is insignificant and immaterial from the point of view of users of financial statements should not be reported. But, what is material and what is immaterial depends upon size and nature of the organization. In other words materiality refers to relative nature importance of an item or event, which differs from company to company. The treatment of certain expenditure as capital by one firm and revenue by the other is a clear example of it. The omission of insignificant and immaterial pieces of information helps to avoid waste of time, money and efforts. However, materiality is purely a matter of personal judgment and should be left to the discretion of the accountant.

3. Convention of Consistency

The consistency assumes that accounting policies are consistent from one period to other. It implies that rules, policies principles, methods adopted by a firm for the purpose of preparation and presentation of accounts are not subject to frequent changes. If it is done so, the comparison of its financial statements over a period of years and with other firms would be difficult. According to IAS-1 consistency is a fundamental assumption and it is assumed that accounting policies are consistent form one period to another. Where this assumption is not followed, the fact should be disclosed. In order to bring uniformity of preparation, presentation, understanding and to enhance usefulness of financial statements it is essential that the precise rules or conventions are continuously adhered to from year to year. It does not mean it is rigid in approach. It allows adoption of new improved accounting policies to bring about a qualitative change in reporting accounting data. Had it been a rigid convention there would not have been any development in the national and international accounting standards. Consistency aims to eliminate personal bias through uniformity of recording and reporting of accounting information. Following examples are also considered simply an application of convention of consistency.

(a) The valuation of stock at cost or market price whichever is less
(b) Valuation of investment at market price or cost whichever is less
(c) Change of methods of charging depreciation due to change in expected life of an asset or any other reason.

According to E.L. Kohler there are three types of consistencies, which should be adhered to :

(i) *Vertical consistency* : It refers to the use of similar measurement, concepts and procedures for related items within the statement of firm for a single period.

(ii) *Horizontal consistency* : It implies the use of same accounting procedures practice by a single firm from one period to other. It facilitates comparison of the operating efficiency of a firm from one period to other.

(iii) *Third dimensional consistency* : It connotes the application of same principles, methods, and procedures by different firms of the same industry.

4. Convention of Conservatism

This is also known as doctrine of prudence. It refers to the policy of playing safe by providing for all possible losses but not for the anticipated gains. Due to business uncertainties and risk it is wiser to account for possible losses. IAS-I states "Uncertainties inevitably surround many transactions. This should be recognized by exercising prudence in financial statements. Prudence does not, however, justify the creation of secret or hidden reserves". According to ASB (USA) statement[4], "Frequently, assets and liabilities are measured in a context of significant uncertainties. Historically, managers, investors and accountants have generally preferred that possible efforts in measurement be made in the direction of understatement rather than overstatement of net income and net assets. This has led to the convention of conservatism."

Thus conservatism does not mean a deliberate and consistent understatement of income or undervaluation of assets but it refers to an approach which safeguards the interest of all those concerned. It is applied when there is uncertainty inherent in the activity such as uncertainty regarding realization of income, estimated liability or occurrence of loss etc. Following are the examples of the application of the convention of conservatism :

(i) Valuing inventories at cost or market price whichever is less.
(ii) Providing for doubtful debts and discount on debtors.
(iii) Not providing for discount on creditors.
(iv) Creating provision against fluctuation in the price of investments.
(v) Treating small capital items like crockery, waste bins to revenue.
(vi) Amortisations of intangible assets like goodwill, which has indefinite life.
(vii) Showing joint life policy at its surrender value as against the amount paid.
(viii) Providing for loss on issue of debentures when these are to be redeemed at premium.

However, a more cautious approach is required with regard to the application of doctrine of conservatism so that it does not distort the actual earnings of the firm, and balance sheet exhibits true and fair view of state of affairs of the business enterprise.

ACCOUNTING STANDARDS

Introduction

Accounting is the language of business and all other organizations, institutions, associations, firms and families involving financial transactions and events. It communicates the result of operations to the users through financial statements, which should show true and fair state of affairs of organization concerned. These financial statements are expected to meet varied needs of users of accounting information. Hence, in order to meet the expectations of interested parties and to make accounting information more meaningful and useful, accounting standards act as guides to processing, preparation and presentation of financial statements. These standards in the form of rules have to be used with reasonable degree of flexibility in view of changing economic, social, legal requirements and technological developments. Therefore, these rules cannot be rigid. However, this does not imply that such rules can be used arbitrarily. It simply means application of rules rationally within the parameters prescribed by various accounting standards. Hence, it becomes quite imperative to develop proper "Accounting Standards" so as to make accounting as true language of all business and non-business organizations who use accounting for recording and reporting purposes. In order to avoid the possibility of financial statements being misleading or presenting distorted picture and to ensure transparency, comparability, consistency, adequacy and reliability of information-contents of financial statements, it is a must that a regulatory force must work to regulate the processing, preparation and presentation of accounting information. The foremost objective of setting accounting standards is to ensure that financial statements are transparent and adequate information-wise, consistent and comparable period-wise and entity-wise so as to improve the overall quality of preparation, presentation and reporting of accounting information.

Meaning of Accounting Standards

Accounting Standards are uniform rules to ensure uniformity of preparation, presentation and reporting of accounting information and thus deal mainly with financial measurements and disclosures. According to Kohler, "Accounting Standard is mode of conduct imposed by custom, law or professional body for the benefit of public accountants and accountants generally.

Littleton defines standard, "as an agreed upon criteria of what is proper practice in a given situation. A basis of comparison and judgment, a point of departure when variation is justifiable by the circumstances and reported as such. Standards are no designed to confine practice within rigid limit but rather to serve as a guide posts to truth, honesty and fair dealing. "These accounting standards aim to improve credibility and reliability of financial statements through reform in theory and practice within the legal framework to cater to the needs of changing socio-economic requirements of the corporate world. These standards are in the form of detailed rules, procedures, and policies to be adopted for the accounting treatment of various items of expenditure and revenue and to eliminate the effect of diverse accounting policies and practices. Hence, accounting standards facilitate uniformity of processing, presentation and reporting accounting information to make it more meaningful and comparable. In the absence of any definite rules or standards the accounting information cannot be interpreted for the purpose of decision-making by the users. If each company develops its own standards or policies of preparation and presentation of financial statements then the users cannot draw right conclusion because of non-comparability of financial position as well as operating efficiency of the various firms. Glautier, Undertown and Clark have rightly stated, "Although, accountants have been able to formulate their own conventions about what is 'true and fair, their interpretation of truth and fairness has not seemed convincing to the public. In the wake of public concern and the fear that government might intervene to impose a measure of state of control in the affairs of the profession, the presence for standardization has become overwhelming." In view of globalization and liberalization of trade there is now a greater need to adherence of International Accounting Standards.

Type of Accounting Standards

Standards may be classified by their "subject matter" and by the process of their "preparation and enforcement".

(A) Classification by "Subject Matter"

(1) **Disclosure standards :** These standards are the rules for external reporting which deal with the disclosing the material information on a uniform pattern so as to help in the decision-making process of the users of financial statements. Application of uniform set of rules brings about a total transparency for the outsiders who interpret accounting information for certain conclusions. Since these standards require explicit disclosure of accounting methods used and assumptions made in preparing financial statements, it helps to restore and boost the confidence of outsiders in the companies adhering to disclosure standards.

(2) **Presentation standards :** Such standards are in the form of methods and policies governing the presentation of accounting information. These standards specify the type and form of accounting information to be presented. In the absence of any set rules of presentation, different entities may follow their own norm of presentation and thus making inter-firm or company comparisons very difficult. Theses standards facilitate a comparative, complete and a better understanding of financial statements of various entities.

(3) **Contents standards :** These standards determine the magnitude or contents of accounting information which is to be included in the financial statements for reporting purposes. Such standards specify the categories of information to be disclosed, how specific items to be reported, and the treatment of items based upon standard accounting practices. Contents standards ensure that each interested party gets fully satisfied with the information contents of financial statements.

(B) Classification by "Methods of Preparation and Enforcement"

(1) **Government standards :** These standards are formulated by government agencies in the form of laws and regulations to ensure uniform accounting practices and disclosures. Company Law Board (CLB), SEBI (Securities Exchange Board of India) and CBDT (Central Board of Direct Taxes) work cohesively to develop standard accounting practices for the purpose of preparation, presentation and reporting accounting information.

(2) **Privately set standards :** These standards are set by the trade associations, stock exchanges, companies or other private accounting bodies whose members ensure effective enforcement.

(3) **Voluntary compliance standards :** Such standards are generally accepted accounting practices and conventions. Generally acceptability implies voluntary compliance by the various enterprises.

SCOPE OF ACCOUNTING STANDARDS

Salient Features

(1) **Standards to conform to rule of law :** Accounting standards must conform to the rule of law, customs, usages and business environment. In case of contradiction or confrontation the rule of law shall prevail and the financial statements shall be prepared accordingly.

(2) **Standards to follow local regulations :** The accounting standards cannot over-ride local regulations governing the preparation and presentation of financial statements. However, the regulatory body (Institute of Chartered Accountant of India) can determine the extent of disclosure to be made in the financial statements including Auditor's report. It may be in the form of clarification with reference to any specific or particular item also.

(3) **Standards to apply to material items only :** Accounting Standards are intended to be applied to items having significant (material) value. The institute will make clear the limitations of any specific standard with regard to its applicability as and when required. The Institute will also specify the date when a particular standard will be made effective. However, no standard will have retroactive application except when otherwise stated.

(4) **Standards are recommendatory unless otherwise stated :** In the initial years some Accounting Standards are not mandatory but recommendatory in nature. The Institute uses its best office to persuade business and industrial world, Government and appropriate authorities to adopt these standards to bring about uniformity of preparation and presentation financial statements.

(5) **Standards are to be simple and flexible :** Standards are formulated to concentrate on basics and essentials to be applied effectively without any complexity on nation-wide basis. However, these standards will continue to be revised to meet the changing requirements of the business world in general, and above all, the expectations of the users of accounting information in particular. Hence, these are likely to gain general acceptability on voluntary basis.

Objectives of accounting standards : The main objective of "Accounting Standards" is to bring about uniformity in recording and classification of business transactions, preparation, presentation and interpretation thereof. The application of accounting standards at these levels will bring about a qualitative change in the financial statements, which in turn enhance the creditability and reliability thereof. This will create a sense of confidence among users of accounting information viz., Shareholders, Investors, Trade Unions, Bankers, Creditors and Government agencies. The Financial Accounting Standard Board (FASB) U.S.A. has listed nine qualitative improvements in the accounting information if the accounting standards are strictly adhered to. These are usefulness, relevance, reliability, understandability, verifiability, neutrality, consistency and comparability, timeliness and completeness of financial statements. The other objectives of Accounting Standards can be short listed as under :

(i) To provide "guides to action" in the matter of processing of accounting information at all levels.

(ii) To provide the norms on the basis of which financial statements are prepared.

(iii) To bring about a qualitative improvement in the accounting information as listed by F.A.S.B. (USA).

(iv) To facilitate accountants to work with speed and accuracy.

(v) To help Auditors to pinpoint shortcomings in the financial statements and prepare a reliable audit report.

INDIAN ACCOUNTING STANDARDS

Since there is widespread diversity of accounting practices in different countries, most countries have their own accounting standards. While most Indian Accounting Standards are mandatory, the International Accounting Standards are recommendatory. To support and propagate international Accounting Standards, the Council of Institute of Chartered Accountants of India set-up an Accounting Standards Board (ASB) on April 21, 1977. The Board (ASB) first prepares and issues "Exposure Drafts" to various professional bodies like ICAI, ICWA, ICS and regulatory agencies and stock exchanges. These "exposure drafts" are finalized in standards after taking into account various observations and comments of various bodies and agencies. While formulating the accounting standards the Board (ASB) takes into consideration the applicable laws, usages customs and business environment. Besides, ASB gives due consideration to International Accounting Standards and tries to integrate them to the possible extent in the light of prevailing national conditions and practices. The Accounting Standards are issued by ASB who is entrusted with the task of propagating Accounting Standards and persuading the concerned parties to adopt them in the preparation and presentation of financial statements. ASB is also responsible for issuing guidance notes, clarification on the Accounting Standards and to review them periodically. This will ensure standardization of accounting practices in the country.

ASB also enumerates and describes the basic concepts to which accounting principles should be oriented and the practices and procedures should conform.

Compliance with the Accounting Standards

It is the duty of the members of the Institute to ensure that the Accounting Standards are implemented. In the event of any deviation from the standards, it will be duty of the members of Institute to make adequate disclosures in their reports (audit) for the benefits of the users by making them aware of any deviation or departure from set standards.

Initially, the standards are issued to be recommendatory in character. The Institute is to give wide publicity among the users and educate members about the utility of Accounting Standards and the need for compliance. Later on, steps are taken to enforce compliance with accounting standards and make them mandatory.

Companies (Amendment) Act 1999, section 211 makes it compulsory on the part of enterprises to report any deviation from the Accounting Standards and reasons for such deviations. Such a practice will certainly have a salutary effect and bring-about a qualitative improvement in the matter of reporting and disclosure of accounting information. The council has, so far, issued the following "Standards".

AS – 1		Disclosure of Accounting Policies
AS – 2	(Revised)	Valuation of Inventories
AS – 3	(Revised)	Cash Flow Statement
AS – 4	(Revised)	Contingencies and Events occurring after the Balance Sheet date
AS – 5	(Revised)	Net Profit or Loss for the period, Prior period items and changes in the Accounting policies
AS – 6	(Revised)	Depreciation Accounting
AS – 7	(Revised)	Construction Contracts
AS – 9	(Revised)	Revenue Recognition

AS – 10	Accounting for Fixed Assets
AS – 11 (Revised)	The Effect of Changes in Foreign Exchange Rates
AS – 12	Accounting for Government Grants
AS – 13	Accounting for Investments
AS – 14 (Revised)	Accounting for Amalgamation
AS – 15	Accounting for Retirement Benefits in the Financial Statements of Employers
AS – 16	Borrowing Costs
AS – 17	Segment Reporting
AS – 18	Related Party Disclosures
AS – 19	Leases
AS – 20	Earnings per share
AS – 21	Consolidated Financial Statements
AS – 22	Accounting for Taxes on Income
AS – 23	Accounting for Investments in Associates in Consolidated Financial Statement
AS – 24	Discontinuing Operations
AS – 25	Interim Financial Reporting
AS – 26	Intangible Assets
AS – 27	Financial Reporting of Interests in Joint Ventures
AS – 28	Impairment of Assets
AS – 29	Provisions, Contingent Liabilities and Contingent Assets [Issued w.e.f. 1-4-2004]
AS – 30	Financial Instruments: Disclosure and Presentation.
AS – 31	Financial Instruments: Presentation

Despite setting of quite good number of "Standards" the process of setting Accounting Standards, however, is not yet over. There are certain areas where new and revised "Standards" are required and this process will go a long way to bring about a qualitative improvement in the areas of disclosure, presentation and reporting. The ICAI is working on the formulation of following new Accounting Standards.

1. Accounting by Insurance Companies
2. Agriculture

However, AS – 1, AS – 5, AS – 10, AS – 11 and AS – 14 are in the process of revision. AS – 8 has been withdrawn after AS – 26 was made mandatory. Due to on-set of liberalization and globalization process in India, the Indian Accounting Standards should continue to foster for improvement in the financial reporting and disclosures to meet the diverse needs of 'global' Individual and Institutional investors. This is a challenging task and hence there is a need on the part of all those concerned viz., Institute of Chartered Accountants of India, Government, Public Sector Undertakings, Industry, Regulatory Agencies such as SEBI and Company Law Board and the whole corporate world to work cohesively to improve overall quality of disclosure and reporting of financial information to make it more meaningful and trustworthy. However, these accounting standards will be done away with as government has made its intention clear that w.e.f 1st April, 2011 the International Financial Reporting Standards (IFRS) shall be made mandatory for the corporate world.

QUESTIONS

1. Explain the Convention of consistency. **[B.Com. (H) DU. (1995), (1987)]**
2. Explain cost concept. **[B.Com (H), DU, (1986)]**
3. Explain the accounting concept of periodic matching of cost and revenue. **[B.Com (H), DU, 1988]**
4. State the meaning and significance of 'going concern concept' in accountancy. **[B.Com. (H), DU, 1989]**
5. Explain briefly the concept of materiality. Give examples. **[B.Com. (H), DU, 1990]**
6. Revenue is recognized when a 'sales' transaction is made or when services are rendered'. State three exceptions to this general rule. **[B.Com (H), DU, 1993]**
7. Explain the matching principle of accounting. Describe in brief the difficulties involved in its application. **[B.Com (H), DU, 1994]**
8. Explain the 'Money Measurement Concept' **[B.Com (H), DU, 1995]**
9. Write short notes on Fundamental Accounting Assumptions. **[C.A. Foundation, May 1996]**
10. Briefly explain 'Dual Aspect Concept'. **[C.S. Foundation, Dec. 1996]**
11. Briefly explain 'Money Measurement Concept'. **[C.S. Foundation, June 1987]**
12. Briefly explain 'Realisation Concept'. **[C.S. Foundation, Dec. 1994]**
13. What are " Accounting Standards"? Why these Standards are required?
14. Explain the procedure for formulation of "Accounting Standards".
15. Mention any seven areas of disclosures as per AS – 1.
16. Write a short note on :

    AS – 2; AS – 3

    AS – 4; AS – 5

    AS – 6; AS – 9

❑❑❑

3 RECORDING BUSINESS TRANSACTIONS - I

The main objective of accounting is to ascertain profit or loss during a specific period and to determine financial position of a business enterprise on a particular date. Besides, it provides necessary business information to the interested parties (users) for the purpose of decision-making. Hence there is a need of a proper and systematic process to keep and present business information. For this purpose the business transactions occurring during an accounting year are recorded, classified, summarized and the results thereof are reported. However there are two approaches to attain the desired objectives :

1. Traditional Approach   2. Accounting Equation Approach

Traditional Approach involves the following :

(i) Recording of business transactions either in Journal or subsidiary books.

(ii) Classifying business transactions by posting them to Ledger Accounts.

(iii) Closing the Ledger Accounts and preparation of summary of all ledger accounts called Trial Balance.

(iv) Preparation of final accounts viz. Trading and Profit and Loss Accounts and Balance Sheet.

JOURNAL

Journal is a book of original entry because the transactions are first recorded in the journal. It shows the daily record of business transactions in a chronological order. The process of recording is known as journalising. There are five columns in the journal, which are as under:

Journal (Format)

Date	Particulars	L.F.	Debit (Rs.)	Credit (Rs.)

First column shows the date of the transaction.

Second column 'particulars' – shows the name of the Account to be debited is written along with 'Dr' on the firss line and the name of the Account to be credited is written along with the word 'Cr' on the second line. An explanation of the entry called 'narration' is followed thereafter within parentheses.

Third column 'L.F.' stands for Ledger Folio, which shows the page number on hich the various accounts appear in the ledger.

Fourth column 'Amount (Dr)' shows the amount, which is to be adjusted to the debit of Account involved in the transaction.

Last column 'Amount (Cr)' shows the amount, which is to be adjusted by crediting the Account involved in the transaction.

According to Kohler, an account is the individual record of a person, firm, a thing, an item of an expense or an item of an income. There may be hundreds of accounts involved under various transactions which can be short listed and grouped as under:

I. Accounts involving persons, firms or companies called **Personal Accounts**. A business enterprise has to enter into business dealings with number of persons or firms. Therefore it becomes imperative to open each and every account of the person or firm involved in the business transactions to determine the amount of receivables and payables.

II. Accounts of each property or assets acquired by the firm named **Real Accounts**. Every business enterprise must have such assets, which are necessarily required in connection with running of business enterprise. It may be stock, cash, furniture, plant and machinery, equipments or any other assets whose account has to be opened in the books of accounts.

III. Accounts of each head of expenses incurred and income earned are classified as **Nominal Accounts**

The business has to incur certain expenses to earn certain income or to meet the requirements of certain business transactions. These may include salaries and wages of employees, rent of shop or factory, telephone, electricity, stationery, advertisement and other office and selling and distribution expenses. These accounts become of vital importance to be operated by the business enterprise, as these are the main ingredients of income statement.

CLASSIFICATION OF ACCOUNTS AND RULES OF RECORDING TRANSACTION (JOURNALISATION)

As discussed earlier, there are basically three types of Accounts :

A. Personal Accounts

(1) Natural Persons Accounts

(2) Artificial Persons Accounts

(3) Representative Persons Accounts

B. Real Accounts

(1) Tangible Real Accounts

(2) Intangible Real Accounts

C. Nominal Accounts

A-1* Natural Persons Account refers to an account of an individual human being such as creditors (Ram, Shyam etc.), Debtors (Ramesh, Mohan etc.), proprietors (x) Accounts.

A-2* Artificial persons account records business transactions of an artificial person created by law such as A & Co. Account, Bank Account, Brown Brothers & Co. Accounts, Insurance Co. Account, Club or any Institution Account etc.

A-3* Representative persons account refers to an account representing large number of accounts of similar nature grouped together such as salaries or wages due to workers belong to similar account (nominal) which is put under salaries or wages outstanding account. This account is representative of employees. The same rules apply to other accounts of this nature such as rent outstanding, rent prepaid, interest accrued, interest outstanding etc.

B-1* Tangible Real Account includes the account of all those things which can be touched, felt, seen, measured and have physical appearance such as land and building, plant and machinery, furniture and fixtures, tools and equipment, motor vehicles etc.

B-2* Intangible Real Accounts do not have physical existence but can be measured in terms of money. For example, goodwill, copyright, trade marks, patents etc.

C. Nominal Accounts are those accounts which record expenses, incomes, gains, profits or losses, salaries, wages, interest paid, interest received, rent paid, rent received, dividend received, commission, discount etc. are examples of nominal accounts.

Note : When an item of nominal account becomes due or accrued it is treated as personal Account i.e. salaries – nominal a/c but salaries o/s is a personal account.

The rules for journalisation are as under :

Name of Account	Debit (Dr)	Credit (Cr)
1. Personal Account	The Receiver	The Giver
2. Real Account	What comes in	What goes out
3. Nominal Account	All expenses & losses	All incomes and gains

Illustration 1

Classify the following accounts :

(i) Capital A/c, (ii) Drawings A/c (iii) Goodwill A/c, (iv) Bank A/c, (v) Cash A/c, (vi) Rent paid A/c, (vii) Interest A/c, (viii) Dividend Received A/c, (ix) Building A/c, (x) Stock A/c, (xi) Machinery A/c, (xii) Discount A/c, (xiii) A & Co. A/c, (xiv) Salaries A/c, (xv) Bills receivable A/c, (xvi) Bills Payable A/c, (xvii) Provision for bad debts (xviii) Bad debts (xix) Unexpired Insurance, (xx) Bank overdraft (xxi) Sales A/c, (xxii) Purchase A/c, (xxiii)Patents A/c, (xxiv) Carriage A/c, (xxv) Salaries o/s, (xviii) Prepaid Rent A/c.

Solution :

(i)	Capital A/c	=	Personal A/c
(ii)	Drawings A/c	=	Personal A/c
(iii)	Goodwill A/c	=	Real A/c
(iv)	Bank A/c	=	Personal A/c
(v)	Cash A/c	=	Real A/c

(vi)	Rent A/c	=	Nominal A/c
(vii)	Interest A/c	=	Nominal A/c
(viii)	Dividend A/c	=	Nominal A/c
(ix)	Building A/c	=	Real A/c
(x)	Stock A/c	=	Real A/c
(xi)	Machinery A/c	=	Real A/c
(xii)	Discount A/c	=	Nominal A/c
(xiii)	A & Co. A/c	=	Personal A/c
(xiv)	Salaries A/c	=	Nominal A/c
(xv)	Bills Receivable A/c	=	Real A/c
(xvi)	Bills Payable A/c	=	Real A/c
(xvii)	Provision for Bad Debts A/c	=	Nominal A/c
(xviii)	Bad Debts	=	Nominal A/c
(xix)	Unexpired Insurance	=	Personal A/c
(xx)	Bank Overdraft	=	Personal A/c
(xxi)	Sales A/c	=	Real A/c
(xxii)	Purchase A/c	=	Real A/c
(xxiii)	Patents A/c	=	Real A/c
(xxiv)	Carriage A/c	=	Nominal A/c
(xxv)	Salaries O/s	=	Personal A/c
(xxvi)	Prepaid Rent A/c	=	Personal A/c

Types of Entries

There are two types of entries, which are recorded in Journal :

1. Simple Entry 2. Compound Entry

A simple entry involves two accounts only, one affecting the debit side and other affecting the credit side with an equal amount.

When a simple entry is recorded for a transaction involving more than two accounts simultaneously or when many transactions of similar nature occurring on the same day are recorded by means of a combined entry, such a simple entry is known as compound entry. There may be three possibilities when a compound entry is recorded.

Only one account to be debited and several accounts are to be credited

Several accounts are to be debited and only one account is to be credited.

Several accounts are to be debited and several accounts are to be credited.

Example of Simple Entry	Examples of Compound Entry
1. Tarted business and introduced Rs. 2,00,000 as capital Cash A/c Dr. 20,00,000 To Capital A/c 2,00,000	1. Started business and introduced Rs. 1,00,000 as capital and stock wroth Rs. 1,00,000 Cash A/c Dr. 1,00,000 Stock A/c Dr. 1,00,000 To Capital A/c 2,00,000

2. Purchased Machinery from X and company for Rs. 50,000 for cash Machinery A/c Dr. 50,000 To Cash A/c 50,000	2. Purchased machinery from X & company for Rs. 50,000 and paid Rs. 20,000 Machinery A/c Dr. 50,000 To Cash A/c 20,000 To X & company A/c 30,000
3. Received Rs. 10,000 from Akash. Cash A/c Dr. 10,000 To Akash A/c 10,000	3. Received Rs. 10,000 from Akash in full settlement of his accounto f Rs. 10,500 Cash A/c Dr. 10,000 Discount A/c Dr. 500 To Akash A/c 10,500
4. Purchased goods for Rs. 20,000 from X & company A/c Purchases A/c Dr. 20,000 To X & company A/c 20,000	4. Purchased goods for Rs. 20,000 from Z & company and paid Rs. 8,000 only. Purchases A/c Dr 20,000 To Z & company A/c 12,000 To Cash A/c 8,000
5. Sold goods to Adam for Rs. 25,000 Adam A/c Dr. 25,000 To Sales A/c 25,000	5. Sold goods to Adam for Rs. 25,000 and received Rs. 10,000 only Adam A/c Dr. 15,000 Cash A/c Dr. 10,000 To Sals A/c 25,000

Illustration 2

Record journal entries in the books of A Ltd.

Jan. 2007, Opening Balances (Dr) Building 2,00,000, Machinery Rs. 80,000, Furniture Rs.20,000, Debtors Rs. 30,000, Stock Rs. 50,000, Bank Rs. 20,000, Cash Rs. 5,000 (Cr), Capital Rs.3,75,000, Creditors Rs. 25,000, Salaries o/s Rs. 5,000.

Transactions During January, 2007

Jan.		Rs.	Jan.		Rs.
1.	Goods Purchased from X & Co.	15,000	22.	Sold goods to Hari and allowed trade discount 10%	20,000
2.	Goods sold	40,000	25.	Paid for postage	500
3.	Paid to Creditors	5,000	26.	Paid for telephone	1,500
4.	Received from Debtors	18,000	27.	Sold old furniture (Book value Rs. 1,500)	1,200
5.	Goods sold to Ram	5,000			
6.	Goods sold to Shyam	15,000	29.	Paid freight	200
7.	Paid commission	1,000	31.	Paid salasries	12,000
8.	Purchased goods from Y & Co.	25,000	31.	Paid for rent	2,000

9.	Purchased stationery	7,000	31.	Purchased motor cycle for son of proprietor	10,000
10.	Paid Cash to X & company Discount allowed by them	14,800 200	31.	Drawing for Household Expenses	5,000
15.	Received from Shyam	10,000	31.	Deposited in the Bank	13,000
20.	Cash received from Ram in full settlement of Account	4,900			

JOURNAL ENTRIES

Date	Particulars		L.F.	(Dr.) Rs.	(Cr.) Rs.
2007 Jan. 1	Building A/c	Dr.		2,00,000	
	Machinery A/c	Dr.		80,000	
	Furniture A/c	Dr.		20,000	
	Stock A/c	Dr.		50,000	
	Debtors A/c	Dr.		30,000	
	Bank A/c	Dr.		20,000	
	Cash A/c	Dr.		5,000	
	To Creditors A/c				25,000
	To Salaries o/s A/c				5,000
	To Capital A/c				3,75,000
	(Being balances for last year brought foward)				
1	Purchases A/c	Dr.		15,000	
	To X & company (Creditors)				15,000
	(Being goods purchased on credit)				
2	Cash A/c	Dr.		40,000	
	To Sales A/c				40,000
	(Being goods sold for cash)				
3	Credtiors A/c	Dr.		5,000	
	To Cash A/c				5,000
	(Being cash paid to Creditors)				
4	Cash A/c	Dr.		18,000	
	To Debtors A/c				18,000
	(Being cash received from Debtors)				
5	Ram's (Debtors) A/c	Dr.		5,000	
	To Sales A/c				5,000
	(Being goods sold to Ram on Crdit)				

6	Shyam's (Debtors) A/c To Sales A/c (Being goods sold to Shyam on credit	Dr.		15,000	15,000
7	Commission A/c To Cash A/c (Being commission paid)	Dr.		1,000	1,000
8	Purchases A/c To Y & and company (Creditors) (Being goods purchased on credit)	Dr.		25,000	25,000
9	Stationery A/c To Cash A/c (Being stationer purchased)	Dr.		7,000	7,000
10	X & company (Creditors) A/c To Cash A/c To Discount received A/c (Beingcash paid to Ceditors (X & Co.) who allowed discount)	Dr.		15,000	14,800 200
15	Cash A/c To Shyam (Debtor) Being cash received from Shyam)			10,000	10,000
20	Cash A/c Discount Allowed A/c To Ram (Debtor) A/c (Being cash received from Shyam)	Dr. Dr.		4,900 100	5,000
22	Hari's A/c (Debtor) To Sales A/c (Being goods sold at 10% trade discount)	Dr.		18,000	18,000
25	Postage A/c To Cash A/c (Being cash paid for postage)	Dr.		500	500
26	Telephone A/c To Cash A/c (Being telephone bill paid)	Dr.		1,500	1,500
27	Cash A/c P & L A/c (Loss on sale of furntiure) To Furniture A/c (Being old furniture sold at loss)	Dr. Dr.		1,200 300	1,500

29	FreightA/c Dr. To Cash A/c (Being freight paid)		200	200
31	Salaries A/c Dr. To Cash A/c (Being Salaries Paid)		12,000	12,000
31	Rent A/c Dr. To Cash A/c (Being rent paid)		2,000	2,000
31	Drawing A/c Dr. To Cash A/c (Being cash drawn fro purchase of motor cycle for private use)		10,000	10,000
31	Drawing A/c Dr. To Cash A/c (Being drawings made for household expenses)		5,000	5,000
31	Bank A/c Dr. To Cash A/c (Being cash deposited in bank)		13,000	13,000

Ledger : Ledger is the book of analytical record which classifies the business transitions. A ledger is an account of an asset, expense, income, or a person showing a summary of all transactions taken place during a specific period of time. It gives an account-wise result of various transactions recorded in the book of original entry i.e. Journal. Once the transactions are recorded in journal, these are transferred to their respective ledger accounts. This process of transfer entries is known as posting. A ledger is in the form of a register where different accounts are opened on different pages. An index of various accounts is maintained at the beginning of the ledger for the purpose of easy reference. This number is shown in journal also as (L.F.) Ledger Folio. Each and every account maintained in the ledger book is closed by balancing which shows the difference between the totals of debit side and credit side. It provides us the information relating to :

(1) Total sale made on credit basis to an individual (debtor) customer
(2) Total credit purchases made from an individual supplier (creditor)
(3) Amount owed from different individual customers (debtors)
(4) Amount owed to different individual suppliers (creditors)
(5) Book value of each and every asset
(6) Total expenses incurred under different individual heads
(7) Individual incomes received under different heads
(8) Individual items of outstanding or accrued.

The ledger consists of two sides, the debit and the credit, which are shown on left side and right side of the ledger respectively. Each side is divided in to four columns viz. date, particulars, folio (page number) and amount. It may be kept in (i) Bound ledger or (ii) Loose leaf form.

LEDGER FORMAT

Date	Particulars	Folio	Rs.	Date	Particulars	Folio	Rs.

Procedure for Posting to Ledger Account

As discussed earlier posting is the process of transferring the transactions recorded in the Journal to the respective ledger accounts. As we know under double entry system each transaction is transferred in two different ledger accounts, affecting the debit side of one and credit side of the other one. The process can be summarized as follows :

1. Open separate ledger account for posting transactions relating to different accounts. Each item under real, personal or nominal account will have separate ledger account such as Land & Building A/c, Plant & Machinery A/c, Sales A/c, Ram's A/c, Bank A/c, Rent A/c, Salaries A/c etc.
2. Consider each transaction separately for posting purposes such as purchase of goods, sales of goods, receipt from customers, payment to creditors etc.
3. Debit the account in the Ledger book, which has been debited in the journal, and credit the account, which has been credited in the journal. Take the case of salaries paid. In journal, Salaries A/c will be debited and Cash A/c will be credited. In the Ledger, Salaries Account shall be debited and shown as 'To Cash A/c to the debit side and in the cash book it will be shown as 'By Salaries' to the credit side of the cashbook.
4. Write the date of transaction in the "date column" and page number of the journal in the "Folio column".
5. Put the appropriate amount of transaction to the debit or credit side of ledger Account in the "Amount" column as shown below.

JOURNAL FOLIO 12

Date	Particulars		LF	(Dr.) Rs.	(Cr.) Rs.
	Salaries A/c	Dr.	25	12,000	
	To Cash A/c		7		12,000

LEDGER ACCOUNTS

(i) Salaries Acount Folio 25

Dr. Cr.

Date	Particulars	Folio	Rs.	Date	Particulars	Folio	Rs.
Jan. 31	To Cash A/c	12	12,000				

(ii) Cash Account Folio 7

Dr. Cr.

Date	Particulars	Folio	Rs.	Date 2007	Particulars	Folio	Rs.
				Jan. 31	By Salaries	12	12,000

DIFFERENCE BETWEEN JOURNAL AND LEDGER

Journal	Ledger
1. Journal is a book of **original** entry.	1. Ledger is the book of **Second** entry.
2. It is a **Subsidiary** book of accounts.	2. It is a **main** book of accounts.
3. It records daily transactions of business in chronological order.	3. It is updated **periodically** either weekly, fortnightly or monthly.
4. The process of maintaining journal is known as **journalizing.**	4. The process of ledger maintaining is known as **posting.**
5. It is a book of prime entry.	5. It is a book of **final** entry.
6. The unit of classification is a transaction.	6. The unit of classification is an **account**.

Balancing of Ledger Accounts or Closing of Accounts

After posting entries in the relevant accounts, the next step involved in the process is that of balancing or closing of ledger accounts. The following steps should be taken for the purpose :

1. Total both the debit amount column and credit amount column separately.
2. Find out the difference between the two sides if there is no difference, close the account by showing the totals of both the sides, which are equal.
3. If there is an excess of debit side total it is called debit balance, the same must be put to credit side as 'By balance c/d' to make the totals of both sides equal. Conversely if there is an excess of credit side total it is called credit balance, the same must be put to debit side as 'To balance c/d.'
4. Carry forward the balance c/d to the opposite side of the Accounts as balance b/d in the beginning of the following year.

Illustration 3

Form the information given in the illustration 2, prepare (ledger) necessary accounts.

CASH A/C

Date	Particulars	LF	Dr.	Date	Particulars	LF	Dr.
2007			Rs.				Rs.
Jan. 1	To Balance b/d		5,000	Jan. 3	By Credtiors A/c		5,000
2	To Sales A/c		40,000	7	By Commission		1,000
4	To Debtors A/c		18,000	8	By Stationery A/c		7,000
15	To Shyam		10,000	10	By X & Co.		14,800
20	To Ram		4,900	25	By Postage A/c		500
27	To Furniture A/c		1,200	26	By Telephone A/c		1,500

				29	By Freight A/c		200
				31	By Rent A/c		2,000
				31	By Drawings A/c		10,000
				31	By Salaries A/c		12,000
				31	By Drawings A/c		5,000
				31	By Bank A/c		13,000
				31	By Balance c/d		7,100
			79,100				79,100
Feb. 1 To Balance b/d			7,100				

BANK A/C

Date	Particulars	LF	Rs.	Date	Particulars	LF	Rs.
2007				2007			
Jan. 1	To Balance b/d		20,000	Jan. 31	By Balance c/d		33,000
Jan. 31	To Cash A/c		13,000				
			33,000				33,000

PURCHASES A/C

Date	Particulars	LF	Rs.	Date	Particulars	LF	Rs.
2007				2007			
Jan. 2	To X & Co. A/c		15,000				
Jan. 8	To Y & Co. A/c		25,000	Jan. 31	By Balance c/d		40,000
			40,000				40,000

SALES A/C

Date	Particulars	LF	Rs.	Date	Particulars	LF	Rs.
2007				2007			
Jan. 31	To Balance c/d		78,000	Jan 2	By Cash A/c		40,000
				Jan 5	By am		5,000
				Jan 5	By Shyam		15,000
				Jan 22	By Hari		18,000
			78,000				78,000
				Feb. 1	By Balance b/d		78,000

X & CO. A/C

Date	Particulars	LF	Rs.	Date	Particulars	LF	Rs.
2007				2007			
Jan 10	To Cash A/c		14,800	Jan. 1	By Purchases A/c		15,000
	To Discount A/c		200				
			15,000				15,000

Y & CO.'S A/C

Date	Particulars	LF	Rs.	Date	Particulars	LF	Rs.
2007				2007			
Jan. 31	To Balance Transferred to Creditors A/c		25,000	Jan. 8	By Purchase A/c		25,000
			25,000				25,000

CREDITORS' A/C

Date	Particulars	LF	Rs.	Date	Particulars	LF	Rs.
2007				2007			
Jan. 3	To Cash A/c		5,000	Jan. 1	By Balance b/d		25,000
Jan. 31	To Balance c/d		45,000	Jan. 31	By Y & Co. b/d		25,000
			50,000				50,000
				31	By Balance b/d		45,000

RAM'S A/C

Date	Particulars	LF	Rs.	Date	Particulars	LF	Rs.
2007				2007			
Jan. 5	To Sales A/c		5,000	Jan. 20	By Cash A/c		4,900
				Jan. 20	By Discount		100
			5,000				5,000

SHYAM & CO. A/c

Date	Particulars	LF	Rs.	Date	Particulars	LF	Rs.
2007				2007			
Jan. 5	To Sales A/c		15,000	Jan. 5	By Cash A/c		10,000
				Jan. 31	By Balance Transferred to Debtors A/c		5,000
			15,000				15,000

HARI'S A/C

Date	Particulars	LF	Rs.	Date	Particulars	LF	Rs.
2007				2007			
Jan. 22	To Sales A/c		18,000	Jan. 31	By Balance Transferred to Debtors A/c		18,000
			18,000				18,000

DEBTORS' A/C

Date	Particulars	LF	Rs.	Date	Particulars	LF	Rs.
2007				2007			
Jan. 1	To Balance b/d		30,000	Jan. 4	By Cash A/c		18,000
31	To Shyam's A/c		5,000	Jan. 31	By Balance c/d		35,000
31	To Hari's A/c		18,000				
			53,000				53,000
Feb. 1	To Balance b/d		35,000				

FURNITURE A/C

Date	Particulars	LF	Rs.	Date	Particulars	LF	Rs.
2007				2007			
Jan. 1	To Balance b/d		20,000	Jan. 27	By Cash A/c		1,200
				Jan. 31	By Loss on Sale of furniture A/c		300
				Jan. 31	By Balance c/d		18,500
			20,000				20,000

COMMISSION A/C

Date	Particulars	LF	Rs.	Date	Particulars	LF	Rs.
2007				2007			
Jan. 1	To Cash A/c		1,000	Jan. 31	By Balance c/d		1,000
			1,000				1,000
Feb. 1	To Balance b/d		1,000				

STATIONERY A/C

Date	Particulars	LF	Rs.	Date	Particulars	LF	Rs.
2007				2007			
Jan. 8	To Cash A/c		7,000	Jan. 31	By Balance c/d		7,000
			7,000				7,000
Feb. 1	To Balance c/d		7,000				

POSTAGE A/C

Date	Particulars	LF	Rs.	Date	Particulars	LF	Rs.
2007				2007			
Jan. 26	To Cash A/c		500	Jan. 31	By Balance c/d		500
			500				500
Feb. 1	To Balance b/d		500				

TELEPHONE A/C

Date	Particulars	LF	Rs.	Date	Particulars	LF	Rs.
2007				2007			
Jan. 26	To Cash A/c		1,500	Jan. 31	By Balance c/d		1,500
			1,500				1,500
Feb. 1	To Balance b/d		1,500				

FREIGHT A/C

Date	Particulars	LF	Rs.	Date	Particulars	LF	Rs.
2007				2007			
Jan. 29	To Cash A/c		200	Jan. 31	By Balance c/d		200
			200				200
Feb. 1	To Balance b/d		200				

RENT A/C

Date	Particulars	LF	Rs.	Date	Particulars	LF	Rs.
2007				2007			
Jan. 31	To Cash A/c		2,000	Jan. 31	By Balance c/d		2,000
			2,000				2,000
Feb. 1	To Balance b/d		2,000				

DRAWINGS A/C

Date	Particulars	LF	Rs.	Date	Particulars	LF	Rs.
2007				2007			
Jan. 31	To Cash A/c		10,000	Jan. 31	By Balance b/d		15,000
Jan. 31	To Cash A/c		5,000				
			15,000				15,000
Feb. 1			15,000				

SALARIES A/C

Date	Particulars	LF	Rs.	Date	Particulars	LF	Rs.
2007				207			
Jan. 31	To Cash A/c		12,000	Jan. 31	By Balance c/d		12,000
			12,000				12,000
Feb. 1	To Balance b/d		12,000				

BUILDING A/C

Date	Particulars	LF	Rs.	Date	Particulars	LF	Rs.
2007				2007			
Jan. 1	To Balance b/d		2,00,000	Jan. 31	By Balance c/d		2,00,000
			2,00,000				2,00,000
Feb. 1	To Balance b/d		2,00,000				

MACHINERY A/C

Date	Particulars	LF	Rs.	Date	Particulars	LF	Rs.
2007				2007			
Jan. 1	To Balance b/d		80,000	Jan. 31	By Balance A/c		80,000
			80,000				80,000
Feb. 1	To Balance b/d		80,000				

STOCK A/C

Date	Particulars	LF	Rs.	Date	Particulars	LF	Rs.
2007				2007			
Jan. 1	To Balance b/d		50,000	Jan. 31	By Balance c/d		50,000
			50,000				50,000
Feb. 1	To Balance b/d		50,000				

DISCOUNT ALLOWED A/C

Date	Particulars	LF	Rs.	Date	Particulars	LF	Rs.
2007				2007			
Jan. 20	To Ram's A/c		100	Jan. 31	By Balance c/d		100
			100				100
Feb. 1	To Balance b/d		100				

DISCOUNT RECEIVED A/C

Date	Particulars	LF	Rs.	Date	Particulars	LF	Rs.
2007				2007			
Jan. 31	To Balance c/d		200	Jan. 10	By X & Co.		200
			200				200
				Feb. 1	By Balance b/d		200

LOSS ON SALE OF FURNITURE A/C

Date	Particulars	LF	Rs.	Date	Particulars	LF	Rs.
2007				2007			
Jan. 27	To Furniture A/c		300	Jan. 31	By Balance c/d		300
			300				300
Feb. 1	Balance b/d		300				

SALARIES O/S A/C

Date	Particulars	LF	Rs.	Date	Particulars	LF	Rs.
2007				2007			
Jan. 27	To Balance c/d		5,000	Jan. 31	By Balance b/d		5,000
			5,000				5,000
Feb. 1	By Balance b/d		5,000				

Note : Fixed assets accounts are usually closed on the last date of accounting year after charging depreciation, if any. For the sake of clarification and convenience these have been closed on January. 31.

TRIAL BALANCE

Trial Balance is a statement prepared periodically from the balances taken from the different ledger accounts on a particular day so as to verify arithmetical accuracy. Since the entire system of accounting is based on the double entry system, it should have debit and credit totals equal to each other in the absence of any error. Initially, the business transactions are first recorded in the books of original entry (Journal/subsidiary books) and then posted to ledger accounts concerned. At the end of the accounting period these ledger accounts are closed or balanced. A list of these ledger accounts with its debit/credit balance is prepared to make sure that posting has been done correctly. Hence trial balance is not a part of any journal entry or ledger account, it is simply a summary of various debit and credit balances pertaining to all the accounts operated and maintained by a business enterprise. It serves the following objectives :

1. To provide arithmetical accuracy of various ledger accounts.
2. To provide base for preparing final accounts.
3. To provide 'at a glance information' relating to ledger accounts since it gives the net impact of numerous transactions taken place during an accounting period.

Methods of preparing Trial Balance

There are three methods of preparing trial balance :

(1) Total Method (2) Balance Method

(3) Total-cum-Balance or Compound Method.

1. **Under Total Method** debit totals and credit totals of each account are transferred to the trial balance without finding out the difference of the two sides. The excess of debit side over credit side or *vice versa* is automatically adjusted and both the sides tally. For example if the total of debit items of cash account is Rs. 1,25,000 and the total of credit items is Rs. 95,000, these both totals will be shown in the trial balance to their respective side as given below.

TRIAL BALANCE

Particulars	Debit	Credit
Cash	1,25,000	95,000

Thus both the totals of each ledger account will be taken to trial balance to make both the sides, debit and credit, in agreement with each other.

2. **Under Balance Method** the difference of two sides i.e. debit and credit, of each ledger account is taken to the trial balance. The excess of debit total over credit is put to the debit column and the excess of credit total over debit items is put to credit column of the trial balance. Taking the above example of 'cash account' the trial balance will show Rs. 30,000 as debit balance.
3. **Under Third Method** Trial Balance is prepared by taking totals as well as balances from each ledger account.

Illustration 4

Using the information given in the illustration 2 & 3 prepare Trial Balance.

Solution: **TRIAL BALANCE AS ON JANUARY 31, 2007**

Particulars	(Dr.) Rs.	(Cr.) Rs.
Cash	7,100	
Bank	33,000	
Purchases	40,000	
Stock	50,000	
Sales	...	78,000
Debtors	35,000	
Creditors	...	45,000
Furniture	18,500	
Loss on sale of furniture	300	
Commission	1,000	
Stationery	7,000	
Postage	500	
Telephone	1,500	
Freight	200	
Rent	2,000	
Drawings	15,000	
Salaries	12,000	
Discount allowed	100	
Building	2,00,000	
Discount received		200
Machinery	80,000	
Salaries o/s		5,000
Capital		3,75,000
	5,03,200	5,03,200

Problems : 1. Redraft the following Trial Balance after detecting errors.

Particulars	Rs.	Particulars	Rs.
Opening Stock	18,000	S. Creditors	15,000
Fax Machine	31,300	Loan from X	7,000
Debtors	16,000	Capital	25,000
Cash in Hand	600	Sales	1,30,000
Cash at Bank	2,400	Return outward	2,000
Purchases	90,000	Bills payable	8,300
Bad debts	500	Commission paid	700
Return inwards	5,000	Postage	400
Salaries	8,000		
Wages	11,000		
Rent	3,600		
Discount allowed	900		
Discount earned	1,100		
	Rs. 1,88,400		Rs. 1,88,400

2. A Book-keeper has submitted the following Trial Balance for your observation and suggestions and to correct the mistakes to make the Trial Balance agree.

Particulars	Rs.	Particulars	Rs.
Land	60,000	Drawings	4,000
Plant & Machinery	80,000	Insurance premium	800
Office furniture	4,000	S. Creditors	31,000
Office computer	8,000	Sales	2,20,000
Debtors	36,000	Capital	80,000
Purchases	1,00,000	Carriage outward	900
Loan on Mortgage	40,000	Discount allowed	400
Cash in Hand	600	Stock (Opening)	16,300
Cash at Bank	34,000	Rent and Rates	2,400
Bad debts	1,700		
Purchases return	1,600		
Trade expenses	900		
Wages	15,000		
Interest on loan	1,600		
Salaries	3,000		
Factory power	3,600		

Discount received	600		
	3,90,600		3,55,800

Ans. Trial Balance Totals Rs. 3,73,200.

3. Mr. X started business on 1st Jan 2002 with a capital of Rs. 1,20,000, the following is the first trial balance on 31st December, 2002.

Particulars	Rs.	Particulars	Rs.
Computer	32,000	X' Capital	1,20,000
Fax & Telephone	60,000	Sales	2,60,000
Stock	40,000	Creditors	24,000
Purchases	1,60,000	Returns inward	10,000
Salaries	44,800	Bad debts W/o	800
Debtors	40,800	Insurance Premium	1,600
Returns outward	4,000	Travelling expenses	1,000
Stationery	3,000	Sundry expenses	600
Rent and taxes	7,200	Discount received	1,200
Loan from Z	10,000		
Interest on loan from Z	400		
Trade expenses	300		
Cash in Hand	6,10		
Cash at Bank	10,600		
	4,19,200		4,19,200

Read and check the Trial Balance carefully. Make your observations and re-draft the Trial Balance, if necessary.

❑❑❑

4

SUBSIDIARY BOOKS

In order to save time, efforts and avoid inconvenience of classifying transactions for posting purposes, similar types of transactions are recorded in special journals called subsidiary books. This would facilitate not only the division of journal but it would also make easier the job of posting in the ledger as the postings are done in the form of totals being transactions of similar nature. These books are known as books of original entry because transactions are first recorded in these books and later on transferred or posted to respected ledger accounts.

The various subsidiary books are as follows :

1. Cash Book
2. Sales Book
3. Purchases Book
4. Sales Returns Book
5. Purchases Returns Book
6. Bills Receivable Book
7. Bills Payable Book and
8. Journal Proper.

CASH BOOK

It is a book of original entry. It records all cash transactions of receipts and payments in chronological order i.e. as and when these occur. Since numbers of cash transactions are usually large, it would have been an uphill task to classify and post them to their respective ledger accounts had these transactions would have been recorded in the journal proper. Though cashbook is a book of prime entry yet it serves as a Ledger Account. Because cash book is supposed to contain one Account, like any other Ledger A/c, .namely Cash Account. That is why it is treated as a Ledger Account. But the real nature of Cash Book is to make an original entry of cash transactions; it also serves as a Subsidiary Book. However there are four types of Cash Books :

1. Simple Cash Book - with Cash column only (Single column C/B)
2. Cash Book - with cash and discount columns (Two column C/B)
3. Cash Book - with cash, Bank and discount columns (Three column C/B)
4. Petty Cash Book for Petty expenses.

1. Simple Cash Book or Single Column Cash Book

It records all types of receipts and payments whether such receipts or payments are in the form of currency notes, coins, cheques, drafts or postal orders. Its format is exactly like a ledger account. Cash received is recorded in the debit side of cash book and cash payment is entered on the credit side. The Cash Book is balanced after a specific interval on a regular basis. It may be daily, weekly or monthly closing depending upon the frequency of cash transactions. A physical verification should be made, preferably, on daily basis to avoid fraud and embezzlement.

The format of Simple Cash Book is as follows :

CASH BOOK

Date	Particulars	R.No.	LF	Amount	Date	Particulars	V.No.	LF	Amount

R. No. = Receipt No. V. No. = Voucher No.

Illustration 1

Enter the following transactions in Cash Book :

2007 April		Rs.
1	Balance of Cash	4,000
4	Cash Sales	3,000
5	Received from Anand	1,400
7	Paid for Cash Purchases	2,600
9	Sold goods for Cash	1,400
10	Deposited into Bank	1,000
12	Sold goods for Cash	700
15	Bought Stationery	250
20	Withdrew from Bank for office	600
24	Purchased goods	4,000
25	Paid to Kishan	600
30	Paid Salaries	160
30	Cash Sales	1,800
30	Paid Rent	300

CASH BOOK

Dr. Cr.

Date	Particulars	R.No.	LF	Amount	Date	Particulars	V.No.	LF	Amount
2007				Rs.	2007				Rs.
April 1	To Balance b/d			4,000	April 7	By Purchases A/c			2,600
4	To Sales A/c			3,000	10	By Bank A/c			1,000
5	To Anand's A/c			1,400	15	By Stationery A/c			250
9	To Sales A/c			1,400	24	By Purchases A/c			4,000
12	To Sales A/c			700	25	By Kishan's A/c			600
20	To Bank A/c			600	30	By Salaries A/c			160
30	To Sales A/c			1,800	30	By Rent A/c			300
						By Balance c/d			3,990
				12,900					12,900

2. Two Column Cash Book (Cash and Discount Column)

In a business all transactions are not made in cash. There are large number of credit transactions for various reasons especially to push up sales in view of ongoing competition. In order to induce prompt payment of credit sales a special concession is allowed to credit customers, which in accounting terminology, is known as discount. Thus "Cash discount" is an allowance by a creditor to his debtor in consideration of the amount of the debt being paid either immediately or within the specified period as per the terms of credit.

Therefore, a Cash Book must contain each side an additional column for the accounting treatment of discount. A discount column on the 'debit side' of Cash Book represents cash discount allowed and on the "credit side" discount received. These discount columns in the cash book are not balanced but simply added up and posted to the "Discount Allowed" and "Discount Received" Account.

However, it should be noted that "Cash discount" is different from 'Trade discount'. A discount deducted from the "amount due" is known as cash discount whereas discount deducted from the price is treated as 'Trade discount'. Distinction between "Cash Discount" and "Trade Discount" is as follows :

S.No	Trade Discount	Cash Discount
1.	Trade discount is not recorded in the Books of Accounts at all.	It is recorded and shown in the Books of Accounts.
2.	It is allowed by the manufacturers or wholesaler to retailer only.	It is allowed by a creditor to a debtor.
3.	It is deducted from the price.	It is deducted from the amount due.
4.	It is an incentive to enhance sale.	It is an incentive for prompt payment.
5.	Trade discount is unconditional	It is conditional as it is allowed only when payment is made within specified period.
6.	It is adjusted from any goods returned	There is no adjustment for goods returned.
7.	It is calculated at certain percentage on list or catalogue price.	It is calculated on net amount payable.
8.	The trade discount rate is fixed to all retailers.	The cash discount rate varies from case to case depending upon the duration (Time Limit) of payment.

Illustration 2

Enter the following transactions in double column Cash Book :

2007 Jan. 1 Balance of Cash in hand Rs. 18,800

2 Received from Soni Rs. 2,740 and allowed him Rs. 60 as discount

3 Bought furniture for Rs. 1,350

8 Purchased goods for Cash Rs. 19,500

11 Paid Rashmi Rs. 1,200 who allowed a discount of Rs. 120

14 Cash sales Rs. 5,700

16 Paid for Stationery Rs. 225

21 Rao paid Rs. 2,040 in full settlement of the amount due Rs. 2,250

25 An amount Rs. 2,400 received from A. Chopra who was allowed Rs. 120. as discount.

31 Paid Salaries Rs. 1,200

31 Paid Rent Rs. 1,500

31 Paid for Postage stamps Rs. 65.

Two Column Cash Book

CASH BOOK

Dr. Cr.

Date	Particulars	R.No.	LF	Discount	Amount	Date	Particulars	VN	LF	Discount	Amount
2007						2007					
Jan. 1	To Balance b/d				18,800	Jan. 3	By Furniture A/c				1,350
2	To Soni's A/c			60	2,740	8	By Purchases A/c				19,500
14	To Sales A/c				5,700	11	By Rashmi's A/c			120	1,200
21	To Rao's A/c			210	2,040	16	By Stationery A/c				225
25	To A. Chopra's A/c			120	2,400	31	By Salaries A/c				1,200
						31	By Rent A/c				1,500
						31	By Postage Stamps A/c				65
						31	By Balance c/d				6,640
				390	31,680					120	31,680
Feb. 1	To Balance b/d			6,640							

3. Three Column Cash Book (i.e. Cash, Bank and Discount Column)

It has become quite customary to receive and make payments through cheques only. This done to minimise the risk of misappropriation of cash. Now-a-days even Income Tax rules ha\ made it mandatory to make payments to parties exceeding Rs. 20,000 through cheques failing which no deduction shall be allowed in respect of such expenditure. Hence it has become quite common t maintain Triple Column Cash Book.

Method of Maintaining : This cashbook has two balances one representing cash in hand and the other representing Cash at Bank. These balances are shown in the Cash and Bank Column respectively.

All cash or cheques received are entered on debit side of the cash book in the cash column Then these cheques are sent to Bank for collection. However if all cheques are banked same day some parties make payment directly to the Bank — such entries are recorded in 'Bank Column' only

Contra Entries : A transaction affecting both Cash and Book column, is given effect in the Cash Book through contra entry. It happens under three situations.

1. Cash paid into Bank : Whenever money received from parties exceeds the cash balance limit, the excess money is deposited into bank. Thus the amount so deposited is debited to Ban Account by entering the amount in the bank column on the debit side of Cash Book as "To Cash" an credited to Cash Account by entering the amount in the cash column on the credit side of the Cash Book as 'By Bank'. In fact the following entry has to be given effect in Cash Book :

Bank A/c Dr (Bank Column)

To Cash A/c (Cash Column)

(Being Cash deposited to Bank)

2. Cash withdrawn from bank : To meet the day-to-day cash requirements of routine nature and in case of shortfall of cash in hand, money is withdrawn from the Bank for office use. The process of recording is reversed according to following entry.

Cash A/c Dr (Cash Column)

To Bank A/c (Bank Column)

(Being Cash withdrawn for office use)

3. Cheques deposited in to bank : If cheques received are banked immediately same day there shall be no "CONTRA ENTRY". However, if cheques are received one day and sent to bank for collection other day, in such a case 'Contra Entry' shall be recorded. For all other transactions there shall be no contra entry, such as payment made through cheque or cheque deposited is dishonored, or payment made by customer direct to Bank or payment made by the Bank on behalf of the customers. Such transactions require single entry of receipt or payment.

Illustration 3

From the following particulars prepare a Three Column Cash Book.

2007		Rs.
Jan. 1	Cash in Hand	450
	Cash at Bank	21,000
4	Received from Akash	2,970
	Discount Allowed to him	30
5	Purchased goods by cheque	7,500
6	Deposited into Bank	1,500
7	Sold goods to Vimal a on credit	2,100
8	Received from Vimal a cheque and sent to bank for collection same day	21,00
10	Cash Sales	2,000
12	Paid to Mahesh by cheque in full settlement of his Account Rs. 3,000	2,940
14	Purchased goods for Cash	1,200
16	Withdraw from bank for office use	3,000
17	Paid cash to Dinesh	555
	Discount received from him	45
17	Purchased Goods and payment was Made by cheque	2,200
20	Sold goods and received payment by cheque and deposited into Bank A/c	1,500
25	Received from Sanjeev	1,770
	Discount Allowed to him	30
26	Purchased postage stamp	45

28	Deposited into Bank	900
31	Paid rent by cheque	210
31	Paid Telephone charges	180
31	Paid Salary to peon	300

Three Column Cash Book

CASH BOOK

Dr. Cr.

Date	Particulars	F	Discount	Cash Rs.	Bank Rs.	Date	Particulars	F	Discount	Cash Rs.	Bank Rs.
2007						2007					
Jan. 1	To Balance b/d			450	21,000	Jan. 5	By Purchases A/c				7,500
4	To Akash A/c		30	2,970		6	By Bank A/c	C		1,500	
6	To Cash A/c	C			1,500	12	By Mahesh's A/c		60		2,940
8	To Vima's A/c				2,100	14	By Purchases A/c			1,200	
10	To Sales A/c			2,000		16	By Cash A/c	C			3,000
16	To Bank A/c	C		3,000		17	By Dinesh A/c		45	555	
20	To Sales A/c				1,500	17	By Purchases A/c				2,200
25	To Sanjeev's A/c		30	1,770		26	By Postage stamp			45	
28	To Cash A/c	C			900	28	By Bank A/c	C		900	
						31	By Rent A/c				210
						31	By Telephone Charges A/c			180	
						31	By Salary A/c			300	
						31	By Balance c/d			5,510	11,150
			60	10,190	27,000				105	10,190	27,000
Feb. 1	To Balance b/d			5,510	11,150						

Illustration 4

Enter the following transactions in the Cash Book with Three columns :

2007		Rs.
April 1	Commenced Business with cash	1,50,000
2	Incurred opening expenses	5,000
3	Paid into Bank	1,35,000
4	Paid Rakesh by cheque	34,500
	Discount allowed to him	500
6	Bought furniture by cheque	7,000
8	Received cheque from Kamini	33,000
	Discount allowed by her	600
10	Cash Sales	25,000
10	Deposited Kamini's cheque into bank	
11	Deposited into Bank	24,000
12	Cheque purchases	50,500
13	Received commission	1,500

13	Paid freight on goods	850
15	Paid publicity expenses	1,200
17	Withdraw Cash from Bank for office use	5,000
20	Received cheque from Ali	12,500
	Discount allowed to him	500
21	Deposited Ali's cheque into bank	
22	Withdraw for private use	5,000
25	Office expenses	11,250
30	Salaries paid by cheque	5,000
30	Purchased a Computer by cheque	32,000

[B.Com., Madurai – Modified]

THREE COLUMN CASH BOOK

Dr. Cr.

Date	Particulars	F	Discount	Cash Rs.	Bank Rs.	Date	Particulars	F	Discount	Cash Rs.	Bank Rs.
2007						2007					
Jan. 1	To Capital A/c			1,50,000		Jan. 1	By Expenses A/c			5,000	
3	To Cash A/c	C			1,35,000	3	By Bank A/c	C		1,35,000	
8	To Kamini's A/c		600	33,000		4	By Rakesh's A/c		500		34,500
10	To Sales a/c			25,000		6	By Furniture A/c				7,000
10	To Cash A/c	C			33,000	10	By Bank A/c	C		33,000	
11	To Cash A/c	C			24,000	11	By Bank A/c			24,000	
13	To commission			1,500		12	By Purchases A/c				50,000
17	To Bank A/c	C		5,000		13	By Freight A/c			850	
20	To Ali's A/c		500	12,500		15	By Publicity A/c			1,200	
21	To Cash A/c	C			12,500	17	By Cash A/c	C			5,000
						21	By Bank A/c	C		12,500	
						22	By Drawings				5,000
						25	By Office Exp. A/c			11,250	
						30	By Salaries A/c				5000
						30	By Computer A/c				32,000
						30	By Balance c/d			4,200	66,000
			1,100	2,27,000	2,04,500				500	2,27,000	2,04,500

4. Petty Cash Book

In every type of business whether large or small there are numerous small expenses which have to be incurred quite frequently. These expenses relate to stationery, cartage, railway time table, newspapers & magazines, refreshments, telegrams and conveyance etc., are known as petty expenses which can be recorded in the Cash Book at the expense of precious time, efforts of the main cashier who will definitely be overburdened. To avoid inconvenience to cashier and save time, such petty expenses are paid and recorded by petty cashier who works under the supervision of main cashier. The petty cashier maintains petty cash book which is multi-columnar cash book where each expense is recorded in separate column.

Amount received from the cashier is debited in petty cash book and payments are credited. Periodic total of each column is posted to respective ledger account. The petty cash book is treated as book of original entry.

There are two system of petty cash :

1. **Simple petty cash :** Under this method petty cashier is given any specific amount to be spent on petty expenses. Once the amount given is exhausted he submits his petty cash book to chief cashier who verifies and grants further money for the next period. The amount so given as advance may differ from period to period.
2. **Imprest system of petty cash :** Under this system the petty cashier is given a certain sum (fixed Amount) of money in the beginning of a fixed period — it may be monthly or quarterly advance to meet the petty cash requirements. At the end of that fixed period the accounts are checked, verified and again cash equivalent to expenses incurred is reimbursed to him. It means the petty cash book's opening and closing balance remains the same i.e. balance held by petty cashier in the beginning and at the end does not change.

Illustration 5

M/s Dinesh Brothers maintain a columnar Petty Cash Book on imprest system. The petty cashier maintains a monthly imprest balance of Rs. 600. From the following details prepare Petty Cash Book for the month of July 2007.

July 2007		Rs.
1	Opening imprest Balance	600
5	Postage	25
7	Refreshment	65
9	Traveling expenses	35
10	Postage	45
12	Repairs of typewriter	38
15	Refreshment	42
17	Stationery	17
20	Telegram	12
22	Cartage	38
23	Newspaper	42
25	Conveyance	24
27	Stationery	25
30	Telegram	18
31	Postage	19
31	Railway Time Table	14

PETTY CASH BOOK (IMPEREST SYSTEM)

Dr. Cr.

Amount Received	Date	VN	Particulars	Total Paym -ents	Post- age	Refre- shment	Trave -lling	Rep- airs	Stati- onary	Tele- gram	Cart- age	Misce- llanous
Rs.	2007			Rs.	Rs.	Rs.	Rs.	Rs.	Rs.	Rs.	Rs.	Rs.
600	1-Jul		To Balance b/d									
	5		To Postage A/c	25	25							
	7		By Refreshment A/c	65		65						
	9		By Travelling Exp. A/c	35			35					
	10		By Postage A/c	45	45							
	12		By Repairs A/c	38				38				
	15		By Refreshment A/c	42		42						
	17		By Stationary	17					17			
	20		By Telegram	12						12		
	22		By Cartage	39							39	
	23		By Newspapers	42								42
	25		By Conveyance	24			24					
	27		By Stationary	25					25			
	30		By Telegram	18						18		
	31		By Postage	19	19							
	31		By Railway T.T	14								14
				460	89	107	59	38	42	30	39	56
			By Balance c/d	140								
600				600								
140	1-Aug		To Balance b/d	140								
460			To Cash	460								

* Newspapers & Railway Time Table hae been considered under Miscellaneous head.

SALES BOOK

It is also known as "Day Book", "Sales Journal", "Sold Book", "Sales Day Book". It records transactions relating to credit sales of the goods in which the firm deals. Credit sale of any other item other than the "trading goods" will not be recorded in the Sales Book. Thus, a transaction, which is to be recorded in "Day Book", must qualify two tests :

(a) That the transaction relates to sale on credit basis, cash sales to be ignored.

(b) And that the credit sales relate to "goods" in which the business enterprise deals in e.g. if a company is trading in computers their credit sale of computers only shall be recorded in the Day Book.

It should be noted that entries in "Day Book" are recorded only when the credit sale has been made and goods have been sent to customer. Any forward sale the delivery of which is to be made in future will not find place in the Day Book. However, the entries are made with the net amount after allowing for trade discount, if any.

SPECIMEN OF SALES BOOK

Date	Invoice No.	Particulars	Folio	Details (Rs.)	Amount (Rs.)	Remark
2007 Mar. 1		Oxford Industries, Delhi				

Sales Day Book is a book of original entry and hence periodic posting must be completed to ledger accounts concerned either on weekly basis or monthly basis. Credit customer's account is debited with the amount of individual sale and sales ledger is credited with total sales of the period.

Illustration 6

Record the following transactions in the "Sales Book" of M/s A & Co. who deals in readymade garments.

2007

March

1 Sold 50 shirts @ Rs. 250 each to Rahul & Co. Trade discount allowed 10%

5 Sold 40 shirts @ Rs. 200 each to Dinesh Brothers. Trade discount allowed @ 8%

8 Sold for cash 60 shirts @ Rs. 220 each X & Co. Trade discount allowed @ 12.5%

10 Sold 30 shirts @ Rs. 150 each to Ramani & Sons. Trade discount allowed @ 5%

15 Sold old furniture for Rs. 2,500 having a book value of Rs. 3,000

20 Sold on credit to M/s Durgesh Nandini 100 shirts @ Rs. 280 each less trade discount @10%

25 Sold 150 shirts @ Rs. 120 each to Zed Sons

30 Sold 20 shirts @ Rs. 400 each to Mehra Sons less trade discount @ 20%

Solution :

SALES BOOK

Date	Invoice No.	Particulars	Folio	Details Rs.	Rs.	Remarks
2007		M/s Rahul & Co.				
March 1		50 shirts @ Rs. 250 each		12,500	11,250	10 days credit
		Less 10% trade discount		–1,250		
5		M/s Dinesh Brothers				
		40 shirts @ Rs. 200 each		8,000		
		Less 8% discount		–320	7,680	1 week credit
10		M/s Ramani & Sons				
		30 shirts @ Rs. 150 each		4,500		
		Less 5% trade discount		–225	4,275	10 days credit
20		M/s Durgesh Nandini		28,000		
		Less 10% trade discount M/s		–2,800	25,200	12 days credit
25		M/s Zed Sons				
		150 shirts @ Rs. 120 each			18,000	15 days credit
31		M/s Mehra Sons				
		20 shirts @ Rs. 400 each		8,000		
		Less 20% trade discount		–1,600	6,400	3 days credit
					72,805	

M/S RAHUL & CO. A/C

Dr. Cr.

Date	Particulars	F	Rs.	Date	Particulars	F	Rs.
2007							
Mar. 1	To Sales A/c		11,250				

M/S DINESH BROTHERS A/C

Dr. Cr.

Date	Particulars	F	Rs.	Date	Particulars	F	Rs.
2007							
Mar. 5	To Sales A/c		7,680				

M/S RAMANI & SONS A/C

Dr. Cr.

Date	Particulars	F	Rs.	Date	Particulars	F	Rs.
2007							
Mar. 10	To Sales A/c		4,275				

M/S DURGESH NANDINI A/C

Dr. Cr.

Date	Particulars	F	Rs.	Date	Particulars	F	Rs.
2007							
Mar. 20	To Sales A/c		25,200				

M/S ZED SONS A/C

Dr. Cr.

Date	Particulars	F	Rs.	Date	Particulars	F	Rs.
2007							
Mar. 25	To Sales A/c		18,000				

M/S MEHRA SONS A/C

Dr. Cr.

Date	Particulars	F	Rs.	Date	Particulars	F	Rs.
2007							
Mar. 31	To Sales A/c		6,400				

SALES LEDGER A/C

Dr. Cr.

Date	Particulars	F	Rs.	Date	Particulars	F	Rs.
2007				2007			
				Mar. 1	By Sundries		72,805
				Mar. 8	By Cash A/c		11,550

PURCHASE BOOK

It is also known as 'Bought Day Book', 'Purchases Day Book', Purchase Journal or Invoice Book. It maintains the record of transactions relating to goods purchased on credit basis in which the firm deals in, i.e. transactions relating to goods or materials purchased on credit basis for the purpose of resale or conversion in the finished goods are recorded in the Purchases Book. Such entries are posted periodically, say daily, weekly or monthly, to respective ledger's Accounts. For posting purposes purchases account is debited with the total of periodical purchases and individual Supplier A/c is credited with the individual amount of purchases made during the period.

SPECIMEN OF PURCHASES BOOK

Dr. Cr.

Date	Invoice No.	Particulars	Folio	Details (Rs.)	Rs.	Remark

Illustration 7

Enter the following transactions in Purchases Book and post them into Ledger Accounts.

2007

Jan.

1 Purchased on credit from Ambani & Co. 100 shirts @ Rs. 125 each less 5% trade discount.

3 Purchased from Behri Brothers 60 shirts @ Rs. 200 each, trade discount allowed by them 10%

10 Purchased a type writer from Big Brothers for Rs. 5,000

12 Purchased 300 shirts @ Rs. 175 each from Rehman & Co.

15 Purchased 150 shirts @ Rs. 150 each less 20% trade discount

20 Purchased a Computer's Printer for Rs. 2,500

22 Purchased 50 shirts @ Rs. 350 each less 10% trade discount

31 Bought 100 shirts @ Rs. 220 each less 15% trade discount

PURCHASES BOOK

Dr. Cr.

Date	Invoice No.	Particulars	Folio	Details (Rs.)	Rs.	Remark
2007						
Jan. 1		M/s Ambani & Co.				
		100 shirts & Rs. 125 each		12,500		
		Less 5% trade discount		–625	11,875	1 week credit
3		M/s Behri Brothers				
		60 shirts @ Rs. 200 each		12,000		
		Less 10% trade discount		–1,200	10,800	10 days credit
12		M/s Rehman & Co.				
		300 shirts @ Rs. 175 each		52,500	52,500	12 days credit
					75,175	

M/S AMBANI & CO. A/C

Dr. Cr.

Date	Particulars	F	Rs.	Date	Particulars	F	Rs.
				2007			
				Jan. 1	By Purchase A/c		11,875

M/S BEHRI BROTHERS A/C

Dr. Cr.

Date	Particulars	F	Rs.	Date	Particulars	F	Rs.
				2007			
				Jan. 3	By Purchases A/c		10,800

M/S REHMAN & CO. A/C

Dr. Cr.

Date	Particulars	F	Rs.	Date	Particulars	F	Rs.
				2007			
				Jan. 12	By Purchases A/c		52,500

PURCHASES A/C

Dr. Cr.

Date	Particulars	F	Rs.	Date	Particulars	F	Rs.
2007							
Jan. 15	To Cash A/c		18,000				
22	To Cash A/c		15,750				
31	To Cash A/c		18,700				
31	To Sundries A/c		75,175				
			1,27,625				

SALES RETURNS BOOK

It is also known as 'Return Inward Book' or 'Sales Return Journal'. It records the transactions relating to goods returned by credit customers only. Cash sales returns are not entered in this book. On receipt of the goods returned by a customer following procedure is followed :

1. **Preparation of 'Credit Note' :** When the goods are returned by credit customers, the company prepares a credit note in the customer's name. This note mentions that the account of the customer who has returned the goods has been credited with the amount stated therein. The original copy of 'credit note' is sent to the customer concerned and the duplicate copy is retained by the company which provides basis for recording entries in the Sales Returns Book.
2. **Recording of entries in the Sales Returns Book :** It shows the date, Name of the customer and the value of goods returned.
3. **Posting from the Sales Returns Book :** The total value of the goods returned by customers are posted to various ledger accounts concerned periodically.

Illustration 8

From the following transactions prepare Returns Inward Book and post them to respective Ledger accounts.

2007

March 7 Returned by M/s Rahul & Co. 5 shirts @ Rs. 225 each

27 Returned by M/s Durgesh Nandini 10 shirts @ Rs. 252 each

31 Returned by M/s Mehra Sons 2 shirts @ Rs. 320 each

Solution :

RETURNS INWARD BOOK

Date	Credit Note No.	Particulars	L.F.	Rs.	Remarks
2007					
March 7		M/s Rahul & Co.			
		5 shirts @ Rs. 225 each		1,125	
27		M/s Durgesh Nandini		2,520	
		10 shirts @ Rs. 252			
31		M/s Mehra Sons			
		2 shirts @ Rs. 320 each		640	
				4,285	

SALES RETURNS/RETURNS INWARD A/C

Dr. Cr.

Date	Particulars	Folio	Rs.	Date	Particulars	Folio	Rs.
2007							
Mar. 31	To Sundries (Total value of goods returned)		4,285				

M/S RAHUL & CO. A/C

Dr. Cr.

Date	Particulars	Folio	Rs.	Date	Particulars	Folio	Rs.
				2007			
				Mar. 7	By Sales Returns A/c		1,125

M/S DURGESH NANDINI A/C

Dr. Cr.

Date	Particulars	Folio	Rs.	Date	Particulars	Folio	Rs.
				2007			
				Mar. 27	By Sales Returns A/c		2,520

M/S MEHRA SONS A/C

Dr. Cr.

Date	Particulars	Folio	Rs.	Date	Particulars	Folio	Rs.
				2007			
				Mar. 31	By Sales Returns A/c		640

RETURNS OUTWARD & PURCHASES RETURN BOOK

This maintains the record of transactions relating to goods returned to credit suppliers i.e. those goods which were purchased on credit basis earlier now being returned either due to defective quality, inferior quality, excess price charged than the agreed upon or due to excess quantity. The following procedure is adopted on dispatch of goods returned to credit suppliers.

1. **Preparation of 'Debit Note' :** When goods are to be returned to supplier, a 'Debit Note' is prepared and is sent to supplier along with the goods to be returned. The 'Debit Note' contains the date of the return, name of supplier and value of goods returned as well as the reasons for returning goods. The only difference between the format of Purchases Book and Purchases Return's Book is that the former contains the 'Invoice No.' and the latter 'Debit Note' number which is prepared in duplicate. Original is sent to supplier and other is retained for recording purposes.
2. Recording of transactions in the Purchases Returns Book as and when the goods are returned.
3. Posting of entries in the ledger accounts concerned. The original entry shall be :

    Returns Outward A/c Dr

    To Purchases A/c

    (Being goods returned to supplier)

Illustration 9

From the following transactions prepare Returns Outward Book and other necessary Ledger: Accounts.

2007 Jan.	7	Returned 10 shirts @ Rs. 118.75 each to Ambani & Co.
	25	Returned 50 shirts @ Rs. 175 each to Rehman & Co.
	31	Returned to Behri Brothers 6 shirts @ Rs. 180 each

Solution :

RETURNS OUTWARD BOOK

Date	Debit Note No.	Particulars	L.F.	Rs.	Remarks
2007					
7		M/s Ambani & Co. 10 shirts @ Rs. 118.75 each		1,187.50	
25		M/r Rehman & Co. 50 shirts @ Rs. 175 each		8,750.00	
31		M/s Behri Brother 6 shirts @ Rs. 180 each		1,080.00	
				11,017.50	

RETURNS OUTWARD A/C

Dr. Cr.

Date	Particulars	Folio	Rs.	Date	Particulars	Folio	Rs.
				2007			
				Jan. 31	By Sundries (as per Ret. o/w Books)		11,017.50

M/S AMBANI & CO. A/C

Dr. Cr.

Date	Particulars	Folio	Rs.	Date	Particulars	Folio	Rs.
2007							
Jan. 7	To Purchases Returns A/c		1,187.50				

M/S REHMAN & CO. A/C

Dr. Cr.

Date	Particulars	Folio	Rs.	Date	Particulars	Folio	Rs.
2007							
Jan. 25	To Purchases Returns A/c		8,750				

M/S BEHRI BROTHERS A/C

Dr. Cr.

Date	Particulars	Folio	Rs.	Date	Particulars	Folio	Rs.
2007							
Jan. 31	To Purchases Returns A/c		1,080				

BILLS RECEIVABLE BOOK

This book maintains the record of all bills received from credit customers who have promised to make payment in future. It contains all information relating to bills drawn and accepted, the name of customer, amount of the bill, the date of acceptance, the date of maturity, the duration of the bill and the treatment meted out to bills if any. The total of the Bills Receivable Book is taken to 'Bills Receivable A/c' and there from posted to the credit of customers account from whom the bills are received. The specimen of Bills Receivable Book is as under :

SPECIMEN OF BILLS RECEIVABLE BOOK

SI No. of Bill	Date of Receipt	From Whom Received	Name of the Drawer	Name of the Acceptor	Date of Bill	Terms of Bill	Due Date	Where Receivable	LF	Rs.	Remarks

BILLS PAYABLE BOOK

This book records the details of the bills accepted by the firm. The particulars of the Bills Payable Book are almost the same as that of Bills Receivable Book. Once the information relating to bills payable recorded, there from it is posted to the debit of respective creditor's account and the total of the Bills Payable Book is transferred to Bills Payable Account. The format of Bills Payable Book is given below :

SPECIMEN OF BILLS PAYABLE BOOK

SI No. of Bill	Date of Receipt	Name of Drawer	Name of the Payee	Terms	Due Date	Where Payable	Rs.	LF	How Met	Remarks

Illustration 10

From the following particulars prepare Bills Receivable & Bills Payable Books.

2007

Jan. 2	A Bill of Rs. 2,100 was drawn by Anil at 2 months.
6	Drew a bill on Raman at 3 months for Rs. 1,500.
10	Accepted a bill of Rs. 2,250 at 3 months drawn by Bhanu.
15	Accepted a bill at 3 months for 1,500 drawn by Chaman Lal.
20	Bill for Rs. 1,200 at 2 months drawn on Manoj which was duly accepted by him.
25	Ramesh drew a bill at 3 months for Rs. 3,000 which is duly accepted.
30	Somesh gave his acceptance at 4 months bill for Rs. 3,000

Solution :

BILLS RECEIVABLE BOOK

SI No. of Bill	Date of Receipt	From Whom Received	Name of the Drawer	Name of the Acceptor	Dae of Bill	Terms of Bill	Due Date	Where Receivable	LF	Rs.	Remarks
	2007				2007		2007				
1	6-Jan	Raman		Raman	6-Jan	3 months	9-Apr			1,500	
2	20-Jan	Manoj		Manoj	20-Jan	2 months	23-Mar			1,200	
3	30-Jan	Samesh		Samesh	30-Jan	4 months	2-Jun			3,000	
										5,700	

BILLS PAYABLE BOOK

SI No. of Bill	Date of Receipt	Name Drawer	Name of the Payee	Terms	Due Date	Where Payable	Rs.	LF	How Met	Remarks
	2007				2007					
1	2-Jan	Anil		2 months	5-Apr		2,100			
2	10-Jan	Bhanu		3 months	13-Apr		2,250			
3	15-Jan	Chamanlal		3 months	18-Apr		1,500			
4	25-Jan	Ramesh		3 months	28-Apr		3,000			
							8,850			

JOURNAL PROPER

Recording of daily business transactions only in one book that is in "General journal" creates lot of problems of classification and proper posting especially when the number of daily transactions is very large. Therefore, for the sake of convenience, simplicity and to save time the transactions are recorded in various subsidiary books. However there remains various other types of transactions which do not find a place in any of the subsidiary books. Thus, journal proper is a book of original entry that records residuary transactions. Broadly speaking, the journal proper is used to record the following types of entries :

1. Opening entries
2. Closing entries
3. Adjusting entries
4. Transfer entries
5. Rectification entries
6. Other residuary entries

1. Opening Entries

Opening entries are recorded for opening accounts in the beginning of a financial year. That is when the balances of various assets and liabilities pertaining to last accounting year are brought forward in the beginning of the current accounting year by recording journal entry in the books, such an entry is known as opening entry. Since each year's accounts are closed at the end of accounting year and most of these accounts show a balance. These balances are shown in the Balance Sheet and represent assets, or liabilities and capital. Such balances become the opening balances of the new financial year.

Illustration 11

Record the opening entry in the books of Adnan & Co. Land and Building Rs. 5,00,000, Plant and Machinery Rs. 1,50,000, Furniture Rs. 50,000, Stock Rs. 60,000, Debtors Rs. 40,000, Bank Rs.35,000, Cash in hand Rs. 5,000, Bills payable Rs. 15,000, S. Creditors, Rs. 65,000, Short Term Investments Rs. 75,000, Outstanding Salaries Rs. 5,000.

Solution : **JOURNAL**

Date	Particulars		LF	Amount (Dr.)	Amount (Cr.)
2007 Jan.	Land and Building A/c	Dr		5,00,000	
	Plant and Machinery A/c	Dr		1,50,000	
	Furniture A/c	Dr		50,000	
	Stock A/c	Dr		60,000	
	Debtors A/c	Dr		40,000	
	Short Term Investment A/c	Dr		75,000	
	Bank A/c	Dr		35,000	
	Cash A/c	Dr		5,000	
	To S. Creditors				65,000
	To Bills payable				15,000
	To Outstanding Salaries				5,000
	To Capital				8,30,000
	(Being balances brought forward from last year)				

2. Closing Entries

For the purpose of ascertaining the profits or losses the items of revenue receipts and revenue expenditures are transferred to income statement or Profit & Loss account which is debited with the debit items and credited with credit items. Such entries are known as closing entries.

1. Trading A/c Dr
   To Opening Stock
   To Purchases
   To Direct expenses*
   *Productive wages, Freight, carriage inward etc.
   (Being balances of above accounts transferred to Trading A/c)
2. Sales A/c Dr
   Closing Stock A/c Dr
   To Trading A/c
   (Being credit items transferred to Trading A/c)
3. Trading A/c Dr
   To Profit and Loss A/c
   (Being gross profit transferred)
4. Profit & Loss A/c Dr.
   To Indirect Expenses **
   **(Salaries, rent, other office expenses, selling and distribution expenses etc.)
   (Being indirect expenses transferred to P & L A/c)

5. Rent Received A/c Dr.
   Interest Received A/c Dr.
   Discount Received A/c Dr.
   To Profit & Loss A/c
   (Being non-operating incomes transferred to Profit & Loss A/c)
6. Profit & Loss A/c Dr
   To Capital A/c***
   (Being profit transferred to Capital A/c)
   ***In case of Loss Capital A/c will be debited.

3. Adjustment Entries

Under mercantile system, accounting policies and practices strictly require companies to follow accounting period concept i.e. preparation of final accounts periodically covering a specific period. For this purpose it is necessary to recognise revenue and expenses pertaining to accounting period, whether such expenses are paid or not and incomes received or not. Thus the matching of revenues and expenses for the purpose of determining the net income, the accrued incomes and outstanding expenses must be accounted for. That is why adjustment entries must be made for depreciation, bad debts and accruals to calculate correct profit and losses and to ascertain true financial position of business.

Examples :

1.	Salaries outstanding :	Salary A/c	Dr
		To Salary o/s A/c	
2.	Prepaid Insurance Premium :	Prepaid Insurance A/c	Dr
		To Insurance Premium A/c	
3.	Accrued Interest :	Interest A/c	Dr
		To Accrued Interest A/c	
4.	Bad debts :	Bad debts A/c	Dr
		To Debtors A/c	
5.	Depreciation :	Depreciation A/c	Dr
		To Asset A/c	
6.	Closing Stock :	Closing Stock A/c	Dr
		To Trading A/c	

The transactions and events which have not been accounted for so far up to the Trial Balance but the information is given in the 'adjustments' such as interest on Capital, Interest on drawings, Goods lost by fire or accident and even rectified entries are also treated as "adjusting entries".

4. Transfer Entries

When certain sum of money is transferred from one account to other account through journal entries such entries are known as transfer entries. If it is in the nature of appropriation then Profit and Loss Appropriation A/c is debited and account concerned is credited.

Transfer to General Reserve, Reserve fund, Dividend Equalisation fund, Sinking fund, Capital redemption reserve, charging of drawings to Capital etc. are in the nature of appropriations.

1.	Transfer to any specific head	P & L Appropriation A/c	Dr
		To Specific Head A/c	
2.	Drawings	Capital A/c	Dr
		To Drawings A/c	

Whenever any transfer is made out of Profit and Loss Account which is in the nature of charge, then Profit & Loss Account is debited and concerned account is credited. For creating Provision for doubtful debts, Provision for legal damages, Provision for repairs, Provision for discount on debtors etc., following entries shall be recorded.

P& L A/c Dr
To Provision for Doubtful Debts
To Provision for Legal damages
To Provision for Repairs
To Provision for Discount on Debtors

5. Rectification Entries

When an error is committed in recording the original entry it is corrected by passing another entry which is known as rectification entry.

For example :

1. A sum of Rs. 500 received from Z credited to Y's A/c

Y's A/c	Dr	500	
To Z's A/c			500

2. Purchase of stationery for office Rs. 1,000 recorded in the Purchases Day Book.

Stationery A/c	Dr	1,000	
To Purchases A/c			1,000

3. A Sale of Rs. 5,000 made to X & Co. entered in the Purchases Book

Z's A/c	Dr	10,000	
To Sales A/c			5,000
To Purchases A/c			5,000

6. Other Entries

If there are other entries which have not been recorded in any other book of original entry, it is recorded in journal proper.

QUESTIONS

1. What is a Journal? Why is it called book of original entry. Give its ruling.
2. "Ledger is the principal book of accounts", do you agree?
3. Explain the procedure of passing entries in the Journal.
4. What is a ledger? Distinguish it from Journal.
5. Narrate the uses of "Folioing" in Journal and Ledger.
6. Define ledger and explain the procedure of posting.
7. Explain the rules governing the process of journalising.

PROBLEMS

1. Journalise the following transactions :

On 1st January 2007, a trader started business with a capital of Rs. 2,00,000. During the month of January following transactions took place :

				Rs.
Jan. 1	Deposited in to Bank			1,30,000
3	Purchased a computer and issued a cheque			56,000
5	Bought furniture worth			15,000
7	Bought goods from X & Co.			15,000
8	Cash Purchases			10,000
9	Cash Sales			12,000
10	Goods sold to	Rama & Co		5,000
		Shyama & Co		7,500
		Co-operative Store		6,000
12	Paid for stationery			1,550
15	Paid to X & Co. in full settlement			14,80
17	Received from Ram & Co. in full settlement.			4,900
18	Received from Shyama & Co.			7,500
20	Purchased goods from Ambani Sons			25,000
21	Sold goods to Zhaveri Sons for			18,000
22	Received cash from Co-operative Store Rs. 5,900, discount allowed		100	
23	Paid Sundry expenses			500
25	Paid to Ambani Sons by cheque			17,000
26	Received Bill receivable from Zhaveri Sons for Rs. 8,000 and cash			10,000
27	Purchased Fax machine by cheque			22,500
31	Paid :	Electricity Charges		500
		Salaries		12,800
		Shop Rent		4,200

2. Record Entries in the Books of Universal Stores for the month of March 2007 during which following transactions took place.

2007		Rs.
March 1	Started business with a capital	1,50,000
2	Bought furniture	10,000
3	Purchased goods	20,000
5	Sold goods for cash	15,000
6	Sold goods to Universal Agencies	1,20,000
8	Purchased goods from Ambika Sons	35,000
10	Goods returned to Ambika Sons	2,000
12	Paid postage and telegram charges	650
15	Paid Ambika Sons half the amount due and availed cash discount 2%	

March 15	Accepted bill of the remaining amount of 1 month duration from Ambika Sons.
17	Purchased stationery worth Rs. 2,750 from Mohan Lal on credit
20	Made credit purchases for Rs. 15,000
22	Made credit sales at 10% trade discount and 2% cash discount to X Rs. 1,500, Y Rs. 2,750 and Z Rs. 3,750
25	Purchased a Computer for office work for Rs. 70,000
30	Purchased an old van for distribution of goods Rs. 23,000 and spent Rs. 7,000 for its haulage and repairs
31	Rent due but not paid Rs. 5,000; Salaries paid Rs. 6,500 and due but not paid Rs. 3,500
31	Deposited in a Bank Account leaving a cash balance of Rs. 2,500.

3. Journalise the following transactions, post them in to Ledger Account and prepare a Trial Balance.

2002		Rs.
April 1	Commenced business with an initial capital	2,50,000
2	Deposited in newly opened Bank A/c	1,00,000
3	Bought Computer	75,000
4	Purchased furniture	25,000
5	Purchased goods from Mehra Sons	70,000
7	Sold goods for Cash	40,000
10	Purchased goods	30,000
12	Sold goods to Green Brothers	25,000
13	Sold goods to White Brothers	18,000
15	Paid to Mehra Sons	50,000
17	Received from Green Brothers	24,500
	Discount allowed	500
18	Bought a fax machine (by cheque)	27,500
19	Purchased goods from Mehra Sons	32,500
22	Goods returned by White Brothers	1,000
25	Cheque received from White Brothers and the same was paid in the Bank A/c	7,000
26	Purchased goods from Husain Sons	12,500
27	Sold goods to Anil & Co.	17,500
30	Issued cheque to Ramesh the landlord for rent	3,000
30	Paid : Salaries to staff	7,500
	Salesman Commission	6,000
	Stationery	225
	Postage	250
30	Withdrawn for household expenses	5,000

4. Journalise the following transactions in the Books of A & Co.

Jan. 1, 2007

Debit Balances : Building Rs. 4,50,000, Furniture Rs. 4,20,000, Stock Rs. 1,00,000, Computer Rs. 75,000, Bank Balance Rs. 53,000, Debtors Rs. 40,500, Cash Rs. 40,000 (debtors include Anand Rs. 13,500, Amresh Rs. 7,500, Satya Rs. 10,000, Jaggi Rs. 9,500).

Credit Balances : Creditors Rs. 91,500, B's Loan A/c Rs. 50,000 (Creditors include Ramesh Rs. 27,000, X & Co. Rs. 38,500, Big Brothers Rs. 26,000).

During the month of January 2002 following transactions took place

2007 Jan. 2	Purchased goods for Rs. 25,000 less 20% trade discount and 5% cash discount
4	Received from Anand Rs. 13,225 in full settlement of his account
6	Goods worth Rs. 2,500 were fully damaged in transit, a claim was made on the carrier of goods Z Transporters.
7	Paid Ramesh Rs. 26,500 in full settlement of his account
10	Satya became insolvent and dividend of 50 paise in a rupee was received in full settlement of her account.
12	Bought a van for Rs. 25,000 for delivering goods to customers I
14	Bought 300 units of UTI US-64 scheme @ Rs. 14 per unit, the payment was made by cheque,
16	Sold goods worth Rs. 29,500 less trade discount @ 10%
20	Purchased stationery for Rs. 1,500
22	Paid for Commission Rs. 1,550, Postage 450, Repairs 650
25	Purchased a cooler for office Rs. 3,000 and for the house Rs. 2,500
30	Paid salaries Rs. 5,000, Rent of shop Rs. 4,500
30	Paid Insurance Premium for the year 2002 Rs. 4,200

5. Record Journal entries to make the following adjustments as on 31st March 2007.

1. Interest on capital @ 5% p.a. is to be allowed on the initial capital of Rs. 2,50,000
2. Insurance premium has been paid for the year ending on 30th June 2002 next Rs. 6,000
3. Telephone rent for one year was paid on 1st July 2001 Rs. 2,000
4. Charge depreciation @ 10% p.a. on Machinery Rs. 50,000, on computer @ 15% p.a. Rs.1,00,000 on Furniture @ 20% p.a. Rs. 15,000.
5. Provide for outstanding expenses :

	Rs.
Salaries	12,000
Water	1,000
Office expenses	5,000
Selling expenses	8,000

6. Record one Journal Entry for each of the following :

(i) Acquired a running business for Rs. 3,50,000 by cheque. The following assets & liabilities were taken over. Computer Rs. 6,500, Stock Rs. 1,20,000, Furniture Rs. 35,000, Debtors Rs. 56,000, Machinery Rs. 83,000, Creditors Rs. 25,000.

(ii) Bought goods from Green Grocers for Rs. 50,000 at 20% trade discount and 2% cash discount and paid half the amount in cash,

(iii) A new machine costing Rs. 50,000 was purchased in exchange for old machine (W.D.V.20,000) valued at Rs. 15,000.

(iv) Goods worth Rs. 2,500 were destroyed during transit. A claim was admitted by the carrier for Rs. 1,400. The goods were fully insured and hence balance was made good by Insurance Company,

(v) Sold the car used for private purposes for Rs. 85,000 and the amount was invested in the business.

7. (i) To clear overdraft of Rs. 50,000 a 10% short-term loan was arranged from the bank Rs. 40,000. However the overdraft was paid off.

(ii) Goods worth Rs. 1,500 used as samples and worth Rs. 2,000 taken by the employees and worth Rs. 5,000 for self-consumption.

(iii) Insurance company paid a claim of Rs. 4,500 only for goods destroyed by fire worth Rs. 7,000.

(iv) Received Rs. 4,200 in cash, a bill receivable or Rs. 3,500 in full settlement of Mohan's account of Rs. 8,000 being the amount due on account of credit sale,

(v) A cheque of Rs. 2,500 was received from a credit customer whose account was written off last year,

(vi) Cashed a Bill receivable of Rs. 2,000 of 3 months duration at 6% discount.

"SUBSIDIARY BOOKS"

1. From the following information prepare 'Sales Day Book' and 'Sales Returns Book' :

2007		Rs.
Oct. 1	Sold goods to Moderm Agencies	17,500
3	Sold goods for Cash	3,750
5	Sold goods to Remington Ltd.	7,500
7	Goods returned by Modern Agencies	1,250
10	Sold goods to Mani Ram Sons	17,500
12	Sold goods to Sushma Stores who sent the cheque immediately	3,500
15	Mani Ram Sons returned the defective goods	3,625
17	Goods sold to Pawan Stores	3,750
20	Pawan Stores informed of short supply which was acknowledged through credit note	625
22	Goods sold to Rama Krishnan	6,250
25	Sold goods to Modern Agencies	8,750
27	Goods returned by Rama Krishnan	1,875
31	Sold goods to Shivani Stores	7,500
31	Sold goods for cash	12,500

Ans. Total of Sales Book Rs. 70,000, Total of Sales Return Book Rs. 7,375.

2. From the following particulars prepare "Purchases Book" and "Purchases Returns Book" :

2007		Rs.
Jan.1	Purchased goods from Jeevan Sons	15,000
3	Goods Purchased from Sonali Stores	7,500
5	Purchased goods for cash from Akash Sons	5,250
7	Goods returned to Jeevan Sons	4,500
10	Invoice of Sonali Stores was found over charged and a debit note was sent to them which was acknowledged	405
13	Purchased goods from Mahajan Stores	10,500
14	Cheque sent to Mahajan Stores	7,500
15	Cheque sent to Jeevan Sons	11,000
17	Bought goods from Ved Kumar Sons	13,500
19	Returned defective goods to Ved Kumar Sons	1,050
23	Goods sold to Prabhakar & Co	37,500
25	Cash Sale	55,000
28	Cash paid to Sonali Stores	7,095
30	Cheque sent to Ved Kumar Sons	7,500

Ans. Purchases Book: Rs. 57,750

Purchases Returns Book: Rs. 5,955

3. Enter the following transactions is proper Subsidiary Books :

2007	
Sept. 1	Purchased goods from Arvind Mills for Rs. 3,200 less 20% trade discount
3	Purchased goods from Bansi Stores for Rs. 2,800 less 20% trade discount
5	Returned goods to Arvind Mills worth Rs. 400
7	Goods returned to Bansi Stores worth Rs. 320.
10	Goods sold to Chandni Stores for Rs. 2,000 less 10% trade discount
13	Goods returned by Chandni Stores Rs. 400
15	David Sons purchased goods from us for Rs. 1,200 less trade discount @ 10%
17	Goods returned by David Sons worth Rs. 200
20	Elite Brothers sold us goods worth Rs. 1,200
25	Famous Agencies purchased goods from us Rs. 600
30	Purchased goods from Ghan Shyam & Co. for Rs. 600 less 20% trade discount s
30	Goods returned to Ghan Shyam & Co. worth Rs. 200

Ans. Purchases Book Rs. 6,480; Purchases Returns Book Rs. 736 Sales Book Rs. 3,480; Sales Returns Book Rs. 540

4. Record the following transactions in proper Subsidiary Books, post them to ledger and prepare the trial balance.

2007		Rs.
April 1	Goods sold to Ramesh & Co. at 10% trade discount	15,000
2	Bought goods from Karim Sons at 20% trade discount	9,000
3	Goods sold to Naresh Agencies	3,000
5	Purchased goods from Man Mohan Stores at 15% trade discount	6,000
8	Goods returned by Ramesh & Co	1,500
10	Bought goods from Gharib Das & Co.	5,100
12	Goods returned to Karim Sons	900
15	Goods sold to Naresh Agencies at 10% trade discount	4,500
16	Purchases made from Karim Sons	3,000
19	Naresh Agencies returned goods	900
21	Goods returned to Karim Sons	300
25	Maheshwari Brothers sold goods to us	1,200
30	Goods sold to Naresh Agencies at 10% trade discount	1,500
30	Goods returned to Maheshwari Brothers	120

Ans. Trial Balance Total 43,500

5. Enter the following transactions in a Two column Cash Book :

2007		Rs.
March 1	Opening balance of cash	15,750
2	Purchased furniture	14,000
3	Received cash from Ambani & Co	2,000
5	Cash paid to Sunil Sons Rs. 2,750 discount allowed by them	100
7	Received from Rahim Sons	1,350
	Discount allowed to them	50

10	Paid into Bank	8,700
15	Cash sales	12,500
18	Stationery purchased	250
20	Paid to S. Ray & Co.	4,900
	Discount allowed	100
25	Cash received from Rahim Sons	1,900
	Discount allowed	100
28	Paid wages	3,000
30	Paid salaries	4,750
31	Purchased Computer for office	50,000

Ans. Dr. Balance Rs. 10,850

6. Enter the following transactions in three column Cash Book :

2007		Rs.
April 1	Cash in hand	2,800
	Cash at Bank	3,600
2	Received cash from Pawan Agencies	3,160
	Discount allowed	40
3	Paid in to Bank account	3,200
5	Paid to Lal Sons Rs. 2700 in full settlement of their account for	2,800
7	Cash sales	3,600
10	Purchased goods and paid by cheque	2,000
12	Deposited into Bank	2,400
15	Received a cheque from Manohar Sons which was sent to Bank for collection	1,600
16	Received cash from Rana Agencies	2,780
	Discount allowed	20
April 18	Sharma Corporation purchased goods from us and sent a cheque for the same which was deposited in the Bank Account same day	4,000
20	Cash Sales	3,600
20	Cash purchases	2,800
25	Purchased stationery & paid by cheque	600
27	Withdrawn from Bank for office use	2,000
28	Paid for rent in cash	2,180
30	Paid to Soni Brothers by cheque	2,600
	Discount allowed by them	80

Ans. Bank Balance (Dr) 4,900; Discount (Dr) 60 Cash Balance (Dr) 4,660; Discount (Cr) 180

7. From the following particulars prepare a Cash Book for the month of March 2000 after taking in to account the following points :

(a) Cheques are received and deposited the same day.

(b) If the cash in hand on any day is less then Rs. 1000, necessary amount should be withdrawn from the bank to maintain the minimum cash in hand of Rs. 1000 and if the cash in hand at any day is more than Rs.2000, the excess should be deposited into bank.

2007		Rs.
March 1	Cash in hand	1,500
	Cash at bank	25,000
2	Cash sales made to A.K. Sons and received cash	1,000
	and a cheque of	5,000
3	Satyam corporation were paid cash Rs. 500 and by cheque	2,000
4	Money paid to land lord for rent by cheque	1,000
	and cash	1,500
5	Received from Atam Sons Cash	3,500
	and a cheque of	1,000
10	Paid in Cash for office expenses	1,000
15	Withdrew from Bank for personal use	750
	Took from office cash	500
20	Cash sales	500
22	Sold goods to A.K.Raman who paid into our Bank account immediately	1,000
23	Drew from Bank Rs. 500 and from office cash	1,250
25	ABC Corporation cleared their dues and paid us cash	2,500
	By cheque	5,000
25	Cash Sales	500
25	Carriage outward paid in Cash	250
30	Cash Sales	1,000
30	Paid Telephone Bill by cheque	500
30	Paid Salaries in cash	1,750

Ans. Cash Balance Rs. 1,250, Bank Balance Rs. 31,750

8. Mr Ram operates two Bank Accounts which are maintained in the columnar Cash Book you are required to draw up a proforma of the Cash Book and record therein the following transactions relating to February and close the Cash Book.

2007		Rs.
Feb.1	Cash in hand	150
	National Bank (Overdraft)	11,240
	Overseas Bank	35,460

2 Received cheque for Rs. 1,250 in respect of sales, for realising of which the National Bank charged Rs. 12 and credited the balance.

5 Purchased goods for Rs. 13,210 and a cheque issued on Overseas Bank. The Bank charged Rs. 13 for collection of cheque to the concerned party.

7 Paid Rs. 45 and Rs. 16 for office expenses and stationery respectively

10 Out of cash sales of Rs. 13,265 a sum of Rs. 10,000 deposited in the National Bank

12 Withdrew Rs. 5,000 from the Overseas Bank

15 A purchase of Rs. 15,000 made from Mr Martin who sent the documents relating to goods through the Overseas Bank for 90% of their value. The Bank charged Rs. 115 for realising documents.

15 A Bill Receivable for Rs. 10,000 was discounted with the Overseas Bank which charged 1% for discounting.

19 Deposited Rs. 5,000 in National Bank

21 A demand draft was purchased for Rs. 3,000 from a Bank after paying Rs. 2 towards their charges and paid to the Electricity Department as deposit.

25 An amount of Rs. 1,500 was withdrawn from the Overseas Bank and paid salaries

27 Manager's salary Rs. 1,000 was paid by cheque drawn on National Bank

28 Interest of Rs. 122 and Rs. 50 was credited and debited respectively by Overseas Bank and National Bank.

29 Overseas Bank collected dividends of Rs. 1,250 and sent a credit note

29 An amount of Rs. 1,500 was transferred from Overseas Bank to National Bank.

Ans. Cash in hand Rs. 352, Cash at National Bank Rs. 5,448, Cash at Overseas Bank Rs. 11,907.

Unit-II

5 FINAL ACCOUNTS (FINANCIAL STATEMENTS) OF TRADING AND MANUFACTURING ORGANISATIONS

The first and foremost objective of accounting is to determine profit or loss made by business concern during any accounting period and to ascertain financial position as on a given date. This can be done by preparing final accounts or financial statements, which includes Manufacturing Account, Trading Account, Profit and Loss Account and the Balance Sheet. The Trial Balance, discussed earlier, provides the necessary base (input) for the preparation of these accounts or statements. These statements provide necessary information to various interested groups viz. shareholders, investors, creditors, employees, management and government agencies etc. Therefore, these financial statements are prepared to serve the information needs of these diverse groups to enable them to make appropriate decisions.

TRADING ACCOUNT

Trading Account is prepared to know the result of trading operation. It shows the gross profit or gross loss arising from buying and selling of goods or/and services in which the business deals in; Gross profit or gross loss is the difference between 'sales' and 'cost of goods sold'. The 'total sales' for any given period are taken from Sales Account whereas 'cost of goods sold' is worked out as under :

Opening Stock	....
Add Purchases made during the period covered	....
Less Return, if any	....
Less Closing stock	....
Add Direct expenses*	....
Cost of goods sold	....

*Direct expenses are those expenses which are incurred by the trader in connection with purchases and procurement of goods and bringing them up to the point of sale. These include freight, carriage inward, octroi, transit-insurance, excise duty, loading charges, import duty, wages, royalty, coal, gas, fuel, power and water etc.

The Trading Account helps in ascertaining the operating efficiency of the concern under normal conditions only. Thus abnormal loss, if any, such as loss due to fire, accident etc., are totally credited to Trading Account. The format of Trading Account is given as under.

TRADING ACCOUNT
For the year ended 31st December 2008 ...

Dr. Cr.

	Particulars	Rs.		Particulars	Rs.
To	Opening Stock	......	By	Sales	......
To	Purchased Less Returns	......		Les Returns	......
To	Direct Expenses :	......	By	Abnormal Loss :	......
	Carriage/Cartage Inward	......		Loss by fire	......
	Freight	......		Loss by accident	......
	Insurance-in-Transit	......		Loss by theft	......
	Wages	......	By	Closing Stock	......
	*Fuel & Power	......	By	Gross Loss c/d	......
	*Coal, gas, water	......		**(Balancing figure)	......
	Packing (essential)	......			
	Import duty, Octroi	......			
	Custom duty	......			
	*Consumable Stores	......			
	Royalty (output)	......			
	*Manufacturing expenses	......			
	*Excise duty	......			
	Dock dues	......			
To	Gross Profit c/d	......			
	**(Balancing figure)	......			
		Total			Total

*Concerns not preparing Manufacturing Account seperately.

**Balancing figure will be either gross profit or gross loss.

Trading account helps to determine the sales policy, price policy and gross profit margin to sales. A comparative study over the years will pinpoint the defects or effectiveness of trading policy. It also helps to determine the optimum level of stock of goods.

Analysis of items appearing to the debit side of Trading Account

1. **Opening Stock :** It refers to the value of goods at hand at the end of last accounting year. It becomes the opening stock for the current accounting year. It contains the value of goods in which business deals in.
2. **Purchases :** It denotes the value of goods (in which the concern deals in) purchased either for cash or on credit for the purpose of resale. However, if the goods so purchased are returned 06 used by proprietor for self-consumption or distributed as free samples or taken up by the employees for their use or given as charity or to be sent on consignment or used for any other purpose except for resale, such amounts shall be deducted from the total purchases.

3. **Direct Expenses :** These expenses are incurred in connection with purchase, procurement or production of goods. It also includes expenses, which bring the goods upto the point of sale as shown in Trading Account (Format) above.

Analysis of items appearing to the Credit side of Trading Account

1. **Sales :** It refers to the sale of goods in which the business deals in and includes both cash and credit sales. It does not include sale of old, obsolete or depreciated assets, which were acquired for use in business. Further, goods returned by customers or goods sent to customers on approval basis VAT or sales tax, if any, included in the sales price should be excluded.
2. **Abnormal Loss :** It refers to abnormal loss of stock due to fire, theft or accident. Since Trading Account is prepared under normal conditions of the business, abnormal loss if any is credited fully to the Trading Account.
3. **Closing Stock :** It refers to the value of goods lying unsold at the end of any accounting year. The stock at the end is valued either at cost or market price whichever is Less. Since Trial Balance generally does not include closing stock, the following entry is recorded to incorporate the effect of closing stock in the Trading Account.

   Closing Stock A/c Dr

   To Trading A/c

   However, if closing stock forms the part of Trial Balance, it will not be transferred to Trading Account but taken to Balance Sheet only.

   In case the goods have been sent to customers on approval (Sale/Return) basis, such goods should be included in the value of closing stock.

Illustration 1

From the following particulars ascertain Cost of goods sold, Gross Profit and prepare Trading Account for the year ending 31st December 2007.

	Rs.		Rs.
Opening Stock	30,000	Office Expenses	5,000
Purchases	2,70,000	Octroi	12,500
Sales	3,50,000	Selling Expenses	6,700
Return Inward	10,000	Packing (essential)	1,500
Return Outward	7,500	Depreciation	10,800
Carriage Inward	2,500	Rent Paid	12,000
Carriage Outward	8,000	Rent Received	5,000
Freight	6,000	Salaries	15,000
Wages	4,000	Advertisement	7,000
Goods distributed as samples	12,000		

Closing stock as on 31st December 2007 amounted to Rs. 50,000.

Solution :

Cost of goods Sold =

Opening Stock

Add Purchases *Less* Returns

Add Direct Expenses

Less Closing Stock

Cost of Goods Sold (COGS)	Rs.	Rs.
Opening Stock		30,000
Add : Purchases (Net)		
Total Purchases	2,70,000	
Less : Returns o/w	(7,500)	
Less : Distributed as samples	(12,000)	2,50,500
		2,80,500
Add : Direct Expenses :		
Carriage Inward	2,500	
Freight	6,000	
Wages	4,000	
Octroi	12,500	
Packing (essential)	1,500	26,500
		3,07,000
Less : Closing Stock		50,000
Cost of goods sold		2,57,000

Gross Profit = Sales (Net) – Cost of goods sold

Sales	Rs. 3,50,000
Less Return I/w	Rs. 10,000
	Rs. 3,40,000
Less COGS	Rs. 2,57,000
Gross Profit	Rs. 83,000

TRADING ACCOUNT

For the year ended 31st December 2007

Particulars		Rs.	Particulars		Rs.
To Opening Stock		30,000	By Sales	3,50,000	
To Purchases	2,70,000		*Less* Returns I/w	(10,000)	3,40,000
Less : Returns O/W	(7,500)		By closing Stock		50,000
Less : Samples' goods	(12,000)	2,50,500			
To Direct Expenses :					
Carriage Inward		2,500			
Freight		6,000			
Wages		4,000			
Octroi		12,500			
Packing (essential)		1,500			
To Gross Profit c/d		83,000			
		3,90,000			3,90,000

Notes : 1. All indirect expenses have been ignored while preparing Trading Account.

2. Goods distributed as samples have been credited to Purchases Account.

3. Packing charges which are essential to make the product saleable are treated as direct expenses.

PROFIT & LOSS ACCOUNT

This account is prepared to ascertain the net profit earned or net loss incurred by the business concern during the accounting period. It starts with gross profit or gross loss as disclosed by Trading Account. It takes into account all the remaining indirect (normal and abnormal) expenses and losses related to or incidental to business. These operating and non-operating expenses are charged to Profit and Loss Account and shown to the debit side of the account. The operating expenses relate to office and administration, selling and distribution, whereas non-operating expenses include financial expenses such as interest, bank charges etc. and other expenses and losses such as loss on sale of fixed assets and abnormal losses (Theft, Fire & Accident) which are credited to Trading Account, will now be debited to Profit and Loss Account to arrive at the actual figure of profit or loss. Besides, if there are non-operating incomes such as Rent, Interest or dividend, the same are credited to Profit and Loss Account. The format of Profit and Loss Account is given below.

PROFIT & LOSS ACCOUNT (Format)
For the year ended...

Dr. Cr.

Particulars	Rs.	Particulars	Rs.
To Gross Loss b/d*	......	By Gross Profit b/d*	......
To Office and Administrative Expenses:	......	By Interest Received	......
Salaries Office Staff	......	By Dividend Received	......
Office Rent, Rates & Taxes	......	By Rent Received	......
Printing and Stationery	......	By Discount Received	......
Postage and Telephones	......	By Profit on sale of fixed asets	......
Fire Insurance Premium	......	By Profit on sale of Investments	......
Audit Fees	......	By Insurance Claims	......
Repairs & Maintenance	......	By Duty Drawbacks	......
Legal Expenses	......	By Apprenticeship Premium	......
Office Lighting	......	By Miscellaneous Receipts	......
Depreciation Office assets	......	By Bad debts recovered	......
Other office expenses	......	By Net loss transferred to capital account	......
To Selling and Distribution Expenses :	......	(Balancing figure)*	......
Salesmen's Salaries	......		
Selling Commission	......		
Travelling Expenses	......		

* Either Gross Loss or Gross Profit

Brokerage	......		
Trade expenses	......		
Advertisement & Publicity	......		
Sales Promotion Expenses	......		
Carriage Outward	......		
Bed debts	......		
Provision for Bad debts	......		
Repairs of Vehicles	......		
Depreciation of Vehicles	......		
Warehouse Expenses	......		
Warehouse Insurance	......		
Waehouse Rent	......		
Delivery Van Expenses	......		
Packing Expenses	......		
Rebate to Customers	......		
To Royalty (based on units sold)	......		
To Financing Expenses :			
Discount Allowed	......		
Interest on Loan	......		
Interest on Capital	......		
Discounts on bills	......		
Bank Charges	......		
To Other Expenses and Losses :	......		
Abnormal losses transferred			
From Trading A/c	......		
(Loss by fire, accident, theft etc.)			
To Loss on sale of Fixed assets	......		
To Miscellaneous Expenses	......		
To Net Profit transferred to Capital A/c	......		
(Balancing figure)*			

*Balancing figure either may be net profit or net loss.

Note : If a concern does not prepare Manufacturing Account then all the factory expenses will be charged to Trading Account.

Explanation and clarification regarding certain items :

1. **Salaries :** Salaries paid/payable to employees including Directors Salaries, Manager's Salaries (except Work Manager's Salaries) are charged to Profit and Loss Account. Works Manager's salaries should be debited to Manufacturing Account. In case a concern does not

prepare Manufacturing Account, the same should be charged to Trading Account. Similarly, salaries and. wages should also be charged to Profit and Loss Account. But wages and salaries be charged to Trading Account.

2. **Brokerage :** This refers to brokerage paid on the items in which the business trades in. Such brokerage on buying and selling of goods in which the enterprise deals in is shown to the debit of Profit and Loss Account. However, any brokerage paid on sale or purchase of assets is treated as of capital nature and hence it is deducted from sale proceeds of the asset sold or added to the cost of the asset acquired.
3. **Trade expenses :** These expenses are of miscellaneous nature and of small amount and sometimes termed as Sundry expenses or Miscellaneous expenses or even Petty expenses. These are debited to Profit and Loss A/c.
4. **Advertisement :** Expenses on advertisement which are of revenue and recurring nature are charged to Profit and Loss Account. Whereas cost of heavy advertisement the benefit of which is likely to cover more than one accounting year, is treated as deferred revenue expenditure. For example, a company incurs Rs. 1,00,000 on advertisement and it is estimated that the benefit of this advertisement expenditure is likely to extend over a period of four years. In this case Rs. 25,000 i.e. 1/4th of total cost of advertisement will be charged to current year's Profit and Loss Account whereas 3/4th i.e. (Rs. 75,000) will be taken to Balance Sheet to be treated as 'Deferred Revenue Expenditure'. However, advertisement expenses incurred for purchase of goods should be charged to Trading Account.
5. **Rebate to customers :** It is an allowance given to a customer when his purchases from the concern exceeds the certain limits say Rs. 200. In such cases all those customers who make purchases from the company exceeding Rs. 200 will be entitled to rebate of 1% or 2% depending upon the policy declared by the company. The amount of rebate so allowed is charged to Profit and Loss A/c.
6. **Duty drawback and subsidy :** It is a refund of duties levied on purchases made by exporters. It serves as an incentive to exporters. The duty drawback and cash subsidy should be deducted from the purchases. But in practice it is treated as 'Income'.
7. **Apprenticeship premium :** It is the fee charged by the business enterprise to train persons in various trades. It is treated as revenue receipts and credited to Profit & Loss Account.
8. It is not necessary to show various expenses under different heads viz. "Office or Administrative Expenses", Selling and Distribution Expenses and Financing Expenses. The classification has been shown to make students familiar with the nature of all indirect expenses to be charged to Profit and Loss Account.
9. **Factory expenses :** Factory expenses are of two types, viz. direct and indirect and both are shown in the Manufacturing Account. If a concern does not prepare Manufacturing Account, then direct expenses are charged to Trading Account and indirect expenses are debited to Profit and Loss Account.
10. **Royalties :** Royalties are paid by the business concerns to the landlord, author or a patentee for the right to use their land, copyrights or patents right. Payment of such royalty sum based on sales is debited to Profit and Loss Account. However, if royalty is paid on the basis of production, it is charged to Trading Account.

11. **Advertisement and publicity :** These expenses are incurred to attract customers for increasing the volume of sales and as such are charged to Profit and Loss Account. Similarly, money spent on prizes given to customers under the scheme of 'sales promotion' such as 'Bumper sales', 'Dhamaka sales' are treated as selling and distribution expenses. If a large sum is incurred on heavy advertisement under a contract or whose benefits may accrue over a period of more than one year, say four years, such expenses are spread over the period of its benefits and a proportionate part is charged to Profit and Loss Account and remaining is taken to Balance Sheet as deferred revenue expenditure.

    However, advertisement expenses incurred for purchasing goods are charged to Trading Account. Whereas advertisement expenses paid for acquiring a capital asset are capitalised. Again cost of advertisement in respect of sale of any capital asset is deducted from the sale proceeds of the asset concerned, hence not charged to Trading or Profit and Loss Account.

12. **Abnormal Losses and Insurance claims :** As a rule, the entire amount of abnormal losses either arising from accident, fire or theft are credited to Trading Account and debited to Profit and Loss Account irrespective of the insurance claims. The amount so received/settled/receivable from the insurance company is credited to Profit and Loss Account.

Alternatively, Trading Account may be credited with the net abnormal loss (abnormal loss, less insurance claims, if any) and Profit and Loss Account may be debited by net abnormal loss only.

DIFFERENCE BETWEEN TRADING A/C AND PROFIT & LOSS A/C

1. Trading Account shows the result of trading operation of an enterprise whereas Profit and Loss Account shows the overall result of the business as a whole.
2. Trading Account takes into account only the direct cost involved including direct expenses whereas Profit and Loss Account deals with the remaining costs and expenses which are of indirect nature.
3. Trading Account is prepared under normal conditions of the business and hence abnormal loss if any, is credited to this account. Profit and Loss Account accounts for all normal and abnormal losses.

Illustration 2

From the following balances extracted from the books of a Trader at the close of the accounting year ended on 31st December 2007, prepare Profit and Loss Account.

	Rs.		Rs.
Gross Profit	1,53,000	Apprenticeship Premium	5,000
Salaries	46,500	Dividend Received	12,000
Rent (Office)	12,300	Interest Received	8,000
Fire Insurance Premium	2,700	Rent Received	5,000
Discount Allowed	1,500		
Carriage Outward	7,500		
Bad debts	6,300		
Printing and Statinoery	750		

Selling Expenses	21,500		
Rent, Rates and Taxes	1,050		
Loss by Fire (not coveed by Insurance)	8,000		
Legal Charges	2,000		
Go down Rent	12,700		
Depreciation on Office Equipments	5,500		
Repairs and Maintenance	4,800		
Bank Charges	1,200		

Salaries due but not paid Rs. 2,500. Fire Insurance Premium has been paid in advance to the extent of Rs. 300. Rent, Rates and Tax outstanding Rs. 150.

Solution :

PROFIT & LOSS ACCOUNT
For the year ended 31st December 2007

Particulars		Rs.	Particulars	Rs.
To Salaries	46,500	49,000	By Gross Profit b/d	1,53,000
Add : O/s	2,500		By Apprentice Premium	5,000
To Rent (Office)		12,300	By Dividend Received	12,000
To Fire Insurance Premium	2,700		By Interest Received	8,000
Less : Prepaid	300	2,400	By Rent Received	5,000
To Bank Charges		1,200		
To Carriage Outward		7,500		
To Printing and Stationery		750		
To Rent, Rates & Taxes	1,050			
Add : Outstanding	150	1,200		
To Legal Charges		2,000		
To Loss by Fire		8,000		
To Discount Allowed		1,500		
To Bed debts		6,300		
To Selling Expenses		21,500		
To Go down Rent		12,700		
To Repairs and Maintenance		4,800		
To Depreciation on (Office Equipments)		5,500		
To Net Profit Transferred to Capital Account		46,350		
		1,83,000		1,83,000

PROFIT AND LOSS APPROPRIATION ACCOUNT

This account shows the distribution or appropriation of profits after the same has been earned and computed. In case of sole proprietor since entire amount of profit belongs to him no Profit and Loss Appropriation is prepared. However, this account is prepared in case of Partnership firms and Joint Stock

Companies where there are several and varied claimants in the net profits. Since company's final accounts are to be studied under corporate accounting present Profit and Loss Appropriation Account deals exclusively for partnership form of business only. The profit distribution under partnership takes various forms. A partner shares earnings of the firm in the form of salary, commission, interest and profit as per the partnership deed. Besides, a partner also pays interest on drawings made by him during the accounting year. All these transactions of the firm with the partners are treated under Profit and Loss Appropriation Account as given below in the format.

PROFIT AND LOSS APPROPRIATION ACCOUNT (FORMAT)

Dr. Cr.

Particualrs	Rs.	Particulars	Rs.
To Profit and Loss A/c* (Net Loss)		By Profit and Loss A/c* (Net Profit)	
To Interest on Capitals of Partners		By Interest on Drawings	
To Salaries to Partners		By Balance transferred to Partners' Capital A/c**	
To Commission to Partners			
To Balance transferred to Partners' Capial A/c**			

*There will either be Profit or Loss

**Represents residual profit or loss.

Illustration 3

X, Y and Z are partners sharing profits and losses in the ratio of 3:2:1. From the following particulars prepare Profit and Loss Appropriation Account.

		Rs.
Net Profit transferred from Profit and Loss Account		72,000
Salaries to X and Z @		9,000 each
Commission to Y		12,000
Interest on Capital is allowed @ 5% p.a.		
Interest on drawings is to be charged @ 6%		
Drawings made during the year :		
	X	10,000
	Y	15,000
	Z	10,000
Capitals in the beginning of the year :		
	X	2,00,000
	Y	1,00,000
	Z	60,000

Solution : **PROFIT & LOSS APPROPRIATION A/C**

Dr. Cr.

Particualrs	Rs.	Particulars	Rs.
To Salaries :		By Net Profit transferred	
X's Capital A/c	9,000	from P & L A/c	72,000
Z's Capital A/c	9,000	By Interest on Drawings :	
To Commission (Y's Capital A/c)	12,000	X's Capital A/c	600
To Interest on Capital		Y's Capital A/c	900
X's Capital A/c	10,000	Z's Capital A/c	600
Y's Capital A/c	5,000		
Z's Capital A/c	3,000		
To Profit transferred to :			
X's Capital A/c	13,050		
Y's Capital A/c	8,700		
Z's Capial A/c	4,350		
	74,100		74,100

MANUFACTURING ACCOUNT

Business concerns engaged in the activities of manufacturing or production of goods prepares Manufacturing Account, which shows the cost of raw materials consumed. Cost of goods produced and the cost of conversion of raw-materials in to finished product. This is prepared in addition to Trading Account. The cost of goods so completed is transferred to Trading Account.

Manufacturing Account accounts for opening stock of raw material purchases of raw materials and closing stock of raw material.

PROFORMA MANUFACTURING ACCOUNT
For the year ending 31st December 200....

Particulars	Rs.	Particulars	Rs.
To Opening Work-in-progress		By Closing Work-in-Progress	
To Raw-Material consumed		By Sale of scrap	
Opening Stock of Raw-materials		By Cost of goods produced	
Add : Purchase *Less* : Returns		transferred to Trading A/c	
Less : Closing stock of Raw-materials			
To Direct Expenses :			
Productive wages			
Freight inward (R/m)			
Cartage/Carriage inward			
To Factory overheads or indirect expnses :			
Salary of works Manager			

Gas, fuel and Power Factory light Rent, Rates and Taxes Insurance of Factory assets Repairs of factory assets Depreciation on factory assets Other factory expenses			

To work out cost of materials consumed, all expenses incurred in connection with purchases of raw-materials and production are debited to Manufacturing Account. However this account starts with opening work-in-progress, closing work-in-progress and sale of scrap if any, are shown to credit side of manufacturing account. The total cost of goods manufactured is transferred to Trading Account.

Points to Note Regarding Manufacturing Account

1. **Work-in-progress :** It refers to the value of incomplete or semi-finished goods which includes cost of raw-materials, and proportionate wages and direct expense incurred till this stage of semi-completion. Opening and closing balances of the same are shown to the debit and credit side respectively.
2. **Raw-materials consumed :** This shows the cost of materials used in the production process. This is arrived at by Adding the net purchases to the opening balance of raw-materials and deducting the closing balance of raw-materials at hand by the end of accounting period.
3. **Direct expenses :** These expenses are incurred either on procurement or purchases of raw-materials and on conversion thereof into finished product. It includes productive wages, freight inward, cartage or carriage inward etc. That is, it includes direct labour and direct expenses (factory).
4. **Factory overheads or indirect expenses :** Factory overheads refers to indirect material, indirect labour and indirect expenses. These include cotton waste, lubricating or machine oil, works manager, supervisor or foreman's salary, Fuel and power, Repairs and maintenance of factory machine, depreciation of factory assets. Rent, rates and taxes of the factory building, factory insurance etc.
5. **Scrap :** It denotes the value of material residue coming out of certain types of processes. It is sold as scrap and credited to Manufacturing account to arrive at the correct cost of production.
6. **Cost of production :** Manufacturing Account ascertains the cost of goods manufactured during any accounting period as shown in the format of Manufacturing account. The cost of production of goods produced is transferred to Trading A/c.

DIFFERENCE BETWEEN TRADING ACCOUNT AND MANUFACTURING ACCOUNT

1. Trading account discloses the result of trading operation while Manufacturing account simply gives the cost of goods produced during any accounting period.
2. Trading Account may have opening and closing balances of finished stock only while Manufacturing Account may have opening and closing balances of raw-materials, work-in-progress and finished goods as well.

3. The closing balance of Trading Account (difference) i.e. excess of debit side over credit (gross profit) or vice versa (gross loss) is transferred to Profit and Loss Account while a Manufacturing Account always have debit balance which is transferred to Trading account either at cost or cost plus profit.

Illustration 4

From the following particulars, prepare a Manufacturing and a Trading Account for the year ended 31st December 2007.

	Rs.
Raw-materials (1.1.2007)	18,000
Work-in-progress (1.1.2007)	9,000
Finished Stock (1.1.2007)	15,000
Raw-materials purchased	1,20,000
Direct wages	15,000
Indirect wages	12,000
Carriage inwards	1,500
Returns outward	3,000
Purchase of finished goods	12,000
Carriage paid on them	800
Royalty on production	1,200
Fuel and power	3,800
Repairs and Maintenance (factory)	2,500
Sales	2,75,000
Returns inward	5,000
Depreciation on factory assets	9,000
Rent, Rates and Taxes	2,000
Fire Insurance Premium	1,000
Balances as on 31-12-2007	
Raw-materials	9,000
Work-in-progress	5,000
Finished Stock	17,500

Adjustments : Direct wages o/s Rs. 5,000, Fuel and power prepaid Rs. 800.

Solution : **MANUFACTURING AND TRADING ACCOUNT OF .....**

For the year ended 31st December 2007

Particulars	Rs.	Particulars	Rs.
To Opening Stock of Raw Material	18,000	By Trading A/c (Cost of production)	1,79,200
Add : Purchases less Returns	1,17,000		
(1,20,000 – 3,000)	1,35,000		
**Less* : Closing Stock of Raw Material	9,000		

To Raw-materials used		1,26,000			
To Carriage Inward		1,500			
To Direct wages	15,000				
Add : Outstanding	5,000	20,000			
To Royalty on Production		1,200			
To Factory or Production O/H :					
Indirect Wages		12,000			
Repairs and Maintenance		2,500			
Fuel and Power	3,800				
Less : Prepaid	800	3,000			
Depreciation		9,000			
		1,75,200			
Add : Opening Work-in-progrss		9,000			
Less : Closing Work-in-progress		(5,000)			
		1,79,200			1,79,200
To Opening Finished Stock		15,000	By Sales	2,75,000	
To Cost of goods produced		1,79,200	*Less* : Returns	5,000	2,70,000
To Purchase of goods		12,000	By Closing Stock		17,500
To Carriage on Purchases		800			
To Gross Profit c/d		80,500			
		2,87,500			2,87,500

*Alternatively, these can be shown to the credit side of Manufacturing Account.

Illustration 5

From the following particulars prepare a Manufacturing Account and a Trading Account for the ended 31st December 2007.

	Rs.
Raw-materials (1-1-2007)	9,000
Work-in-progress (1-1-2007)	6,000
Finished goods (1-1-2007)	6,750
Raw-materials purchased	60,000
Productive wages	7,500
Indirect wages	6,000
Carriage inward	250
Return outward	1,500
Freight on Raw-materials purchased	750
Fuel, Gas & Power	2,000
Repair of factory machines	1,200
Depreciation on factory assets	3,000
Purchase of finished goods	6,000
Carriage paid on finished goods	400
Warehouse wages	1,000
Sales	1,55,000

Raw-materials (31-12-2007)	4,500
Work-in-Progress (31-12-2007)	1,800
Finished goods (31-12-2007)	4,000

Goods are transferred from production department to sales department at cost plus 20%.

There are no outstanding expenses. There is no credit sales. All the goods have been sold on cash basis. Depreciation has been charged on machinery @ 10% p.a. on straight-line basis. You are required to calculate cost of goods transferred to Trading Account and amount of gross profit made.

Solution : **MANUFACTURING AND TRADING ACCOUNT**

For the year ended 31st December, 2007

Particulars		Rs.	Particulars	Rs.
To Raw material Consumed :			By Closing Work-in-progress	1,800
To Opening Stock (R M)	9,000		By Transferred to Trading A/c	1,05,480
Add Purchases-Returns	58,500			
(60,000 – 1,500)	67,500			
Less : Closing stock of Raw-materials	(4,500)	63,000		
To Carriage inwards		250		
To Freight		750		
To Productive wages		7,500		
To Factory Overheads :				
To Indirect wages		6,000		
To Fuel Gas & Power		2,000		
To Repairs of Factory Machine		1,200		
To Depreciation factory Machine		3,000		
To Opening Work-in-progress		6,000		
To Factory profit (@ 20% on 87,900)		17,580		
		107,280		107,280
To Opening Stock (FG)		6,750	By Sales	1,55,000
To Purchases (FG)		6,000	By Closing Stock (FG)	4,000
To Cost of goods produced		1,05,480		
To carriage on (FG)		400		
To Warehouse wages		1,000		
To Profit transferred to Profit and Loss A/c		39,370		
		1,59,000		1,59,000

	Rs.
*Cost of goods transferred to Trading Account	105480
* Gross Profit	39.370

BALANCE SHEET

Balance Sheet is a statement of assets and liabilities, which helps us to ascertain the financial position of a concern on a particular date, i.e. on a date when financial statements or final accounts are prepared or books of accounts are closed. In fact it treats the balances of all those ledger accounts which have not yet been squared up. These accounts relate to assets owned, expenses incurred but not paid or not due, expenses due but not paid, incomes accrued but not received, or certain receipts which are not due or accrued. In other words it deals with all those real and personal accounts, which have not been accounted for, in the Manufacturing, Trading or Profit and Loss Accounts. Besides, balance sheet also treats all those items given in the adjustments, which affect Real or Personal Accounts. The Nominal accounts are treated in the income statement in the usual manner. It aims to ascertain nature and amount of different assets and liabilities so that the financial position (such as liquidity or solvency position) could clearly be known to all those interested. Thus the main function of the Balance Sheet is to depict the true picture of the concern on a particular date.

DIFFERENCE BETWEEN A TRIAL BALANCE AND A BALANCE SHEET

1. Trial Balance consists of Debit (Dr) and Credit (Cr) side, whereas a Balance Sheet shows the assets and liabilities side.
2. Trial Balance is a statement showing balance of all (Real, Personal and Nominal) ledger accounts. A Balance Sheet considers and shows the accounting treatment of Real and Personal accounts only.
3. Trial Balance is the first step in the preparation of final accounts and a Balance Sheet is the last step.
4. Trial Balance is prepared from various ledger accounts while a Balance Sheet is based on the Trial Balance.
5. A Trial Balance is prepared to check the arithmetical accuracy of the accounting records whereas a Balance Sheet is prepared to know the financial position of the concern.
6. Opening stock forms the part of Trial Balance while closing stock is shown in the Balance Sheet.
7. There is no specific format and arrangement of various ledger accounts in a Trial Balance. But, a Balance sheet shows all the concerned account in a systematic way, either in the order of liquidity or in the order of permanence.
8. A Trial Balance is complete even without stock-taking process whereas a Balance Sheet cannot be completed without stock-taking.

PREPARATION AND PRESENTATION OF BALANCE SHEET

The process of preparation and presentation of Balance Sheet involves two steps :

(i) Grouping and (ii) Marshalling

The first step refers to proper grouping of the various items which are to be shown in the Balance Sheet as assets and liabilities. For this purpose items of similar nature are grouped under one head so that the Balance Sheet could convey true message to its users. For example, stock, debtors, lBills receivables, Bank, Cash in hand etc. are grouped under the heading 'Current Assets' and Land and Building, Plant and Machinery, Furniture and Fixtures, Tools and Equipments under "Fixed Assets", similarly 'Sundry creditors' for goods must be shown separately and distinguished from creditors for furniture or of any other asset. Likewise, 'Sundry debtors' are distinguished from money owing other than due to credit sales of goods.

The second step involves marshalling of assets and liabilities. It means orderly arrangement in which various assets and liabilities are presented or shown in the Balance Sheet. There are two method of presentation :

(i) In the order of liquidity

(ii) In the order of permanence

Under liquidity order, assets are shown on the basis of liquidity or reliability. These are rearranged in an order of most liquid, more liquid, liquid, least liquid and not liquid (Fixed) assets. Similarly, liabilities are arranged in the order in which these are to be paid or discharged.

Under the "order of permanence" the assets are arranged on the basis of their useful life. The assets which are to serve business for the longest period of time are shown first. In other words, this method puts the first method in the reverse gear. Similarly, in case of liabilities, after capital, the liabilities are arranged as long term, medium term, short term and current liabilities.

Following are the respective formats of Balance Sheets to bring out the clarity of concept.

I. Liquidity Order

BALANCE SHEET OF....

As on ....

Liabilities	Rs.	Assets	Rs.
Current Liabilities		*Current Assets* :	
Bank Overdraft		Cash in hand	
Outstanding Expenses		Cash at Bank	
Bills Payable		Marketable Securities	
Sundry Creditors		Short term Investment	
Income Received in Advance		Bills Receivables	
Long term Liabilities		Sundry Debtors	
Mortgaged Loan		Prepaid Expenses	
Loan from Bank		Accrued Income	
Capital		*Long term Investment* :	
Add : Profit		*Fixed Assets*	
Less : Loss		Furniture & Fixtures	
Less : Drawings		Motor Vehicles	
Add : Capital introduced during the year		Tools & Equipments	
		Plant & Machinery	
		Land and Building	

		Intangible Assets Patents Copy rights Trademarks Goodwill	

II. Order of Permanence

BALANCE SHEET OF.... As on ....

Liabilities	Rs.	Assets	Rs.
Capital		*Fixed Assets*	
Add Profit		Goodwill	
or (*Less* Loss)		Land and Building	
Less Drawings		Plant & Machinery	
Add Capital introduced		Tolls & Equipments	
during the year		Motor Vehicles	
Long Term Liabilities		Furniture & Fixtures	
Mortgage loan		Patents Trademarks	
Loan from Bank		*Investment (Long Term)*	
Current Liabilities		*Current Assets*	
Income Received in Advance		Stock	
Sundry Creditors		Accrued Income	
Bills Payable		Prepaid Expenses	
Outstanding Expenses		Sundry Debtors	
Bank Overdraft		Bills Receivable	
		Short term Invstments	
		Marketable Securities	
		Cash and Bank Balance	
		Facilitious Assets	
		Advertisement	
		Profit & Loss Account	
		Miscellaneous Expenses	

Explanation and clarification of certain items : In order to understand proper placement of various items it is necessary to know the type and nature of classification of assets and liabilities which are to be arranged in either of two orderly manner discussed earlier. For the purpose of presentation of assets in the Balance Sheet assets are classified as under :

(i) Fixed Assets

(ii) Intangible Assets (These are generally shown under 'fixed assets')

(iii) Current Assets

(iv) Fictitious Assets

(v) Wasting Assets

(vi) Contingent Assets

Fixed assets : Fixed assets are those assets which are acquired for the purpose of producing goods or rendering services. These are not held for resale in normal course of business. Fixed assets are used for the purpose of earning revenue and hence these are held for a longer period of time. These are also treated as 'Gross Block' (Fixed assets before depreciation) and "Net Block" (Fixed assets after depreciation). Investment in these assets is known as 'Sunk Cost'. Examples of fixed assets are Land & Building, Plant and Machinery, Furniture and Fixtures, Tools and Equipments, Motor vehicles etc. All fixed assets are 'tangible' by nature.

Intangible assets : Intangible assets are those capital assets which do not have any physical existence. Though cannot be touched or seen yet they have long life and help to generate income. Such assets have value by virtue of the rights conferred upon the owner by mere possession. Goodwill, trademarks, copyrights and patents are the examples of intangible assets.

Current assets : Current assets include cash and other assets which are converted or realised into cash within a normal operating cycle or say within a year. These are acquired either for the purpose of resale, or assisting and helping process of production or rendering of service or supplying of goods. These assets constantly keep on changing their form and contribute to routine transactions and operations of business. Examples are, Cash, Bank, Bills Receivables, Debtors, Stock, Prepaid expenses etc. Current assets are also known as floating assets or circulating assets.

Liquid or quick assets : Those current assets which can be converted into cash at a very short notice or immediately without incurring much loss or^exposing to high risk. Quick assets can be worked out by deducting Stock (Raw-materials, work-in-progress or finished goods) and prepaid expenses out of total current assets.

Fictitious assets : These are the non-existent worthless items which represent unwritten off losses or cost incurred in the past which cannot be recovered in future or realised in cash. Examples of such assets are preliminary expenses (formation expenses), Advertisement suspense, Underwriting commission, Discount on issue of shares and debentures, Loss on issue of debentures and Debit balance of Profit and Loss Account. These fictitious assets are written off or wiped out by debiting to Profit and Loss Account.

Wasting assets : Assets with limited useful life by nature deplete over a limited period of time are called wasting assets. These assets become worthless once its utility is over or exhaust fully. Such assets are natural resources like, timber forests, coalmines, oil wells, and mineral deposits etc.

Contingent assets : Contingent assets are probable assets which may or may not become assets as it depends upon occurrence or non-occurrence of a specified event or performance or non-performance of a specified act. For example, a suit is pending in the court of law against ownership title of any disputed property and if the suit is decided in favour of the business concern it becomes the asset of the concern. On the other hand if the decision goes against the concern, the company cannot claim to enjoy ownership rights. Thus it remains a contingent asset as long as the judgment is not pronounced by court. Such assets are shown by means of footnote and hence do not form part of assets shown in the Balance Sheet. Beside this hire-purchase contract, uncalled share capital etc. are the other example of contingent assets.

Classification of Liabilities

Long term liabilities: These are the obligations which are to be met by the business enterprise after a relatively long period of time. Such liabilities do not become due for payment in the ordinary course of business operation or within normal operating cycle. Debentures, long term loans from Banks or financial Institutions are the examples of long-term liabilities.

Current liabilities: Current liabilities are those liabilities which are payable within normal operating cycle i.e. within an accounting year. These may arise either out of realisation from current assets or by creating fresh current liability (obligation). Trade creditors, Bills payable, Bank overdraft, Outstanding expenses, Short-term loans (payable within twelve months or within accounting year) are examples of current liabilities.

Contingent liability: It is not an actual liability but an anticipated (probable) liability which may or may not become payable. It depends upon happening of certain events or performance of certain acts. An element of uncertainly is always attached. A contingent liability, thus, may or may not become a sure liability. Examples are, liability for bills discounted, liability for acting as surety, liability arising on a suit for damages pending in the court of law, liability for calls on partly paid shares etc. Contingent liabilities are shown as footnote under the Balance Sheet.

Vertical Format

Under vertical form various items of incomes and expenses, assets and liabilities are arranged vertically to get some additional information about the operating efficiency and financial position of the business enterprise. The vertical form of Income Statement shows the gross profit, operating profit and net profit. The impact of non-operating incomes and expenses cannot be ascertained if the Trading and Profit and Loss Account is not prepared under vertical form. Similarly the Balance Sheet discloses owner's Capital, borrowed Capital, net working capital etc. It is to be noted that sole traders and partnership firms hardly adopt vertical form of financial statements. Following formats will bring-about a clarity of understating of vertical form of financial statements.

INCOME STATEMENT (A FORMAT)
For the year ending 31st March ....

Particulars	Figures at the end of	
	Previous year	Current year
	Rs.	Rs.
Sale/Turnover	......	......
Less : Cost of Goods sold*	......	......
Gross Profit	***	***
Less : Administrative Expenses*		
Less : Selling & Distribution Expenses*	......	......
Operating Profit	......	......
Add : Other Incomes* (Non-operating Incomes)	***	***
Less : Financial Expenses (Non-operating Expenses)	......	......
Net Profit	......	......

Less : Transfer to General Reserve	***	***
and/or Capital Account/Accounts (in the form of profit,		
salary, commission, etc.	......	......
salary, commission etc.)	......	......

*Explained earlier under conventional form

OPERATING VS. NON-OPERATING ITEMS

Operating Profit/Loss

The excess of operating incomes over operating expenses represents operating profit, whereas when operating expenses exceed operating income it results in operating loss.

Operating incomes are those incomes which arise from operating activities in which the enterprise deals in. For a trading concern, revenue arising from "sale of goods in which the enterprise deals in is treated as operating income. In fact operating activities are the principal revenue-producing activities of the enterprise. Operating income measures the efficiency of a business enterprise, because these activities make-up the main business of the enterprise and are of recurring in nature. The operating activities may be :

- Manufacturing and distribution of goods by manufacturing and trading enterprises.
- Purchasing and selling of goods, services and securities by a Trading concern.
- Exploration of natural resources by Extracting and Trading entity.
- Granting of loans and advances by a Financial Institution.
- Construction and development of colonies by a construction enterprise.

Operating expenses are those expenses which are incurred in connection with main revenue producing activities. These operating expenses may be classified under various heads — such as office and administrative expenses and selling and distribution expenses. A detailed list of these expenses has already been given under horizontal format of Profit and Loss Account. These expenses are necessary to run the business enterprise but the same are not directly related to trading or manufacturing activities. These directly related expenses are termed as direct expenses, which are charged to Manufacturing/ Trading/Account.

Hence operating profit = Gross Profit-Operating Expenses (Office and Selling Distribution).

NON-OPERATING INCOMES

Such incomes arise from other major or principal revenue earning activities. These are in the form of, in case of a manufacturing and trading concerns, rent received, interest received, dividend received which are credited to Profit and Loss Account. Profit on sale of fixed assets and the revenue arising from activities which are incidental to main business, are treated as non-operating incomes. Such types of income arise when unused portion of building used for business purposes is let-out or idle funds of business invested either in shares, debentures, and government securities or deposited in a fixed deposit account. Since such incomes have nothing to do with the business operation of the enterprise — these incomes are treated as non-operating incomes.

It is to be noted that "Interest," and "Dividend" received by a "Financial Institution" is treated as operating income because these incomes arise from main/principal revenue earning activity.

NON-OPERATING EXPENSES

These expenses are incurred on activities other than main or principal revenue earning activities. These may be in the form of non-operating losses. Interest paid on borrowings (financial overheads), loss on sale of fixed assets, loss on sale of investment (held as an asset) are some of the examples of' non-operating expenses. Such expenses are also charged to Income Statement to ascertain the overall net profit.

BALANCE SHEET OF.... (A VERTICAL FORMAT)
As on 31st March....

Assets	Figures at the end of	
	Previous year	**Current year**
Fixed Assets/Gross Block		
Less : Depreciation	...	...
Nex Fixed Assets/Net Block	...	...
Current Assets		
Stock-in-Trade	...	...
S. Debtors	...	...
Bills Receivable	...	...
Cash & Bank Balance	...	...
Total Current Assets*	...	...
Total Assets	***	***
Liabilities & Capital		
Capital		
Add : Profit (Retained Earnings)	...	...
Less : Drawings	...	...
Owner's Equity	...	...
S. Creditors	...	
Bills Payable		
o/s Expenses		
Total current liabilities*		
Total	***	***

*The list is not exhaustive.

REVENUE RECOGNITION (AS-9)

Revenue arises in the ordinary course of business activities of an enterprise from :

- sale of goods
- rendering of services and
- use by others of enterprise resources yielding interest, royalties and dividends.

Revenue recognition is mainly concerned with the timing of recognition of revenue in the statement of profit and loss. According to AS-9, "revenue is the gross in-flow of cash, receivable, or other consideration arising in the course of ordinary activities of an enterprises."

The basic problem of revenue recognition lies in identifying of the "accounting period" during which revenues are earned. There are several stages or activities in a business before the revenues are earned and realised. Hence problem arises — should revenue be recognised at the point of production, sale, delivery or receipt of cash. According to "Realisation Concept" revenues are recognised at the point of sale or services are rendered. However, there is no single uniform practice to recognise various types of revenues according to one common principle. There are guidelines which help us in recognising operating revenues and non-operating revenues. Non-operating revenues include interest dividend and rent and other incomes, which are not related to normal course of operation of the enterprise. It is advisable to show operating and non-operating revenues separately in the Profit and Loss Account.

Following are some of the established practices to recognise revenue as per AS-9.

(A) Sale of Goods

Trading and Manufacturing organisations, in general, recognise revenue when sale is effected. However, the following conditions should be satisfied :

(i) The "property in goods" is transferred for a price.

(ii) All significant risks and rewards have been transferred and no effective control is retained by the seller.

(iii) No significant uncertainty exists regarding the collection of amount of consideration. Special Cases of "Sale of Goods" and Applicability of AS-9

(a) **Delivery of goods delayed at buyer's request and buyer takes title and accepts billing**. Revenue should be recognised and the "goods to be delivered" at any subsequent date should not be included in the inventory.

(b) **Goods delivered subject to installation and inspection**. Revenue should be recognised only) after the installation and inspection is completed.

(c) **Sale on approval.** In case of sale on approval or return basis, revenue should be recognised only when acceptance is received from buyer.

(d) **Sale subject to a warranty.** If sales are subject to a warranty, revenue recognition should not be deferred but a provision should be made to cover the liability, which may arise under the terms and period of warranty.

(e) **Guaranteed sales.** Sometimes goods are sold and delivery is made giving the buyer an unlimited right to return. That is under "Money back guarantee," if not completely satisfied. Under this situation it is apparent to recognise the 'revenue' at the point of sale and to make provisions for returns as well.

(f) **Consignment sales**. Revenues are recognised when the goods are sold to customers by the consignee and not at the time of dispatch of goods by consignor.

(g) **Cash on delivery sales.** If a sale has been effected under the terms of "Cash-on-delivery," revenue should be recognised only when cash is received by seller.

(h) **Installment sales.** Revenues are recognised on delivery to the extent of normal cash down price. However, interest on deferred payment should be recognised in the ratio of amount outstanding.

(i) **Special order.** Where payment is received against the specific order of goods, which are not in the stock, revenue from such sale should be recognised only when goods are purchased or manufactured and are ready for delivery.

(j) **Sale/Repurchase agreement.** Where seller concurrently agrees to repurchase the same goods at some later date, the flow of cash under such a situation will not be recognised as revenue.

(k) Sales to distributors or dealers for resale. Revenues are recognised only if significant risks of ownership have passed on distributors/dealers.

(B) Revenue Recognition in Case of Rendering of Services Conditions

(i) Revenue are recognised either on completed service method or 'proportionate' completion method.

(ii) No significant uncertainty exists regarding amount of consideration,

(iii) It is reasonable to expect ultimate collection of consideration.

Under completed service method revenue are recognised only on completion of service. In cases there are more than one act involved, revenue are recognised on execution of all these acts.

Proportionate completion method recognises revenue proportionate with the degree of completion of services. If there are more than one act involved revenue are recognised on execution of certain acts. Some examples of recognition of service revenue are :

1. **Installation fee.** In cases where installation fees are other than incidental to sales, the revenue should be recognised only when the equipment is installed and accepted by the customer.
2. **Advertising and Insurance Agency Commission.** Revenue should be recognised when service is completed. For advertising agencies, media commission will normally be recognised when the related advertisement or commercial appears before the public and the necessary intimation is received by the agency. Insurance agency commission should be recognised on the effective commencement or renewal dates of the related policies.
3. **Financial service commissions.** A financial service may be rendered as a single act or may be provided over a period of time. Similarly charges for such services may be made as a single amount or in stages over the period of the service or the life of the transaction to which it relates. Such charges may be settled in full when made or added to a loan or other account and settled in stages. The recognition of revenue should therefore have regard to :

   (a) Whether the service has been provided once and for all or on continuing basis.

   (b) The incidence of cost relating to service.

   (c) Commission charged for arranging and granting of loan or other facilities, should be recognised when a binding obligation has been entered into. Commitment, facility or loan management fees which relate to continuing obligations or service should normally be recognised over the life of the loan or facility having regard to the amount of the obligation outstanding, the nature of the service provided and timing of the costs relating thereto.

Admission Fees : Revenue from artistic performance, banquets and other special events should be recognised when the event takes place. When fees relate to a number of events, it should be allocated to each event on a systematic and rational basis.

Tuition Fees : Revenue should be recognised over the period of instruction.

Entrance and Membership Fees : AS-9 recommends capitalisation of entrance fees. If membership fee permits only membership and all other services or products are paid for separately or if there is a separate annual subscription, the fee should be recognised when received. If the membership fee entitles the member to services or publications to be provided during the year, it should be recognised on a systematic and rational basis having regard to the timing and nature of all services provided.

Subscription for Publications

Revenue received or billed should be deferred and recognised either on straight-line basis over time or where the items delivered vary in value from period to period revenue should be based on the sales value of the items delivered in relation to total sales value of all items covered by the subscription.

EXCEPTIONS OF GENERAL RULE

1. **Revenue recognition at the point of production (Completed Production Method) :** Under this method revenue are recognised at the point of production. It applies in case of agriculture. Extractive industries like gold, silver", uranium, other metals and oil (crude). In all these cases revenue are recognised just after completion of production even before the sales take place.
2. **Cash Basis :** Under this, revenue are not recognised at the point of sale but when cash is realised including outstanding if any. This basis is applicable in case of hire-purchase system where revenue are recognised on the basis of cash received and instalments due during the year.
3. **Revenue recognition during the production period on Percentage of Completion Method :** Under this method revenue are recognised on the basis of contract value, associated costs, number of acts or other suitable basis. It is applicable in case of long term construction contracts where revenue are recognised on the basis of degree of completion or what work certified bears to cash received by the contractor.
4. **Time Basis :** In many cases revenue are realised on the basis of time or period. For example, interest on fixed deposits is credited to Profit and Loss Account on time proportion basis i.e., interest accrued yet not payable.

(C)

It is to be noted that revenue in case of "Royalties" are recognised on an accrual basis in accordance with terms of agreement and Dividends are recognised when the right to receive payment is established.

Illustration 6

Following is the Trial Balance of a Trader as on 31st December 2007

Dr. Cr.

	Rs.		Rs.
Land and Building	2,70,000	Sales	5,30,000
Plant & Machinery	1,80,000	Returns Outwards	2,500
Furniture and Fixtures	45,000	Discount Received	500
Opening Stock	37,500	Commission Received	1,500
Purchases	4,25,000	Interest Received	2,000
Returns Inwards	5,000	Creditors	60,000
Carriage Inwards	500	Bills payable	28,500
Carriage OUtwards	1,000	Loan from Bank	1,50,000
Bank Balance	15,500	Sales Tax Collected	25,000
Wages	2,000	Capital	4,75,000
Salaries	10,000		
Cash in Hand	6,250		
Discount allowed	1,000		
Commission	750		
10% Investments (1-7-2007)	40,000		
Interest	1,500		
Rent, Rates & Taxes	5,000		
Repairs & Maintenance	2,500		
Printing and Stationery	500		
Power and Water	1,000		
Office Expenses	5,500		
Staff Welfare Expenses	1,500		
Publicity and Advertisement	2,500		
Bad debts	500		
Depreciation	55,000		
Debtors	1,35,000		
Drawings	25,000		
	12,75,000		12,75,000

Closing Stock as on 31-12-2007 was Rs. 50,000.

Record Closing and Adjustment entries and prepare Trading, Profit and Loss Account for the year ending 31st December 2007 and the Balance Sheet as on that date.

Solution : CLOSING AND ADJUSTMENT ENTRIES

Date 2007	Particulars		LF	(Dr) Rs.	(Cr) Rs.
Dec. 31	Trading A/c	Dr		4,71,000	
	To Opening Stock				37,500
	To Purchases				4,25,000
	To Returns Inwards				5,000
	To Carriage Inwards				500
	To wages				2,000
	To Power and Water				1,000
	(Being balances transferred to debit of Trading A/c)				
	Sales A/c	Dr		5,30,000	
	Returns Outwards A/c	Dr		2,500	
	To Trading A/c				5,32,500
	(Being balances transferred to credit of Trading A/c)				
	Closing Stock A/c	Dr		50,000	
	To Trading A/c				50,000
	(Being closing stock transferred Trading A/c)				
	Trading A/c	Dr		1,11,500	
	To Profit and Loss A/c				1,11,500
	(Being Gross Profit transferred to Profit and Loss A/c)				
	Profit & Loss A/c	Dr		87,250	1,000
	To Carriage Outwards				10,000
	To Salaries				1,000
	To Discount Allowed				750
	To Commission				1,500
	To Interest				5,000
	To Rent, Rates & Taxes				2,500
	To Repairs & Maintenance				500
	To Pringing & Stationery				5,500
	To Office Expenses				1,500
	To Publicity and Advertisement				2,500
	To Bad debts				500
	To Depreciation				55,000
	(Being expenses transferred to Profit & Loss A/c)				
	Discount Received	Dr		500	
	Commission Received	Dr		1,50	
	Interest Received	Dr		2,000	

	To Profit and Loss A/c (Being other incomes transferred to Profit and Loss A/c)			4,000
	Profit and Loss A/c Dr To Capital A/c (Being Net Profit transferred to Capital A/c)		28,250	28,250
	Capital A/c Dr To Drawings A/c (Being drawings charged to Capital A/c)		25,000	25,000

TRADING AND PROFIT & LOSS ACCOUNT
For the year ended 31st December 2007

Particulars		(Rs.)	Particulars		(Rs.)
To Opening Stock		37,500	By Sales	5,30,000	
To Purchase	4,25,000		Less : Returns	5,000	5,25,000
Less : Returns	2,500	4,22,500	By Closing Stock		50,000
To Carriage Inwards		500			
To Wages		2,000			
To Power and Water		1,000			
To Gross Profit transferred to Profit and Loss A/c		1,11,500			
		5,75,000			5,75,000
To Carriage Outwards		1,000	By Gross Profit b/d		1,11,500
To Salaries		10,000	By Discount Received		500
To Discount Allowed		1,000	By Commission Received		1,500
To Commission		750	By Interest Received		2,000
To Interest		1,500			
To Rent, Rates & Taxes		5,000			
To Repairs & Maintenance		2,500			
To Printing & Stationery		500			
To Office Expenses		5,500			
To Staff Welfare Expenses		1,500			
To Publicity and Advertisement		2,500			
To Bad Debts		500			
To Depreciation		55,000			
To Net Profit transferred to Capital A/c		28,250			
		1,15,500			1,15,500

BALANCE SHEET
As on 31st December, 2007

Liabilities		Rs.	Assets	Rs.
Capial	4,75,000		Land and Building	2,70,000
Add : Net Profit	28,250		Plant and machinery	1,80,000
	5,03,250		Furniture and Fixture	45,000
Less : Drawings	25,000	4,78,250	10% Investments	40,000
Loan from Bank		1,50,000	Closing Stock	50,000
Creditors		60,000	Debtors	1,35,000
Bills Payable		28,500	Bank Balance	15,500
Salex-Tax payable		25,000	Cash in Hand	6,250
		7,41,750		7,41,750

TREATMENT OF ADJUSTMENTS IN FINAL ACCOUNTS

The Final Accounts are prepared on the basis of information disclosed by trial balance which shows the summary of balances extracted from different ledgers accounts. Some ledgers accounts show the expenses actually paid or income received during an accounting year but do not show or disclose the amount actually incurred or earned during that accounting period. In other words no adjustment is made pertaining to outstanding expenses or accrued incomes. Hence these balances do not reflect the true value in relation to accounting period. Under Mercantile system of accounting, the 'accrual basis' is followed for matching the cost with revenue. Hence it becomes imperative to account for all expenses relating to an accounting year whether these are paid or not and similarly account for all incomes pertaining to an accounting year whether received or not. This will help us to calculate correct amount of profit and loss and show true financial position or state of affairs of business enterprise. Besides there are certain policy decisions which are to be implemented and the effect of which has to be reflected in the books of accounts. For example charging of depreciation, provision for bad debts, interest on capital, Interest on drawings, writing off certain expenses etc. are the adjustments which have to be made while preparing final accounts. Accounting treatment of these adjustments is being given below.

Note : Items appearing in the Trial Balance require single treatment while adjustments items are to be treated in two different Accounts, such as :

(i) Trading A/c and Balance Sheet or

(ii) Trading A/c and Profit & Loss A/c or

(iii) Profit and Loss A/c and Balance Sheet

Adjustments

1. Closing stock : Stock at the end is valued at market price or cost price whichever is Less. Usually it is not shown in the Trial Balance. An adjustment entry is recorded to give its effect in the final accounts. Following entry is recorded :

Closing Stock A/c Dr
To Trading A/c

This suggests that closing stock is taken to the credit side of Trading A/c and Assets side of the Balance Sheet. The closing stock of this year becomes the opening stock of the next year and is shown as part of Trial Balance. This opening stock is transferred to the debit of Trading A/c. However, when closing stock appears as a part of Trial Balance, it is directly shown to the assets side of Balance Sheet.

2. Expenses outstanding : Expenses due or incurred during an accounting period but not paid, are treated as expenses outstanding. Since these relate to an accounting year, the same are adjusted or Added to expenses due and paid. Following entry is made :

Expenses (Salary, Rent or any name of expenses) A/c Dr

To Expense Outstanding A/c (Salary, Rent or any other expenses)

e.g. office salaries @ Rs. 5,000 p.m. are incurred but during an accounting year salaries for 11 months have been paid and one month's salary is outstanding i.e. due but not paid. Salaries due and paid plus salaries due but not paid (both) will be debited to Profit and Loss A/c whereas outstanding salaries will again be shown to the liability side of balance sheet.

3. Prepaid expenses : This refers to the expenses paid the benefit of which shall be availed in the next accounting year e.g. if the accounting year ends on 31st December 2000 and the payment of any expense, any salary or insurance premium, has been made up to 31st March 2001 in such a case the payment made beyond the closing of books of accounts represents prepaid expense. While preparing final accounts prepaid is deducted from the actual amount paid in the Profit and Loss A/c and is shown to the Assets side of the Balance Sheet. Following entry is recorded for adjustment purposes.

Prepaid Expense* A/c Dr

To Expense A/c

*(Name of Expense, Salary or Insurance)

4. Accrued income : This refers to the income earned but not received during the accounting period or up to the date of closing of books of accounts. For example interest on investments, interest on fixed deposits, interest on debentures of other companies or rental income, a commission on sales etc. earned during the accounting year might have not been received till the date of preparation of final accounts. Following adjustment entry is recorded :

Accrued Income* A/c Dr

To Income A/c

*Name of income (Interest, Rent, Dividend or Commission) Effect

Accrued income is credited to Profit & Loss A/c and it is shown on the asset side of Balance Sheet.

5. Income received in advance : When an income is received before it has become due, is treated as a liability of the business on the date of preparation of final accounts. This advance income (unearned income) is deducted from the actual receipt of the concerned income on the credit side of Profit and Loss A/c and there from it is taken to liability side of Balance Sheet. Following entry is recorded :

*Income Received A/c Dr

To Income Received in Advance A/c

(*Name of Income)

6. Depreciation : Depreciation is an expired cost of the asset resulting in reduction in its value due to usage and normal wear and tear. It is treated a charge on Profit and Loss A/c and shown as a deduction from the book value (cost/W.D.V.) of the asset in the Balance Sheet. Following entry is recorded :

Depreciation A/c Dr
To Asset A/c

However, in case, depreciation is shown in the Trial Balance, it is given only single treatment and is debited to Profit and Loss A/c. No deduction is made out of the book value of the concerned asset in the Balance Sheet.

7. Bad debts : When credit customers fail to clear their accounts either due to insolvency, negligence, dishonesty, change in ownership or management etc., such an amount standing to their debit becomes irrecoverable and treated as loss. This loss is treated as bad debts and totally charged to Profit and Loss A/c. Following adjustment entry is recorded :

Bad debts A/c Dr
To Sundry Debtors

The effect of this entry is double :

1. It is debited in the Profit & Loss A/c
2. The amount of bad debt is deducted from the Debtors in the Balance Sheet.

If 'Bad Debts' appear in the Trial Balance, it means bad debts have already been adjustec (deducted) in the Debtor's A/c and require single treatment in Profit & Loss A/c only. No adjusting entry is required.

8. Provision for bad and doubtful debts : Besides actual bad debts, there may be certain debts whose recovery may be doubtful. Doubtful debts may or may not be recovered and hence these represent expected loss for which a provision is created on debtors to meet such a loss in case it occurs. However, expected loss cannot be treated as a loss before it actually occurs. Such debts cannot be written off as bad debts because non recovery of debts is not yet certain. That is why a provision for doubtful debts is maintained. This is done to show the amount of debtors at the true value without deducting the amount of estimated expected loss. The adjusting entry creates provision which is charged to Profit and Loss A/c.

Provision for Doubtful debts A/c Dr
To Debtors A/c

Effect of this entry is :

1. The amount of the provision required is debited to Profit and Loss A/c
2. It is deducted from the debtors in the Balance Sheet.

However, when actual bad debts and "Provision for doubtful" exists, necessary adjustments are required to find out the amount to be charged to Profit and Loss A/c and amount to be deducted from the debtors in the Balance Sheet.

Following illustrations will make the points clear.

Illustration (A-I)

Following figures are taken from the Trial Balance of a Trader on the last of accounting year :

	Rs.
Sundry Debtors	60,000
Bad debts	2,000

Create Provision for doubtful debt at 5% on debtors.

Solution : **Adjustment entry**

			Dr		
	(i)	Provision for Doubtful debts A/c	Dr	3,000	
		To Debtors A/c			3,000
		(Being Provision for Doubtful debts created)			
and	(ii)	Profit and Loss A/c	Dr	3,000	
		To Provision for Doubtful debt			3,000
		(Being Provision for Doubtful debts @ 5% on Rs. 60,000 transferred to P & L A/c)			

PROFIT & LOSS A/C

	Rs.	
To Bad Debts	2,000	
To Provision for Doubtful debts	3,000	

BALANCE SHEET AS ON...(only relevant item)

	Assets		Rs.
	Sundry Debtors	60,000	
	Less : Provision for Doubtful debts	3,000	57,000

Illustration (A-2)

EXTRACT FROM TRIAL BALANCE AS ON 31ST MARCH 2008

	Dr. (Rs.)	Cr. (Rs.)
Sundry Debtors	40,000	
Bad debts	1,500	

Additional information :

There was further bad debt of Rs. 800

Provide 5% provision for doubtful debts.

Solution : Provision for Doubtful debt is to be created on Rs. 39,200 (40,000 - 800) i.e. Debtors Less additional bad debts. It should be noted that debts, which are definitely good or definitely bad, do not require any provision as such. Thus 5% of Rs. 39,200 i.e. Rs. 1,960 are to be provided for.

PROFIT & LOSS A/C

		Rs.	
To Bad debts	1,500		
Add : Additional Bad debts :	800		
Add : Provision for doubtful debts	1,960	4,260	

BALANCE SHEET OF AS ON .....

	Assets		Rs.
	Debtors	40,000	
	Less : Additional Bad debts	800	
		39,200	
	Less : Provision	1,960	37,240

Illustration (A-3)

EXTRACTS FROM A TRIAL BALANCE

	Dr. (Rs.)	Cr. (Rs.)
Sundry Debtors	62,000	......
Provision for Doubtful debts	......	2,500
Bad debts	18,000	......

There were further bad debts of Rs. 1,000 Create 5% Provision for doubtful debts.

Solution : In this case provision for doubtful debt is to be made on Rs. 61,000 (62,000 - 1,000) i.e. debtors as per Trial Balance Less Additional or further bad debts as given in the adjustments. Thus 5% of Rs. 61,000 i.e. Rs. 3,050 is to be maintained for the next accounting year.

The amount to be charged to Profit and Loss A/c can be worked out as under :

	Rs.
Bad dets as per Trial Balance	1,800
Add further Bad debts	1,000
	2,800
Add New provision i.e. 5% on Rs. 61000	3,050
	5,850
Less old Provision as per Trial Balance	2,500
Amount to be charged to Profit & Loss A/c	3,350

This amount can also be worked out by preparing 'Provision for doubtful debts' account as shown under :

PROVISION FOR DOUBTFUL DEBTS A/C

	Rs.		Rs.
To Bad debts (as per T/B)	1,800	By Balance b/d (as per T/B)	2,500
To Bad debts (Additional)	1,000	By Profit and Loss A/c	3,350
To Balance c/d	3,050	(B.F.)	
	5,850		5,850

BALANCE SHEET......
As On..........

	Assets		
	S. Debtors	62,000	
	Less : Further Bad debts	1,000	
		61,000	
	Less : Provision	3,050	57,950

Illustration (A-4)

EXTRACTS FROM A TRIAL BALANCE

	(Dr) Rs.	(Cr) Rs.
Sundry Debtors	85,000	
Provision for Doubtful debts		3,500
Bad debts	2,850	

Sundry debtors include on amount of Rs. 5,000 due from 'X' who became insolvent. A dividend of 40 paisa in a rupee is likely to be received from him. Prepare "Provision for Bad and Doubtful Debts Account and show the amount of Sundry Debtors to be shown in the Balance Sheet.

Solution : PROVISION FOR BAD & DOUBTFUL DEBTS A/C

	Rs.		Rs.
To Bad debts	2,850	By Balance b/d	3,500
To Bad debts (Additional)	3,000	By Profit and Loss A/c	6,350
To Balance c/d	4,000	(Balancing figue)	
	9,850		9,850

BALANC SHEET AS ON ......

	Assets	Rs.	Rs.
	S Debtors	85,000	
	Less : Further Bad debts	3,000	
		82,000	
	Less : Provision for D. Debts	4,000	78,000

9. Provision for Discount on Debtors : Generally, a business enterprise encourages credit customers to make prompt payment for which they are allowed discount. Hence a concern maintains "provision for discount on debtors" account to find out cash discount expected to be availed by the existing debtors during on accounting year. It is an expected loss and charged to Profit and Loss A/c.

Illustration (A-5)

EXTRACTS FROM A TRIAL BALANCE

	(Dr) Rs.	(Cr) Rs.
Sundry debtors	82,000	
Provision for Bad debts		3,000
Provisionf or Discount		1,000
Bad debts	2,800	
Discount Allowed	1,400	

Required : Make a provision for bad and doubtful debts @ 5% on debtors and Create a provision for discount on debtors @ 2%. A customer who had to pay Rs. 2,000 became insolvent. Nothing could be recovered from him. Show how these items will appear in the Profit and Loss A/c and Balance Sheet.

Solution : **PROVISION FOR BAD & DOUBTFUL DEBTS A/C**

Dr. Cr.

	Rs.		Rs.
To Bad debts	2,800	By Balance b/d	3,000
To Bad debts (further)	2,000	By Profit and Loss A/c (Blancing Figure)	5,800
To Balance c/d 5% on (82,000 – 2,000)	4,000		
	8,800		8,800

PROVISION FOR DISCOUNT A/C

Dr. Cr.

	Rs.		Rs.
To Discount Allowed	1,400	By Balance b/d	1,000
To Balance c/d 2% on (82,000 – 2,000 – 4,000)	1,520	By Profit and Loss A/c (Balancing Figure)	1,920
	2,920		2,920

PROFIT & LOSS A/C

Dr. Cr.

	Rs.	
To Provision for Doubtful debts	5,800	
To Provision for Discount	1,920	

BALANCE SHEET OF AS ON ...

Dr. Cr.

	Assets	Rs.	
	Sundry Debtors	82,000	
	Less : Irrecoverable debts	2,000	
		80,000	
	Less : 5% Provision for Doubtful debts	4,000	
		76,000	
	Less : 2% Provision for discount	1,520	74,480

It should be noted that 'Provision for discount' is calculated on the net amount, which will definitely be recovered from debtors. Thus debts which are bad, and which are doubtful, should be deducted before calculating provision for discount on debtors.

Illustration (A-6)

A Trader maintains 'Provision for Bad and Doubtful Debts Account' @ 5% and "Provision for Discount" on debtors @ 2%. Following particulars are available :

	2006	2007
	Rs.	Rs.
Bad debts	1,600	3,000
Discount allowed	2,400	1,000
Recovery of Bad debts Written off in earlier years	1,000	600

Sundry debtors (before writing off bad debts and discount) amount to Rs. 1,20,000 on 31st December 2006 and Rs. 84,000 on 31st December 2007. On 1-1-2006 Provision for Bad debts and Provision for Discount on debtors had balance of Rs. 9,100 and Rs. 1,600 respectively. Show the provision for bad debts account and provision for discount on debtors account for 2006 and 2007.

[I.C.W.A. Inter, 1989-Modified]

Solution : PROVISION FOR BAD AND DOUBTFUL DEBTS A/C

Date	Particulars	Rs.	Date	Particulars	Rs.
2006			2006		
Dec. 31	To Bad debts	1,600	Jan. 1	By Balance b/d	9,100
Dec. 31	To Profit & Loss A/c				
	(Balancing figure)	1,700			
Dec. 31	To Balance c/d	5,800			
		9,100			9,100
2007			2007		
Dec. 31	To Bad debts	3,000	Jan. 1	By Balance bd	5,800
Dec. 31	To Balance c/d	4,000	Dec. 31	By Profit & Loss A/c	1,200
		7,000		(Balancing figure)	7,000
			2008 Jan. 1	By Balance b/d	4,000

PROVISION FOR DISCOUNT ON DEBTORS A/C

Date	Particulars	Rs.	Date	Particulars	Rs.
2006			2006		
Dec. 31	To Discount Allowed	2,400	Jan. 1	By Balance b/d	1,600
Dec. 31	To Balance c/d	2,204	Dec. 31	By Profit & Loss A/c	3,004
				(Balancing figure)	
		4,604			4,604
2007			2007		
Dec. 31	To Discount Allowed	1,000	Jan. 1	By Balance b/d	2,204
Dec. 31	To Balance c/d	1,520	Dec. 31	By Profit & Loss A/c	316
				(Balancing figure)	
		2,520			2,520
			2008 Jan. 1	By Balance b/d	1,520

Working Notes :

			Rs.
(1)	Debtors as on 31-12-2006		1,20,000
	(Before Bad debts and Discount allowed)		
	Less Bad debts	1,600	
	Less Discount Allowed	2,400	4,000
			1,16,000
	Provision for Bad debts @ 5% on Rs. 1,16,000		(5,800)
	Provision for discount @ 2% on Rs. 1,10,200 (1,16,000 – 5,800)		(2,204)
	Amount to be shown in the Balance Sheet		1,07,996
(2)	Debtors (before Bad debts and discount allowed) as on 31-12-2007		84,000
	Less Bad debts	3,000	
	Less Discount Allowed	1,000	4,000
			80,000
	Provision for Bad debts @ 5% on Rs. 80,000		4,000
	Provision for discount @ 2% on Rs. 76,000		76,000
	Amount to be shown in the Balance Sheet		1,520
			74,480

Illustration (A-7)

EXTRACTS FROM A TRIAL BALANCE

	Dr (Rs.)	Cr (Rs.)
Sundry Debtors	60,000	
Bad debts	4,500	
Provision for Bad and Doubtful debts		5,000

Adjustments :

1. Write off further bad debts Rs. 1,200, 2. Provide for doubtful debts at 5% on Debtors.

Record journal entries and prepare necessary ledger accounts and show the relevant items in the final accounts.

Solution : **JOURNAL ENTRIES**

			Rs.	Rs.
Bad Debts A/c	Dr		1,200	
To Sundry Debtors A/c				1,200
(Being additional bad debts provided)				
Provision for Bad & Doubtful debts	Dr		5,700	
To Bad Debts A/c				5,700
(Being additional bad debts transferred to Provision A/c)				
Profit and Loss A/c	Dr		3,640	
To Provision for Bad & Doubtful A/c				3,640
(Being amount charged to Profit & Loss A/c)				

PROVISION FOR BAD & DOUBTFUL DEBTS A/C

To Bad Debts	4,500	By Balance b/d	5,000
To Bad Debts (Additional)	1,200	By Profit & Loss A/c (Balancing figure)	3,640
To Balance c/d	2,940		
	8,640		8,640

PROFIT & LOSS A/C
For the year ended ——————

To Provision for Bad and Doubtful debts	3,640	

BALANCE SHEET OF ———AS ON——————

		S. Debtors	60,000	
		Bad debts	1,200	
			58,800	
		Provision for Doubtful debts	2,940	55,860

10. Provision for discount on creditors : The policy of 'prompt payment' to creditors enhances reputation and goodwill of the business. Besides credit worthiness, the firm also avails and earns discount from creditors. When it becomes a regular feature, the business concern creates and maintains a "Provision for Discount" Account, which is credited to Profit and Loss Account.

Following adjustment entries are recorded :

(1) S. Creditors A/c Dr
    Provision for Discount A/c

(2) Provision or Reserve for Discount on Creditors A/c Dr
    To Profit and Loss A/c

The effect of this entry is double.

1. The amount of reserve is credited to Profit and Loss Account and
2. Such amount is deducted out of the Sundry creditors, which appear on the liability side of Balance Sheet.

11. Transfer to other Reserves : There is a general practice to transfer each year, a certain percentage of net profit earned to other reserves to meet certain unforeseen contingencies. These transfers are also charged to Profit & Loss Account by means of following entry.

Profit and Loss A/c Dr
    To Reserve or Reserve Fund A/c
    To Repairs and Renewals A/c or any other reserve

such reserves are shown on the liability side of Balance Sheet.

12. Deferred revenue expenditure : When a concern incurs heavy expenditure on advertisement, sales promotion schemes or on Research projects and the benefit thereof lasts many years to come, such expenditure is treated as deferred revenue expenditure which is written off over a period of its benefits. For example, if a company spends Rs. 50,000 on sales promotion or advertisement and estimates its impact on sales to last for 5 years, then an amount of Rs. 10,000 (Rs. 50,000 + 5) will be charged to Profit and Loss Account and the balance of Rs. 40,000 be treated as deferred revenue expenditure to be shown on the assets side of Balance Sheet.

13. Interest on capital : It is a common practice, in case of sole trade and partnership firm, to allow interest on capital. Such interest is treated as an expense and charged to Profit and Loss Account and credited to Capital Account. Following adjustment entries are recorded :

Interest on Capital A/c Dr
    To Capital A/c
Profit and Loss A/c Dr
    To Interest on Capital A/c

It should be noted that interest on capital is a non-cash charge and simply adjusted to Capital Account.

14. Interest on drawings : When a proprietor or partners withdraw cash from the business for personal use it is treated as drawings. In order to check reckless drawings interest on drawing is charged which is credited to Profit and Loss Account and debited to Capital Account. Following adjustment entries are recorded :

(i) Capital A/c Dr
    To Interest on Drawings A/c
(ii) Interest on Drawings A/c Dr
    To Profit & Loss Account

15. Abnormal losses : Losses arising on account of goods destroyed by fire, theft, pilferage or due to accident in transit are treated as abnormal losses. Since Trading A/c shows the result of trading operations under normal conditions, hence the entire amount of abnormal loss is credited to Trading A/c, which is equivalent to cost of goods destroyed or pilfered.

However if goods are fully insured, the amount of insurance claim is shown to the asset side of Balance Sheet.

In case goods are partly insured then, claims admitted will be taken to the asset side of the Balance Sheet and the difference between actual cost of goods destroyed and claims admitted will be charged to Profit and Loss A/c.

Again, in case goods (Stock) not insured at all, the total loss shall be charged to Profit and Loss A/c only. Following adjustment entries are recorded :

(a) When goods are fully insured

Abnormal Loss A/c Dr
    To Trading A/c
Or
* Insurance Claims A/c Dr
    To Trading A/c

(b) When goods are partly insured

* Insurance Claims A/c	Dr	
Profit and Loss A/c	Dr	
To Trading A/c		

* To be shown on the "Asset side" of Balance Sheet

(c) Goods not at all insured

Profit and Loss A/c	Dr	
To Trading A/c		

Example : Goods costing Rs. 25,000 were destroyed by fire on 1-11-2007. Record necessary adjustment entries on 31-12-2007, the daybooks of accounts are closed if,

(i) Stock was not at all insured

(ii) Stock was partly insured and claim of Rs. 10,000 was admitted by the insurance company,

(iii) Stock was fully covered by insurance.

Solution :

(1)	Profit and Loss A/c	Dr	25,000	
	To Trading A/c			25,000
(2)	Insurance Claims A/c	Dr	10,000	
	Profit and Loss A/c	Dr	15,000	
	To Trading A/c			25,000
(3)	*Insurance Claims A/c	Dr	25,000	
	To Trading A/c			25,000

*To be shown on the asset side of Balance Sheet.

16. Payment of "Life Insurance Premium" on the life of proprietor or partner, or payment of "Income Tax" out of concern's cash or bank balance : Payment or discharge of any personal liability of proprietor or partner such as life insurance premium, income tax or installment of personal loan etc. is treated as drawings. Following adjustment entries are record :

(1)	Drawings A/c To Cash or Bank A/c	Dr	**Effect :** Bank or Cash Balance will decrease
	Capital A/c To Drawings A/c	Dr	**Effect :** Capital will decrease and shown on the Balance Sheet

17. Goods taken by proprietor or partners for self-consumption are treated as drawings :

(1)	Drawings A/c To Purchases A/c	Dr	**Effect :** A decrease in Purchases to be shown in the Trading A/c
(2)	Capital A/c To Drawings A/c	Dr	**Effect :** A decrease in Capital to be shown in the Balance Sheet

18. Goods distributed as 'samples' and given to employees for their personal use : Goods distributed as samples are charged to "advertisement" and goods given to employees for their personal use are debited to "salaries" account. And the total cost of goods so distributed as samples and given to employees is credited to Purchases A/c. For example a manufacturer of toothpaste distributed toothpaste as 'samples' worth Rs. 2,500 and gave to office staff worth Rs. 1,500 for their personal use. Following adjustment entry will be recorded :

Advertisement A/c	Dr	2,500	
Salaries A/c	Dr	1,500	
To Purchases A/c			4,000

19. Goods sent on approval basis : Sometimes the goods are sent to customers on sale or return basis. If goods are approved by customers it is treated as sold and if not, these are returned to the firm. However when goods are sent on approval basis it is credited to "Sales" Account and debited to customer's Account. If on the date of closing of books of accounts, such goods are still lying with the customers who have the right to return the goods, the following adjustment entries are recorded :

(1)	Sales A/c	Dr	with the Actual sales price
	To Debtors A/c		

This entry shows the cancellation of sales recorded at the time goods were sent on approval basis.

(2)	Closing Stock A/c	Dr	at cost price
	To Trading A/c		

The effect of above entries will decrease the sales in the Trading A/c and increase the closing stock at cost price.

In the Balance Sheet 'Debtors' shall be reduced by sales price of such goods and a stock will be increased by cost price of such goods.

Illustration 8

Sales include goods worth Rs. 2,500 sent to customers on approval basis which include profit @ 25% on cost. Till the date of closing of books of accounts no intimation has been received so far. Pass adjustment entries.

Solution :

(1)	Sales A/c	Dr	2,500		with the sales value
	To Debtors A/c			2,500	
(2)	Closing Stock A/c	Dr	2,000		with the cost price
	To Trading A/c			2,000	

20. Treatment of hidden transactions : Extract of Trial Balance as on 31-12-2007

	Dr	Cr
12% Loan		30,000
Interest on Loan	2,000	

The above information shows that on Loan of Rs. 30,000 only Rs. 2,000 have been paid till the date of closing of books of accounts as against the total interest due of Rs. 3,600 (12% on Rs. 30,000) Following adjustment entries will be recorded.

Interest A/c	Dr	1,600	
To Interest Outstanding A/c*			1,600
Profit and Loss A/c	Dr	3,600	
To Interest A/c			3,600

""'Interest outstanding will be shown to the liabilities side of Balance Sheet.

PROFIT & LOSS A/C

Dr.

		Rs.	
To Interest	2,000		
Add : Outstanding	1,600	3,600	

BALANCE SHEET AS ON 31ST DEC. 2007

Liabilities	Amount (Rs.)	Assets	Amount (Rs.)
12% Loan	30,000		
Interest Outstanding	1,600		

21. Extract of a Trial Balance as on 31-12-2007

	Dr	Cr
9% Investments	50,000	
Interest on Investments		3,000

The information in the Trial Balance suggests that the interest received should have been Rs. 4,500 (9% on Rs.50,000) whereas the amount shown in the Trial Balance is Rs. 3,000 only which means an amount of Rs. 1,500 (4,500 - 3,000) is accrued but not yet received. Following adjustment entries will be recorded :

Interest Accrued A/c	Dr	1,500	
To Interest Received A/c			1,500
Interest Received A/c	Dr	4,500	
To Profit and Loss A/c			4,500

'Interest accrued will be shown to the Assets side of the Balance Sheet.

PROFIT & LOSS A/C

			Rs.
	By Interest Received	3,000	
	Add : Accrued	1,500	4,500

BALANCE SHEET AS ON 31ST DEC. 2007

	Assets	Rs.
	9% Investments	50,000
	Interest Accrued	1,500

22. Extract of a Trial Balance as on 31st Dec. 2007

	(Dr) Rs.	(Cr) Rs.
Income Tax	25,000	
Advance Income Tax	5,000	
Interest on Advance Tax		100

Show the treatment in the final accounts.

Solution : Income Tax or advance income tax is the personal liability (expense) of the proprietor or partner hence it is treated as drawings and interest earned thereon is the private income brought into business, which will be regarded as Additional Capital. Following adjustment entries will be recorded :

	Drawings A/c	Dr		30,000	
	To Income Tax A/c				25,000
	To Advance Income Tax A/c				5,000
	Capital A/c	Dr		30,000	
	To Drawings A/c				30,000
	Interest on Advance Tax A/c	Dr		100	
	To Capital A/c				100

BALANCE SHEET AS ON 31ST DEC. 2007

Liabilities		Rs.	
Capital	....		
Less : Drawings	(30,000)		
Add : Additional Capital	100	....	

23. Mutual transactions : When a concern enters into dual transactions with the same party it is said to have entered into dual transactions. For example a concern may be dealing with other concern who is the debtor and creditor of the business at the same time. In such a situation following adjustment entry is recorded :

Sundry Creditors A/c Dr
    To Sundry Debtors A/c

It is to be noted that while creating provision for doubtful debts and reserve for creditors such amount of mutual debt should be adjusted against debtors and creditors before creating provision or reserve.

24. Manager's Commission : When a manager is entitled a commission based on fixed percentage of the net profits earned, it is treated as a charge on the profits and thus debited to Profit and Loss Account. If commission remains unpaid it is taken to the liabilities side of the Balance Sheet. Following adjustment entries are recorded :

Commission A/c Dr
    To Commission Payable A/c
Profit and Loss A/c Dr
    To Commission A/c

While calculating Manager's commission it should be made clear whether commission payable on net profits is to be calculated before charging such commission or after charging such commission. For example if net profit earned by the business is Rs. 63,000 and Manager is entitled a commission of 5% of net profit after charging such commission, the amount of commission will be Rs. 3,000 $\left(\frac{5}{105} \times 63{,}000\right)$.

And in case it is 5% of net profit before charging such commission, then the Amount of commission will be Rs. 3,150 $\left(\frac{5}{100}\times 63{,}000\right)$.

Thus, the formula for calculating the commission payable as a percentage of net profit before charging such commission will be as follows :

$$= \frac{\text{Net Profit Commission} \times \text{Rate of Commission}}{100}$$

And if the commission is payable as a percentage of net profit after charging such commission, following formula shall be applied :

$$= \frac{\text{Net Profit before Commission} \times \text{Rate of Commission}}{100 + \text{Rate of Commission}}$$

Sometime Works Manager and General Manager both are entitled commission as a percentage of net profit after charging each other's commission. For example, Works Manager is entitled @ 5%°A commission on net profit after charging General Manager's and his own commission and Genera Manager is entitled @ 10% commission on net profit after Works Manager's commission and his own commission in such a case the formula will be :

For Works Manager's commission :

$$= \frac{\text{Net Profit before Commission} \times 5\,(\text{Rate of Work Manager's Commission})}{100 + 5 + 10\,(\text{Rate of Work Manager's Commission} + \text{General Manager's commission})}$$

and for General Manager's commission :

$$= \frac{\text{Net Profit before Commission} \times 10\,(\text{Rate of General Manager's Commission})}{100 + 5 + 10\,(\text{Rate of Work Manager's Commission} + \text{Rate of General Manager's commission})}$$

"MISCELLANEOUS ADJUSTMENTS"

25. On 1-1-2007 Tools and Equipments Account disclosed a balance of Rs. 6,300. During the year a further addition was made worth Rs. 2,700 in respect of which Rs. 500 were paid as freight and handling charges which were debited to Purchases and Freight Account respectively. on 31st December 2007 the Tools and Equipments were valued at Rs. 8,000.

Solution :

Tools and Equipments A/c	Dr	3,200	
To Purchases A/c			2,700
To Freight A/c			500
Depreciation A/c	Dr	1,500	
To Tools & Equipment A/c			1,500

Dep. = (6,300 + 2,700 + 500 – 8,000) 1,500

26. On 1-1-2007 the balance standing to the debit of investment account was Rs. 19,200 On 31-12-2007 these were valued at Rs. 11,700. During the year some investments were sold for Rs. 4,500, realising a profit of Rs. 1,020. This was passed through sales Book.

Solution :

(i)	Sales A/c	Dr	4,500	
	To Investment			3,480
	To Profit & Loss A/c*			1,020

Alteratively it can be transferred to Investment Fluctuation fund,

(ii)	Profit and Loss A/c	Dr	4,020	
	To Investment Fluctuation Fund A/c**			4,020

**If there is no investment fluctuation fund, the same can be credited to Investment A/c. as shown below.

Working Notes	Rs.	Rs.
Sale price of investment	4,500	
Less Profit	1,020	
Cost of Investment (Book Value)	3,480	
Total Value of Investment as on 1-1-2007		19,200
Less Book Value of Investment sold		3,480
		15,720
Less Value as on 31-12-2007		11,700
Loss or Provision Required		4,020

27. A Plant of the book value of Rs. 1,60,000 was disposed of for Rs. 56,000 in part exchange for a new machine costing Rs. 1,30,000. The net invoice of Rs. 74,000 was passed through the invoice book.

Solution :

New Plant A/c	Dr	1,30,000	
Profit & Loss A/c	Dr	1,04,000	
To Old Plant A/c			1,60,000
To Purchases A/c			74,000

New plant acquired has to be debited with the actual price and Old Plant sold, to be credited with the Book Value appearing in the books. The Difference between Book Value of plant sold and sale price of plant is the resultant loss, which will be debited to Profit and Loss A/c. The purchases wrongly debited earlier will be credited to rectify the mistake.

GRADED PROBLEMS WITH SOLUTIONS

Problem 1 (Abnormal Loss and Insurance Claims)

From the following Trial Balance you are required to prepare Trading and Profit and Loss Account for the year ended 31st March 2007 and a Balance Sheet as on that date.

TRIAL BALANCE AS ON 31ST MARCH 2007

Dr. Cr.

Particulars	Rs.	Particulars	Rs.
Drawings Account	7,500	Capital Account	1,50,000
Plant and machinery (1-4-2006)	1,25,000	Returns Outward	1,250
Plant and machinery (1-10-2006)	6,250	Sundry Creditors	22,500
Stock (1-4-2006)	19,250	Sales	2,00,000
Purchases	1,02,500	Provision for Bad & Doubtful debts	500

Returns Inward	2,500	Discount Received	1,000
Sundry Debtors	25,750	Rent (upto 30-9-2007)	1,500
Furniture	6,200		
Freight	12,500		
Carriage Outwards	625		
Rent, Rates & Taxes	5,750		
Printing and Stationery	1,000		
Trade Expenses	500		
Insurance Charges	875		
Salaries and Wages	26,625		
Cash at Bank	25,675		
Cash in hand	7,250		
Postage & Telegram	1,000		
	3,76,750		3,76,750

Adjustments :

(i) Stock on 31st March 2007 was valued at Rs. 15,000

(ii) Write off Rs. 750 as bad debts.

(iii) Provision for Bad and Doubtful debts is to be maintained at 5% on Sundry debtors.

(iv) Create a provision for discount on debtors and also reserve for discount on creditors @ 2%.

(v) Charge depreciation @ 20% p.a. on Plant and Machinery and @ 5% on Furniture,

(vi) Insurance prepaid was Rs. 125.

(vii) Goods worth Rs. 6,250 were totally damaged in an accident. The Insurance Company admitted a claim of Rs. 5,000 on 28-3-2007.

Solution :

TRADING ACCOUNT
For the year ended 31st March 2007

Dr. Cr.

Particulars		Rs.	Particulars		Rs.
To Opening Stock		19,250	By Sales	2,00,000	
To Purchases	1,02,500		*Less* : Returns	2,500	1,97,500
Less : Returns	1,250	1,01,250			
			By Closing Stock		15,000
To Freight		12,500	By Insurance Claims		5,000
To Gross Profit transferred to Profit & Loss A/c		85,750	By Profit & Loss A/c (Abnormal Loss)		1,250
		2,18,750			2,18,750

PROFIT & LOSS ACCOUNT

Particulars		Rs.	Particulars		Rs.
To Rent, Rates & Taxes		5,750	By Gross Profit b/d		85,750
To Printing and Statinoery		1,000	By Discount Received		1,000
To Trade xpenses		500	By Rent Received	1,500	
To Insurance	875		Less : Prepaid	750	750
Less : Prepaid	125	750	By Reserve for Discount on Creditors		450
To Salaries & Wages		26,625			
To Postage & Telegram		1,000			
To Provisionf or Bad and Doubtful		1,500			
To Provision for Discount on debtors		475			
To Carriage Outward		625			
To Abnormal Loss (Accident)		1,250			
To Depreciation on :					
Furniture	310				
Plant & Machinery	25,625	25,935			
To Net Profit transferred to Capital		22,540			
		87,950			87,950

BALANCE SHEET AS ON 31ST MARCH 2007

Liabilities		Rs.	Assets		Rs.
Capital	1,50,000		Plant & Machinery	1,25,000	
Add : Net Profit	22,540		Additions	6,250	
	1,72,540		*Less* : Depreciation	1,31,250	
Less : Drawings	7,500	1,65,040		25,625	1,05,625
Sundry Creditors	22,500		Furniture	6,200	
Less : Provision	450	22,050	*Less* : Depreciation	310	5,890
Advance Rent		750	Closing Stock		15,000
			Debtors	25,750	
			Less : Bed debts	750	
				25,000	
			Less : Provision	1,250	
				23,750	
			Less : Provision	475	23,275
			Cash at Bank		25,675
			Cash in hand		7,250
			Insurance Claims		5,000
			Prepaid Insurance		125
		1,87,840			1,87,840

Problem 2 (Treatment of Provident Fund)

The following is the Trial Balance of Mr. M as on 31st December 2007. Prepare a Trading and Profit & Loss Account for the year ended 2007 and Balance Sheet as on 31st December 2007.

Dr. Cr.

	Rs.		Rs.
Purchases	1,80,000	Sales	2,05,000
Opening Stock	10,000	Loan (10% interest)	10,000
Salaries Less : Provident Fund	5,400	Creditors	15,000
Drawings	5,000	Capital	55,000
Provident Fund remittances including proprietor's contribution 50%	1,200		
Rent Rs. 250 per month	2,750		
Machinery	29,000		
Wages	3,000		
Furniture & Fittings	5,000		
Electricity	550		
Trade Expenses	1,500		
Debtors	10,500		
Interest on Loan	900		
Commission	200		
Building	30,000		
	2,85,000		2,85,000

On 1-1-2007 machinery worth Rs. 5,000 was sold for Rs. 4,000 and credited to machinery account Wages include Rs. 1,000 paid for machinery erection charges. Purchases include cost of moped scooter for Rs. 5,000. Proprietor has taken goods costing Rs. 1,000 for which no entry has been made. Sundry Debtors include Rs. 500 which have become bad. Provide 10% reserve for bad debts. Electricity outstanding Rs. 50 Goods costing Rs. 5,000 were destroyed by fire and insurance claim to be received for Rs. 4,000. Provide depreciation at 10% on machinery, furniture and moped. Provide depreciation 5% on Building. Closing stock is Rs. 12,000. **[C.A. Ent., Dec. 1985, Modified]**

Solution :

TRADING AND PROFIT & LOSS ACCOUNT
For the year ended 31st December 2007

Particulars		Rs.	Particulars	Rs.
To Opening Stock		10,000	By Sales	2,05,000
To Purchases	1,80,000		By Loss by fire transferred	
Less : Purchase of Scooter	5,000		to P & L A/c	5,000
Less : Drawings (goods used)	1,000	1,74,000	By Closing Stock	12,000
To Wages	3,000			
Less : Erection charges	1,000	2,000		

To Gross Profit c/d		36,000		
		2,22,000		2,22,000
To Salaries	5,400		By Gross Profit b/d	36,000
Add : Subscription	600		By Insurance Claims	4,000
Contribution	600	6,600		
To Rent	2,750			
Add : Outstanding	250	3,000		
To Electricity	550			
Add : Outstanding	50	600		
To Commission		200		
To Trade Expenses		1,500		
To Bad debts		500		
To Interest	900			
Add : Outstanding	100	1,000		
To Provision for Bad debts		1,000		
To Loss on sale of Machinery		1,000		
To Loss by fire (Trading A/c)		5,000		
To Depreciation on :				
Building		1,500		
Machinery		2,900		
Furniture		500		
Scooter		500		
To Net Profit		14,200		
		40,000		40,000

BALANCE SHEET
As on 31st December 2007

Liabilities		Rs.	Assets		Rs.
Capital	55,000		Building	30,000	
Add : Net Profit	14,200		*Less* : Depreciation	1,500	28,500
Less : Drawings (5000 + 1000)	6,000	63,200	Machienry	29,000	
10% Loan		10,000	*Add* : Erection Charges	1,000	
Creditors		15,000	*Less* : Loss on Sale	(1,000)	
Rent Outstanding		250	*Less* : Depreciation	(2,900)	26,100
Interest Outstanding		100	Furniture	5,000	
Electricity Charges O/S		50	*Less* : Depreciation	500	4,500
			Scooter	5,000	
			Less : epreciation	500	4,500
			Closing Stock		12,000

		Debtors	10,500	
		Less : Bad debts	(500)	
		Less : Provision @ 10%	(1,000)	9,000
		Insurance Claims		4,000
	88,600			88,600

Problem 3 (Remission of liability)

A shopkeeper has prepared the following Trial Balance as on 31st March 2007 :

	Rs.		Rs.
Purchases	6,20,000	Sales	8,30,000
Cash in hand	4,200	Cash at Bank	24,000
Stock (1-4-2006)	1,00,000	Capital	5,77,200
Drawings	8,000	Salaries	64,000
Postage & Telephone	23,000	Salesmen's Commission	70,000
Insurance	18,000	Advertising	34,000
Furniture	44,000	Printing & Stationery	6,000
Motor Car	96,000	Bad debts	4,000
Cash Discount Allowed	8,000	General Expenses	60,000
Carriage Inwards	20,000	Carriage Outwards	44,000
Wages	40,000	Creditors	80,000
Debtors	2,00,000		

Prepare Trading and Profit & Loss A/c for the year ended 31st March 2007 and Balance Sheet as on that date. You are also given the following information :

1. Cost of goods in stock on 31st March 2007 Rs. 1,45,000.
2. The proprietor had withdrawn goods worth Rs. 5,000 during the year.
3. Purchases include purchase of furniture worth Rs. 10,000.
4. Debtors include Rs. 5,000 bad debts.
5. Creditors include a balance of Rs. 4,000 to the credit of Mr. B in respect of which it has been decided and settled with the party to pay only Rs. 1,000.
6. Sales include goods worth Rs. 15,000 sent to Ram & Co. on approval and remaining unsold on 31st March 2007, the cost of goods was Rs. 10,000.
7. Provision for Bad debts is to be created at 5% on Debtors.
8. Depreciate furniture by 15%, Motor Car by 20%.
9. Salesmen are entitled Commission @ 10% on total sales. **[C.A. (Inter), 1989-Modified]**

Solution :

TRADING AND PROFIT AND LOSS ACCOUNT
For the year ended 31st March 2007

Dr. Cr.

Particulars		Rs.	Particulars		Rs.
To Opening Stock		1,00,000	By Sales	8,30,000	
To Purchases	6,20,000		*Less* : Goods on approval	15,000	8,15,000
Less : Drawings	(5,000)		By Closing Stock	1,45,000	
Less : Furniture	(10,000)	6,05,000	*Add* : Cost of goods		
To Carriage Inwards		20,000	sent no approval	10,000	1,55,000
To Wages		40,000			
To Gross Profit transferred to Profit & Loss A/c		2,05,000			
		9,70,000			9,70,000
To Salaries		64,000	By Gross Profit b/d		2,05,000
To Salesmen's Commission	70,000		By Remission of Liability		3,000
Add : Outstanding	11,500	81,500	By Net Loss transferreted to Capital A/c		1,75,800
To Advertising		34,000			
To Printing & Stationery		6,000			
To Bad debts		9,000			
To Provisionf or Bad debts 5% on 1,80,000		9,000			
To General Expenses		60,000			
To Carriage Outwards		44,000			
To Postage & Telephone		23,000			
To Insurance		18,000			
To Cash Discount		8,000			
To Depreciation on :					
Furniture @ 15% on Rs. 54,000 (44,000 + 10,000)		8,100			
Motor Car @ 20%		19,200			
		3,83,800			3,83,800

BALANCE SHEET
As on 31st March 2007

Liabilities		Rs.	Assets		Rs.
Capital	5,77,200		Furniture	44,000	
Less : Net Loss	(1,75,800)	3,88,400	*Add* : Purchased	10,000	
Less : Drawing (Cash)	(5,000)		*Less* : Depeciation	54,000	
Less : Drawings (Cash)	(8,000)			(8,100)	45,900
Creditors	80,000		Motor Car	96,000	
Less : Waived Off (Remission)	(3,000)	77,000	*Less* : Depreciation	(19,200)	76,800
Salesmen Commission O/S		11,500	Closing Stock	1,45,000	
			Add : goods sent on approval	10,000	1,55,000
			Debtors	2,00,000	
			Less : Additional Bed debts	(5,000)	
				1,95,000	
			Less : Sale on approval	(15,000)	
				1,80,000	
			Less : Provision @ 5%	(9,000)	1,71,000
			Cash at Bank		24,000
			Cash in Hand		4,200
		4,76,900			4,76,900

Problem 4 (Calculation of Commission)

From the following balances and information extracted from the books of Mr. X on 31st March 2007, prepare Trading, Profit and Loss Account for the year ended 31st March 2007 and the Balance sheet as on that date

	Rs.		Rs.
X's Capital Account	60,000	Plant and Machinery	18,000
Depreciation on Plant & Machinery	2,000	Repairs to Plant	1,600
Wages	28,000	Salaries	4,000
Income Tax	500	Cash in hand	2,000
Land	24,500	Depreciation on Building	2,500
Purchases Less : Returns	1,23,500	Sales	2,49,000
Bank Overdraft	13,800	Accrued Income	1,500
Salaries Outstanding	2,000	Bills Receivable	30,000
Bills Payable	3,000	Discount on Purchases	4,000
Bad debts	1,000	Sundry Creditors	23,300
Sundry Debtors	35,000	Building	50,000
Stock (1-4-2006)	37,000	Provision for Bad debts	6,000

Additional Information :

(i) Stock on 31st March 2007 was Rs. 30,000.

(ii) Write off Rs. 3,000 bad debts and maintain a provision for bad and doubtful debts at 5% on Sundry Debtors.

(iii) Goods costing Rs. 5,000 were sent to customers on sale on approval basis on 31-3-2007. These were recorded as actual sale. The rate of gross profit was l/6th of sale.

(iv) Rs. 1,200 paid as rent of the office was debited to Landlord's account and were included in sundry debtors.

(v) General Manager is to be given commission at 10% after charging the commission of Works Manager and his own on net profit. Works Manager is to be given commission at 5% after charging commission of General Manager and his own on net profits. Such commission shall be calculated to the nearest rupee. **[C.A. Foundation, 1990-Modifted]**

Solution : **TRADING AND PROFIT & LOSS ACCOUNT**

For the year ended 31st March 2007

Dr. Cr.

Particulars	Rs.	Particulars		Rs.
To Opening Stock	37,000	By Sales	2,49,000	
To Purchases *Less* : Returns	1,23,500	*Less* : Goods sent on approval	6,000	2,43,000
To Wages	28,000	By Closing Stock	30,000	
To Gross Profit transferred to Profit & Loss A/c	89,500	*Add* : Cost of Goods on approval	5,000	35,000
	2,78,000			2,78,000
To Salaries	4,000	By Gross Profit b/d		89,500
To Rent	1,200	By Provision for Bad debts**		760
To Repairs to Plant	1,600	By Discount on Purchases		4,000
To Depreciation on : Plant	2,000			
Building	2,500			
To Works Manager's Commission	3,607*			
To General Manager's Commission	7,214*			
To Net Profit transferred to Capital A/c	72,139			
	94,260			94,260

*Commission of Works Manager and General Manager has been calculated as under :

Works Manager's commission is 5% of net profit after charging General Manager's commission and his own commission.

General Manager is entitled @ 10% of net profit after charging Works Manager's commission and his own commission.

Thus Works Manager's commission would be :

$$= \frac{\text{Net Profit before Commission} \times \text{Rate of Works Manager's Commission}}{100 + \text{Rate of Work Manager's Commission} + \text{Rate of General Manager's commission}}$$

$$= \frac{82{,}960 \times 5}{100 + 5 + 10} = \frac{82{,}960 \times 5}{115} = \text{Rs. } 3{,}607$$

and similarly General Manager's commission will be :

$$= \frac{82{,}960 \times 10}{100 + 5 + 10} = \text{Rs. } 7{,}214.$$

****PROVISION FOR BAD DEBTS A/C**

Dr. Cr.

Particulars	Rs.	Particulars	Rs.
To Bad debts	1,000	By Balance b/d	6,000
To Bad debts (Additional)	3,000		
To Profit & Loss A/c (B/F)	760		
To Balance c/d	1,240		
	6,000		6,000

BALANCE SHEET OF X, As on 31st March 2007

Liabilities		Rs.	Assets		Rs.
Capital	60,000		Land		24,500
Add : Net Profit	72,139		Building	52,500	
	1,32,139		*Less* : Dep.	2,500	50,000
Less : Drawings (I. Tax)	500	1,31,639	Plant & Machinery	20,000	
Works Manager's Commission o/s		3,607	*Less* : Dep.	2,000	18,000
General Manager's Commission o/s		7,214	Closing Stock		35,000
Salaries O/s		2,000	Sundry Debtors*	24,800	
Bank Overdraft		13,800	*Less* : Provision	1,240	23,560
Sundry Creditors		23,300	Bills Receivable		30,000
Bills Payable		3,000	Accrued Income		1,500
			Cash in hand		2,000
		1,84,560			1,84,560

	Rs.
*Sundry Debtors	35,000
Less : Sale on approval	6,000
	29,000
Less : Bad debts (Additional)	3,000
	26,000
Less : Rent debited to Debtor's A/c	1,200
Provision required on	24,800

Problem 5 (Goods on Approval and Rectification)

The following is the Trial Balance of Shri Madan Lal as on 31st March 2007 you are required to prepare the Trading and Profit and Loss Account for the year ended 31st March 2007 and the Balance Sheet as on that date after making necessary adjustments.

Debit balances	Rs.	Credit balances	Rs.
Sundry Debtors	5,00,000	Sundry Creditors	2,00,000
Outstanding Liability for Expenses	55,000	Capital	14,43,000
Purchases	15,50,000	Sales	19,87,500
Stock (1-4-2000)	2,50,000		
Wags	1,00,000		
Cariage Outwards	10,000		
Carriage Inwards	50,000		
General Expenses	70,000		
Cash Discount	20,000		
Bad debts	10,000		
Cash at bank	60,000		
Motor Car	2,40,000		
Printing & Stationery	15,000		
Cash in hand	10,500		
Furniture and Fitting	1,10,000		
Advrtisement	85,000		
Insurance	45,000		
Salesmen's Commission	87,500		
Postage and Telephone	57,500		
Salaries	2,60,000		
Rates & Taxes	25,000		
Drawings	20,000		
	36,30,500		36,30,500

Adjustments :

1. Stock on 31st March 2007 was valued at Rs. 7,25,000
2. Make a provision for Doubtful Debts equal to 5% on sundry debtors.
3. Depreciate Motor Car by 20%, Furniture and Fittings by 10%.
4. Shri Madan Lal had withdrawn goods worth Rs. 25,000 during the year.
5. Sales include goods worth Rs. 75,000 sent out to Shanti and Company on approval and remaining unsold on 31st March 2007. The cost of goods was Rs. 50,000 (The customer was still having the right to return the goods).
6. The salesmen are entitled to a commission of 5% on total sales.
7. Debtors include Rs. 25,000 bad debts.

8. Printing and Stationery expenses of Rs. 55,000 relating to 2006-2007 had not been provided in that year but was paid in this year by debiting outstanding liabilities account.
9. Purchases include purchase of furniture Rs. 50,000. **[C.A. Entrance, 1991-Adapted]**

[B.Com. (H) DU 2007]

TRADING AND PROFIT & LOSS ACCOUNT
For the Year ended 31st March 2007

Particulars		Rs.	Particulars		Rs.
To Opening Stock		2,50,000	By Sales	19,87,500	
To Purchases	15,50,000		*Less* : Goods on approval	75,000	19,12,500
Less : Drawings	(25,000)		By Closing Stock	7,25,000	
Less : Purchase of Furniture	(50,000)	14,75,000	*Add* : Cost of goods sent on approval	50,000	7,75,000
To Carriage Inwards		50,000			
To Wages		1,00,000			
To Gross Profit transferred to P & L A/c		8,12,500			
		26,87,500			26,87,500
To Salaries		2,60,000	By Gross Profit		8,12,500
To Postage & Telephone		57,500			
To Insurance		45,000			
To Rates & Taxes		25,000			
To Printing & Stationery		15,000			
To Advertisement		85,000			
To Carriage Outwards		10,000			
To Bad debts		35,000			
To Provisionf or Bad debts		20,000			
To Cash Discount		20,000			
To General Expenses		70,000			
To Salesmen's Commission*		95,625			
Paid	87,500				
Outstanding	8,125				
To Depreciation on :					
Furniture & Fitting		16,000			
Motor Car		48,000			
To Net Profit transferred to Capital A/c		10,375			
		8,12,500			8,12,500

*5% on 19,12,500 = Rs. 95,625.

BALANCE SHEET
As on 31st March 2007

Liabilities		Rs.	Assets		Rs.
Capital	14,43,000		Motor Car	2,40,000	
Add : Net Profit	10,375		*Less* Depreciation	48,000	1,92,000
Less : Drawings	(45,000)		Furniture & Fitting	1,10,000	
Less : Last year's expenses			Additions	50,000	
wrongly debited	(55,000)	13,53,375	*Less* : Dep.	(16,000)	1,44,000
Sundry Creditors		2,00,000	Closing Stock	7,25,000	
O/s Salesmen's Commission		8,125	*Add* : Goods sent on approval	50,000	7,75,000
			Sundry Debtors	5,00,000	
			Less : Goods on approval	(75,000)	
				4,25,000	
			Less : Bad debts (additional)	(25,000)	
			Less : Provision	(20,000)	3,80,000
			Cash at Bank		60,000
			Cash in hand		10,500
		15,61,500			15,61,500

Problem 6 (Adjustment in Closing Stock and Provident Fund)

From the following particulars prepare the Trading and Profit and Loss Account for the year ended 31 st December 2007 and a Balance Sheet as on that date.

Particulars	Rs.	Particulars	Rs.
Building	50,000	Loans (1-1-2007)	30,000
Machinery	22,000	Capital	52,000
Furniture	10,000	Creditors	40,000
Bank	9,000	Purchase Returns	10,000
Cash	1,000	Sales	3,22,000
Debtors	50,000	Provident Fund deducted from salaries	1,000
Opening Stock	12,000		
Purchases	2,50,000		
Sales Returns	12,000		
Rent	6,000		
Establishment	16,000		
Interest (10%)	2,000		
Electricity	1,000		
Phone	1,000		
Commission	6,000		
Insurance Premium	1,000		
Bad debts	2,000		
Bills Receivable	4,000		
	4,55,000		4,55,000

Provide depreciation on Building @ 5%, Machinery, @ 15% and Furniture @ 10%. Stock was not taken on 31st December 2007 but only on 7-1-2008. The transactions from 1-1-2008 to 7-1-2008 are : Sales Rs. 25,000, Purchases Rs. 15,000. Stock on 7-1-2008 Rs. 18,000 and Gross Profit 20%. During the year machinery of the value of Rs. 10,000 was destroyed by fire and the insurance claim was settled at Rs. 8,000 and credited to Machinery A/c. Also provide: Employer's share of P.F. Rs. 1,000, Provision for Bad debts 5%, Commission of the Manager @ 10% on net profit after providing such commission.

[C A Ent. Modified]

TRADING AND PROFIT & LOSS ACCOUNT
For the year ended 31st December 2007

Particulars		Rs.	Particulars		Rs.
To Opening Stock		12,000	By Sales	3,22,000	
To Purchases	2,50,000		*Less* : Returns	(12,000)	3,10,000
Less : Returns	(10,000)	2,40,000	By Closing Stock	18,000	
To Gross Profit c/d		81,000	*Add* : Cost of goods		
			sold after closing	20,000	
			Less : Goods purchased		
			after closing	(15,000)	23,000
		3,33,000			3,33,000
To Rent		6,000	By Gross Proit b/d		81,000
To Establishment		16,000			
To Interest	2,000				
Add : O/s	1,000	3,000			
To Phone		1,000			
Electricity		1,000			
To Insurance		1,000			
To Commision		6,000			
To Bad debts		2,000			
To Provision for Bad debts		2,500			
To Loss due to fire (Machine)		2,000			
To Employer's Contribution to Provident Fund		1,000			
To Depreciation on :					
Building		2,500			
Machinery		3,000			
Furniture		1,000			
To Manager's Commission		3,000			
To Net Profit c/d		30,000			
		81,000			81,000

BALANCE SHEET
As on 31st December 2007

Liabilities		Rs.	Assets		Rs.
Capital	52,000		Building	50,000	
Add : Net Profit	30,000	82,000	*Less* : Depreciation	(2,500)	47,500
Loan		30,000	Machinery	22,000	
Interest on Loan O/s		1,000	*Less* : Loss by fire[(1)]	(2,000)	
Creditors		40,000	*Less* : Depreciation	(3,000)	17,000
Manager's Commission O/s		3,000	Furniture	10,000	
Provident Fund[(2)]			*Less* : Depreciation	(1,000)	9,000
Employee's Share	1,000		Stock		23,000
Contribution	1,000	2,000	Debtors	50,000	
			Less : Provision for Bad debts	(2,500)	47,500
			Bills Receivable		4,000
			Cash at Bank		9,000
			Cash in hand		1,000
		1,58,000			1,58,000

Working Notes :

1. Since insurance claim of Rs. 8,000 has already been credited to machinery account, only actual loss of Rs. 2,000 (10,000 - 8,000) has been adjusted against the machinery account. Thus "insurance claim" has not been shown in the Balance Sheet.
2. Provident Fund is shown as a liability. Employer and employee's contribution has been put together.

Problem 7 (Adjustment in Purchases)

The following Trial Balance was extracted from the books of Mr. Anil as on 30th September 2007 :

Particulars	Rs.	Particulars	Rs.
Plant & Machinery	78,000	Capital	1,00,000
Furniture	2,000	Sales	1,27,000
Purchases	60,000	Returns	750
Returns	1,000	Discount	800
Opening Stock	30,000	Provision for Bad debts	525
Discount	425	Sundry Creditors	25,000
Sundry Debtors	45,000		
Salaries	7,550		
Manufacturing Wages	10,000		
Carriage Outward	1,200		
Rent, Rates & Taxes	10,000		
Advertisement	2,000		
Cash	6,900		
	2,54,075		2,54,075

Prepare Trading and Profit and Loss Account for the year ended 30th September 2007 and a Balance Sheet as on that date after taking into account the following adjustments :

(1) Closing Stock was valued at Rs. 34,220

(2) Provision for Bad debts is to be kept at Rs. 500

(3) Allow interest on Capital at 10% p.a.

(4) Furniture was old and the same was disposed off for Rs. 760 in exchange of a new furniture costing Rs. 1,680. The net invoice of Rs. 920 was passed through Purchase-Register (No depreciation need to be charged on old and new furniture)

(5) Depreciate Plant and Machinery by 10% p.a.

(6) The proprietor Mr. Anil has taken goods worth Rs. 5,000 for personal use and distributed goods worth Rs. 1,000 as samples. **[C.A. Entrance, May 1989-Modified]**

Solution : **TRADING AND PROFIT & LOSS ACCOUNT**

For the year ended 31st September 2007

Particulars		Rs.	Particulars		Rs.
To Opening Stock		30,000	By Sales	1,27,000	
To Purchases	60,000		Less : Returns	(1,000)	1,26,000
Less : Drawings			By Closing Stock		34,220
(goods for personal use)	(5,000)				
Less : Goods used for samples	(1,000)				
Less : Puchase of furniture					
wrongly debited	(920)				
Less : Returns	(750)	52,330			
To Manufacturing Wages		10,000			
To Gross Profit c/d		67,890			
		1,60,220			1,60,220
To Salaries		7,550	By Gross Profit b/d		67,890
To Rent, Rates & Taxes		10,000	By Excess Provision for Bad debts		
To Carriage Outward		1,200	(Existing less New) (525 – 500)		25
To Advertisement	2,000		By Discount		800
Add : Samples	1,000	3,000			
To Discount		425			
To Depreciation on Plant & Machinery		7,800			
To Loss on sale of furniture		1,240			
To Interest on Capital		10,000			
To Net Profit transferred to Capital A/c		27,500			
		68,715			68,715

BALANCE SHEET
As on 30th September 2007

Liabilities		Rs.	Assets		Rs.
Capital	1,00,000		Plant and Machinery	78,000	
Add : Interest @ 10%	10,000		*Less* : Depreciation	(7,800)	70,200
Add : Net Profit	27,500		Furniture (New)		1,680
Less : Drawings (goods)	(5,000)	1,32,500	Stock		34,220
Sundry Creditors		25,000	Sundry Debtors	45,000	
			Less : Provision	(500)	44,500
			Cash in hand		6,900
		1,57,500			1,57,500

Problem 8 (Adjustments in Debtors and Purchases)

From the following balances, which are extracted from the books of Mr. X, prepare Trading and Profit Loss Account for the year ended 31st December 2007 and a Balance Sheet as on that date.

Particulars	Rs.	Particulars	Rs.
Computer at Cost	18,380	X's Capital Account	60,000
Purchases	71,280	Sundry Creditors	13,000
Cash at Bank	4,000	Bills Payable	10,220
Cash in hand	2,836	Discount Received	22,000
Furniture & Fitting at Cost	1,540	Sales	60,720
Rent	12,540	Returns Outwards	11,432
Bills Receivable	6,720	Rent due	320
Trade Charges	920		
Sundry Debtors	34,156		
Drawings	5,200		
Discount	540		
Wages	1,800		
Salaries	16,780		
Returns Inwards	1,000		
	1,77,692		1,77,692

Adjustments :

(i) Closing Stock on 31st December 2007 was valued at Rs. 25,600 at cost (Market Value Rs. 26,200).

(ii) Rs. 6,000 paid to Mr. Y against 'Bills payable' were debited by mistake to Mr. Z's account and included in the list of sundry debtors,

(iii) Travelling expenses paid to sales representative Rs. 5,000 for the month of December 2007 were debited to his personal account and included in the list of sundry debtors,

(iv) Depreciation on furniture and fitting shall be provided at 10% per annum.

(v) Provide for doubtful debts at 5% on Sundry debtors.

(vi) Goods costing Rs. 1,500 used by the proprietor.

(vii) Salaries include Rs. 12,000 paid to sale representative who is further entitled to a commission of 5% on net sales.

(viii) Stationery charges Rs. 1,200 due on 31 st December 2007.

(ix) Purchases include opening stock valued at Rs. 7,000 (cost price),

(x) Sales representative further entitled to an extra commission of 5% on net profits after charging his extra commission,

(xi) No depreciation need to be provided for computer as it had been purchased on 31 st December 2007 and not put into use. **[C.A. (Inter), May 1991-Modified]**

Solution : **TRADING AND PROFIT & LOSS ACCOUNT**

For the year ended 31st December 2007

Dr. Cr.

Particulars		**Rs.**	**Particulars**		**Rs.**
To Opening Stock		7,000	By Sales	60,720	
To Purchases	71,280		*Less* : Returns	(1,000)	59,720
Less : Stock (Opening)	(7,000)		By Closing Stock		25,600
Less : Returns	(11,432)				
Less : Drawings	(1,500)	51,348			
To Wages		1,800			
To Gross Profit c/d		25,172			
		85,320			85,320
To Salaries		16,780	By Gross Profit b/d		25,172
To Traveling Expenses		5,000	By Discount		22,000
To Salesmen's Commission (5% on 59,720)		2,986			
To Rent		12,540			
To Discount		540			
To Stationery Charges		1,200			
To Trade Charges		920			
To Provision for Doubtful debts		1,158			
To Depreciation on Furniture & Fittings		154			
To Salesmen's Commission (extra)		281			
To Net Profit transferred to Capital A/c		5,613			
		47,172			47,172

BALANCE SHEET
As on 31st December 2007

Liabilities		Rs.	Assets		Rs.
Capital	60,000		Furniture & Fittings		1,386
Less : Drawings (goods used),	(1,500)		Computer at Cost		18,380
Less : Drawings (cash)	(5,200)		Stock in Trade		25,600
Add : Net Profit	5,613	58,913	Sundry Debtors	34,156	
Sundry Creditors		13,000	*Less* : Amount wrongly Included	(6,000)	
Bills Payable (10,220 – 6,000)		4,220	*Less* : Traveling expenses wrongly debited	(5,000)	
Rent Outstanding		320		23,156	
Statioary Charges due		1,200	*Less* : 5% Provision for Doubtful debts	(1,158)	21,998
Salesmen's Commission O/s			Bills Receivable		6,720
(2,986 + 281)		3,267	Cash at Bank		4,000
			Cash in hand		2,836
		80,920			80,920

Problem 9 (Workers Insurance and their Contribution)

From the following Trial Balance of Shri Goyal prepare Trading and Profit and Loss Account for the year ending 31st December 2007 and a Balance Sheet as on that date after taking in to account the adjustments given at the end of Trial Balance.

Particulars	Rs.	Particulars	Rs.
Purchases (Adjusted)	3,49,600	Sales	3,70,000
Wages	10,450	Capital Account	34,250
National Insurance	150	Discount Earned	300
Carriage Inwards	200	Creditors	10,000
Carriage Outwards	250	Dividends Received	150
Lighting	300		
Rates and Insurance (including premium) @ Rs. 150 p.a. paid on 30-6-2007	200		
Closing Stock	30,625		
Cash in hand & at Bank	875		
Plant & Machinery	15,000		
Discount Allowed	50		
Debtors	3,000		
Furniture	4,000		
	4,14,700		4,14,700

Adjustments :

1. National Insurance also includes employee's contribution of Rs. 75. Wages are shown 'Net' after deducting National Insurance contribution borne by employee.
2. Owing to nature of employment,' some employees are housed in the building of business. The Rental value of the portion is assessed at Rs. 250 per annum. The benefit to the employee is treated as wages and the rental as income.
3. Depreciate Plant and Machinery at 15% p.a. and Furniture and 10% p.a.
4. Goods worth Rs. 2,000 given by Shri Goyal to his son at cost.
5. The Manager is entitled to a commission of 20% of the net profit after charging his commission. **[C.A. Entrance, Nov. 1987-Modified]**

Solution : **TRADING AND PROFIT & LOSS ACCOUNT**

For the year ended 31st December 2007

Particulars		**Rs.**	**Particulars**	**Rs.**
To Purchases (adjusted)	3,49,600		By Sales	3,70,000
Less : Drawings (goods given to Proprietor's son)	(2,000)	3,47,600		
To Wages	10,450			
Add : National Insurance	75			
Add : Accommodation	250	10,775		
To Carriage Inwards		200		
To Gross Profit c/d		11,425		
		3,70,000		3,70,000
To Carriage Outwards		250	By Gross Profit b/d	11,425
To Lighting		300	By Discount earned	300
To National Insurance (Employer's Share)		75	By Dividend Received	150
To Rates & Insurance	200		By Notional Rent for	
Less : Prepaid Insurance	(75)	125	Accommodation	250
To Discount Allowed		50		
To Depreciation on :				
Plant and Machinery		2,250		
Furniture		400		
To Manager's Commission		1,446		
To Net Profit transferred to Capital A/c		7,229		
		12,125		12,125

BALANCE SHEET OF SHRI GOYAL
As on 31st December, 2007

Liabilities		Rs.	Assets		Rs.
Capital	34,250		Plant & Machinery	15,000	
Add Net Profit	7,229		*Less* Depreciation	(2,250)	12,750
	41,479		Furniture	4,000	
Less Drawings (goods)	(2,000)	39,479	*Less* Depreciation	(400)	3,600
Creditors		10,000	Closing Stock		30,625
Manager's Commission o/s		1,446	Debtors		3,000
			Cash in hands at Bank		875
			Prepaid Insurance		75
		50,925			50,925

Problem 10 (Interest on Investment)

From the following particulars extracted from the books of Mr. Yogesh Gupta prepare Trading and Profit & Loss Account and a Balance Sheet as on 31 st March 2007 after making necessary adjustments.

Particulars	Rs.	Particulars	Rs.
Stock (1-4-2006)	23,400	Capital	54,050
Sales Returns	4,300	Sales	1,44,800
Purchases	1,21,550	Purchases Returns	2,900
Carriage Inwards	9,300	Sundry Creditors	7,400
Rent	2,850	12% Loan from Dena Bank Ltd.	10,000
Salaries	4,650	Interest Received	725
Drawings	5,000	Discount Received	1,495
Sundry Debtors	12,000		
Interest Paid	450		
Printing & Stationery	1,700		
Advertising	5,600		
Cash with Traders Bank Ltd.	4,000		
5% Investments (as on 1-4-06)	2,500		
Furnitue (as on 1-4-06)	900		
Discount Allowed	3,770		
General Expenses	1,960		
Audit Fees	350		
Fire Insurance Premium	300		
Traveling Expenses	1,165		
Postage and Telegrams	435		
Cash in hand	190		
10% Deposit (1-4-06)	15,000		
	2,21,370		2,21,370

Adjustments :

1. Value of stock as on 31st March 2007 is Rs. 39,300. This includes goods returned by customers on 31st March 2007 to the value of Rs. 1,500 for which no entry has been passed in the books.
2. Purchases include furniture purchased on 1st January 2007 for Rs. 1,000.
3. Depreciation should be provided on furniture at 10% p.a.
4. The Loan Account from Dena Bank in the books of Yogesh Gupta appears as follows :

31-3-2007	To Balance c/d	10,000	1-4-2006	By Balance b/d	5,000
			31-3-2007	By Bank	5,000
		10,000			10,000

5. Sundry Debtors include Rs. 2,000 due from Robert and Sundry Creditors include Rs.1,000 due to him.
6. Interest paid include Rs. 300 paid to Dena Bank Ltd. Interest received represent Rs.100 from S. Debtors and the balance on investments and deposits.
7. Provide for interest payable to Dena Bank and interest receivable on investments and deposits.
8. Make a provision for doubtful debts at 5% on the balance under 'Sundry Debtors'. No such provision need to be made for deposits. **[C.A. Foundation, Nov. 1994-Modified]**

Solution : **TRADING AND PROFIT & LOSS ACCOUNT**

For the year ended 31st March 2007

Particulars		Rs.	Particulars		Rs.
To Opening Stock		23,400	By Sales	1,44,800	
To Purchases	1,21,550		*Less* : Sales Returns		
Less : Purchase of furniture	(1,000)		(4300 + 1500)	(5,800)	1,39,000
Less : Returns	(2,900)	1,17,650	By Closing Stock		39,300
To Carriage Inwards		9,300			
To Gross Profit c/d		27,950			
		1,78,300			1,78,300
To Salaries		4,650	By Gross Profit b/d		27,950
To Rent		2,850	By Interest Received(3)		1,725
To Printing & Stationery		1,700	By Discount Received		1,495
To Fire Insurance Premium		300			
To Postage & Telegrams		435			
To Audit Fees		350			
To General Expenses		1,960			
To Discount Allowed		3,770			
To Interest(1)	450				
Add : O/s	300	750			
To Advertisement		5,600			
To Travelling Expenses		1,165			
To Provision for D. Debts(2)		475			
To Depreciation on Furniture		115			
To Net Profit transferred to Capital		7,050			
		31,170			31,170

		Rs.
(1)	12% interest on Bank Loan of Rs. 5000 =	600
	Less Paid to Dena Bank	(300)
	Outstanding interest	300
(2)	Sundry Debtors	12,000
	Less Sales Returns not received	(1,500)
		10,500
	Less Mutual Owings	(1,000)
		9,500
	Provision @ 5% on 9,500	475
(3)	Interest accrued on Investments & Deposits	
	Interest @ 5% p.a. on Rs. 2,500 investment	125
	Interest @ 10% p.a. on Deposit of Rs. 15,000	1,500
		1,625
	Less Interest received on investments and deposits (725 – 100)	(625)
		1,000

(Total interest received Less interest received from Debtors)

BALANCE SHEET of Mr. Yogesh Gupta
As on 31st March 2007

Liabilities		Rs.	Assets		Rs.
Capital	54,050		Furniture	900	
Add : Net Profit	7,050		*Add* : Purchased during the yr.	1,000	
Less : Drawings	(5,000)	56,100	*Less* : Depreciation	(115)	1,785
Loan from Dena Bank		10,000	5% Investments		2,500
O/s Interest on Loan		300	10% Deposits		15,000
Sundry Creditors		6,400	Interest Accrued on Deposits		1,000
			Stock in Trade		39,300
			Sundry Debtors	9,500	
			Less : Provision	(475)	9,.025
			Cash with Traders Bank		4,000
			Cash in hand		190
		72,800			72,800

Problem 11 (General)

From the following Trial Balance of Nidhi and Additional information, prepare Trading & Profit and Loss Account for the year ended 31st March 2008 and a Balance Sheet as on that date :

Particulars	Rs.	Particulars	Rs.
Furnitue	20,000	Capital	1,00,000
Purchases	1,50,000	Interest Earned	4,000
Debtors	2,00,000	Sales	3,21,000
Salaries	30,000	Purchase Returns	5,000
Wages	20,000	Creditors	1,20,000
Rent	15,000	Provision for Bad debts	6,000
Sales Returns	10,000	Provision for Depreciation	2,000
Bad debts written off	7,000		
Drawings	24,000		
Printings & Stationery	8,000		
Insurance	12,000		
Opening Stock	50,000		
Office Expenses	12,000		
	5,58,000		5,58,000

Additional Information :

1. Depreciate Furniture by 10% on original cost.
2. A provision for Doubtful debts is to be created to the extent of 5% on Sundry debtors.
3. Salaries for the month of March 2008 amounting to Rs. 3,000 were un-paid which must be provided for. However, salaries included Rs. 2,000 paid in advance.
4. Insurance amounting to Rs. 2,000 is prepaid.
5. Provide for outstanding office expenses Rs. 8,000.
6. Stock used for private purposes Rs. 6,000.
7. Closing stock in Trade Rs. 60,000. **[C.A. Foundation, May 1995-Modified]**

Solution : **TRADING AND PROFIT & LOSS ACCOUNT**

For the year ended 31st March 2008

Dr. Cr.

Particulars		Rs.	Particulars		Rs.
To Opening Stock		50,000	By Sales	3,21,000	
To Purchases	1,50,000		*Less* : Returns	(10,000)	3,11,000
Less : Returns	(5,000)		By Closing Stock		60,000
Less : Drawings (goods for private use)	(6,000)	1,39,000			
To Wages		20,000			
To Gross Profit c/d		1,62,000			
		3,71,000			3,71,000

TRADING AND PROFIT & LOSS ACCOUNT (Contd.)

Dr. Cr.

Parti culars		Rs.	Particulars	Rs.
To Salaries	30,000		By Gross Profit b/d	1,62,000
Add : Outstanding	3,000		By Interest Received	4,000
Less : Prepaid	(2,000)	31,000		
To Rent		15,000		
To Printing & Stationery		8,000		
To Office Expenses	12,000			
Add : Outstanding	8,000	20,000		
To Insurance	12,000			
Less : Prepaid	2,000	10,000		
To Provision for Bad Debts(1)		11,000		
To Depreciation on Furniture		2,000		
To Net Profit transferred to Capital		69,000		
		1,66,000		1,66,000

BALANCE SHEET
As on 31st March 2008

Liabilities		Rs.	Assets		Rs.
Capital	1,00,000		Furniture at Cost	20,000	
Add : Net Profit	69,000		*Less* : Provision for Dep.	(4,000)	16,000
Less : Drawings			Stock in Trade		60,000
(24,000 + 6,000)	(30,000)	1,39,000	Debtors	2,00,000	
Creditors		1,20,000	*Less* : Provision	(10,000)	1,90,000
Salaries O/s		3,000	Salaries Prepaid		2,000
Office Expenses O/s		8,000	Insurance Prepaid		2,000
		2,70,000			2,70,000

Working Note :

PROVISION FOR BAD & DOUBTFUL DEBTS A/C

Particulars	Rs.	Particulars	Rs.
To Bad debts w/o	7,000	By Balance b/d (1-4-2007)	6,000
To Balance (31-3-2008)	10,000	By Profit & Loss A/c (B.F.)	11,000
	17,000		17,000

Problem 12 (Mutual Owings)

The following is the Trial Balance of Shri Bajaj as on 31st December 2007.

Particulars	Rs.	Particulars	Rs.
Stock (1-1-2007)	46,800	Capital Account	76,690
Returns Inwards	8,600	Sales	3,89,600
Purchases	3,21,700	Returns Outwards	5,800
Carriage Inwards	19,600	Sundry Creditors	14,800
Rent & Taxes	4,700	Bank Loan @ 14% p.a.	20,000
Salaries & Wages	9,300	Discount Earned	4,440
Sundry Debtors	24,000		
Bank Interest	1,100		
Cash Balance	380		
Bank Balance	8,000		
Printing & Stationery	14,400		
Discount Allowed	1,800		
Furniture & Fittings	5,000		
General Expenses	11,450		
Insurance	1,300		
Postage & Telegram	2,330		
Travelling Expenses	870		
Drawings	30,000		
	5,11,330		5,11,330

Additional Information :

1. Included amongst the debtors is Rs. 3,000 due from Ram and included amongst the creditors Rs. 1,000 due to him.
2. Provision for bad and doubtful debts be created @ 5% and for discount @ 2% on Sundry Debtors.
3. Depreciation on Furniture & Fitting shall be written off @ 10%.
4. Personal purchases of Shri Bajaj amounting to Rs. 600 had been recorded in the Purchases Day Book.
5. Interest on Bank Loan shall be provided for the whole year.
6. A quarter of the amount of Printing and Stationery Expenses is to be carried forward to the next year.
7. Credit Purchase invoice amounting to Rs. 400 had been omitted to be recorded.
8. Stock on 31st December 2007 was Rs. 78,600.

Prepare :

(i) Trading and Profit and Loss Account for the year ended 31st December 2007 and

(ii) Balance Sheet as on 31st December 2007. **[C.A. Foundation, Nov. 1995-Modifted]**

Slution :

TRADING AND PROFIT & LOSS ACCOUNT
For the year ended 31st December 2007

Dr. Cr.

Particulars		Rs.	Particulars		Rs.
To Opening Stock		46,800	By Sales	3,89,600	
To Purchases	3,21,700		*Less* : Returns	(8,600)	3,81,000
Less : Returns	(5,800)		By Closing Stock		78,600
Less : Drawings (Personal use)	(600)				
Add : Purchase not recorded	400	3,15,700			
To Freight & Carriage		19,600			
To Gross Profit c/d		77,500			
		4,59,600			4,59,600
To Salaries & Wages		9,300	By Gross Profit b/d		77,500
To Rent and Taxes		4,700	By Discount Earned		4,440
To Printing & Stationery	14,400				
Less : Prepaid 1/4	(3,600)	10,800			
To Postage & Telegram		2,330			
To General Expenses		11,450			
To Insurance		1,300			
To Discount Allowed		1,800			
To Travelling Expenses		870			
To Bank Interest	1,100				
Add : Due	1,700	2,800			
To Provision for Bad debts(1)		1,150			
To Provision for Discount(2)		437			
To Depreciation		500			
To Net Profit transferred to Capital		34,503			
		81,940			81,940

Working Notes :

	Rs.		Rs.
(1) Sundry Debtors	24,000	(2) Debtors after B/D	21,850
Less Mutual owing	(1,000)	*Less* Discount @ 2%	(437)
	23,000	Debtors to be shown in B/s	21,413
Less 5% Provision for Bad debt	(1,150)		
	21,850		

BALANCE SHEET OF SHRI BAJAJ
As on 31st December 2007

Liabilities		Rs.	Assets		Rs.
Capital	76,690		Furniture & Fittings	5,000	
Add : Net Profit	34,503		*Less* : Depreciation	(500)	4,500
Less : Drawings (Cash + goods)			Sundry Debtors (2)		21,413
(30,000 + 600)	(30,600)	80,593	Stock		78,600
Bank Loan		20,000	Bank Balance		8,000
Bank Interest due		1,700	Cash Balance		380
Sundry Creditors	14,800		Printing & Stationery Prepaid		3,600
Less : Mutual owing	(1,000)				
Add : Unrecorded Purchases	400	14,200			
		1,16,493			1,16,493

Problem 13 (Ascertainment of Closing Stock)

From the following particulars, prepare Trading and Profit & Loss" Account of Mr. X for the* year ended 31st March 2008 and a Balance Sheet as on that date.

Particulars	Rs.	Particulars	Rs.
Building	5,00,000	18% Loan (1-6-2007)	
Machineries	2,00,000	on Mortgage of Building	3,00,000
Furniture	1,00,000	X's Capital	5,20,000
Cash at Bank	90,000	Sundry Creditors	4,00,000
Cash in hand	10,000	Sales	32,20,000
Sundry Debtors	5,00,000	Purchases Returns	1,00,000
Stock (1-4-2007)	1,20,000		
Purchases	25,00,000		
Sales Return	1,20,000		
Rent	60,000		
Establishment Expenses	1,80,000		
Electricity Charges	15,000		
Telephone Charges	10,000		
Commission on Sales	30,000		
Insurance Premium	10,000		
Bad debts	20,000		
Bills Receivable	75,000		
	45,40,000		45,40,000

Additional Information :

You are required to provide for depreciation on building at 5% p.a., on machineries at 25%, on furniture at 10% p.a. Provision for doubtful debts is to be made at 5% on sundry debtors. The manager is entitled a commission of 10% on the net profit after charging his commission. Closing stock was not taken on 31st March 2008 but on 7-4-2008. Following transactions took place during the period from 1-4-2008 to 7-4-2008.

Sales Rs. 2,50,000, Purchases Rs. 1,50,000, Stock on 7th April 2008 was Rs. 1,80,000 and the rate of gross profit on sales was 20%, Insurance Premium mentioned in the Trial Balance was in respect of Building and machineries. Interest on Loan to be provided upto 31st March 2008.

[C.A. Foundation, May 97-Modified)

Solution : **TRADING AND PROFIT & LOSS ACCOUNT**

For the year ended 31st March 2008

Dr. Cr.

Particulars		Rs.	Particulars		Rs.
To Opening Stock		1,20,000	By Sales	32,20,000	
To Purchases	25,00,000		*Less* : Returns	(1,20,000)	31,00,000
Less : Returns	(1,00,000)	24,00,000	By Closing Stock (1)		2,30,000
To Gross Profit c/d		8,10,000			
		33,30,000			33,30,000
To Rent		60,000	By Gross Profit b/d		8,10,000
To stablishment Expenses		1,80,000			
To Telephone Charges		10,000			
To Electricity Charges		15,000			
To Insurance Premium		10,000			
To Commission on Sales		30,000			
To Bad debts		20,000			
To Provision for Bad debts		25,000			
To Interest on Loan		45,000			
To Depreciation on :					
Building		25,000			
Machineries		50,000			
Furniture		10,000			
To Manager's Commission		30,000			
To Net Profit transferred to Capital A/c		3,00,000			
		8,10,000			8,10,000

BALANCE SHEET OF Mr. X
As on 31st March 2008

Liabilities		Rs.	Assets		Rs.
Capital	5,20,000		Building	5,00,000	
Add : Net Profit	3,00,000	8,20,000	*Less* : Depreciation	(25,000)	4,75,000
18% Mortgage Loan		3,00,000	Machineries	2,00,000	
Interest Accrued on Loan		45,000	*Less* : Depreciation	(50,000)	1,50,000
Sundry Creditors		4,00,000	Furniture	1,00,000	
Manager's Commission due		30,000	*Less* : Depreciation	(10,000)	90,000
			Closing Stock		2,30,000
			Sundry Debtors	5,00,000	
			Less : Provision for Bad debts	(25,000)	4,75,000
			Bills Receivable		75,000
			Cash at Bank		90,000
			Cash in hand		10,000
		15,95,000			15,95,000

Working Note : Valuation of Closing Stock

		Rs.
Stock as on 7th April 2008		180,000
Add cost of goods sold during		
1-4-2008 to 7-4-2008	Rs.	
Sales	250,000	
Less Profit Margin @ 20% on sales	(50,000)	200,000
		3,80,000
Less Purchases made during		
1-4-2008 to 7-4-2008		150,000
Stock as on 31-3-2008		230,000

Problem 14 (Unrecorded Purchases and Dishonor of Bill)

Mr. Sugandh has extracted the following Trial Balance from his books as on 31st March 2008.

Dr. Cr.

Particulars	Rs.	Particulars	Rs.
Purchases	4,00,000	Sundry Creditors	50,000
Sundry Debtors	1,50,000	Sales	7,00,000
Cash in hand	4,000		
Cash at Bank	8,000		
Rent, Rates & Taxes	3,000		

Insurance Premium	9,000		
Salaries	42,000		
Carriage Outward	21,000		
Carriage Inward	18,000		
Claim Recoverable	5,000		
Advertisement Suspense	9,000		
Furniture & Fittings	23,000		
Deposit with Supplier	6,000		
Office Equipment	10,000		
Bills Receivable	6,000		
Bad debts	4,000		
Opening Stock	30,000		
Electricity Expenses	2,000		
	7,50,000		7,50,000

The following further information is provided :

(1) A purchase invoice of Rs. 15,000, received from a creditor has not been entered through oversight.

(2) The claim recoverable has been settled with the Insurance company for Rs. 2,000.

(3) 50% of the advertisement suspense account is to be written off this year. The amount represents the cost of an advertising campaign conducted this year.

(4) Depreciation is to be charged on Straight Line Method on furniture and fittings and office equipments @ 5%.

The original costs were :

Furniture and fittings	Rs. 30,000
Office equipment	Rs. 15,000

(5) Goods costing Rs. 5,000 were dispatched out on 29th March. The sale, however, took place on 3rd April 2008 when an invoice for Rs. 7,500 was raised against a customer.

(6) Insurance premium includes a prepaid amount of Rs. 1,000.

(7) The Deposit with a supplier was made on 1-10-2007. It carried interest @ 12% p.a.

(8) Two bills receivable from customer of Rs. 700 and Rs. 1,300 were dishonored on 30th March 2008. These had earlier been discounted with the Bank.

(9) Provide 2% on Sundry Debtors for doubtful debts.

(10) Physical stock of goods on hand on 31st March 2008 at cost was Rs.1,00,000.

Prepare Trading & Profit and Loss Account and Balance Sheet from the above information.

[C.A., Inter-Modified]

Solution :

TRADING AND PROFIT & LOSS ACCOUNT
For the year ended 31st March 2008

Dr. Cr.

Particulars		Rs.	Particulars		Rs.
To Opening Stock		30,000	By Sales		7,00,000
To Purchases	4,00,000		By Closing Stock	1,00,000	
Add : Unrecorded	15,000	4,15,000	*Add* : Goods with customers	5,000	1,05,000
To Carriage Inward		18,000			
To Gross Profit c/d		3,42,000			
		8,05,000			8,05,000
To Rent, Rates & Taxes		3,000	By Gross Profit b/d		3,42,000
To Salaries		42,000	By Interest Accrued on Deposit		360
To Insurance Premium	9,000				
Less : Prepaid	(1,000)	8,000			
To Electricity Charges		2,000			
To Carriage Outward		21,000			
To Advertisement (1/2 to 9,000)		4,500			
To Bad debts		4,000			
To Provision for Bad debts		3,040			
To Insurance Claims		3,000			
To Depreciation on Furniture		1,500			
To Depreciation on Office		750			
To Net Profit		2,49,570			
		3,42,360			3,42,360

Balance Sheet
As on 31st March 2008

Liabilities		Rs.	Assets		Rs.
Capital			Furniture	23,000	
Net Profit	2,49,750	2,49,750	*Less* : Depreciation	(1,500)	21,500
			Office Equipments	10,000	
Sundry Creditors	50,000		*Less* : Depreciation	(750)	9,250
Add : Unrecorded purchases	15,000[(1)]	65,000	Closing Stock[(2)]		1,05,000
			Debtors[(3)]		1.48,960
			Bills Receivable		6,000
			Deposit with Supplier		6,000
			Interest Accrued on Deposit		360
			Cash at Bank[(3)]		6,000
			Cash in hand[(4)]		6,000
			Prepaid Insurance		1,000
			Advertisement Suspense		4,500
		3,14,750			3,14,750

Working Notes :

(1) Unrecorded purchases will increase the creditors and purchases as well.

(2) Stock includes stock with customers.

(3) Dishonour of discounted bills will increase the debtors and reduce the Bank Balance at the same time.

(5) Since claims recoverable are reduced to Rs. 2,000 from Rs. 5,000 the difference being charged to Profit & Loss Account and Rs.2,000 have been added to cash-in-hand.

(6) Provision on Debtors has been calculated on the gross debtors.(15,0,000 + 2,000).

Problem 15 (Deferred Revenue Expenditure & Change of Method of Depreciation)

Dinesh has extracted Trial Balance from his books as on 31st March 2008.

Dr. Cr.

Particulars	Rs.	Particulars	Rs.
Drawings	16,000	Capital	34,000
Cash	6,760	Sundry Creditors	35,000
Petty Cash	1,000	Sales	6,00,000
Leasehold Land	20,000	Suspense Account	10,000
Opening Stock at Market Value	50,000		
Salary	12,000		
Sundry Debtors	50,000		
Wages	40,000		
Bank	21,000		
Rent	9,000		
Electricity	6,000		
Motor Car	10,240		
Advertising	9,000		
Purchases	4,00,000		
Postage & Telephone	3,000		
Discounts	11,400		
General Charges	4,000		
Petty Cash Expenses	9,600		
	6,79,000		6,79,000

You are required to prepare a Trading, Profit and Loss Account and Balance Sheet using the following Additional information :

(1) Closing stock at market value as on 31 st March 2008 was Rs. 80,000 (cost Rs. 75,000). Stock is being valued on a consistent basis of cost or market prices whichever is lower.

(2) The petty cash balance represents the month end imprest amount. As on the closing date the petty cashier had vouchers totaling Rs. 400 for which he had not received reimbursement from the main cashier

(3) Discount allowed amounting to Rs. 1,000 had been posted to the debit of Sundry Debtors.

(4) Cash withdrawn from the Bank Rs. 4,000 had not been entered in the Bank column of Cash Book.

(5) Sales account had been under-cast on the credit side by Rs. 4,000.

(6) Motor car which had been purchased in 2004-05 was depreciated at 20 per cent on the reducing balance method. The original cost of the car is Rs. 20,000. It is now decided to charge depreciation at 6% on the straight line method and to make this change effective from the year of purchase of ear.

(7) The leasehold land was purchased during the year. On the date of purchase the unexpired period of the lease was five years.

(8) No entry has been passed in the books for goods withdrawn from the business by the proprietor valued at Rs. 10,000.

(9) Advertising includes cost of campaign run during the year Rs. 6,000. It is expected that the effect of this campaign will be felt at least for three years.

(10) Telephone bill amounting to Rs. 1,000 remains unpaid. **[C.A., Inter-Modified]**

Solution : **TRADING AND PROFIT & LOSS ACCOUNT**

For the year ended 31st March 2008

Dr. Cr.

Particulars		Rs.	Particulars		Rs.
To Opening Stock (1)		50,000	By Sales	6,00,000	
To Purchases	4,00,000		*Add* : Under-casting	4,000	6,04,000
Less : Drawings	(10,000)	3,90,000	Closing Stock		75,000
To Wages		40,000			
To Gross Profit c/d		1,99,000			
		6,79,000			6,79,000
To Salary		12,000	By Gross Profit b/d		1,99,000
To Rent		9,000			
To Electricity		6,000			
To Postage & Telephone	3,000				
Add : Outstanding	1,000	4,000			
To Petty Expenses	9,600				
Add : Expenses not reimbursed	400	10,000			
To General Charges		4,000			
To Discount		11,400			
To Advertising	9,000				
Less : Deferred	(6,000)				
	3,000				
Add : 1/3 of Deferred	2,000	5,000			
To Depreciation on Car		1,200			
To Leasehold written off					
(1/5 of 20,000)		4,000			
To Net Profit transferred to Capital A/c		1,32,400			
		1,99,000			1,99,000

(1) Petty expenses will increase by Rs. 400, or account of petty expenses not reimbursed and petty cash balance will be reduced by Rs. 400.

BALANCE SHEET
As on 31st March 2008

Liabilities		Rs.	Assets		Rs.
Capital	34,000		Leasehold	20,000	
Add : Net Profit	1,32,400		*Less* : Written off	(4,000)	16,000
Add : Excess Depreciation	6,160(1)		Motor Car	20,000	
Less : Drawings	(26,000)	1,46,560	*Less* : Dep. (3,600 + 1,200)	(4,800)	15,200
Creditors		35,000	Stock at Cost		75,000
Telephone Expenses o/s		1,000	Debtors	50,000	
			Less : Discount wrongly Debited	(2,000)	48,000
			Bank	21,000	
			Less : Withdrawn amount not entered	(4,000)	17,000
			Cash		6,760
			Petty Cash	1,000	
			Less : Expenses not reimbursed	(400)	600
			Deferred Advertisement		4,000
		1,82,560			1,82,560

(1) Excess depreciation has been calculated as under :

	Rs.	
Original Cost of Car	20,000	
Depreciation @ 6% p.a. on Original cost for three years (1,200 × 3)	3,600*	
W.D.V. as on 1-4-2007 (as per S.L. Method)	16,400	
W.D.V. as per Reducing Balance Method (as per Trial Balance)	10,240	
	6,160	Excess Depreciation to be credited to P & L A/c or earlier years of Capital A/c

Problem 16 (Works Manager's and General Manager's Commission)

The following Trial Balance was extracted from the Books of Mr X as on 31st December 2007 :

Dr. Cr.

Particulars	Rs.	Particulars	Rs.
Plant & Machinery	40,000	Capital	1,60,000
Manufacturing Wages	69,000	Sundry Creditors	89,120
Salaries	31,700	Bank Loan	30,000

Furniture	20,000	Purchases Returns	3,480
Freight on Purchases	3,720	Sales	5,01,700
Freight on Sales	4,280	Provision for Bad debts	4,000
Building	48,000		
Motor Car	24,000		
Purchases	2,04,000		
Sales Returns	6,200		
Bad debts	2,800		
Interest & Bank Charges	800		
Cash at Bank	8,400		
Cash in hand	2,240		
Manufacturing Expenses	19,000		
Insurance & Tax	8,500		
Goodwill	50,000		
General Expenses	16,400		
Factory, Fuel & Power	2,560		
Sundry Debtors	1,56,400		
Factory Lighting	1,900		
Opening Stock	68,400		
	7,88,300		7,88,300

Prepare Trading and Profit & Loss Account for the year ended 31st December 2007 and the Balance Sheet as on that date taking into consideration the following information :

(1) Stock in hand on 31 st December 2007 was valued at Rs. 61,000.

(2) Depreciate Plant & Machinery by 10%; Furniture by 5%; Motor Car by Rs. 2,000.

(3) Bring provision for Bad debts to 5% on Sundry Debtors.

(4) A Commission of 1% on the gross profit is to be provided for works manager.

(5) A commission of 2% on the net profit (after charging works manager's commission) is to be credited to the General Manager. **[C.A. Entrance-Adapted]**

Solution : **TRADING AND PROFIT & LOSS ACCOUNT**

For the year ended 31st December 2007

Dr. Cr.

Particulars		**(Rs.)**	**Particulars**		**(Rs.)**
To Opening Stock		68,400	By Sales	5,01,700	
To Purchases	2,04,000		*Less* : Returns	(6,200)	4,95,500
Less : Returns	(3,480)	2,00,520	By Closing Stock		61,000
To Freight on Purchases		3,720			
To Manufacturing Wages		69,000			
To Factory, Fuel & Power		2,560			

To Factory Lighting	1,900		
To Manufacturing Expenses	19,000		
To Gross Profit c/d	1,91,400		
	5,56,500		5,56,500
To Salary	31,700	By Gross Profit b/d	1,91,400
To General Expenses	16,400		
To Insurance & Tax	8,500		
To Proision for Bad debts	6,620		
To Interest and Bank Charges	800		
To Freight on Sales	4,280		
To Depreciation on :			
Plant & Machinery	4,000		
Furniture	1,000		
Motor Car	2,000		
To Works Manager's Commission	1,914		
To General Manager's Commission	2,284		
To Net Profit	1,11,902		
	1,91,400		1,91,400

BALANCE SHEET OF MR. X
As on 31st December 2007

Liabilities		Rs.	Assets		Rs.
Capital	1,60,000		Goodwill		50,000
Add : Net Profit	1,11,902	2,71,902	Building		48,000
Bank Loan		30,000	Plant & Machinery	40,000	
Sundry Creditors		89,120	*Less* : Depreciation	4,000	36,000
Works Manager's Commission o/s		1,914	Motor Car	24,000	
General Manager's Commission o/s		2,284	*Less* : Depreciation	2,000	22,000
			Furniture	20,000	
			Less : Depreciation	1,000	19,000
			Closing Stock		61,000
			Sundry Debtors	1,56,400	
			Less : Provision	7,820	1,48,580
			Cash at Bank		8,400
			Cash in hand		2,240
		3,95,220			3,95,220

Working Notes : **PROVISION FOR BAD DEBTS**

Date	Particulars	Rs.	Date	Particulars	Rs.
31-12-07	To Bad debts	2,800	1-1-2007	By Balance b/d	4,000
	To Balance c/d	7,820		By Profit & Loss A/c (B.F.)	6,620
		10,620			10,620

*Works Manager's Commission @ 1% on Gross Profit Rs. 1914.

*General Manager's Commission @ 2% on Net Profit before charging his own commission *Rs. 2,284.

Problem 17 (Apportionment of Expenses and Manufacturing A/c)

From the following Trial Balance and information prepare Manufacturing, Trading and Profit & Loss Account for the year ended 31st December 2007 and a Balance Sheet as on that date.

Dr. Cr.

Particulars	Rs.	Particulars	Rs.
Drawings	32,000	Capital A/c	1,40,000
Power (Factory)	14,456	Current Account	6,492
Furniture	3,600	Discount	1,648
General Expenses (Factory)	820	Sales	3,16,696
General Expenses (Office)	1,384	Provision for Bad debts	4,000
Insurance	3,608	Creditors	24,600
Light & Heat	1,928		
Plant & Machinery (1-1-05)	60,000		
Plant & Machinery (30-6-05)	8,000		
Bank Charges	480		
Purchases	1,34,672		
Packing & Transport	4,340		
Rent & Rates	5,944		
Repairs to Plant	3,140		
Salaries (Office)	14,760		
Bad debts	2,420		
Opening Stock :			
Raw Materials	20,920		
Work-in-Progress	6,680		
Finished goods	29,520		
Wages (Factory)	82,800		
Debtors	42,240		
Cash at Bank	15,704		
Cash in hand	700		
Advertising	3,320		
	4,93,436		4,93,436

Stock on 31st December 2007 were as follows :

	Rs.
(1) Raw-materials	14,240
(2) Work-in-progress	6,960
(3) Finished goods	38,600
(4) Packing Materials	500
The following liabilities are to be provided for:	
(5) Factory Power	2,248
(6) Rent and Rates	1,544
(7) Light and heat	640
(8) General Expenses—Factory	100
(9) General Expenses—Office	160
(10) Insurance prepaid	680

Provide depreciation @ 10% p.a. on Plant & Machinery and 5% p.a. on Furniture. Increase Bad debts provision by Rs. 2,000. Five-sixth of Rent and Rates, Lights & Heat and insurance are to be allocated to the factory and one-sixth to the office. **[ICWA-Adapted]**

Solution :

MANUFACTURING ACCOUNT
For the year ended 31st December 2007

Dr. Cr.

Particulars		Rs.	Particulars	Rs.
To Raw-materials used :			By Transfer to Trading A/c	2,61,856
Opening Stock	20,920		(Cost of goods manufactured)	
Add : Purchases	1,34,672			
Less : Closing Stock	(14,240)	1,41,352		
To Factory Wages		82,800		
To Factory Power	14,456			
Add : O/s	2,248	16,704		
To Rent & Rates (Factory) 5/6th of	{ 5,944			
Add : O/s	1,544	6,240*		
To Light & Heat (5/6th) of	{ 1,928			
Add : O/s	640	2,140*		
To Repairs to Plant		3,140		
To General Expenses (Factory)	820			
Add : O/s	100	920		
To Insurance (F-5/6th) of	{ 3,608			
Less : Prepaid	(680)	2,440*		
To Depreciation on :				
Plant & Machinery		6,400		

* 5/6th of the total have been charged

	2,62,136		
Add : Opening Work-in-progress	6,680		
	2,68,816		
Less : Closing Work-in-progress	6,960		
Cost of goods & manufactured	2,61,856		2,61,856
F = Factory			
O/s = Outstanding			

TRADING AND PROFIT & LOSS ACCOUNT
For the year ended 31st December 2007

Dr. Cr.

Particulars	Rs.	Particulars	Rs.
To Opening Stock of Finished goods	29,520	By Sales	3,16,696
To Transfer from Manufacturing A/c	2,61,856	By Closing Stock (F.G.)	38,600
To Gross Profit c/d	63,920		
	3,55,296		3,55,296
To Salaries (Office)	14,760	By Gross Profit b/d	63,920
To Rent and Rates (1/6)	1,248	By Discount	1,648
To Light & Heat (1/6)	428		
To Insurance (1/6)	488		
To General Expenses (0)	1,544		
To Bank Charges	480		
To Advertising	3,320		
To Bad Debts	2,420		
To Provision for Bad debts	2,000		
To Packing & Transport 4,340			
Less : Stock (500)	3,840		
To Depreciation on Furniture	180		
To Net Profit transferred to Current A/c	34,860		
	65,568		65,568

BALANCE SHEET
As on 31st December 2007

Liabilities		Rs.	Assets		Rs.
Capital		1,40,000	Plant & Machinery	60,000	
Current Account	6,492		*Add* : Purchased	8,000	
Add : Net Profit	34,860			68,000	
	41,352		*Less* : Depreciation	(6,400)	61,600

Less : Drawings	(32,000)	9,352	Furniture	3,600	
Creditors		24,600	*Less* : Depreciation	(180)	3,420
Factory Power o/s		2,248	Stock :		
Rent & Rates o/s		1,544	Raw Materials		14,240
			Work-in-progress		6,960
Light & Heat o/s		640	Finished goods		38,600
General Expenses (F) o/s		100	Packing Materials		500
General Expenses (O) o/s		160	Debtors	42,240	
			Less : Bad debts Provision	(6,000)	36,240
			Insurance Prepaid		680
			Cash at Bank		15,704
			Cash in hand		700
		1,78,644			1,78,644

Problem 18 (Joint Venture's Profit and Suspense A/c)

Zed gives you the following Trial Balance as on 31st December 2007 :

Dr. Cr.

Particulars		Rs.	Particulars	Rs.
Purchased (Adjusted)		6,89,200	Capital	48,500
Salaries		11,900	Sales	7,40,000
Carriage Inward		900	Discount	900
Building		30,000	Expenses	700
Furniture		6,000	Sundry Creditors	21,200
Sundry Debtors		8,000		
Prepaid Expenses		200		
General Expenses		900		
Stock (31-12-2007)		56,250		
Depreciation : Building	600			
Furniture	600	1,200		
Cash		1,750		
Tee's Suspense A/c		5,000		
		8,11,300		8,11,300

Tee's suspense account represents cash sent to 'Tee' for a joint venture. Tee has sent intimation that the venture has resulted in a profit of Rs. 4,000 of which Zed's share is Rs. 1,000. This remains to be adjusted. Prepare final accounts in the books of Zed. **[B.Com. (H) 1st yr.-Modified]**

Solution :

TRADING AND PROFIT & LOSS A/C
For the year ended 31st December 2007

Dr. Cr.

Particulars	Rs.	Particulars	Rs.
To Purchases (Adjusted)	6,89,200	By Sales	7,40,000
To Carriage Inward	900		
To Gross Profit c/d	49,900		
	7,40,000		7,40,000
To Salaries	11,900	By Gross Profit b/d	49,900
To General Expenses	900	By Discount	900
To Depreciation on :		By Profit on Joint Venture	1,000
Building	600		
Furniture	600		
To Net Profit	37,800		
	51,800		51,800

BALANCE SHEET
As on 31st December 2007

Liabilities		Rs.	Assets	Rs.
Capital	48,500		Building	30,000
Add : Net Profits including			Furniture	6,000
that of joint venture	37,800	86,300	Stock (Closing)	56,250
Sundry Creditors		21,200	Debtors	8,000
Expenses O/s		700	Prepaid Expenses	200
			Cash	1,750
			Tee's Suspense A/c*	6,000
		1,08,200		1,08,200

The total amount due from Tee is Rs. 6,000 (5,000 + 1,000), cash sent for joint venture and the share of profit therefrom.

Problem 19 (Elimination of Suspense Account)

From the following particulars prepare a Trading and Profit & Loss Account for the year ended 31st Dec. 2007 and a Balance Sheet as on that date after taking additional information given below :

Dr. Cr.

Particulars	Rs.	Particulars	Rs.
Purchases	1,20,000	Sales	4,00,000
Land & Machinery	80,000	Capital	1,00,000
Plant & Machinery	1,00,000	Creditors	40,000
Drawings	36,000	Bills Payable	16,000
Sundry Debtors	80,000	Bank Overdraft	20,000
Wages	20,000	Cash Credit	20,000
Salaries	44,000	Provision for Bad debts	4,000
Rent	12,000		
Carriage Inward	6,000		
Repairs	6,000		
Insurance	10,000		
Opening Stock	24,000		
Furniture	20,000		
Discount	10,000		
Suspense Account	32,000		
	6,00,000		6,00,000

Additional Information :

1. Closing Stock on 31 st December 2007 has been valued at Rs. 60,000.
2. Purchases include purchase of materials used for the construction of building Rs. 10,000.
3. Wages include Rs. 6,000 incurred for the erection of a Machinery.
4. Sales include sale of furniture for Rs. 2,000 (Book value Rs. 4,000).
5. Goods worth Rs. 2,000 were used by the proprietor.
6. Purchased a plant for Rs. 10,000 wrongly debited to Purchases Account.
7. Rent included Rs. 2,000 paid for proprietor's residential portion.
8. Purchase of stationery for Rs. 200 was debited to Repairs Account.
9. A customer's cheque returned dishonoured wrongly debited to Discount Account Rs.2,000.
10. A sale of goods not debited to Customers Account Rs. 32,000.
11. Stock destroyed by fire amounted to Rs. 20,000 Insurance Company admitted a claim of Rs.16,000. only.

Solution : **TRADING AND PROFIT & LOSS ACCOUNT**

For the year ended 31st December 2007

Dr. Cr.

Particulars		Rs.	Particulars		Rs.
To Opening Stock		24,000	By Sales	4,00,000	
To Purchases	1,20,000		*Less* : Sale of furniture	(2,000)	3,98,000
Less : Purchase of			By Loss by fire (Insurance claims)		16,000
Building Materials	(10,000)		By P & L A/c		4,000

Less : Goods used by proprietor	(2,000)		By Closing Stock	60,000
Less : Plant wrongly debited	(10,000)	98,000		
To Wages	20,000			
Less : Erection charges	(6,000)	14,000		
To Carriage Inward		6,000		
To Gross Profit c/d		3,36,000		
		4,78,000		4,78,000
To Salaries		44,000	By Gross Profit b/d	3,36,000
To Rent	12,000		By Provision for Bad Debts	4,000
Less : For self-occupied	(2,000)	10,000		
To Repairs	6,000			
Less : Stationery	(200)	5,800		
To Insurance		10,000		
To Discount	10,000			
Less : Debtors	(2,000)	8,000		
To Stationary		200		
To Loss by fire		4,000		
To Loss on sale of furniture		2,000		
To Net Profit		2,56,000		
		3,40,000		3,40,000

BALANCE SHEET
As on 31st December 2007

Liabilities		Rs.	Assets		Rs.
Capital	1,00,000		Land & Building	80,000	
Add : Net Profit	2,56,000		Additions	10,000	90,000
	3,56,000		Plant & Machinery	1,00,000	
Less : Drawings	(36,000)		*Add* : Wages for erection of		
Less : Goods used by prop.	(2,000)		Machines	6,000	
Less : Building used by prop.	(2,000)	3,16,000	*Add* : Additions	10,000	1,16,000
Creditors		40,000	Furniture	20,000	
Bills Payable		16,000	*Less* : Sold	(4,000)	16,000
Bank Overdraft		20,000	Closing Stock		60,000
Cash Credit		20,000	Sundry Debtors	80,000	
			Add : Discount	2,000	
			Add : Suspense	32,000	1,14,000
			Insurance claims		16,000
		4,12,000			4,12,000

Working Note :

(a) It is assumed that provision for bad debt is no longer required, therefore, it is credited to Profit & Loss Account. Alternatively it could have been shown to the liability side of Balance Sheet.

(b) Do you have any suggestion regarding the fixed assets?

Ans. Yes, the depreciation should have been charged on fixed assets.

Problem 20 (Partnership)

A & B are partners is a firm sharing profits & losses in the ratio of their opening capitals. Below is their Trial Balance as on 31st March 2008.

Particulars	Rs.	Particulars	Rs.
Freehold Property	1,02,000	Sales	2,88,000
Plant & Machinery	60,000	Discount	2,400
Opening Stock	36,000	Sundry Creditors	24,000
Purchases	96,000	Bills Payable	12,900
Carriage Inwards	2,040	A's Loan A/c	60,000
Carriage Outwards	3,000	A's Capital A/c	60,000
Wages	19,200	B's Capital A/c	30,000
Sundry Debtors	60,000		
Salaries	14,400		
Furniture	21,600		
Trade Expenses	7,200		
Returns Inwards	1,140		
Advertisement suspense	15,000		
Discount	1,080		
Drawings : A	3,600		
B	2,400		
Blls Receivable	24,000		
Insurance	1,440		
Bad debts	1,200		
Cash at Bank	6,000		
	4,77,300		4,77,300

Adjustments :

(1) Closing stock is valued at Rs. 54,000.

(2) Depreciate Plant @ 10% and Furniture @ 20%. Appreciate Freehold property to Rs.1,08,000.

(3) Bad debts reserve is to be raised to 2.5% on Sundry Debtors.

(4) Advertisement Suspense A/c is to be written off over five years.

(5) Partners' drawings are to be charged interest @ 10% per annum. Amounts were withdrawn at 31st December 2007.

(6) Annual charge for insurance is Rs. 1,200 the balance represents amount paid in advance.

(7) A gave loan to the firm on 30th September 2007.

(8) B was to be allowed a partnership salary of Rs. 300 per month.

(9) The partners agree to contribute 50% of the distributable profits to National Defence Fund.

[B.Com. (H), D.U-Adapted]

Solution :

TRADING AND PROFIT & LOSS ACCOUNT
For the year ended 31st March 2008

Dr. Cr.

Particulars	Rs.	Particulars		Rs.
To Opening Stock	36,000	By Sales	2,88,000	
To Purchases	96,000	*Less* : Returns	1,140	2,86,860
To Wages	19,200	By Closing Stock		54,000
To Carriage Inwards	2,040			
To Gross Profit c/d	1,87,620			
	3,40,860			3,40,860
To Salaries	14,400	By Gross Profit b/d		1,87,620
To Carriage Outwards	3,000	By Discount		2,400
To Trade Expenses	7,200	By Appreciation of Freehold Property		6,000
To Advertisement Suspense	3,000			
To Insurance *Less* Prepaid (1,440 – 240)	1,200			
To Bad Debts	1,200			
To Provision for Bad debts	1,500			
To Discount	1,080			
To Depreciation on Plant	6,000			
To Depreciation on Furniture	4,320			
To Interest on A's Loan	1,800			
To Net Profit Transferred to P & L App. A/c	1,51,320			
	1,96,020			1,96,020

PROFIT & LOSS APPROPRIATION A/C
For the year ended 31st March 2008

Particulars		Rs.	Particulars	Rs.
To A's Salary @ 300 p.m.		3,600	By Transfer from P & L A/c (Net Profit)	1,51,320
To Contribution to National Defence Fund (50% of 1,51,320 + 90 + 60 – 3,600)		73,935	By Interest on Drawings :	
			A's Capital A/c	90
To Capital A/cs	A 49,290		B's Capital A/c	60
	B 24,645	73,935		
		1,51,470		1,51,470

BALANCE SHEET OF A & B
As on 31st March 2008

Liabilities		Rs.	Assets		Rs.
A's Capital	60,000		Freehold Property	1,02,000	
Add : Net Profit	49,290		*Add* : Appreciation	6,000	1,08,000
	1,09,290		Plant & Machinery	60,000	
Less : Drawings	(3,600)		*Less* : Depreciation	(6,000)	54,000
and Interest thereon	(90)	1,05,600	Furniture	21,600	
B's Capital	30,000		*Less* : Deprecaition	(4,320)	17,280
Add : Net Profit	24,645		Closing Stock		54,000
	54,645		Sundry Debtors	60,000	
Add : Salary	3,600		*Less* : Provision	(1,500)	58,500
Less : Drawings	(2,400)		Bill Receivable		24,000
and Interest thereon	(60)	55,785	Cash at Bank		6,000
A's Loan	60,000		Prepaid Insurance		240
Interest on Loan	1,800	61,800	Advertisement Suspense		12,000
Sundry Creditors		24,000			
Bills Payable		12,900			
Contribution to NDF		73,935			
		3,34,020			3,34,020

QUESTIONS

1. What are final accounts? Why are these accounts prepared?
2. What is the need of making adjustments while preparing final accounts.
3. What are operating and non-operating profits? **[B.Com. (H) D. U., 1988]**
4. Distinguish between accrued income and outstanding income. **[B.Com. (H) D.U., 1989]**
5. Explain the limitations of financial statements. **[B. Com. (H) D. U., 1988]**
6. Write short note on uses and limitation of financial statements. **[B.Com. (H) D.U., 1991]**
7. What do you understand by "Grouping and Marshalling" of Balance Sheet? Explain the methods of arranging assets and liabilities.
8. Write note on 'adjustment' entries. Give adjustment entries for the following when :
   (a) appearing in the Trial Balance
      (i) Outstanding expenses
      (ii) Accrued incomes
      (iii) Closing stock
      (iv) Bad debts
      (v) Income tax
   (b) when appearing in adjustments.
      (vi) Adjusted purchases
      (vii) Goods distributed as samples
      (viii) Goods destroyed in-transit
      (ix) Manager's commission
      (x) Depreciation.
9. What are intangible fictitious assets? Give examples.

PROBLEMS

1. Make the adjustment entries from the following matters while preparing the annual accounts for the year ended 31st December 2005.
   (a) Goods sold and recorded as sales for Rs. 5,000 were packed and invoice was sent to customer. Stock-taking intervened and the parcel of goods not dispatched but was included in the stock on hand.
   (b) A purchase was made for a staff member of Rs. 15,000 and the cost was included in purchases. A deduction of similar amount was made from his salary and the net payment to him posted to salaries account.
   (c) Several employees took their salary in advance in the month of December 2005 which was payable to them in January 2006 amounting to Rs. 25,000.
   (d) Wages paid to the firm's own workmen for making certain additions to furniture amounting to Rs. 4,000 were posted to wages account.
   (e) A dishonoured bill receivable for Rs. 1,000 returned by the bank with whom it had been discounted, had been credited to Bank Account and debited to Bills Receivable Account.
   (f) A cheque amounting to Rs. 850 received from a customer was dishonoured. The returned cheque correctly entered in the Cash Book but was posted there-from to Allowance Account.
   (g) A duplicate invoice for a purchase of machinery costing Rs. 25,000 was erroneously passed again and entered in the books.
   (h) A sum of Rs. 6,000 drawn by the proprietor was debited to Traveling Expenses.

[C.A. (Entrance) Adapted]

2. A trader maintained Provisions for Doubtful Debts @ 5%, Provision for Discount @ 2% on Sundry Debtors and Reserve for Discount @ 2% on creditors which on 1st January 2006 stood at Rs. 3,000, Rs. 1,000 and Rs. 8,000 respectively. His balances on 31st December 2006 and 31st December 2007 were as follows :

	31-12-2006	31-12-2007
	Rs.	Rs.
Sundry Debtors	40,000	12,000
Sundry Creditors	30,000	20,000
Bad debts written off	3,600	600
Discount Allowed	1,200	400
Discount Received	600	100

Show necessary ledger Accounts. **[ICWA, June 1985, Adapted]**

3. From the following particulars prepare :
   (i) Provision for Doubtful Debts Account
   (ii) Provision for Discount on Debtors and
   (iii) Provision for Discount on Creditors for the year ending 31st December 2006 and 2007

   Balances on 1st January 2006 :

   Provision for Doubtful Debt Rs. 1,750, Provision for Discount on Debtors Rs. 875, Provision for Discount on Creditors Rs. 700

   Debtors as on 31st December 2006 were Rs. 43,750 after writing off bad debts Rs. 1,050 and allowing discount Rs. 350

   Debtors as on 31st December 2007 were Rs. 35,000 after writing off bad debts Rs. 1,050 and allowing discount of Rs. 87.50

   Total creditors as on 31st December 2006 and 2007 were Rs. 26,250 and Rs. 17,500 respectively.

Discount received during the years were Rs. 525 and Rs. 87.50

Provide 5% for doubtful debts, 2.5% as provision for discount on debtors and 2% for discount on creditors.

		2006	2007
Ans.	Provision for Doubtful debts	1487.50	612.5
	Provision for Discount	514	120
	Provision for Discount on Creditors	350	87.5

4. From the following particulars, prepare Provision for Doubtful debts Account, Provision for Discount Account and show relevant extract for Profit & Loss Account and Balance Sheet.

TRIAL BALANCE (EXTRACT)

	Dr	Cr
Sundry Debtors	70,000	
Bad debts	4,200	
Provision for Bad & Doubtful debts		4,900
Discount Allowed	500	
Provision for Discount		700

Additional Information :

Sundry Debtors include Rs. 7,000 due from a customer who became insolvent and a dividend of 50 paise in a rupee was received from him. Maintain provision for bad & doubtful debts @ 5% on Debtors and provision for discount on debtors @ 2%.

Ans. Rs. 5,950 to be debited to P & L A/c on account of Provision for Doubtful debts.

Rs. 997 to be debited to P & L A/c on account of Provision for Discount.

5. From the following balances prepare Trading and Profit & Loss Account for the year ended 31st March 2009 and a Balance Sheet as on that date.

	Rs.		Rs.
Capital	1,50,000	Drawings	13,000
Bills Receivable	17,800	Rent Owing (Dr)	800
Bills Payable	13,450	Interest & Discount (Dr)	1,350
Creditors	19,600	Salaries	6,000
Furniture	2,500	Return Inwards	12,300
(including Purchase of Rs. 1,000		Return Outwards	8,750
On 30th September, 2008)		Sales	146,800
Rent & Tax	3,500	Debtors	85,390
Purchases	1,78,200	Trade Charges	2,300
Cash at Bank	17,090		

Additional Information :

(i) Stock at the end was valued at Rs. 64,000 (Market Value Rs. 65,500) (ii) Rs. 1,500 paid to X against our acceptances were debited by mistake to Y's A/c and from there it was included in the list of Sundry Debtors (iii) Goods costing Rs. 2,500 were used by the proprietor (iv) Traveling expenses paid to our sales representative Rs. 1,250 for the month of March were debited to his personal account (v) Depreciate furniture at 10% p.a. (vi) Provide for doubtful debts @ 5% on Debtors.

Ans. Gross Profit Rs. 31,580, Net Loss Rs. 215, Balance Sheet Rs. 1,66,635.

6. From the following Trial Balance, prepare Trading and Profit & Loss Account and Balance Sheet as on 31st December 2008.

	Rs.		Rs.
Opening Stock	28,800	Capital	40,000
Postage	640	Loan	11,200
Commission	1,120	Sales	2,08,000
Discount Allowed	1,440	Bills Payable	13,280
Rent	5,760	Returns Outwards	3,200
Wages	17,600	Discount Received	1,760
Salaries	12,800	Sundry Creditors	24,000
Furniture	1,600		
Type writer	480		
Motor Car	48,000		
Sundry Debtors	25,600		
Cash in hand & at Bank	4,800		
Purchases	1,44,000		
Bad debts	800		
Return Inwards	8,000		
	3,01,440		3,01,440

Adjustments :

(a) Closing stock was valued at Rs. 38,400

(b) Outstanding salaries Rs. 2,400

(c) Provide for interest on Capital @ 5%

(d) Create provision for Bad & Doubtful debt @ 5% on debtors and 1% provision for discount on Sundry Creditors.

(e) Depreciate furniture by 10%, Motor Car by 20% and Typewriter at 5%.

Ans. Gross Profit Rs. 51,200; Net Profit Rs. 15,176; Balance sheet Rs. 1,07,816

7. From the following Trial Balance and additional information prepare Trading and Profit Loss Account for the year ended 30th June 2008 and a Balance sheet as on that date.

	Rs.		Rs.
Goodwill	24,000	Capital	2,61,000
Furniture	32,000	Sales	7,42,400
General Expenses	41,360	Creditors	31,200
Purchases	6,49,600		
Wages	57,600		
Drawings	41,040		
Debtors	1,53,600		
Stock	28,000		
Cash in hand	8,000		
	10,35,200		10,35,200

Additional Information :

1. Stock at the end was valued at Rs. 36,000. In view of constant falling prices, it has been decided to write off stock by 10%.
2. Sales book was overcast by Rs. 400.
3. Wages outstanding Rs. 400 though included in the Wages A/c was not included in the Trial Balance.
4. Private purchases worth Rs. 800 were passed through the purchase day book.
5. Furniture (Book value on 1-7-2007 Rs. 3,200) was sold on 31st December 2005 for Rs.3,600 was passed through daybook
6. Depreciate furniture at 20% p.a.

Ans. Gross Profit Rs. 36,400; Net Profit Rs. 7,440; Balance sheet Rs. 2,43,920.

8. The following balances are extracted from the ledgers of a Trader for the year ending 31st December 2008. You are required to prepare final accounts to be presented in the Shareholders' meeting.

	Rs.		Rs.
Computer (W.D.V.)	9,600	Capital	1,87,500
Motor Vehicles	93,750	Provision for Bad debts	3,000
Premises	1,12,500	Sundry Creditors	37,500
Bad debts	1,875	Bank Over draft	42,750
Sundry Debtors	57,000	Sales	2,31,750
Stock on 1st January 2001	51,900	Purchase Return	1,875
Purchases	82,125	Commission	5,625
Sales Return	3,000		
Advertising	6,750		
Interest on Overdraft	1,770		
Cash in hand	9,750		
Taxes and Insurance	18,750		
General Expenses	11,730		
Salaries	49,500		
	5,10,000		5,10,000

Additional Information :

(i) Stock as on 31st December 2008 was Rs. 48,750.

(ii) Depreciate building @ 5%, Computer @ 10% and Motor Vehicles @ 20%.

(iii) Insurance amounting to Rs. 1,500 is prepaid,

(iv) Salaries Rs. 4,500 and Taxes Rs. 1,800 are outstanding,

(v) Rs. 1,275 is due for interest on bank overdraft,

(vi) Write off a further sum of Rs. 1,500 as bad debts and provision for bad and doubtful debts to be made equal to 10% on debtors.

Ans. Gross Profit Rs. 1,45,350, Net Profit Rs. 23,265, Balance sheet Total Rs. 3,00,465.

9. From the following Trial Balance of X, prepare final accounts for the year ended 31st March 2008.

	Rs.		Rs.
Opening Stock	86,800	Sales	3,22000
Furniture & Fittings	29,960	Capital	2,26,800
Office Equipments	22,400	Sundry Creditors	60,200
Sundry Debtors	1,20,400	12% Loan (1-5-2005)	42,000
Cash at Bank	3,640	Provision for bad debts	4,200
Cash in hand	1,960	Purchase Returns	3,640
Electric Charges	3,080	Discount Received from Creditors	2,240
Printing & Stationery	2,520		
Drawings	16,800		
Carriage Outwards	2,800		
Freight on Purchases	1,680		
Discount Allowed to Debtors	3,360		
Rates and Taxes	2,940		
Interest on Loan	3,780		
Rent for go down	7,700		
Salaries	15,400		
Sales Returns	5,880		
Purchases	1,96,000		
Insurance Premium	7,700		
General Office Expenses	4,200		
Bad debts	2,800		
Bank Charges	2,240		
Building	84,000		
Motor Car	28,000		
Car Expenses	5,040		
	6,61,080		6,61,080

Adjustments :

(i) Stock at the end was valued at Rs. 61,600.

(ii) One month's rent and one month's salary are outstanding.

(iii) Provision for Bad debts is to be maintained at 5% on S. Debtors.

(iv) Insurance premium includes Rs. 5,600 paid towards proprietor's Life Insurance Policy and the balance of the insurance charges cover the period from 1-4-2007 to 30-6-2008.

(v) Half of building is used for residential purposes of proprietor,

(vi) Depreciate : Building used for business by 5%, Furniture and Fittings by 10%. One steel table purchased during the year for Rs. 1,960 was sold for same price but the sale proceeds were wrongly credited to sales account,

(vii) Depreciate : Equipments by 15%, Motor Car by 20%, purchase of a type writer during the year for Rs. 5,600 has been wrongly debited to purchases, Motor Car by 20%. **[C.A. (Entrance) Adapted]**

Ans. Gross Profit Rs. 1,00,520, Net Profit Rs. 25,760, Balance sheet Total Rs. 3,33,200.

10. From the following Trial Balance and additional information, prepare Trading and Profit & Loss Account for the year ended 31st March 2009 and a Balance sheet as on that date.

	Rs.		**Rs.**
Drawings	16,000	Capital	1,60,000
Debtors	80,000	Creditors	38,400
Purchases	1,92,000	Sales	3,20,320
Return Inwards	16,000	Returns Outward	24,000
Bills Receivable	24,000	Bills Payable	35,200
Opening Stock	49,920	Dividend Received	1,600
6% Loan to X	16,000		
Salaries	32,000		
Furniture & Fixtures	24,000		
Machinery	80,000		
Machinery (1-1-2009)	16,000		
General Expenses	1,600		
Factory Wages	16,000		
Office light	8,000		
Cash in hand	8,000		
	5,79,520		5,79,520

Additional Information :

(a) Stock on 31st March 2009: Goods Rs. 64,000, Stationery Rs. 320.

(b) General Expenses include stationery purchased for Rs. 720.

(c) Included in the sales Rs. 4,000 being sale of fixture (Book value Rs. 6,400), Depreciation thereon to the date of sale Rs. 320.

(d) Bad debts during the year amounted to Rs. 960.

(e) Depreciate Machinery and Fixtures & Furniture by 10% p.a.

(f) Goods destroyed but covered by insurance amounted to Rs. 8,000 but amount is not yet received.

(g) The Manager is entitled to receive a commission of 10% on the net profit before charging such commission.

Ans. Gross Profit Rs. 1,38,400, Net Profit Rs. 77,544, Commission Rs. 8,616, Balance Sheet, Rs.3,03,760.

Hint. Provide for interest on loan. Profit before commission Rs. 86,160.

11. Following balances have been extracted from the books of a Trader as on 31st March 2009 :

	Rs.		Rs.
Rent, Rates and Taxes	1,800	Sales	4,20,000
Salaries	25,200	Sundry Creditors	30,000
Insurance Premium	5,400		
Carriage Inwards	10,800		
Carriage Outwards	12,600		
Claims Receivable	3,000		
Bad debts	2,400		
Advertisement Suspense	5,400		
Purchases	2,40,000		
Sundry Debtors	90,000		
Cash in hand	2,400		
Cash at Bank	4,800		
Electricity Charges	1,200		
Opening Stock	18,000		
Bills Receivable	3,600		
Office Equipments	6,000		
Deposit with Supplier	3,600		
Computer	13,800		
	4,50,000		4,50,000

Adjustments :

1. Goods costing Rs. 3,000 were dispatched on 27th March. The sale, however, took place on 2nd April 2009 when on invoice of Rs. 4,500 was raised against a customer.
2. A purchase invoice for Rs. 9,000 received from a Sundry Creditor, has not been entered through oversight.
3. A claim recoverable has been settled with the Insurance company for Rs. 1,200.
4. 50% of Advertisement Suspense Account is to be written off this year. The amount represents cost of advertising campaign conducted this year.
5. Insurance premium includes a prepaid amount of Rs. 600.
6. Deposit with supplier was made on 1-10-2008 and carries interest @ 12% p.a.
7. Two bills received from customers of Rs. 450 and 750 were dishonoured on 30th March. These had earlier been discounted with the Bank.
8. Provide 2% on Sundry Debtors for doubtful debts.
9. Physical stock of goods as on 31st March 2009 was Rs. 60,000.
10. Depreciate Computer by 10% and on Office Equipments by 5% on Straight Line Method. The original cost was Rs. 18,000 and Rs. 9,000 for the Computer and office equipments respectively.

Prepare Final Accounts. **[C.A. (Inter) Adapted]**

12. From the following Trial Balance and additional information you are required to prepare Trading and Profit and Loss Account for the year ended 31 st March 2009 and a Balance Sheet as on that date.

	Rs.		Rs.
Opening Stock	25,000	Capital	50,000
Drawings	12,500	Overdraft	2,500
Telephone	7,500	Sundry Creditors	9,250
Machinery	25,000	Sales	1,20,000
Sundry Debtors	25,000	Mortgage	30,000
Sales Return	2,500	Bills Payable	5,500
Computers	52,500		
Purchases	50,000		
Bills Receivable	3,750		
Furniture	1,500		
Trade Expenses	1,000		
Bad debts	1,000		
Wages	10,000		
	2,17,250		2,17,250

Additional Information :

(a) Stock on 31st March 2009 was valued at Rs. 27,500.

(b) Goods worth Rs. 500 returned by a customer were included in purchases.

(c) The proprietor used the goods worth Rs. 7,500.

(d) The telephone was obtained under "Own your Telephone Scheme" and free of rent for five years.

(e) Machine worth Rs. 2,500 has not been entered in the books and no payment has been made so for.

(f) Included among the debtors Rs. 2,500 due from X and included in creditors' list Rs. 2,500 due to him.

(g) Proprietor's wife works in the firm and is allowed a salary of Rs. 250 per month. This amount has been included in drawings,

(h) It was discovered that stock on 1-4-2008 was overcast by Rs.5,000.

(i) Further bad debts Rs. 500.

(j) A commission of 10% on the net profit is due to Manager after charging such commission.

Ans. Gross Profit Rs. 72,500

Net Profit Rs. 59,550

Commission Rs. 5,955

Balance Sheet Rs. 1,48,250

13. Mr. Ashwani is a Trader. His Trial Balance as on 31 st March 2009 was as follows. You are required to prepare final accounts after talking into consideration the adjustments.

	Rs.		Rs.
Drawings	2,800	Capital	2,02,020
Carriage Inwards	7,000	Sales	2,90,500
Purchases	2,17,000	Creditors	28,000
Carriage Outwards	15,400		
Stock	35,000		
Cash in hand & at Bank	9,870		
Debtors	70,000		
Salaries	22,400		
Rent & Taxes	3,500		
Postage & Telephone	8,050		
Salesman's Commission	24,500		
Insurance	6,300		
Advertising	11,900		
Furniture & Fittings	15,400		
Fittings & Stationery	2,100		
Motor Car	33,600		
Bad debts	1,400		
Cash Discounts	2,800		
General Expenses	9,800		
Wages	14,000		
O/s Liability for Expenses	7,700		
	5,20,520		5,20,520

Adjustments :

(1) Cost of goods in Stock on 31st March 2009 was Rs. 1,01,500.

(2) Ashwani had withdrawn goods worth Rs. 3,500 during the year.

(3) Sales include goods worth Rs. 10,500 sent out to party on approval and remaining unsold as on 31st March 2009. This includes profit of 50% on cost.

(4) Debtors include Rs. 3,500 bad debts. Provision for bad debts is to created at 5%.

(5) Purchases include purchase of furniture worth Rs. 7,000.

(6) Printing and stationery expenses worth Rs. 7,700 relating to previous year had not been provided in that year but is paid in this year by debiting outstanding liability.

(7) Creditors include a balance of Rs. 2,800 to the credit of a Private Company of which it has been decided and settled with the party to pay only Rs. 700.

(8) The Salesmen are entitled to a commission of 10% on total sales.

(9) Depreciate furniture and fittings by 10% & Motor Car by 20%. **[C.A. (Inter) Adapted]**

Ans. Gross Profit Rs. 1,26,000; Net Profit Rs. 1,190; Balance Sheet Rs. 2,18,610.

14. The following Trial Balance is extracted from the books of X as on 31st December 2008.

	Rs.		**Rs.**
Building	60,000	Sundry Creditors	1,11,400
Goodwill	62,500	Capital	2,00,000
Purchases	2,55,000	Bank Loan	37,500
Plant & Machinery	50,000	Provision for Bad debts	5,000
Manufacturing Wages	86,250	Sales	6,27,125
Salaries	39,625	Purchase Returns	4,350
Furniture	25,000		
Freight on Purchases	4,650		
Freight on Sales	5,350		
Computer	30,000		
Sales Returns	7,750		
Bad debts	3,500		
Interest & Bank Charges	1,000		
Manufacturing xpenses	23,750		
Insurance & Tax	10,625		
General Expenses	20,500		
Factory Fuel & Power	3,200		
Opening Stock	85,500		
Factory lighting	2,375		
Sundry Debtors	1,95,500		
Cash in hand & at Bank	13,300		
	9,85,375		9,85,375

Prepare Trading and Profit & Loss Account for the year ended 31st December 2008 and a Balance sheet as on that date after taking into consideration the following adjustments :

1. Stock on 31st December 2008 was valued at Rs. 76,250.
2. Depreciate : Furniture by 5%, Plant & Machinery by 10% and Computer by Rs. 2,500.
3. Bring Provision for Bad debts to 5% on Sundry Debtors.
4. A commission of 1% on gross profit is to be provided for Works Manager.
5. A commission of 2% on net profit (after charging the Works Manager's commission) is to be credited to the General Manager. **[C.A. (Entrance) Adapted]**

Ans. Gross Profit Rs. 2,39,250;
Net Profit Rs. 1,39,878;
Balance sheet Rs. 4,94,025.

15. From the following prepare Final Accounts for the period mention.

Particulars	**Rs.**	**Rs.**
Purchases/Sales	1,30,295	1,80500
Cash in Hand	500	–
Cash at bank	9,500	–
Stock on 1-04-2007	40,000	–
Wages	22,525	–
Returns	2,400	195
Repairs	1,675	–
Debtors/Creditors	30,000	30,305
Bad Debts	2,310	–
Loan (12% p.a.)	–	20,000
Discounts	800	530
Capital	–	37,500
Interest on Loan	600	–
Salaries	8,000	–
Sales Tax	800	–
Octroi	500	–
Insurance	1,000	–
Charity	125	–
Rent	2,000	–
Machinery	16,000	–
	269,030	269,030

Adjustments :

(i) Wages include Rs 2,000 for erection of new machinery installed on 1-04-2007
(ii) Provide depreciation on Machinery @ 5% p.a
(iii) Stock on 31-03-2008 is Rs 40,925.
(iv) Salaries unpaid Rs 800.
(v) Further bad debts Rs 400.
(vi) Make a provision of 5% on debtors for doubtful debts
(vii) Rent is paid up to 30th June 2008
(viii) Unexpired insurance Rs 300.

Ans. Gross Profit – Rs. 27,900; Net Profit- Rs. 6,440; Total of Balance Sheet – Rs. 96845.

[B.com (Pass), D.U. 2004 (Modified)]

16. From the following balance taken from the ledgers of a trader on 31st March 2008. Prepare the Trading and Profit & Loss Account for the year ending 31st March 2008 and the Balance Sheet on that date :

	Rs.		Rs.
Sundry Creditors	19,000	Bad Debts	100
Building	15,000	Loan from Ram	2,500
Income Tax	1,025	Sundry Debtors	9,500
Loose Tools	1,000	Investments	6,500
Cash at Bank	16,200	Bad debts reserve	1,600
Sundry Expenses	1,990	Rent and Rates	850

Bank Interest (Credit)	75	Furniture	3,000
Purchases	1,57,000	Stock (01-04-2007)	27,350
Wages	10,000	Capital	47,390
Carriage Inwards	1,120	Discount allowed	630
Sales	1,85,000	Discount received	535
Motor Van	12,500	Drawings	2,000
Cash in hand	335	Bills payable	10,000

Adjustments :

(i) Write off further Rs. 300 as bad debts and create a provision for bad debts at 20% on debtors

(ii) Dividend accrued and due on investments is Rs. 135. Rates paid in advance Rs. 100 wages owing Rs. 450.

(iii) On 31-03-2008 stock was valued at Rs. 15,000 and loose tools were valued at Rs. 800.

(iv) Write off 5% for depreciation on building and 40% on motor van.

(v) Provide for interest at 12% p.a. due on loan taken on 01-06-2007

(vi) Manager is entitled to a commission of 5% on net profits after charging his commission.

[B.Com (P), DU, 2006- Category 'B']

Ans. Gross Profit – Rs. 4080; Net Loss – Rs. 5385; Total of Balance Sheet. Rs. 71,180

17. From the following, prepare Trading, Profit & Loss Account for the year ended 31st March 2008 & a Balance Sheet as at date.

Particulars	Rs.	Particulars	Rs.
Capital Account	1,00,000	Rent (Credit)	2,100
Drawings	17,600	Railway frieight and other expenses on goods sold	16,940
Purchases	80,000	Carriage Inwards	2,310
Sales	1,40,370	Office Expenses	1,340
Purchase Returns	2,820	Printing & Stationery	660
Opening Stock	11,460	Postage & Telegrams	820
Bad debts	1,400	Sundry Debtors	62,070
Bad debts provision on 1-4-2008	3,240	Sundry Creditors	18,920
Rates & Insurance	1,300	Cash at bank	12,400
Discounts (Cr.)	190	Cash in hand	2,210
Bills Receivable	1,240	Office Furniture	3,500
Sales Returns	4,240	Salary & commission	9,870
Wages	6,280	Additions to Building	7,000
Buildings	25,000		

Prepare Trading Profit and Loss Account for the year ending 31st March 2008 and balance sheet as on 31st March 2008 after keeping in view these adjustments :

(1) Depreciate old building @ 1 ½ % and new addition to the building @ 2% and office furniture @ 5%

(2) Write off further bad debts Rs. 570

(3) Increase the bad debts provision on debtors to 6%

(4) Outstanding salary Rs. 570.

(5) Rent receivable Rs. 200.
(6) Interest on Capital @ 5%.
(7) Stock is valued at Rs. 14,290 on 31st March 2008.
(8) Unexpaired Insurance Rs. 240.

Ans. Gross Profit-Rs. 53,190; Net Profit – Rs. 16060; Total Balance Sheet- Rs. 1,22,950.

[B.Com (P), DU-2005]

18. From the following Trial Balance of a trader on March 31, 2008, prepare Trading and Profit & Loss Account for the year ending 31st March, 2008 and Balance Sheet as at date after giving effect to the under mentioned adjustments :

Debit Balances	Rs.	Credit Balances	Rs.
Drawings	60,000	Bank Overdraft	2,50,000
Wages	1,55,000	Interest on Investment	58,000
Stock	1,28,000	Bills Payable	46,000
Loan to X	40,000	Interest on Loan to X	3,200
Rent	50,000	Capital	10,00,000
General Expenses	14,800	Reserve for Bad and doubtful debts	2,500
Investments	6,00,000	Sales	23,00,000
Purchases	16,00,000	Sundry Creditors	1,25,900
Freight and Carriage	21,000		
Goodwill	4,00,000		
Bills Receivable	62,000		
Rates and Taxes	18,000		
Sales Returns	21,000		
Insurance	9,000		
Cash & Bank balances	37,000		
Postage & Telegram	38,000		
Land & Buildings	2,50,000		
Plant & Machinery	1,00,000		
Sundry Debtors	1,65,000		
Packing Charges	4,000		
Bad debts	12,800		
	37,85,600		37,85,600

Adjustments :

(i) Closing stock as on 31-03-2008 was Rs. 1,60,000.
(ii) Goods worth Rs. 7,000 were sent on 25-03-2008 as "Sale on Approval Basis" for Rs. 8,000 and the approval was not received before the end of the month.
(iii) 20% of the goodwill is to be written off.
(iv) Further bad debts were estimated at Rs. 3,500 Increase reserve for bad debts to the extent of Rs. 15,000.
(v) Depreciate land and building by 3% and Plant & Machinery by 10%.
(vi) Goods worth Rs. 8,000 were distributed as free samples. **[B.Com (P), D.U. 2006 (Regular) Modified]**

Ans. Gross Profit – Rs. 54,200; Net Profit Rs. 33,510; Total Balance Sheet Rs 1,69,700.

19. From the following Trial Balance of a Trader prepare Trading and Profit & Loss Account for the year ending 31st March 2008 and Balance Sheet after. Giving effect to the under mentioned adjustment :

	Rs.		Rs.
Drawings	32,500	Capitals	1,50,000
Stock (1-4-2007)	1,74,450	Returns Outward	8,400
Returns Inwards	5,540	Interest on Loan to Ashok	350
Carriage Inwards	12,500	Rent Outstanding	1,300
Deposit with Anand	13,750	Creditors	30,000
Carriage Outward	7,250	Provision for Doubtful Debts	12,000
Loan to Ashok @ 5% p.a. given on 1-4-2004	10,000	Sales	2,79,140
Rent	8,200		
Purchases	1,29,700		
Debtors	40,000		
Goodwill	17,300		
Advertisement expenses	9,540		
Bad Debts	4,000		
Patents & Patterns	5,000		
Cash	620		
Discount allowed	3,300		
Wages	7,540		
	4,81,190		4,81,190

Adjustments :

(i) The Manager is entitled to a commission of 10% of net profit, calculated after charging such commission

(ii) Increase bad debts by Rs. 6,000 make provision for doubtful debts @ 10% and provision for discount on debtors @ 5%

(iii) Stock valued at Rs. 15,000 destroyed by fire on 25-03-2008 but the insurance company admitted a claim for Rs 9,500 only and the same would be paid in May, 2008.

(iv) Rs. 2,000 out of the advertisement expenses are to be carried forward to the next year.

(v) The value of closing stock is Rs. 1,87,920. **[B.Com (P) D.U, 2006 Modified]**

Ans. Gross Profit Rs. 1,60,730; Net Profit – Rs. 1,15,010; Total Balance Sheet- Rs. 2,75,310.

❑❑❑

6

FINAL ACCOUNTS OF NON-PROFIT MAKING ORGANISATIONS

Besides, profit making organisations, there are certain other types of concerns, organisations or institutions which aim to render service with or without profit motive. These may be :

1. Professional organisations with profit motive such as firms of Chartered Accountants, Solicitors, Tax Consultants, Management Consultants, Doctors and Architects etc.
2. Charitable and religious concerns without profit motive such as Educational Institutions, Hospitals, Public Libraries, and Missionary Organisations.
3. General welfare organisations without profit motive such as Clubs, Unions, Societies and Associations.

These organisations and institutions are created to promote Arts & Culture, Sports and Games, Science and Commerce, Health and Education, Charity & Religion etc. Because of the distinct and different nature of operating activities, their accounting system is entirely different from Trading organisations in terms of preparation, presentation and perceptions. The main source of revenue or income stems from subscriptions, donations, or government grants in case of Non-Trading organisation rather than from sales (in case of Trading organisations). Similarly non-trading organisations spend their incomes on achieving the objectives for which these were formed whereas Trading organisations incur on buying of goods and services in which these deal in. Thus, these non-profit making organisations prepare :

1. Receipts and Payments Account
2. Income and Expenditure Account and
3. Balance Sheet.

1. RECEIPTS & PAYMENTS ACCOUNT

It is a real account by nature and shows the summary of cash transactions taken place during the accounting period. It is equivalent to Cashbook of Trading organisations. It records all cash receipts on the debit side and all cash payments on the credit side in a chronological order. It does not make any distinction between capital receipts or revenue receipts, capital expenditure or revenue expenditure, recurring items of receipts or payments and non-recurring items of receipts or payments. Similarly these may relate to current year, last year, next year. However, outstanding, due or accrued are not considered under receipts and payments account. In other words, the process of preparation of Receipts & Payments Account is exactly the same as that of Cash Book of Trading Organisations. The format of Receipts & Payments Account is given as follows :

RECEIPTS AND PAYMENTS ACCOUNT OF...
For the year ended...

Dr. Cr.

Receipts	Rs.	Payments	Rs.
To Balance b/d	—	By Balance b/d (Overdraft)	—
Cash	—	By Honorarium	—
Bank : Fixed Deposit	—	By Salaries and Wages	—
Current Account	—	By Rent, Rates & Taxes	—
Savings Bank A/c	—	By Printing and Stationery	—
To Subscriptions	—	By Postage and Telegrams	—
To Donations	—	By Repairs and maintenance	—
To Entrance Fees	—	By Audit Fees	—
To Government Grant/ Subsidy	—	By Newspaper, Magazines etc.	—
To Life membership Fees	—	By Gas, Water, Electricity etc.	—
To Legacies	—	By Purchase of assets (Furniture, Computer,	
To Dividend, Interest & Rent etc.	—	Typewriter, Printer etc.)	—
To Sale of old Newspapers	—	By Purchase of Sports material	—
To Locker's Rent Received	—	By Purchase of Bar/Restaurant materials	—
To Sale from Bar/Restaurant	—	By Bank Charges & Insurance etc.	—
To Fees from Clients	—	By Sundry Expenses	—
To Sundry Receipts	—	By Balance c/d	
To Balance c/d (Overdraft)	—	Cash	—
		Bank: Fixed Deposit	—
		Saving Bank A/c	—
		Current A/c	—
	Total		Total

2. INCOME AND EXPENDITURE ACCOUNT

It is a nominal account by nature and similar to Profit and Loss Account of Trading organisations. This account is prepared on accrual basis and it incorporates all adjustments relating to outstanding or prepaid items of incomes and expenses. It is based on the same rules, which are applicable to Profit and Loss Account. It accounts for the incomes and expenses relating to current accounting year only whether received or not, or whether paid or not. It ignores items of income and expenses relating to last year or next year. Again, items of capital nature whether income or expenses, are totally excluded. Incomes of recurring nature are treated whereas non-recurring and specific receipts are ignored while preparing Income & Expenditure Account. It follows the concepts of accounting period, accrual or matching concept.

Following is the format of Income and expenditure account.

INCOME AND EXPENDITURE ACCOUNT OF
... For the year ended...

Dr. Cr.

Expenditure	Rs.	Income	Rs.
To Salaries/Honorarium	—	By Subscription Donations (General)	—
*Add Outstanding	—	By Entrance Fees #	—
*Less Prepaid	—	By Government Grants (Recurring)	—
To Rent, Rates & Taxes	—	By Sale of old newspapers	—
To Printing and Stationery	—	By Sales of used sports materials	—
To Insurance	—	By Profit on sale of Assets	—
To Newspaper, Magazines	—	By Rent, Interest or dividend	—
To Sports Material used		By Fees	—
Opening Stock	—	By Profit from Bar/Restaurant	—
Add Purchases	—	By Sundry Receipt	—
Less Closing Stock	—	By *Excess of Expenditure over income	—
To Gas, Water, Electricity	—		
To Repairs and maintenance	—		
To Bank Charges	—		
To Loss on Sale of assets	—		
To Depreciation	—		
To Sundry Expenses	—		
To *Excess of Income over Expenditure	—		
	Total		Total

*Whichever is applicable? # If so desired in the question

DISTINCTION BETWEEN RECEIPTS AND PAYMENTS ACCOUNT AND INCOME AND EXPENDITURE ACCOUNT

Basis	Receipts and Payments A/c	Income & Expenditure
1 Nature of Account	It is a Real Account by nature just like a Cash Book.	It is a Nominal Account by nature. It is like a trading and Profit and Loss A/c
2 Nature of items	It includes both capital and revenue items.	It accounts for only revenue items.
3 Balance	It always starts with opening balance of Cash /bank and closes with closing balance of Cash /Bank.	It does not have either opening or closing balance.
4 Sides of Account	Debit side shows the receipts while payments are shown on credit side	Expenses are shown on debit side and incomes on the credit side.

5 Basis of Accounting	It is prepared on cash basis and thus Ignores all outstanding, due or accrued.	It is prepared on accrual basis.It considers all outstanding, due or accrued.
6 Period	It includes items relating to proceeding, current or succeeding year.	It considers items of current year only.
7 Non Cash items	Non Cash items such as depreciation, loss on sale of assets are not recorded.	It records all non-cash items.
8 Difference	The difference between the two sides of account represents Cash and Bank balance or Overdraft .	The difference between two sides of account represents surplus or deficit.
9 Balance Sheet	It is not accompanies by a Balance Sheet because it is not necessary to prepare a Balance Sheet along with this account.	It is accompany by a Balance Sheet.

Accounting Treatment of "Special Items"

There are certain items, which are peculiar and distinct from items explained and considered under final accounts of profit-making organisation, require special treatment while preparing final accounts of non-trading organisations. The accounting treatment of special items is being explained below :

1. Subscription

Subscription is received by the non-trading organisations from its members regularly each year. It is a recurring receipt of revenue nature and hence treated as a main source of income. This is shown to the debit of Receipts and Payments Account and to the credit side of Income and Expenditure Account As already explained, Receipts & Payments account shows the subscription (or any other item of income) on actual receipt basis while it is taken on accrual basis in the Income and Expenditure Account. Subscription outstanding is treated as an asset and subscription received in advance as a liability, which are shown in the Balance Sheet after due adjustments in the Income & Expenditure Account. It is explained as under.

	Rs.
Subscription received during the year	_____
(As per Receipts and Payments Account)	_____
Add : Outstanding subscription of the current year	_____
Less : Subscription in advance received during the current year	_____
Add : Subscription in advance received last year	_____
Less : Subscription outstanding of last year received this year	_____
Subscription to be shown in Income/Expenditure Account	_____

SUBSCRIPTION A/C (A Format)

	Rs.		**Rs.**
To Balance b/d (Outstanding of last year)	—	By Balance b/d (Advance received last year)	—
To Income and Expenditure A/c (Balancing figure)	—	By Cash (as per Receipts and Payments A/c)	—
To Balance c/d (Advance received for next year)	—	By Income and Expenditure A/c (Subscription written off)	—
	—	By Balance c/d (Outstanding of the current year)	—
	—		—

Illustration 1

From the following information, calculate the amount of subscriptions for the year ending 31 st December 2007 and show the same in Income and Expenditure Account and Balance Sheet of a club.

RECEIPTS AND PAYMENTS ACCOUNT
For the year ending 31st December 2007

Receipts	Rs.	Payments	Rs.
To Subscriptions	26,000		

Additional Information :

	Rs.
1. Subscriptions outstanding on 31st December 2006	5,200
2. Subscription outstanding on 31st December 2007	8,400
3. Subscription received in advance on 31st December 2006	4,800
4. Subscription received in advance on 31st December 2007	4,000

Solution :

	Rs.
Subscriptions as per Receipts and Payments Account	26,000
Add : Subscriptions outstanding on 31st Dec. 2007. (Current year)	8,400
	34,400
Less : Subscription outstanding on 31st Dec. 2006 (Last year)	5,200
	29,200
Add : Subscriptions received in advance in 2006 for the year 2007 (Current year)	4,800
	34,000
Less : Subscriptions received in advance 2007 for the year 2008 (Next Year)	4,000
Amount to be credited to Income and Expenditure Account for the year ending 31st December 2007	30,000

SUBSCRIPTION A/C

		Rs.			Rs.
2007			2007		
Jan. 1	To Balance b/d	5,200	Jan. 1	By Balance b/d	4,800
	To Income and Expenditure A/c (B/F)	30,000		By Cash (Receipts & Payments A/c)	26,000
Dec. 31	To Balance c/d	4,000	Dec. 31	By Balance c/d	8,400
		39,200			39,200

INCOME AND EXPENDITURE A/C
For the year ending 31st December 2007

Expenditure	Rs.	Income	Rs.
		By Subscriptions	30,000

BALANCE SHEET OF A CLUB
As on 31st December 2006

Liabilities	Rs.	Assets	Rs.
Subscription in Advance	4,800	Subscription Outstanding	5,200

BALANCE SHEET OF A CLUB
As on 31st December 2007

Liabilities	Rs.	Assets	Rs.
Subscription in Advance	4,000	Subscription Outstanding	8,400

Illustration 2

From the following extracts of Receipts and Payments Account and additional information, you are required to calculate the income from subscriptions for the year ending 31st March 2008 and show them in Income and Expenditure Account and the Balance Sheet of a club.

RECEIPTS AND PAYMENTS ACCOUNT
For the year ending 31st March 2008

Receipts	Rs.	Payments	Rs.
To Subscriptions :			
2006-2007	5,000		
2007-2008	30,000		
2008-2009	6,000		

Additional information :

	Rs.
1. Subscription outstanding on March 31st, 2007	6,000
2. Subscription outstanding on March 31st, 2008	5,000
3. Subscription received in advance on March 31st, 2007	6,000

[B.Com. (H), Delhi Univ., 1988, Modified]

Solution : The amount to be credited to Income and Expenditure Account can be worked out by preparing Subscription Account.

SUBSCRIPTION A/C

		Rs.				Rs.
2007			2007			
April 1	To Balance b/d	6,000	April 1	By Balance b/d		6,000
	To Income and Expenditure Account (B.F.)	40,000		By Cash (Receipts & Payment A/c)		41,000
2008	To Balance c/d	6,000	2008	By Balance c/d		
Mar. 31			Mar. 31	L.Y. -	1,000	
				C.Y. -	4,000	5,000
		52,000				52,000

INCOME AND EXPENDITURE A/C
For the year ending 31st March 2008

Expenditure	Rs.	Income	Rs.
		By Subscriptions	40,000

BALANCE SHEET OF A CLUB
As on 31st March 2007

Liabilities	Rs.	Assets	Rs.
Subscription in Advance	6,000	Subscription Outstanding	6,000

BALANCE SHEET OF A CLUB
As on 31st March 2008

Liabilities	Rs.	Assets		Rs.
Subscription in Advance	6,000	Subscription Outstanding		5,000
		Last Year	- 1,000	
		Current Year	- 4,000	

Illustration 3

Prepare the 'Subscription Account' from the following items for the year ending on 31st March 2008 and show the relevant items in Income and Expenditure Account and Balance Sheet.

	Rs.
1. Subscription in arrears on 31st March 2007	500
2. Subscription received in advance on 31st March 2007	1,100
3. Total Subscriptions received during 2007-2008 including Rs. 400 for 2006-2007 Rs. 1,200 for 2008-2009	35,400
4. Subscriptions Outstanding for 2007-2008	400

[B.Com. (Hons.), D.U. 1993, Modified]

Solution : **SUBSCRIPTION ACCOUNT**

Date	Particulars	Rs.	Date	Particulars		Rs.
2007			2007			
April 1	To Balance b/d	500	April 1	By Balance b/d		1,100
2008			2008			
Mar. 31	To Income & Expenditure A/c (B.F.)	35,300	Mar. 31	By Cash (Receipts & Payments A/c)		35,400
2008			2008	To Balance c/d		
Mar. 31	To Balancd c/d	1,200	Mar. 31	L.Y.	- 100	
				C.Y.	- 400	500
		37,000				37,000

INCOME AND EXPENDITURE A/C
For the year ending 31st March 2008

Particulars	Rs.	Particulars	Rs.
		By Subscriptions	35,300

BALANCE SHEET OF A CLUB
As on 31st March 2007

Liabilities	Rs.	Assets	Rs.
Subscription in Advance	1,100	Subscription Outstanding	500

BALANCE SHEET OF A CLUB
As on 31st March 2008

Liabilities	Rs.	Assets	Rs.
Subscription in Advance	1,200	Subscription Outstanding L.Y. - 100 C.Y. - 400	500

Illustration 4

	Rs.
Subscriptions income for the year 2007-2008 as per Income and Expenditure A/c	82,000
Advance subscriptions received during 2006-2007	4,000
Subscriptions outstanding at the end of 2007-08. (including Rs. 1,000 for 2006-07)	9,500
Advance Subscriptions received for 2008-09	2,000
Subscriptions written off during 2007-08	500
Subscription receivable on 1-4-2007	5,000
Subscriptions collected by Secretary but not deposited	1,000

Prepare a statement showing subscriptions received 2007-08 as per Receipts and Payment A/c

[LC.W.A (Inter), June 1993-Modified]

Solution : **SUBSCRIPTION ACCOUNT**

	Rs.		Rs.
To Balance b/d (1-4-2007) (due in the beginning)	5,000	By Balance b/d (1-4-2007) (Advance in the beginning)	4,000
To Income & Expenditure A/c	82,000	By Secretary	1,000
To Balance c/d (Advance at the end) (for 2008-09)	2,000	By Income and Expenditure A/c (Written off)	500
		By Cash (Subscription received as per Receipts and Payments A/c) (Balancing figure)	74,000
		By Balance c/d (Due at the end) for L.Y. 1,000 C.Y. 8,500	9,500
	89,000		89,000

Important Note : Students must note carefully the language of the question and make it clear as to whether the subscription outstanding relates to current year only or other than the current year's also. If the subscription outstanding "as on" or "as at" is given, it means subscription outstanding refers to total amount of subscription due till date including that for current year as well as for earlier year's also. Whereas subscription due "for the year" suggests outstanding for the year mentioned (usually current year) only (Refer to illustration 2 & 3).
Where subscription for any year becomes irrecoverable and if it is decided to write off, the same should be debited to Income and Expenditure Account and credited to Subscription A/c.

2. Donations

Donations represent the amount received by these non-trading organisations from the members or from any other person, firm or a company by way of gift. It may be in cash or in kind. Donations in cash may be of two types :

(i) General Donations (ii) Specific Donations

(i) General donations refer to those donations, which are received without any specific purpose, instruction or condition. These are not earmarked to be spent on particular head or item of expenditure. These general donations may further be classified as donations of "recurring nature" and that of "non-recurring nature". As a rule or convention "small amount donations" are treated as recurring items of income and "large amount donations" are treated as "non-recurring items or capital receipt".

(ii) Specific donations are meant for some specific purpose and are earmarked for a specific head or activity e.g. donation received for construction/extension of hospital building or for purchase of 'X' ray machine etc. Such donations are treated as non-recurring or capital receipts.

It should be noted that non-recurring or capital receipts are taken to the liabilities side of Balance Sheet, whereas recurring or revenue items are treated as income and hence credited to Income and Expenditure Account. It is further explained with the help of following Illustration.

Illustration 5

Following information has been extracted from the Receipts and Payments Account of a Hospital. You are required to show the appropriate amount to be shown in the Income and Expenditure Account and Balance Sheet.

RECEIPTS & PAYMENTS ACCOUNT (EXTRACT)
For the year ending 31st December 2007

Receipts	Rs.	Payments	Rs.
To Donation for Construction of Operation theater	80,000		
To Donations	6,000		

Additional Information :

(1) During the year a sum of Rs. 25,000 has been spent on the construction of Operation Theater.

Solution :

INCOME AND EXPENDITURE A/C
For the year ending 31st December 2007

Expenditure	Rs.	Income	Rs.
		By Donations	6,000

BALANCE SHEET
As on 31st December 2007

Liabilities	Rs.	Assets	Rs.
Building Fund (OT)	80,000	Building (OT)	25,000

Notes :

(a) The amount of donation received for the construction of operation theater is a specific donation and, therefore, has been capitalised and shown to the liabilities side of Balance Sheet.

(b) Expenditure incurred of Rs. 25,000 on the construction of operation theater is a Capital expenditure and shown as asset in the Balance Sheet. However, this will not affect the "Building Fund" created for the purpose. Alternatively, it may be merged with the Capital Fund after the amount is fully exhausted.

(c) Donations of Rs. 6,000 which are received without any earmarked or specific purpose are of recurring nature and hence treated as income which has been credited to Income and Expenditure Account.

3. Legacy

When any donation is received by these non-profit making entities as per the will of a deceased person, it is called legacy. Since it is of non-recurring nature it is capitalised and taken to the liabilities side of Balance Sheet.

4. Entrance Fee

It is also known as "Admission Fees" which is collected from the new members only once at the time of admission or joining the club, society or institution. There is no consensus as to the accounting treatment of entrance fee. Some authorities treat it as an item of capital receipt on the ground that it is received and collected from members once in the lifetime of their membership and hence it is of non-recurring nature and thus taken to the liabilities side of Balance Sheet. Where as others contend that since every year new members join the organisation, the receipt of entrance fees becomes regular feature or a recurring source of revenue and hence it is treated as income and credited to Income and Expenditure Account. Sometime, there are specific instructions for the treatment of entrance fees. Such instructions must be noted carefully. In the absence of any specific instructions the entrance fees may be given either of two treatments justifying by a footnote. However, AS-9 recommends capitalisation of entrance fees.

5. Life-membership

It is a "once in a life", lump sum payment made by the members to the organisation in lieu of their monthly, quarterly or yearly fee or subscription. This makes them life time beneficiary of membership without paying any further fee. There are two methods of its treatment in the books of accounts.

(i) The amount so received as "Life membership Fee" may be treated as capital receipt and taken to the liabilities side of Balance Sheet under the heading "Life Membership Fee".

(ii) The amount received may be credited to separate account called "Life Membership Fee Account", and out of this account an amount equal to annual subscription of the concerned members may be transferred to Income and Expenditure Account and the balance may be carried forward till it is completely exhausted. In case of death of a member the balance, if any, standing to the credit of Life Membership Fee Account equivalent to deceased's share, be transferred to Capital Fund Account.

6. Government Grants and Subsidy

Some non-profit making organisations also receive grants or subsidy from government agencies. These grants may be specific or general. When a grant is received for a specific purpose it is capitalised and taken to the liabilities side of the balance Sheet. For example grant received by a school (from the government) for the purpose of purchasing and installing computers, such grant shall be capitalised. If a grant is released without any specific instruction or earmarked purpose, it is treated as income and credited to Income and Expenditure Account. Such grants are also known as "Maintenance Grant",. which are meant to meet day-today expenses.

7. General Fund

It is also known as Capital Fund. It is the excess of assets over liabilities of the concern. The excess of income over expenditure (surplus) is added and excess of expenditure over income (deficit) is deducted there-from. It is shown on the liabilities side of the Balance sheet.

8. Special Funds

Some institutions also maintain various funds to meet specific expenses against specific receipts and its income thereon. The incomes of special funds are credited to such special funds account and expenses are deducted there from, the balancing figure is shown to the liability side of Balance Sheet. Thus the expenses or incomes pertaining to special funds are not taken to Income and Expenditure Account. Examples of special funds are Tournament Fund, Prize Fund, Charity Fund and Building Fund etc. The receipts of such funds are invested outside the organisation in securities. This brings regular income for the special fund created for the purpose. On completion of the specific purpose for which fund was set up the balance is transferred to Capital Fund.

Illustration 6

Show the accounting treatment of the following items appearing in the Trial Balance of a club as on 31st December 2007.

Particulars	Debit (Rs.)	Credit (Rs.)
Tournament Fund		25,000
Tournament Expenses	8,000	
Receipt from Tournament		10,000
Prize Fund		12,000
Prize Fund Investment	12,000	
Income from Prize Fund Investment		1,000
Prizes awarded	800	

BALANCE SHEET OF .... (EXTRACTS)
As on 31st December 2007

Liabilities		Rs.		Rs.
Tournament Fund	25,000		Prize Fund Investment	12,000
Add Receipts from Tournament	10,000			
	35,000			
Less : Expenses	(8,000)	27,000		
Prize Fund	12,000			
Add : Income from Prize F. Inv.	1,000			
	13,000			
Less : Prizes awarded	(800)	12,200		

Illustration 7

Following information is extracted from the Trial Balance of a Club. You are required to show them in the Income and Expenditure Account and the Balance Sheet of the Club as on 31st December 2007.

Particulars	Debit (Rs.)	Credit (Rs.)
Donation received for Building		500,000
Expenditure on construction up to 31st December 2007	3,50,000	
Estimated Cost (Rs. 10,00,000)		
Life Membership Fee received during the year		10,000
Sports Fund as on 1-1-2007		15,000
Sports Fund Investment	15,000	
Income from Sports Fund Investment		1,500
Donation for Sports Fund		2,800
Sports Prizes awarded	4,000	
General Fund		50,000
General Fund Investment	50,000	
Interest on General Fund Investment		5,000

Solution : **INCOME AND EXPENDITURE A/C**
For the year ending 31st December 2007

Expenditure	Rs.	Income	Rs.
		Interest on General Fund Investment	5,000

BALANCE SHEET OF...
As on 31st December 2007

Liabilities		Rs.	Assets	Rs.
Building Fund		5,00,000	Building	3,50,000
Life-membership Fee		10,000	Sports Fund Investment	15,000
General Fund		50,000	General Fund Investment	50,000
Sports Fund	15,000			
Add Donation for Sports	2,800			
Add Income from S.F. Investments	1,500			
	19,300			
Less Prizes awarded	4,000	15,300		
General Fund		50,000		

9. Endowment Fund

It is a receipt of capital nature and therefore, it is taken to the liability side of the Balance Sheet. According to Kohler, "it is a fund, usually of a non-profit institution, arising from be quest or gift the income of which is devoted to a specified purpose". In fact, it provides for the permanent means of support of income for a non-profit concern.

10. Sale of Old Assets

Any amount received on sale or disposal of any old/obsolete/worn out asset is treated as capital receipt and debited to Receipts and Payments A/c. However, profit (Excess of sale proceeds of asset over Written down value) is credited to Income and Expenditure Account while loss on sale (Excess of Written down value over Sale price) is debited to Income and Expenditure Account in the year of sale or disposal.

11. Sale of Old Newspapers and Magazines

Such receipts are of recurring or revenue nature and thus treated as income of the concerned institution and credited to Income and Expenditure Account.

12. Sale of Old (used) Sports Materials

Sale proceeds of condemned sports materials such as used up old bats, balls and other old sports material, is treated as income of recurring nature. It is, therefore, taken to Income and Expenditure Account.

13. Other Revenue Receipts

These include income from rent, dividend and interest from investments (general) A/c. These are taken from the debit of Receipts and Payments Account to the credit of Income and Expenditure Account. Outstanding or accrued are shown to the assets side of Balance Sheet after due adjustment.

14. Sale and Purchase of Consumable Items or Running a Canteen or Bar

Usually a hospital, school or a club runs a canteen or, a Bar for its members and hence buys and sells refreshments, cigarettes, and bar materials etc. The cost of items purchased is a revenue expenditure and proceeds from sale is treated as revenue receipt. Therefore, these are taken to Income and

Expenditure Account. The unsold stock of these items is shown on the assets side of Balance Sheet. Likewise outstanding expenses or payments on these accounts are treated as liability.

However, sometimes examination problem requires preparation of Bar Trading Account or Refreshment or Canteen Trading Account. Under such a situation all items pertaining to Bar, Refreshment a Canteen are treated together under Bar or Canteen Trading Account and the net result thereof (Profit or Loss) is transferred to Income and Expenditure Account.

Illustration 8

Following information has been extracted from the Trial Balance of a Club, you are required to prepare Canteen & Bar Trading Account for the year ended 31st December 2008.

	Rs.
Stock at Canteen including Bar on 1-1-2007	25,000
Stock at Canteen including Bar on 31 -12-2007	20,000
Bar Takings	48,000
Sale Proceeds of Canteen	60,000
Purchases for Canteen & Bar	70,000
Barman's Wages	5,000
Bearers (Canteen) Wages	7,500

Solution : **CANTEEN & BAR TRADING ACCOUNT**

Particulars	Rs.	Pariculars	Rs.
To Opening Stock	25,000	By Bar Takings	48,000
To Purchases	70,000	By Sale Proceeds of Canteen	60,000
To Barman's Wages	5,000	By Stock (Closing)	20,000
To Bearers Wages	7,500		
To Surplus/Profit transferred to Income and Expenditure A/c	20,500		
	1,28,000		1,28,000

15. Consumable Supplies and Materials

Usually, the office supplies such as stationery or postage stamps and other requirements of club such as sports materials etc. are purchased during the year are not fully exhausted by the end of accounting year. Under these situations the amount, which should be charged to Income and Expenditure Account, has to be worked out as under :

Opening Balance (Stock) of such item	xxx
Add : Purchases* made during the year	xxx
Less : Closing Stock of such item	xxx
Actual Expenditure to be charged to Income and Expenditure account	xxx

*(Cash purchases as per Receipts and Payments Account)

Sometimes, when purchases of above items are made on credit bases and the payment to suppliers is either made in advance or subsequently leaving a balance to be paid in the next accounting year, the adjustment has to be made with regard to the amount due to the suppliers (creditors), both at the beginning and at the end of the accounting year as shown under :

Opening Stock of such item	xxx
Add : Payments made to Suppliers (creditors) as per Receipts and Payment Account	xxx
	xxx
Less : Closing Stock of such item	xxx
	xxx
Add : Creditors at the end	xxx
	xxx
Less : Creditors at the beginning	xxx
Amount to be charged to Income and Expenditure A/c	xxx

Alternatively, the amount can be worked out systematically through creditors and Stock Accounts, where creditors or suppliers Account will disclose the actual amount of purchases made during the year and Stock Account will show the amount to be charged to Income and Expenditure Account. This is given as under :

CREDITORS' (SUPLIERS') ACCOUNT

Particulars	Rs.	Particulars	Rs.
To Balance b/d (Advance at beg.)	—	By Balance b/d	
To Receipts and payments A/c		(Creditors at the beginning)	—
(Cash Paid)	—	By Purchases*	
To Balance c/d		(Balancing figure transferred	
(Creditors at the end)	—	to Stock A/c)	—
		By Balance c/d	
		(Advance at the end)	—
	—		—

STOCK ACCOUNT

To Balance b/d		By Income and Expenditure A/c	
(Opening Stock)	—	(Item Consumed)	—
To Purchases*		By Balance c/d	
(transfer from Creditor's A/c)	—	(Closing Stock)	—

Illustration 9

From the following information, calculate the amount to be charged to Income and ExpenditureAccount for the year ended 31st December 2007.

	Rs.
Stock of Stationery on 1st January 2007	3,000
Creditors for Stationery on 1st January 2007	2,000
Amount Paid for Stationery during the year	10,800
Stock of Stationery on 31st December 2007	500
Creditors for Stationery on 31st December 2007	1,300

[B.Com (H), D.U. 1985- Modified]

CREDITORS FOR STATIONERY ACCOUNT

	Rs.		Rs.
To Cash	10,800	By Balance c/d	2,000
To Balance c/d	1,300	By Stationery Purchased transferred to stock of stationery A/c (B.F.)	10,100
	12,100		12,100

STOCK OF STATIONERY ACCOUNT

To Balance b/d	3,000	By Income and Expenditure A/c (B.F.)	
To Creditors for Stationery A/c (Purchases)	10,100	(Stationery used)	12,600
		By Balance c/d	500
	13,100		13,100

Illustration 10

Calculate the amount to be debited to Income and Expenditure Account for the year ended 31st December 2007.

	Rs.
Stock of Stationery on 1-1-2007	3,000
Creditors of Stationery on 1-1-2007	2,000
Advance Paid for stationery carried from 2006	200
Amount Paid for stationery during the year	10,800
Stock of Stationery on 31-12-2007	500
Creditors of Stationery on 31-12-2007	1,300
Advance paid for stationery on 31-12-2007	1,300

CREDITORS FOR STATIONERY ACCOUNT

	Rs.		Rs.
To Balance b/d (Advance in the beginning)	200	By Balance b/d	2,000
To Receipts & Payments A/c (Cash Paid to Creditors)	10,800	By Stock of Stationery A/c (B.F.) (Being purchases made)	9,000
To Balance c/d	1,300	By Balance c/d (Advance at the end)	1,300
	12,300		12,300

STOCK OF STATIONERY ACCOUNT

	Rs.		Rs.
To Balance b/d	3,000	By Income and Expenditure A/c (Bal. figure)	11,500
To Creditors for Stationery A/c (being stationery purchased)	9,000	By Balnce c/d	500
	12,000		12,000

Illustration 11

From the following, calculate the amount of "Sports Materials" to be debited to Income and Expenditure A/c for the year ended 31st December 2007.

	Rs.
1. Amount paid for Sports Materials during the year 2007	14,000
2. Stock of Sports Materials as on 1-1-2007	1,200
3. Advance paid for Sports Materials on 31-12-2007	1,600
4. Advance paid for Sports Materials during December 2006 for the Sports Materials received during 2007	2,000
5. Creditors for Sports Materials on 1-1-2007	2,560
6. Stock of Sports Materials on 31-12-2007	3,320
7. Amount due to Creditors 31-12-2007	2,400

Solution : CREDITORS FOR SPORTS MATERIAL ACCOUNT

		Rs.			Rs.
2007			2007		
Jan. 1	To Balance b/d	2,000	Jan. 1	By Balance b/d	2,560
	To Cash-Receipts & Payment A/c	14,000		By Stock of Sports Material A/c (b/f)	14,240
Dec. 31	To Balance c/d	2,400	Dec. 31	By Balance c/d	1,600
		18,400			18,400

STOCK OF SPORTS MATERIAL ACCOUNT

		Rs.			Rs.
2007			2007		
Jan. 1	To Balance b/d	1,200	Dec. 31	By Income and Expenditure A/c (Sports Material used)	12,120
	To Creditors for Sports Material A/c (Purchases)	14,240		By Balance c/d	3,320
		15,440			15,440

3. BALANCE SHEET

There is no special process of preparation of balance Sheet of non-trading organisations. It is prepared as usual and on the same principles which are applicable to profit making or trading organisations. However, when Capital fund or General Fund is not given, an opening Balance Sheet is also prepared to determine the Capital fund which represents excess of assets over liabilities. The Capital fund is made of Capital receipts, receipts which are Capitalised and surpluses generated from Income and Expenditure Accounts of the preceding years since the inception of the organisation. The Closing Balance Sheet shows the financial position of the institution as on that date. The format of the Closing Balance Sheet is given below :

BALANCE SHEET OF... (A Format)
As on....

Liabilties		Rs.	Assets		Rs.
Capital Fund in the beginning	—		Fixed Assets		
Add : Surplus	—		Pavilion & Land		
Or			Building	—	
Less : Deficit	—		*Less* : Depreciation	—	—
Add : Receipts to be Capitalised	—		Furniture/Computer etc.	—	
	—	—	*Less* : Depreciation	—	—
(Entrance Fee, Life-Membership Fee etc.)			Surgical Equipments	—	
Special Fund			*Less* : Depreciation	—	—
(Building Fund, *Match Fund, Sports Fund,			Library Books	—	
Tournament Fund etc.)	—		*Less* : Depreciation	—	—
Add : Income from special fund			Investments**		
Investments	—	—	Special Fund Investments		
Add : Donation for Special fund	—	—	*Current Assets*		
Less : Expenses on account of special fund		—	Stock of Sports Materials		—
Outstanding Expenses		—	Stock of Stationery		—
Subscription in Advance		—	Stock of Bar Supplies		—
Creditors for Suppliers		—	Subscription Outstanding		—
Creditors for Furniture etc.		—	Interest Accrued		—
Bank Overdraft		—	Prepaid Insurance		—
			Prepaid Rent		—
			Cash in hand		—
			Cash at Bank		—
		Total			Total

* General Investments and Special Fund Investments must be shown separately.

** Building Fund is not affected by expenditure on construction.

A. Preparation of Income and Expenditure Account and Balance Sheet from Receipts and Payments Account and other additional information

I. Preparation of Income and Expenditure Account

Steps :

1. Make a single treatment of all REVENUE, items given in the Receipts and Payments Account relating to Current accounting year only. Double treatment for adjustment items.
2. Add up outstanding and accrued items to their respective heads, which relate to current year.
3. Deduct advance receipts and advance payments made during the current year for the next year from their respective heads of income and expenditure.
4. Adjust (add) the "advances" made during the last year for the current year in respect of revenue items.

5. Ensure that the income received and expenditure incurred do not extend beyond 'twelve months' of the accounting year covered.
6. Provide for depreciation as required to be debited to Income and Expenditure Account.
7. Adjust the loss or gain on sale of fixed asset, if any.
8. Close the Income and Expenditure Account by transferring the difference to General Fund or Capital Fund.

II. Preparation of Balance Sheet

Steps :

1. Ascertain the Capital Fund in the beginning by preparing a statement of assets and liabilities as on the first day of accounting year. The excess of assets over liabilities represents Capital Fund.
2. Adjust the Capital Fund against Surplus/Deficiency of Income & Expenditure A/c.
3. Add the amounts capitalised during the year, if any.
4. Treat the remaining items (Assets and Liabilities) in the Balance Sheet.
5. Assets as shown in the beginning must be adjusted against sale, addition and depreciation made during the year.
6. Show all outstanding expenses as current liability and all accrued incomes as current assets in the Balance Sheet.
7. If fixed assets are acquired on credit basis the amount due to vendor of assets (such as computer, equipments and furniture etc.) must be shown to the "liability" side of Balance Sheet
8. Special Funds must be taken to liability side of Balance Sheet after making necessary adjustments of the current year as shown in the format.
9. Closing Bank balances (such as Savings Bank A/c, Current A/c or Fixed Deposits A/c) along with the Cash in hand must be shown to the assets side of the Balance Sheet.

GRADED ILLUSTRATIONS

Illustration 1 (General)

Following is the Receipt and Payments Account of a Literary Club for the year ended on March 31, 2008 :

Receipts	Rs.	Payments	Rs.
To Cash at Bank	12,500	By Salaries	2,500
To Subscription	52,500	By Printing and Stationery	1,250
To Annual Day Receipts	26,800	By Annual day expenses	2,500
To Receipts from concert	22,000	By Telephone charges	2,500
To Dividend receipts	2,000	By Sundry expenses	2,000
		By Investment in Shares	75,000
		By Postage and Telegrams	2,250
		By Building maintenance	6,000
		By Rent of Theatre	10,000
		By Cash at Bank	11,800
	1,15,800		1,15,800

Additional information :

(i) On April 1,2007, building stood in the books at Rs. 50,000 and Investments in shares at Rs. 5,000 Buildings are subject to depreciation @ 5% p.a.

(ii) There were 200 members paying subscription at the rate of Rs. 250 per annum each. Some members have paid their annual subscription in advance during the year.

(iii) As on 1st April, 2007, no subscription had been received in advance but subscriptions were outstanding to the extent of Rs. 1,000 as at March 31, 2007. Subscription accrued as on 31st March, 2008 was Rs. 1,500.

(iv) Postage stamps worth Rs. 250 were in stock with the secretary as on April 1, 2007 and as on 31st March, 2008 they were valued at Rs. 150.

(v) Telephone charges paid in advance were Rs. 300.

You are required to prepare the Income and Expenditure Account for the year ended on March 31, 2008 and the Balance Sheet as at that date. **[B.Com (P),D.U, 1996.Adapted]**

Solution :

Literary Club
Balance Sheet
As on 31-3-2007

Liabilities	Rs.	Assets	Rs.
Capital Fund (Balancing Figure)	68,750	Cash at Bank	12,500
		Subscription	1,000
		Buildings	50,000
		Postage Stamps	250
		Investments	5,000
	68,750		68,750

INCOME AND EXPENDITURE ACCOUNT
For the year ended March 31, 2008

		Rs.			Rs.
To Salaries		2,500	By Subscription (52,500-4,000 + 1,500)		50,000
To Printing and Stationery		1,250	By Annual Day Income		
To Telephone	2,500		Receipts	26,800	
Less : Prepaid	(300)	2,200	*Less* : Payments	(2,500)	24,300
To Sundry expenses		2,000	By Receipts from concert		22,000
To Postage and telegram	2,250		By Dividend received		2,000
Add : Stamps in Hand on 1-4-2007	250				
	2,500				
Less : Stamps in Hand on 31-3-2008	(150)	2,350			
To Building Maintenance		6,000			
To Depreciation on Building		2,500			
To Rent of Theatre		10,000			
To Excess of Income over Expenditure		69,500			
		98,300			98,300

BALANCE SHEET
As on 31st March, 2008

Liabilities		Rs.	Assets		Rs.
Capital Fund	68,750		Building at cost	50,000	
Add : Excess of Income over Expenditure	69,500	1,38,250	*Less* : Depreciation	2,500	47,500
Subscription in advance		3,000	Investment (In Shares) (75,000 + 5,000)		80,000
			Postage Stamps		150
			Telephone Advance		300
			Subscription O/s		1,500
			Cash at Bank		11,800
		1,41,250			1,41,250

SUBSCRIPTION A/C

	Rs.		Rs.
To balance b/d (o/s)	1,000	By Receipts & Payments A/c	52,500
To Income & Expenditure A/c	50,000	By Balance c/d (O/s)	1,500
To Balance c/d	3,000		
	54,000		54,000

Illustration 2 (Specific Funds)

Following is the Trial Balance of a School as on 31st March, 2008 :

Debit Balances	Rs.	Credit Balances	Rs.
Land	50,000	Capital Fund	15,60,000
Building	15,00,000	Tuition Fees received	25,10,000
Furniture	3,00,000	Salaries Payable	1,75,000
Salaries			
Teaching Staff	12,00,000	Prize Fund	2,00,000
Administrative Staff	2,60,000	Tournament Fund	3,00,000
Investments	7,00,000	General Reserve Fund	2,00,000
Stationery, Postage	1,73,000	Interest Received on Investments	77,000
Lighting	36,000	Donations for the Hall	1,50,000
General Expenses	65,000		
Tournament expenses	30,000		
Bank balance	4,63,000		
Prize Awarded	20,000		
Library books	3,75,000		

Depreciation is to be provided as follows :

Building 20%; Furniture 10%; and Library Books 20%.

The investments were made against the various funds commonly.

Prepare the Income and Expenditure Account for 2007-08, and the Balance Sheet as on the 31st March, 2008. **[B.Com (P), D.U, Adapted]**

Solution : **INCOME AND EXPENDITURE ACCOUNT**
For the year ended March 31, 2008

Expenditure	Rs.	Income	Rs.
To salaries		By Tuition Fees	25,10,000
Teaching Staff	12,00,000	By Interest on investments	77,000
Administrative Staff	2,60,000		
To Stationery, Postage, etc.	1,73,000		
To Lighting	36,000		
To General expenses	65,000		
To Depreciation			
Building	3,00,000		
Furniture	30,000		
Library Books	75,000		
To Excess of Income over expenditure	4,48,000		
	25,87,000		25,87,000

BALANCE SHEET
As at 31st March, 2008

Liabilities		Rs.	Assets		Rs.
Salaries Payable		1,75,000	Bank balance		4,63,000
Prize Fund	2,00,000		Investments		7,00,000
Less : Prizes	(20,000)	1,80,000	Library Books	3,75,000	
Tournament fund	3,00,000		*Less* : Depreciation	(75,000)	3,00,000
Less : Expenses	(30,000)	2,70,000	Land		50,000
Donation		1,50,000	Building	15,00,000	
General Reserve Fund		2,00,000	*Less* : Depreciation	(3,00,000)	12,00,000
Capital fund			Furniture	3,00,000	
Balance	15,60,000		*Less* : Depreciation	(30,000)	2,70,000
Add : Surplus	4,48,000	20,08,000			
		29,83,000			29,83,000

Illustration 3 (Revanue vs. Capital expenditure)

From the following particulars, prepare Income and Expenditure Account.

		Rs.
1	Fees collected including Rs. 80,000 on account of previous year	3,80,000
2	Fees for the year outstanding	10,000
3	Salary paid, including Rs. 3,000 on account of previous year	28,000
4	Salary outstanding at the end of the year	1,000

5 Entertainment expenses 3,000
6 Tournament expenses 12,000
7 Meeting expenses 18,000
8 Traveling expenses 6,000
9 Purchase of books and periodicals including Rs. 19,000 for purchase of books 29,000
10 Rent 10,000
11 Postage, telegram and telephones 15,000
12 Printing and stationery 4,000
13 Donations received 20,000

[C.S. (Foundation), June 1995-Modified]

Solution : **INCOME AND EXPENDITURE A/C**

For the year ended...

Expenditure		**Rs.**	**Income**		**Rs.**
To Salary	28,000		By Fees	3,80,000	
Less : For previous year	(3,000)		*Less* : For previous year	(80,000)	
	25,000			3,00,000	
Add : Outstanding	1,000	26,000	*Add* : Outstanding	10,000	3,10,000
To Entertainment Expenses		3,000	By Donations		20,000
To Tournament Expenses		12,000			
To Meeting Expenses		18,000			
To Traveling Expenses		6,000			
To Purchase of Periodicals					
(29,000 – 19,000)		10,000			
To Rent		10,000			
To Postage, Telegram & Telephone		15,000			
To Printing & Stationery		4,000			
To Excess of Income over Expenditure		2,26,000			
		3,30,000			3,30,000

Illustration 4 (Tournament Fund and Tournament Expenses)

From the following Receipts and Payments Account of a Sports Club and the subjoined information, prepare Income and Expenditure Account for the year ended 31st December 2007 and a Balance Sheet as on that date.

Receipts	**Rs.**	**Payments**	**Rs.**
To Balance :		By Crockery Purchased	2,650
Cash	3,520	By Maintenance	6,820
Bank - Current A/c	27,380	By Match Expenses	13,240
6% Fixed Deposit	30,000	By Salaries	11,000

To Membership Subscription	40,000	By Conveyance	820
(including Rs. 6,000 for 2006)		By Upkeep of Lawn	4,240
To Entrance Fees	2,750	By Postage Stamps	1,050
To Donation	5,010	By Purchase of Cricket goods	9,720
To Interest on Fixed Deposit	900	By Sundries	2,000
To Tournament Fund	20,000	By Investments	5,700
To Sale of Crockery		By Tournament Expenses	18,800
(Book Value Rs. 1,200)	2,000	By Balance :	
		Cash in hand	2,200
		Current Accound	23,320
		Fixed Deposit	30,000
	1,31,560		1,31,560

Information :

	Rs.
(a) Monthly Salary	1,000
(b) The Value of unused postage stamp is follows :	
31st December 2006	750
31st December 2007	900
(c) Stock of cricket equipments is as follows :	
31st December 2006	3,210
31st December 2007	2,800
(d) Arrears of membership subscription :	
2006	6,600
2007	8,000

[B.Com. (H), D.U., 1983-Adapted]

Solution :

INCOME AND EXPENDITURE ACCOUNT
For the year ended 31st December 2007

Expenditure		Rs.	Income		Rs.
To Maintenance		6,820	By Subscription(3)		42,000
To Match Expenses		13,240	By Interest on Fixed Deposit	900	
To Salaries	11,000		*Add* : Accrued	900	1,800
Add : O/s	1,000	12,000			
To Conveyance		820			
To Upkeep of Lawn		4,.240	By Profit on Sale of Crockery		800
To Postage Stamp used(1)		900	By Excess of Expenditure		
To Cricket goods used(2)		10,130	over Income		5,550
To Sundries		2,000			
		50,150			50,150

BALANCE SHEET
As on 1st January 2007

Liabilities	Rs.	Assets	Rs.
Capital Fund	72,660	Cash in hand	3,520
(Balancing Figure)		Current Account	27,380
		Fixed Deposit 6%	30,000
		Subscription O/s	6,600
		Postage Stamps	750
		Cricket Equipments	3,210
		Crockery	1,200
	72,660		72,660

BALANCE SHEET
As on 31st December 2007

Liabilities		Rs.	Assets			Rs.
Salaries O/s		1,000	Cash in hand			2,200
Entrance Fees*		2,750	Current Account			23,320
Tournament Fund	20,000		Fixed Deposit 6%			30,000
Less : Tournament Expenses	(18,800)	1,200	Subscription O/s**	2006	600	
				2007	8,000	8,600
Capital Fund	72,660		Interest Accrued			900
Add : Donation*	5,010		Stock of Postage Stamps			900
	77,670		Stock of Cricket goods			2,800
Less : Deficit	(5,550)	72,120	Crockery			2,650
			Investment			5,700
		77,070				77,070

		Rs.
(1)	Postage Stamp used = Opening Stock of Postage Stamp	750
	Add : Purchased	1,050
		1,800
	Less : Closing Stock	(900)
		900
(2)	Cricket goods used = Opening Stock of Cricket goods	3,210
	Add : Purchased	9,720
		12,930
	Less : Closing Stock	(2,800)
		10,130

(3)	Subscriptions as per R/P Account	40,000
	Less : Subscription of last year	(6,000)
		34,000
	Add : Subscription O/s of current year	8,000
		42,000

*Entrance Fees and Donation have been Capitalised.

**Since subscription relating to last year Rs. 6,000 has been received this year out of the total amount due of Rs. 6,600 an amount of Rs. 600 is still outstanding as shown in the Balance Sheet.

Illustration 5 (General Fund Investments and Specific Fund Investments)

From the following Receipts and Payments Account, of a Club and from the information supplied, you are required to prepare Income and Expenditure Account for the year ended 31st December 2007 and the Balance Sheet as on that date.

RECEIPTS AND PAYMENTS ACCOUNT
For the year ending 31st December 2007

Receipts		Rs.	Payments	Rs.
To Balance b/d (1-1-2007)		7,000	By Tournament Expenses	1,100
To Subscriptions			By Furniture	4,000
2006	600		By Curtains	800
2007	14,000		By Crockery	400
2008	800	15,400	By Sports Materials	1,200
To Donation for Building		8,000	By Salaries	1,300
To General Donations		2,000	By Honorarium	2,600
To Legacies		6,000	By Charities	8,000
To Sale of old furniture		750	By Advertisements	250
(Costing Rs. 800)			By Rent and Rates	1,400
To Endownment Receipts		10,000	By Advance Against Construction of Building	5,000
To Sale of Newspapers		400	By Cost of Entertainment	1,450
To Rent Received		1,500	By Payment to Creditors of last year	400
To Advertisement Receipts		400	By Electric Installation expenses	3,000
To Proceeds of Concert		1,200	By Library Books	800
To Tournament		1,500	By Newspapers	1,300
To Sale of Sports materials		80	By Postage	700
			By Bar Expenses including purchase	1,600
			By 7% Investments (1-7-2007)	10,000
			By Balance c/d	8,.930
		54,230		54,230

Additional Information :

	Rs.
1. Balances on 31st December 2007	
Sports Materials	100
Bar Stock	120
Postage Stamps	20
2. Subscription Outstanding on 31st December 2007	700
3. Salary Outstanding on 31st December 2007	50

4. Salary Paid included Rs. 80 for the year 2006 and Rs. 10 for 2008
5. Investments included investments out of Building donation for Rs. 8,000

[B.Com. (H), D.U., 1970-Modified]

Solution :

INCOME AND EXPENDITURE ACCOUNT
For the year ended 31st December 2007

Expenditure		Rs.	Income		Rs.
To Salaries	1,300		By Subscription		
Less : Paid for last year	(80)		for the year 2005	14,000	
Less : Paid for next year	(10)		*Add* : Outstanding	700	14,700
Add : Outstanding	50	1,260	By General Donation		2,000
To Honorarium		2,600	By Sale of Newspapers		400
To Charities		8,000	By Sale of Sports Materials		80
To Advertisement		250	By Rent Received		1,500
To Rent and Rates		1,400	By Advertisement		400
To Cost of Entertainment		1,450	By Interest Accrued on general		
To Newspapers		1,300	investment		70
To Postage	700		By Proceeds of Concerts		1,200
Less : Stock (Unused)	(20)	680			
To Bar Expenses & Purchases	1,600				
Less : Stock	(120)	1,480			
To Sports Materials	1,200				
Less : Stock	(100)	1,100			
To Loss on sale of furniture		50			
To Excess of Income over					
Expenditure (Surplus)		780			
		20,350			20,350

BALANCE SHEET
As on 1st January 2007

Liabilities	Rs.	Assets	Rs.
Creditors	400	Cash in hand	7,000
Salary Outstanding	80		
Capital Fund (Balancing Figure)	7,120	Subscription Oustanding	600
	7,600		7,600

BALANCE SHEET OF A CLUB
As on 31st December 2007

Liabilities		Rs.	Assets		Rs.
Capital Fund	7,120		Furniture	4,000	
Add : Surplus	780	7,900	*Less* : Sold	(800)	3,200
Donation for Building	8,000		Curtains		800
Add : Interest accrued on			Crockery		400
Investment	280	8,280	Electric Installations		3,000
Endownment Fund		10,000	Library Books		800
Legacies		6,000	7% Investments against :		
Tournament Fund	1,500		Building Fund	8,000	
Less : Expenses	(1,100)	400	General Investments	2,000	10,000
Subscription in Advance		800	Building Advance		5000
Salary Outstanding		50	Stock of Sports Materials		100
			Bar Stock		120
			Postage Stamp		20
			Subscription Outstanding		700
			Interest Accrued on :		
			Building Fund Investment	280	
			General Investment	70	350
			Salaries Paid in Advance		10
			Cash Balance		8,930
		33,430			33,430

Notes :

1. Interest on Specific Fund (Building Fund) Investment has been capitalised and interest on general investment has been treated as income (revenue) which is credited to Income and Expenditure A/c, Interest on Building Fund Investment

$$= 8{,}000 \times \frac{7}{100} \times \frac{6}{12} = \text{Rs. } 280.$$

2. Interest on General Investment $= 2{,}000 \times \frac{7}{100} \times \frac{6}{12} = \text{Rs. } 70.$

3. Electric installation expenses and Advance for construction of Building are capital expenditures and hence capitalised.

4. Tournament fund is a specific fund hence expenses thereof have been charged to Tournament Fund Account as shown in the Balance Sheet.

Illustration 6 (Calculation of Loss and Depreciation on Furniture)

The following is the Receipts and Payments Account of an Amusement Club for the year ended 31st December 2007 :

Receipts		Rs.	Payments	Rs.
To Balance b/d			By Salary of Secretary	36,000
Cash	600		By Honorarium	4,500
Bank	30,000	30,600	By Wages	24,000
To Subscriptions (including Rs. 1,500			By Charities	20,000
for 2,006)		90,000	By Printing & Stationery	3,000
To Sale of Old furniture (1-1-2007)		7,500	By Postage	1,000
To Sale of Newspapers		500	By Rent and Taxes	12,000
To Legacies		30,000	By Upkeep of the land	5,000
To Interest on Investments		12,000	By Sports materials	25,000
(Cost of Investments Rs. 2,00,000)			By Balance c/d	1,48,500
To Endowment Fund Receipts		1,00,000		
To Proceeds of Concerts		8,000		
To Advertisement in the year book		400		
		2,79,000		2,79,000

Some assets and liabilities as on 31st December 2006 and 31st December 2007.
Were as follows :

	31 st December 2006	31 st December 2007
	Rs.	Rs.
Subscriptions in Arrears	2,000	4,500
Subscriptions in Advance	3,000	6,000
Furniture	20,000	10,800

Depreciation was 10% p.a. on the furniture left after selling a part of it. It was decided that half of the legacies may be capitalised.

Prepare Income and Expenditure Account and the Balance Sheet as on that date.

[B.Com. (H), DU, 1983-Adapted]

Solution :

INCOME AND EXPENDITURE ACCOUNT
For the year ended 31st December 2007

Expenriture	Rs.	Income		Rs.
To Salaryof Secretary	36,000	By Subscription*(1)		89,500
To Honorarium	4,500	By Legacies	30,000	
To Wages	24,000	*Less* : Capitalised	(15,000)	15,000
To Charities	20,000	By Sale of Old Newspapers		500
To Printing & Stationery	3,000	By Interest on Investments		12,000
To Postage	1,000	By Proceeds of Concert		8,000
To Rent and Taxes	12,000	By Advertisement in the year book		400
To Upkeep of Land	5,000	By Deficit-Excess of Expenditure		
To Sports materials	25,000	over Income		6,800
To Loss on sale of old furniture	500			
To Depreciation of furniture*(2)	1,200			
	1,32,200			1,32,200

BALANCE SHEET OF AMUSEMENT CLUB
As on 31st December 2007

Liabilities		Rs.	Assets		Rs.
Capital Fund*(3)	2,49,600		Furniture		10,800
Less : Deficit	6,800	2,42,800	Investments		2,00,000
Endowment Fund		1,00,000	Cash and Bank Balance		1,48,500
Legacies		15,000	Subscriptions due for 2006	500	
Subscription in Advance		6,000	2007	4,000	4,500
		3,63,800			3,63,800

Working Notes :

(1) SUBSCRIPTION ACCOUNT

	Rs.			Rs.
To Balance b/d (Due)	2,000	By Balance b/d (Adv.)		3,000
To Income and Expenditure A/c	89,500	By Cash (Receipts & Payments A/c)		90,000
(Balance figure)	6,000	By Balance c/d (Due) 2006	500	4,500
To Balance c/d (Advance)		2007	4,000	
	97,500			97,500

(2) FURNITURE ACCOUNT

	Rs.		Rs.
To Balance b/d	20,000	By Cash (Sale as per Receipts & Payments A/c)	7,500
		By Loss on Sale	500
		By Depreciation	1,200
		By Balance c/d	10,800
	20,000		20,000

(3) BALANCE SHEET
As on 31st December 2006

Liabilities	Rs.	Assets	Rs.
Capital Fund		Furniture	20,000
(Balancing figure)	2,49,600	Investments	2,00,000
Subscription in Advance	3,000	Subscription due	2,000
		Bank Balance	30,000
		Cash	600
	2,52,600		2,52,600

(4) W.D. Value of furniture on 31-12-2007 Rs. 10,800 and rate of Depreciation is 10%

W.D.V. of furniture on 1-1-2007 $\frac{10,800 \times 100}{90} = 12,000$

	Rs.
W.D.V. of furniture before sale	20,000
W.D.V. of furniture after sale	12,000
Book Value of furniture sold	8,000 - Sale Proceeds 7,500
Loss on sale of furniture	5,00

Illustration 7 (Depreciation by Revaluation)

A Club gives you the following Receipts and Payments Account for the year ended 31st March 2008 :

Receipts	Rs.	Payments	Rs.
To Balance b/d	4,820	By Salaries	12,000
To Subscriptions	28,600	By Rent and Electricity	7,220
To Miscellaneous Income	700	By Library Books	1,000
To Interest on Fixed Deposit	2,000	By Magazines and Newspapers	2,172
		By SundryExpenses	10,278
		By Sports Equipments	1,000
		By Balance c/d	2,450
	36,120		36,120

Figures of other assets and liabilities

	31st March 2007	31st March 2008
	Rs.	Rs.
Outstanding Salaries	710	170
Outstanding rent & electricity	864	973
Outstanding magazines & newspaper	226	340
Fixed Deposits (10%) with Bank	20,000	20,000
Interest Accrued thereon	500	500

Subscription receivable	1,263	1,575
Prepaid expenses	417	620
Furniture	9,600	
Sports equipments	7,200	
Library Books	5,000	

The closing value of furniture and sports equipments are to be determined after charging depreciation at 10% and 20% p.a. respectively inclusive of additions, if any, during the year. The library books are revalued at the end of every year and the value at the end of 31st March 2008 was Rs. 5,250.

Required :

(i) Balance Sheet as on 31st March 2007

(ii) Income and Expenditure Account for the year ending on 31st March 2008

(iii) Balance Sheet as on 31st March 2008 **[C.A. (Entrance), December 1982-Modified]**

Solution : Income and Expenditure Account for the year ended 31st March 2008 :

To Salaries	12,000		By Subscription	28,600	
Add : O/s of current year	170		*Add* : Outstanding	1,575	
	12,170			30,175	
Less : Outstanding of last year	(710)	11,460	*Less* : O/s of last year's	(1,263)	28,912
To Rent & Electricity	7,220		By Interest on Fixed Deposit	2,000	
Add : Outstanding	973		*Less* : Accrued last year	(500)	
	8,193			1,500	
Less : O/s of last year	(864)	7,329	*Add* : Accrued during Current year	500	2,000
To Magazine & Newspapers	2,172		By Miscellaneous Income		700
Add : O/s of current year	340		By Deficit-excess of Expenditure over Income		2,888
	2.512				
Less : O/s of last year	(226)	2,286			
To Sundry Expenses	10,278				
Add : Prepaid of last year	417				
	10,695				
Less : Prepaid of Current year	(620)	10,075			
To Depreciation on :					
Furniture @ 10% on 9,600	960				
Sports Equipments @ 20% on (7,200 + 1,000)	1,640				
Books (5,000 + 1,000 – 5,250)	750	3,350			
		34,500			34,500

BALANCE SHEET
As on 31st March 2007

Liabilities	Rs.	Assets	Rs.
Capital Fund (Balancing figure)	47,000	Furniture	9,600
Outstanding Salaries	710	Sports Equipments	7,200
Outstanding Rent & Electricity	864	Library Books	5,000
Outstanding for Magazine & Newspapers	226	Fixed Deposit with bank	20,000
		Interest Accrued	500
		Subscription Receivable	1,263
		Prepaid Expenses	417
		Cash Balance	4,820
	48,800		48,800

BALANCE SHEET
As on 31st March 2008

Liabilities		Rs.	Assets		Rs.
Capital Fund	47,000		Furniture	9,600	
Less : Deficit	(2,888)	44,112	*Less* : Depreciation	(960)	8,640
Outstanding Salaries		170	Sports Equipments	8,200	
Outstanding Rent & Electricity		973	*Less* : Depreciation	(1,640)	6,560
O/s Magazine & Newspapers		340	Library Books		5,250
			Fixed Deposits with Bank		20,000
			Interest Accrued		500
			Subscription Receivable		1,575
			Prepaid Expenses		620
			Cash Balance		2,450
		45,595			45,595

Illustration 8 (Opening balance of Assets not given)

From the following data of a Hospital prepare an Income and Expenditure Account for the year ended 31st December 2007 and a Statement of Affairs as on that date.

Receipts		Rs.	Payments	Rs.
To Balance			By Salaries (Rs. 3,600 for 2,006)	15,600
Cash	400		By Hospital Equipments	8,500
Bank	2,600	3,000	By Furniture Purchased	3,000
To Subscriptions :			By Additions to Building	25,000
For 2006		2,550	By Printing & Stationery	1,200
For 2007		12,250	By Diet Expenses	7,800
For 2008		1,200	By Rent (Rs. 150 for 2008)	1,000
To Govt. Grant :			By Electricity & Water Charges	1,200
For Building		40,000	By Office Expenses	1,000
For Maintenance		10,000	By Investments	10,000

	Rs.			Rs.
To Fees from Sundry Patients	2,400	By Balance :		
To Donations (General)	4,000	Cash	700	
To Net Collection from benefit shows	3,000	Bank	3,400	4,100
	78,400			78,400

Additional Information :

	Rs.
Value of building under construction as on 31-12-2007	70,000
Value of hospital equipment on 31-12-2007	25,500
Building Fund as on 1-1-2007	40,000
Subscriptions in Arrears as on 31-12-2006	3,250

Investment in 8% Govt. Securities were made on 1-7-2007 **[C.A. (Inter), May 1984-Modified]**

Solution : **INCOME AND EXPENDITURE ACCOUNT**

For the year 31st December 2007

Expenditure		Rs.	Income	Rs.
To Salaries	15,600		By Subscription	12,250
Less : For last year	(3,600)	12,000	By Govt. Grants (Maintenance)	10,000
To Diet Expenses		7,800	By Fees from Patients	2,400
To Printing & Stationery		1,200	By Donation (General)	4,000
To Rent	1,000		By Net Collection from benefit show	3,000
Less : Prepaid	(150)	850	By Interest on Govt. Securities	400
To Electricity & Water		1,200		
To Office Expenses		1,000		
To Surplus-Excess of Income over Expenditure		8,000		
		32,050		32,050

BALANCE SHEET

As on 31st December 2007

Liabilities		Rs.	Assets	Rs.
Building Fund	40,000		Value of Building under construction	70,000
			Value of Hospital Equipments	25,500
Add : Govt. Grant for Building	40,000	80,000	Furniture	3,000
Capital Fund	24,650*		8% Govt. Securities	10,000
Add : Surplus	8,000	32,650	Interest Accrued	400
Subscriptions in Advance		1,200	Subscription due for the year 2006 (3,250 – 2,550)	700
			Prepaid Rent	150
			Cash	700
			Bank	3,400
		1,13,850		1,13,850

*see the working notes

Working Notes :

(1) STATEMENT OF AFFAIRS
As on 31st December 2006

Liabilities	Rs.	Assets	Rs.
Outstanding Salaries	3,600	Cash	400
Building Fund	40,000	Bank	2,600
Capidal Fund	24,650	Subscription due	3,250
(Balancing figure)		Value of Building under construction	45,000*
		Value of Hospital Equipments	17,000**
	68,250		68,250

(2) BUILDING A/C

	Rs.		Rs.
To Balnce b/d* (Balancing figure)	45,000	By Balance c/d (Given)	70,000
To Cash	25,000		
(Addition made as per R & P A/c)			
	70,000		70,000

(3) HOSPITAL EQUIPMENTS A/C

	Rs.		Rs.
To Balance b/d** (B.F.)	17,000		
To Cash	8,500	By Balance c/d (Given)	25,500
(Addition made as per R & P A/c)			
	25,500		25,500

Illustration 9 (Adjustment of expense items with reference to last year)

Following is the Receipts and Payments Account of a club for the year ended 31st March 2007 :

Receipts	Rs.	Payments	Rs.
To Balance b/d	20,000	By Salaries	30,000
To Subscriptions		By Stationery	10,000
2005-2006	30,000	By Rates and Taxes	3,000
2006-2007	40,000	By Telephone Charges	15,000
2007-2008	10,000	By 8% Securities at Par	50,000
To Profit on Sports Fair	30,000	By Sundry Expenses	2,000
To Interest on 8% Securities	10,000	By Balance c/d	30,000
	1,40,000		1,40,000

The following additional facts are ascertained :

(i) There are 500 members, each paying an annual subscription of Rs. 100. Rs. 35,000 being in arrears for the year 2005-2006 at the beginning of 2006-2007. Subscriptions were paid in advance by 30 members for 2006-2007.

(ii) Stock of stationery at 31st March 2006 was Rs. 4,000 and at 31 st March 2007 was Rs.5,000.

(iii) At 31 st March 2007, the rates and taxes were prepaid to the following 31 st January, the yearly charges being Rs. 3,000.

(iv) A quarter charge for telephone is outstanding; the amount accrued being Rs. 3,000. The charge for each quarter is same for both 2005-2006 and 2006-2007.

(v) Sundry expenses accruing on 31st March 2006 were Rs. 500 and on 31st March 2007, Rs.600.

(vi) At 31st March 2006, Building stood in the books at Rs. 3,00,000 and it is required to write off depreciation at 10% p.a.

(vii) Value of 8% securities at 31st March 2006 was Rs. 1,50,000 which were purchased at par. Additional securities worth Rs. 50,000 were purchased on 31st March 2007.

You are required to prepare :

(i) An Income and Expenditure Account for the year ended 31st March 2007

(ii) And a Balance Sheet on that date. **[ICWA (Inter), Dec. 1983-Adapted]**

Solution : **INCOME AND EXPENDITURE ACCOUNT**

For the year ended 31st March 2007

Expenditure		Rs.	Income		Rs.
To Salaries		30,000	By Subscriptions	40,000	
To Stationery used	10,000		*Add* : O/s of current of year	7,000	
Add : Opening Stock	4,000			47,000	50,000
	14,000		*Add* : Adv. Received last year	3,000	
Less : Closing Stock	(5,000)	9,000	By Interest on Securities*	10,000	
To Rent and Taxes	3,000		*Add* : Accrued	2,000	12,000
Less : Prepaid	(2,500)		By Profits on Sports Fair		30,000
	500				
Add : Prepaid of last year	2,500	3,000			
To Telephone Charges**	15,000				
Less : O/s of last year	(6,000)				
	9,000				
Add : O/s of current year	3,000	12,000			
To Sundry Expenses	2,000				
Add : O/s of current year	600				
	2,600				
To *Less* : O/s of last year	(500)	2,100			
To Depreciation on Building		30,000			
To Surplus-Excess of Income over-Expenditure		5,900			
		92,000			92,000

*8% on 1,50,000 = Rs. 12,000

** Quarterly Telephone charges are Rs. 3,000, hence yearly Rs. 12,000. Since current year's quarter charges (Rs. 3,000) are outstanding it means Rs. 9,000 have been paid on account of current year. Thus Rs. 15,000 - Rs. 9,000 i.e. Rs. 6,000 relate to last year.

Calculation of Capital Fund

BALANCE SHEET
As on 31st March 2006

Liabilities	Rs.	Assets	Rs.
Subscription in Advance	3,000	Cash Balance	20,000
Outstanding Sundry Expenses	500	Prepaid Rent & Taxes	2,500
Telephone Charges O/s	6,000	Subscription due	35,000
Capital Fund	5,02,000	Stock of Stationery	4,000
(Balancing figure)		8% Investment in Securities	1,50,000
		Building	3,00,000
	5,11,500		5,11,500

BALANCE SHEET
As on 31st March 2007

Liabilities		Rs.	Assets		Rs.
Subscription in Advance		10,000	Cash Balance		30,000
Outstanding Sundry Expenses		600	Prepaid rent & Taxes		2,500
O/s Telephone Charges		3,000	Subscription due		
Capital Fund	5,02,000		2005-2006		5,000
Add : Surplus	5,900	5,07,900	2006-2007		7,000
			Sock of Stationery		5,000
			8% Investment		2,00,000
			Interest Accrued		2,000
			Building	3,00,000	
			Less : Depreciation	(30,000)	2,70,000
		5,21,500			5,21,500

Illustration 10 (Hidden Value of Investments)

The following is the Receipts and Payments Account of a Cricket Club for the year ended 31st December 2007.

Receipts	Rs.	Payments	Rs.
To Balace b/d		By New Building Constructed	75,000
Cash	290	By Souvenir	2,000
Bank	3,710	By Salaries	6,000
To Subscriptions	12,000	By Postage	500
To Donations	13,000	By Telephone	500
To Activities Collection	6,900	By Electricity	600
To Sale of old Newspapers	300	By Maintenance Expenses	12,000

To Souvenir Advertisement	5,800	By Newspapers	500
To Endownment Income	3,000	By Balance c/d	
To Sale Proceeds of old		Cash	300
Building at Book value	60,000	Bank	11,600
To Income from Investments @ 10%	4,000		
	1,09,000		1,09,000

Subscriptions :

	Rs.
For 2006 (due as at 31-12-2006, Rs. 1,500) received	1,000
For 2008 Advance	1,200
Due for 2007	800
Expenses Outstanding :	
Salary	1,200
Electricity	100
Telephone	100
Postage	100

Provide depreciation on Building @ 5% **[C.A. Entrance, Dec. 1985-Modified]**

Solution :

INCOME AND EXPENDITURE ACCOUNT
For the year ended 31st December 2007

Expenditure		Rs.	Income		Rs.
To Salaries	6,000		By Subscriptions	12,000	
Add : Outstanding	1,200	7,200	*Add* : O/s for current year	800	
To Postage	500			12,800	
Add : Outstanding	100	600	*Less* : Received for last year	(1,000)	
To Souvenir		2,000		11,800	
To Telephone	500		*Less* : Received in Advance	(1,200)	10,600
Add : Outstanding	100	600	By Donations		13,000
To Electricity	600		By Activities Collection		6,900
Add : Outstanding	100	700	By Sale of old Newspapers		300
To Maintenance Expenses		12,000	By Souvenir Advertisement		5,800
To Newspapers		500	By Income fom Investment @ 10%		4,000
To Depreciation on Building		3,750	By Endowment Income		3,000
(@ 5% on Rs. 75,000)					
To Surplus-Excess of Income					
over Expenditure		16,250			
		43,600			43,600

BALANCE SHEET
As on 31st December 2006

Liabilities	Rs.	Assets	Rs.
Capital Fund	1,05,500	Cash	290
(Balancing figure)		Bank	3,710
		Investments 10%*	40,000
		Building	60,000
		Subscription Receivable	1,500
	1,05,500		1,05,500

*Income from investments (10%) has been taken basis for calculating the value of investment as under :

$$\frac{\text{Interest} \times 100}{\text{Rate}} = \text{Rs. } 4{,}000 \times \frac{100}{10} = 40{,}000$$

BALANCE SHEET OF A CRICKET CLUB
As on 31st December 2007

Liabilities		Rs.	Assets		Rs.
Expenses Outstanding :			Cash		300
Salary		1,200	Bank		11,600
Electricity		100	Subscription due :		
Telephone		100	2006		500
Postage		100	2007		800
Subscription in Advance		1,200	10% Investments		40,000
Capital Fund	1,05,500		New Building	75,000	
Add : Surplus	16,250	1,21,750	*Less* : Depreciation	(3,750)	71,250
		1,24,450			1,24,450

Illustration 11 (Capital Fund and Revenue Fund)

Following is the Receipts and Payments Account of a Charitable Trust for the year ending 31st March 2007 :

Receipts	Rs.	Payments	Rs.
To Balance b/d		By Capital Payments :	
Cash	1,000	Investment	10,000
Bank	14,000	Furniture	4,000
To Capital Funds :		Clinical Equipments	5,000
Donation for Clinic Fund	6,000	By Revenue Payments :	
To Revenue Receipts :		Salaries	6,200
Interest	30,000	Medicines	14,000
Rent	12,000	Scholarships	10,000
Sundries	3,000	Printing etc.	800
		Traveling	1,000
		By Balance c/d	
		Cash	1,600
		Bank	13,400
	66,000		66,000

Trust Fund originally consisted of : Building valued at Rs. 1,50,000,9% Govt. Securities Rs. 3,20,000 (Nominal value Rs.3,50,000) and Bank Balance Rs. 10,000.

Bank interest receivable at the end of the year was Rs. 2,500. Interest accrued on investments on 1-4-2006 Rs. 3,500 and on 31-3-2007 Rs. 5,000. The Trust owed suppliers of medicines Rs. 1,200 and Rs. 800 on 1-4-2006 and 31-3-2007 respectively. Furniture stood in the books at Rs. 3,000 on 1-4-2006.

You are required to prepare final accounts of the Trust for the year ending 31st March 2007 after providing $2\frac{1}{2}$% depreciation on the book value of the building and 20% on other assets.

[ICWA (Final), Dec. 1987-Modified]

Solution :

INCOME AND EXPENDITURE ACCOUNT
For the year ended 31st March 2007

Expenditure		Rs.	Income		Rs.
To Salaries		6,200	By Revenue Receipt	30,000	
To Medicines	14,000		Interest on Investment	5,000	
Add : O/s of current year	800			35,000	
	14,800		*Less* : Accrued last year	(3,500)	31,500
Less : O/s of last year	(1,200)	13,600	By Sundry Receipts		3,000
To Scholarships		10,000	By Bank Interest Receivable		2,500
To Printing etc.		800	By Rent		12,000
To Traveleing		1,000			
To Depreciation on :					
Building @ $2\frac{1}{2}$%		3,750			
Furniture @ 20%		1,400			
Clinical Equipments		1,000			
To Surplus-Excess of Income over - Expenditure		11,250			
		49,000			49,000

BALANCE SHEET
As on 1st April 2006

Liabilities	Rs.	Assets	Rs.
Creditors for Supplies	1,200	Cash	1,000
Trust Fund	4,80,000	Bank	14,000
*Revenue Fund (Balancing figure)	10,300	Accrued Interest on Investment	3,500
		Investments at Cost	3,20,000
		Furnitue	3,000
		Building	1,50,000
	4,91,500		4,91,500

*Alternatively Trust Fund and Revenue Fund may be treated under Capital Fund. Since Capital and revenue items are shown separately in the Receipts and Payments Account the same have been treated separately. Trust Fund as given is Rs. 4,80,000 which consist of :

	Rs.
Building	1,50,000
9% Govt. Securities	3,20,000
Bank Balance	10,000

BALANCE SHEET
As on 31st March 2007

Liabilities		Rs.	Assets		Rs.
Trust Fund	4,80,000		Building	1,50,000	
Add : Donations	6,000	4,86,000	*Less* : Depreciation	(3,750)	1,46,250
Revenue Fund	10,300		Furniture	3,000	
Add : Surplus	11,250	21,550	Addition	4,000	
Creditors for Supplies		800		7,000	
			Less : Depreciation	(1,400)	5,600
			Clinical Equipments	5,000	
			Less : Depreciation	(1,000)	4,000
			Investments	3,20,000	
			Addition	10,000	3,30,000
			Interest Accrued on Investment		5,000
			Bank Interest Accrued		2,500
			Cash at Bank		13,400
			Cash in hand		1,600
		5,08,350			5,08,350

Illustration 12 (Restaurant and Bar Trading Account)

Following is the Receipts and Payments Account of a Sydney Club for the year ended on 31st March 2007.

Receipts	Rs.	Payments		Rs.
To Balance b/d		By Salaries		1,20,000
Cash	3,850	By Creditors		15,20,000
Bank	10,000	By Printing & Stationery		70,000
To Subscriptions	2,02,750	By Postage		40,000
To Entrance Donations	1,00,000	By Telephone & Telex		52,000
To Interest Received	58,000	By Repairs & Maintenance		48,000
To Sale of Assets	8,000	By Glass and Table Linen		12,000
To Miscellaneous Income	9,000	By Crockery and Cutlery		14,000
To Receipts from :		By Garden Upkeep		8,000
Coffee Room	10,70,000	By Membership Fees		4,000
Wines & Soda	5,10,000	By Insurance		5,000
Swimming Pool	80,000	By Electricity		28,000
Tennis Court	1,02,000	By Balance c/d	Cash	8,000
			Bank	2,24,600
	21,53,600			21,53,600

The assets and liabilities as on 1-4-2006 were as follows :

	Rs.
Fixed Assets (Net)	5,00,000
Stock	3,80,000
Investments in 12% Govt. Securities	5,00,000
Outstanding Subscriptions	12,000
Prepaid Insurance	1,000
Sundry Creditors	1,12,000
Subscription received in Advance	15,000
Entrance Donations Received pending membership	1,00,000
Gratuity Fund	1,50,000

The following adjustments are to be made while drawing up accounts :

(i) Subscription received-in-advance as on 31st March 2007 was Rs. 18,000.

(ii) Outstanding subscriptions as on 31st March 2007 was Rs. 7,000.

(iii) Outstanding expenses are :

Salaries	Rs. 8,000
Electricity	Rs. 15,000

(iv) 50% of Entrance Donations are to be capitalised. There is no pending membership as on 31st March 2007.

(v) The cost of asset sold net as on 1-4-2006 was Rs. 10,000.

(vi) Depreciation is to be provided at the rate of 10% on assets.

(vii) A sum of Rs. 20,000 received in October 2006 as Entrance donation from an applicant was to be refunded, as he had not fulfilled the requisite membership qualification. The refund was made on 3-6-2007.

(viii) Purchases made during the year amounted to Rs. 15,00,000.

(ix) The value of closing stock was Rs. 2,10,000.

(x) The club as a matter of policy charges off to Income and Expenditure Account all purchases made on account of crockery, cutlery, glass and linen in the year of purchase.

You are required to prepare an Income and Expenditure Account for the year ended 31st March 2007 and the Balance Sheet as on that date. **[C.A. (Foundation), June 1993-Modified]**

Solution : **INCOME AND EXPENDITURE ACCOUNT**

For the year ended 31st March 2007

Expenditure		**Rs.**	**Income**		**Rs.**
To Salaries	1,20,000		By Subscription*[(1)]		1,94,750
Add : Outstanding	8,000	1,28,000	By Entrance Donations*[(2)]		90,000
To Printing & Stationery		70,000	By Profit from Bar & Pool etc.* [(3)]		92,000
To Postage		40,000	By Interest Received	58,000	
To Telephone & Telex		52,000	*Add* : Accrued	2,000	60,000
To Repairs and Maintenance		48,000	By Miscellaneous Income		9,000

To Glass & Table Linen		12,000	By Deficit-Excess of	
To Crockery & Cutlery		14,000	Expenditure over Income	30,250
To Garden Upkeep		8,000		
To Membership Fee		4,000		
To Insurance	5,000			
Add : Prepaid of last year	1,000	6,000		
To Electricity	28,000			
Add : Outstanding	15,000	43,000		
To Loss on Sale of Asset*[(4)]		2,000		
To Depreciation*[(4)]		49,000		
		4,76,000		4,76,000

Working Notes :

(1)* SUBSCRIPTION A/C

	Rs.		Rs.
To Balance b/d(O/s)	12,000	By Balance b/d (Adv.)	15,000
To Income and Expenditure A/c	1,94,750	By Cash-Receipts and Payments A/c	2,02,750
(Balancing figure)		By Balance c/d (O/s)	7,000
To Balance c/d (Adv.)	18,000		
	2,24,750		2,24,750

(2)* Entrance donations have been worked out as under :

	Rs.
Entrance donations received pending membership on 1-4-2006	1,00,000
Add : Received during the current year	1,00,000
	2,00,000
Less : Refund to disqualified member	20,000
	1,80,000
Less : 50% Capitalised	90,000
Amount to be credited to Income & Expenditure A/c	90,000

(3)* RESTAURANT & BAR TRADING ACCOUNT

	Rs.		Rs.
To Opening Stock	3,80,000	By Proceeds from	
To Purchases	15,00,000	Coffee Room	10,70,000
To Profit transferred to		Wines & Soda	5,10,000
Income & Expenditure A/c	92,000	Swimming Pool	80,000
		Tennis Court	1,02,000
		By Closing Stock	2,10,000
	19,72,000		19,72,000

SUNDRY CREDITORS ACCOUNT

	Rs.		Rs.
To Bank (as per Receipts & Payments A/c)	15,20,000	By Balance b/d	1,12,000
		By Purchases	15,00,000
To Balance c/d (B.F.)	92,000		
	16,12,000		16,12,000

(4)* FIXED ASSETS ACCOUNT

	Rs.		Rs.
To Balance b/d	5,00,000	By Cash (Sale)	8,000
		By Loss on Sale (10,000-8,000)	2,000
		By Depreciation	49,000
		By Balance c/d	4,41,000
	5,00,000		5,00,000

Calculation of Capital Fund

BALANCE SHEET
As on 31st March 2006

Liabilities	Rs.	Assets	Rs.
Sundry Creiditors	1,12,000	Cash	3,850
Subscription in Advance	15,000	Bank	10,000
Entrance Donations in Advance	1,00,000	Prepaid Insurance	1,000
Gratuity Fund	1,50,000	Subscriptions Receivable	12,000
Capital Fund (Balancing figure)	10,29,850	Stock	3,80,000
		Investments	5,00,000
		Fixed Assets	5,00,000
	14,06,850		14,06,850

BALANCE SHEET OF SYDNEY CLUB
As on 31st March 2007

Liabilities		Rs.	Assets	Rs.
Outstanding Salaries		8,000	Cash	8,000
O/s Electricity Charges		15,000	Bank Balance	2,24,600
Sundry Creditors		92,000	Interest Accrued	2,000
Subscription in Advance		18,000	Subscriptions Receivable	7,000
Entrance Donation Refundable		20,000	Stock	2,10,000
Gratuity Fund		1,50,000	Investments	5,00,000
Capital Fund	10,29,850		Fixed Assets* (4)	4,41,000
Add : Donation	90,000			
	11,19,850			
Less : Deficit	(30,250)	10,89,600		
		13,92,600		13,92,600

Illustration 13 (Un-presented Cheques and Affiliation Fees)

From the following Receipts and Payments Account of a Football Club and additional information, prepare Income and Expenditure Account for the year ended 31st March 2007

Receipts	Rs.	Payments	Rs.
To Balances b/d : Cash	10,200	By Purchase of Bills	65,000
Bank	30,000	By Tournament Fees	10,000
To Subscriptions	2,45,000	By Affiliation Fee for five years	2,000
To Interest on Investment	1,800	By Rent of Playground	6,000
To Sale of tickets for		By Travelling Expanses	20,000
Variety Programme	20,000	By Expenses on Variety Programme	15,000
To Sale of Furniture (30-9-2006)	9,000	By Refreshment Expense	4,000
To Donation for Building	50,000	By Furniture bought on 1-10-06	5,000
To Legacy	11,000	By Advance to Building contractor	50,000
		By Repairs	5,000
		By Salary	15,000
		By Telephone Bill	1,500
		By Miscellaneous Expenses	8,000
		By 12% Investments (F.V. 1,70,000) (1-1-07)	1,50,000
		By Balances : Cash	8,500
		Bank	12,000
	3,77,000		3,77,000

Additional Information :

(i) Miscellaneous Expenses include Rs. 3,000 for the honorarium.

(ii) Subscriptions received include Rs. 9,000 outstanding subscription for the year 2005-06. Subscription for the year 2006-07 amounting to Rs. 16,000 is still outstanding. Some members have paid subscription for the year 2007-08 amounting to Rs. 8,000, which is included in the subscriptions received.

(iii) Face value of 12% Investments on 31st March 2006 was Rs. 15,000 (cost price Rs.12,000).

(iv) Book value of the furniture sold on 1-4-2006 was Rs. 12,000 depreciation being 20% p.a. Provide depreciation on new furniture at the same rate.

(v) Telephone bill for one quarter is outstanding, the amount outstanding being Rs. 300. The charge for each quarter is same both for 2005-06 and 2006-07.

(vi) Un-presented cheques for repairs to building being Rs. 4,000 for 2005-06 and 12,000 for 2006-07.

(vii) Bank balance represents 'Balance as per Bank Pass Book'.

(viii) Stock of Balls with the club on 31st March 2007 amounted to Rs. 6,000.

[B Com. (H), DU, 1993 – Modified]

Solution :

INCOME AND EXPENDITURE ACCOUNT
For the year ending 31st March 2007

Expenditure		Rs.	Income		Rs.
To Balls used	65,000		By Subscriptions	2,45,000	
Less : Stock	(6,000)	59,000	*Add* : Outstanding	16,000	
To Tournament Fees		10,000		2,61,000	
To Affiliation Fees (1/5 of 2,000)		400	*Less* : O/s of last year	(9,000)	
To Rent of Playground		6,000		2,52,000	
To Refreshment Expenses		4,000	*Less* : Adv. For next Yr .	(8,000)	2,44,000
To Traveling Expenses		20,000	By Interest on Investments	1,800	
To Repairs to Building*		13,000	*Add* : Accrued	5,100	6,900
To Salaries		15,000	By Income From Variety -		5,000
To Telephone Bill	1,500		Programme (20,000 - 15,000)		
Add : outstanding	300				
	1,800				
Less : paid for last year	(600)	1,200			
To Honorarium		3,000			
To Miscellaneous Expenses		5,000			
To Loss on Sale of furniture		1,800			
To Depreciation on furniture (1,200+500)		1,700			
To Excess of Income over Expenditure		1,15,800			
		2,55,900			2,55,900

	Rs.
*Repairs to Building as per Receipts and Payment A/c	5,000
Add : Unpresented Cheques of the Current year being O/s	12,000
	17,000
Less : Un-presented Cheques of the last year	4,000
Amount Charged to Income & Expenditure A/c	13,000

BALANCE SHEET
As on 1st April 2006

Liabilities	Rs.	Assets	Rs.
Telephone Bill O/s	600	Cash in hand	10,200
Capital Fund (Balancing figure)	68,600	Bank Balance* (30,000-4,000)	26,000
		Subscriptions O/s	9,000
		12% Investments at cost (F.V. 15,000)	12,000
		Furniture	12,000
	69,200		69,200

BALANCE SHEET
As on 31st March 2007

Liabilities		Rs.	Assets	Rs.
O/s Telephone Bills		300	Cash in hand	8,500
Subscriptions in Advance		8,000	Bank Balance*	—
Donation for Building		50,000	Subscriptions O/s	16,000
Legacy		11,000	Affiliation Fee (Unexpired)	1,600
Capital Fund	68,600		Stock of Balls	6,000
Add : Surplus	1,15,800	1,84,400	Interest Accrued	5,100
			12% Investments at Cost	
			(12,000 + 1,50,000)	1,62,000
			(Face Value 1,85,000)	
			Furniture	4,500
			Advance for Pavilion Building	50,000
		2,53,700		2,53,700

	1-4-2006	31-3-2007
*Bank Balance as per Pass Book	30,000	12,000
Less : Unpresented Cheque	4,000	12,000
Balance as per Cash Book	26,000	—

Illustration 14 (Accumulated Depreciation)

The Accountant of the City Club gave the following information about receipts and payments for the year ended 31st March 2008.

Receipts	Rs.	Payments	Rs.
To Subscriptions	62,130	By Premises	30,000
To Fair Receipts	7,200	By Rent	2,400
To Variety Show Receipts (Net)	12,810	By Rates & Taxes	3,780
To Interest	690	By Printing & Stationery	1,410
To Bar Collections	22,350	By Sundry Expenses	5,350
		By Wages	2,520
		By Fair Expenses	7,170
		By Honorarium to Secretary	11,000
		By Payment for Bar Purchases	17,310
		By Repairs	960
		By New Car (Less Sale Proceeds of old car Rs. 9,000)	37,800

Additional Information :

	1-4-2007	31-3-3008
	Rs.	Rs.
Cash in hand	450	—
Balance as per Pass Book	24,420	10,350

Cheques issued for Sundry Expenses not yet presented for payment	270	90
Subscriptions due	3,600	2,940
Premises at cost	87,000	?
Accumulated depreciation	56,400	?
Car at cost	36,570	?
Accumulated Depreciation	30,870	?
Bar Stock	2,130	2,610
Creditors for Bar Purchases	1,770	1,290

Annual Honorarium to Secretary is Rs. 12,000. Depreciation on premises is to be provided @ 5% p.a. and on Car @ 20% p.a. Prepare Income and Expenditure A/c for the year ended for the 31st March 2008 and a Balance Sheet as on that date. **[C.A. (Foundation), June 1999-Modified]**

Solution : **INCOME AND EXPENDITURE ACCOUNT**

For the year ended 31st March 2008

Expenditure		**Rs.**	**Income**		**Rs.**
To Rent		2,400	By Subscriptions	62,130	
To Rates & Taxes		3,780	*Add* : O/s of current year	2,940	
To Printing & Stationery		1,410		65,070	
To Sundry Expenses	5,350		*Less* : O/s of last year	(3,600)	61,470
Add : Outstanding	90		By Fair Receipts		7,200
	5,440		By Variety Show Receipts		12,810
Less : O/s of last year	(270)	5,170	By Interest		690
To Wages		2,520	By Profit from Bar* (1)		6,000
To Honorarium	11,000		By Profit on sale of old car* (2)		3,300
Add : Outstanding	1,000	12,000			
To Repairs		960			
To Fair Expenses		7,170			
To Depreciation on:					
Premises		3,030			
Car		9,360			
To Surplus-Excess of Income		43,670			
		91,470			91,470

(1) BAR TRADING ACCOUNT

	Rs.		**Rs.**
To Opening Stock	2,130	By Sales (Collection)	22,350
To Purchases	16,830	By Closing Stock	2,610
To Profit transferred to I/E A/c	6,000		
	24,960		24,960

BAR CREDITORS ACCOUNT

	Rs.		Rs.
To Cash	17,310	By Balance b/d	1,770
To Balance c/d	1,290	By Purchases (B.F.)	16,830
	18,600		18,600

PREMISES ACCOUNT

	Rs.		Rs.
To Balance b/d	87,000	By Balance c/d	1,17,000
To Cash (Addition)	30,000		
	1,17,000		1,17,000

(2) CAR DISPOSAL ACCOUNT

	Rs.		Rs.
To Car Account	36,570	By Accumulated Dep.	30,870
To Profit transferred to Income & Expenditure A/c	3,300	By Cash (Sale Proceeds)	9,000
	39,870		39,870

BALANCE SHEET
As on 1st April 2007

Liabilities	Rs.	Assets		Rs.
Creditors for bar Supplies	1,770	Cash in hand		450
Capital Fund (Balancing figure)	64,860	Bank Balance	24,420	
		Less : Unpresented cheque	(270)	24,150
		Subscription due		3,600
		Stock		2,130
		Car at Cost	36,570	
		Less : Ace. Depreciation	(30,870)	5,700
		Premises at Cost	87,000	
		Less : Ace. Depreciation	(56,400)	30,600
	66,630			66,630

BALANCE SHEET
As on 31st March 2008

Liabilities		Rs.	Assets		Rs.
Creditors for Bar Supplies		1,290	Cash at Bank	10,350	
Capital Fund	64,860		*Less* : Unpresented Cheque	(90)	10,260
Add : Surplus	43,670	1,08,530	Subscription due		2,940
O/s Honorarium		1,000	Bar Stock		2,610
			New Car at Cost	46,800*	
			Less : Dep. @ 20%	(9,360)	37,440
			Premises at Cost	1,17,000	
			Less : Ace. Depreciation	(59,430)	57,570
		1,10,820			1,10,820

*Amount paid plus proceeds of old car (Rs. 37,800 + 9,000) = Rs. 46,800.

Depreciation :

		Rs.
Premises (old) W.D.V		
(87,000 - 56,400)	=	30,600
New Premises		30,000
		60,600
Depreciation @ 5%		3,030

ACCUMULATED DEPRECIATION A/C

	Rs.		Rs.
To Balance c/d	59,430	By Balance b/d	56,400
		By Depreciation A/c	3,030
	59,430		59,430

Illustration 15 (General)

From the following Receipts and Payment Account prepare Income and Expenditure Account for the year ended 31st December 2007 and a Balance Sheet as on that date.

Receipts	Rs.	Payments	Rs.
To Balance b/d		By Salary	2,000
Cash in hand	4,000	By Repair Expenscs	500
Cash at Bank	10,000	By Purchase of Furniture	6,000
To Donations	5,000	By Miscellaneous Expenses	500
To Subscriptions	12,000	By Purchase of Investments	6,000
To Entrance Fees	1,000	By Insurance Premium	200
To Interest on Investment	100	By Billiard Table	8,000
To Interest from Bank	400	By Paper, Ink etc.	150
To Sale of Old Newspapers	150	By Drama Expenses	500
To Sale of Drama Tickets	1,050	By Balance c/d	
		Cash in hand	2,650
		Cash at Bank	7,200
	33,700		33,700

Additional Information :

1. Subscriptions in arrear for 2007 Rs. 900 and subscriptions in advance for 2008 Rs. 350
2. Insurance Premium Outstanding Rs. 40
3. Miscellaneous Expenses prepaid Rs. 90
4. 50% of donations to be Capitalised
5. Entrance Fees are to be treated as revenue income
6. Interest on 8% investments has accrued for five months
7. Billiard Table costing Rs. 30,000 was purchased during the last year and Rs.22,000 were paid for it. **[C.A. (Foundation), Nov. 1997-Modified]**

Solution :

INCOME AND EXPENDITURE ACCOUNT
For the year ended 31st December 2007

Expenditure		Rs.	Income		Rs.
To Salary		2,000	By Subscriptions	12,000	
To Repair Expenses		500	*Add* : Outstanding	900	
To Insurance Premium	200			12,900	
Add : Outstanding	40	240	*Less* : Advance for next year	(350)	12,550
To Paper Ink etc.		150	By Donations (50%)		2,500
To Miscellaneous Expenses	500		By Entrance Fees		1,000
Less : Prepaid	(90)	410	By Interest on 8% Investment	100	
To Surplus-Excess of Income			*Add* : Accrued for 5 months	200	300
Over Expenditure		14,150	By Profit from Drama		
			By Sale of Ticket)	1,050	
			Less : Expenses	(500)	550
			By Interest from Bank		400
			By Sale of old Newspapers		150
		17,450			17,450

BALANCE SHEET
As on 1st January 2007

Liabilities	Rs.	Assets	Rs.
Creditors for Billiard Table	8,000	Cash in hand	4,000
Capital Fund (B.F.)	36,000	Cash at Bank	10,000
		Billiard Table	30,000
	44,000		44,000

BALANCE SHEET
As on 31st December 2007

Liabilities		Rs.	Assets	Rs.
Subscriptions in Advance		350	Cash in hand	2,650
Outstanding Insurance Premium		40	Cast at Bank	7,200
Capital Fund	36,000		Subscriptions Due	900
Add : Surplus	14,150		Prepaid Expenses	90
	50,150		Interest Accrued on Investment	200
Add : Donations	2,500	52,650	8% Investments	6,000
			Billiard Table	30,000
			Furniture	6,000
		53,040		53,040

Illustration 16 (Specific Fund and Bar Trading Account)

ABC Sports Club's financial year ends on 31st March. The assets and liabilities of the club at dates stated were as follows :

	As on 31-3-2007	As on 31-3-2008
	Rs.	Rs.
Equipments	25,000	28,000
Subscriptions in Arrears	2,000	1,800
Subscriptions in Advance	1,300	1,100
Creditors for Bar Stock	3,500	4,300
Bar Stock	8,000	6,000
Electricity owing	1,050	14,000
Raffle (Lottery) Fund	500	?
Bank Balance	7,230	?

In the year ending 31st March 2008 the cash receipts were :

Subscriptions (including Rs. 600 of arrears from previous year)	21,000
Bar-takings	41,000
Annual Dinner/dance sale of tickets	24,000
Sale of Raffle tickets	1,800

In the same period the following payments were made :

Affiliation Fee (for four years)	1,000
Purchase of Equipments	8,000
Bar Stock	20,500
Barman's Wages	7,500
Catering (Dinner/dance)	14,400
Hire of Band (Dinner/dance)	3,000
Raffle Prizes	600
Printing and Postage	2,000
Electricity	5,810
Secretary's Honorarium	1,220
Repairs to Equipments	3,000
Hire of Hall	15,000

Note : Subscriptions arrears of previous year written off Rs. 400.

Prepare Bar Trading Account, Income and Expenditure Account for the year ended 31st March 2008 and a Balance Sheet as on that date. **[B.Com. (Hons.), DU, 1994-Modified]**

Solution :

BAR TRADING ACCOUNT
For the year ended 31st March 2008

Particulars	Rs.	Particulars	Rs.
To Opening Bar Stock	8,000	By Bar Takings	41,000
To Purchases- 1	21,300	By Closing Bar Stock	6,000
To Wages	7,500		
To Profit transferred to Income and Expenditure A/c	10,200		
	47,000		47,000

INCOME AND EXPENDITURE ACCOUNT
For the year ended 31st March 2008

Expenditure		Rs.	Income	Rs.
To Affiliation Fees	1,000		By Subscriptions (3)	21,400
Less : Prepaid	(750)	250	By Annual Dinner/Dance	
To Catering Expenses		14,400	tickets sale proceeds	24,000
To Hire of Band		3,000	By Profit from Bar	10,200
To Hire of Hall		15,000		
To Printing & Postage		2,000		
To Electricity (5,810 + 1,400 – 1,050)		6,160		
To Secretary's Honorarium		1,220		
To Repairs to Equipments		3,000		
To Subscriptions Written off		400		
To Depreciation (2)		5,000		
To Surplus-Excess of Income Over Expenditure		5,170		
		55,600		55,600

CALCULATION OF CAPITAL FUND
Balance Sheet as on 1st April 2007

Liabilities	Rs.	Assets	Rs.
Creditors for Bar Stock	3,500	Bank	7,230
Electricity O/s	1,050	Subscriptions Due	2,000
Subscription in Advance	1,300	Equipments	25,000
Raffle Fund	500	Bar Stock	8,000
Capital Fund (B.F.)	35,880		
	42,230		42,230

BALANCE SHEET
As on 31st March 2008

Liabilities		Rs.	Assets	Rs.
Electricity O/s		1,400	Bank (4)	13,000
Creditors for Bar Stock		4,300	Subscription Receivable	1,800
Subscriptions in Advance		1,100	Affiliation Fee Prepaid	750
Raffle Fund	500		Bar Closing Stock	6,000
Add : Receipt	1,800		Equipments	28,000
	2,300			
Less : Prizes	(600)	1,700		
Capital Fund	35,880			
Add : Surplus	5,170	41,050		
		49,550		49,550

Working Notes :

(1) CREDITORS FOR BAR STOCK A/c

	Rs.		Rs.
To Bank	20,500	By Balance b/d	3,500
To Balance c/d	4,300	By Purchases (B.F.)	21,300
	24,800		24,800

(2) EQUIPMENTS A/c

	Rs.		Rs.
To Balance b/d	25,000	By Depreciation (B.F.)	5,000
To Bank (Purchased during the year)	8,000	By Balance c/d	28,000
	33,000		33,000

(3) SUBSCRIPTIONS ACCOUNT

	Rs.		Rs.
To Balance b/d (Due)	2,000	By Balance b/d (Advance)	1,300
To Income & Expenditure A/c	21,400	By Bank-Receipts & Payments A/c	21,000
To Balance c/d (Advance)	1,100	By Income & Exp. A/c (Written off)	400
		By Balance c/d (Due)	1,800
	24,500		24,500

(4) BANK ACCOUNT

	Rs.		Rs.
To Balance b/d	7,230	By Receipts & Payments A/c (Total Payments)	82,030
To Receipts & Payments A/c (Total Receipts)	87,800	By Balance c/d (B.F.)	13,000
	95,030		95,030

B. Preparation of Receipts and Payments Account from Income and Expenditure Account

Steps :

(i) All receipts irrespective of their nature (Capital or revenue) whether relate to previous year, current year or next year are taken to receipts side of the account,

(ii) All expenditures, whether Capital or revenue by nature, irrespective of the year these belong to are shown to the credit (Payments) side of the account,

(iii) Cash in hand, Cash at Bank (Whether under Current A/c, Saving A/c or Deposit A/c) is shown as opening balance or closing balance depending upon the date to which these relate to. These opening balances are shown to the debit side of Receipts and Payments Account and closing balances to the credit side,

(iv) In case, there is overdraft in the beginning, the same should be shown to the credit side of the Receipts and Payments Account as the opening balance and conversely overdraft at the end to be taken to the debit side of the Account.

(v) All adjustments with reference to out-standings and prepaids are to be neutralised (ignored),

(vi) All Fixed Assets Accounts be prepared to find out actual receipts (inflow) or actual payments (outflow) involved on account of sale and purchase of the asset concerned.

Illustration 17 (Calculation of Missing Figures)

From the following particulars relating to Excel Hospital prepare : (i) Receipts and Payments Account for year ended 31st March 2008 and (ii) a Balance Sheet as on 31st March 2008.

INCOME AND EXPENDITURE ACCOUNT
For the year ended 31st March 2008

Expenditure	Rs.	Income		Rs.
To Medicines Used	29,980	By Subscriptions		56,000
To Honorarium to Visiting Doctors	12,000	By Donations		9,500
To Salaries	27,500	By Interest on Investments @ 11% p.a.		11,000
To Printing & Stationery	1,100	By Income from Film Show		
To Electricity & Water	475	Proceeds	11,450	
To Rent	6,000	*Less* : Expenses	(780)	10,670
To Depreciation on :				
Furniture & Fixture	2,100			
Equipment	3,250			
To Surplus-Excess of Income over Expenditure	4,765			
	87,170			87,170

Additional Information :

		31.3.2007	31.3.2008
		Rs.	Rs.
(i)	Subscription Due	120	160
(ii)	Subscription received in Advance	64	100

(iii)	Electricity & Water bills unpaid	92	115
(iv)	Stock of Machine	7,820	9,750
(v)	Estimated Value of Equipment	11,600	13,900
(vi)	Furniture and Fixture (Cost less Depreciation)	21,000	18,900
(vii)	Land	—	10,000
(viii)	Interest Accrued on Investment in 11% Debentures Costing Rs. 1,02,500 (Face Value Rs. 1,00,000)	3,750	3,750
(ix)	Cash in hand	340	160
(x)	Cash at Bank	9,000	?

[B.Com. (H), DU, 2001; 1986-Modified]

Solution :

RECEIPTS AND PAYMENTS ACCOUNT
For the year ended 31st March 2008

Receipts	Rs.	Payments	Rs.
To Balance b/d		By Medicines(2)	31,910
Cash in hand	340	By Honorarium to Visiting Doctors	12,000
Cash at Bank	9,000	By Purchase of Land	10,000
To Subscriptions(1)	55,996	By Salaries	27,500
To Donations	9,500	By Printing & Stationery	1,100
To Interest on Investments	11,000	By Electricity & Water(3)	452
To Proceeds form Film Show	11,450	By Purchase of Equipments(4)	5,550
		By Rent	6,000
		By Expenses on Film Show	780
		By Balance c/d	
		Cash in hand	160
		Cash at Bank (B.F.)	1,834
	97,286		97,286

(1) SUBSCRIPTIONS ACCOUNT

	Rs.		Rs.
To Balance b/d (Due in the beginning)	120	By Balance b/d (Advance in the beg.)	64
To Income and Expenditure A/c	56,000	By Cash-Receipts & Payments A/c (B.F.)	55,996
To Balance c/d (Advance at the end)	100	By Balance c/d (Due at the end)	160
	56,220		56,220

The actual payment made on account of various expenses has been worked out as under :

		Rs.
(2)	**Medicines :** Expenses charged to I/E Account	29,980
	Add : Closing Stock of Medicines	9,750
		39,730
	Less : Opening Stock of Medicines	(7,820)
		31,910

(3)	**Electricity and Water** as per I/E Account	475
	Add : O/s of last year paid this year	92
		567
	Less : O/s current year	(115)
		452

(4) EQUIPMENTS ACCOUNT

	Rs.		Rs.
To Balance b/d	11,600	By Depreciation	3,250
To Cash (Purchased during the year)	5,550	By Balance c/d	13,900
	17,150		17,150

(5) FURNITURE & FIXTURES ACCOUNT

	Rs.		Rs.
To Balance b/d	21,000	By Depreciation	2,100
		By Balance c/d	18,900
	21,000		21,000

(6) LAND ACCOUNT

	Rs.		Rs.
To Balance b/d	—	By Balance c/d	10,000
To Cash (Acquired during the year B.F.)	10,000		
	10,000		10,000

BALANCE SHEET
As on 31st March 2007

Liabilities	Rs.	Income	Rs.
Subscription in Advance	64	Cash in hand	340
O/s Electricity & Water Bill	92	Cash at Bank	9,000
Capital Fund (Balancing figure)	15,974	Subscription O/s	120
		Interest Accrued	3,750
		Stock of Medicines	7,820
		Investments at Cost	1,02,500
		Furniture & Fixture	21,000
		Equipments	11,600
	1,56,130		1,56,130

BALANCE SHEET
As on 31st March 2008

Liabilitis		Rs.	Assets	Rs.
Subscription in Advance		100	Cash in hand	160
O/s Electricity & Water Bill		115	Cash at Bank	1,834
Capital Fund	1,55,974		Subscriptions O/s	160
Add : Surplus	4,765	1,60,739	Interest Accrued on Investment	3,750
			Stock of Medicines	9,750
			11% Investment at Cost	1,02,500
			Furniture & Fixture	18,900
			Equipments	13,900
			Land	10,000
		1,60,954		1,60,954

Illustration 18 (Opening Cash Balance is not given)

The Income and Expenditure Account of a Club for the ended on 31 st December 2007 is as follows :

Expenditure	Rs.	Income	Rs.
To Salaries	1,20,000	By Subscriptions	1,70,000
To Printing & Stationery	6,000	By Entrance Fees	4,000
To Postage	500	By Contribution for Dinner	36,000
To Telephone.	1,500		
To General Expenses	12,000		
To Interest & Bank Charges	5,500		
To Audit Fees	2,500		
To Annual Dinner Expenses	25,000		
To Depreciation	7,000		
To Surplus-Excess of Income over Expenditure	30,000		
	2,10,000		2,10,000

The Income and Expenditure Account has been prepared after following adjustments :

	Rs.
Subscriptions outstanding on 31-12-2006	16,000
Subscriptions outstanding on 31-12-2007	18,000
Subscriptions received in Advance on 31-12-2006	13,000
Subscriptions received in advance on 31-12-2007	8,400
Salaries outstanding on 31-12-2006	6,000
Salaries outstanding on 31 -12-2007	8,000
Audit Fees for 2006 paid during 2007	2,000
Audit Fees outstanding for 2007	2,500

The Club owned building since 2005	1,90,000
The Club had sports equipments on 31 -12-2006 valued at	52,000
Value of sports equipments (after charging depreciation of Rs. 7,000) as on 31 -12-2007	63,000
In 2006 the Club had raised a bank loan, which is still not paid	30,000
Cash in hand on 31-12-2007	28,500

Prepare Receipts and Payments Account for the year 2007 and the Balance Sheet as on 31st December 2007.

Solution :

RECEIPTS AND PAYMENTS ACCOUNT
For the year ended 31st December 2007

Receipts	Rs.	Payments	Rs.
To Balance b/d (Balancing figure)	13,600	By Salaries (2)	1,18,000
To Subscriptions (1)	1,63,400	By Printing & Stationery	6,000
To Entrance Fee	4,000	By Postage	500
To Contribution for Dinner	36,000	By Telephone	1,500
		By General Expenses	12,000
		By Interest & Bank Charges	5,500
		By Audit Fees (3)	2,000
		By Annual Dinner Expenses	25,000
		By Sports Equipments (4)	18,000
		By Balance c/d	28,500
	2,17,000		2,17,000

Working Notes :

(1) SUBSCRIPTION A/C

	Rs.		Rs.
To Balance b/d (due)	16,000	By Balance b/d (Advance.)	13,000
To Income & Expenditure A/c	1,70,000	By Cash-Receipts & Payment A/c (B.F.)	1,63,400
To Balance c/d (Advance at the end)	8,400	By Balance c/d (due at the end)	18,000
	1,94,400		1,94,400

		Rs.
(2)	Salaries as per I/E Account	1,20,000
	Add : Due of last year paid this year	6,000
		1,26,000
	Less : Outstanding of current year	(8,000)
	Cash paid	1,18,000
(3)	Audit Fees paid for last year	2,000

(4) SPORTS EQUIPMENTS A/C

	Rs.		Rs.
To Balance b/d	52,000	By Depreciation	7,000
To Cash-Receipts & Payments A/c (Sports equipment purchased)	18,000	By balance c/d	63,000
	70,000		70,000

Illustration 19 (Omission and Rectification)

Following is the Income and Expenditure Account of the United Club for the year ended 30th June 2007.

Expenditure	Rs.	Income	Rs.
To Salaries	15,750	By Subscriptions	45,000
To Stationery	1,250	By Donations	7,500
To Postage	800	By Profit on sale of furniture	1,000
To Sundry Expenses	4,700	By Govt. Grants	4,000
To Repairs & Maintenance	3,600	By Interest on Fixed Deposit	800
To Sports Expenses	1,800		
To Swimming Pool Expenses and Maintenance	2,000		
To Affiliation Fee	500		
To Electricity	3,250		
To Billiard Room Expenses	1,250		
To Periodicals	1,200		
To Audit Fee	250		
To Depreciation on :			
Sports Equipments	1,000		
Building	2,500		
Furniture	450		
To Surplus : Excess of Income over Expenditure	18,000		
	58,300		58,300

The above account is prepared after considering the information given below :

	As on 1-7-2006 Rs.	30-6-2007 Rs.
1 Building	1,00,000	97,500
2 Sports Ground	1,00,000	1,00,000
3 Sports Equipments	6,000	9,000
4 Furniture	5,000	—
5 Fixed Deposit in Bank	8,000	8,000
6 Saving Bank Account	—	25,000
7 Subscriptions O/s	5,000	2,000
8 Subscriptions in Advance	3,000	1,000
9 Stock of Stationery	250	500

10	Audit Fee Outstanding	200	250
11	Salaries Outstanding	500	1,000
12	Affiliation Fee paid in Advance	—	250

Cash in hand on 1-7-2006 was Rs. 1,250. New furniture of Rs. 9,000 has been purchased on credit but not entered in the books. Depreciation has been charged on this furniture at 5%, you are required to prepare :

(a) Receipts and Payments Account for the year ended 30-06-07 and

(b) Balance Sheet as on 30th June 2007. **[I.C.W.A. (Inter), Dec. 1984-Modified]**

Solution : **RECEIPTS AND PAYMENTS ACCOUNT**

For the year ended 30th June 2007

Receipts	Rs.	Payments	Rs.
To Balance b/d		By Salaries[(2)]	15,250
Cash in hand	1,250	By Stationery[(3)]	1,500
Saving Bank	—	By Postage	800
Fixed Deposit	8,000	By Sundry Expenses	4,700
To Subscriptions[(1)]	46,000	By Repairs & Maintenance	3,600
To Donations	7,500	By Sports Expenses	1,800
To Govt. Grants	4,000	By Swimming Pool Expenses	
To Interest on Fixed Deposit	800	and Maintenance	2,000
To Sale of old Furniture	6,000	By Affiliation Fee[(4)]	750
		By Electricity	3,250
		By Billiards Room Expenses	1,250
		By Periodicals	1,200
		By Audit Fee[(5)]	200
		By Sports & Equipments	4,000
		By Balance c/d	
		Cash in hand	250
		Saving Bank	25,000
		Fixed Deposit	8,000
	73,550		73,550

BALANCE SHEET

As on 1st July 2006

Liabilities	Rs.	Assets	Rs.
Salaries O/s	500	Cash in hand	1,250
Audit Fees O/s	200	Fixed Deposit	8,000
Subscriptions in Advance	3,000	Subscriptions Receivable	5,000
Capital Fund		Stock of Stationery	250
(Balancing Figure)	2,21,800	Sports Equipments	6,000
		Furniture	5,000
		Building	1,00,000
		Sports Ground	1,00,000
	2,25,500		2,25,500

BALANCE SHEET
As on 30th June 2007

Liabilities		Rs.	Assets		Rs.
Salaries O/s		1,000	Cash in hand		250
Audit Fees O/s		250	Saving Bank A/c		25,000
Subscription in Advance		1,000	Deposit Bank A/c		8,000
Creditors for Furniture		9,000	Stock of Stationery		500
Capital Fund	2,21,800		Subscription Receivable		2,000
Add : Surplus	18,000	2,39,800	Affiliation Fee		250
			Furniture	9,000	
			Less : Depreciation	(450)	8,550
			Sports Equipments		9,000
			Building		97,500
			Sports Ground		1,00,000
		2,51,050			2,51,050

Working Notes :

(1) SUBSCRIPTIONS A/C

	Rs.		Rs.
To Balance b/d (Due)	5,000	By Balance b/d (Advance)	3,000
To Income and Expenditure A/c	45,000	By Cash-Receipts & Payments A/c	46,000
To Balance c/d (Advance)	1,000	By Balance c/d (Due)	2,000
	51,000		51,000

(2) SALARIES A/C

	Rs.		Rs.
To Cash-Receipts & Payments A/c (B.F)	15,250	By Balance b/d (O/s)	500
To Balance c/d (O/s)	1,000	By Income & Expenditure A/c	15,750
	16,250		16,250

(3) STOCK OF STATIONERY A/C

	Rs.		Rs.
To Balance b/d	250	By Income & Expenditure A/c	1,250
To Cash-Receipts & Payments A/c (B.F.)	1,500	By Balance c/d	500
	1,750		1,750

4. The total of affiliation fee paid for the year Rs. 500 and Rs. 250 as advance to be taken to Receipts & Payments A/c.
5. Audit Fees paid for the last year only Rs. 200 to be taken to Receipts & Payments Account.

Illustration 20 (Missing Figures)

Prepare Receipts and Payments Account for the year 31st March 2008 and also the Balance Sheet as on that date from the following :

INCOME AND EXPENDITURE ACCOUNT
For the year ending 31st March 2008

Expenditure	Rs.	Payments	Rs.
To Salaries	29,500	By Subscriptions	25,000
To Stationery	5,000	By Donations	15,000
To Rent & Taxes	2,500	By Interest	10,000
To Insurance	1,200	By Miscellaneous Receipts	300
To Other Expenses	1,800		
To Depreciation on :			
Properties	3,750		
Books	100		
Furniture	120		
To Surplus-Excess of Income over Expenditure	6,330		
	50,300		50,300

Other Information :

	31-3-2007	21-3-2008
	Rs.	Rs.
Cash in hand and at Bank	?	23,700
Shares and Debentures		
(Face Value Rs. 3,00,000)	2,80,000	2,80,000
Subscriptions Outstanding	7,000	10,000
Subscriptions Received in Advance	1,200	1,600
Salaries Outstanding	500	1,000
Furniture	2,000	1,980
Properties	3,00,000	2,96,250
Investments	1,000	1,000
Books	3,500	3,900
Stationery Expenses due	200	300
Stock of Stationery	1,000	800

[B.Com. (Hons.), D.U., 2000-Modified]

Solution :

RECEIPTS AND PAYMENTS ACCOUNT
For the year ended 31st March 2008

Receipts	Rs.	Payments	Rs.
		By Salaries	29,000
To Balance b/d		By Rent & Taxes	2,500
(Balancing figure)	15,800	By Insurance	1,200
To Subscriptions[(1)]	22,400	By Office Expenses	1,800
To Donations	15,000	By Stationery[(2)]	4,700
To Interest	10,000	By Furniture Purchased[(3)]	100
To Miscellaneous Receipts	300	By Books Purchased[(4)]	500
		Balance c/d	23,700
	63,500		63,500

BALANCE SHEET
As on 1-4-2007

Liabilities	Rs.	Assets	Rs.
Salaries O/s	500	Cash in hand & at Bank	15,800
Subscription in Advance	1,200	Subscription O/s	7,000
Stationery Expenses O/s	200	Stock of Stationery	1,000
Capital fund (B.F.)	6,08,400	Shares & Debentures (at cost)	2,80,000
		(F.V. 3,00,000)	
		Investment	1,000
		Books	3,500
		Furniture	2,000
		Properties	3,00,000
	6,10,300		6,10,300

BALANCE SHEET
As on 31st March 2008

Liabilities		Rs.	Assets		Rs.
Salary O/s		1,000	Cash & Bank Balance		23,700
Subscriptions in Advance		1,600	Subscriptions O/s		10,000
Stationery Expenses o/s		300	Stock of Stationery		800
Capital fund	6,08,400		Shares & Debentures		2,80,000
Add : Surplus	6,330	6,14,730	(F.V. 3,00,000)		
			Investment		1,000
			Books		3,900
			Furniture		1,980
			Properties	3,00,000	
			Less : Depreciation	(3,750)	2,96,250
		6,17,630			6,17,630

Working Notes :

(1) SUBSCRIPTIONS A/C

	Rs.		Rs.
To Balance b/d (Due)	7,000	By Balance b/d (Advance)	1,200
To Income and Expenditure A/c	25,000	By Cash-Receipts & Payments A/c (B.F.)	22,400
To Balance c/d (Advance)	1,600	By Balance c/d (Due)	10,000
	33,600		33,600

(2) STATIONERY EXPENSES O/S (CREDITORS) A/C

	Rs.		Rs.
To Cash-Receipts & Payments A/c (B.F.)	4,700	By Balance b/d	200
To Balance c/d	300	By Purchases	4,800
	5,000		5,000

STOCK OF STATIONERY A/C

	Rs.		Rs.
To Balance c/d	1,000	By Income & Expenditure A/c	5,000
To Purchases A/c	4,800	By Balance b/d	800
	5,800		5,800

(3) FURNITURE A/C

	Rs.		Rs.
To Balance b/d	2,000	By Depreciation	120
To Cash (Purchased) (B.F.)	100	By Balance c/d	1,980
	2,100		2,100

(4) BOOKS A/C

	Rs.		Rs.
To Balance b/d	3,500	By Depreciation	100
To Cash (Purchased) (B.F.)	500	By Balance c/d	3,900
	4,000		4,000

Illustration 21 (Opening and Closing Balance Sheets given)

City Sports Club gives you the following information :

INCOME AND EXPENDITURE ACCOUNT
For the year ended 31st March 2007

Expenditure	Rs.	Income		Rs.
To Coach Remuneration	9,000	By Subscription		50,000
To Staff Salaries	12,000	By Bar Receipts	12,000	
To Rent of Ground	6,000	*Less* : Expenses	(10,000)	2,000
To Repairs	6,500	By Sale of used Kits		2,000
To Sundry Expenses	3,500	By Rent of Hall		6,000
To Ground Maintenance	9,000			
To Depreciation on Furniture	1,500			
To Excess of Income over Expenditure	12,500			
	60,000			60,000

BALANCE SHEET
As on 31st March 2006 & 31st March 2007

Liabilities	31-3-2006 Rs.	31-3-2007 Rs.	Assets	31-3-2006 Rs.	31-3-2007 Rs.
Rent of ground	3,000	2,000	Cash in hand	5,000	4,000
Staff Salaries	2,000	3,000	Cash at Bank	—	10,000
Sundry Expenses	1,500	1,000	Fixed Deposit	22,500	30,000
Subscriptions in Advance	4,000	3,000	Furniture	21,000	19,500
Capital Fund	44,000	62,500	O/s Subscription	6,000	8,000
	54,500	71,500		54,500	71,500

Staff Salaries, Sundry Expenses, and Ground Rent due in March 2006 had been paid during the year ended 31-3-2007. Subscriptions received in advance is in respect of subsequent year. Subscriptions due in March 2006 received in full before March 2007. The increase in Capital Fund was due to the inclusion of the entrance fee of Rs. 6,000 and "surplus" earned during the year.

Prepare Receipts and Payments Account of the City Club for the year ended 31st March 2007.

[C.A. (Inter), May 1991 (Modified)]

RECEIPTS AND PAYMENTS ACCOUNT
For the year ended 31st March 2007

Receipts	Rs.	Payments	Rs.
To Balance b/d		By Coach Remuneration	9,000
Cash in hand	5,000	By Staff Salaries (2)	11,000
To Subscription (1)	47,000	By Rent for Ground (3)	7,000
To Bar Receipts	12,000	By Repairs	6,500

To Sale of used Kits	2,000	By Sundry Expenses (4)	4,000
To Rent of Hall	6,000	By Ground Maintenance	9,000
To Entrance Fees	6,.000	By Bar Expenses	10,000
		By Fixed Deposit	7,500
		By Balance c/d	
		Cash in hand	4,000
		Bank Balance	10,000
	78,000		78,000

Working Notes :

(1) SUBSCRIPTION A/C

	Rs.		Rs.
To Balance b/d (Due)	6,000	By Balance b/d (Advance)	4,000
To Income and Expenditure A/c	50,000	By Cash Receipts & Payments (B.F.) A/c	47,000
To Balance c/d (Advance)	3,000	By Balance c/d (Due)	8,000
	59,000		59,000

(2) STAFF SALARIES A/C

	Rs.		Rs.
To Cash-Receipts & Payments A/c (B.F.)	11,000	By Balance b/d	2,000
To Balance c/d	3,000	By Income & Expenditure A/c	12,000
	14,000		14,000

(3) RENT OF GROUND A/C

	Rs.		Rs.
To Cash-Receipts & Payments A/c (B.F.)	7,000	By Balance b/d (O/s)	3,000
To Balance c/d	2,000	By Income & Expenditure A/c	6,000
	9,000		9,000

(4) SUNDRY EXPENSES A/C

	Rs.		Rs.
To Cash-Receipts &Payments A/c (B.F.)	4,000	By Balance c/d	1,500
To Balance c/d	1,000	By Income and Expenditure A/c	3,500
	5,000		5,000

Illustration 22 (Sale & Purchase of Provisions)

The following is the Income and Expenditure Account of a club for the year ending 31st March 2008 :

Expenditure		Rs.	Income	Rs.
To Provision used :			Bu Subscriptions	34,000
Opening Stock	10,000		By Sale of Provisions	1,63,000
Add : Purchases	1,40,000			
Less : Closing stock	1,50,000			
	(5,000)	1,45,000		
To Salaries		18,000		
To General Expenses		5,000		
To Depreciation on Equipments		1,000		
To Surplus		28,000		
		1,97,000		1,97,000

The Following Balance Sheets are given to you :

Liabilities	On 31-3-2007	On 31-3-2008
	Rs.	Rs.
Creditors for Provisions	8,000	10,000
Capital Fund	47,000	75,000
	55,000	85,000
Assets		
Equipments (Cost less Depreciation)	10,000	25,000
Stock of Provisions	10,000	5,000
Subscriptions Receivable	5,000	10,000
Cash at Bank and in hand	30,000	45,000
	55,000	85,000

Prepare the Receipts and Payments Account of the Club for the year ended 31st March 2008.

[C.S. (Foundation), 1997-Modified]

Solution : **RECEIPTS AND PAYMENTS ACCOUNT**
For the year ended 31st March 2008

Receipts	Rs.	Payments	Rs.
To Balance b/d	30,000	By Payment to Creditors of Provisions(1)	1,38,000
To Subscriptions(3)	29,000	By Salaries	18,000
To Sale of Provisions	1,63,000	By General Expenses	5,000
		By Purchase of Equipments(2)	16,000
		By Balance c/d	45,000
	2,22,000		2,22,000

(1) CREDITORS FOR PROVISIONS A/C

	Rs.		Rs.
To Cash (Paymens) (B.F.)	1,38,000	By Balance b/d	8,000
To Balance c/d	10,000	By Purchases	1,40,000
	1,48,000		1,48,000

(2) EQUIPMENTS ACCOUNT

	Rs.		Rs.
To Balance b/d	10,000	By Depreciation	1,000
To Cash-Addition made during the year	16,000	By Balance c/d	25,000
	26,000		26,000

		Rs.
(3)	Subscriptions as per Income & Expenditure A/c	34,000
	Less : Outstanding of current year	(10,000)
		24,000
	Add : O/s of last year received this year	5,000
	Subscriptions received	29,000

Illustration 23 (General)

The following is the Income and Expenditure Account of a Youth Club for the year ended 31st March 2007 :

Expenditure	Rs.	Income	Rs.
To Salaries	19,500	By Subscriptions	68,000
To Rent	4,500	By Donations	5,000
To Printing	750		
To Insurance	500		
To Audit Fees	750		
To Games & Sports	3,500		
To Subscriptions Written off	350		
To Miscellaneous Expenses	14,500		
To Loss on Sale of Furniture	2,500		
To Depreciation on :			
Sports Equipments	6,000		
Furniture	3,100		
To Excess of Income over Expenditure	17,050		
	73,000		73,000

Additional Information :

	31-3-2006	31-3-2007
	Rs.	Rs.
Subscriptions in Arrear	2,600	3,700
Advance Subscriptions	1,000	1,500
Outstanding Expenses :		
Rent	500	800
Salaries	1,200	350
Audit Fees	500	750
Sports Equipments less Depreciation	25,000	24,000

Furniture less Depreciation	30,000	27,900
Prepaid Insurance	—	150

Book Value of furniture sold is Rs. 7,000. Entrance fees capitalised Rs. 4,000. On 1-4-2006, there was no cash in hand but Bank overdraft for Rs. 15,000. On 31-3-2007 Cash in hand amounted to Rs. 850 and the rest was Bank balance. Prepare Receipts and Payments Account of the Club for the year ended 31st March 2007. **[ICWA (Inter), Dec. 1988-Modifled]**

Solution : **RECEIPTS AND PAYMENTS ACCOUNT**
For the year ended 31st March 2007

Receipts	Rs.	Payments	Rs.
To Balance b/d		By Balance b/d	
Cash in hand	—	Overdraft	15,000
To Subscriptions[(1)]	67,050	By Salaries[(2)]	20,350
To Donations	5,000	By Rent[(3)]	4,200
To Entrance Fees	4,000	By Printing	750
To Sale of old Furniture	4,500	By Insurance[(4)]	650
		By Audit Fee[(5)]	500
		By Games & Sports	3,500
		By Miscellaneous Expenses	14,500
		By Purchase of Sports Equipments[(6)]	5,000
		By Purchase of Furniture[(7)]	8,000
		By Balance c/d	
		Cash in hand	850
		Bank Balance (B.F.)	7,250
	80,550		80,550

(1) SUBSCRIPTIONS ACCOUNT

	Rs.		Rs.
To Balance b/d (Due)	2,600	By Balance b/d (Advance)	1,000
To Income and Expenditure A/c	68,000	By Receipts & Payments A/c (Cash)	67,050
To Balance c/d (Advance)	1,500	By Income & Expenditure A/c (Subs. w/o)	350
		By Balance c/d	3,700
	72,100		72,100

		Rs.
(2)	Salaries as per Income and Expenditure A/c	19,500
	Less : Outstanding of the Current year	(350)
		19,150
	Add : O/s of last year paid this year	1,200
		20,350

(3)	Rent as per Income & Expenditure A/c	4,500
	Less : Outstanding of the current year	(800)
		3,700
	Add : Outstanding of last year paid this year	500
		4,200
(4)	Insurance as per Income and Expenditure A/c	500
	Add : Prepaid	150
		650

(5) Audit fee is due for current year and paid for the last year.

(6) SPORTS EQUIPMENTS ACCOUNT

	Rs.		Rs.
To Balance b/d	25,000	By Depreciation	6,000
To Cash-Purchased during the year (B.F.)	5,000	By Balance c/d	24,000
	30,000		30,000

(7) FURNITURE ACCOUNT

	Rs.		Rs.
To Balance b/d	30,000	By Cash (R/P A/c) (Sale)	4,500*
To Cash-Purchased during the year (B.F.)	8,000	By Income & Exp. A/c (Loss)	2,500
		By Depreciation (I/Exp.)	3,100
		By Balance c/d	27,900
	38,000		38,000

*(Book value less loss on sale) Rs. 7,000 - Rs. 2,500.

Illustration 24 (Prize Fund and General Fund)

From the following Income and Expenditure Account and the Balance Sheet of a Club, prepare Receipts and Payments Account and Subscriptions Account of the year ended 31st March 2007.

INCOME AND EXPENDITURE ACCOUNT
For the year ended 31st March 2007

Expenditure	Rs.	Income	Rs.
To Upkeep of lawn	10,000	By Subscriptions	17,320
To Printing	1,000	By Sale of old Newspapers	260
To Salaries	11,000	By Lectures	1,500
To Rent	600	By Entrance Fees	1,300
To Depreciation on Furniture	1,000	By Miscellaneous Income	400
		By Deficit	2,820
	23,600		23,600

BALANCE SHEET AS ON 31ST MARCH 2007

Liabilities	Rs.	Assets	Rs.
Subscription in Advance (2007-08)	100	Furniture	9,000
Prize Fund :		Grounds and Building	47,000

Last Balance	25,000		Prize Fund Investment	20,000
Add : Interest	1,000		Cash in hand	2,300
	26,000		Subscription O/s (2006-07)	700
Less : Prizes	(2,000)	24,000		
General Fund Balance	56,420			
Less : Deficit	(2,820)			
	53,600			
Add : Entrance Fee	1,300	54,900		
		79,000		79,000

The following adjustments have been made in the above accounts :

(i) Upkeep of ground Rs. 600 and Printing Rs. 240 relating to 2005-06 were paid in 2006-07.

(ii) One half of entrance fee has been capitalised by transfer to General Fund.

(iii) Subscriptions outstanding in 2005-06 were Rs. 800 and for 2006-07 Rs. 700.

(iv) Subscription received in advance in 2005-06 was Rs. 200 and in 2006-07 for 2007-08 Rs.100.

[C.A. (Entrance), Dec. 1983-Modified]

Solution : **RECEIPTS AND PAYMENTS ACCOUNT**
For the year ended 31st March 2007

Receipts	Rs.	Payments		Rs.
To Balance b/d (B.F.)	4,660	By Upkeep of Ground	10,000	
To Subscriptions	17,320	*Add* : Paid for last year	600	10,600
To Sale of Old Newspapers	260	By Printing	1,000	
To Lectures	1,500	*Add* : Paid for last year	240	1,240
To Entrance Fee	2,600	By Salaries		11,000
To Miscellaneous Income	400	By Rent		600
To Interest on Prize Fund Investments	1,000	By Prizes		2,000
		By Balance c/d		2,300
	27,740			27,740

SUBSCRIPTIONS ACCOUNT

	Rs.		Rs.
To Balance b/d (Due)	800	By Balance b/d (Advance)	200
To Income and Expenditure A/c	17,320	By Cash-Receipts & Payments A/c	17,320
To Balance c/d (Advance)	100	By Balance c/d (Due)	700
	18,220		18,220

Illustration 25 (Calculation of Closing Balance of Assets)

The following is the Income and Expenditure Account of a Sports Club for the year ended on 31st March 2008.

Expenditure	Rs.	Income	Rs.
To Salaries	24,000	By Subscriptions	72,000
To Rent	10,800	By Entrance Fees	8,000
To Taxes	600	By Surplus on Publication of brochure	4,500
To Postage	720	By Profit on Sale of Sport Materials	1,200
To Affiliation Fees to Lawn Tennis Association	1,200	By Interest on 5% Investments	600
		By Other Incomes	225
To Sports Materials	15,750		
To Electricity Charges	1,200		
To Repairs and Maintenance to Tennis Court	9,600		
To Depreciation @10% of Book Value at the end of year	4,800		
To Surplus	17,855		
	86,525		86,525

Additional Information as on :

		31-3-2007 Rs.	31-3-2008 Rs.
(i)	Sundry Assts (Including sports Material)	44,000	?
	Bank Balance	4,800	?
	Subscriptions in Arrear	4,750	3,500
	Subscriptions received in advance	1,400	2,600
	5% Investments	12,000	12,000
(ii)	Expenses Outstanding: Salaries	600	1,200
	Rent	900	1,800
	Rates and Taxes	Nil	600
	Tennis Court Maintenance	780	320
(iii)	Outstanding for purchase of sports materials	1,400	2,950
(iv)	Prize Fund	4,600	3,250

(v) The book value as on 1-4-2007 of sports materials sold in the year was Rs. 4,000.

(vi) Prize Fund is separately maintained. All receipts are credited to it and expenditure is met out of the fund directly. During the year, credits to the account amounted to Rs. 2,800.

(vii) Interest received this year was only for two quarters.

(viii) The Club was admitted as a member of the All India Lawn Tennis Federation on 1-10-2007 when it paid subscription till 30-9-2008.

(ix) Advertisement charges on brochure-yet to be collected Rs. 450.

(x) A fixed deposit of Rs. 25,000 was made on 31-3-2008.

Prepare Receipts and Payments Account for the year ended on 31st March 2008 and a Balance Sheet as on that date. **[B.Com. (H), DU, 1996-Modified & 2002]**

Solution :

RECEIPTS AND PAYMENTS ACCOUNT
For the year ended 31st March 2008

Receipts	Rs.	Payments	Rs.
To Balance b/d		By Salaries*	23,400
Bank Balance	4,800	By Rent*	9,900
To Subscriptions (1)	74,450	By Rates and Taxes	Nil
To Entrance Fees	8,000	By Postage	720
To Net Receipt from Brochure Publications*	4,050	By Affiliation Fees to Lawn Tennis Association (2)	2,400
To Sale of Sports Materials		By Sports Materials*	14,200
(Profit + Book value) (1,200 + 4,000)	5,200	By Electricity Charges	1,200
To Interest on 5% Investments	300	By Repairs and Maintenance of	
To Prize Fund Receipts	2,800	Tennis Court*	10,060
To Other Income	225	By Sundry Assets (3)	8,000
		By Prizes Awarded (4)	4,150
		By Fixed Deposit	25,000
		By Balance c/d (Bank)	795
	99,825		99,825

*These items show the figures after adjustments for the out standings.

BALANCE SHEET AS ON 31ST MARCH 2007

Liabilities	Rs.	Assets	Rs.
Outstanding for Sports Materials	1,400	Bank Balance	4,800
Expenses Outstanding :		Subscriptions in Arrear	4,750
Salaries	600	5% Investments	12,000
Rent	900	Sundry Assets including	
Maintenance (Tennis Court)	780	Sports Materials	44,000
Subscription in Advance	1,400		
Prize Fund	4,600		
Capital Fund (B.F.)	55,870		
	65,550		65,550

BALANCE SHEET OF SPORTS CLUB
As on 31st March 2008

Liabilities		Rs.	Assets	Rs.
Outstanding for Sports Material		2,950	Bank Balance	795
Expenses Outstanding :			Subscriptions in Arrear	3,500
Salaries		1,200	Interest Accrued on Investment	300
Rent		1,800	Advertisement Charges Receivable	450
Rates & Taxes		600	Affiliation Fee Prepaid	1,200
Maintenance (Tennis Court)		320	5% Investments	12,000
Subscriptions in Advance		2,600	Fixed Deposit	25,000
Prize Fund		3,250	Sundry Assets(3)	43,200
Capital Fund :	55,870			
Add : Surplus	17,855	73,725		
		86,445		86,445

Working Notes :

(1) SUBSCRIPTION ACCOUNT

	Rs.		Rs.
To Balance b/d (Due)	4,750	By Balance b/d (Advance)	1,400
To Income and Expenditure A/c	72,000	By Bank-Receipts & Payments A/c	74,450
To Balance c/d (Advance)	2,600	By Balance c/d (Due)	3,500
	79,350		79,350

(2) Since Affiliation Fees has been paid for one year (From 1-10-2007 to 30-9-2008) only expired amount relating to current accounting period (From 1-10-2007 to 31-3-2008) has been shown in the Income and Expenditure Account, it means an amount of Rs. 2,400 must have actually been paid for whole the year.

(2) SUNDRY ASSETS ACCOUNT
(Including Sports Materials)

	Rs.		Rs.
To Balance b/d	44,000	By Bank-Sale	
To Income & Expenditure A/c		(Book Value + Profit)	5,200
(Being Profit on sale)	1,200	By Depreciation (I/Exp. A/c)	4,800
To Bank-Purchased during the		By Balance c/d*	
year (B.F.)	8,000	$(100/10 \times 4,800 = 48,000 - 4,800)$	43,200
	53,200		53,200

* $\frac{\text{Depreciation} \times 100}{\text{Rates}}$ = Book value before Depreciation

Book value before Depreciation – Depreciation = W.D.V.

(4) PRIZE FUND ACCOUNT

	Rs.		Rs.
To Bank (R/P A/c) (Prizes Awarded-(B.F.)	4,150	By Balance b/d	4,600
To Balance c/d	3,250	By Receipts-Bank (R/P A/c)	2,800
	7,400		7,400

Illustration 26

The following is the Income & Expenditure Account of a Club for the year ended 31st March 2008.

Expenditure		**Rs.**
To provision used : Opening Stock	10,000	
Add : Purchases	1,40,000	
	1,50,000	
Less : Closing Stock	(5,000)	1,45,000
To Salaries		18,000
To General expenses		5,000
To Depreciation on equipments		1,000
To Surplus, i.e., excess of Income over Expenditure		28,000
		1,97,000
Income		
By Subscription		34,000
By Sale of Provisions		1,63,000
		1,97,000

The following balance sheets are also given to you

Liabilities	**On 31.3.2007**	**On 31.3.2008**
	Rs.	**Rs.**
Creditors for provisions	8,000	10,000
Capital fund	47,000	75,000
	55,000	85,000
Assets		
Equipments (Cost Less Depreciation)	10,000	25,000
Stock of provisions	10,000	5,000
Subscription receivable	5,000	10,000
Cash at Bank in Hand	30,000	45,000
	55,000	85,000

Prepare the Receipts and Payments Account of the Club for the year ended 31st March, 2008.

[C.S Foundation, Dec, 1997, Adapted]

Solution :

RECEIPTS & PAYMENTS ACCOUNT
For the year ended 31st March, 2008

Receipts	Rs.	Payments	Rs.
To Balance b/d	30,000	By Salaries	18,000
To Sale of Provisions	1,63,000	By General Expenses	5,000
To Subscriptions	29,000	By Equipments Purchased	16,000
		By paid for the Provisions	1,38,000
		By Balance c/d	45,000
	2,22,000		2,22,000

Working notes :

(1) EQUIPMENTS ACCOUNT

	Rs.		Rs.
To Balance b/d	10,000	By Depreciation	1,000
To Cash-Purchase (Bal. figure)	16,000	By Balance c/d	25,000
	26,000		26,000

(2) Calculation of cash paid for the provisions :

	Rs.
Creditors for provisions (Opening balance)	8,000
Add : Purchase of provisions during the year	1,40,000
	1,48,000
Less : Creditors for provision (Closing Balance)	10,000
Cash Paid	1,38,000

Alternatively :

Creditors A/c

	Rs.		Rs.
To Cash (b/f)	1,38,000	By Balance b/d 8,000	
To Balance c/d	10,000	By Purchases1,40,000	
	1,48,000		1,48,000

(3) SUBSCRIPTION ACCOUNT

	Rs.		Rs.
To Balance b/d (o/s)	5,000	By Cash (b/f) (Receipts & Payments)	29,000
To Income & Expenditure A/c	34,000	By Balance c/d (o/s)	10,000
	39,000		39,000

Illustration 27 (Calculation of closing balances)

Following are the Receipts & Payments and Income & Expenditure Account of Delhi Club for the year ending 31st March 2007.

Receipts		Rs.	Payments	Rs.
To Balance b/d		1,000	By Ground Maintenance	1,200
To Subscriptions			By Salaries & Honorarium	
2005-06	400		(Including salary of 05-06 Rs. 700/-)	1,800
2006-07	10,300		By Water & Electricity	350
2007-08	500	11,200	By Books out of Donation	3,000
To Legacy		800	By Fixed Deposit out of Donation	4,000
To Donation for Library		7,000	By Match Expenses	2,200
To Match Fund		3,300	By Crockery	1,000
To Sale of Furniture		500	By Food	2,000
			By Entertainment	2,000
			By Sports Materials	2,000
			By Balance c/d	4,250
		23,800		23,800

INCOME & EXPENDITURE ACCOUNT
For the year ending 31st March, 2007

Expenditure	Rs.	Income	Rs.
To Ground Maintenance	1,200	By Subscription	10,400
To Salary & Honorarium	1,800		
To Entertainment	2,000		
To Loss on Sale of Furniture	300		
To Electricity & Water	350		
To Sports Material Used (75% of total stock in hand during the year)	2,010		
To Food Consumed (80% of total stock in Hand)	1,500		
To Excess of income over Expenditure	1,240		
	10,400		10,400

Additional Information :

(a) Subscription outstanding on 31.3.2006 Rs. 550- estimated at Rs. 500-.

(b) Subscription outstanding on 31.3.2007 Rs. 120-.

(c) Furniture on 31.03.2006 Rs. 3,000-.

(d) Crockery on 31.03.2006 Rs. 2,500-.

You are requested to prepare Balance Sheet as on 1.4.2006 and 31.3.2007.

[B.com (P) 2006, D.U, Category 'A']

Solution : **Balance Sheet as on 31st March 2006**

Liabilities	Rs.	Assets	Rs.
Salary Outstanding	700	Cash Balance	1,000
Subscription Received in Advance	80*	Subscription outstanding	500
Capital Fund		Stock of Crockery	2,500
(Balancing Figure)	8,775	Furniture	3,000
		Sports Materials(1)	680
		Food(2)	1,875
	9,555		9,555

Balance Sheet as on 31st March 2007

Liabilities		Rs.	Assets	Rs.
Capital Fund	8,775		Cash Balance	4,250
Add : Surplus	1,240	10,015	Subscription Outstanding	120
Salary Outstanding		700	Books	3,000
Match Fund (Rs. 3,300-2,200)		1,100	Fixed Deposits	4,000
Advance Subscription		500	Furniture	2,200**
Legacy		800	Sports Material	670
Donation		7,000	Crockery	3,500
			Food	2,375
		20,115		20,115

Working notes :

*** SUBSCRIPTION ACCOUNT**

	Rs.		Rs.
To Balance b/d (Outstanding)	500	By Balance b/d (Advance)	80*
To Income & Expenditure A/c	10,400	By Bank A/c (R.P. A/c)	11,200
To Balance c/d (Advance)	500	By balance c/d (o/s)	120
	11,400		11,400

1. *** Sports Materials**

75% of total stock in hand during the year = 2,010

Total stock during the year $= 2{,}010 \times \frac{100}{75} = \text{Rs.}\,2{,}680$

Less : Purchased during the year = Rs. 2,000

Opening Balance 680

Closing Balance = Rs. 680 + Rs. 2,000 – Rs. 2,010

= Rs. 670

2. **Food**

80% of total stock in hand = Rs. 1,500

stock in hand $= \text{Rs.}\,1{,}500 \times \frac{100}{80} = 1{,}875$

Closing stock = Rs. 1,875 + Rs. 2,000 – 1,500
= Rs. 2,375

Illustration 28

A Charitable Dispensary shows the following information.

INCOME & EXPENDITURE ACCOUNT
For the year ended 31st December, 2007

Expenditure		Rs.	Income	Rs.
To Salaries		23,500	By Subscriptions	25,000
To Surgery & Dispensary		3,000	By Interest	9,000
To Rent Taxes		500	By Donations	4,000
To Insurance		200	By Miscellaneous Receipts	300
To Office Expenses		800		
To Depreciations				
Building	3,750			
Furniture	120			
Instruments	100	3,970		
To Surplus		6,330		
		38,300		38,300

Other information :

	31.12.2006 Rs.	31.12.2007 Rs.
Cash in Hand and at Bank		18,700
Government securities (Face value Rs. 2,00,000)	1,80,000	1,80,000
Subscription outstanding	7,000	10,000
Subscription received in advance	200	600
Salaries Unpaid	1,000	1,500
Furniture	2,000	1,980
Land and buildings	2,00,000	1,96,250
Instruments	3,500	3,900
Surgery expenses due	200	300
Stock of medicines	300	100

Prepare Receipts and Payments Account for the year ending 31st December, 2007.

[B.com(P), D.U, 2006 (F.C.)]

Solution :

RECEIPTS AND PAYMENTS ACCOUNT
For the year ending 31st December, 2007

		Rs.			Rs.
To balance b/d		10,800*	By Salaries	23,500	
To Subscription	25,000		*Add* : Unpaid for the last year	1,000	
Add : O/s 2006	7,000			24,500	
Advance 2007	600		*Less* : Unpaid (Current year)	(1,500)	23,000
	32,600		By Surgery Expenses & Dispensary	3,000	
Less : O/s 2006	(10,000)		*Add* : Due (Last year)	200	
Less : Advance for 2008	(200)	22,400		3,200	
To Interest		9,000	*Less* : Due (Current year)	(300)	
To Donations		4,000		2,900	
To Miscellaneous Receipts		300	*Add* : Closing Stock	100	
				3,000	
			Less : Opening Stock	(300)	2,700
			By Rent and Taxes		500
			By Insurance		200
			By Office Expenses		800
			By Furniture (1,980+120-2,000)		100
			By Instruments (3,900+100-3,500)		500
			By Balance c/d		18,700
		46,500			46,500

QUESTIONS

1. Distinguish between Income and Expenditure Account and Receipts and Payments Account. **[B.Com. (H), D.U., 1982, 1985]**
2. How would you deal with :
   (i) Donations — general & specific and
   (ii) Legacy — in the final accounts of non-trading organisation. **[B.Com. (H), D.U., 1990]**
3. Explain conversion of Receipts and Payments Account into an Income and Expenditure Account. **[B.Com. (H), D.U., 1995]**
4. Differentiate between Income Outstanding & Income Accrued. **[B.Com. (H), D.U., 1989]**
5. How will you treat Donation and Legacy in the financial statements of non-profit making entities? **[B.Com. (H), D.U., 1998]**
6. Write short notes on :
   (i) Entrance Fees vs. Professional Fees
   (ii) Subscriptions in Advance vs. Subscription in Arrears
   (iii) Capital Fund vs. Endowment Fund
   (iv) Life Membership Fee vs. Membership Fee

PROBLEMS

1. Prepare Income & Expenditure A/c and Balance Sheet from the following Receipts & Payments A/c and Balance Sheet as on 31-12-2007. **[B.Com. (H), DU, Adapted]**

RECEIPTS & PAYMENTS A/C
For the year ending 31st December 2007

Receipts		Rs.	Payments		Rs.
To Balance b/d		50,000	By Expenses :		
To Subscription :			2006	6,000	
2006	1,000		2007	10,000	16,000
2007	10,500		By Land		20,000
2008	500	12,000	By Interest		2,000
To Entrance Fees		4,000	By Miscellaneous Expenses		10,000
To Lockers Rent		3,500	By Balance c/d		41,500
To Miscellaneous Income		20,000			
		89,500			89,500

BALANCE SHEET AS ON 31ST DEC. 2006

Liabilities	Rs.	Assets	Rs.
Capital Fund	1,68,100	Building	1,50,000
Subscription Received in Advance	3,000	Outstanding Subscriptions	1,900
Outstanding Expenses	7,000	Outstanding Locker Rent	1,200
Loan	25,000	Cash	50,000
	2,03,100		2,03,100

Ans. Excess of Income over Expenditure: Rs. 17,800; Balance Sheet Total: Rs. 2,12,400.

2. Following is the Receipts and Payments A/c of Delhi Club for the year ended 31st Dec. 2007 :

Receipts		Rs.	Payments		Rs.
To Balance b/d			By Secretary Remuneration		25,000
Cash	10,000		By Salary to Staff		25,000
Bank	50,000	60,000	By Canteen Expenses		60,000
To Subscriptions :			By Newspaper & Magazines		5,000
2006	25,000		By Construction of Building		75,000
2007	1,000		By Balance c/d		
2008	500	26,500	Cash	4,000	
To Interest from 5% Govt.			Bank	10,000	14,000
Security (Purchased in the past)					
@ 1% Discount		10,000			

To Sale of old Furniture	5,000		
To Sale of old Newspapers	2,500		
To Canteen Collections	50,000		
To Donations for Building Fund	50,000		
	2,04,000		2,04,000

With the additional information given below, prepare the Income and Expenditure Account for the year ended 31st Dec. 2007 and the Balance Sheet as on that date.

	As on 31st Dec. 2006	As on 31st Dec. 2007
	Rs.	Rs.
(a) Subscriptions Receivable	5,000	?
(b) Subscriptions received in advance	1,000	500
(c) Salary to Staff O/s	10,000	5,000
(d) Canteen Expenses Prepaid	5,000	2,500
(e) Furniture etc.	50,000	?
(f) Construction Expenses O/s	—	10,000
(g) Subscriptions due for the year 2007	—	27,500

(h) The book value of Furniture sold in December was Rs. 15,000.

(i) Charge depreciation on Furniture @ 10% on the closing net balance.

Ans. Excess of Expenditure over Income Rs. 10,000; Balance Sheet Total Rs. 3,62,500.

[C.A. (Inter), Adapted]

3. The following is the Receipts and Payments A/c of Sun Club in respect of the year 31st March 2008 :

RECEIPTS & PAYMENTS A/C
For the year ended 31st March 2008

Receipt		Rs.	Payments	Rs.
To Balance b/d			By Salaries	3,000
Cash-in-hand		2,000	By Stationery	1,000
To Subscriptions :			By Rent & Taxes	300
2006-07	3,000		By Telephone Charges	1,500
2007-08	4,000		By 8% Securities at par	5,000
2008-09	1,000	8,000	By Sundry Expenses	200
To Profit on Sports		3,000	By Balance c/d	
To Interest on 8% Securities		1,000	Cash-in-hand	3,000
		14,000		14,000

The following additional facts are ascertained :

1. There are 500 members, each paying an annual subscription of Rs. 10; Rs. 3,500 being in arrears for 2006-2007, at the beginning of 2007-2008. During 2006-2007, subscriptions were paid in advance by 30 members for 2007-2008.
2. Stock of Stationery at 31st March 2007 was Rs. 400 and at 31st March 2008 Rs. 500.
3. At 31st March 2008, the Rent and Taxes was prepaid to the following 31st January the yearly charge being Rs. 300.

4. A quarter's charge for telephone is outstanding the amount accrued being Rs. 300. The charges for each quarter is same both for 2006-2007 and 2007-2008.
5. Sundry Expenses accruing at 31st March 2007 were Rs. 50 and at 31st March 2008 Rs. 60.
6. At 31st March 2007, Building stood in the books at Rs. 30,000 and it is required to write off depreciation at 10% p.a.
7. Value of 8% Securities at 31st March 2007 was Rs. 15,000 which were purchased at that date at par, additional Securities worth Rs. 5,000 were purchased on 31st March 2008.

You are required to prepare :

(a) An Income & Expenditure Account for the year ended 31st March 2008.

(b) A Balance Sheet as at that date.

Ans. Excess of Income over Expenditure Rs. 590; Balance Sheet Total Rs. 52,150; Capital Fund Rs. 50,200.

[I.C.W.A., Adapted]

4. The following particulars relate to the 'X' club for the year ended 31-12-2007 and you are required to prepare there from an Income & Expenditure A/c for the year and a Balance Sheet as on 31-12-2007.

SUMMARY OF CASH BOOK

		Rs.		Rs.
To Balance b/d		23,500	By Salaries	12,000
To Entrance Fees		3,000	By Electricity	1,200
To Subscriptions :			By Newspapers & Journals	5,250
2006	500		By Fixed Deposits	25,000
2007	35,000		By Crockery	2,000
2008	750	36,250	By Payment to Creditors	10,000
To Profit from Refreshment		1,000	By Balance c/d	11,500
To Lockers Rent		2,000		
To Sundry Income		1,200		
		66,950		66,950

The Assets and Liabilities on 1-1-2007 were Crockery Rs. 8,000; Furniture Rs. 25,000; Consumable Stores Rs. 3,500; Creditors Rs. 12,000. On 31-12-2007 value of Consumable stores was Rs. 7,000; Creditors amounted to Rs. 5,500; the Subscriptions outstanding were Rs. 750 and the Interest accrued on Fixed deposits was Rs. 250.

Ans. Surplus-Rs. 24,750; Capital Fund Rs. 48,500; Balance Sheet Total Rs. 79,500.

5. From the following information relating to Apollo Cricket Club, prepare Income & Expenditure A/c for the year ended 31st March 2008, Balance Sheet as at 31st March 2008 and Balance Sheet as at 31st March 2007 :

Dr. **Cr.**

Receipts	Rs.	Payments	Rs.
Members' Subscriptions	90,000	Upkeep of Field & Pavilion	36,000
Members' Admission Fees	5,400	Expenses for Tournament	12,600
Sale of old Balls, Bats etc.	900	Rates & Insurance	3,600
Hire of Ground	5,400	Telephones	900
Subscription for H.S. Tournament	18,000	Printing & Stationery	1,800

Cash drawn from Bank	72,000	General Expenses	900
Donations	1,80,000	Honorarium to Secretary	3,060
		Grass Seeds	540
		Bats & Balls etc.	12,600
		Cash Deposited into Bank	2,99,700
	3,71,700		3,71,700

Assets as on 1st April 2007 :

	Rs.
Cash-at-bank	54,000
Stock of Balls, Bats etc.	2,700
Printing & Stationery	3,600
Subscription Due	9,000
Liabilities	Nil

Donations received and surplus on account of H.S. Tournament should be kept in Reserve for a permanent Pavilion. Subscriptions due at 31st March 2008 were Rs. 13,500. Write off 50% of Bats, Balls Account and 25% of Printing & Stationery Account.

Ans. Excess of Income over Expenditure - Rs. 40,050; Total of B/s for 2007 - Rs. 93,600; Total of B/s for 2008 - Rs. 3,19,050. **[C.A. (I), Adapted]**

6. Following are the assets and liabilities of a Public Library on 31st December 2007 :

Liabilities	Rs.	Assets		Rs.
Outstanding for Expenses	3,900	Cash		19,200
Ccapital fund :		Furniture		29,100
Excess of Income over Expenditure	2,66,100	Debtors :		
		O/s Subscription :	4,500	
		Amount to be received for the use of Lecture Hall	2,100	6,600
		Library Books		1,01,100
		Investments		30,000
		Buildings		84,000
	2,70,000			2,70,000

CASH BOOK (FOR THE YEAR 2008)

Dr. **Cr.**

Receipts	Rs.	Payments	Rs.
Balance b/d	19,200	Salaries	14,400
Entrance Fees	15,600	Municipal Taxes	4,200
Subscriptions	51,000	Insurance on Building	3,000
Receipts from Sale of Old Newspapers	360	Increase in the Books of Library	7,500
Rent of Library Hall	6,240	Payment to last year's Creditors	3,900
Proceeds from Lectures and Entertainment	18,000	Repairs	1,500

Sale of Old Furniture	3,600	Electric Fittings	27,000
		Printing & Stationery	2,400
		Postal Charges	300
		Sundry Expenses	900
		Balance c/d	48,900
	1,14,000		1,14,000

It was found out at the end of the year that amount to be received for subscriptions were Rs.6,600 and for use of Library Hall were Rs. 2,250, prepaid insurance on Building was Rs. 1,050, and Outstanding Sundry Expenses were Rs. 4,800. Provide for Depreciation 2½ % on building and write off 5% on Investments and 10% on the opening amount of Library Books. Whole of the Entrance Fee is to be treated as revenue income. Prepare Income & Expenditure A/c and Balance Sheet for the year ending at 31st Dec. 2008.
Ans. Excess of Income over Expenditure—Rs. 49,290; Balance Sheet Total—Rs. 3,20,190.

7. The following particulars relate to Maggie Club for the year ended 31st December 2007 :

RECEIPTS & PAYMENTS A/C
For the year ended 31-12-2007

Receipts		Rs.	Payments	Rs.
To Balance c/d		9,000	By Salaries	18,675
To Subscriptions :			By Stationery	3,600
2006	360		By Rates & Taxes	5,400
2007	18,990		By Telephone	900
2008	720	20,070	By Investments	11,250
To Profit from Canteen		13,500	By Advertisements	1,575
To Miscellaneous		675	By Postage	1,500
To Sale of Old Newspapers		1,680	By Sundries	5,250
To Dividends		7,275	By Balance c/d	4,050
		52,200		52,200

You are required to prepare an Income & Expenditure A/c and Balance Sheet after making the following adjustments :

1. There are 450 members each paying an annual subscription of Rs. 45; Rs. 405 being in arrears for 2006 at the beginning of this year.
2. Stock of Stationery on 31st December 2006 was— Rs. 450; on 31st December 2007 — Rs.810.
3. Cost of Buildings is Rs. 90,000. Depreciate @ 5%.

Ans. Surplus— Rs. 2,340; Capital Fund— Rs. 99,855; Balance Sheet Total — Rs.1,02,915.

8. The following is the Receipts & Payments A/c of the Sophia Sports Club for the year ending December 31, 2007 :

Receipts		Rs.	Payments	Rs.
To Opening Balance		30,000	By Wages	6,000
To Subscriptions :			By Furniture	18,000
2006	3,000		(Purchased on 1-10-2007)	
2007	90,000		By Sports Expenses	15,000

2008	6,000	99,000	By Sundry Expenses	91,200
To Life Members' Fees		72,000	By Closing Balance	84,000
To Sale of Scrap		1,200		
To Interest on Sports Fund Investments		12,000		
		2,14,200		2,14,200

The Club has 1,600 members each paying annual subscription of Rs. 60. Subscription of Rs.2,700 is still in arrears for 2006. On 1-1-2006 the Club's assets and liabilities included Furniture of Rs. 12,000, Sports Fund Rs. 1,80,000, Sports Fund Investment Rs. 1,80,000. The Investment was at 10%. Provide depreciation on Furniture at 20%.

Prepare Income & Expenditure A/c from the year ended December 31st, 2007, and the Balance Sheet as on that date.

Ans. Deficit—Rs. 300; Capital Fund—Rs. 47,700; Balance Sheet Total—Rs. 3,05,400.

9. From the following particulars relating to a Missionary Charitable Hospital, prepare Income & Expenditure A/c for the year ended 31st December 2007 and Balance Sheet as at that date.

RECEIPTS & PAYMENTS A/C

Dr. For the year ended 31st Dec. 2007 Cr.

Receipts	Rs.	Payments	Rs.
To Cash-in-hand (1-1-07)	8,556	By Medicines	36,708
To Subscription	57,594	By Doctor's Honorarium	10,800
To Donation	17,400	By Salaries	32,400
To Sale of Old Equipment (Cost Rs. 240)	120	By Newspapers	480
To Interest on Investment (@ 7% p.a.)	8,400	By Stationery	120
To Proceeds from Charity Show	12,300	By Petty Expenses	552
To Sale of Newspapers	120	By Equipments	18,000
		By Expenses on Charity Show	900
		By Cash-in-hand	4,530
	1,04,490		1,04,490

Additional Informations :

	On 1-1-2007 Rs.	On 31-12-2007 Rs.
(i) Subscription Due	288	336
(ii) Subscription received-in-advance	78	120
(iii) Stock of medicines	10,572	11,688
(iv) Estimated value of Equipment	25,440	37,920
(v) Building (Less Depreciation)	48,000	45,600
(vi) Salaries Outstanding	120	240
(vii) Prepaid Salaries	—	360

Ans. Surplus—Rs. 7,416; Capital Fund—Rs. 2,12,659.20; Balance Sheet Total—Rs. 2,20,434.

10. Given below is Income & Expenditure A/c and Receipts & Payments A/c of Delhi Sports Club for the year ended 31st December 2007 :

INCOME & EXPENDITURE A/C

Dr. **For the year ended 31st Dec. 2007** **Cr.**

Expenditure	Rs.	Income	Rs.
To Salaries	12,900	By Entrance Fees	18,000
To Printing & Stationery	3,600	By Subscriptions	28,200
To Advertising	1,800	By Rent	7,500
To Audit Fees	1,200		
To Fire Insurance	1,500		
To Miscellaneous Expenses	7,350		
To Depreciation on Sports Equipments	4,500		
To Excess of Income over Expenditure	20,850		
	53,700		53,700

RECEIPTS & PAYMENTS A/C

For the year ended 31st Dec. 2007

Receipts		Rs.	Payments	Rs.
To Balance b/d		8,850	By Salaries	12,300
To Entrance Fees		18,000	By Printing & Stationery	4,500
To Subscriptions :			By Advertising	1,800
2006	1,425		By Fire Insurance	1,800
2007	27,300		By Investments	22,500
2008	1,050	29,775	By Sports Equipments	7,500
To Rent Received		6,750	By Miscellaneous Expenses	7,050
			By Balance c/d	5,925
		63,375		63,375

Additional Information :

The assets on 1st Jan. 2007 included Club Ground and Pavilion Rs. 72,000; Sports Equipments Rs. 37,500 and Furniture & Fixtures Rs. 9,000. On that date, subscriptions in arrears were Rs. 1,950 and subscriptions paid-in-advance were Rs. 300 and Creditors for Stationery were Rs. 900.

You are required to prepare Balance Sheet as at 31-12-2007. **[C.A. (Inter), Adapted]**

Ans. Capital Fund Rs. 1,28,100; Balance Sheet Total Rs. 1,52,100.

11. ABC Club was registered in a city and the Accountant prepared the following Receipts & Payments A/c for the year ended 31st October 2007 and showed a deficit of Rs. 20,328.

ABC CLUB RECEIPTS & PAYMENTS A/C
For the year ended 31st October 2007

Dr. Cr.

Receipts	Rs.	Payments	Rs.
To Subscriptions	86,982	By Premises	42,000
To Fair Receipts	10,080	By Honorarium to Secretary	16,800
To Variety Show Receipts (Net)	17,934	By Rent	3,360
To Interest	966	By Rates & Taxes	5,292
To Bar Collection	31,290	By Printing & Stationery	1,974
To Cash Spent more	1,400	By Sundry Expenses	7,490
To Deficit	20,328	By Wages	3,528
		By Fair Expenses	10,038
		By Bar Purchase Payment	24,214
		By Repairs	1,344
		By New Car (*Less* : Proceeds of old Car Rs. 12,600)	52,920
	1,68,980		1,68,980

The following additional information is obtained :

		1-11-2006 Rs.	31-10-2007 Rs.
1	Cash in hand	630	—
2	Bank balance as per Pass – Book	34,566	14,616
3	Cheques issued not presented for Sundry Expenses	378	126
4	Subscriptions due	5,040	4,116
5	Premises at cost	1,21,800	1,63,800
6	Accumulated Depreciation on Premises	78,960	—
7	Car at cost	51,198	65,520
8	Accumulated Depreciation on Car	43,218	—
9	Bar Stock	2,982	3,654
10	Creditors for Bar purchases	2,478	1,806

Cash over spent represent Honorarium to Secretary not withdrawn due to cash deficit. His annual honorarium is Rs. 16,800. Depreciation on premises and Car is to be provided @ 5% and 20% on W.D.V.

You are required to prepare the correct Receipts & Payments A/c, Income & Expenditure A/c and Balance Sheet as at 31st October 2007. **[ICWA (Adapted)]**

Ans. Balance Cash-in-hand Rs. 14,490; Surplus Rs. 60,886; Capital Fund Rs. 91,182; Balance Sheet Total Rs. 1,55,274.

12. The following summary of the Cash Book has been prepared by the Treasurer of the Club.

RECEIPTS & PAYMENTS A/C

For the year ended 31st March 2008

Dr. Cr.

	Rs.		Rs.
To Balance b/d	4,110	By Wages Outdoor Staff	20,070
To Subscriptions	44,580	By Restaurant Purchases	75,600
To Entrance Fees	4,800	By Rent (18 Months to July 08)	11,250
To Restaurant Receipts	85,200	By Rates	3,300
To Games Competitions Receipts	20,460	By Secretary's Salary	4,680
		By Lighting	11,550
		By Competition Prizes	6,000
		By Printing & Postage etc.	9,000
		By Fixed Deposit	12,000
		By Balance c/d	8,700
	1,62,150		1,62,150

On 1st April 2007, the Club's assets were :

Furniture	Rs.	72,000
Restaurant Stock	Rs.	3,900
Stock of Prizes	Rs.	1,200

Rs. 7,800 was owing for supplies to the restaurant. On 31st March 2008, the Restaurant Stock was Rs. 4,500 the prizes in hand were Rs. 750. While the Club owed Rs. 8,400 for restaurant supplies. It was also found that subscriptions unpaid at 31st March 2008 amounted to Rs. 1,500 and that of the figure of Rs. 44,580 shown in the Cash Book included Rs. 1,050 in respect of previous year and Rs. 600 paid in advance for the following year.

Prepare an Account showing Profit & Loss made on the Restaurant and a General Income & Expenditure A/c for the year ended 31st March 2008, together with Balance Sheet as at that date, after writing 10% off the Furniture.

Ans. Surplus Rs. 4,740; Capital Fund Rs. 75,585 (1-4-2007); Balance Sheet Total Rs. 94,125 (31-3-2008).

13. The following informations were obtained from the books of Delhi Club as on 31st March 2006, at the end of the first year of the club. You are required to prepare Receipts and Payments Account, Income and Expenditure Account for the year ended 31st March 2006 and a Balance Sheet as at 31st March 2006 on mercantile basis.

(i) Donations received for Building and Library Room Rs. 2,00,000

(ii) Other revenue income and actual receipts :

	Revenue Income Rs.	Actual Receipts Rs.
Entrance Fees	17,000	17,000
Subscriptions	20,000	19,000
Locker's Rent	600	600
Sundry Income	1,600	1,060
Refreshment Account	—	16,000

(iii) Other revenue expenditure and actual payments :

	Revenue Income Rs.	Actual Receipts Rs.
Land (Cost Rs. 10,000)	—	10,000
Furniture (Cost Rs. 1,46,000)	—	130,000
Salaries	5,000	4,800
Maintenance of Playground	2,000	1,000
Rent	8,000	8,000
Refreshment Account	—	8,000

Donations to the extent of Rs. 25,000 were utilised for the purchase of Library Books, balance was still unutilised. In order to keep it safe 9% Government Bonds of Rs. 1,60,000 were purchased on 31st March 2006. Remaining amount was put in the Bank on 31st March 2006 under the term deposit. Depreciation at 10% p.a. was to be provided for the whole year on Furniture and Library Books.

[C.A.(Foundation), Nov. 1998, Modified]

Ans. Closing balance of Receipts and Payments Account Rs. 1,08,140 (Overdraft)
Excess of Income over Expenditure (Surplus) Rs. 15,100
Total of Balance Sheet Rs. 3,40,440

14. The following Income and Expenditure Account of a club is given for the year ended on 31st March 2006 :

INCOME AND EXPENDITURE ACCOUNT
For the year ended 31st March 2006

	Rs.		Rs.
To Opening Stock of Provisions	17,500	By Subscriptions	1,50,500
To Purchase of Provisions	1,40,000	By Donations	52,500
To Salaries	1,05,000	By Entrance Fees	14,000
To Printing and Stationery	8,750	By Sale of Provisions	1,19,000
To General Expenses	5,250	By Closing Stock of Provisions	8,750
To Depreciation on Equipments	1,750		
To Surplus Excess of Income over Expenditure	66,500		
	3,44,750		3,44,750

The following further information is given :

BALANCE SHEET OF THE CLUB
As on 31st March 2005

Liabilities	Rs.	Assets	Rs.
Creditors for Provisions	14,000	Equipments (at written down value)	17,500
General Fund	64,750	Stock of Provisions	17,500
		Cash in hand and at Bank	35,000
		Subscriptions Receivable	8,750
	78,750		78,750

BALANCE SHEET OF THE CLUB
As on 31st March 2006

Liabilities	Rs.	Assets	Rs.
Creditors for Provisions	17,500	Equipments (at written down value)	26,250
General Fund	1,31,250	Stock of Provisions	8,750
		Cash in hand & at Bank	78,750
		Subscriptions Receivable	35,000
	1,48,750		1,48,750

Prepare a Receipts and Payments Account of the Club for the year ended 31st March 2006 from the above information. **[C.A. (Inter), Adapted]**

Ans. Total of Receipts and Payments Account Rs. 3,44,750.

❑❑❑

7 SINGLE ENTRY SYSTEM (ACCOUNTING FROM INCOMPLETE RECORDS)

It is a system of accounting which does not follow the 'Double Entry System' of accounting in its entirety. According to Kohler, "Single Entry System is a system of book keeping in which as a rule only records of cash and of personal accounts are maintained. It is always incomplete double entry varying with the circumstances." In other words, single entry system follows double entry system in respect of certain transactions where cash and personal accounts are involved as it is evident from the definition itself that "it maintains cash and personal accounts". Whereas in certain cases only single 'entry' (account) record is maintained in respect of transactions involving 'Cash' and 'nominal' or real accounts. And also it ignores transactions not involving cash and are of 'nominal' nature. Hence it is clear that single entry system follows different methods of recording in different circumstances of cases. For example cash paid to creditors and cash received from debtors involve cash and 'personal accounts' and help to determine amount due to creditors and amount due from customers and hence are recorded in the cash book and in the personal accounts of creditors and debtors. Similarly cash purchases, cash sales, expenses paid and purchase of assets for cash are recorded in the "Cash Book" only. There is no corresponding entry is any other book. Likewise purchases of goods on credit and sale of goods on credit basis are recorded in the personal accounts of creditors and debtors only without having any other separate record of such transactions. Whereas other transactions such as depreciation and bad debts are totally ignored and not recorded at all.

Thus it is clear single entry system maintains 'cash' and personal accounts and ignores real and nominal accounts.

Salient Features

(i) It maintain Cash Book which records personal and business transactions both. It maintains personal accounts and avoids real and nominal.

(ii) There is no system of keeping record of total sales or total purchases the same has to be ascertained from original vouchers.

(iii) It does not follows uniform policy or rule of recording all type of transactions. Its method of recording differs from transaction to transaction.

(iv) To prepare final accounts, this system is incomplete and does not provide all the necessary information which is required for the purpose.

(v) It maintains only fewer books of accounts and is suitable for sole traders (petty traders) only because they can manage with Cash Book and Personal Accounts only. However, it is simple and economical to follow.

Limitations :

(i) Since it does not provide complete information regarding most of the transactions, the final accounts cannot be prepared.

(ii) In the absence of double entry system in respect of all transactions arithmetical accuracy cannot be ensured as no Trial balance can be prepared.

(iii) This system is more prone to risk of fraud or errors as there is no other method to detect fraud or manipulation of books especially in the absence of double entry system.

(iv) It does not show the result of business operation in the absence of Trading Account which cannot be prepared, likewise true profits cannot be ascertained without preparing Profit & Loss Account.

(v) Since this system does not keep record of all assets and liabilities, a Balance Sheet cannot be prepared to know the financial position of the business.

(vi) It does not satisfy the information needs of users of accounting information such as of employees, management, investors, bankers etc. This system provides little information but for self-consumption of proprietor. Managerial decisions relating to future market, its trend, production planning and control cannot be taken with surety. Reasons of variations in the profits or sales cannot be ascertained.

(vii) Income Tax Authorities do not recognise single entry system of accounting for income tax purposes.

Distinction between Single Entry System and Double Entry System

Basis of Distinction	Single Entry System	Double Entry System
1. Recording of transactions	It records both the aspects of certain transactions, single aspect of some transactions and some other transactions are totally ignored.	It records both aspects of all transactions without any exception.
2. Maintenance of accounts	Cash, Bank and other Personal Accounts (Debtors and Creditors) are maintained. Nominal and real accounts are not maintained.	It maintains all types of accounts viz. real, personal and nominal
3. Maintenance of subsidiary books	It does not maintain Subsidiary Books like Purchases Book or bought ledger, Sales Book or Sold Ledger, B.R.. book and B.P. book. Single entry system maintains only Cash Book.	Under double entry system all types of subsidiary books are maintained.

4.	Arithmetical accuracy	Under single entry system the arithmetical accuracy of accounts cannot be checked as no Trial Balance can be prepared.	Under double entry system the arithmetical accuracy of the books of accounts can be cheked by preparing Trial Balance.
5.	Ascertainment of profits or losses	Profit or losses are ascertained rather estimated by preparing statement of affairs. In the absence of record of nominal accounts, trading and P & L account cannot be prepared.	Under double entry system the profits and losses are ascertained systematically by preparing Trading and Profit and Loss Account.
6.	Financial position	Under single entry system, the financial position of the business cannot be ascertained because in the absence of real accounts the balance sheet cannot be prepared. However a vague idea can be made.	Under this system the financial position is ascertained by preparing Balance Sheet since double entry system keeps complete and systematic record of all assets and liabilities.
7.	Cost involved	It does not involve much cost in terms of money, efforts and time because only a few books are maintained. It is economical as compared to double entry system	It involves greater cost as compared to single entry system because it is a complete scientific system of maintaining all business records.
8.	Suitability	It is suitable for small and petty sole traders	It is suitable for all types of organisations, sole trade, partnership and joint stock companies

Distinction between Balance Sheet and Statement of Affairs

	Basis of Distinction	Balance Sheet	Statement of Affairs
1.	Basis of preparation	It is prepared from the balances taken from ledger Accounts of various assets and liabilities. The balances form part of Trial Balance and there from are transferred to Balance Sheet.	It is prepared partly from balances taken from ledger accounts of some items, which are maintained on double entry basis and partly from estimates.
2.	Capital Balance	Capital Account is prepared separately or within Balance Sheet adjustments relating to drawings and profits are shown.	Capital is a balancing figure. It represents excess of assets over liabilities
3.	Accuracy	Balance Sheet ensures arithmetical accuracy as both sides of Balance Sheet agree. Any omission of any asset or liability can easily be traced.	As both the sides of statement of affairs do not agree automatically, it s is difficult to locate any error of omission of any item of asset or liability.
4.	Purpose	It aims to ascertain financial position of the enterprise and hence shows the true financial position as on the date of preparation.	It is prepared to ascertain the capital

ACCOUNTING PROCEDURE

Ascertainment of Profit or Losses

There are two methods of profit or loss calculations under single entry system:
(1) Statement of Affairs Method (2) Conversion Method.

(1) Statement of Affairs Method

This method is also known as "Net Worth" method. A statement of affairs is a statement of 'Assets & liabilities' of business on a particular date. Under this method two statements of affairs are prepared. First statement of affairs is based on the assets and liabilities on the first day of accounting year i.e. in the beginning and the second statement of affairs is prepared on the basis of assets and liabilities at the end. From these statements capital in the beginning and capital at the end is ascertained. If there are no drawings or capital introduced during the year, the difference between these two capitals is either Profit or Loss. This can be explained stepwise:

1. In case of new business, only statement of affairs at the end is prepared because capital in the beginning is given.
2. In case of an existing old business, firstly, the statement of affairs in the beginning is prepared in order to ascertain capital in the beginning.
3. Likewise a statement of affairs at the end is prepared to ascertain the capital at the end.
4. Capital at the end is increased by the amount of drawings made during the year and decreased by the amount of further capital introduced during the year.
5. Out of the balance (after step no. 4) capital in the beginning is compared and if there is excess of balance over initial capital, it is taken as profit whereas if the initial capital exceeds the balance or adjusted capital, it is treated as loss.

This profit or loss so ascertained is further adjusted for depreciation, interest on capital, interest on drawings, provision for bad and doubtful debts, the remainder is net profit or net loss. This can be shown as under:

STATEMENT OF PROFIT OR LOSS (A FORMAT)

		Rs.
Capital at the end before any adjustment		......
Add Drawings made during the year		......
		......
Less Capital introduced during the year, if any		......
Adjusted capital at the end		......
Less Capital in the beginning		......
Less Bad debts	......	
" Provision for Bad debts	......	
" Depreciation etc.	......	......
Net Profit		......

Illustration 1 (Simple)

On 1-1-2007 Mr. X started a business with Rs. 2,50,000. From the following prepare a statement of profit or loss for the ending 31st December 2007.

	Rs.
Cash and Bank Balance	15,000
Machinery	50,000
Computer	36,000
Debtors	1,90,000
Creditors	1,50,000
Investments	1,85,000
Bills Payable	85,000
Stock in trade	1,68,500
Bank Overdraft	56,000

The drawings during the year amounted to Rs. 1,25,000 and further capital introduced in the business Rs. 75,000. Write off Rs. 10,000 as bad debts and create a reserve for doubtful debts at 5%. Depreciate computer by 10% and machinery by 5%. There were outstanding salaries of Rs. 6,000 and prepaid rent of Rs. 2,500.

Solution :

Statement of Affairs
As on 31st December 2007

Liabilities	Rs.	Assets	Rs.
Sundry Creditors	1,50,000	Cash & Bank Balance	15,000
Bills Payable	85,000	Debtors	1,90,000
Bank Overdraft	56,000	Stock	1,68,500
Salaries O/s	6,000	Investment	1,85,000
Capital (Balancing figure)	3,50,000	Prepaid Rent	2,500
		Computer	36,000
		Machinery	50,000
	6,47,000		6,47,000

Statement of Profit or loss
For the year ended 31st December 2007

	Rs.	Rs.
Capital as per statement of affairs as on 31st Dec. 2007		3,50,000
Add drawings made during the year		1,25,000
		4,75,000
Less Capital introduced during the year		(75,000)
Adjusted Capital		4,00,000
Less Capital in the beginning (1-1-2007)		(2,50,000)
Profit before adjustments		1,50,000
Less Bad debts	10,000	
Provision for doubtful debts	9,000	
@ 5% on (1,90,000 – 10,000)		
Depreciation on computer @ 10%	3,600	
Depreciation on machinery @ 5%	2,500	(25,100)
Net profits for the year		1,24,900

Statement of Affairs (Adjusted)
As on 31st December 2007

Liabilities		Rs.	Assets		Rs.
Capital (1-1-2007)	2,50,000		Machinery	50,000	
Add Net Profit	1,24,900		*Less* Depreciation	(2,500)	47,500
	3,74,900		Computer	36,000	
Add Capital Introduced			*Less* Depreciation	(3,600)	32,400
during the year	75,000		Stock		1,68,500
	4,49,900		Debotrs	1,90,000	
Less Drawings	(1,25,000)	3,24,900	*Less* Bad debts	(10,000)	
Ceditors		1,50,000		1,80,000	
Bills Payable		85,000	*Less* 5% Provision	(9,000)	1,71,000
Bank Overdaraft		56,000	Investments		1,85,000
Salary O/s		6,000	Prepaid Rent		2,500
			Cash & Bank Balance		15,000
		6,21,900			6,21,900

Illustration 2 (Bank Balance not given)

Mr. Z had Rs. 5,10,000 in Bank on 1-1-2007. With this amount he started business. He keeps his records on Single Entry basis. His particulars of business were as under:

	As on 31-3-2007 Rs.	As on 31-3-2008 Rs.
Cash in Hand	3,400	5,100
Debtors	8,500	10,200
Stock	25,500	42,500
Creditors	6,800	3,400

On 1st February 2007 he began drawing Rs. 2,500 p.m. for his private expenses. His bank statement showed the following entries.

	Deposits Rs.	Withdrawls Rs.
1-1-2007	5,10,000	—
1-1-2007 to 31-3-2007	—	3,79,100
1-4-2007 to 31-3-2008	3,91,000	4,59,000

The above withdrawals included payments by cheque of Rs. 3,40,000 and Rs. 1,02,000 respectively during the periods from 1st January 2007 to 31st March 2007 and from 1st April 2007 to 31st March 2008 for the purchase of machinery for the business and deposits after 1st January 2007 consisted wholly sales price received from customers by cheques. Draw up statement of affairs of Mr. Z as on 31st March 2007 and on 31st March 2008 respectively and worked out his profit or loss for the year ended 31st March 2008. **[Company Secretaries-Adapted]**

Solution :

Statement of Affairs
As on 31st March 2007

Liabilities	Rs.	Assets	Rs.
Creditors	6,800	Cash in hand	3,400
Capital (Balancing figure)	5,01,500	Cash at Bank*1	1,30,900
		Debtors	8,500
		Stock	25,500
		Machinery	3,40,000
	5,08,300		5,08,300

*1 (5,10,000 – 3,79,100)

Statement of Affairs
As on 31st March 2008

Liabilities	Rs.	Assets		Rs.
Creditors	3,400	Cash in hand		5,100
Capital (Balancing figure)	5,59,300	Debtors		10,200
		Stock		42,500
		Bank Balance*2		62,900
		Machinery	3,40,000	
		Addition	1,02,000	4,42,000
	5,62,700			5,62,700

*2 (1,30,900 + 3,91,000 – 4,59,000)

Statement of Profit or loss

	Rs.
Capital as on 31-3-2008	5,59,300
Add Drawings @ 2,500	30,000
	5,89,300
Less Capital as on 1-4-2007	(5,01,500)
Profit earned during the year	87,800

Illustration 3 (Partnership Firm)

A, B and C carrying on business in partnership keep their books by 'Single Entry' on 31st December 2006, the statement of affairs was as under.

Liabilities	Rs.	Assets	Rs.
Creditors	54,500	Cash at Bank	35,250
A's Capital	2,19,000	Debtors	1,32,000
B's Capital	1,03,250	Stock	1,04,000
		Computers	71,250
		C's Capital	34,250
	3,76,750		3,76,750

On 31st December 2007 firm's assets and liabilities were as under:

	Rs.
Cash at Bank	11,750
Debtors	1,78,500
Stock	95,000
Computers	1,05,000
Creditors	87,750

A, B & C share profits and losses in the proportion of 3 : 2 : 2 and have drawn Rs. 1,750, Rs.1,000 and Rs. 750 per week respectively. Interest on capital and partner's overdraft at 6% per annum is to be provided.

You are required to calculate profit or loss for the year ended 31st December 2007 and the financial position of the firm as on that date.

Solution :

STATEMENT OF AFFAIRS

As on 31st December 2007

	Rs.		Rs.
Creditors	87,750	Cash at Bank	11,750
Capital (Balancing figure)	3.02,500	Debtors	1,78,500
		Stock	95,000
		Computers	1,05,000
	3,90,250		3,90,250

STATEMENT OF PROFIT OR LOSS

		Rs.
Capital as on 31st December 2007		3,02,500
Add Drawings:		
A 1,750 × 52	91,000	
B 1,000 × 52	52,000	
C 750 × 52	39,000	1,82,000
		4,84,500
Less Capital as on 31st December 2006		
A	2,19,000	
B	1,03,250	
	3,22,250	
Less Debit Balance of C	(34,250)	
	2,88,000	2,88,000
Profit before Adjustments		1,96,500

PROFIT & LOSS APPROPRIATION A/C

		Rs.		Rs.
To Interest on Capital :			By Profit	196,500
A	13,140		By Interest on Overdraft	2,055
B	6,195	19,335	(Debit Balance of C)	
To Net Profit transferred to:			(On Rs. 34,250 @ 6%)	
A's Capital		76,810		
B's Capital		51,205		
C's Capital		51,205		
		1,98,555		1,98,555

STATEMENT OF AFFAIRS (ADJUSTED)
As on 31st December 2007

Liabilities		Rs.	Assets		Rs.
A's Capital	2,19,000		Computer		1,05,000
Add Interest on Capital	13,140		Stock		95,000
Add Profit	76,810		Debtors		1,78,500
	3,08,950		Cash at Bank		11,750
Less Drawings	(91,000)	2,17,950	C's Capital	34,250	
B'S Capital	1,03,250		*Add* Drawings	39,000	
Add Interest on Capital	6,195			73,250	
Add Profit	51,205		*Add* Interest on O/D/	2,055	
	1,60,650			75,305	
Less Drawings	(52,000)	1,08,650	*Less* Net profit	(51,205)	24,100
Creditors		87,750			
		4,14,350			4,14,350

Conversion of Single Entry in to Double Entry

In view of limitations of single entry system, such as absence of the details of gross profit and net profit, a vague financial position presented by statement of affairs, non-disclosure of arithmetical inaccuracies, it becomes incumbersome to rely upon these accounting data for the purpose of decision-making. Thus it defeats the very purpose of accounting. In order to make accounting information more reliable and meaningful it is necessary to make single entry system in the perfect double entry. It is done through locating and finding out the various missing figures. It is to be noted that under single system only cash and personal accounts are maintained. Therefore in order to ensure arithmetical accuracy, to calculate gross and net profit in a systematic way, and to ascertain true financial position of the business, it is essential that the missing figures must be worked out. These missing figures include, credit purchases, credit sales, various items of nominal accounts (such as salaries, rent, stationery and other trading or manufacturing expenses whether these relate to factory, office or sales department) and various assets including old and new and the liabilities as such. This required a post mortem of Cash Book transactions and therefrom preparation of various ledger accounts. Thus it involves:

(i) Preparation of Cash book from the given information.

(ii) Sundry Debtors and Creditors Accounts including B/R & B/P accounts.

(iii) Opening and closing of various nominal accounts.

(iv) Preparation of various assets accounts such as Building, plant, furniture, stock etc. (i.e. Fixed Assets & Other Assets Accounts)

This can be done systematically according to the following steps:

(I) Prepare Statement of Affairs to calculate capital in the beginning. In case the statement of affairs cannot be prepared for want of information such as cash or Bank balance, debtors or creditors, Bills Receivables and Bills Payable, then the concerned accounts must be opened.

(II) Prepare Cash Book and find out opening or closing balance. In case these balances are given then the missing link may be either cash sales, cash collected from debtors, drawings, capital introduced during the year on an item of expense or income (Nominal Accounts).

(III) Prepare Sundry Debtors and B/R account, to calculate credit sales or opening or closing balance to ascertain credit purchases, opening or closing balance of creditors or B/P.

(IV) Cash book will provide the necessary details relating to various nominal accounts and other information will provide for outstanding and accrued besides the Real Account's balances.

Once these steps are completed, the Trial Balance can be drawn and Final Accounts prepared.

CALCULATION OF "MISSING FIGURES"

Illustration 4

From the following particulars you are required to ascertain credit purchases and credit sales.

	Rs.
Sundry Creditors as on 1-1-2006	43,500
Sundry Debtors as on 1-1-2006	68,900
Sundry Creditors as on 31-12-2006	35,700
Sundry Debtors as on 31-12-2006	65,750
Cash paid to creditors during the year	1,71,250
Cash received from credit customers during the year	3,82,000
Discount allowed to credit customers	5,600
Discount received from Suppliers	2,500
Returns Inwards	8,000
Returns Outwards	5,550
Bills Received from Credit Customers	12,500
Bills accepted during the year	7,500
Cash Sales	1,15,000
Cash Purchases	75,800
Bad debts	8,500

Solution : **SUNDRY CREDITORS' ACCOUNT**

	Rs.		Rs.
To Cash Paid	1,71,250	By Balance b/d	43,500
To Bill Payable (Bills Accepted)	7,500	ByCredit Purchases	1,79,000
To Discount Received	2,500	(Balancing figure)	
To Returns Outwards	5,550		
To Balance c/d	35,700		
	2,22,500		2,22,500

SUNDRY DEBTORS' ACCOUNT

	Rs.		Rs.
To Balance b/d	68,900	By Cash Received	3,82,000
To Credit Sales		By Bills Receivables	12,500
(Balancing figures)	4,13,450	By Returns Inwards	8,000
		By Discount Allowed	5,600
		By Bad debts	8,500
		By Balance c/d	65,750
	4,82,350		4,82,350

Illustration 5

From the following calculate Credit Sales and Credit purchases:

	Rs.
Debtors in the beginning	36,000
Creditors in the beginning	28,800
Debtors at the end	27,000
Creditors at the end	43,200
Cash received from Debtors	2,16,000
Cash paid to Suppliers	1,49,000
Discount allowed by suppliers	1,980
Discount allowed to customers	1,080
Bills received during the year	72,000
Bills issued during the year	57,600
Cash return to customers	3,600
Bad debts written off	8,640
Bad debts recovered	2,160
Bills endorsed to creditors	28,800
Bills receivable dishonoured	7,200
Endorsed Bills dishonoured	3,600
Bills receivable discounted	5,040

Discounted Bills dishonoured	5,040
Returns Inwards	4,320
Return Outward	1,440

Solution :

***SUNDRY DEBTORS' ACCOUNT**

	Rs.		Rs.
To Balance c/d	36,000	By Cash Received	2,16,000
To Cash returns	3,600	By Returns Inwards	4,320
To B/R Dishonoured	7,200	By Discount Allowed	1,080
To Creditors (Endorsed B/R dish.)	3,600	By Bills Receivable	72,000
To Bank (Discounted B/R dishonoured)	5,040	Bad Debts	8,640
To Credit Sales (Balancing figure)	2,73,600	By Balance c/d	27,000
	3,29,040		3,29,040

SUNDRY CREDITORS' ACCOUNT

	Rs.		Rs.
To Cash	1,49,000	By Balance b/d	28,800
To Discount Received	1,980	By Debtors (Endorsed Bill dishonoured)	3,600
To Bills Payable Account	57,600	By Credit Purchases	
To Bills Endorsed	28,800	(Balancing figure)	2,49,620
To Returns Outwards	1,440		
To Balance c/d	43,200		
	2,82,020		2,82,020

* **Note :** B/R discounted and Bad debts recovered will not be shown in Sundry Debtors A/c.

MISSING FIGURES AND FINAL ACCOUNTS

Illustration 6

A Trader keeps his records under single entry system. From the following particulars you are required to prepare Trading and Profit and loss Account for the year ended 31st March 2007.

Cash book analysis shows the following:

	Rs.
Cash Sales	1,80,000
Received from Credit Customers	3,00,000
Payments to Suppliers	1,77,000
Salaries	1,55,000
Personal withdrawals	24,000
Interest paid	1,200
Bank Balance (as on 31-3-2007)	29,100
Cash in hand (as on 31-3-2007)	900
Other Business Expenses	44,800

Other particulars were as under:	As on 31-3-2006	As on 31-3-2007
	Rs.	Rs.
Office Building	1,80,000	1,80,000
Furniture	12,000	12,000
Stock	1,08,000	1,22,640
Creditors	96,000	66,000
Debtors	2,64,000	3,60,000

Provide 5% interest on Capital as on 1-4-2006. Provide Rs. 18,000 for doubtful debts and 5% depreciation on all fixed assets. 5% group incentive commission to staff has to be provided for on net profit after meeting all expenses and commission. **[B.Com. (H), DU, Modified]**

Solution :

Calculation of Missing figures

Statement of Affairs

As on 1st April 2006

Liabilities	Rs.	Assets	Rs.
Creditors	96,000	Office Building	1,80,000
Capital (Balancing figure)	4,20,000	Furniture	12,000
Overdraft*	48,000	Stock	1,08,000
		Debtors	2,64,000
	5,64,000		5,64,000

CASH BOOK

	Rs.		Rs.
To Debtors Account	3,00,000	By Balance b/d (Overdraft)*	
To Sales	1,80,000	(Balancing figure)	48,000
		By Creditors (Suppliers)	1,77,000
		By Salaries	1,55,000
		By Drawings	24,000
		By Interest paid	1,200
		By Other Expenses	44,800
		By Balance c/d	
		Cash	900
		Bank	29,100
	4,80,000		4,80,000

SUNDRY DEBTORS' ACCOUNT

	Rs.		Rs.
To Balance b/d	2,64,000	By Cash	3,00,000
To Credit Sales (Bal. Figures)	3,96,000	By Balance c/d	3,60,000
	6,60,000		6,60,000

SUNDRY CREDITORS' ACCOUNT

	Rs.		Rs.
To Cash	1,77,000	By Balance b/d	96,000
To Balance c/d	66,000	By Credit Purchases (Bal. figure)	1,47,000
	2,43,000		2,43,000

TRADING AND PROFIT & LOSS ACCOUNT
For the year ended 31st March 2007

	Rs.			Rs.
To Opening Stock	1,08,000	By Sales :		
To Purchases	1,47,000	Cash	1,80,000	
To Gross Profit c/d	4,43,640	Credit	3,96,000	5,76,000
		By Closing Stock		1,22,640
	6,98,640			6,98,640
To Salaries	1,55,000	By Gross Profit b/d		4,43,640
To Other Expenses	44,800			
To Interest paid	1,200			
To Provision for doubtful debts	18,000			
To Depreciation on Office Building	9,000			
To Depreciation on Furniture	600			
To Interest on Capital	21,000			
To Group Commission*	9,240			
To Net Profit	1,84,800			
	4,43,640			4,43,640

(* Net Profit before commission x 5/105) * (1,94,040×5/105)

BALANCE SHEET
As on 31st March 2007

Liabilities		Rs.	Assets		Rs.
Capital	4,20,000		Office Building	1,80,000	
Add Net Profit	1,84,800		Less Depreciation	(9,000)	1,71,000
Add Interest	21,000		Furniture	12,000	
	6,25,800		Less Depreciation	(600)	11,400
Less Drawings	(24,000)	6,01,800	Stock		1,22,640
Creditors		66,000	Debtors (3,60,000–18,000 Provision)		3,42,000
Group Commission		9,240	Cash at Bank		29,100
			Cash in hand		900
		6,77,040			6,77,040

GRADED ILLUSTRATIONS

Illustration 1

Calculate total sales from the following information:

	Rs.
Bills Receivable on 1-1-2007	7,800
Debtors on 1-1-2007	30,800
Cash received on maturity of bills receivable during the month	20,900
Cash received from debtors	70,000
Bad debts written off	4,800
Returns inwards	8,700
Bills receivable dishonoured	1,800
Bills receivable on 31st January 2007	6,000
Debtors on 31st January 2007	25,500
Cash sales during the month	15,900

[C.S. Foundation, June 1998; B.Com. (H), DU, 1999]

Solution : **SUNDRY DEBTORS ACCOUNT**

	Rs.		Rs.
To Balance b/d	30,800	By Cash	70,000
To Bills receivable (Dishonoured)	1,800	By B/R	20,900
To Sales on Credit		By Return Inwards	8,700
(Balancing figure)	94,300	By Bad debts	4,800
		By Balance c/d	22,500
	1,26,900		1,26,900

BILLS RECEIVABLE ACCOUNT

	Rs.		Rs.
To Balance b/d	7,800	By Cash	20,900
To Debtors A/c (Bal. figure)	20,900	By Debtors A/c (Dishonoured)	1,800
		By Balance c/d	6,000
	28,700		28,700

Total sales = 15,900 + 94,300 = Rs. 1,10,200

Illustration 2 (Simple)

Mr. Z owns a general store in Delhi and does not maintain his accounts on Double Entry System. His assets and liabilities on 1st April 2007 were as follows:

	Rs.		Rs.
Bills Payable	2,000	Bank & Cash Balance	6,710
Creditors	3,310	Machinery	15,000
Debtors & Stock	18,600		

His position on 31st March 2008 was as follows:

	Rs.		Rs.
Machine	15,000	Cash in hand	3,000
Debtors	9,320	Bank Balance as per	
Motor cycle	12,000	Bank Statement	5,930
Stock	13,400	Creditors	8,700

During the year he had withdrawn Rs. 4,500 for household requirements and a motorcycle was purchased for business use. A cheque of Rs. 700 issued in March 2008 was not presented up to 31st March 2008.

Ascertain the amount of profit the year ending 31st March 2008 after making following adjustments:

(a) Write off Rs. 400 as bad debts and 5% reserve for bad & doubtful debts.

(b) Provide 8% depreciation on Machine and 10% on Motor cycle.

[B.Com. (Hons), DU, 1998-Modified]

Solution :

STATEMENT OF AFFAIRS
As on 1st April 2007

Liabilities	Rs.	Assets	Rs.
Bills Payable	2,000	Bank & Cash Balance	6,710
Creditors	3,310	Debtors & Stock	18,600
Capital (Balancing figure)	35,000	Machinery	15,000
	40,310		40,310

STATEMENT OF AFFAIRS
As on 31st March 2008

Liabilities	Rs.	Assets		Rs.
Creditors	8,700	Cash in hand		3,000
Capital (Balancing figure)	49,250	Cash at Bank	5,930	
		Less Unpresented	700	5,230
		Debtors		9,320
		Stock		13,400
		Motor cycle		12,000
		Machine		15,000
	57,950			57,950

STATEMENT OF PROFIT OR LOSS
For the year ended 31st March 2008

		Rs.
Capital as on 31st March 2008		49,250
Add Drawings made during the year		4,500
Adjusted Capital as on 31-3-2008		53,750
Less Capital as on 1-4-2007		(35,000)
Profit before Adjustment		18,750
Less	Rs.	
Bad debts	400	
Provision for doubtful debts 5% of (9,320 – 400)	446	
Depreciation on Machine @ 8%	1,200	
Depreciation on Motor cycle @ 10%	1,200	(3,246)
Net profit		15,504

Illustration 3 (Partnership)

A & B started business on 1st January 2007 with Rs. 75,000 as Capital contributed equally but the profit sharing ratio was 3 : 2. Their drawings were Rs. 450 and Rs. 300 per month respectively. They had kept no accounts excepts the following information:

	As on 31-12-2007
	Rs.
Machinery at Cost	30,000
Stock in Trade	45,000
Debtors	75,000
Cash	3,000
Creditors	45,000
Outstanding Expenses	6,000
Bank Balance (as per Pass Book)	9,000

Provision is to be made for depreciation at 10% on the cost of machinery as at the end of year. Debtors on 31st December 2007 include Rs. 7,500 for goods sent on consignment at 25% above cost and goods were not sold by the end of 2007. A cheque for Rs. 1,500 had been deposited on 31st December 2007 but was credited on 2nd January 2008.

Determine the profits for 2007 and draw up a Balance Sheet as on 31st December 2007.

[C.A. (Inter), Nov. 1985-Modified]

Solution :

STATEMENT OF AFFAIRS
As on 31st December 2007

Liabilities	Rs.	Assets		Rs.
Creditors	45,000	Machinery		30,000
O/s Expenses	6,000	Stock in Trade	45,000	
Capital (Balancing figure)	1,11,000	*Add* Goods on Consignment (7,500 – 1,500)	6,000	51,000
		Debtors	75,000	67,500
		Less Goods on consignment	(7,500)	
		Bank	9,000	
		Add deposited but not credited	1,500	10,500
		Cash in hand		3,000
	1,62,000			1,62,000

STATEMENT OF PROFIT
For the year ended 31st December 2007

		Rs.
Capital as per Statement of Affairs as on 31-12-2007		1,11,000
Add Drawings:	Rs.	
A @ 450 p.m.	5,400	
B @ 300 p.m.	3,600	9,000
	Adjusted Capital	1,20,000
Less Capital as on 1-1-2007 (A & B)		75,000
Profit before Depreciation		45,000
Less Depreciation on Machinery @ 10%		3,000
	Net Profit	42,000
A's Share 3/5	25,200	
B's Share 2/5	16,800	

STATEMENT OF AFFAIRS (AFTER ADJUSTMENTS)
As on 31st December 2007

Liabilities		Rs.	Assets		Rs.
A's Capital (1-1-2007)	37,500		Machinery	30,000	
Add Profit	25,200		*Less* Depreciation	(3,000)	27,000
	62,700		Stock in Trade		51,000
Less Drawings	(5,400)	57,300	Debtors		67,500
B's Capital	37,500		Bank Balance		10,500
Add Profit	16,800		Cash in hand		3,000
	54,300				
Less Drawings	(3,600)	50,700			
Creditors		45,000			
O/s Expenses		6,000			
		1,59,000			1,59,000

Illustration 4 (Current Accounts)

A, B and C were in partnership and towards the end of the year 2007 most of their books and records were destroyed by fire. The Balance Sheet as on 31st December 2006 was as under:

Liabilities	Rs.	Assets	Rs.
Creditors	55,000	Cash	24,000
Capitals : A	45,000	Debtors	36,000
B	30,000	Stock	65,000
C	15,000	Machinery	14,400
Current Accounts :		Fixture and Fittings	6,000
A	1,450	Advance Payments	350
B	1,000	C's Current Account	1,700
	1,47,450		1,47,450

The partners drawings during the year 2007 were: A – Rs. 14,000, B – Rs. 10,000 and C – Rs. 6,500. A introduced Rs. 15,000 as additional Capital on July 1, 2007. On 31st December 2007, the cash was Rs. 32,000, Debtors, Rs. 40,250, Stock Rs. 59,000, Advance payments Rs.250 and Creditors Rs. 45,400. Machinery is to be depreciated by 10% and fixture and fittings at 7-½%, 5% interest is to be allowed on initial Capital. No interest is to be charged on drawings. The partners share profits in the proportions of 3 : 2 : 1.

You are required to prepare a statement, showing the net trading profit for the year 2007 and the division of the same between partners, together with the Balance Sheet as on 31st December 2007.

[B.Com. (H), DU, 2001-Modified]

Solution :

STATEMENT OF AFFAIRS
As on 31st December 2007

Liabilities	Rs.	Assets	Rs.
Creditors	45,400	Cash	32,000
Capital (Balancing figure)	1,06,500	Debtors	40,250
		Stock	59,000
		Advance payments	250
		Fixtures & Fittings	6,000
		Machinery	14,400
	1,51,900		1,51,900

STATEMENT OF PROFIT OR LOSS
For the year ended 31st December 2007

				Rs.
Total Capital as per Statement of Affairs as on 31-12-2007				1,06,500
Add Drawings:				
A	14,000			
B	10,000			
C	6,500			30,500
			Adjusted Capital	1,37,000
Less Total Capital as on 1-1-2007				
A	45,000			
B	30,000			
C	15,000			(90,000)
				47,000
Less Credit Balances of Current Accounts:				
A			1,450	
B			1,000	(2,450)
				44,550
Add Debit balance of Current Account: 'C'			1,700	1,700
				46,250
Less Capital introduced during the year (A)				(15,000)
Profit before Adjustments				31,250
Less Interest on Capital:	A	2,250		
	B	1,500		
	C	750	4,500	
Depreciation on Machinery			1,440	
Depreciation on fixtures & fittings			450	(6,390)
			Net Profit	24,860
A's Share 3/6	12,430			
B's Share 2/6	8,287			
C's Share 1/6	4,143			

STATEMENT OF AFFAIRS (ADJUSTED)
As on 31st December 2007

Liabilities		Rs.	Assets		Rs.
A's Capital	45,000		Machinery	14,400	
Add Introduced	15,000	60,000	*Less* Depreciation	(1,440)	12,960
B's Capital		30,000	Fixtures and Fittings	6,000	
C's Capital		15,000	*Less* Depreciation	(450)	5,550
A's Current Accounts:			Stock		59,000
Op. Balance	1,450		Debtors		40,250

Add Profit (Share)	12,430		Advance Payment		250
Add Interest on Capital	2,250		C's Current Account:		
	16,130		Op. Balance	1,700	
Less Drawings	(14,000)	2,130	*Add* Drawings	6,500	
B's Current A/c:				8,200	
Op. Balance	1,000		*Less* Share of Profit	(4,143)	
Add Share of Profit	8,287			4,057	
Add Interest	1,500		*Less* Interest on Capital	(750)	3,307
	10,787		Cash		32,000
Less Drawings	(10,000)	787			
Creditors		45,400			
		1,53,317			1,53,317

Illustration 5 (Unpresented Cheque)

'X' is a small cloth merchant who has not kept full double entry records. His position as on 1-1-2007 stood as under:

	Rs.		Rs.
Cash in hand	3,800	Bank Balance	34,750
Stock	63,000	Debtors	22,500
Furniture	10,000	Creditors	21,550

His Position at the end of 2007 was as follows:

Cash in hand	2,350	Bank Balances as per Pass Book	29,650
Stock	83,500	Debtors	31,600
Furniture	10,000	Mobike	20,000
Creditors	26,500		

During the year he had withdrawn Rs. 2,000 p.m. for his personal expenses and purchased a new Mobike for his business use for Rs. 20,000. A cheque of Rs. 5,000 issued on 31-12-2007 was presented for payment on 5-1-2008.

Prepare statement showing his trading result for the year ended 31st December 2007 and a Balance Sheet as on 31-12-2007 after :

(a) Providing 10% depreciation on furniture and 20% depreciation on Mobike,

(b) Writing off Rs. 1,600 as actual bad debts and

(c) Making a 5% provision for likely bad debts. **[C.A. (Entrance), June 1983-Adapted]**

Solution :

STATEMENT OF AFFAIRS
As on 1st January 2007

	Rs.		Rs.
Sundry Creditors	21,550	Cash in hand	3,800
Capital (Balancing figure)	1,12,500	Bank Balance	34,750
		Debtors	22,500
		Stock	63,000
		Furniture	10,000
	1,34,050		1,34,050

STATEMENT OF AFFAIRS AS ON 31ST DEC. 2007

	Rs.		Rs.
Creditors	26,500	Cash in hand	2,350
Capital (Bal. figure)	1,45,600	Bank Balance	
		(29,650 – 5,000 unpresented Cheque)	24,650
		Debtors	31,600
		Stock	83,500
		Mobike	20,000
		Furniture	10,000
	1,72,100		1,72,100

STATEMENT OF PROFIT OR LOSS
For the year ended 31st December 2007

		Rs.
Capital as per Statement of Affairs as on 31-12-2007		1,45,600
Add Drawings		24,000
Adjusted Capital		1,69,600
Less Capital as on 1st January 2007		(1,12,500)
Gross Profit		57,100
Less Bad debts	1,600	
Provision for Bad debts @ 5% on (31,600 – 1,600)	1,500	
Depreciation on Furniture @10%	1,000	
Depreciation on Mobike @ 20%	4,000	(8,100)
Net Profit		49,000

STATEMENT OF AFFAIRS (ADJUSTED)
As on 31st December 2007

Liabilities		Rs.	Assets		Rs.
Sundry Creditors		26,500	Cash in Hand		2,350
Capital (1-1-2007)	1,12,500		Bank Balance		24,650
Add Profit (Net)	49,000		Sundry Debtors	31,600	
	1,61,500		*Less* Bad debts	(1,600)	
Less Drawings	(24,000)	1,37,500		30,000	
			Less 5% Provision	(1,500)	28,500
			Stock		83,500
			Mobike	20,000	
			Less Depreciation @ 20%	(4,000)	16,000
			Furniture	10,000	
			Less Depreciation @ 10%	(1,000)	9,000
		1,64,000			1,64,000

Illustration 6 (Meeting business expenses out of personal fund)

From the following information, prepare a statement showing the profit of the year ending 31st March 2007 as well as Balance Sheet on that date.

X and Y carrying on business in partnership and sharing profits and losses in proportion of 2 : 1 have the following balances to the credit of their accounts shown in the books of firm as on 1st April 2006.

X Rs. 1,38,000, Y Rs. 72,000

On 31st March 2007, the position of the business was as follows:

	Rs.
Cash in hand	17,160
Cash at Bank	27,000
Sundry Debtors	1,00,000
Stock	1,20,000
Furniture	20,000
Sundry Creditors for goods	38,000
Creditors for Expenses	7,600

During the year, X had drawn Rs. 36,000 from the firm. He had sold some goods of the business for Rs. 10,800 and retained the proceeds himself. He had personally paid to some of employees of the firm Rs. 19,800 towards their salary, which he was entitled to be reimbursed. Y had withdrawn Rs. 15,000 in cash and taken some goods worth Rs. 3,000 for his personal use. He had personally paid towards some of the firm expenses Rs. 9,600 which he was entitled to be reimbursed. **[I.C.W.A. (Inter), 1986-Adapted]**

Solution :

STATEMENT OF AFFAIRS
As on 31st March 2007

Liabilities	Rs.	Assets	Rs.
Creditors for expenses	7,600	Cash in hand	17,160
Creditors for goods	38,000	Cash at Bank	27,000
Capital (Balancing figure)	2,38,560	Debtors	1,00,000
		Stock	1,20,000
		Furniture	20,000
	2,84,160		2,84,160

STATEMENT OF PROFIT OR LOSS

				Rs.
Capital as per Statement of Affairs as on 31st March 2007				2,38,560
Add	Drawings in (Cash)	by X	36,000	
		by Y	15,000	51,000
Add	Drawings in goods	by X (Proceeds Retained)	10,800	
	Drawing in goods	by Y	3,000	13,800
				3,03,360
Less	Salary paid	by X	19,800	
	Expenses paid	by Y	9,600	(29,400)
				2,73,960
Less	Capitals of	X	1,38,000	
		Y	72,000	(2,10,000)
			Profit	63,960

STATEMENT OF AFFAIRS (ADJUSTED)
As on 31st March 2007

Liabilities		Rs.	Assets	Rs.
Expenses O/s		7,600	Cash in hand	17,160
Creditors for Goods		38,000	Cash at Bank	27,000
X's Capita	1,38,000		Debtors	1,00,000
Add Profit	42,640		Stock	1,20,000
Add Salary Paid	19,800		Furniture	20,000
	2,00,440			
Less Drawings*	(46,800)	1,53,640		
Y's Capital	72,000			
Add Profit	21,320			
Add Expenses paid	9,600			
	1,02,920			
Less Drawings*	(18,000)	84,920		
*(Cash + Goods)		2,84,160		2,84,160

CONVERSION

Illustration 7

Mr. Zed keeps his books on single entry system. From the following particulars prepare Trading and Profit & Loss Account for the year ended 31st December 2007 & a Balance Sheet as on that date.

	31-12-2006	31-12-2007
	Rs.	Rs.
Furniture	10,000	12,000
Stock	6,000	2,000
Debtors	12,000	14,000
Prepaid Expenses	—	4,000
Creditors	4,000	?
Outstanding Expenses	1,200	2,000
Cash	2,200	600

Receipts and payments during the year were as follows

Receipts from Debtors	42,000
Paid to Creditors	20,000
Carriage Inwards	4,000
Drawings	12,000
Sundry Expenses	14,000
Furniture purchased	2,000

Other Information : There were considerable amount of cash sales. Credit purchases during the year amounted to Rs. 23,000. Provide for doubtful debts to the extent of 10% on debtors.

[B.Com. (P) D.U, 1997, Adapted]

Solution : **TRADING AND PROFIT AND LOSS ACCOUNT**

For the year ending 31st December 2007

		Rs.			Rs.
To Stock-Opening		6,000	By Sales- Cash	8,400	
To purchases		23,000	Credit	44,000	52,400
To Carriage inwards		4,000	By Stock-closing		2,000
To Gross profit c/d		21,400			
		54,400			54,400
To Sundry expenses	14,000		By Gross profit b/d		21,400
Add Outstanding for 2007	2,000				
	16,000				
Less Outstanding for 2006	(1,200)				
	14,800				
Less Prepaid expenses	(4,000)	10,800			
To Provision for doubtful debts		1,400			
To Net Profit c/d		9,200			
		21,400			21,400

BALANCE SHEET

As on 31st December, 2007

Liabilities		Rs.	Assets		Rs.
Outstanding expenses		2,000	Cash in Hand		600
Creditors		7,000	Debtors	14,000	
Capital:			*Less* Provision	(1,400)	12,600
Op. Balance	25,000		Stock		2,000
Add Net Profit	9,200		Prepaid expenses		4,000
	34,200		Furniture	10,000	
Less Drawings	12,000	(22,200)	Additions	2,000	12,000
		31,200			31,200

Working Notes :

1. Calculation of Sales

TOTAL DEBTORS ACCOUNT

	Rs.		Rs.
To Balance b/d	12,000	By Cash	42,000
To Sales-Credit	44,000	By Balance c/d	14,000
	56,000		56,000

2. Calculation of Closing balance of creditors

TOTAL CREDITORS ACCOUNT

	Rs.		Rs.
To Cash	20,000	By Balance b/d	4,000
To Balance c/d	7,000	By Purchae — Credit	23,000
(bal. fig.)			
	27,000		27,000

3. Calculation of cash sales

CASH ACCOUNT

	Rs.		Rs.
To Balance b/d	2,200	By Creditors	20,000
To Debtors a/c	42,000	By Carriage inwards	4,000
To Sales-cash	8,400	By Drawings	12,000
(bal. fig.)		By Sundry expenses	14,000
		By Furniture	2,000
		By Balance c/d	600
	52,600		52,600

4. Calculation of opening capital

BALANCE SHEET
As on 1st January 2007

Liabilities	Rs.	Assets	Rs.
Outstanding expenses	1,200	Cash	2,200
Creditors	4,000	Debtors	12,000
Capital (bal. fig.)	25,000	Stock	6,000
		Furniture	10,000
	30,200		30,200

Illustration 8

The books of Mr. Brown showed the following figures:

	31-12-2006	31-12-2007
	Rs.	Rs.
Cash at bank	3,500	8,500
Cash in Hand	410	850
Stock in Trade	22,500	25,500
Sundry debtors	18,000	?
Sundry Creditors	8,000	7,300
Bills payable	20,000	18,000
Furniture and fittings	5,000	?
Outstanding salary	200	?

The cash book analysis showed the following figures amongst others :

	Rs.		Rs.
Receipts from customers	1,05,000	Drawings	6,000
Discount allowed to customers	1,300	Payments to creditors	19,000
Salary up to 31-12-2007	2,600	Discount received from creditors	2,600
Rent	3,600	Payments for bills payable	80,000
Sundry trade expenses	8,500		
Furniture Purchased on 1-07-2007	1,000		

Depreciation provided on furniture and fittings @ 10% per annum. No Figures are available for total sales. However he maintains a steady gross profit rate of 25% on sales.

Prepare Trading Profit and Loss account for the year ended 31st December, 2007 and the Balance Sheet as on that date. **[C.S. Foundation, Dec., Adapted]**

Solution :

CASH BOOK

Receipts		Rs.	Payments		Rs.
To Balance b/d			By salaries		2,600
Cash	410		By Rent		3,600
Bank	3,500	3,910	By sundry trade expenses		8,500
To Sundry Debtors		1,05,000	By Drawings		6,000
To Cash sales (bal. fig.)		21,140	By Furniture		1,000
			By Sundry Creditors		19,000
			By Bills payable		80,000
			By Balance c/d		
			Cash	850	
			Bank	8,500	9,350
		1,30,050			1,30,050

BILLS PAYABLE ACCOUNT

	Rs.		Rs.
To Cash	80,000	By Balance b/d	20,000
To Balance c/d	18,000	By Total Creditors A/c (bal. fig.)	78,000
	98,000		98,000

TOTAL CREDITORS ACCOUNT

	Rs.		Rs.
To Cash	19,000	By Balance b/d	8,000
To Discount	2,600	By Purchases-Credit	98,900
To Bills payable	78,000	(bal. fig)	
To Balance c/d	7,300		
	1,06,900		1,06,900

Note: Credit sales have been computed as under:

		Rs.
Opening Stock		22,500
Add Purchases		98,900
		1,21,400
Less closing stock		(25,500)
Cost of sales		95,900
Total sales	= (95,900 × 100/75) =	1,27,867
Cash Sales	=	21140
Credit sales	=	1,06,727

TOTAL DEBTORS ACCOUNT

	Rs.		Rs.
To Balance b/d	18,000	By Cash	1,05,000
To Sales-credit	1,06,727	By Discount	1,300
		By Balance c/d (bal. fig.)	18,427
	1,24,727		1,24,727

STATEMENT OF AFFAIRS
As on 1st January 2007

Liabilities	Rs.	Assets	Rs.
Creditors	8,000	Cash at bank	3,500
Bills Payable	20,000	Cash in hand	410
Outstanding salary	200	Sundry debtors	18,000
Capital (bal. fig)	21,210	Stock in trade	22,500
		Furniture and fittings	5,000
	49,410		49,410

TRADING & PROFIT AND LOSS ACCOUNT
For the year ending 31-12-2007

		Rs.		Rs.
To Opening Stock		22,500	By Sales	1,27,867
To Purchases		98,900	By Closing Stock	25,500
To Gross Profit c/d		31,967		
		1,53,367		1,53,367
To Discount		1,300	By Gross Profit b/d	31,967
To Salaries	2,600		By Discount	2,600
Less o/s of last Yr.	(200)	2,400		
To Rent		3,600		
To Sundry Trade Expenses		8,500		
To Depreciation @ 10% :				
on Furniture on Rs. 5,000 for 1 Yr.	500			
On Rs. 1,000 for 6 months	50	550		
To Net profit transfered to Capital A/c		18,217		
		34,567		34,567

BALANCE SHEET
As on 31st December 2007

Liabilities		Rs.	Assets		Rs.
Bills payable		18,000	Cash in hand		850
Sundry creditors		7,300	Cash at bank		8,500
Capital:			Sundry debtors		18,427
Balance	21,210		Stock		25,500
Add net profit	18,217		Furniture	5,000	
	39,427		Addition	1,000	
Less Drawings	(6,000)	33,427		6,000	
			Less Depreciation	(550)	5,450
		58,727			58,727

Illustration 9 (Making personal payment out of business fund)

Mr. X submits you the following figures relating to his business in respect of year ending 31st December 2007. You are required to prepare a Trading and Profit and Loss Account for the year ended and a Balance Sheet as at 31st December 2007. Any difference in the cash balance is assumed to be drawings.

	Rs.
Cash paid into Bank	1,50,000
Private dividends paid in the Bank	2,000
Private payments out of Bank	26,000
Payment for goods out of Bank	1,22,000
Cash received from Debtors	2,50,000
Payments for goods by Cash & Cheques	1,60,000
Wages	40,000
Delivery Expenses	7,000
Rent & Rate	2,000
Lighting & Heating	1,000
General Expenses	4,600

The assets and liabilities are as follows:

Assets/ Liabilities	As on 1-1-2007 Rs.	As on 31-12-2007 Rs.
Stock	20,000	15,000
Bank Balance	8,000	12,000
Cash in hand	300	400
Trade debtors	14,000	20,000
Trade creditors	27,300	30,000
Investments	50,000	50,000

[C.A. (Inter), Nov. 1986–Modified]

Solution : **(I) CALCULATION OF MISSING FIGURES**

Cash Book

	Rs.		Rs.
To Balance b/d	300	By Bank	1,50,000
To Debtors	2,50,000	By Wages	40,000
		By Creditors for goods (1,60,000 – 1,22,000)	38,000
		By Delivery Expenses	7,000
		By Rent & Rates	2,000
		By Lighting & Heating	1,000
		By General Expenses	4,600
		By Drawings (Bal. Figure)	7,300
		By Balance c/d	400
	2,50,300		2,50,300

BANK ACCOUNT

	Rs.		Rs.
To Balance b/d	8,000	By Drawings (Pvt. Payments)	26,000
To Cash (Deposit)	1,50,000	By Creditors (by cheque)	1,22,000
To Dividend transferred to Capital A/c	2,000	By Balance c/d	12,000
	1,60,000		1,60,000

SUNDRY CREDITORS' ACCOUNT

	Rs.		Rs.
To Cash	38,000	By Balance b/d	27,300
To Bank	1,22,000	By Purchases (Balancing figure)	1,62,700
To Balance c/d	30,000		
	1,90,000		1,90,000

DEBTORS' ACCOUNT

	Rs.		Rs.
To Balance b/d	14,000	By Cash	2,50,000
To Sales (Bal. figure)	2,56,000	By Balance c/d	20,000
	2,70,000		2,70,000

BALANCE SHEET
As on 1st January 2007

Liabilities	Rs.	Assets	Rs.
Creditors	27,300	Cash	300
Capital (Balancing figure)	65,000	Bank Balance	8,000
		Debtors	14,000
		Stock	20,000
		Investment	50,000
	92,300		92,300

II. TRADING AND PROFIT & LOSS ACCOUNT
For the year ended 31st December 2007

	Rs.		Rs.
To Opening Stock	20,000	By Sales (as per Debtors A/c)	2,56,000
To Purchases (as per Creditors A/c)	1,62,700	By Closing Stock	15,000
To Wages	40,000		
To Gross Profit c/d	48,300		
	2,71,000		2,71,000
To Delivery Expenses	7,000	By Gross Profit b/d	48,300
To Rent & Rates	2,000		
To Lighting & Heating	1,000		
To General Expenses	4,600		
To Net – Profit	33,700		
	48,300		48,300

BALANCE SHEET AS ON 31ST DECEMBER 2007

			Rs.		Rs.
Capital as per Op. B/s		65,000		Investments	50,000
Add Net Profit		33,700		Stock	15,000
Add Capital brought in		2,000		Debtors	20,000
		1,00,700		Bank Balance	12,000
Less Drawings	- Cash	(7,300)		Cash	400
	- Goods	(26,000)	67,400		
Creditors			30,000		
			97,400		97,400

Illustration 10 (Gift in Cash)

Mr. X commenced business on 1-1-2007 with a Capital of Rs. 99,000. He immediately purchased computer for Rs. 52,800. During the year he received from his uncle a gift of Rs. 6,600 and he borrowed Rs. 11,000 from his father. He had withdrawn Rs. 1,320 per month for his household expenses. He had no bank account and dealings were in cash. He did not maintain any books but following information is given:

	Rs.
Sales (including cash Sales of Rs. 66,000)	2,20,000
Purchases (including, Cash purchases of Rs. 22,000)	1,65,000
Carriage Inwards	1,540
Wages	660
Discount Allowed to Debtors	1,760
Salaries	13,640
Bad debt written off	3,300
Trade Expenses	2,640
Advertisement	4,840

He used goods worth Rs. 2,860 for personal purposes and paid Rs. 1,100 to his son for examination and College fees.

On 31st December 2007 his debtors were worth Rs. 46,200 and creditors Rs. 33,000. Stock in trade was valued at Rs. 22,000 computer to be depreciated by 10% p.a.

Prepare Trading and Profit & Loss Account for the year ended 31st December 2007 and Balance Sheet as at 31st December 2007. **[ICWA (Inter), June 1987-Adapted]**

Solution : **I. CALCULATION OF MISSING FIGURES**

(1) Cash Book

	Rs.		Rs.
To Capital	99,000	By Computer	52,800
To Loan from Father	11,000	By Purchases (Cash)	22,000
To Gift from Uncle	6,600	By Carriage Inwards	1,540
To Sales (Cash)	66,000	By Wages	660
To Debtors (Collection)*	1,02,740	By Salaries	13,640
		By Trade Expenses	2,640
		By Advertisement	4,840
		By Drawings (son's fees)	1,100
		By Creditors* (payment)	1,10,000
		By Drawings (Cash)	15,840
		By Balance c/d	60,280
	2,85,340		2,85,340

(2) TOTAL DEBTORS ACCOUNT

	Rs.		Rs.
To Sales (Credit)		By Cash (Bal. Figure)	1,02,740
(2,20,000 – 66,000)	1,54,000	By Discount Allowed	1,760
		By Bad debts	3,300
		By Balance c/d	46,200
	1,54,000		1,54,000

(3) TOTAL CREDITORS' ACCOUNT

	Rs.		Rs.
To Cash (Bal. figure)	1,10,000	By Balance b/d	—
To Balance c/d	33,000	By Purchases (Credit) (1,65,000 – 22,000)	1,43,000
	1,43,000		1,43,000

TRADING AND PROFIT & LOSS ACCOUNT
For the year ended 31st December 2007

		Rs.		Rs.
To Purchases	1,65,000		By Sales	2,20,000
Less Drawings (Self use)	(2,860)	1,62,140	By Closing Stock	22,000
To Carriage Inwards		1,540		
To Wages		660		
To Gross Profit c/d		77,640		
		2,42,000		2,42,000
To Salaries		13,640	By Gross Profit b/d	77,640
To Trade Expenses		2,640		
To Advertisement		4,840		
To Discount Allowed		1,760		
To Bad debts		3,300		
To Depreciation on Computer		5,280		
To Net Profit		46,200		
		77,640		77,640

BALANCE SHEET
As on 31st December 2007

Liabilities			Rs.	Assets		Rs.
Capital as on 1-1-2007		99,000		Computer	52,800	
Add Gift from Uncle		6,600		*Less* Depreciation	(5,280)	47,520
Add Net Profit		46,200		Stock		22,000
		1,51,800		Debtors		46,200
Less Drawings for:				Cash in hand (as per Cash Book)		60,280
Household	15,840					
Fees	1,100					
Goods	2,860	(19,800)	1,32,000			
Creditors			33,000			
Loan from Father			11,000			
			1,76,000			1,76,000

Illustration 11 (General)

The following facts have been ascertained from the records of M who maintains his books of accounts under single entry system:

Receipts for the year ended 31st March 2007:

	Rs.
From Sundry Debtors	88,125
Cash Sales	20,625
Paid in by proprietor	12,500
	1,21,250

Payments made during the year:	
New Plant purchased	3,125
Drawings	7,500
Wages	33,625
Salaries	5,625
Interest paid	375
Telephone	625
Rent	6,000
Light and Power	2,375
Sundry Expenses	10,625
Sundry Creditors	38,125
	1,08,000

It may be noted that 'M' banks all receipts and makes all payments by cheques. The assets and liabilities were as under:

	As on 31-3-2006 Rs.	As on 31-3-2007 Rs.
Sundry Creditors	12,625	12,000
Sundry Debtors	18,750	30,625
Bank Balance	3,125	?
Stock in Trade	31,250	15,625
Plant	37,500	36,575

From the above prepare Trading and Profit and Loss Account for the year ended 31st March 2007 and a Balance Sheet as on that date. **[C.S. (Foundation), Dec. 1994-Modified]**

[B.Com. (H) D.U., 2007]

Solution :

I. CALCULATION OF MISSING FIGURES

(1) STATEMENT OF AFFAIRS

As on 1st April 2006

	Rs.		Rs.
Sundry Creditors	12,625	Cash at Bank	3,125
Capital (Bal. figure)	78,000	Sundry Debtors	18,750
		Stock in Trade	31,250
		Plant	37,500
	90,625		90,625

(2) BANK ACCOUNT

	Rs.		Rs.
To Balance b/d	3,125	By Plant	3,125
To Sundry Debtors	88,125	By Drawings	7,500
To Sales	20,625	By Wages	33,625
To Capital (Additional)	12,500	By Salaries	5,625
		By Interest paid	375
		By Telephone	625
		By Rent	6,000
		By Light & Power	2,375
		By Sundry Expenses	10,625
		By Creditors	38,125
		By Balance c/d (Balancing figure)	16,375
	1,24,375		1,24,375

(3) SUNDRY DEBTORS ACCOUNT

	Rs.		Rs.
To Balance b/d	18,750	By Cash	88,125
To Credit Sales (Balancing figure)	1,00,000	By Balance c/d	30,625
	1,18,750		1,18,750

(4) SUNDRY CREDITORS ACCOUNT

	Rs.		Rs.
To Bank	38,125	By Balance b/d	12,625
To Balance c/d (Balancing figure)	12,000	By Credit Purchases	37,500
	50,125		50,125

II. TRADING AND PROFIT & LOSS ACCOUNT
For the year ended 31st March 2007

	Rs.			Rs.
To Opening Stock	31,250	By Sales:		
To Purchases (4)	37,500	Cash	20,625	
To Wages	33,625	Credit (3)	1,00,000	1,20,625
To Gross Profit c/d	33,875	By Closing Stock		15,625
	1,36,260			1,36,250
To Salaries	5,625	By Gross Profit b/d		33,875
To Interest paid	375			
To Telephone	625			
To Rent	6,000			
To Light & Power	2,375			
To Sundry Expenses	10,625			
To Depreciation (5)	4,050			
To Net Profit	4,200			
	33,875			33,875

BALANCE SHEET
As on 31st March 2007

Liabilities		Rs.	Assets		Rs.
Capital (1)	78,000		Plant	37,500	
Add Additional Capital	12,500		Addition made	3,125	
Add Net Profit	4,200			40,625	
	94,700		*Less* Depreciation*	(4,050)	36,575
Less Drawings	(7,500)	87,200	Closing Stock		15,625
Sundry Creditors		12,000	Sundry Debtors		30,625
			Bank Balance (2)		16,375
		99,200			99,200

* Being the Balancing figure-because closing balance of plant is already given. Alternatively, Plant Account may be prepared as follows:

PLANT ACCOUNT

	Rs.		Rs.
To Balance b/d	37,500	By Dep. (Bal. figure)	4,050
To Bank (Addition)	3,125	By Balance c/d	36,575
	40,625		40,625

Illustration 12

Mr. X is a tobacco merchant. He follows the practice of paying creditors for goods purchased through his Bank Account and making payments in cash on all nominal accounts.

	As on 1-1-2007	As on 31-12-2007
	Rs.	Rs.
Cash in hand	30	50
Cash at Bank	1,000	1,500
Sundry Debtors	1,750	2,500
Sundry Creditors	3,410	3,750
Investments	6,250	6,250
Stock	2,500	1,870
Transactions during the year:		
Salaries Paid		1,500
General Expenses Paid		3,500
Payment of Stationery		870
Payment of Rent & Rates		700
Lighting Charges paid		250
Cash Receipts from Debtors		31,250
Payment to Creditors through Bank and Trade expenses in Cash		20,000
Payment into bank—Business		18,750

Payment into Bank—Additional Capital	250
Payment into Bank—Personal	3,250
Cash payment—Personal	910
Stock taken for personal use	140

You are required to prepare Trading & Profit & Loss A/c for the year ended 31st December 2007 and a Balance Sheet as on that date. **[B.Com. (H), DU, 1995-Modified]**

Solution : **I. CALCULATION OF MISSING FIGURES**

(1) STATEMENT OF AFFAIRS AS ON 1-1-2007

Liabilities	Rs.	Assets	Rs.
Sundry Creditors	3,410	Cash in hand	30
Capital (Balancing figure)	8,120	Cash at Bank	1000
		Sundry Debtors	1,750
		Stock in Trade	2,500
		Investments	6,250
	11,530		11,530

(2) BANK ACCOUNT

	Rs.		Rs.
To Balance b/d	1,000	By Drawings	3,250
To Cash (Deposited)	18,750	By Creditors	15,250
To Capital (Additional)	250	By Balance c/d	1,500
	20,000		20,000

(3) CASH ACCOUNT

	Rs.		Rs.
To Balance b/d	30	By Salaries	1,500
To Debtors	31,250	By General Expenses	3,500
		By Payment for Stationery	870
		By Rent & Rates	700
		By Lighting Charges	250
		By Drawings	910
		By Bank (Deposited)	18,750
		By Trade Expenses (Balancing figure)	4,750
		By Balance c/d	50
	31,280		31,280

(4) SUNDRY DEBTORS' ACCOUNT

	Rs.		Rs.
To Balance b/d	1,750	By Cash	31,250
To Credit Sales (Balancing figure)	32,000	By Balance c/d	2,500
	33,750		33,750

(5) SUNDRY CREDITORS' ACCOUNT

	Rs.		Rs.
To Bank (20,000 – 4,750)	15,250	By Balance b/d	3,410
To Balance c/d	3,750	By Credit Purchases (Balancing figure)	15,590
	19,000		19,000

II. TRADING AND PROFIT & LOSS ACCOUNT
For the year ended 31st December 2007

		Rs.		Rs.
To Opening Stock		2,500	By Sales (Credit)	32,000
To Purchases	15,590		By Closing Stock	1,870
Less Drawings (goods used by X)	(140)	15,450		
To Gross Profit c/d		15,920		
		33,870		33,870
To Salaries		1,500	By Gross Profit b/d	15,920
To General Expenses		3,500		
To Stationery		870		
To Rent & Rates		700		
To Lighting Charges		250		
To Trade Expenses		4,750		
To Net Profit		4,350		
		15,920		15,920

BALANCE SHEET OF X
As on 31st December 2007

Liabilities		Rs.	Assets	Rs.
Capital (As on 1-1-2007)	8,120		Investments	6,250
Add Net Profit	4,350		Stock in Trade	1,870
	12,470		Sundry Debtors	2,500
Add Capital (Additional)	250		Cash at Bank	1,500
Less Drawings (Bank 3,250 + Cash 910 + Goods 140)	(4,300)	8,420	Cash in hand	50
Sundry Creditors		3,750		
		12,170		12,170

QUESTIONS

1. What do you understand by "accounting from incomplete records"? Explain its salient features and limitations.
2. Distinguish between 'Single entry system' and 'Double entry system'.
3. What is a 'statement of affairs'? How is it prepared? How far it is different or similar to Balance Sheet.
4. Explain the procedure of Conversion of single entry system into double entry system.
5. Explain the merits and demerits of single entry system. **[B.Com. (H), DU, 1995]**

PROBLEMS

1. Mr. A keeps his books by single entry system. On 1-1-2007, his position was as follows:
Sundry Creditors Rs. 30,000; Cash in hand Rs. 450; Cash at Bank Rs. 15,750; Sundry Debtors Rs. 60,000; Stock Rs. 15,000; Plant Rs. 30,000.
On 31-12-2007, the position was as indicated as below:
Sundry Creditors Rs. 52,500; Cash in hand 750; Cash at Bank Rs. 33,000; Sundry Debtors Rs. 73,500; Stock Rs. 18,000; Plant Rs. 67,500.
Mr. A drew Rs. 750 at the end of every month. He introduced Rs. 37,500 by way of additional capital. Depreciate Plant @ 10% and raise a reserve of 2½% against Sundry Debtors.
You are required to prepare a statement of Profit & Loss for the year and a statement of affairs for the year ending.
Ans. Capital as on 1-1-2007: Rs. 91,200; Capital as on 31-12-2007: Rs. 1,40,250; Net Profit: Rs. 13,838.
2. Following is the Statement of Affairs as at 31-3-2008, prepared by the accounts clerk of Mr. A, the wholesale dealer in Hosiery goods:

STATEMENT OF AFFAIRS AS AT 31-3-2008

	Rs.		Rs.
Sundry Creditors	24,375	Petty Cash	100
Capital	877,00	Stock	7,150
		Sundry Debtors	25,525
		Cash at Bank	4,225
		Furniture & Fixture	9,825
		Plant & Machinery	65,250
	1,12,075		1,12,075

It is now decided that the stock is overvalued by Rs. 775 that a debt of Rs. 1,050 owed by Mr. X is irrecoverable and that the furniture should have been reduced in value of Rs. 1,575. Redraft the statement after necessary corrections, showing separately the amount of current assets and the amount of fixed assets, state also the amount of working capital of the business.
Ans. Working Capital: Rs. 10,800.
3. Mr. X does not maintain complete double entry books of accounts. From the following details determine profit for the year statement of affairs as at the end of the year.
Rs. 2,200 (Cost) furniture was sold for Rs. 11,000 on 1-1-2007. 10% Depreciation is to be charged on furniture. Mr. X has drawn Rs. 2,200 p.m. Rs. 4,400 was invested by Mr. X in 2007.

	1-1-2007	31-12-2007
	Rs.	Rs.
Stock	88,000	1,32,000
Debtors	66,000	88,000
Cash	4,400	2,200
Bank	22,000	11,000 (Overdraft)
Creditors	33,000	55,000
Outstanding Expenses	11,000	17,600
Furniture (Cost)	6,600	4,400

Bank Balance on 1-1-2007 is as per Cash Book, but Bank overdraft on 31-12-2007 is as per Bank Statement. Rs. 4,400 cheques drawn in December 2007 have not been encashed within the year.

Ans. Capital as on 1-1-2007: Rs. 1,43,000; Net Profit: Rs. 17,160;
Total of statement of Affairs: Rs. 2,26,160.

4. Mr. Raman, a trader, does not keep proper books of accounts. However he provides the following particulars:

	31-12-2006	31-12-2007
	Rs.	Rs.
Cash at bank	45,000	30,000
Cash in hand	3,000	40,000
Stock in trade	4,00,000	4,50,000
Debtors	1,20,000	2,00,000
Equipments	50,000	50,000
Creditors	3,00,000	2,00,000
Furniture	40,000	40,000

During the year Raman introduced Rs. 60,000 as additional capital and withdrew Rs. 40,000 as drawings. Write off depreciation on furniture at 10 % and on equipment at 5%.

Prepare a statement showing the profit or loss made by him for the year ended on 31-12-2007.

[B.Com (P), D.U, 1998, adapted]

Ans. Opening Balance of Capital Rs. 3,58,000
Closing Balance of Capital Rs. 6,03,500
Profit Rs.- 2,25,500

5. A and B are partners in a firm sharing profits and losses as 5/8 and 3/8. They keep their books on Single Entry System. On 31-3-2007 a Statement of Affairs was prepared from their books and the following position was disclosed:

Liabilities		Rs.	Assets	Rs.
Capital :			Plant & Equipment	1,25,000
A	1,00,000		Stock	50,000
B	75,000	1,75,000	Debtors	1,00,000
Loan A/c-A		75,000	Cash	25,000
Creditors		50,000		
		3,00,000		3,00,000

The Assets and Liabilities as on 31-12-2007 were as follows:

Plant & Equipment Rs. 1,50,000; Stock Rs. 60,000; Debtors Rs. 1,25,000; Cash Rs. 65,000; Creditors Rs. 75,000; A's loan A/c Rs. 75,000.

(1) You are required to ascertain the profit or loss of the firm for the period ended 31-12-2007. The following adjustments are required:

(a) Depreciate Plant & Equipment @ 5% p.a. (assume additions to it were made on 31-12-2007). (b) Reserve for Bad Debts @ 2½%. (c) Allow Interest on A's Loan @ 6% p.a. (d) Partners Drawings amounted to: A: Rs. 4,500, B: Rs. 3,375 (e) Allowed interest on Capital @ 4% p.a.

(2) Draw up the Final Statement of Affair as at 31-12-2007.

Ans. Profit — A: Rs. 41,520, B: Rs. 24,915, Total of Statement of Affairs: Rs. 3,92,185.

6. Following is the Statement of Affairs of X, Y & Z as on 1-1-2007.

Liabilities		Rs.	Assets	Rs.
Sundry Creditors		41,400	Cash	2,300
Bills Payable		14,720	Stock	44,620
Capital A/cs:			Sundry Debtors	82,800
X	82,800		Plant & Machinery	55,200
Y	55,200	1,38,000	Capital A/c: Z	9,200
		1,94,120		1,94,120

During 2007, X & Y withdrew Rs. 2,760 & Rs. 2,300 per month respectively. On 31-12-2007 their assets and liabilities were as follows:

Cash Rs. 6,348; Stock Rs. 46,920; Sundry Debtors Rs. 53,360; Plant & Machinery Rs. 55,200; Sundry Creditors Rs. 27,600; Bills Payable Rs. 5,428.

You are required to prepare the Statement of Affairs as on 31-12-2007 after considering the following information:

(a) Depreciation is to be charged @ 5% on Plant & Machinery.

(b) Partners are entitled to interest on Capital @ 5% and partner having debit balance in capital A/c is to pay interest @ 5% also.

(c) X, Y & Z share profits & losses in the ratio 5 : 3 : 2.

Ans. Profit — X: Rs. 25,760; Y: Rs. 15,456; X: Rs. 10,304; Total of Statement of Affairs: Rs. 1,59,068.

7. X, Y and Z were in partnership, and towards the end of 2006, most of their books of records were destroyed by fire. The Balance Sheet as at 31-12-2007 was as follows:

Liabilities		Rs.	Amount	Rs.
Creditors		13,200	Cash at Bank	5,760
Capital A/cs:			Debtors	8,640
X	10,800		Stock	15,600
Y	7,200		Machinery & Plant	3,456
Z	3,600	21,600	Fixtures & Fittings	1,440
Curent A/cs :			Advance Payment	84
X	348		Current A/c: Z	408
Y	240	588		
		35,388		35,388

The partners' drawings during 2007 were – X: 3,360; Y: Rs. 2,400; Z : Rs. 1,560. On 31-12-2007: Cash at Bank was Rs. 7,680; Debtors Rs. 9,660; Advance payment Rs. 60; Creditors Rs. 14,496. Machinery is to be depreciated @ 10% p.a. and Fixtures & Fittings @ 7½% p.a. 5% interest is to be allowed on Capital, and partners share profit in the respective proportion of ½, 1/3 and 1/6.

You are required to prepare a statement showing the net trading profit for the year 2007 and the division of same between the partners, together with the Balance Sheet as at 31-12-2007.

Ans. Profit X: Rs. 2,983, Y: Rs. 1,988, Z: Rs. 995; Total of Balance Sheet: Rs. 36,796.

8. From the information given below, prepare a Trading and Profit & Loss A/c for the year ended 30th June 2001 and a Balance Sheet as at that date:

	Balance on 1-7-2007 Rs.	Balance on 30-6-2008 Rs.
Debtors	28,800	26,640
Creditors for purchases	10,800	8,640
Rent payable (Outstanding)	180	108
Cash	2,700	11,700
Stock	27,000	28,800
Plant	18,000	21,600

Cash transactions:

Receipts : Cash Sales – Rs. 1,800; Debtors – Rs. 1,27,800

Payments : Purchase of Plant – Rs. 3,600; Rent – Rs. 2,232; Cash Purchases – Rs. 3,600; Payment to Creditors – Rs. 56,160; Salaries – Rs. 36,000; Wages – Rs. 10,800; Electricity – Rs. 3,600. (Shortage is Cash Balance to be treated as Drawings). Bad Debts already written off Rs. 360. Depreciation on Plant has to be provided at 10%.

Ans. Capital as on 1-7-2007: Rs. 65,520; Net Profit: Rs. 17,100; Total of Balance Sheet: Rs. 86,760.

9. Mr. A keeps his books under Single Entry System. His Capital as at 1-1-2007 was Rs.1,50,000. An abstract of his cash transactions for the year ended 31-12-2007 was as follows:

	Rs.		**Rs.**
Balance b/d	25,000	Cash Purchases	37,500
Cash Sales	1,00,000	Wages	50,000
Collection from Debtors	1,50,000	Payment to Creditors	70,000
Capital Introduced	25,000	Bills Payable Paid	35,000
Bills Receivable Collected	50,000	Salaries	20,000
		General Expenses	10,000
		Drawings	37,500
		Plant Purchases	25,000
		Balance c/d	65,000
	3,50,000		3,50,000

Other particulars of his assets & liabilities were as follows:

	1-1-2007	31-12-2007
	Rs.	Rs.
Plant	50,000	75,000
Furniture	5,000	5,000
Bills Payable	20,000	25,000
Bills Receivable	22,500	32,500
Sundry Debtors	55,000	62,500
Sundry Creditors	37,500	40,000
Stock-in-trade	50,000	37,500

Your are required to draft a Trading and Profit & Loss A/c for the year ended 31-12-2007 and a Balance Sheet as at that date after providing for 5% interest on initial Capital and 2½% of further introduction, 5% reserve for doubtful debts, 2½% Reserve on Bills Receivable, 10% depreciation on Plant and 6% depreciation on furniture. **[C.A. Adapted]**

Ans. Capital on 1-1-2007: Rs. 1,50,000; Net Profit: Rs. 56,388; Total of Balance Sheet: Rs. 2,67,012.

10. From the following figures drawn from the books of Mr. B, who maintains his accounts as per Single Entry System, you are required to calculate total Sales:

	Rs.
Bills Receivable in the beginning of the year	35,100
Debtors in the beginning of the year	1,38,600
Bills Receivable encashed during the year	94,050
Cash Received from Debtors	3,15,000
	Rs.
Bad Debts written off	12,600
Returns Inwards	39,150
Bills Receivable Dishonoured	8,100
Bills Receivable at the end of the year	27,000
Debtors at the end of the year	1,14,750
Cash Sales as per Cash Book	1,26,702

[B.Com., Delhi-Adapted]

Ans. Credit Sales: Rs. 4,28,850; Total Sales Rs. 5,55,552; Bills received during the year Rs. 94,050.

11. From the following particulars extracted from the books kept under Single Entry System, you are required to find out the figures for credit sales and credit purchases by showing the Total Debtors A/c and Total Creditors A/c. Show also the Bills Receivable and Bills Payable A/c

	Rs.
Total Debtors on 1st January	22,125
Total Creditors on 1st January	13,455
Bills Receivable on 1st January	8,000
Bills Payable on 1st January	2,500
Cash Received from Debtors	86,175
Discount allowed to Customers	870
Bad Debts written off	1,275

Return Inward	1,725
Bills Receivable accepted by Customers	14,400
Cash paid to Creditors	59,070
Discount allowed by Creditors	645
Cash Received against Bills Receivable	15,000
Returns to Suppliers	780
Bills Payable accepted	9,600
Payments made against Bills Payable	7,000
Total Debtors on 31st December	20,835
Total Creditors on 31st December	14,175

[ICWA, Adapted]

Ans. Bills Receivable A/c balance on 31st Dec. Rs. 7,400; Bills Payable A/c Balance on 31st Dec. Rs. 5,100; Credit Sales: Rs. 1,03,155; Credit Purchases: Rs. 56,415.

12. X and Y are carrying on business in partnership sharing profit and losses in 1 : 1 ratio. They were unable to maintain full and complete records. From the following available information calculate the profits of the firm and prepare a Balance Sheet:

	As on 1-1-2007	As on 31-12-2007
	Rs.	Rs.
Land and Building (at cost)	1,25,000	1,25,000
Machinery (at cost)	1,50,000	1,87,500
Furniture (at cost	50,000	62,500
Stock	30,000	75,000
Debtors	42,500	55,000
Bank	12,250	12,500
Cash	2,750	12,500
Insurance Policy Premium Paid	12,500	–
Bills Receivable	–	20,000
Creditors	1,50,000	1,25,000
Bills Payable	25,000	–

At the beginning of the year the Capitals of the partners were equal. During the year X brought in Rs. 37,500 and B has withdrawn Rs. 12,500. Insurance Policy matured during the year for Rs. 25,000. A sum of Rs. 10,000 has become bad out of debtors. Debtors of Rs. 55,000 are before writing off bad debts. Provision has to be made for depreciation @ 10% on Land & Building, Machinery and Furniture.

[C.A. Entrance, Adapted]

Ans. Net Profit: Rs. 90,000; Balance Sheet: Rs. 5,02,500.

13. Following are the assets and liabilities of X and Y on 1-4-2000 (where X contributing $1\frac{1}{2}$ times of Y's Capital): Plant & Machinery Rs. 19,200; Stock Rs. 9,600; Debtors Rs. 19,200; Cash in hand and at Bank Rs. 12,000; Creditors Rs. 15,600.

Their position as on 31-3-2001 was as follows:

Cash in hand and at Bank: Rs. 1,920; Creditors Rs. 24,240; Debtors Rs. 10,560; Stock Rs. 10,080. X's drawings during the year had been Rs. 9,600 and Y's had drawn Rs. 7,440. Besides this X had withdrawn

Rs. 4,800 on 30-09-2000 from his Capital A/c. Depreciate Plant and Machinery by 10% and allow interest on Capital @ 5% p.a. Interest on drawings is to be ignored. You are required:

(1) To calculate Gross Profit, Net Profit before interest on Capitals and Net Profit after interest on Capitals.

(2) To prepare final Statement of Affairs showing Capitals of X and Y separately.

[C.S. Preliminary-Adapted]

Ans. Net Profit before interest on Capitals: Rs. 3,840; Divisible Profit after interest on Capitals: Rs. 2,280; Total of Final Statement of Affairs: Rs. 39,840.

14. A trader keeps his books by Single Entry. During the year 2007, he kept a Cash Book of which the following is the analysis:

	Rs.
Received from Sundry Debtors	96,000
Additional Capital introduced on 1-10-2007	12,000
Loan from X @ 16% p.a. on 1-7-2007	15,750
Paid to Sundry Creditors	86,550
General Expenses paid	5,850
Salaries Paid	4,500
Drawings	6,000
Deposits in the bank during the year	75,000
Withdrawals from the bank during the year	54,000

The following balances existed on 1-1-2007: Sundry Debtors Rs. 22,950, Sundry Creditors Rs. 17,250, Bank Overdraft Rs. 12,000, Building Rs. 63,750, Stock Rs. 32,700 and Cash Balance Rs. 900.

The following balances existed on 31-12-2007: Sundry Debtors Rs. 24,000, Sundry Creditors Rs. 17,850, and Stock Rs. 39,000.

Depreciate Building by 4% and Provide interest on X's loan.

Prepare Trading and Profit & Loss A/c for the year ended 31-12-2007 and Balance Sheet as on that date. Also prepare Sundry Debtors A/c. Sundry Creditors A/c, Cash A/c, Bank A/c, and Working notes in full, as part of your answer. **[C.A. Entrance, Adapted]**

Ans. Gross Profit: Rs. 16,200; Net Profit: Rs. 2,040; Balance Sheet: Total Rs. 1,33,950; Credit Sales: Rs. 97,050; Credit Purchases: Rs. 87,150; Cash Balance at the end: Rs. 750; Bank Balance at the end: Rs. 9,000; Opening Capital: Rs. 91,050.

15. From the following particulars prepare Bills Receivable Account and Total Debtor's Account for the year ended 31st December 2006

	Rs.
Total Debtors Account Balance on 1-1-2006	36,000
Bills Receivable Account Balance on 1-1-2006	10,000
Sales including cash sales Rs. 20,000 made during the year	3,00,000
Returns inward	15,000
Cash Received from Debtors during the year	2,00,000
Discount allowed to debtors	10,000
Bills receivable Endorsed to creditors during the year	10,000

Cash received for Bills matured during the year	15,000
Bad Debts written off during the year	3,000
Bills Receivable Account Balance on 31-12-2006	15,000

[B.Com (Hons.) D.U]

(Bills received from Debtors during the year Rs. 30,000 Debtors balance at end Rs. 61,000)

16. The position of Lal's business as on 1st January 2008 was as under:

Sundry creditors Rs. 17,000; Freehold Premises Rs. 50,000; Stock Rs. 25,000;

Sundry Debtors Rs. 20,000; Furniture Rs. 2,000.

An abstract of the Cash Book is appended below:

Receipts	**Rs.**	**Payments**	**Rs.**
Sundry Debtors	15,000	Overdraft (1-1-2008)	10,000
Cash Sales	80,000	Expenses	50,000
		Drawings	3,000
		Sundry Creditors	20,000
		Cash in Hand	2,000
		Cash at Bank	10,000
	95,000		95,000

The following additional information is available :

Closing Stock Rs. 30,000; Closing Debtors Rs. 25,000; Closing Creditors Rs. 12,000. No additions were made during the year to Premises and Furniture Account, but they are to be depreciated @ 10% and 15% respectively. A Bad Debts Provision of Rs. 2 ½ % is to be raised.

Prepare a Trading and Profit and Loss Account for the year ended 31st December 2008 and a Balance Sheet as on that date.

Ans. Gross Profit Rs. 90,000, Net Profit: Rs. 34,075, Balance Sheet Total Rs. 1,13,075

17. The books of A and B on July 2007 showed the following position:

	Rs.		Rs.
Capital	1,60,000	Goodwill	61,800
Profits undrawn	1,16,100	Fittings	46,700
Sundry creditors	30,700	Debtors	42,200
	3,06,800		3,06,800

During the six months ended December 31, 2007 the account of the business had been very imperfectly recorded, but an analysis of the bank transaction disclosed the following:

	Rs.		Rs.
Receipts from customers	7,08,000	Payments to creditors	3,01,200
Drawings of partners	2,72,000	Payments for Rent	31,500
Payments of salaries	61,000	Sundry expenses	12,800

No account was taken of the stock on December 31, 2007 but a schedule of debtors totalled to Rs. 18,900 and that of the creditors to Rs. 53,500 on that date.

Prepare a bank account, a Trading and Profit & Loss Account and a Balance Sheet as at 31st December 2007.

Ans. Gross Profit : Rs. 4,16,900 ; Net Profit : 3,11,600 ; Balance Sheet Total Rs. 3,69,200.

18. M commenced business as a cloth merchant on 1st January 2007, with a capital of Rs. 2,00,000. On the same day, he purchased furniture for cash Rs. 60,000. He keeps his books under single entry system.

From the following particulars prepare Trading and Profit and Loss Account for the year ended 31st December 2007 and a balance sheet as on that date.

	Rs.
Sales (including cash sales of Rs. 1,40,000)	3,40,000
Purchase (including cash purchase of Rs. 80,000)	3,00,000
M's Drawings	24,000
Salaries	40,000
Bad debts written off	10,000
Business Expenses	14,000
Stock of goods on 31-12-2007	1,30,000
Debtors on 31-12-2007	1,04,000
Creditors on 31-12-2007	72,000

M took cloth worth Rs. 10,000 from the shop for private use and paid Rs. 6,000 cash to his son but forgot to record these transactions in his books. Provide depreciation on furniture at 10%. **[B. Com. (Hons.), D.U]**

Ans. (Gross Profit Rs. – 1,80,000, Net profit Rs.- 1,10,000, Balance Sheet Total Rs. 3,42,000, Cash Balance at end Rs. 45,000 cash received from debtors Rs. 86,000, cash paid to creditors Rs. 1,48,000).

❑❑❑

Unit-III

8

DEPRECIATION ACCOUNTING

Depreciation is one of most important constituents of income determination. Usually a business is confronted with two types of problems. First one deals with the acquisition of capital assets and secondly, the accounting for its usage. That is how the cost of asset so incurred be allocated or apportioned against the annual revenue to justify its usage over its useful life. More rationally and accurately it is done, the more reliable shall be the accounting information for decision-making purposes.

Meaning of Depreciation

Depreciation refers to gradual decrease or loss in the value of asset due to usage, passage of time and normal wear and tear. This gradual fall in the value of the asset is of permanent nature, which cannot be made good by normal repair and maintenance.

International Accounting Standard Committee defines, "Depreciation is the **allocation** of the depreciable amount of an asset over its estimated life."

Whereas Accounting Standard (AS-6) issued by Institute of Chartered Accountants of India defines depreciation as follows :

"Depreciation is a measure of wearing out consumption or other loss of value of depreciable asset arising from use, effuxion of time or obsolescence through technology and market changes. Depreciation is allocated so as to charge a fair proportion of the depreciable amount in each accounting period during the expected useful life of the assets."

However, an extensive definition has been given by the Committee on Terminology of the American Institute of Certified Public Accountants (AICPA), which is stated below :

"Depreciation accounting is a system of accounting which aims to distribute the cost of other basic value of tangible capital asset less salvage if any, over the estimated useful life of the asset in a systematic and rational manner. It is a process of allocation, not of valuation. Depreciation for the year is the portion of the total charge, under such a system, that is allocated to the year. Although the allocation may properly take into account occurrence during the year, it is not intended to be the measurement of the effect of all such occurrences."

All the above definitions treat depreciation as a 'process of allocation of the cost of depreciable assets' over its useful life, but fail to elaborate 'what cost' and its basis of allocation.

However the following 'characteristics' of the depreciation may be noted.

1. Depreciation is charged on fixed and tangible assets only.
2. Depreciation is a gradual decrease in the value of fixed assets. Fall in the value of current assets are outside the preview of depreciation.
3. This gradual decrease is of permanent nature.
4. It is a process of allocation of cost of the asset over its useful life in a systematic way.
5. Depreciation covers not only loss of economic life due to normal wear and tear and usage but due to effluxion of time also.
6. The basis of charging depreciation is economic life of the asset and the cost thereof. Market value has no relevance for calculating depreciation.
7. Depreciation is a charge against profit and hence debited to Profit and Loss Account.
8. Depreciation represents only an estimate and not the exact amount.
9. Total depreciation cannot exceed the cost of the depreciable asset.
10. It is a non-cash charge and hence does not involve outflow of cash.
11. Depreciation is different and distinct from Amortisation, Depletion Obsolescence, Dilapidation and Fluctuation.

DEPRECIATION, DEPLETION, DILAPIDATION, AMORTISATION, OBSOLESCENCE & FLUCTUATION

Depreciation, as discussed earlier, refers to gradual and continuous decrease in the value of depreciable asset arising from usage, normal wear and tear and effluxion of time. This decrease is of permanent nature, which cannot be restored or made good even by routine repairs and maintenance. Depreciation accounting is related to periodic measurement of benefits arising from the asset and charging the same to yearly revenue. Thus, depreciation accounting is simply an application of 'Matching Principle'. In fact it is that part of cost of depreciable asset which is not recoverable.

Depletion refers to the systematic and rational allocation of the acquisition cost of natural resources over the period of their exhaustion during which these natural resources contribute to revenue. This applies to timber forests, coal-mines oil wells and stone quarries etc.

Dilapidation applies to lease hold assets. When such assets are returned to the owner after the expiry of lease period and if, under the terms and condition the leasehold property is to be returned in good condition as and when it was taken on lease. Then, a reasonable sum is set out each year to provide for dilapidation. Such amount is added to the cost of leased property, which is spread over the lease period. Thus dilapidation refers to cost of maintaining leasehold property.

Amortisation is the process of writing off the cost of intangible assets over a future period covering its expected useful life. This applies to writing off goodwill, patents, copyrights, trademarks and heavy organisation costs.

Obsolescence : Obsolescence refers to sudden and imminent fall in the value of assets due to technological changes or use of improved and new technology of production. The asset in use is rendered redundant and becomes economically unviable and unprofitable. In such a situation asset has to be discarded suddenly. Hence obsolescence is not gradual decrease in the value of the asset like that of depreciation but it is sudden and imminent.

Fluctuation : Fluctuation refers to a purely temporary variation in the market price of the asset. This variation may represent either fall or rise in the market price (value) of the floating assets and not fixed assets. Unlike depreciation, fluctuation is not a ongoing or continuing process. Fluctuation is worked out on the basis of change in market price as compared to cost price of the current asset concerned especially that of marketable securities or short term investments. Hence fluctuation is entirely different from depreciation and these two have no relationship with each other at all.

AT A GLANCE RECAPITULATION

S. No.	Nature of Assets	Type of Assets	Term used/Process of writing off
1.	Tangible assets A :	Land	Not applicable
	Tangible assets B :	Building, Plant & Machinery, Vehicles, Tools & Equipments etc.	Depreciation
	Tangible assets C : (Wasting assets)	Oil wells, Timber Forests, Coalmines, Mineral Deposits etc.	Depletion
2.	Intangible assets :	Goodwill, Copyrights, Trademarks, Patents etc.	Amortisation
3.	Leasehold assets :	Leasehold Building etc.	Dilapidation
4.	Floating assets :	Investments Marketable securities	Fluctuation

CAUSES OF DEPRECIATION

There is no one factor which can be held responsible solely causing depreciation but there are host of factors contributing to depreciation. However, the main factor which can be pointed out as the most decisive factor is the usage which reduces the service potential of an asset. Besides, there are many factors that cause decline in the service potential of the asset and hence requiring depreciation to be accounted for during its useful life.

1. **Usage :** Normal usage of any tangible fixed asset such as building, plant and machinery, furniture and fixtures, or motor vehicle bring physical deterioration which is caused by friction, movement, strain, vibration or even by weathering and chemical reaction. This physical deterioration of the asset cannot be made good by repairs and maintenance. Thus depreciation is that part or service potential of the asset which is expired and cannot be regained or recovered.
2. **Passage of time :** There are certain assets such as patents, copyrights and leasehold assets, which decrease in value with the effluxion of time. These assets generate revenue for a stipulated period of time for which these are acquired or paid for. After such period these assets lose their value even if the same are not used at all. Hence, such assets are written off during its stipulated life.
3. **Obsolescence :** When due to innovation or technological changes an existing asset in use becomes economically unviable it is said to have become obsolete and hence has to be abandoned. Obsolescence is also caused by change in fashion, government policy, customer's

demand/taste which render the asset useless to be discarded. Present era is witnessing fast or overnight changing technology and with rapid and quick changes in demands, plant and machinery and building structures often become obsolete before they wear out. Day-to-day challenges of the rival also keep the management on their toes to update their technology.

4. **Exhaustion or depletion :** This applies to the wasting assets which get physically exhausted due to continuous extraction. For instance natural deposits such as oils or mineral deposits, coalmines, timber forest and quarries are bound to be fully exhausted after some period of time. The amount to be written off depends upon the magnitude of consumption of wasting assets.
5. **Inadequacy :** When any asset fails to cope with the increasing volume of business activity and considered inadequate to meet the present requirement, such assets lose their usefulness and hence require replacement. However, these assets may lose usefulness for the existing company but may be useful for other business having relatively lower volume of business activity. Hence these assets should not be scrapped but sold to other business concern. Again a firm has to use its plant capacity to the optimum level. If production level does not permit to operate at optimum capacity, the plant or machinery or any other asset has to be abandoned for replacement.

OBJECTIVES OR NEED FOR PROVIDING DEPRECIATION

1. To ascertain true value of assets and financial position

Accounting, through Balance Sheet, aims to disclose true state of affairs or financial position as it shows the correct and proper value of assets after charging appropriate depreciation. If depreciation is not provided the value of assets will be shown at inflated value in the Balance Sheet thereby fixed assets will not represent true and correct state of affairs of business.

2. To calculate correct amount of profits or losses

Matching principle states that the expenses or cost (expired), which are incurred to earn revenue, must be charged to profit and loss account for the purpose of correct computation of profit. Depreciation on fixed assets represents expired cost of the assets which have been used for generating revenue and hence should be charged to P & L A/c. Like any other operating expenses as such. If depreciation is not provided the profits will be inflated and losses understated.

3. To make provision for replacement of worn-out assets

All the fixed assets used in the business need replacement after the expiry of their useful life. Sometime rapid change in technology, taste, fashion or demand renders the assets useless causing permanent loss in the value of assets requiring replacement. Annual charge to Profit and Loss Account makes it possible to retain necessary amount by way of depreciation to provide for replacement of the depreciating asset. The amount so provided either may be retained in business by ploughing back or invested in outside securities to make the funds available for replacement purposes. Practically the provisions so provided for depreciation help to recover the expired cost of the assets used, depleted or exhausted.

4. To compute cost of production

Depreciation not only helps in financial accounting in computation of profits but it is also an important element of cost determination process. In the absence of depreciation, it is very difficult to ascertain actual cost of production, process, batch, contract, order or of a product. Although the method , of charging (allocating) depreciation is totally different yet without depreciation no costing system is complete.

5. To comply with legal provisions of the Companies Act

Section 205 of the Companies Act 1956 provides that depreciation on fixed assets must be charged and necessary provision be made before the company distributes dividends to its shareholders. Hence depreciation is charged to comply with the provisions of the Companies Act.

6. To avail tax benefits

Income Tax Act also provides the deductibility of depreciation while computing business income. Hence charging of depreciation brings a net savings of cash resources equivalent to tax rate. The general rate for partnership firms, domestic companies and foreign companies 30% (including surcharge 10% & education cess 3%). However, for sole proprietors the slab rate of taxation is applicable.

COMPUTATION OF DEPRECIATION

Calculation of depreciation is not an easy process. There are several factors which affect the computation of depreciation. Some of the factors are given below.

1. Cost of the depreciable asset

Cost of the asset plays a decisive role in determining the amount of depreciation. Cost means historical cost of the asset. This notion is also supported by cost concept which states that the fixed assets should be recorded at cost to the firm. Cost for this purpose includes the catalogue price (less discount if any), freight or handling charges, legal charges, installation charges or transfer charges, sales tax, insurance in transit etc. which help in acquisition and putting the asset into working condition. When a second hand asset is purchased, the initial cost of putting the asset in working position such as cost of new parts, repairs/renovation etc. are added to the cost of assets.

However, interest on loan taken to purchase an asset, will not form part of cost of asset. But interest paid on a loan during construction period will be treated part of cost of an asset. According to AS-6 (Revised) "historical cost of depreciable asset represents money outlay or its equivalent in connection with its acquisition, installation and commissioning as well as additions to or improvement thereof. The historical cost of a depreciable asset may undergo subsequent changes arising as a result of increase or decrease in long term liability on account of exchange fluctuation, price adjustments, changes in duties or similar factors."

2. Useful life of the depreciable asset

According to AS-6 (7) the useful life of a depreciable asset is shorter than its physical life and is:

(i) Pre-determined by legal or contractual limits, such as expiry dates of related leases;

(ii) Directly governed by extraction or consumption;

(iii) Dependent on the extent of use and physical deterioration on account of wear and tear which again depends upon on operational factors such as number of the shifts the asset is to be used, repair and maintenance policy of the enterprise etc., and

(iv) Reduced by obsolescence arising from such factors as :

(a)Technological changes;

(b) Improvement in production method;

(c) Change in market demand for the product or service output of the asset; or

(d) Legal or other restrictions.

Further, the determination of useful life of a depreciable asset is a matter of estimation and is normally based on various factors including experience with similar types of assets. Such estimation is more difficult for an asset using new technology or used in the production of a new product on in provision of a new service but is nevertheless required on some reasonable basis.

Hence it is quite clear that the useful or economic life of a depreciable asset depends upon intensity of use, repairs and maintenance policy and other factors such as technological, legal or demand factors causing obsolescence.

With regard to addition or extension AS-6 (Revised) states "that such capital expenditure becomes an, integral part of the existing asset and is depreciated over the remaining useful life of that asset. As a practical measure, however, depreciation is sometimes provided on such addition or extension at the rate which retains a separate identity and is capable of being used after the existing asset is disposed off. These additions/extensions are depreciated independently on the basis of an estimate of its own useful life."

Residual value

It is an estimated amount, which is likely to be recovered when the asset is discarded and sold as scrap. However, the expenses incurred on sale or disposal must be deducted from the sale proceeds of discarded asset. According to AS-6, 'determination of residual value of an asset is normally a difficult matter. If such value is considered as insignificant, it is normally regarded as nil. On the contrary, if the residual value is likely to be significant, it is estimated at the time of acquisition/ installation or at the time of subsequent revaluation of the asset. One of the basis of determining the residual value would be the realizable value of similar assets which have reached the end of their useful lives and have operated under the conditions similar to those in which asset will be used.

Thus, the amount of depreciation is the function of three variables—the cost of asset, useful or economic life of the depreciating asset and the residual value thereof.

METHODS OF CHARGING DEPRECIATION

Depreciation accounting aims to allocate the cost of the depreciable asset in a rational and systematic manner over its useful life. Original cost of the asset is considered as deferred expenses, which are charged to Profit & Loss Account. There are several methods of allocation of cost of the asset which are known as methods of charging depreciation. These methods of depreciation are as under :

1. Straight Line Method

(b) Service Hours Method

(c) Productive Output/Depletion Method

2. Written Down Value Method
   (a) Sum of Year's Digit Method
   (b) Double Declining Method
3. Revaluation Method
4. Group Depreciation Method
5. Replacement Method
6. Annuity Method
7. Sinking Fund Method
8. Insurance Policy Method

1. Straight Line Method

Under this method a fixed amount is written off as depreciation and charged to Profit and Loss Account every year over the useful life of the depreciating asset. Thus the amount so charged year after year as depreciation does not change and remains constant except in the year of acquisition or disposal when the asset is used for lesser period than for twelve months. This suggests that this method depends upon the passage of time. The depreciable cost is allocated for each accounting year by dividing the total depreciable cost (C-S)* by the number of years of estimated life of the asset. As already stated the depreciation is the function of three valuables viz. cost of the asset, residual value and economic life of the depreciating asset. The formula for calculating annual depreciation and the rate thereof is as under :

$$\text{Annual Depreciation} = \frac{\text{*Cost of the asset} - \text{Residual value}}{\text{Number of years of useful life}}$$

or

$$D = \frac{C - S}{n}$$

$$\text{Rate of Depreciation} = \frac{\text{Annual Depreciation}}{\text{Cost of the asset}} \times 100$$

$$R = \frac{D}{C} \times 100$$

Example : A company purchased a Computer for Rs. 1,00,000 on 1-1-2005. The useful life is estimated ten years, whereas salvage value is considered to be nil. Calculate the amount and rate of depreciation.

$$D = \frac{C - S}{n} = \frac{\text{Rs. } 1,00,000 - \text{Nil}}{10}$$

$$\text{Annual Depreciation} = \text{Rs. } 10,000$$

$$R = \frac{D}{C} \times 100 = \frac{10,000}{1,00,000} \times 100 = 10\%$$

Suppose the salvage or residual value of the computer is Rs. 10,000 the amount and rate of depreciation will be as under :

$$\text{Depreciation} = \frac{\text{Rs. } 1,00,000 - 10,000}{10} = 9,000$$

$$\text{Rate} = r = \frac{9,000}{1,00,000} \times 100 = 9\%$$

Advantages :

1. This method is simple to understand, easy to apply and calculate amount of depreciation to be charged for each accounting year. Even additions or disposal does not pose any problem.
2. It reduces the written down value of the depreciating asset to zero if so desired. It means asset can be fully exhausted through use. No other method reduces the written down value to zero.
3. Since a fixed sum is charged each year it hardly distorts the profits after depreciation and thus makes profit figures comparable year after year.

Disadvantages :

1. The main drawback of this method is that whereas the depreciation of each year is equal, the expenses incurred on account of repairs and maintenance keep on increasing as the asset becomes older. As a result the Profit and Loss Account in the later years is charged heavily as compared to initial years. Thus it ignores effectiveness of the asset.
2. Interest on capital invested in the depreciating asset is totally ignored i.e. cost of capital is not considered under straight-line method.
3. The method does not take into account the usage of asset, but allocates depreciation on the basis of passage of time, which sounds illogical and improper. Even seasonal fluctuations or variations in output do not affect amount of depreciation to be charged.
4. This method allocates cost over useful life of the asset but does not provide for replacement thereof. It does not make any provision for availability of cash resources.

Suitability : Straight Line Method is suitable for those assets, which do not require regular repairs and renewals such as patents, copyrights, trademarks, leasehold rights. This method can also suit to furniture and fixtures also, which require very small amount of maintenance charges.

The straight line method can be applied on the basis of (a) Service Hours method and (b) Productive Output method.

(a) Service Hours Method

Under this method depreciation is charged on the basis of running time of the asset. This method measures the use of asset in terms of effective productive hours for which an asset can be put to used; throughout its economic life. That is the utility of the asset is directly related to working time. This method is useful where there are no chances of obsolescence. For instance, the cost of an asset is Rs. 4,50,000 and salvages value is Rs. 50,000 and life in terms of effective working hours is 20,000 hours.

$$D = \frac{C - S}{n} = \frac{4,50,000 - 50,000}{20,000} = \text{Rs. } 20 \text{ per service hour}$$

If the asset worked for 2,500 hours in a year the annual depreciation will be:

$$(2,500 \times 20) = \text{Rs. } 50,000$$

(b) Productive Output Method (or depletion method)

This method measures the effective or useful life of the depreciating asset in terms of physical output, thereby directly relating the utility of the asset to its productive use. This method is useful where output can effectively be measured. It is applicable for the exhaustion of natural resources. These natural resources exhaust or deplete by exploitation. The cost of natural resources is the price paid for its acquisition plus price paid for the development of such asset.

$$\text{Depletion per unit} = \frac{\text{Cost of Acquisition} + \text{Cost of Development}}{\text{Estimated physical output during the lease priod}}$$

It is suitable in case of extracting minerals from mines or stone quarries etc. where the output is easily estimated. Depreciation is calculated by multiplying the units of output by the cost per unit of output. For instance, if a coal-mine is taken on lease for 5 years at a price of Rs. 4,00,000 with an estimated total output of coal 5,000 tones, the rate of depreciation would be Rs. 80 per tone. If the output for the current year amounts to 800 tones, the depreciation to be charged to Profit and Loss Account would be Rs. 64,000 (800×80).

DECLINING DEPRECIATION CHARGE METHOD

2. Written Down Value or Diminishing Balance Method

Under this method a fixed percentage of written down value (cost less depreciation) of the asset is written off as depreciation every year till the amount is reduced to its scrap value. It should be remembered that while percentage of depreciation remains fixed but amount of depreciation goes on declining year after year. For example if an asset is acquired for Rs. 50,000 and depreciation is to be written off @ 20% p. a. on diminishing balance, then the depreciation will be calculated as under:

Cost/W.D.V.		**Depreciation**
Depreciation for the first year 20% of Rs. 50,000	=	Rs. 10,000
Depreciation for the second year 20% of (50,000 – 10,000 = 40,000)	=	Rs. 8,000
Depreciation for the third year 20% of (40,000 – 8,000 = 32,000)	=	Rs. 6,400
Depreciation for the fourth year 20% of (32,000 – 6,400 = 25,600)	=	Rs. 5,120

Since depreciation is charged on the book value or written down value, which keeps on decreasing year after year that is why the depreciation also declines gradually. Hence more depreciation is charged during the initial years of use as compared to subsequent years. Thus this method is known as reducing installment system of charging depreciation.

For the purpose of calculating rate of depreciation following formula shall be applied.

$$r = 1 - n\sqrt{\frac{S}{C} \times 100}$$

Where, r = rate of depreciation, n = expected useful life in years

S = Scrap or Salvage value, C = Cost of the asset

This method is suitable in respect of those assets, which require an increasing amount of repairs and renewals with the passage of time, such as plant and machinery, aircraft & Motor Car etc.

Merits :

(i) The impact of obsolescence is reduced to minimum as major portion of cost is written off in earlier years.

(ii) This method justifies the charging of less and less depreciation because of gradual decrease in service potential of the asset.

(iii) The Profit and Loss Account is charged almost uniformly because of declining depreciation and increasing cost of repairs and maintenance.

(iv) It is recognised by Income Tax Authorities.

Limitations :

(i) It is difficult to calculate the rate of depreciation and impossible when scrap value is presumed to be zero.

(ii) This method neither provides for replacement of asset nor makes any provision for any loss of interest on capital invested in depreciating assets.

(iii) The asset's written down value is never reduced to zero which implies that the asset is hardly to be depreciated to the fullest possible extent.

The written, down value method can also be applied on the following basis :

(a) Sum of Year's Digits Method (SYD)

(b) Double declining Method.

(a) This method is also based on diminishing balance but the basis of charging depreciation year after year is entirely different. It does not use mathematical formula for calculating rate of depreciation but it sums up years' digits of an asset's life span to be used as denominator and individual year's digit as numerator to be put in reverse order.

Example

A company purchased an asset costing Rs. 50,000. It is estimated to have a useful life of 5 years and expected to realise Rs. 5,000 as scrap. Calculate the yearly depreciation based on sum of years-digit method.

Solution : Sum of years-digits can be computed with the help of following formula :

Since life of assest is 5 years, $SYD = \frac{n(n+1)}{2} = 15$

$$\text{Depreciation} = \frac{\text{Number of years of the remaining life}}{\text{SYD}}$$

TABLE SHOWING CALCULATION OF DEPRECIATION UNDER SYD METHOD

Year Rs.	Opening Book Value	Depreciable cost (C – S) Rs.	Rate	Amount of Depreciation = (Depreciable Cost × Rate) Rs.
1	50,000	(50,000 – 5,000) 45,000	$\frac{5}{15}$	15,000
2	35,000	45,000	$\frac{4}{15}$	12,000
3	23,000	45,000	$\frac{3}{15}$	9,000
4	14,000	45,000	$\frac{2}{15}$	6,000
5	8,000	45,000	$\frac{1}{15}$	3,000

Hence scrap value is Rs. 5,000 (8,000 – 3,000).

(b) Double Declining Balance Method

Under this method, depreciation is charged on diminishing balance at double of the rate computed on the basis of straight-line method. However, scrap value of the depreciating asset is totally ignored and presumed to be zero for calculating depreciation. However, total depreciation should not exceed cost less scrap value. During the last year only the difference between the written down value and scrap value will be taken as amount to be charged as depreciation.

Example

A plant was acquired at a cost of Rs. 80,000. It is estimated to realise Rs. 6,200 as scrap at the end of its useful life of 5 years. Calculate depreciation for each year according to Double Declining Method.

Solution : *Step Ist* : Computation of rate of depreciation on the basis of straight line method, scrap value to be ignored.*

$$D = \frac{C-S}{n} = \frac{80,000 - \text{Nil}}{5} = 16,000$$

$$r = \frac{D}{C} \times 100 = \frac{16,000}{80,000} \times 100 = 20\%$$

Step IInd : Rate as per straight-line method × 2 = 20% × 2 = 40%

Year	Book Value in the beginning (Rs.)	Rate of Dep. %	Amount of Depreciation (Rs.)
1	80,000	40%	32,000
2	48,000	40%	19,200
3	28,800	40%	11,520
4	17,280	40%	6,912
5	10,368	40%	4,147**

** Depreciation in the fifth year will be taken to be the difference between written down value and the scrap value i.e. (10,368 – 6,200) = Rs. 4,168 and similarly if the salvage value of asset is estimated at Rs. 6,500, the depreciation in the fifth year will be taken at Rs. 3,868 (10,368 - 6,500) and not Rs. 4,147 as shown in the table.

3. Revaluation Method or Inventory System of Depreciation

This method is adopted when there are large-numbers of small value items of the assets or where the life of the assets is uncertain and calculation of depreciation is an uphill task. Separate account cannot be opened for each asset in the books of accounts. Hence these assets are valued on Balance Sheet date. The difference between the opening value of assets and closing value of assets is treated as depreciation as in case of loose tools. Those tools, which are in perfectly good condition, are valued at cost and rest are treated as scrap having no value.

Suitability : This method is applied in case of loose tools, live stock etc. because of their short and uncertain useful life and it is not possible to calculate depreciation on each item separately.

Example

On 01-01-2005 X Ltd. had a stock of loose tools worth Rs. 15,000. During the year loose tools worth Rs. 12,000 were purchased. On 31-12-2005 the loose tools were valued at Rs. 20,500. Calculate depreciation.

	Rs.
Opening Balance of loose tools as on 1-1-2005	15,000
Add : loose tools acquired during the year	12,000
	27,000
Less : loose tools at the end	(20,500)
Depreciation	6,500

Appraisal : It is easy to operate and apply. At the same time it is difficult to value each and every item of loose tools individually, because market value is totally ignored. Appreciation in the value is not taken into account at all.

Each year, Profit and Loss Account is charged with different figures of depreciation whereas asset serves more or less equally throughout its lifetime.

However, in case of unscrupulous person, the chances of fraud and dishonesty are more likely.

4. Group Depreciation

A business enterprise usually use numerous similar type of assets which have almost same life span and are of same value. Such assets are grouped together for the purpose of charging depreciation. Under this method average life expectancy determines the rate of depreciation. Hence depreciation is not calculated on the basis of individual life of an asset but on the basis of group as a whole. Any addition made during the year is added at cost and sale or disposal out of the group is credited to group account at its sales price. Depreciation is charged on the balance. The difference between the cost of the asset sold and its sales price is transferred to accumulated depreciation account.

Example

A company purchased 10 air conditioners @ Rs. 25,000 each. It is estimated that the salvage value of the air-conditioner after the useful life of eight years will be Rs. 5,000 each. At the end of the first year the company sold away one air-conditioner at Rs. 10,000 and at the beginning of second year it purchased 2 new air-conditioners in the group at Rs. 30,000 each. Calculate rate and amount of depreciation for the first, second, and third year.

Solution : Calculation of depreciation rate

	Rs.
Cost of 10 air-conditioners in the group	2,50,000
Less : scrap value of 10 ACs	50,000
Depreciable cost for 8 years	2,00,000

Depreciation per year 2,00,000 ÷ 8 = Rs. 25,000

$$\text{Rate of Depreciation} = \frac{25{,}000}{2{,}50{,}000} \times 100 = 10\%$$

Depreciation for the first year 10% of Rs. 2,50,000 =	25,000
Depreciation for the second year =	28,500
(2,50,000 – 25,000 + 60,000) = 2,85,000)	
Depreciation for the third year	28,500

Suitability : It is suitable for fans, cars, air-conditioners or numerous similar identical machines of the same value.

5. Replacement Method

This method of charging depreciation is usually used by Public Utility Corporations such as Water or Electricity companies. Under this system depreciation is not recorded during the lifetime of assets put to use but when it requires replacement. An amount equivalent to the cost of the new assets acquired less salvage value of the old worn out asset is charged as depreciation.

Example

On 1 -1 -2005 Delhi Vidyut Board intends to replace 100 worn-out electric poles which were installed in 1970 @ Rs. 200 each. At present each electric pole cost Rs. 500. It is estimated that each old pole will be sold as scrap @ Rs. 75 each. Find out the depreciation to be charged during the current year.

Solution : Cost of new poles :	Rs.
100 poles @ Rs. 500 each	50,000
Less scrap value of 100 poles @ Rs. 75	(7,500)
Depreciation to be charged during the 2005	42,500

6. Annuity Method

This method takes into account notional interest on the amount invested in the assets. It assumes that had the amount been invested outside it would have earned or yielded certain amount of interest. Thus such a notional interest calculated on reducing balance is debited to Asset Account and depreciation which is worked out on the basis of annuity table is credited to asset account by the end of each year. The amount of depreciation remains fixed but interest amount goes on declining.

In other words this method considers the loss of notional interest on the capital, which is invested and blocked in an asset, and thus this loss is included in the cost of asset by debiting the same to asset account. This is evident from the fact that depreciation charged includes not only the original cost but also the interest thereon.

It is suitable for leasehold assets where large sums are invested.

Merits :

(i) This method recognises the acquisition of assets as investment in business and thus charges interest thereon.

(ii) Depreciation calculation is more rational because it includes a part of capital plus interest on unexpired cost.

Demerits :

(i) Additions made during the year create lot of problems because calculations are difficult and complicate.

(ii) The combined cost of depreciation and repairs and maintenance is never the same year after year during the useful life of the asset.

(iii) It contradicts with the cost concept because assets are shown more than its cost price in the Balance Sheet.

Accounting Entries :

(i) On purchase of asset :	Asset A/c	Dr	at Cost Price
	To Bank A/c		
(ii) On charging of Notional Interest	Asset A/c	Dr	(Interest on initial/
	To Interest A/c		or opening balance)
(iii) On charging Depreciation	Depreciation A/c	Dr	(Amount ofDepreciation)
	To Asset A/c		

7. Sinking Fund or Depreciation Fund Method

All the methods of charging depreciation discussed so far, none of the methods provides for the replacement provisions. This method not only charges depreciation but also makes provision for replacement of asset on the expiry of its useful life. Under this method a certain sum, calculated on the basis of cost of the asset and sinking fund table, is written off every year by debiting Profit and Loss Account and crediting Sinking Fund or Depreciation Fund Account throughout the useful life of the asset. The amount so transferred to Sinking Fund Account is invested outside securities every year. The interest on such investment is also invested in similar securities, which enjoy high liquidity. The amount that is annually set aside as depreciation is such that this, with compound interest will be sufficient to provide a sum equal to the cost of the asset less residual value if any, by the end of the useful life of the asset. When the asset becomes useless, the investments are sold and money so received is utilised for purchasing a new asset. The old Asset Account standing at the original cost is closed by setting it off against the Depreciation Fund Account.

The asset (at cost) is shown on the assets side of the Balance Sheet. Depreciation Fund Account appears on the Liabilities side and Depreciation Fund Investment on the assets side.

The amount of depreciation can also be calculated by using the following formula:

$$\text{Depreciation} = \frac{1}{\frac{(1+r)\,n-1}{r}}$$

r = Rate of Interest

n = Life in number of years

Merits :

(i) Sinking Fund method provides necessary amount for the replacement of asset at the end of its useful life, because of annual investment in marketable securities. No other method provides funds for replacement.

(ii) This method continues to show the original cost of the asset and total depreciation charged till date, which may be of great importance for 'certain decision-making purpose'.

Limitations :

(i) Investment in securities is always subject to certain risk of price fluctuations which creates uncertainly about the actual amount at hand at the time of replacement.

(ii) Annual investment in securities does affect the working capital within the business because of yearly outflow of cash for the purchase of securities.

Accounting entries at the end of first year :

(i) Profit and Loss A/c Dr
To Sinking Fund A/c or Depreciation Fund A/c
(Being amount of annual depreciation transferred to sinking fund account)

(ii) Sinking Fund or Depreciation Fund Investment A/c Dr
To Bank A/c
(Being investment purchased out of amount of yearly depreciation)

Entries at the end of subsequent years except the last year :

(i) Bank A/c Dr
To Interest on Sinking Fund Investment A/c
(Being interest on investment received)

(ii) Interest on Sinking Fund Investment A/c Dr
To Sinking Fund A/c
(Being interest on Sinking Fund Investment transferred to Sinking Fund Account)

(iii) Profit & Loss Account Dr
To Sinking Fund A/c
(Being depreciation provided and transferred to Sinking Fund Account)

(iv) Sinking Fund Investment A/c Dr
To Bank A/c
(Being Sinking Fund Investment purchased out of amount of yearly depreciation including interest)

Entries at the end of useful life of asset :

(i), (ii) and (iii) entries shall be recorded as usual but the (IVth) entry will not be recorded because in the last year investments are not purchased but sold for the purpose of replacement o asset.

Bank A/c Dr
To Sinking Fund Investment A/c
(Being investments sold)

Sinking Fund Investment A/c Dr
To Sinking Fund A/c
(Being profit on sale of investments credited to Sinking Fund Account)

or

Sinking Fund A/c Dr
To Sinking Fund Investment A/c
(Being loss on sale of investments charged to Sinking Fund Account)

8. Insurance Policy Method

Under this method an insurance policy is effected for the sum sufficient to replace the asset when it is worn-out at the end of its useful life. An amount equivalent to the amount of yearly depreciation is paid to the insurance company by way of insurance premium each year. The lump sum amount so insured is paid back by the insurer to the insured on the maturity of policy. Thus it provides a risk free amount enough to replace the old worn out asset.

Merits :

(i) This method provides fund for replacement of old asset for the new one, which may be costlier than the previous one.

(ii) There is no need to work and think about portfolio management with regard to selection of securities. Efforts relating to buying and selling are totally eliminated. Risk arising due to price fluctuations in securities is fully averted.

Demerits :

(i) It is expensive because insurance premium is generally higher than the actual cost involved therein.

(ii) It puts additional burden and loss when there is need of replacement before the maturity date because of obsolescence etc.

1. Entry at the time of effecting a policy :

Depreciation Fund Policy A/c Dr
  To Bank A/c

2. Entry for annual depreciation :

Profit & Loss Account Dr
  To Depreciation Fund A/c

Both these entries shall be recorded during the policy period (or useful life of asset) each year.

On the maturity of policy :

Bank A/c Dr
  To Depreciation Fund Policy A/c

For Profit made on policy :

Depreciation Fund Policy A/c Dr
  To Depreciation Fund A/c

Closing entry :

Depreciation Fund A/c Dr
  To Old Asset A/c

On sale of asset as scrap :

Bank A/c Dr
  To Old Asset A/c

On Purchase of New Asset :

New Asset A/c Dr
  To Bank A/c

CHANGE OF METHOD OF CHARGING DEPRECIATION

The depreciation method once selected should be applied consistently to ensure comparison over the years. AS-6 states that "the method of depreciation is applied consistently to provide comparability of the results of the operations of the enterprise from period to period. A change from one method of providing depreciation to another is made only if the adoption of next method is required by statute or for compliance with an accounting standard or if it is considered that the change would result in more appropriate preparation or presentation of the financial statements of the enterprise. When such a change in the method of depreciation is made, the un-amortized depreciable amount of the asset is charged to revenue over the remaining useful life by applying the new method".

Hence it is quite clear that a business enterprise may change the method either :

(i) To comply with statutory requirements or

(ii) To enhance or improve quality of preparation or presentation of financial statements.

There are two ways to change the method of the depreciation :

*(i) A change made effective from the current year only

**(ii) A change in method with retrospective effect.

*When a change is made effective from the current year only, then unexpired cost of the asset should be charged to Profit & Loss Account over the remaining useful life of the asset by applying the new method of depreciation. Such a change is treated as a change in accounting policy and as such it is disclosed in the financial statements.

**When a change in the method of depreciation is made with retrospective effect then following steps must be taken.

(i) Find out the book value/cost of the assets in the beginning of year, from that date the change is to be made effective. For example if on 31st March 2001 it is decided to change the method with effect from 1st April 1998, then the book value of the assets on 1-4-1998 has to be worked out. And similarly if the change is to be made from the date of acquiring of such assets then cost of the assets has to be found out.

(ii) Find out total depreciation charged on the assets till date on the basis of old rate i.e. depreciation already provided.

(iii) Calculate the depreciation on the basis of new method with retrospective effect up to the end of previous year.

(iv) Find out the difference between (ii) and (iii) as above.

(v) Debit or credit the asset account by adjusting the difference. If there is an excess of old accumulated depreciation over the total depreciation calculated in accordance with the new rate, asset account will be debited with the difference. And if it is otherwise, asset account will be credited with the differential figure.

(vi) Charge depreciation according to new method for the current year.

METHODS OF RECORDING DEPRECIATION

There are two methods of recording depreciation in the books of accounts :

(1) When only "Asset Account" is maintained and Provision or Depreciation Account" is not maintained.

Under this method all entries relating to charging of depreciation, purchase or disposal of asset, profit or loss arising from disposal etc. are recorded in the asset account. The cost or book-value of the asset keeps on decreasing by the amount of yearly depreciation because the depreciation so calculated for the accounting period, is directly charged to asset account which is shown at its written down value (cost less depreciation) in the Balance Sheet. However, depreciation account is closed by transferring to Profit & Loss Account. Following entries are recorded :

(a) Depreciation A/c Dr
To Asset A/c
(Being depreciation charged)

(b) Profit & Loss A/c Dr
To Depreciation A/c
(Being depreciation transferred to Profit & Loss A/c)

Note : On sale or disposal of asset no separate account is opened. The profit or loss arising there-from is adjusted in the asset account itself.

(2) When a "Provision for Depreciation Account" is maintained and Asset Account is maintained at cost.

Under this method depreciation is not directly charged to Asset Account which continues to appear at original cost. The yearly depreciation keeps on accumulating under "Provision for depreciation account". However the closing entry for the depreciation does not change at all. It remains the same as was under first method. The total accumulated depreciation charged till date appears on the liabilities side of the Balance Sheet. In case any asset is discarded and disposed off, a separate account named 'Asset Disposal A/c' is opened. The asset at cost and accumulated depreciation charged till date on the discarded asset are transferred to "Asset Disposal Account" to ascertain the amount of profit or loss arising from sale of such asset. Following entries are recorded :

(a) Depreciation A/c Dr
To Provision for Depreciation A/c
(Being depreciation provided transferred to provision for depreciation A/c)

(b) Profit & Loss A/c Dr
To Depreciation A/c
(Being depreciation charged to Profit & Loss A/c)

(c) On disposal of asset

(i) Asset Disposal A/c Dr At Cost
To Asset A/c

(ii) Provision for Depreciation A/c Dr Total accumulated depreciation
To Asset Disposal A/c on the asset discarded
(Being accumulated depreciation on the asset discarded transferred to Asset Disposal A/c)

(iii) Bank A/c Dr
To Asset Disposal A/c With sale proceed
(Being discarded asset sold for cash)

(iv) Asset Disposal A/c Dr
To Profit and Loss A/c
(Being profit made on sale of asset)

or

Profit and Loss A/c Dr
To Asset Disposal A/c
(For loss incurred)

CHOICE OF METHOD OF DEPRECIATION OR SELECTION OF DEPRECIATION POLICY

The choice of method of depreciation depends upon various factors and considerations as it affects the result of trading operations, financial position and replacement policy and even expansion and diversification plan. A depreciation policy in a true sense aims to achieve managerial objectives as well as to protect and safeguard the interest of users of accounting information in general and company in particular. Management, while selecting the method of depreciation, analyses its financial and accounting implications especially in the light of organisational goals. An effective depreciation policy not only allocates the expired cost over the useful life of the asset in a rational and systematic way but it also ensures a uniform rate of return, a proper and adequate provision for replacement, availing maximum tax-advantage while complying the various legal provisions of Companies Act. Besides, it requires periodical review of depreciation policy in the light of changing technical, financial, economic, accounting and legal requirements of the business enterprises. Hence a continuous appraisal of the depreciation policy is a must to meet the fast changing requirements of the enterprise. This calls for the selection of a suitable method of charging depreciation. However, while selecting a depreciation policy following factors must be taken into account.

(1) Managerial Considerations

Depreciation policy is considered as an instrument of financial policy. It should aim to match the cost with revenue in more scientific and rational manner, because it has direct bearing on the income stream. Although it does not affect cash flow before tax, yet it has greater policy implications. A depreciation method which under-charges the Profit and Loss Account makes greater part available by way of distributable profits. However, an unwise dividend policy may distribute a large chunk of cash available hence affecting the process of replacement adversely. A depreciation method or a policy which helps management in arriving at appropriate decision shall be taken as a healthy and effective depreciation policy.

(2) Reporting Factor

Accounting Standard (AS-6) on reporting or disclosure states 'that the depreciation methods used, the total depreciation for the period for each class of assets, the gross amount of each class of depreciable assets and related accumulated depreciation are disclosed in the financial statements along with the disclosure of other accounting policies. The depreciation rates or useful lives of the assets are disclosed only if they are different from the principal rates specified in the statute governing the enterprise'.

Hence depreciation policy should be such which allocates depreciation as fairly as possible over the economic life of assets which is the most appropriate to the type of asset and its use in business. This will enhance the reliability of accounting information and credibility of the management.

(3) Technical Considerations

Depreciation decides the replacement policy, which in turn depends upon economic life or effective usage within the enterprise along with the availability of enough funds to meet the cost of replacement. However, in a present-day situation when technology is fast changing it is very difficult to estimate with precision the exact life of an asset or when the asset requires replacement. Now-a-days the economic life of machines is decided by technological advancement. Thus, a good depreciation policy should be able to recover depreciation at its earliest so that the company adapts to the new technology to compete with rivals to survive. The accumulated depreciation to replace old technique for new one depends not only on the rate of depreciation but also on the availability of profits to provide for depreciation. Business enterprises with high rate of profits during the earlier years should provide more depreciation initially as compared to later part of life when profits are less. Rapid technological changes demand an early accumulation of depreciation otherwise company will not have the enough resources to buy new technology.

(4) Legal Provisions

In case of a company, depreciation has to be charged either as per the provisions of Companies Act 1956 or Income Tax Act 1961. However, in case of a company any departure from such provisions can be made only when there is prior approval from Central Government. If the management's estimate of economic life of the asset is either longer or shorter than that provided under statute, depreciation rate lower or higher than that provided in the statute can be applied in accordance with the legal requirements (provisions).

From tax point of view depreciation is a deductible expense and hence profits which are set aside as depreciation become tax free. Business enterprises earning higher rate of profits should adopt, accelerated method of depreciation and amortisation so as to enjoy tax concession and save tax.

(5) Impact of Price Level Change

The price level change render most of the depreciation methods ineffective, because the accumulated depreciation at the end of the economic life of the asset is found insufficient for replacement purposes. Rising prices erode the value of money. An asset acquired, for instance, for Rs. 25,000 in 1998 may cost Rs. 40,000 in the year 2003 on the expiry of useful life. Hence total accumulated depreciation can provide only Rs. 25,000 whereas cost of replacement of the asset is Rs. 40,000. The gap of Rs. 15,000 is the impact of price level change due to inflationary pressure. Therefore, depreciation policy should be devised in a manner, which enhances the replacement capability of the business enterprise. However, these aspects are studied under 'Inflation Accounting' which provides depreciation on current cost rather than on historical cost.

Therefore, whichever method of charging depreciation is selected, it should be applied consistently from period to period. AS-6 clearly states that 'a change from one method of providing depreciation to another should be made only if the adoption of new method is required by statute for compliance with an accounting standard or if it is considered that the change would result in more appropriate preparation, presentation of the financial statements of the enterprises.

However, there is no one method, which satisfies and fulfils all the criterion discussed above. The selection strategy depends upon the type of asset, nature of the use of asset and the circumstances prevailing in the business. AS-6 recognises both simple (straight line) and accelerated (written down value) methods of depreciation.

Any how the use of accelerated methods of depreciation provide certain advantages over simple method of depreciation which are as under :

1. **Inflow of cash :** Depreciation is an expense, which does not result in outflow of cash. Accelerated Method provides larger amount of inflow of cash in the form of depreciation (being a non-cash charge) during the initial years. This way depreciation under Accelerated

Method, provides interest free loan, postpones tax liability and leaves lesser amount in the form of divisible profits to be used for paying dividends. The company will have lesser dependence on capital market for raising funds to meet its long term financial needs.

2. **Tax-benefit :** Depreciation is a deductible expense. Income Tax rules allow deducibility of depreciation on accelerated basis (written down value). Higher depreciation charges mean lower income and lesser tax liability. If accelerated method is used for tax shield purposes, these should not be used for reporting or presentation purposes. This method provides larger tax shield initially but higher tax at the end of useful life of the asset. Because total tax deducibility cannot exceed the cost of the asset.
3. **Facilitates expansion :** Accelerated method of charging depreciation provides funds to the growing companies who require large sum to be invested in fixed assets in the wake of expansion or modernisation programme. When a company is expanding, the higher depreciation amount will help and finance investment activities.
4. **Replacement of assets :** This method enhances the replacement capabilities of the company because it works as an incentive to replace old machinery and buy new one before the end of economic life in the event of any technological changes.

SALIENT FEATURES OF AS-6 : DEPRECIATION ACCOUNTING

1. Depreciable amount of a depreciable asset is its historical cost which should be allocated over the useful life of the asset.
2. The useful life depends upon :
   - Physical wear and tear,
   - Obsolescence,
   - Legal or other limits on the use of the asset.
3. The useful life, however, should be reviewed periodically. In case of any change in the life span of an asset, the unamortised depreciable amount should be spread over the revised remaining life of the asset concerned.
4. In case of change in the historical cost due to increase or decrease in long-term liability on account of exchange fluctuations/price adjustments, depreciation on unamortised depreciable amount should be provided prospectively.
5. Where there is a change in the written down value due to revaluation, the provision for depreciation should be based on the revalued amount and on the estimated remaining useful life of such asset.
6. Where any depreciable asset is disposed of, discarded, demolished or destroyed, the net surplus on deficiency, if material, should be disclosed separately.
7. The two popularly used and legally acceptable methods are :
   - Straight Line Method (SLM)
   - Written Down Value Method (WDVM)

   Any method so chosen should be applied consistently. However a change in method should be effected if :
   - It is required by statute or
   - For compliance with an accounting standard or
   - It is more appropriate in preparation and presentation of financial statements.

Necessary adjustment must be made in the accounts in the year in which method is changed. Such a change in accounting policy should be quantified and disclosed.

8. The following should be disclosed :
   - Historical cost or any other amount (revised cost due to revaluation) substituted for historical cost of each class of depreciable assets.
   - Depreciation charged for the period for each class of assets.
   - Total accumulated depreciation.
   - Method of charging depreciation.
   - Rates of depreciation/useful lives of the assets.

It is to be noted that disclosure requirements are meant for joint stock companies who must apply the rates of charging depreciation as per schedule XIV. Any variation from the specified rates, proper disclosure must be made by the reporting enterprise.

STRAIGHT LINE METHOD

Illustration 1 (Simple)

On 01-1-2006 company acquired Plant & Machinery for Rs. 64,000. On 01-04-2007 a part of plant costing Rs. 8,000 was sold for Rs. 4,800. The company acquired a new plant costing Rs. 16,000 on 01-10-2007.

Record journal entries and prepare Plant Account for the year ending on 31st December 2006 and 2007. Depreciation is charged @ 10% p.a. on straight-line method.

	Calculation of depreciation Rs.	Amount of Depreciation Rs.	
1. Depreciation for the year 2006 @ 10% for 12 months	Book Value (cost) $\frac{64,000 \times 10}{100}$	6,400	
2. Accounting year 2007			
Depreciation on part of plant sold @ 10% p.a. for 3 months	$\frac{8,000 \times 10 \times 3}{100 \times 12} = 200$	200	
Depreciation on the balance of the plant @ 10% p.a.	$\frac{56,000 \times 10}{100} = 5,600$	5,600	6,200
Depreciation on New plant for 3 months	$\frac{16,000 \times 10 \times 3}{100 \times 12} = 400$	400	

Loss on sale of part of Plant =	Written down value as on the date of disposal	Cost – total depreciation Rs. 8,000 – Rs. (800 + 200) = 7,000
	Less Sale Price	Rs. 7,000 – 4,800 = 2,200
		Loss = 2,200

JOURNAL ENTRIES

Date	Particular		LF	(Dr) Rs.	(Cr) Rs.
2006	Plant and Machinery A/c	Dr		64,000	
Jan. 1	To Bank A/c				64,000
	(Being Plant & Machinery purchased)				
Dec. 31	Depreciation A/c	Dr		6,400	
	To Plant & Machinery A/c				6,400
	(Being depreciation charged)				
	Profit & Loss A/c	Dr		6,400	
	To Depreciation A/c				6,400
	(Being depreciation debited to P & L A/c)				
2007	Bank A/c	Dr		4,800	
April 1	To Plant & Machinery A/c*				4,800
	(Being part of plant sold)				
	Depreciation A/c	Dr		200	
	To Plant & Machinery A/c*				200
	(Being depreciation charged for 3 months)				
	Loss on Sale of Plant A/c	Dr		2,200	
	To Plant & Machinery A/c*				2,200
	(Being loss on sale of part of plant)				
Oct. 1	Plant & Machinery A/c	Dr		16,000	
	To Bank A/c				16,000
	(Being new plant purchased)				
Dec. 31	Depreciation A/c	Dr		6,000	
	To Plant & Machinery A/c				6,000
	(Being depreciation charged)				
	Profit & Loss A/c	Dr		8,400	
	To Depreciation A/c				6,200
	To Loss on sale of Plant A/c				2,200
	(Being depreciation and loss on sale of part of plant charged to Profit & Loss A/c)				

*Alternatively one combined entry could have been recorded :

Bank A/c	Dr.	4,800	
Depreciation A/c	Dr.	200	
Loss on Sale of Plant A/c	Dr.	2,200	
To Plant & Machinery A/c			7,200

PLANT AND MACHINERY A/C

Date	Particular	Rs.	Date	Particular	Rs.
2006			2006		
Jan. 1	To Bank	64,000	Dec. 31	By Depreciation A/c	6,400
				By Balance c/d	57,600
		64,000			64,000
2007			2007		
Jan. 1	To Balance b/d	57,600	Apr. 1	By Bank A/c	4,800
Oct. 1	To Bank A/c	16,000	"	By Depreciation A/c	200
			"	By Loss on Sale of Plant A/c	2,200
			Dec. 31	By Depreciation A/c	6,000
			" "	By Balance c/d	60,400
		73,600			73,600
2008					
Jan. 1	To Balance b/d	60,400			

Illustration 2 (Provision for Depreciation A/c)

On 01-04-2006 X Ltd. purchased a Computer for Rs. 90,000 including Printer. It purchased another Computer on 01-10-2006 costing Rs. 60,000 and on 01-07-2007 costing Rs. 30,000. On 01-01-2008 the printer of the computer purchased on 01-04-2006 costing Rs. 30,000 became ineffective and was sold for Rs. 10,000.

(a) Prepare Computer A/c in the books of X Ltd. whose accounting year is the calendar year and charges depreciation @ 10% p.a. on Straight Line Method.

(b) Will it make any difference if 'Provision for Depreciation A/c' is maintained?

Solution : (a) **COMPUTER A/C**

Dr. Cr.

Date	Particulars	Rs.	Date	Particulars	Rs.
2006 Apr. 1	To Bank A/c	90,000	2006 Dec. 31	Dec. Depreciation A/c	8,250
Oct. 1	To Bank A/c	60,000		By Balance c/d	1,41,750
		1,50,000			1,50,000
2007 Jan. 1	To Balance b/d	1,41,750	2007 Dec. 31	By Depreciation A/c	16,500
July. 1	To Bank A/c	30,000		By Balance c/d	1,55,250
		1,71,750			1,71,750
2008 Jan. 1	To Balance b/d	1,55,250			
			2008 Jan. 1	By Bank A/c	10,000
				By Profit & Loss A/c	14,750
			Dec. 31	By Depreciation A/c	15,000
				By Balance c/d	1,15,500
		1,55,250			1,55,250
2009 Jan. 1	To Balance b/d	1,15,500			

(b) When 'Provision for Depreciation A/c' is maintained.

COMPUTER A/C

Dr. Cr.

Date	Particulars	Rs.	Date	Particulars	Rs.
2006			2006		
Apr. 1	To Bank A/c	90,000	Dec. 31	By Balance c/d	1,50,000
Oct. 1	To Bank A/c	60,000			
		1,50,000			1,50,000
2007			2007		
Jan. 1	To Balance b/d	1,50,000	Dec. 31	By Balance c/d	1,80,000
July 1	To Bank A/c	30,000			
		1,80,000			1,80,000
2008			2008		
Jan. 1	To Balance b/d	1,80,000	Jan. 1	By Computer Disposal A/c	30,000
			Dec. 31	By Balance c/d	1,50,000
		1,80,000			1,80,000
2009					
Jan. 1	To Balance B/d	1,50,000			

PROVISION FOR DEPRECIATION A/C

Dr. Cr.

Date	Particulars	Rs.	Date	Particulars	Rs.
2006			2006		
Dec. 31	To Balance c/d	8,250	Dec. 31	By Depreciation A/c(1)	8,250
		8,250			8,250
2007			2007		
Dec. 31	To Balance c/d	24,750	Jan. 1	By Balance b/d	8,250
			Dec. 31	By Depreciation A/c(2)	16,500
		24,750			24,750
2008			2008		
Jan. 1	To Computer Disposal A/c	5,250	Jan. 1	By Balance b/d	24,750
Dec. 31	To Balance c/d	34,500	Dec. 31	By Depreciation A/c(4)	15,000
		39,750			39,750
			2009		
			Jan. 1	By Balance b/d	34,500

COMPUTER DISPOSAL A/C

Dr. Cr.

Date	Particulars	Rs.	Date	Particulars	Rs.
2006			2006		
Jan. 1	To Computer A/c	30,000	Jan. 1	By Provision for Depreciation A/c*	5,250
				By Bank A/c	10,000
				By Profit & Loss A/c(3)	14,750
		30,000			30,000

Working Notes :

		Rs.
1.	Depreciation on Rs. 90,000 @ 10% p.a. for 9 months	6,750
	Depreciation on Rs. 60,000 @ 10% p.a. for 3 months	1,500
		8,250
2.	Depreciation on first Computer for one year	9,000
	Depreciation on second Computer for one year	6,000
	Depreciation on third Computer for 6 months	1,500
	(on Rs. 30,000 @ 10% p.a.)	16,500
3.	Loss on sale of printer :	
	Cost price of Printer	30,000
	Less Accumulated Depreciation	(5,250)
		24,750
	Less Sale Proceeds	(10,000)
		14,750
4.	Depreciation on First Computer excluding Printer	6,000
	Depreciation on Second Computer	6,000
	Depreciation on Third Computer	3,000
		15,000
	* Depreciation on Rs. 30,000 @ 10% p.a. for 9 months for the year 2006 (1-4-2006 to 31-12-2006)	2,250
	Depreciation for the 2007 (Rs. 30,000 @ 10% p.a.)	3,000
		5,250

Illustration 3 (Different Rates of Depreciation)

A company acquired the following assets as under :

1. On 01-01-2006 a plant costing Rs. 75,000 and having estimated life of 15 years.
2. On 01-04-2006 a plant costing Rs. 37,500 with an estimated life of 10 years.
3. On 01-07-2007 a plant costing Rs. 30,000 and its estimated life 8 years.
4. On 01 -05-2008 a plant costing Rs. 50,000 having an estimated life of 6 years.

On 01-07-2008 a part of the plant costing Rs. 15,000 on 01-01-2006 was sold for Rs. 8,400. Residual value of each of the plant acquired is 10% of its original cost. Company charges depreciation on Straight Line Method and closes its books of accounts on 31st December each year.

Prepare Plant Account for the years 2006, 2007 and 2008.

Working Note : $D = \frac{C-S}{n}$

		Rs.
1. Depreciation on Plant No. 1	$= \frac{75{,}000 - 7{,}500}{15}$	4,500 p.a.
2. Depreciation on Plant No. 2	$= \frac{37{,}500 - 3{,}750}{10}$	3,375 p.a.
3. Depreciation on Plant No. 3	$= \frac{30{,}000 - 3{,}000}{8}$	3,375 p.a.
4. Depreciation on Plant No. 4	$= \frac{50{,}000 - 5{,}000}{6}$	7,500 p.a.

5. Loss on Sale Plant No. 1 = Cost less Depreciation charged till the date of sale.
Rs. 15,000 - Depreciation @ 900* p.a. for 2 ½years (2,250) (Being 1/5 of yearly depreciation Written down value Rs. 12,750 - less Sales proceeds Rs. 8,400 = Rs. 4,350) i .e. $\frac{\text{Part of Plant sold}}{\text{Cost of the plant}}$

Solution : **PLANT A/C**

Dr. Cr.

Date	Particular	Rs.	Date	Particulars	Rs.
2006			2006		7,031
Jan. 1	To Bank A/c	75,000	Dec. 31	By Depreciation A/c	
				4,500 + (3,375 × 9/12)	
	To Bank A/c	37,500		By Balance c/d	1,05,469
		1,12,500			1,12,500
2007			2007		
Jan. 1	To Balance b/d	1,05,469	Dec. 31	By Depreciation A/c	9,563
				4,500 + 3,375 + (3,375 × 6/12)	
Oct.1	To Bank A/c	30,000		By Balance c/d	1,25,906
		1,35,469			1,35,469
2008			2008		
Jan. 1	To Balance	1,25,906	July 1	By Bank A/c	8,400
May 1	To Bank A/c	50,000		By Depreciation	450
				By Profit & Loss a/c	4,350
			Dec.	By Depreciation*	15,350
				By Balance c/d	1,47,356
		1,75,906			1,75,906

*Depreciation for the year 2008 has been worked out as follows :

On Ist plant (only 4/5 of 4,500)	3,600
(out of Rs. 75,000 worth Rs. 15,000 sold away	
On IInd Plant	3,375
On IIIrd Plant	3,375
On IVth Plant (Only for 8 months) (7,500 × 8/12)	5,000
	15,350

Illustration 4 (Insurance Claims)

Roshan Transport Company purchased 5 Lorries at Rs. 5,40,000 each on 1-1-2004. On 1-7-2007 one of the Lorries was involved in an road-accident and was completely destroyed. A sum of Rs. 1,75,000 was received from the Insurance Co. in full and final settlement. On the same date, another lorry was purchased by the company for Rs. 6,50,000. The company writes off 20% per annum on original cost and closes its books of accounts on 31st March each year.

Prepare Lorries Account & Depreciation A/c for ending 31st March 2007 and 2008 only.

Solution : **LORRIES A/C**

Dr. Cr.

Date	Particulars	Rs.	Date	Particulars	Rs.
2006			2007		
April 1	To Balance b/d(1)	14,85,000	March 31	By Depreciation A/c	5,40,000
				By Balance c/d	9,45,000
		14,85,000			14,85,000
2007			2007		
April 1	To Balance b/d	9,45,000	July 1	By Bank A/c	1,75,000
July 1	To Bank A/c	6,50,000		(Insurance claims)	
July 1	To Profit and Loss A/c(2)	13,000		By Depreciation A/c	27,000
			2008	By Depreciation A/c(3)	5,29,500
			March 1	By Balance c/d	8,76,500
		16,08,000			16,08,000

Working Notes :

1. Written down value of lorries on 01 -04-2006

		Rs.
Cost price of 5 lorries	Rs. 27,00,000	
Less Depreciation @ 20% p.a.		
For 2 years and 3 months	Rs. 12,15,000	14,85,000

2. Profit on Lorry involved in accident

Cost - Depreciation for 3 years and 6 months (Rs. 5,40,000 – Rs. 3,78,000) = 1,62,000

(Profit = Insurance Claims – Written down value)

Profit (Rs. 1,75,000 - 1,62,000) = 13,000

3. Depreciation for the year ending 31 st March 2008.

Full year's depreciation on 4 lorries	4,32,000
9 months depreciation on New lorry $\frac{6{,}50{,}000 \times 20 \times 9}{100 \times 12}$	97,500
Purchased on 01-07-2007	5,29,500

DEPRECIATION A/C

Dr. Cr.

Date	Particulars	Rs.	Date	Particulars	Rs.
2007			2007		
March 31	To Lorries A/c	5,40,000	March 31	By Profit & Loss A/c	5,40,000
		5,40,000			5,40,000
2007			2008		
July 1	To Lorries A/c	27,000	March 31	By Profit & Loss A/c	5,56,500
2008					
March 31	To Lorries A/c	5,29,500			
		5,56,500			5,56,500

DIMINISHING BALANCE METHOD

Illustration 5 (General)

On 1st January 2005 a plant was purchased for Rs. 2,00,000. On 01-01-2006 additions were made to plant of Rs. 1,00,000. On 31st March 2007, the plant purchased on 01-01-2006 costing Rs.30,000 was sold for Rs. 27,500 and on 30th June 2007, plant purchased on 01-01-2005 costing Rs.80,000 was sold for Rs. 66,750. On 1st October 2007 additions were made to the amount of Rs.50,000. Depreciation is provided @ 10% p.a. on Diminishing Balance Method.

Show the Plant Account for three years from 2005 to 2007. Books of Accounts are closed 31st December each year. **[ICWA (Inter) Modified]**

Solution :

PLANT A/C

Dr. Cr.

Date	Particulars	Rs.	Date	Particulars	Rs.
2005			2005		
Jan. 1	To Bank A/c	2,00,000	Dec. 31	By Depreciation A/c	20,000
				By Balance c/d	1,80,000
		2,00,000			2,00,000
2006			2006		
Jan. 1	To Balance b/d	1,80,000	Dec. 31	By Depreciation A/c	28,000
Jan. 1	To Bank A/c	1,00,000		By Balance c/d	2,52,000
		2,80,000			2,80,000

2007			2007		
Jan. 1	To Balance b/d	2,52,000	Mar. 31	By Bank A/c	27,500
Mar. 31	To Profit & Loss A/c(2)	1,175		By Depreciation A/c(1)	675
June 30	To Profit & Loss A/c(4)	5,190	June 30	By Bank A/c	66,750
Oct. 1	To Bank A/c	50,000		By Depreciaton A/c(3)	3,240
			Dec. 31	By Depreciation A/c(5)	17,270
				By Balance c/d	1,92,930
		3,08,365			3,08,365

Working Notes :

	Plant No. 1	Plant No. 2	Plant No. 3
Date of Acquisition	1-1-2005	1-1-2006	1-10-2007
	Rs.	Rs.	Rs.
Cost of Plant	2,00,000	1,00,000	50,000
Less Depreciation (2005)	20,000		
W.D.V. 1-1-2006	1,80,000		
Less Depreciation (2006)	18,000	10,000	
W.D.V. 1-1-2007	1,62,000	90,000	
Less W.D.V.* of part of plant on (1-1-2007)	64,800*	27,000*	
	97,200	63,000	
Less Depreciation (2007)	9,720	6,300	1,250
W.D.V. on 1-1-2008	87,480	56,700	48,750

Working Notes :

		Rs.	
I.*	Cost price of part of Plant purchased on 1-1-2006	30,000	
	Less Depreciation for the year 2006	3,000	
	W.D.V. on 1-1-2007	27,000	
	Less Depreciation for 3 months	675	(1)
	W.D.V. on 3 1-3-2007	26,325	
	Less Sale proceeds	27,500	
	Profit on sale	1,175	(2)
II	Cost price of part of plant purchased on 1-1-2005	80,000	
	Less Depreciation for the year 2007	8,000	
	W.D.V. on 1-1-2006	72,000	
	Less Depreciation for 2006	7,200	
	W.D.V. on 1-1-2007	64,800	
	Less Depreciation for 6 months	3,240	(3)
	W.D.V. on 1.7.2007	61,560	

	Sale Proceeds	66,750	
	Profit on sale	5,190	(4)
III	Depreciation for the year 2007 = (Rs. 9,720 + 6,300 + 1,250)	17,270	(5)
IV	W.D.V. on 31-12-2007 (87,480 + 56,700 + 48,750)	1,92,930	(6)

Illustration 6 (Exchange)

On 1-1-2006 X Ltd. purchased a Computer for Rs. 1,00,000. On 1-7-2008 the Computer was replaced by a new Computer of Rs. 75,000, the vendor taking the old computer in part exchange at a valuation of Rs. 40,000.

Prepare Computer Account up to 31st December 2008. Depreciation is charged @ 10% on the diminishing balance on the Computer at the end of each year.

COMPUTER A/C

Dr. Cr.

Date	Particulars	Rs.	Date	Particulars	Rs.
2006			2006		
Jan. 1	To Bank A/c	1,00,000	Dec. 31	By Depreciation A/c	10,000
				By Balance c/d	90,000
		1,00,000			1,00,000
2007			2007		
Jan. 1	To Balance b/d	90,000	Dec. 31	By Depreciation A/c	9,000
				By Balance c/d	81,000
		90,000			90,000
2008			2008		
Jan. 1	To Balance b/d	81,000	July 1	By Vendor's A/c	40,000
July 1	To Vendor's A/c	75,000		By Profit & Loss A/c (Loss on exchange)	41,000
			Dec. 31	By Depreciation*	7,500
				By Balance c/d	67,500
		1,56,000			1,56,000
2009					
Jan. 1	To Balance b/d	67,500			

Working Note :

*As depreciation is to be charged on computer installed at the end of the year, full year's depreciation has been charged irrespective of the date of purchase and none in the year of disposal. It is again evident from the rate @ 10% and not 10% p.a. Loss on exchange is (W.D.V.-Exchange value) Rs. 81,000 - 40,000 = 41,000.

Illustration 7 (Exchange & Loss by Fire)

On 1-1-2005 a company purchased two machines costing Rs. 1,20,000 and Rs. 80,000 respectively. On 1-1-2006 another machine was purchased forRs. 2,00,000. On 1-1-2007 the first machine purchased on 1-1-2005 costing Rs. 1,20,000 got out of order and a new machine was purchased costing Rs. 2,40,000 after surrendering the old machine and paying Rs. 1,80,000 in cash. On 1-1-2008 the machine purchased on 1-1-2006 was destroyed by fire and Insurance Company paid Rs. 1,20,000 only.

Show the Machinery Account for 2005, 2006, 2007 and 2008. Charge depreciation @ 10% p.a. on W.D.V. method. Books of accounts are closed on 31st December each year.

[C.A. (Entrance), 1986-Modified]

Solution :

MACHINERY A/C

Dr. Cr.

Date	Particulars	Rs.	Date	Particulars	Rs.
2005			2005		
Jan. 1	To Bank A/c		Dec. 31	By Depreciation A/c	20,000
	M_1 1,20,000			By Balance c/d	1,80,000
	M_2 80,000	2,00,000			
		2,00,000			2,00,000
2006			2006		
Jan. 1	To Balance b/d	1,80,000	Dec. 31	By Depreciation A/c	38,000
Jan. 1	To Bank (M_3)	2,00,000		By Balance c/d	3,42,000
		3,80,000			3,80,000
2007			2007		
Jan. 1	To Balance b/d	3,42,000	Jan. 1	By Vendor's A/c	60,000
Jan. 1	To Vendor's A/c (M_4)	2,40,000		(Agree value on Exchange)	
			Dec. 31	By Profit & Loss A/c(1)	37,200
				(Loss on exchange)	
				By Depreciation A/c(2)	48,800
				By Balance c/d	4,36,320
		5,82,000			5,82,000
2008			2008		
Jan. 1	To Balance b/d	4,36,320	Jan. 1	By Bank (Insurance claims)	1,20,000
				By Profit & Loss A/c(3)	42,000
				By Depreciation A/c(4)	27,432
				By Balance c/d(5)	2,46,888
		4,36,320			4,36,320

Working Notes :

Particulars	M1	M2	M3	M4	Total Depreciation	Balance
Date of Acquisition	1-1-2005	1-1-2005	1-1-2006	1-1-2007		
	Rs.	Rs	Rs.	Rs.	Rs.	Rs.
Cost of Acquisition	1,20,000	80,000	2,00,000	2,40,000		
Less Depreciation year ending 3 1-12-2005	12,000	8,000	—	—	20,000	
W.D.V. 1-1-2006	1,08,000	72,000				1,80,000
Less Depreciation year ending 31-12-2006	10,800	7,200	20,000		38,000	
W.D.V. as on 1-1-2007	97,200	64,800	1,80,000			3,42,000
M1 exchanged for M4 at an agreed value	60,000					
(1) P & L A/c (Loss)	(37,200)					
(2) Depreciation (2007)		6,480	18,000	24,000	48,480	
W.D.V. 1-1-2008		58,320	1,62,000	2,16,000		4,36,320
Destroyed by fire, claims received			1,20,000			
(3) P & L A/c (Loss)			(42,000)			
(4) Less Depreciation 2008		5,832		21,600	27,432	
(5) W.D.V. 31-12-2008		52,488		1,94,400		2,46,888

Illustration 8 (Part-exchange & Rectification)

On 1-1-2006 the Machinery Account of a company had a balance of Rs. 1,40,000. On 1-7-2006 a part of the above Machinery whose book value on 1-1-2006 was Rs. 28,000 was surrendered to the vendor at an agreed price of Rs. 11,200 in part exchange for a new machinery costing Rs. 23,800. The net invoice of Rs. 12,600 was passed through the Purchases Book. At the same time Rs. 1,400 incurred on installation of new machine wrongly debited to wages account.

Record Journal Entries and Prepare Machinery Account for the year ended 31st December 2006. Depreciation is charged @ 10% p.a. on Diminishing Balance.

Solution : **JOURNAL ENTRIES**

Date 2006	Particulars		LF	(Dr) Rs.	(Cr) Rs.
July 1	Vendors A/c	Dr		11,200	
	Depreciation A/c	Dr		1,400	
	P & L A/c (Loss on sale)	Dr		15,400	
	To Machinery A/c				28,000
	(Being part of old Machinery transferred to vendor)				

	Machinery A/c Dr		23,800	
	To Vendor's A/c			11,200
	To Purchases A/c			12,600
	(Being new machinery acquired)			
	Machinery A/c Dr		1,400	
	To Wages A/c			1,400
	(Being installation expenses debited to wages A/c corrected)			
Dec. 31	Depreciation A/c Dr		12,460	
	To Machinery A/c			12,460
	(Being depreciation charged)			

MACHINERY A/C

Date	Particulars	Rs.	Date	Particulars	Rs.
2006			2006		
Jan. 1	To Balance b/d	1,40,000	July 1	By Vendor's A/c	11,200
July 1	To Vendor's A/c	11,200		By Depreciation A/c (1)	1,400
	To Purchases A/c	12,600		By P & L A/c (Loss) (2)	15,400
	To Wages A/c	1,400	Dec. 31	By Depreciation A/c (3)	12,460
				By Balance c/d	1,24,740
		1,65,200			1,65,200
2007					
Jan. 1	To Balance b/d	1,24,740			

Working Notes :

Depreciation on part of machinery surrendered

Book value as on 1-1-2006	28,000	
Less Depreciation @ 10% p.a. for 6 months	1,400	(1)
	26,600	
Less Exchange value	11,200	
*Loss on surrender of machine	15,400	(2)
Depreciation for the year ending 31st Dec. 2006		
Depreciation @ 10% p.a. on Rs. 1,12,000 (Rs. 1,40,000 - Rs. 28,000)	11,200	
Depreciation on new machine of Rs. 25,200 (Cost 23,800 + Installation 1,400) @ 10% p.a. for 6 months	1,260	
	12,460	(3)

CHANGE OF METHOD

Illustration 9 (Change from W.D.V. to S.L.M.)

X Ltd. commenced business on 1st January 2003. On the same date a plant costing Rs. 3,50,000 was purchased. Depreciation was charged @ 15% p.a. on diminishing balance basis and charging full year's depreciation on additions. Over the years following additions were made :

On 1-8-2004 Rs. 75,000

On 30-9-2007 Rs 1,00,000

On 1-1-2007 it was decided to change the method and rate of depreciation to 10% on straight line basis with retrospective effect from 1-1-2003, the adjustment being made in the account for the year ending 31st December 2007.

Prepare plant account for the year 2007 only. **[B.Com. (H) D.U., 2007]**

Solution :

PLANT A/C

Dr. Cr.

Date	Particulars	Rs.	Date	Particulars	Rs.
2007			2007		
Jan. 1	To Balance c/d (1)	2,28,761	Dec. 31	By Depreciation (3)	52,500
	To Excess depreciation charged adjusted (2)	33,739	"	By Balance c/d	3,10,000
Sept 30	To Bank A/c	1,00,000			
		3,62,500			3,62,500
2008					
Jan.	To Balance b/d	3,10,000			

Working Notes :

1. Calculation of written down value of the plant on 1 -1 -2007

	Rs.	
Book value (cost) as on 1-1-2003	3,50,000	
Less Depreciation @ 15% on diminishing Balance	52,500	
W.D.V. as on 1-1-2004	2,97,500	
Addition made during 2004	75,000	
	3,72,500	
Less Depreciation for the year 2004 @ 15%	55,875	
W.D.V. on 1-1-2005	3,16,625	
Less Depreciation for the year 2005 @ 15%	47,494	
W.D.V. on 1-1-2006	2,69,131	
Less Depreciation for the year 2006 @ 15%	40,370	
W.D.V. as on 1-1-2007	2,28,761	(1)

2. Difference in Depreciation

	Rs.	
Depreciation already charged @ 15% as per Diminishing Balance Method (52,500 + 55,875 + 47,494 + 40,370)	1,96,239	
Depreciation as per New Method i.e. Straight Line Method @ 10%	1,62,500*	
	33,739	(2)

	Rs.
*Cost of 1st Plant	3,50,000
Depreciation @ 10% for 4 years (i.e. 2003, 2004, 2005 & 2006)	1,40,000*
Cost of second plant	75,000
Depreciation for 3 years @ 10% on second plant (2004, 2005 and 2006)	22,500*
Total Depreciation = (Rs. 1,40,000 + 22,500) =	1,62,500

3. Depreciation for the year 2007

	Rs.
Cost of First Plant	3,50,000
Cost of Second Plant	75,000
Cost of Third Plant	1,00,000
	5,25,000
Depreciation @ 10% on original cost	52,500 (3)

Illustration 10 (Change with retrospective effect)

M Ltd. which depreciated its machinery @ 10% p.a. according to diminishing balance method, had on 1-4-2006 Rs. 4,86,000 balance in the Machinery Account. During the year ended 31st March 2007, the machinery purchased on 1-4-2004 for Rs. 60,000 was sold for Rs. 40,000 on 1-10-2006 and a new machinery costing Rs. 70,000 was purchased and installed at the same date, installation charges being Rs. 5,000. The company wants to change its method of depreciation from diminishing balance method to straight-line method w.e.f. 1-4-2004 and adjust the difference before 31-3-2007, the rate of depreciation remaining the same as before.

Show the Machinery Account for the year ended 31st March 2007. **[C.S. Foundation, June 1997]**

Solution : **MACHINERY A/C**

Dr. Cr.

Date	Particulars	Rs.	Date	Particulars	Rs.
2006			2006		
Apr. 1	To Balance b/d	4,86,000	Oct. 1	By Bank A/c	40,000
Oct. 1	To Bank A/c	70,000		By Depreciation A/c (1)	2,430
	To Bank A/c (Installation charges)	5,000		By P & L A/c (Loss) (2)	6,170
			2007		
			Mar. 31	By Additional Depreciation (3) (due to change in Method)	5,400
				By Depreciation (4) (54,000 + 3,750)	57,750
				By Balance c/d	4,49,250
		5,61,000			5,61,000

Working Notes : W.D.V. of Machine sold :

	Rs.			
Cost of the Machine (on 1-4-2004)	60,000		W.D.V.	4,86,000
Less Depreciation for (2004-05) @ 10%	6,000		*Less* W.D.V. of Machine sold*	48,600
W.D.V. on 1-4-2005	54,000		W.D.V. after sale of Machinery	4,37,400**
Less Depreciation for (2005-06)	5,400			
W.D.V. on 1-4-2006	48,600*			
Less Depreciation (from 1-4-2006 to 1-10-2006) for 6 months	2,430	(1)		
	46,170			
Sale Proceed	40,000			
Loss on sale of Machine	6,170	(2)		

W.D.V. as on 1-4-2005 $\frac{4,86,000 \times 100}{90} = 5,40,000$

W.D.V. as on 1-4-2004 $= 5,40,000 \times \frac{100}{90} = 6,00,000$

W.D.V. of rest of machines Rs. 5,40,000 after sale (6,00,000 – 60,000)

Depreciation as per Straight Line @ 10% on	5,40,000	
i.e. 54,000 p.a.		
Depreciation for 2004-05 and 2005-06 (54,000 × 2) =	1,08,000	
Depreciation already charged (Cost 5,40,000 – W.D.V. 4,37,400)** (as on 1-4-2004 - as on 1-4-2006)	1,02,600	
Additional Depreciation to be provided	5,400	(3)
Current year's Depreciation		
10% on cost of remaining assets (5,40,000)	54,000	
& on Rs. 75,000 (New addition for 6 months)	3,750	
	57,750	(4)

Illustration 11 (Preparation of Account Retrospectively)

The Plant and Machinery Account of a company had a debit balance of Rs. 1,47,390 on 1-1-2007. The company was incorporated in 2004 and has been following the practice of charging depreciation every year on the Diminishing Balance System @ 15%. In the year 2007 it was, however decided to change the method from reducing system to Straight Line with retrospective effect from 2004 and to give effect of the change while preparing the final accounts for year ended 31st December 2007, the rate of depreciation remaining the same as before.

In the year 2007 a new machine was purchased at a cost of Rs. 50,000. All the other machineries were acquired in 2004. Show the Plant & Machinery A/c from 2004 to 2007.

[I.C.W.A., Dec. 1988, Modified]
[B.Com. (H) D.U., 2007]

Solution : **PLANT & MACHINERY A/C**

Dr. Cr.

Date	Particulras	Rs.	Date	Particulars	Rs.
2004			2004		
Jan. 1	To Balance A/c (1)	2,40,000	Dec. 31	By Depreciation A/c	36,000
				By Balance c/d	2,04,000
		2,40,000			2,40,000
2005			2005		
Jan. 1	To Balance b/d	2,04,000	Dec. 31	By Depreciation A/c	30,600
				By Balance c/d	1,73,400
		2,04,000			2,04,000
2006			2006		
Jan. 1	To Balance b/d	1,73,400	Dec. 31	By Depreciation A/c	26,010
				By Balance c/d	1,47,390
		1,73,400			1,73,400
2007			2007		
Jan. 1	To Balance b/d	1,47,390	Dec. 31	By Depreciation A/c (2)	15,390
	To Bank A/c	50,000		(Additional due to change	
				in method)	43,500
				By Depreciation A/c	
				(Current year's)	1,38,500
				By Balance c/d	
		1,97,390			1,97,390
2008					
Jan. 1	To Balance	1,38,500			

Working Note :

Calculation of Cost of Plant & Machinery

1. W.D.V. as on 1-1-2006 $= \frac{1,47,390 \times 100}{85}$ Rs. 1,73,400

   W.D.V. as on 1-1-2005 $= \frac{1,73,400 \times 100}{85}$ Rs. 2,04,000

   Cost as on 1-1-2004 $= \frac{2,04,000 \times 100}{85}$ Rs. 2,40,000 (original cost)

2. Depreciation charged as per old method

	Rs.
(2,40,000 – 1,47,390) =	92,610
Depreciation as per new method @ 15% straight line	1,08,000
(from 1-1-2004 to 1-1-2007) $\left[\frac{2,40,000 \times 15 \times 3}{100}\right]$	
Additional Depreciation to be provided	15,390

Illustration 12 (Change from SLM to WDV with immediate effect)

On 1-1-2005 A Ltd. purchased a second hand plant for Rs. 45,000 and immediately spent Rs. 30,000 on overhauling and repair. On 1-7-2005 additional machinery of Rs. 37,500 was purchased. On 1-7-2007 the plant purchased on 1-1-2005 became obsolete and was sold for Rs. 15,000. On the same date a new machinery was purchased at a cost of Rs. 90,000.

Depreciation was provided for annually on 31st December each year at 10% p.a. on the original cost. In 2008, however, the company changed this method of providing depreciation and adopted the method of writing off 15% on the diminishing balance.

Show Plant & Machinery A/c for 2005 to 2008. **[C.A., Foundation, Nov. 1994-Modified]**

Solution : **PLANT & MACHINERY A/C**

Dr. Cr.

Date	Particulars	Rs.	Date	Particulars	Rs.
2005			2005		
Jan. 1	To Bank A/c	45,000	Dec. 31	By Depreciation A/c	9,375
	To Bank (Installation & Repairs)	30,000		By Balance c/d	1,03,125
July 1	To Bank A/c	37,500			
		1,12,500			1,12,500
2006			Dec. 2006		
Jan. 1	To Balance b/d	1,03,125		By Depreciation A/c	11,250
				By Balance c/d	91,875
		1,03,125			1,03,125
2007			2007		
Jan. 1	To Balance b/d	91,875	July 1	By Bank A/c	15,000
July 1	To Bank A/c	90,000		By Depreciation A/c	3,750
				By Profit and Loss A/c (Loss on sale)	41,250
			Dec. 31	By Depreciation A/c	8,250
				By Balance c/d	1,13,625
		1,81,875			1,81,875
2008			2008		
Jan. 1	To Balance b/d	1,13,625	Dec. 31	By Depreciation A/c @ 15% on 1,13,625	17,044
				By Balance c/d	96,581
		1,13,625			1,13,625

Illustration 13

Plant & Machinery Account of S Ltd. showed a balance of Rs. 1,62,000 on 1-1-2007, depreciation being provided at 10% p.a. On 1-7-2007 a part of plant purchased for Rs. 50,000 on 1-1-2005 was sold for Rs. 35,000 and on the same date a machinery costing Rs. 1,00,000 was acquired. On 31st December 2007, S Ltd. decided to change the method of depreciation from W.D.V. to SLM with effect from 1-1-2005 rate of depreciation remaining at 10% p.a.

Show Plant & Machinery Account for the year 2007. **[ICWA-1974-Modified]**

Solution :

PLANT & MACHINERY A/C

Dr. Cr.

Date	Particulars	Rs.	Date	Particulars	Rs.
2007			2007		
Jan. 1	To Balance c/d	1,62,000	July 1	By Bank A/c	35,000
July 1	To Bank A/c	1,00,000	"	By Depreciation A/c (1) (On machine sold @ 10% on 40,500 for 6 months	2,025
			"	By Profit & Loss A/c (2) (Loss on sale)	3,475
			Dec. 31	By Depreciation A/c (3) (Additional dep. Provided due to change in method)	1,500
			"	By Depreciation A/c on Rs. 1,50,000 @ 10% p.a. on 1,00,000 @ 10% p.a. for 6 months	20,000
			"	By Balance c/d	200,000
		262,000			262,000

W.D.V. as on 1-1-2007 = Rs. 1,62,000

W.D.V. as on 1-1-2006 $= \frac{1{,}62{,}000 \times 100}{90}$ 1,80,000

W.D.V. as on 1-1-2005 $= \frac{1{,}80{,}000 \times 100}{90}$ 2,00,000 (original cost)

Cost of the Plant & Machinery	2,00,000	
Less Cost of the Plant sold	50,000	
Cost of remaining Plant	1,50,000	
Dep.already provided @ 10% p.a. on W.D.V. method for the years 2005 & 2006 (Rs. 15,000 + Rs. 13,500)	28,500	
Depreciation @ 10% p.a. on original cost (due to change in method) (Rs. 15,000 + Rs. 15,000)	30,000	
Additional Depreciation to be provided	1,500	(3)
Cost of the Plant sold	50,000	
Less Dep. for 2005 @ 10% p.a. on W.D.V	5,000	
	45,000	
Less Dep. for the year 2006	4,500	
	40,500	
Less Dep. for 6 months (1-1-2007 to 1-7-2007)	2,025	(1)
W.D.V. of the plant sold	38,475	
Less Sale proceeds	35,000	
Loss on sale	3,475	(2)

GRADED ILLUSTRATIONS

Illustration 1

On 1st January, 2004, Green Ltd. purchased machinery for Rs. 1,20,000 and on 30th June, 2005, it acquired additional machinery at a cost of Rs. 20,000. On 31st March, 2006 one of the original machines which had cost Rs. 5,000 was found to have become obsolete and was sold as scrap for Rs. 500. It was replaced on that date by a new machine costing Rs. 5,000. Depreciation is to be provided at the rate of 15 percent per annum on the written down value. Accounts are closed on 31st December each year. Show Machinery Account for the first three years. **[B.Com (P), D.U, 2006-Cat 'B']**

Solution :

		Rs.			Rs.
2004			2004		
Jan. 1	To Bank A/c	1,20,000	Dec. 31	By Depreciation A/c	18,000
				By Bal. C/d	1,02,000
		1,20,000			1,20,000
2005			2005		
Jan. 1	To Balance b/d	1,02,000	Dec. 31	By Depreciation A/c	16,800
June 30	To Bank A/c	20,000		(15,300 + 1,500)	
				By Bal. C/d	1,05,200
		1,22,000			1,22,000
2006			2006		
Jan. 1	To Balance b/d	1,05,200	March 31	By Cash A/c	500
March 31	To Bank A/c	5,000		By Depreciation A/c(1)	135
				By P&L A/c(2)	2,977
			Dec. 31	By Depreciation A/c	
				(15,238 + 562)(3)	15,800
				By Balance C/d	90,788
		1,10,200			1,10,200

Working Note :

		Rs.
1. Cost of Machine sold	=	5,000
Depreciation @ 15%	=	(750)
(2004)		4,250
Depreciation For 2005	=	(638)
W.D.V. as on 1.1.2006		3,612
Depreciation For 3 Months (2006)	=	(135)
W.D.V. on 31-03-2006	=	3,477

2. Loss on Sale = (W.D.V – Sale Price)
(3,477 – 500) = Rs. 2,977

3. Depreciation for the current year

	Rs.
W.D.V. as on 1.1.2006	1,05,200
Less W.D.V. on 1.1.2006 of Machinery sold	3,612
	1,01,588
Depreciation @ 15%	15,238
Depreciation on New Machine (on Rs. 5,000 @ 15% for 9 months)	562
	15,800

Illustration 2

A Transport Company purchased 5 trucks at Rs. 10,00,000 each on 1-7-2004. On 1-1-2007, one of the trucks is involved in an accident and is completely destroyed. A sum of Rs. 4,00,000 is received from the insurer in full settlement. On the same date, another truck is purchased by the company for Rs. 12,00,000. The company writes off 20% on original cost per annum and closes its books every year on March 31. Show Motor Trucks Account for two years ending 31st March, 2008.

[B.Com (P), D.U, 2003, External]

Solution : **Motor Trucks Account**

		Rs.			Rs.
1-4-2006	To Balance b/d*[1]	32,50,000	01-01-2007	By Bank A/c (Ins. claim)	4,00,000
1-1-2007	To Bank A/c	12,00,000		By Depreciation A/c[3]	1,50,000
				By P&L A/c[2]	1,00,000
			31-03-2007	By Depreciation A/c[4]	8,60,000
				By Balance c/d	29,40,000
		44,50,000			44,50,000
1-4-2007	To Balance b/d	29,40,000	31-03-2008	By Depreciation A/c	10,40,000
				By Balance c/d	19,00,000
		29,40,000			29,40,000
1-4-2008	To Balance b/d	19,00,000			

Working Notes :

	Rs.
1. Calculation of Book Value on 1.4.2006	
Total Cost on 1.7.2004	50,00,000
Less : Dep. From 1.7.2004 to 31.03.2006	
On Rs. 50,00,000 @ 20%, for 21 months	17,50,000
W.D.V. as on 1.4.2006	32,50,000
2. Calculation of Loss :	
Cost of the Truck	10,00,000
Depreciation for 2 ½ Years @ 20% p.a	5,00,000
(1.7.2004 to 1.1.2007) W.D.V.	5,00,000
Less : Insurance Claim	4,00,000
	1,00,000

3. Cost price of one Truck :	10,00,000
Depreciation for nine months @ 20% (1.4.2006 to 1.1.2007)	1,50,000
4. Depreciation on Rs. 40,00,000 @ 20%	8,00,000
Depreciation on Rs. 12,00,000 @ 20%	60,000
for 3 months	8,60,000

Illustration 3 (Machinery acquired on Installments)

On July 1, 2004 X Ltd. purchased second-hand machinery for Rs. 20,000 and spent Rs. 3,000 on re-conditioning and installing it. On January 1, 2005 the firm purchased new machinery worth Rs. 12,000. On June 30, 2006 the machinery purchased on January 1, 2005 was sold for Rs. 8,000. On July 2006 fresh machinery was purchased on installment basis, payment for this machinery was to be made as follows :

July 1, 2006 Rs. 5,000
June 30, 2007 Rs. 6,000
June 30, 2008 Rs. 5,500

Payment in 2007 and 2008 include interest Rs. 1,000 and Rs. 500 respectively.

The company writes off Deprecation @ 10% on original cost. The accounts are closed every year on 31st March. Show the Machinery A/c for three years ending 31st March 2007.

[B.Com. (H), Delhi, 1985-Modified]

Solution : **MACHINERY A/C**

Date	Particulars	Rs.	Date	Particulars	Rs.
2004			2005		
July 1	To Bank A/c	20,000	Mar. 31	By Depreciation I	1,725
	To Bank (Expenses)	3,000	"	By Depreciation II	300
2005					
Jan. 1	To Bank A/c	12,000	"	By Balance c/d	32,975
		35,000			35,000
2005			2006		
April 1	To Balance b/d	32,975	Mar. 31	By Depreciation I	2,300
				By Depreciation II	1,200
			"	By Balance b/d	29,475
		32,975			32,975
2006			2006		
Apr. 1	To Balance b/d	29,475	June 30	By Depreciation (for 3 months)	300
July 1	To Hire Vendor A/c	15,000	"	By Bank A/c	8,000
				By P & L A/c	2,200
			2007		
			Mar. 31	By Depreciation I	2,300
				By Depreciation II	1,125
				By Balance c/d	30,550
		44,475			44,475

Illustration 4 (Change in life span of an asset)

A Ltd. acquired a machine for Rs. 5,40,000 on April 2004. Depreciation was to be charged @ 20% on Straight-Line Basis. During 2006-07, a modification was made to improve its technical reliability at a cost of Rs. 60,000, which it was considered would extend the useful life of the machine for two years. Routine maintenance during the said accounting period cost Rs. 7,500. Show the Machinery A/c and the amount to be charged a to the Profit and Loss A/c for the year ending 31st March 2007 only.

[B.Com. (H), Delhi-Modified]

Solution : **MACHINERY A/C**

Date	Particulars	Rs.	Date	Particulars	Rs.
2006			2007		
Apr. 1	To Balance b/d	3,24,000	Mar. 31	By Depreciation A/c	76,800
	(5,40,000 – 2,16,000 Dep.)			20% * (3,24,000 + 60,000)	
	To Bank A/c	60,000		By Balance c/d	3,07,200
		3,84,000			3,84,000
2007					
Apr. 1	To Balance b/d	3,07,2000			

Amount Charged to the Profit & Loss A/c for the year ended 31-3-2007

Rs. 76,800 (Dep.) + Rs. 7,500 (Routine Maintenance) = Rs. 84,300

$$* \text{ Life of machine } \frac{100}{20} = 5 \text{ years} \left(\frac{\text{Percent}}{\text{Rate}} \right)$$

Life expired 2 years

$$\text{Life improvement 2 years } (5 - 2 + 2) = 5 \text{ years} = \frac{100}{5} = 20\% \left(\text{Rate} = \frac{100}{\text{Revised life span}} \right)$$

Illustration 5 (Part Exchange, Abnormal Loss and Insurance Claim)

On January 1st, 2004, P purchased Roasting Machine for Rs. 60,000 and Grinding Machine for Rs. 40,000. On January 1, 2005, he purchased an oil expeller for Rs. 1,00,000. On January, 2006, the Roasting Machine got out of order and a new roaster was purchased costing Rs. 1,20,000 after surrendering the old one and paying cash Rs. 90,000. On January 1, 2007, the oil expeller purchased on January 1, 2005, was destroyed by fire and the insurance company paid Rs. 60,000 only. Show the Machinery A/c for 2004, 2005, 2006 and 2007. Charge Depreciation @ 10% p.a. on the W.D.V. method.

[C.A. Entrance, May 1986]

Solution : **MACHINERY A/C**

Date	Particulars	Rs.	Date	Particulars	Rs.
2004			2004		
Jan. 1	To Bank A/c	1,00,000	Dec. 31	By Depreciation A/c	10,000
	(Roasting Mahine 60,000			(6,000 + 4,000)	
	Grinding Machine 40,000)			By Balance c/d	
				RM 54,000	
				GM 36,000	90,000

		1,00,000			1,00,000
2005			2005		
Jan. 1	To Balance b/d (54,000 + 36,000)	90,000	Dec. 31	By Depreciation A/c (5,400 + 3,600 + 10,000)	19,000
	To Bank A/c (Oil Expeller)	1,00,000	"	By Balance c/d (RM 48,600 + GM 32,400 + OE 90,000)	1,71,000
		1,90,000			1,90,000
2006			2006		
Jan. 1	To Balance b/d (48,600 + 32,400 + 90,000)	1,71,000	Jan. 1	By Machinery Disposal A/c (60,000 – 6,000 – 5,400)	48,600
	To Vendor's A/c	1,20,000	Dec. 31	By Depreciation A/c (3,240 + 9,000 + 12,000)	24,240
			"	By Balance c/d (GM29,160 + OE81,000 + NR 1,08,000)	2,18,160
		2,91,000			2,91,000
2007			2007		
Jan. 1	To Balance b/d (29,160 + 81,000 + 1,08,000)	2,18,160	Jan. 1	By Insurance Co. A/c	60,000
			"	By Profit & Loss A/c (Net Loss by fire) (81,000 – 60,000)	21,000
			Dec. 31	By Depreciation A/c (2,916 + 10,800)	13,716
				By Balance c/d	1,23,444
		2,18,160			2,18,160
2008					
Jan. 1	To Balance b/d	1,23,444			

MACHINERY DISPOSAL A/C

Date	Particulars	Rs.	Date	Particulars	Rs.
2006			2006		
Jan. 1	To Machinery A/c	48,600	Jan. 1	By Vendor's A/c (1,20,000 – 90,000)	30,000
				By Profit & Loss A/c (48,600 – 30,000) (Loss on Exchange)	18,600
		48,600			48,600

Note : Alternatively, following entries could have been made at the time of exchange of asset on Jan. 1, 2006 :

			Rs.	Rs.
(a) (i)	Machinery A/c	Dr	120,000	
	To Bank A/c			90,000
	To Part Exchange Allowance A/c			30,000
(ii)	Part Exchange Allowance A/c	Dr	30,000	
	Profit & Loss A/c	Dr	18,600	
	To Machinery A/c			48,600
(b)	Machinery A/c (New)	Dr	120,000	
	Profit & Loss A/c (New)	Dr	18,600 (BF)	
	To Bank A/c			90,000
	To Machinery (old) A/c			48,600

Illustration 6 (Accident & Insurance claim)

A Transport Company purchased 5 Trucks @ Rs. 2,00,000 each on 1-4-2005. The Company writes off depreciation @ 20% p.a. on original cost and observes calendar year as its accounting year.

On October 1, 2007 one of the trucks was involved in an accident and was completely destroyed. Insurance Company paid Rs. 90,000 in full settlement of the claim. On the same day the company purchased an used Truck for Rs. 1,00,000 and spent Rs. 20,000 on its overhauling. Prepare Trucks A/c for the three years ending on 31st December 2007. **[B.Com. (H), Istyr. (DU), 1987-Modified]**

Solution :

TRUCKS A/C

Date	Particulars	Rs.	Date	Particulars	Rs.
2005			2005		
April 1	To Bank A/c	10,00,000	Dec. 31	By Depreciation A/c	1,50,000
				By Balance c/d	8,50,000
		10,00,000			10,00,000
2006			2006		
Jan. 1	To Balance b/d	8,50,000	Dec. 31	By Depreciation A/c	2,00,000
				By Balance c/d	6,50,000
		8,50,000			8,50,000
2007			2007		
Jan. 1	To Balance b/d	6,50,000	Oct. 1	By Bank A/c (Insurance claim)	90,000
Oct. 1	To Bank (Second-hand Truck) including overhauling charges	1,20,000		By P & L A/c [(1)]	10,000
			Dec. 31	By Depreciation A/c [(2)]	1,96,000
				By Balance c/d	4,74,000
		7,70,000			7,70,000
2008					
Jan. 1	To Balance b/d	4,74,000			

Working Notes :

		Rs.	Rs.
(1)	Cost Price of the truck		200,000
	Depreciation charged		
	2005 for 9 months	30,000	
	2006 for 12 months	40,000	
	2007 for 9 months	30,000	100,000
	i.e. up to 1-10-2007		
	Written down value of the truck (destroyed) on 1-10-2007		100,000
	Less Insurance		90,000
	Loss on truck (destroyed) charged to Profit & Loss A/c		10,000
(2)	Depreciation for the year 2007		
	Depreciation on the truck destroyed (for 9 months)		30,000
	Depreciation on 4 remaining trucks for (Full year)		160,000
	Depreciation on second-hand truck for (3 months)		6,000
	(Acquired during the year)		196,000

Illustration 7 (Installation, Overhauling & Dismantling Expenses)

X purchased a second-hand machinery on 1-2-2006 for Rs. 50,000; paid Rs. 11,000 for its overhauling and Rs. 5,000 for its installation which was completed on 31-3-2006.

The company provides depreciation on its machinery at 15% per annum on Diminishing Balance Method from the date it is put to use and closes its books on December 31st each year.

On 1-10-2007, a repair work was carried out on the machine and Rs. 5,000 were paid for the same.

The machine was sold on 31-10-2008 for a sum of Rs. 11,000 and an amount of Rs. 1,000 was paid as dismantling charges. Prepare Machinery Account from 2006 to 2008.

[B.Com. (H), 1st yr. (DU), 1989 Modified]

Solution : **MACHINERY A/C**

Date	Particulars	Rs.	Date	Particulars	Rs.
2006			2006		
Feb.	To Bank	66,000	Dec. 31	By Depreciation A/c (for 9 months)	7,425
	(Including overhauling and installation charges) (1)		"	By Balance c/d	58,575
		66,000			66,000
2007			2007		
Jan. 1	To Balance b/d	58,575	Dec. 31	By Depreciation A/c	8,786
			"	By Balance c/d	49,789
		58,575			58,789

2008			2008		
Jan. 1	To Balance b/d	49,789	Oct. 31	By Depreciation A/c	6,224
				By Bank A/c (2)	10,000
				By Profit & Loss A/c	33,565
		49,789			49,789

Notes :

(1) Installation charges are always capitalised. Overhauling and repair charges on the secondhand machine incurred are capitalised before the machine is put to use. However, all such charges after the installation of machine are treated as revenue charges and hence not capitalised.

(2) Dismantling expenses have been deducted out of the sale proceeds of the machine disposed off.

Illustration 8 (Provision for Depreciation)

Metropol Ltd. acquired a machine for Rs. 5,40,000 on 1st April 2005. Depreciation was to be charged at 20% on Straight Line Method. During 2007-08, a modification was made to improve its technical reliability at a cost of Rs. 50,000 which it was considered would extend the useful life of the machine for two years. At the same time an important component of the machine was replaced at a cost of Rs. 10,000 because of excessive wear and tear. Routine maintenance during the said accounting period cost Rs. 7,500.

Show the Machine A/c, Provision for Depreciation on Machine A/c and charges to Profit & Loss A/c for the year ending 31st March 2008 only. **[B.Com. (II), Istyr. (DU), 1993] Modified**

Solution :

MACHINE A/C

Date	Particulars	Rs.	Date	Particulars	Rs.
2007			2008		
Apr. 1	To Balance b/d	5,40,000	Mar. 31	By Balance c/d	6,00,000
	To Bank A/c	50,000			
	(Modification cost)				
	To Bank A/c	10,000			
	(Component cost)				
		6,00,000			6,00,000
2008					
Apr. 1	To Balance b/d	6,00,000			

PROVISION FOR DEPRECIATION A/C

Date	Particulars	Rs.	Date	Particulars	Rs.
2008			2007		
Mar. 31	To Balance c/d	2,92,800	Apr. 1	By Balance b/d	2,16,000
			2008		
			Mar. 3	By Profit & Loss A/c	76,800*
		2,92,800			2,92,800

Working Notes :

Balance of Provision for depreciation has been worked out as under :

		Rs.
Depreciation @ 20% p.a. on Straight Line Method on cost		5,40,000
i.e. 1,08,000 for (2005 – 06)		
& 1,08,000 for (2006 – 07)		2,16,000
Depreciation for the years 2007-08		
Written down value /Book Value of Machine as on 1-4-2005		5,40,000
Less Depreciation fo 2005–2006 & 2006–07		2,16,000
W.D.V. as 31-3-2007		3,24,000
Add cost of modification and component		60,000
		3,84,000
Total useful life of Machine	5 years	
Less Used up life of machine	2 years	
Remaining useful life of machine	3 years	
Add increase in life span due to modification	2 years	
Total useful life of machine	5 years	
Revised cost of old machine		3,84,000
Revised life of old machine		5 years

Revised amount of Depreciation $D = \frac{C - S}{n} = \frac{3,84,000}{5}$ = Rs. 76,800 p.a.

Notes :

1. Cost of modification which will improve the life span of the asset is capitalised.
2. Cost of component has been charged to Machinery A/c because it is being replaced due to 'excessive' wear and tear. Had this part been replaced because of 'normal' wear and tear, it would not have been capitalised. Further, the replacement will help improve the life span also.

Illustration 9 (Change of Method)

S. J. Enterprises purchased second-hand machinery on 1st April 2004 for Rs. 3,70,000 and installed at a cost of Rs. 30,000. On 1st October 2005, it purchased another machine for Rs.1,00,000 and on 1st October 2006 it sold off the first machine purchased in 2004 for Rs.2,80,000.

On the same date it purchased another machine for Rs. 2,50,000. On 1st October, 2007, the second machinery purchased for Rs. 1,00,000 was sold off for Rs. 20,000.

In the beginning depreciation was provided on machinery @ 10% p.a. on the original cost each year on 31st March. From the year 2005-06, however, the trader changed the method of providing depreciation and adopted the W.D.V. Method, the rate of depreciation being 15% p.a.

Give the Machinery A/c for the period 2004-2008. **[C.A. Entrance, Nov. 1991 Modified]**

Solution :

MACHINERY A/C

Date	Particulars	Rs.	Date	Particulars	Rs.
2004			2005		
April 1	To Bank A/c	3,70,000	Mar. 31	By Depreciation A/c @ 10%	40,000
	To Bank (Installation Cost)	30,000	"	By Depreciation A/c	3,60,000
		4,00,000			4,00,000
2005			2006		
April 1	To Balance b/d	3,60,000	Mar. 31	By Depreciation A/c	61,500
Oct. 1	To Bank A/c	1,00,000		(15% on Rs. 3,60,000 & 15% on Rs. 1,00,000 for 6 months)	
			"	By Balance c/d (Rs. 3,06,000 + Rs. 92,500)	3,98,500
		4,60,000			4,60,000
2006			2006		
Apr. 1	To Balance b/d	3,98,500	Oct. 1	By Bank A/c	2,80,000
	(Rs.3,06,000 + Rs.92,500)		"	By Depreciation A/c	22,950
Oct. 1	To Bank A/c	2,50,000		(15% on Rs. 3,06,000 for 6 months)	
				By P&L A/c (Loss on sale) (1)	3,050
			2007		
			Mar. 31	By Depreciation A/c	13,875
				@ 15% on Rs.92,500 & on Rs.2,50,000 for 6 months	18,750
					3,09,875
			"	By Balance c/d (Rs. 78,625 + Rs. 2,31,250)	
		6,48,500			6,48,500
2007			2007		
April 1	To Balance b/d	3,09,875	Oct. 1	By Bank A/c	20,000
	(Rs.78,625 + Rs.2,31,250)		"	By Depreciation A/c	5,897
				(15% on Rs. 78,625 for 6 months)	52,728
			"	By P & L A/c (Loss on sale) (2)	
			2008		
			Mar. 31	By Depreciation A/c	34,688
				(15% on Rs. 2,31,250)	
			"	By Balance b/d	1,96,562
		3,09,875			3,09,875

Working Notes :

1. Loss on sale of Machinery on 1-10-2006 :

	Rs.	Rs.
W.D.V. on 1-4-2006		3,06,000
Less Depreciation for 6 months	22,950	
Sale price	2,80,000	(3,02,950)
	Loss on Sale	3,050

2. Loss on sale of Machinery on 1.10.2007 :

W.D.V. as on 1.4.2007		78,625
Less Depreciation for 6 months	5,897	
Sale Price	20,000	(25,897)
	Loss on sale	52,728

Illustration 10 (Change of Method with retrospective effect)

R. Ltd. which depreciates its machinery @ 10% p.a. on Diminishing Balance Method, had on 1st January 2005, Rs. 9,72,000 on the debit side of Machinery A/c. During the year 2005, Machinery purchased on 1st January 2003 for Rs. 80,000 was sold for Rs. 45,000 on 1st July 2005 and a new machinery at a cost of Rs. 1,50,000 was purchased and installed on the same date, installation charges being Rs. 8,000. The company wanted to change the method of Depreciation from Diminishing Balance Method to Straight Line Method with effect from 1st January 2003. Difference of depreciation up to 31st December 2005 to be adjusted. The rate of depreciation remains the same as before. Show Machinery A/c. **[C.A. (Foundation), May 1995; B.Com. (H), DU] (Modified)**

Solution : **MACHINERY A/C**

Date	Particulars	Rs.	Date	Particulars	Rs.
2005			2005		
Jan. 1	To Balance b/d	9,72,000	July 1	By Bank A/c (Sale)	45.000
July, 1	To Bank A/c	1,50,000	"	By Depreciation A/c	3,240
"	To Bank A/c (Expenses)	8,000	"	By P&L A/c	
				(Loss on sale) (2)	16,560
			Dec. 31	By P & L A/c (4)	11,200
				(Additional Depreciation)	
			"	By Depreciation A/c (3)	1,19,900
			"	By Balance c/d	9,34,100
		11,30,000			11,30,000

Working Notes :

Rate of Depreciation 10% and W.D.V. being 90% (100 - 10)

1. Calculation of W.D.V. as on 1-1-03 — Rs.

W.D.V. as on 1-1- 05 — 9,72,000

W.D.V. as on 1-1-04 $\frac{9,72,000 \times 100}{90}$ = 10,80,000

Cost price as on 1-1-03 $\frac{10,80,000 \times 100}{90}$ = 12,00,000

2. Calculation of loss on sale of Machinery

	Rs.
Original cost as on 1-1-03	80,000
Less Depreciation @ 10%	8,000
W.D.V. as on 1-1-04	72,000
Less Depreciation @ 10%	7,200
W.D.V. as on 1-1-05	64,800
Less Depreciation up to 1-7-05 for 6 months	3,240
W.D.V. as on 1-7-05	61,540
Less Sale Proceeds	45,000
Loss on sale	16,560

3. Calculation of Depreciation of 2005

	Rs.
On Machines (other than sold one) existing as on 1-1-2005 @ 10% on (Rs. 12,00,000 - 80,000)	1,12,000
On Machine Purchased on 1-7-05 i.e. 10% on Rs. 1,58,000 for 6 months	7,900
	1,19,900

4. Calculation of difference in the amount of depreciation due to change in method.

		Rs.
Depreciation under SLM for 2 years (Rs. 12,00,000 – 80000] × 10% × 2)		2,24,000
Depreciation on W.D.V. Basis for 2 years		
For 2003 on Rs. 11,20,000	112,000	
For 2004 on Rs. 10,08,000	100,800	2,12,800
Deference adjusted		11,200

Illustration 11 (Provision for Depreciation & Depreciation A/c)

On 1st April 2003 a firm purchased a machinery for Rs. 2,00,000. On 1st October in the same accounting year, additional machinery costing Rs. 1,00,000 was purchased. On 1st October 2004, the machinery purchased on 1st April 2003, having become obsolete, was sold off for Rs. 90,000. On 1st October 2005, new machinery was purchased for Rs. 2,50,000 while the machinery purchased on 1st October 2003 was sold for Rs. 85,000 on the same day. The firm provides depreciation on its machinery @ 10% per annum on original cost on 31st March every year. Show Machinery Account, Provision for Depreciation Account and Depreciation Account for the period of three accounting years ending 31st March 2006. **[C. S.. Foundation, June 1996-Modified]**

Solution :

MACHINERY A/C

Date	Particulars	Rs.	Date	Particulars	Rs.
2003			2004		
April 1	To Bank A/c (M-I)	2,00,000	March 31	By Balance c/d	3,00,000
Oct. 1	To Bank A/c (M-II)	1,00,000			
		3,00,000			3,00,000
2004			2004		
April 1	To Balance b/d	3,00,000	Oct. 1	By Bank A/c (M-I)	90,000
			"	By Provision for Depreciation A/c	30,000
			"	By Profit & Loss A/c (Loss on sale)	80,000
			2005 Mar. 31	By Balance c/d (M-II)	1,00,000
		3,00,000			3,00,000
2005			2005		
Apr. 1	To Balance b/d	1,00,000	Oct. 1	By Bank A/c (M-II)	85,000
Oct. 1	To Bank A/c (M-III)	2,50,000	"	By Provision for Depreciation A/c	20,000
	To Profit & Loss A/c	5,000			
			2006 Mar 31	By Balance c/d (M-III)	2,50,000
		3,55,000			3,55,000

DEPRECIATION A/C

Date	Particulars	Rs.	Date	Particulars	Rs.
2004			2004		
Mar. 31	To Provision for Depreciation A/c	25,000	Mar. 31	By Profit & Loss A/c	25,000
		25,000			25,000
2004			2005		
Oct.1	To Provision for Depreciation A/c (On the Machinery sold for six months)	10,000	Mar. 31	By Profit & Loss A/c	20,000
2005 Oct. 1	To Provision for Depreciation A/c	10,000			
		20,000			20,000

2005 Oct. 1	To Provision for Depreciation A/c (On the machinery sold for six months)	5,000	2006 Mar. 31	By Profit & Loss A/c	17,500
2006 Mar. 31	To Provision for Depreciation A/c	12,500			
		17,500			17,500

PROVISION FOR DEPRECIATION A/C

Date	Particulars	Rs.	Data	Particulars	Rs.
2004 Mar. 31	To Balance c/d	25,000	2004 Mar. 31	By Depreciation A/c MI-20,000 MIl- 5,000	25,000
		25,000			25,000
Oct. 1	To Machinery A/c (M-I) (20,000 + 10,000)	30,000	Apr. 1	By Balance b/d	25,000
			Oct. 1	By Depreciation A/c (M-I)	10,000
2005 Mar. 31	To Balance c/d	15,000	2005 Mar. 31	By Depreciation A/c (M-II)	10,000
		45,000			45,000
2005 Oct. 1	To Machinery A/c (M-I) (5,000 4-10,000 + 5,000)	20,000	2005 Apr. 1	By Balance b/d By	15,000
			Oct. 1	Depreciation A/c (M-II)	5,000
2006 Mar. 31	To Balance c/d	12,500	2006 Mar. 31	By Depreciation A/c (M-III)	12,500
		32,500			32,500
				By Balance b/d	12,500

Illustration 12 (Asset Disposal Account)

X, who closes his books on 30th June every year, operates his factory with two machines purchased from Y under an arrangement by which at the end of three years Y allows him 20% per annum of the cost price as on exchange for a new model.

A provides depreciation at the rate of 30% per annum of original cost for each of the first two years and 20% per annum for the third year.

The following payments to Y have been recorded since X commenced business on 1st June 2004 :

	Rs.
On 1st July 2004 Purchase of Machine A	2,000
On 1st July 2005 Purchase of Machine B	3,000
On 30th June 2007 purchase of Machine C in exchange of Machine A	3,600

On 31st December 2007, X purchased from Y a new model (Machine D) which would do the work of two machines. The cost was Rs. 5,000 and Y allowed Rs. 3,000 for machine B and C in part exchange.

You are required to prepare Plant A/c for four years upto 31st December 2007 in the books of X. Open a separate account for Depreciation Provision and showing the balances on these accounts carried down as on 30th June every year and on 31st December 2007. Also, prepare Plant Disposal A/c clearly differentiating between depreciation and loss on sale. **[B.Com. (H), Delhi, 1996] (Modified)**

Solution :

MACHINERY A/C

Date	Particulars	Rs.	Date	Particulars	Rs.
1-7-04	To Bank A/c (MA)	2,000	30-6-05	By Balance c/d	2,000
		2,000			2,000
1-7-05	To Balance b/d	2,000	30-6-06	By Balance c/d	5,000
1-7-05	To Bank (MB)	3,000			
		5,000			5,000
1-7-06	To Balance b/d	5,000	30-6-07	By Machinery Disposal A/c	2,000
30-6-07	To Vendor's A/c (MC) (3,600 + 400)*	4,000	30-6-07	By Balance c/d	7,000
		9,000			9,000
1-7-07	To Balance b/d	7,000	31-12-07	By Machinery Disposal A/c	7,000
31-12-07	To Vendor's A/c (MD) (2,000 + 3,000)	5,000	31-12-07	By Balance c/d	5,000
		12,000			12,000

* 20 % of original Cost of machine 'A'.

PROVISION FOR DEPRECIATION A/C

Date	Particulars	Rs.	Date	Particulars	Rs.
30-6-05	To Balance c/d	600	30-6-05	By Depreciation A/c (A)	600
		600			600
30-6-06	To Balance c/d	2,100	1-7-05	By Balance b/d	600
			30-6-06	By Depreciation A/c (600 + 900) (A + B)	1,500
		2,100			2,100
30-6-07	To Machinery Disposal A/c	1,600	1-7-06	By Balance b/d	2,100
30-6-07	To Balance c/d	1,800	30-6-07	By Depreciation A/c (400 + 900) (A + B)	1,300
		3,400			3,400

30-12-07	To Machinery Disposal A/c	2,700	1-7-07	By Balance b/d	1,800
			31-12-07	By Depreciation A/c* (300 + 600) (B + C)	900
		2,700			2,700

MACHINERY DISPOSAL A/C (PLANT A)

Date	Particulars	Rs.	Date	Particulars	Rs.
2007 June 30	To Plant A A/c	2,000	2007 June 30	By Provision for Depreciation A/c	1,600
				By Vendor A/c (Exchange value)	400
		2,000			2,000

MACHINERY DISPOSAL A/C (PLANT B&C)

Date	Particulars	Rs.	Date	Particulars	Rs.
2007 Dec. 31	To Plant & Machinery A/c	7,000	2007 Dec. 31	By Provision for Depreciation A/c	2,700
				By Vendor A/c (Exchange value)	3,000
				By P & L A/c (Loss)	1,300
		7,000			7,000

Working Note :

	Cost	Ist year Depreciation @ 30%	IInd year Depreciation @ 30%	IIIrd year Depreciation @ 20%
Machine A	2,000	600	600	400*
Machine B	3,000	900	900	600
Machine C	4,000	1,200	1,200	800

*for 6 months

Illustration 13 (Rate of Depreciation not given)

A firm writes off 95% of the cost of the machine over 10 years following Straight Line Method, leaving the rest 5% as estimated scrap value. Full Depreciation is provided even if an asset is used only for part of the year.

On 31-12-2005, the original costs of the machines in possession were :

	Rs.
(i) Those purchased in 1994 or earlier	2,40,000
(ii) Those purchased in 1997	80,000
(iii) Those purchased in 2001	60,000

On 30-6-2006, a machine purchased in 1994 for Rs. 20,000 was sold for Rs. 1,800. On 30-11-06, a machine purchased in 2001 for Rs. 30,000 was sold for Rs. 10,000 and on the same date a new machine was purchased for Rs. 90,000.

Show the Machinery account, Provision for Depreciation A/c and Machinery Sold Account for the year 2006. **[B.Com. (H), Delhi, 1997; F.C. S. Foundation, Dec. 1994]**

Solution :

MACHINERY A/C

Date	Particulars	Rs.	Date	Particulars	Rs.
2006 Jan. 1	To Balance b/d	3,80,000	2006 June 30	By Machinery Sold A/c	20,000
	(2,40,000+80,000+60,000)		Nov. 30	By Machinery Sold A/c	30,000
Nov. 30	To Bank A/c	90,000	Dec. 30	By Balance c/d	4,20,000
		4,70,000			4,70,000

PROVISION FOR DEPRECIATION A/C

Date	Particulars	Rs.	Date	Particulars	Rs.
2006 Jane 30	To Machinery Sold A/c (I)	19,000	2006 Jan. 1	By Balance b/d (1)	3,24,900
Nov. 30	To Machinery Sold A/c (III)	17,100		2,28,000 + 68,400 + 28,500)	
Dec. 31	To Balance c/d	3,07,800	Nov. 30	By Depreciation A/c (3) (Machinery III)	2,850
			Dec. 31	By Depreciation A/c (4)	
				Machine II 7,600	
				IV 8,550	16,150
		3,43,900			3,43,900

MACHINERY SOLD A/C

Date	Particulars	Rs.	Date	Particulars	Rs.
2006 June 30	To Machinery A/c	20,000	2006 June 30	By Provision for	
"	To P & L A/c (Profit)	800		Depreciation A/c	19,000
			" "	By Bank A/c	1,800
Nov. 30	To Machinery A/c	30,000	Nov. 30	By Provision for	
				Depreciation A/c	17,100
			"	By Bank A/c	10,000
			"	By P & L A/c (Loss)	2,900
		50,800			50,800

Working Notes :

1. *Depreciation Balance on 1-1-2006 — Rs.

   (a) Machinery purchased in 1994 or before (95% of Rs. 2,40,000) — 2,28,000

   (b) Machinery purchased in 1997

*Depreciation for 9 years	$= \frac{95 \times 80{,}000 \times 9}{100 \times 10}$		68,400
Machinery purchased in 2001			
*Depreciation for 5 years	$= \frac{95 \times 60{,}000 \times 5}{100 \times 10}$		28,500
			3,24,900
2. Depreciation on Machinery sold on 30-6-06		Original cost	20,000
*Depreciation	$\frac{95 \times 20{,}000}{100}$		19,000
3. Depreciation on Machinery sold on 30-11-06		Original cost	30,000
*Total Depreciation in 10 years	$= \frac{95 \times 30{,}000}{100}$		28,500
Depreciation charged upto 2005	$= \frac{28{,}500 \times 5}{10}$		14,250
Depreciation for 2006 = 1/10 × 28,500			2,850
Total depreciation on machine sold on 30-11-2006			17,100
4. *Depreciation for 2006			
On Machine II	$= \frac{95 \times 80{,}000 \times 1}{100 \times 10}$		7,600
On Machine IV	$= \frac{95 \times 90{,}000 \times 1}{100 \times 10}$		8,550
			16,150

*Alternatively $\left(\frac{C - S}{n}\right)$ that is Cost less 5% there of divided by 10 would have given yearly depreciation.

PROVISION AND RESERVE

Provision refers to the amount set aside to meet certain expected contingencies which cannot be ascertained. The Companies Act 1956 states that, "Provision means amount written off or retained by way of providing depreciation, renewals or diminution in the value of assets or retained by way of providing for any known liability, the amount of which cannot be determined with substantial accuracy." Thus, the above definition clearly mentions that a provision may be created either for depreciation or for a known liability the amount of which cannot be determined accurately e.g. Provision for Depreciation, Provision for Repairs and Renewals. Provision for Bad & Doubtful debts, Provision for Discount on Debtors or Provision for Taxation.

Reserve refers to the sum set aside out of divisible profits for the purpose of ploughing back or reinvesting with in the business. It is not a charge but appropriation of profits. The profits so retained strengthen the financial position, provide funds for expansion or modernisation, help to maintain stable dividend policy and comply with the legal provisions, such as General Reserve, Capital Redemption Reserve, Debenture Redemption Reserve, Dividend Equalisation Reserve. However, when these revenue reserves are not retained but invested outside business are known as Reserve Funds. A reserve which is created without any known or specific purpose is known as **"General Reserve".** Whereas a reserve which is created for a particular purpose is called **Specific Reserve.** All these reserves are also known as **Revenue Reserves.**

A reserve which is created not out of divisible profits is called **Capital Reserve.** Such reserve is created out of capital profits of the business, such as profits on revaluation or sale of fixed assets, Profits on reissue of forfeited shares, Profits prior to incorporation, Securities Premium, Debenture issue Premium, Profit on redemption of debentures etc.

DISTINCTION BETWEEN PROVISION AND RESERVE

1. A provision is a charge against Profits while Reserve is simply an appropriation of profits.
2. A provision is created to meet a known liability whose amount is uncertain while Reserve is created to strengthen the financial position and not for any specific liability.
3. A provision is shown as a deduction out of the asset concerned whereas Reserve is shown separately on liability side. The sum so set aside as provision is never invested outside business whereas reserves may be invested outside business.
4. Provision is a part of divisible profits but the same cannot be made available for the purpose of distributing dividends while reserves (Revenue) are always available to be distributed as dividends.
5. Provisions have to be created whether there is a profit or loss, while reserve is created only when there are profits.

SECRET RESERVE

A reserve which is not disclosed in the Balance Sheet is known as secret reserve. The Companies Act 1956 prohibits creation of secret reserve because it conceals the actual financial position from the users of accounting information. However, the financial position of the company is definitely better than what it appears from the Balance Sheet. Secret reserve is created by adopting a policy of excessive depreciation, understatement of the value of assets, over-valuation of liabilities, treating capital expenditure as revenue, creating excessive provision for bad debts, or creating provisions which are not required and treating contingent liability as an actual liability.

Objectives : The policy of secret reserve is adopted by the management to achieve the following objectives :

1. To meet the exceptional losses
2. To bring down the market price of the shares within trading range
3. To enhance the availability of working capital
4. To maintain dividend rate
5. To elude competition by concealing large profits
6. To minimize tax liability
7. To keep strong financial position
8. To lessen the dependence upon the capital market or external finance.

"PROVISION FOR REPAIRS AND RENEWALS"

Under this system, the total amount of repairs and renewals is estimated for the entire life of the asset and the same is added back to the cost of asset excluding salvage value. An average amount is debited to Profit and Loss Account every year and credited to "Provision for Repairs and Renewals Account" irrespective of the actual amount incurred on repairs and renewals. The balance of the Provision for Repairs and Renewals Account is carried forward. At the end of working life of the asset, the Provision Account is closed by transferring the balance to the Asset Account.

Illustration 14

X Ltd. purchased a machine on 1-1-2003 for Rs. 50,000. It is estimated to have an useful life of 5 years and realise Rs. 5,000 as scrap. The repairs and maintenance charges are estimated to be Rs. 12,000 during the entire life of the machine. However, actual expenses on repairs and renewals were as follows :

	Rs.
2003	1,500
2004	2,000
2005	3,000
2006	4,500
2007	6,500

At the end of the fifth year the machine realized Rs. 6,500. Show the necessary ledger accounts using equitable method of charging depreciation and maintenance expenses.

Solution :

	Rs.	
Cost of the Machine	50,000	
Less estimated scrap value	5,000	
	45,000	
Add estimated Repairs and Renewals charges	12,000	
	57,000	divided by life span 5
	= Rs. 11,400	

MACHINERY A/C

Date	Particulars	Rs.	Date	Particulars	Rs.
2003			2003		
Jan. 1	To Bank A/c	50,000	Dec. 31	By Balance c/d	50,000
2004			2004		
Jan. 1	To Balance b/d	50,000	Dec. 31	By Balance c/d	50,000
2005			2005		
Jan. 1	To Balance b/d	50,000	Dec. 31	By Balance c/d	50,000
2006			2006		
Jan. 1	To Balance b/d	50,000	Dec. 31	By Balance c/d	50,000
2007			2007		
Jan	To Balance b/d	50,000	Dec. 31	By Bank A/c	6,500

				By Provision for Depreciation & Repairs A/c	39,500
				By Profit & Loss A/c (B.F.)	4,000
		50,000			50,000

PROVISION FOR DEPRECIATION & REPAIRS A/C

Date	Particulars	Rs.	Date	Particulars	Rs.
2003			2003		
Dec. 31	To Repairs & Maintenance A/c	1,500	Dec. 31	By Profit & Loss A/c	11,400
"	To Balance c/d	9,900			
		11,400			11,400
2004			2004		
Dec. 31	To Repairs & Maintenance A/c	2,000	Jan. 1	By Balance b/d	9,900
"	To Balance c/d	19,300	Dec. 31	By Profit & Loss A/c	11,400
		21,300			21,300
2005			2005		
Dec. 31	To Repairs & Maintenance A/c	3,000	Jan. 1	By Balance b/d	19,300
"	To Balance c/d	27,000	Dec. 31	By Profit & Loss A/c	11,400
		30,700			30,700
2006			2006		
Dec. 31	To Repairs & Maintenance A/c	4,500	Jan. 1	By Balance b/d	27,700
"	To balance c/d	34,600	Dec. 31	By Profit & Loss A/c	11,400
		39,100			39,100
2007			2007		
Dec. 31	To Repairs & Maintenance	6,500	Jan. 1	By Balance b/d	34,600
"	To Machinery A/c (B.F.)	39,500	Dec. 31	By Profit & Loss A/c	11,400
		46,000			46,000

Illustration 15

The following particulars are available from the books of a large fleet of transport vehicles : Balance of repairs and renewals account :

	Rs.
As on 31st March, 2007	1,15,000
Annual Repair charges incurred during :	
Year ended 31st March 2007	75,000
Year ended 3 1 st March 2008	32,000

The Company transfers annually a sum of Rs. 40,000 to the repairs and renewals reserve account. Draw up the repairs and renewals reserve account for the years 2006-2007 and 2007-2008.

[C.A. (Inter), November 1974 (Modified)]

Solution : **REPAIRS AND RENEWALS RESERVE A/C**

Date	Particulars	Rs.	Date	Particulars	Rs.
2007			2006		
Mar. 31	To Repair & Renewals A/c	75,000	April 1	By Balance b/d (B.F.)	1,50,000
"	To Balance c/d	1,15,000	2007		
			Mar. 31	By P & L A/c	40,000
		1,90,000			1,90,000
2008			2007		
Mar. 31	To Repairs & Renewals A/c	32,000	April	By Balance b/d	1,15,000
"	To Balance c/d	1,23,000	2008		
			Mar. 31	By P & L A/c	40,000
		1,55,000			1,55,000
			2008		
			April 1	By Balance b/d	1,23,000

QUESTIONS

1. Explain the nature and need for depreciation. **[B. Com. (H), DU, 1994]**
2. What is depreciation? Why is it needed? **[B.Com. (H), DU, 1988]**
3. Define Depreciation, Depletion and Amortisation. **[B. Com. (H), DU, 1988]**
4. What does the term Depreciation mean as used in accounting? What factors determine the amount of annual depreciation expense for a tangible fixed asset?
5. Distinguish depreciation from Depletion, Amortisation, Dilapidation, Fluctuation and Obsolescence.
6. Explain the necessity of providing depreciation.
7. Enumerate and explain the factors determining the amount of depreciation.
8. Distinguish between Straight Line Method and Diminishing Balance Method of providing depreciation. **[B.Com. (H), DU, 1997]**
9. Make a distinction between Annuity Method and Depreciation Fund Method of depreciation. **[B.Com. (H), DU, 1982]**
10. Describe the points of similarity and points of distinction between Depreciation Fund Method and Insurance Policy Method of providing depreciation. **[B.Com. (H), DU, 1992]**
11. Explain Sinking Fund Method of depreciation with an example. **[B.Com. (H), DU, 1998]**

PROBLEMS

1. X Ltd. purchased a Plant for Rs. 4,00,000 on 1-1-2005. Depreciation is charged @ 10% p.a. on written down value basis. The Plant was sold on 1-7-2008 for Rs. 2,26,000. Write up Plant Account assuming that accounting year ends on 31st December each year. **[C.A. Entrance, May 1980-Modified]**

   Ans. Loss on sale of Plant-Rs. 51,020.

2. On 1-7-2006 Z Ltd. purchased a second-hand machinery for Rs. 80,000 and spent Rs.12,000 on reconditioning and installing it. On 1-1-2007 another machine was purchased worth Rs. 48,000. On 30-6-2000 the machine purchased on 1-1-2007 was sold for Rs.32,000. On 1-7-2008 a new plant was purchased for Rs. 60,000.

   Depreciation is charged @ 10% on original cost. The Books of Accounts are closed 31st March each year. Prepare Plant & Machinery A/c for three years ending 31st March 2009.

   [B.Com., Madras, 1982-Modified]

   Ans. Balance in the Plant & Machinery A/c Rs. 1,22,200.

3. X purchased on 1st January 2004 second-hand plant for Rs. 30,000 and immediately spent Rs 20,000 in overhauling it. On first July, 2004. additional machinery costing Rs. 20,000 was purchased. On 1st July, 2006, the plant purchased on 1st January, 2004 became obsolete and was sold for Rs 10,000. On that date new machinery was purchased at a cost of Rs.60,000.

   Depreciation was provided for annually on 31st December, at the rate of 10 per cent per annum on the original cost of asset. With effect from 1-1-07, however, X changed this method of providing depreciation and adopted the method of writing off 15 percent on the diminishing value.

   Show the machinery account as it would appear in the books of X for the Years 2004 to 2007 (both inclusive).

   [B.com (Hons.) D.U.]

   Ans. Machinery account balance on December 31, 2007 Rs. 61,200.

4. On 1-4-2005 a machinery was purchased for Rs. 56,000 and Rs. 2,800 was spent on its installation. On 1-10-2005 another machinery was purchased for Rs. 35,000. On 1-1-2008 the first machinery purchased on 1-4-2005 was totally destroyed due to outbreak of fire in the factory, and the same was sold for Rs. 1,400 only. On 1-1-2009 a second-hand machinery was purchased for Rs. 42,000 and Rs. 7,000 was spent on its reconditioning. The machinery was put to use w.e.f. March 15, 2009.

   Depreciation has been provided at 10% on Straight Line Method. It was the practice to provide depreciation for full year on all additions made at any time during the year and to ignore depreciation on any item sold or discarded during any year. None of the assets were insured. The Accounts are closed on 31st March each year. It is now decided to follow the Diminishing Balance Method, the rate being 15% with retrospective effect and to make necessary adjustment on 31st March 2009.

   Prepare Machinery Account and Provision for Depreciation A/c for the year ending 31st March 2009.

   [C.A. (Inter), 1992-Modified]

   Ans. Rs. 84,000 Balance in Machinery A/c, Loss Rs. 45,640
   Rs. 17,062 Balance in Provision A/c, Additional Depreciation Rs. 5,162

5. On 1-1-2004 Z Ltd. acquired a machinery for Rs. 46,000 and spent Rs. 2,000 on its installation On 1-7-2004 another machinery was purchased for Rs. 16,000. On 1-7-2006, the first machinery having become obsolete was sold to Y Ltd. for Rs. 22,880 and on the same date a new machine was acquired and installed at a cost of Rs. 32,000. Depreciation is provided annually on 31st Dec. @ 10% on Written Down Value. In 2008 Z Ltd. changed to Straight Line @ 5% per annum on original cost

   Prepare Machinery A/c. and Machinery Disposal A/c. Books are closed on 31st Dec. each year

   [C.A. Entrance, 1978-Modified]

   Ans. Balance on 31 -12-2008, Rs. 40,400.

6. Modern Corporation charges depreciation on Plant & Machinery on the basis of Straight Line Method @ 10%.

   On 1-1-2010, it was decided that the Diminishing Balance Method of charging depreciation on Plant & Machinery should be adopted w.e.f. 1-1-2007, the rate of depreciation remaining 10%. The Plant &

Machinery A/c stood in the books at Rs. 67,000 on 1-1-2010. Following are the particulars regarding additions and disposal of plant during the three-year period.

		Rs.
2007	Depreciation charged during the year	8,000
1-4-07	Sale of Machinery Rs. 12,000 (bought on 1-7-2004 for Rs. 18,000)	
1-6-07	Addition made at cost	21,000
2008	Depreciation charged during the year	6,000
1-2-08	Sale of machinery scrap Rs. 600 (bought on 1-1-2008 at Rs. 27,500)	
2009	Depreciation charged during the year	7,000
31-12-09	Depreciation written off (on new machinery acquired) for 3 months	500

Prepare Plant & Machinery A/c for the year ending on 31st December 2007, 2008, 2009.

[C.A. (Inter), 1966-Modified]

Ans. Balance of Plant & Machinery A/c :

1-1-2007 Rs. 60,050

1-1-2008 Rs. 60,000

1-1-2009 Rs. 54,000

Addition made during 2009	Rs.	20,000
Profit on sale of machinery during 2008	Rs.	600
Loss on sale of Machinery 2007	Rs.	1,050

7. On 1-4-2006 S Ltd. Purchased 6 machines of Rs. 30,000 each. On 1-4-2007 one machine became defective and was sold for Rs. 25,000 and again on 1-4-2008 a second machine was also sold for Rs. 25,000. On 1-10-2007 a new machine of higher technical reliability was acquired fa Rs. 56,000. Depreciation is charged @ 10% on initial cost and debited to Profit & Loss A/c am credited to Provision for Depreciation Account on 31st March each year.

Prepare necessary accounts in the Books of the Company.

Ans.	Balance in Machinery A/c	Rs. 1,76,000
	Balance in Provision for Dep.	Rs. 44,400
	Loss on Disposal (2007)	Rs. 2,000
	Profit on Disposal (2008)	Rs. 1,000

8. On 1-1-2008 the balance in the Plant and Machinery A/c was Rs. 3,90,300. The original cost of the various machines and equipment in use was as under :

	Rs.
Machines acquired in 1997 or earlier	1,16,000
Machines acquired in 1998	62,000
Machines acquired in 1999	34,000
Machines acquired in 2000 or after	5,04,000
	7,16,000

During 2008 a new plant costing Rs. 59,000 was purchased and one machine which had cost Rs. 11,000 in 1993 was sold for Rs. 700. During 2009 further additions were made costing Rs.36,000 and a machine which had cost Rs. 14,000 in 2001 was sold for Rs. 3,000.

Depreciation is charged by the company @ 10% on original cost till the whole cost of the asset is wiped off. Full depreciation is written off even if the machinery is put to use for a part of a year. Accounts are closed on 31st December each year.

Show Plant & Machinery A/c for 2008 & 2009.

Ans. Balance in Plant & Machinery A/c Rs. 3,64,300

9. ABC Corporation had a balance of Rs. 1,62,000 to the debit of Plant & Machinery A/c on 1.1-2007. During the year 2007 part of the plant purchased on 1-1-2005 for Rs. 20,000 was sold for Rs. 12,500 on 1-7-2007 and a new machinery at a cost of Rs. 23,500 was purchased and installed at the same date, the installation charges being Rs. 1,500.

The Corporation charges depreciation @ 10% on diminishing balance. It was decided to change the method of charging depreciation to Straight Line Method retrospectively w.e.f. 1-1-2005. The rate of depreciation remaining the same as before.

Prepare Plant & Machinery A/c for the year 2007.

Ans. Balance Plant & Machinery A/c Rs. 1,49,750.

10. X Ltd. maintains its fixed assets at cost. Depreciation is charged @ 10% on written-down value method which is credited to provision for depreciation account. On 31st December 2005 the position was as under :

Asset	Cost	Accumulated Depreciation
	Rs.	Rs.
Plant and Machinery	7,53,550	3,11,750
Computers & Printers	1,32,250	57,500

On 1-4-2006 another machine costing Rs. 50,000 and on 1-6-2006 a Printer of Rs. 15,000 were purchased. A machine costing Rs. 30,000 purchased on.1-1-2004 was sold for Rs.17,500 on 30-6-2006.

During the year 2007 it was decided to change the method of charging depreciation from Written Down Value to Straight Line Method. The rate of depreciation remaining the same as before.

Prepare relevant accounts for the year ended 31st December 2006 and 2007.

[B. Com., Bombay-Modified]

Ans.

Balance as on 31-12-2006	Cost (Rs.)	Provision (Rs.)
Plant & Machinery	7,73,550	3,51,550
Computers & Printers	1,47,250	65,850
Balance as on 31-12-2007		
Plant & Machinery	7,73,550	4,28,905
Computers & Printers	1,47,250	80,875

❑❑❑

Unit-IV

9

ACCOUNTING FOR CONSIGNMENT

In order to cover the ever-expanding market and cater to the requirements of consumers spread over wide range of area the producers, manufacturers, wholesalers appoint agents to sell the goods on commission basis. These agents are usually the local people who are well aware of the local market conditions and thus able to sell goods with little efforts. This exercise is economical and profitable for both — the principal and the agent. The principal (i.e. manufacturer/ producer/ wholesaler) who appoints agent is known as the Consignor and the agent as consignee. The consignor sends the goods to the consignee who sells the goods as per the instructions of the Consignor. The Consignee sends the details of transactions relating to sales along with the expenses incurred by him. This statement of account is also known as "Account Sales". There after the consignee arranges to remit money due to the consignor after deducting for the expenses incurred (on behalf of the Consignor) and the commission as per terms of agreement. The accounting of these transactions is known as Consignment Accounting.

Thus, Consignment is the dispatch of goods (or transfer of goods) to an agent *for the purpose of sale as per the instructions given by the owner, in consideration of Commission as per terms and conditions of mutual agreement between principal and the agent. The goods may be sent either at cost or selling or proforma invoice price.

TERMS USED IN CONSIGNMENT ACCOUNTING

Proforma Invoice and Proforma invoice price:

When the goods are dispatched by the consignor to the consignee, a statement, showing the particulars of goods such as quantity, price, weight, size, grade, code, marking and the amount etc., is also sent along with the goods, is known as proforma invoice.

Whereas proforma invoice price is the amount, which is charged by the consignor, at which goods will be disposed off. It always includes certain minimum amount of profit below which the consignee is not allowed to sell except under certain conditions and as per the approval of consignor. The Proforma Invoice price is always higher than the actual cost price. In case, the goods are sent at Proforma Invoice price, an adjustment' has to be made (at the end of the period) for the loading in order to ascertain the correct amount of the profit.

Non-Recurring Expenses

These are also known as direct expenses, which are incurred in bringing the goods from consignor's place to the place of consignee. These may be paid either by consignor or consignee. Freight. Insurance-in-transit, Carriage, Cartage, Forwarding charges, Packing expenses, Dock dues, Custom duty or landing charges, Octroi, loading and unloading charges, Railway dues, Import duty etc. are the examples of Non-Recurring or direct expenses. These expenses are taken into account for the purpose of determining the value of closing stock or loss of goods-in-transit, if any.

DIFFERENCE BETWEEN CONSIGNMENT AND SALES

Basis of distinction	Consignment	Sale
1. Transfer of goods and Ownership	Consignment involves dispatch of goods from consignor to consignee without transferring ownership of goods	Sales involves transfer of goods and it's ownership from seller to buyer immediately.
2. Relationship	The relationship between the Consignor and consignee is that of Principal and an Agent for the latter acts as per the instructions of former.	The relationship between the seller and buyer is that of creditor and debtor.
3. Contract	There has to be a contract between the Consignor and consignee in writing, which is known as Consignment Deed	There is no need for a contract of sale in writing. It may be oral also.
4. Main Consideration	Commission is the main Consideration of Consignment transactions.	Profit is the main consideration of sale.
5. Incentives	The Consignor may give extra commission to the consignee for boosting sales	The seller may give discount to buyers to enhance sale.
6. Expenses	Expenses incurred by the Consignee after the goods have been received are reimbursed by the Consignor.	The seller has nothing to do with the post sale expenses. The buyer has to meet himself.
7. Order	There is an agreement to send the goods. An order is not required.	An order is a must for sale transaction.
8. Risk	All risks involved in the dispatch of goods, sale of goods, collections of money from customers rest with the consignor.	The risk is immediately transferred from seller to buyer along with the goods.
9. Periodic Statement	The Consignee is required to send a statement of transactions called Account Sales periodically to the Consignor.	There is no such statement of transactions required to be sent by or to either of the parties.
10. Return of goods	The unsold stock with the Consignee may be returned to consignor as per the instructions of the latter or the Consignee may return the goods of his own.	The seller has no right to call back the goods sold to customers. However, customers may return the goods if it is not up to mark, standard or quality.

11. Liability for loss	In case of loss in transit (normal or abnormal), loss at Consignee's godown due to fire or otherwise etc. the consignee is not liable for any such loss.	As soon as the goods are transferred along with the ownership rights, the purchaser is liable for all such losses occurring after sale.

Recurring Expenses

The expenses which are incurred after the goods have been received at Consignee's place of business (godown) are known as Recurring Expenses. These expenses are incurred quite frequently on regular basis. Such expenses are not taken into account for the purpose of determining the value of closing stock or goods-in-transit or loss-in-transit. These are Godown or shop rent, Storage Charges, Insurance charges, Salary of salesmen, selling expenses, Commission, Bank Charges, Advertising, and other Establishment expenses.

Account Sales

It is a statement sent by the consignee periodically to the consignor showing the details of goods sold, expenses incurred, commission charged, advance sent and balance remitted or due to the Consignor, if any. The Account Sales provides the necessary information relating to consignment transactions on the basis of which the Consignor records entries in the books, prepares Consignment Account, Consignee's Account and other accounts to determine the amount of profit or loss and the balance due from consignee, if any. A specimen of "Account Sales" is as under:

ACCOUNT SALES

Particular		Rs.
Gross Sales Proceeds		-------
......articles/items of goods @ Rs. ———		-------
......articles/items of goods @ Rs. ———		
Less Expenses*		
Clearing Charges/Landing Charges	-------	
Dock dues	-------	
Import duty/Custom duty	-------	
Selling Expenses	-------	
Advertising	-------	
Other Expenses	-------	
Less Commission (ordinary)		
@ ——— on Rs.	-------	
Commission (del-creditors/Over-riding)		
@ ——— on Rs.		-------
Less Advance		-------
Balance due/Bank draft		-------

* paid by consignee

Commission

It is the remuneration paid by the Consignor to the consignee for his efforts to effect sales. 1t is normally calculated at fixed percentage of total sales or as per the terms agreed upon between the consignor and consignee. The Commission paid is classified in three categories:

(i) Ordinary or Normal Commission

(ii) Del-Credere Commission

(iii) Over-riding or Special Commission.

Ordinary Commission is usually calculated at a fixed percentage on gross sales.

Del-Credere Commission is paid by the Consignor when the consignee undertakes to bear any loss arising on account of bad debts. Generally, the goods are sold by the consignee on behalf of and at the risk of consignor and hence consignee is not liable to the consignor for the loss arising out of bad debts, if any. Therefore, in order to eliminate risk of collection from customers the consignor agrees to pay extra commission to the Consignee in lieu of risk of bad debts that may arise out of credit sales. This extra commission is known as Del-Credere Commission, which is calculated on gross sale - proceeds. But, sometime del-credere commission is calculated on credit sales only if the terms and conditions of agreement so provide.

Overriding commission is paid in addition to ordinary and del-credere commission. It is allowed on achieving a specified sales target or when new product is introduced and the consignee has to make extra-efforts to sell the new product. It is also calculated at a fixed percentage on gross sales. Thus/it works as an incentive for the consignee.

ACCOUNTING TREATMENT IN THE BOOKS OF CONSIGNOR

The Goods sent on consignment may be recorded either at cost or at invoice price. The Consignor records journal entries and prepares Consignment Account, Consignee's Account, Goods sent on Consignment Account and Stock on Consignment Account. In case of goods damaged, destroyed either in-transit or at Consignee's godown, the Abnormal Loss Account has to be opened in order to ascertain profit or loss arising from Consignment transactions, and to find out amount due from consignee.

Journal Entries in the Books of Consignor (at Cost)

1. When goods are sent on consignment
   Consignment Account A/c Dr. (With the cost of goods sent)
   To Goods sent on Consignment A/c.
   (Being goods sent on Consignment to —— Name of Place)
2. When expenses of consignment are paid by the Consignor
   Consignment A/c Dr.
   To Cash/Bank A/c
   (Being expenses on Consignment paid)
3. When goods are received by Consignee No Entry
4. When an advance is received by Consignor from Consignee
   Cash/Bank/Bill Receivable A/c Dr.
   To Consignee A/c
   (Being an advance of Rs.—— received from consignee in Cash/Chcque/Bill receivable)
5. When the expenses are incurred by the consignee
   Consignment A/c Dr
   To Consignee A/c
   (Being expenses incurred by the Consignee)

6. When the Bill is discounted by the Consignor with his Bank

Bank A/c Dr

Discount A/c Dr

To Bill Receivable A/c.

(Being B/R received from consignee discounted)

7. Profit and Loss A/c Dr.

To Discount A/c

(Being discount transferred to P & L A/c)

8. When goods are sold and reported to Consignor by the Consignee.

Consignee A/c Dr.

To Consignment A/c

(Being sales reported by the Consignee)

9. For Commission on payable to Consignee

Consignment A/c Dr.

To Consignee A/c

(Being Commission due to Consignee)

10. When the goods remain unsold with the Consignee

Stock on consignment A/c Dr (at cost price plus direct proportionate Expenses of consignor and cosignee)

To consignment A/c

(Being goods lying unsold)

11. When there is a loss-in-transit or any other abnormal loss reported by the Consignee

Abnormal loss A/c Dr. (Cost of goods plus direct propor - tionate expenses of cosignor)

To Consignment A/c

(Being loss of goods reported by the Consignee)

12. When goods are insured and a claim is admitted by the insurance company

Insurance Claims A/c Dr.

To Consignment A/c

(Being a claim for loss of goods admitted by the Insurer)

13. On closing the Consignment A/c when there is profit

Consignment A/c Dr.

To Profit and Loss A/c

(Being Consignment profit transferred to P & L A/c)

or

If there is a loss:

Profit and Loss A/c Dr.

To Consignment A/c

(Being loss on consignment transferred to P and L A/c)

14. When final settlement is made and the Consignor receives the balance due from Consignee
    Cash/Bank/Bill Receivable A/c Dr.
    To Consignee A/c.
    (Being amount due from Consignee received)
15. When Goods sent on consignment Account is closed.
    Goods sent on Consignment A/c Dr.
    To Trading A/c or Purchases A/c
    (Being amount of goods sent credited to Trading*/Purchases** A/c)

* Manufacturing Concerns transfer to Trading A/c

** Trading Concerns transfer to Purchases A/c

VALUATION OF CLOSING STOCK

In order to ascertain the true profits it is necessary to make proper valuation of stock on consignment .Usually closing stock is valued either at cost or market price whichever is less. However, in case of consignment accounting cost means cost of goods (purchase price) plus direct proportionate expenses incurred by the consignor and consignee. It is calculated as under,

(i) Cost of goods lying unsold and
(ii) Proportionate non-recurring (direct) expenses incurred by the Consignor
(iii) Proportionate non-recurring (direct) expenses incurred by the Consignee.

Recurring or indirect expenses are not taking into account for the purpose of valuing closing stock.

Example. 1. X Consigned 100 bicycles @ Rs. 1,000 each to Y. He incurred the following expenses:

	Rs.
Freight	2,500
Insurance Charges	1,500
Y sold 80 bicycles @ Rs. 1,500 each and incurred the following expenses	
Clearing charges	1,000
Godown Rent	3,000
Selling and distribution expenses *	2,000

Ascertain the value of stock on consignment.

VALUATION OF STOCK ON CONSIGNMENT

20 bicycles @ Rs. 1,000 each	20,000
Add Direct (Non-recurring) proportionate expenses incurred by the consignor	
Freight and nsurance (Rs. 2,500 + 1,500) $\frac{4,000 \times 20}{100}$	800
Add Direct proportionate expenses incurred by the cosignee	
Clearing Charges Rs. $\frac{1,000 \times 20}{100}$	200
Value of Stock on Consignment	21,000

It is to be noted that while valuing stock on consignment only direct (Non-recurring) expenses are taken into account while Recurring (Indirect) expenses are totally ignored.

Illustration 1.

C of Chennai consigned 500 boxes of tea at Rs. 1,600 per box to D of Delhi. C paid Rs. 5,000 as freight and insurance. D sold 400 boxes @ Rs. 2,000 per box and 50 boxes (@ Rs. 2,200. D spent Rs. 4,000 as clearing charges and octroi. His other expenses amounted to Rs. 1,500. D remitted the amount due to C after deducting his commission @ 5% (normal)(2½% (Del-credere) and 1% (over-riding) on total sales as per the terms and conditions of consignment deed. Record journal entries and prepare Consignment Account, Consignee's Account and Goods sent on Consignment Account in the books of C.

Solution : **In the books of C**

JOURNAL ENTRIES

			Rs.	Rs.
	Consignment A/c To Goods Sent on Consignment A/c (Being goods sent on Consignment to D)	Dr	8,00,000	8,00,000
	Consignment A/c To Cash (Being expenses paid on Consignment)	Dr.	5,000	5,000
	D's A/c To Consignment A/c (Being goods sold by D) 400 boxes @ Rs. 2,000 each, 50 boxes @ "Rs. 2.200 each)	Dr.	9,10,000	9,10,000
	Consignment A/c To D (Being expenses incurred by D)	Dr.	5,500	5,500
	Consignment A/c To D (Being Commission due to D) (Normal Commission 5% + Del-Credcre $2\frac{1}{2}$ % + 1% over-riding commission) on Rs. 9,10,000	Dr.	77,350	77,350
	Stock on Consignment A/c To Consignment A/c (Being goods on consignment lying unsold)	Dr.	80,900	80,900
	Bank A/c To D (Being balance due from D received)	Dr.	8,27,150	8,27,150
	Cosignment A/c To Profit and Loss A/c (Being profit on consignment transferred to P & L A/c)	Dr.	1,03,050	1,03,050
	Goods sent on consignment A/c To Purchases (Being goods sent on consignment transferred to purchases)	Dr	8,00,000	8,00,000

Valuation of Stock on Consignment

	Rs.
Cost of 50 boxes @ Rs. 1,600 each	80,000
Add Direct proportionate expenses of cosigner	
Freight and Insurance $\left(\frac{5{,}000 \times 50}{500}\right)$	500
Add Direct proportioante expenses of consignee	
Clearing Charge $\left(\frac{4{,}000 \times 50}{500}\right)$	400
	80,900

CONSIGNMENT ACCOUNT

		Rs.		Rs.
To Goods sent on Consignment A/c		8,00,000	By D (Sales)	9,10,000
To Cash (Feight and Insurance)		5,000	By Stock on Consignment	80,900
To D (Expenses)				
Clearing Charges	4,000			
Other Expenses	1,500	5,500		
To D (Commission)				
Normal @ 5%	45,500			
Del-Credere @ $2\frac{1}{2}$	22,750			
Over-riding @ 1%	9,100	77,350		
To Profit transferred to P & L		1,03,050		
		9,90,900		9,90,900

D'S ACCOUNT

	Rs.		Rs.
To Consignment A/c (Sales)	9,10,000	By Consignment A/c (Expenses)	5,500
		By Consignment A/c (Commission)	77,350
		By Bank	8,27,150
	9,10,000		9,10,000

GOODS SENT ON CONSIGNMENT A/C

	Rs.		Rs.
To Purchases A/c	8,00,000	By Consignment A/c	8,00,000
	8,00,000		8,00,000

BOOKS OF CONSIGNEE

Consignee is simply an agent who acts in accordance with the instructions given by his principal (Consignor) in consideration of commission as per consignment deed (agreement). He is not the owner of goods he is selling. He is not authorised to make purchases. He receives goods only from the consignor for the purpose of sale on behalf of the consignor. Thus receipt of goods is known as inward consignment and is recorded in consignment Inward Book only. No other accounting entry in respect of goods received is recorded.

JOURNAL ENTRIES INTHE BOOKS OF CONSIGNEE

1. When consignment of goods is received

   No Entry

2. When expenses are incurred by the consignee

   Consignor's A/c Dr

   To Cash/Bank

   (Being Expenses incurred on Consignment)

3. When any advance is sent to Consignor

   Consignor's A/c Dr

   To Cash/Bank/Bills Payable A/c

   (Being advance sent to consignor by Cash/Cheque/Bill)

4. When goods are sold for Cash

   Cash/Bank A/c Dr

   To Consignor's A/c

   (Being sales made for Cash)

5. When goods are sold on credit

   Consignment Debtors A/c Dr

   To Consignor's A/c

   (Being goods sold on credit)

6. When the commission is due

   Consignor's A/c Dr

   To Commission A/c

   (Being commission become due)

7. When collection is made from Consignment debtors

   Cash/Bank A/c Dr

   To Consignment Debtors

   (Being amount collected from debtors)

8. For bad debts

   (a) When del-credere commission is not allowed

   Consignor's A/c Dr

   To Consignment Debtors

   (Being bad debts incurred on consignment debtors)

(b) When del-credere commission is allowed

Bad debts A/c Dr

To Consignment debtors

(Being bad debts incurred on consignment debtors)

Commission A/c Dr

To Bad debts

(Being bad debts adjusted against commission)

9. When Commission is transferred to Profit and Loss A/c

Commission Account Dr

To Profit and Loss A/c

(Being Commission transferred to P & L A/c)

10. When the amount due to Consignor is remitted/paid.

Consignor's Account Dr

To Cash/Bank/Bills Payable A/c.

(Being amount due to consignor paid)

11. For stock on Consignment

No Entry.

Illustration 2.

X of Delhi consigned 1,000 sewing machines to Y of Ludhiana costing Rs. 750 each and incurred Rs. 4,800 on freight, Rs. 1,200 on insurance Rs. 1,000 packing and loading. Immediately after receipt of goods X drew a bill on Y for Rs. 2,50,000 payable after two months. The bill was discounted by X at 9% p.a the next day. Y sent an account sales reporting that he sold 800 machines at Rs. 1,000 per sewing machine and incurred following expenses:

	Rs.
Clearing Charges	1,800
Unloading and Carriage Inward	1,200
Godown rent	5,000
Selling and Other establishment Expenses	2,500

Y is entitled a normal commission @ 5% and 2% del-credere. Y remitted the amount due to X by bank draft.

Record journal entries and necessary ledger accounts in the books of both the parties

Solution : **In the Books of Consignor (X)**

JOURNAL ENTRIES

			Rs.	Rs.
	Consignment A/c Dr. To Goods sent on Consignment A/c (Being goods sent on consignment)		7,50,000	7,50,000

Date	Particulars		L.F.	Dr.	Cr.
	Consignment A/c	Dr.		7,000	
	To Cash				7,000
	(Being expenses on consignment paid) Freight Rs. 4,800 + Insurance Rs. 1,200 + Packing and loading Rs. 1,000				
	Bills Receivable A/c	Dr.		2,50,000	
	To Y				2,50,000
	(Being bill drawn accepted by Y)				
	Bank A/c	Dr.		2,46,250	
	Discount A/c	Dr.		3,750	
	To Bills Receivable				2,50,000
	(Being bill discounted @ 9% p.a.)				
	$2{,}50{,}000 \times \frac{9}{100} \times \frac{2}{12} = 3{,}750$				
	Consignment A/c	Dr.		10,500	
	To Y				10,500
	(Being expenses incurred by Y)				
	(Clearing charges Rs. 1,800 + Unloading and Carriage inward Rs. 1.200 + Godown Rent Rs. 5,000 + Selling and Other establishment expenses Rs. 2,500)				
	Y A/c	Dr.		8,00,000	
	To Consignment A/c				8.00,000
	(Being goods sold by Y)				
	Consignment A/c	Dr.		56,000	
	To Y				56,000
	(Being commission due to Y)				
	Normal commission @ 5% and Del-credere @ 2% or Rs. 8,00,000				
	Stock on Consignment A/c	Dr.		1,52,000	
	To Consignment A/c				1,52,000
	(Being Stock valued on Consigment)				
	Consignment A/c	Dr.		1,28,500	
	To Profit & Loss A/c				1,28,500
	(Being profit on cosignment transferred to P & L A/c)				
	Bank A/c	Dr.		4,83,500	
	To Y				4,83,500
	(Being balance remitted by Y)				

CONSIGNMENT ACCOUNT

		Rs.		Rs.
To Goods sent on Consignment A/c		7,50,000	By Y (Sales)	8,00,000
To Cash (Expenses)			By Stock on Consignment*	1,52,000
Freight	4,800			
Insurance	1,200			
Packing and Loading	1,000	7,000		
To Y (Expenses)				
Clearing Charges	1,800			
Unoloading and Carriage I/W	1,200			
Go-down rent	5,000			
Selling and O.E. Exp.	2,500	10,500		
To Y (Commission)				
Normal @ 5%	40,000			
Del-Credere @ 2%	16,000	56,000		
To Profit & Loss A/c		1,28,500		
		9,52,000		9,52,000

Y A/c

	Rs.		Rs.
To Consignment A/c (Sales)	8,00,000	By Bills Receivable A/c	2,50,000
		By Consignment A/c (Exp.)	10,500
		By Consignment A/c (Comm.)	56,000
		By Bank A/c	4,83,500
	8,00,000		8,00,000

GOODS SENT ON CONSIGNMENT A/c

	Rs.		Rs.
To Trading A/c	7,50,000	By Consignment A/c	7,50,000
	7,50,000		7,50,000

* Stock on Consignment :		Rs.
200 sewing Machines @ Rs. 750 each		1,50,000
Add Direct proportionate expenses :		
Consignor's	7,000	
Consignee's	3,000	2000
	10000 × 200/1000 =	152,000

Books of Consignee (Y)
JOURNEL ENTRIES

				Rs.	Rs.
	X A/c	Dr.		10,500	
	To Cash A/c				10,500
	(Being expenses paid)				
	X A/c	Dr.		2,50,000	
	To Bills payable A/c				2,50,000
	(Being bill drawn by X accepted)				
	Bank A/c	Dr.		8,00,000	
	To X				8,00,000
	(Being sales made)				
	X A/c	Dr.		56,000	
	To Commission A/c				56,000
	(Being Commission due)				
	X A/c	Dr.		4,83,500	
	To Bank				4,83,500
	(Being amount due remitted to X)				
	Commission A/c	Dr.		56,000	
	To Profit & Loss A/c				56,000
	(Being Commission transferred to P &L A/c)				

CONSIGNOR'S (X) A/c

		Rs.		Rs.
To Bills Payable		2,50,000	By Bank	8,00,000
To Cash (Expenses)				
Clearing Charges	1,800			
Unloading and Carriage I/W	1,200			
Go down Rent	5,000			
Selling and O.E. Exp.	2,500	10,500		
To Commission				
Normal @ 5%	40,000			
Del-credere @ 2%	16,000	56,000		
To Bank (balance remitted)		4,83,500		
		8,00,000		8,00,000

COMMISSION A/c

	Rs.		Rs.
To Profit and Loss A/c	56,000	By X A/c	56,000
	56,000		56,000

NORMAL AND ABNORMAL LOSSES

When goods are sent on consignment, sometimes a part of goods may be lost either in transit or at consignee's place such loss may be normal or abnormal depending upon the nature of loss.

1. Normal loss is unavoidable because it is due to inherent characteristics of goods. Such loss is bound to occur in the course of consignment transaction and cannot be controlled. It is due to natural causes such as leakage, shrinkage, breakage or loss of weight due to evaporation, sublimation or drying up of goods etc. Such losses are not shown in the consignment Account. It is treated part of cost of goods and no accounting entry is required for it's adjustment. The only effect the normal loss has, is the higher cost per unit. For example 'A' consigns 1,000 Kg of edible oil to "B" at the rate of Rs. 50 per Kg. and incurs Rs. 960 as freight and forwarding charges. During transit 20 Kg. of oil was lost due to leakage. The consignee sold 750 Kg of oil.

Find out value of closing stock.

	Rs.
Cost of 1,000 Kg of oil @ Rs. 50	50,000
Add Non-Recurring (Direct) expenses	960
But consignee received only 980 Kg. of oil	50,960
Therefore, Rs. 50,960 is the cost of 980 Kg of oil	
Hence, unsold stock of 230 Kg will be valued as under.	
$\text{Stock} = \frac{\text{Rs. } 50{,}960}{980 \text{ kg}} \times 230 \text{ kg} =$	Rs. 11,960

$$\text{i.e.,} = \frac{\text{Total Cost of goods + Non - recurring expenses}}{\text{Goods Units Received by consignee}} \times \text{Unsold Stock in Units}$$

Illustration 3

K of Kolkata consigned 5,000 tones of coal @ Rs. 100 per tone to C of Chennai. K paid Rs. 25,000 as freight and loading charges. C took the delivery and paid Rs. 5.000 as clearing charges. Rs. 4,100 as unloading charges. Godown rent of Rs. 15,000 has already been paid in advance by C. Loss due to evaporation is estimated to be 2% of the coal consigned. C sold 4.500 tones of coal @ Rs. 150 per tone. He was allowed commission @ 5% on gross sales. You are required to prepare Consignment Account, showing the treatment of loss due to evaporation.

Solution :

In the Books of K

CONSIGNMENT CCOUNT

		Rs.		Rs.
To Goods Sent on Consignment		5,00,000	By C (Sales)	6,75,000
To Bank (Freight and loading charges)		25,000	By Stock on Consignment*	43,600
To C (Expenses)				
Clearing Charges	5,000			
Unloading Charges	4,100			
Go down Rent	15,000	24,100		
To C (Commission)		33,750		
To Profit transferred to Profit & Loss A/c		1,35,750		
		7,18,600		7,18,600

* Valuation of Closing Stock	Rs.
Cost of 5,000 Tones @ Rs. 100	5,00,000
Add Direct expenses: of consignor's and	25,000
Consignees (5,000 + 4,100)	9,100
	5,34,100

Rs. 5,34,100 is the Cost of 5,000 Tones of Coal but 100 Tones (i.e. 2% of 5,000 tones) is lost due to evaporation being normal loss by nature. Hence Rs. 5,34,100 is the cost of 4,900 tones of coal. Out of this 4,500 tones was sold leaving a unsold stock of 400 tones of Coal. The Value of Stock on Consignment will be as under

$$\frac{5{,}34{,}100}{5000-100} \times 400 = \frac{5{,}34{,}100}{4{,}900} \times 400 = \text{Rs. } 43{,}600$$

When loss of goods is incurred due to negligence, accident or caused by unnatural and unexpected reasons, it is treated as abnormal loss. Loss of goods due to theft, fire, flood, earth quake, war. or accident in transit etc. are treated abnormal losses. Such losses are adjusted before ascertaining profit or loss on consignment. The amount of abnormal loss is calculated just like value of stock on consignment. Abnormal loss can be ascertained as under :

	Rs.
Cost of goods damaged or destroyed	——
Add Direct proportionate expenses incurred prior to loss	——
	——

It is to be noted that only those direct expenses will be accounted for which arc incurred before the loss. Thus, where an abnormal loss arises in-transit, then only proportionate expenses incurred prior to this loss such as dispatch and forwarding expenses, will be taken in to account for the purpose of determining the value of abnormal loss. These expenses are usually paid by the Consignor. If goods arc destroyed at Consignee's place then proportionate expenses incurred by the consignee will also be added to the value of abnormal loss.

Accounting treatment of abnormal loss :

(i) When goods are not insured at all

Abnormal Loss A/c Dr.

To Consignment A/c

(Being abnormal loss incurred)

Profit & Loss A/c Dr.

To Abnormal loss A/c

(Being abnormal loss charged to P &L A/c)

(ii) When goods are partly insured

Abnormal Loss A/c Dr.

To Consignment A/c

(Being abnormal loss incurred)

Insurance claims/Bank A/c Dr. With the amount} of claim admitted/received

Profit & Loss A/c Dr. (Balancing figure)

To Abnormal loss A/c/

(Being loss partly admitted/recovered and balance transferred to P & L A/c)

(iii) When goods are fully insured

Abnormal loss A/c Dr.

To Consignment A/c

Insurance Claims/Bank A/c Dr.

To Abnormal Loss A/c

(Being amount fully admitted/Recovered from Insurance Co.)

Illustration 4

X consigned 500 bags of rice to Y, each bag costing Rs. 800 and paid Rs. 13,500 towards freight and insurance. During transit 20 bags were damaged and the Insurer paid Rs. 6,000 only.

Y took the delivery of the goods and immediately accepted a bill drawn on him for Rs. 2,00,000 for two months. Y reported that 300 bags were sold @ Rs. 1,200, 100 bags @ Rs. 1,250 and the damaged bags @ Rs. 250 per bag. He incurred the following expenses.

	Rs.
Clearing Charges	2,400
Godown Rent	5,000
Carriage Outwards	500

He is entitled to a commission @ 5% on the sale proceeds excepting damaged goods. Y remitted the balance due to X by bank draft. Prepare necessary ledger accounts in the books of X.

Solution

In the hooks of X

CONSIGNMENT ACCOUNT

	Rs.		Rs.
To Goods sent on Consignment	4,00,000	By X (Sales)	4,85,000
To Bank (Freight and Insurance)	13,500	300 bags @ Rs. 1,200	
To X Rs.		100 bags @ Rs. 1,250	
Clearing Charges 2,400		By Abnormal loss A/c (1)	16,540
Go down Rent 5,000		By Stock on Consignment (2)	66,560
Carriage O/W 500	7,900		
To X (Commission)	24,250		
To Profit transferred to P & L A/c	1,22,450		
	5,68,100		5,68,100

Y ACCOUNT

	Rs.		Rs.
To Consignment A/c (Sales)	4,85,000	By BilllsReceivable	2,00,000
To Abnormal Loss A/c	5,000	By Consignment A/c (Expenses)	7,900
(Sale of damaged bags)		By Consignment A/c (Commission)	24,250
20 bags @ 250 each		By Bank (draft)	2,57,850
	4,90,000		4,90,000

ABNORMAL LOSS A/c

	Rs.		Rs.
To Consignment A/c	16,540	By Y A/c (Sale)	5,000
		By Bank-Insurance claim	6,000
		By Profit & Loss A/c	5,540
	16,540		16,540

Working Notes :

		Rs.
(1)	Calculation of Abnormal loss	16,000
	Cost of 20 bags @ Rs. 800 per bag	
	Add Direct proportionate Expenses of consignor	
	Freight and Insurance $\left(\frac{13{,}500 \times 20}{500}\right)$	540
		16,540
(2)	Valuation of Closing Stock	
	Cost of 80 bags @ Rs. 800 per bag	64,000
	Add Direct proportionate Expenses of Consignor	
	Freight and Insurance $\left(\frac{13{,}500 \times 80}{500}\right)$	2,160

Add Direct proportionate Expenses of Consignce

Clearing charges $\left(\frac{2,400 \times 80}{480}\right)$ 400

66,560

Illustration 5 (Normal and Abnormal loss)

M Ltd. of Mumbai Consigned 1,000, barrels of lubricant oil costing Rs. 1,200 per barrel to Standard Oil Company, Delhi. M Ltd. paid Rs. 60,000 as freight and Rs. 12,000 as insurance. 50 barrels of oil was destroyed in-transit. The insurance claim was settled at Rs. 25.000 and was paid directly to consignor.

Standard Oil Company took delivery of consignment and accepted a bill for Rs. 5,00,000 for three months. An account sale was received and following was reported by the consignee,

(i) 750 barrels of oil was sold @ Rs. 1,750 per barrel

(ii) The Other expenses were

	Rs.
Clearing Charges	13,800
Godown rent	15,000
Wages	35,000
Selling and Advertising Expenses	25,000

(iii) 20 barrels of oil was lost due to leakage which is considered to be normal.

Standard Oil Co. is entitled to a commission of 5% on gross sales. The balance due to consignor was sent by bank draft.

You arc required to prepare necessary ledger accounts in the books of M Ltd.

Solution : **In the books of M Ltd.**

CONSIGNMENT ACCOUNT

		Rs.		Rs.
To Goods Sent Consignment		12,00,000	By Standard Oil Co. (Sales)	
To Bank (Expenses)			750 barrels @ 1,750	13,12,500
Freight	60,000		By Abnormla Loss(1)	63,600
Insurance	12,000	72,000	By Stock on Consignment(2)	2,36,555
To Standard Oil Co. (Expenses)				
Clearing charges	13,800			
Go down Rent	15,000			
Wages	35,000			
Selling and Advt. Exp.	25,000	88,800		
To Standard Oil Co. (Commission)		65,625		
To Profit-transferred to P & L A/c		1,86,230		
		16,12,655		16,12,655

STANDARD OIL COMPANY A/c

	Rs.		Rs.
To Consignment A/c (Sales)	13,12,500	By Bills Receivable	5,00,000
		By Consignment A/c (Expenses)	88,800
		By Consignment A/c (Commission)	65,625
		By Bank (draft)	6,58,075
	13,12,500		13,12,500

ABNORMAL LOSS A/c

	Rs.		Rs.
To Consignment A/c	63,600	By Bank-Insurance Claims	25,000
		By Profit and Loss A/c	38,600
	63,600		63,600

GOODS SENT ON COSIGNMENT

	Rs.		Rs.
To Trading A/c	12,00,000	By Consignment A/c	12,00,000
	12,00,000		12,00,000

Working notes : Rs.

(1) Calculation of Abnormal Loss

		Rs.
50 barrels @ Rs. 1, 200 per barrel		60,000
Add Direct proportionate expenses of Consignor		
Freight	60,000 $\left(\dfrac{\text{Rs. } 72{,}000 \times 50}{1{,}000}\right)$	3,600
Insurance	12,000	63,600

(2) Valuation of Closing Stock

	Rs.
Cost of 1,000 barrels of oil @ Rs. 1,200 per barrel	12,00,000
Add Non-recurring Expenses of Consignor	72,000
(Freight Rs. 60,000 + Insurance Rs. 12,000)	12,72,000
Less Abnormal loss	(63,600)
	12,08,400
Add Non-recurring (Direct) expenses of Consignee	13,800
Value of (1,000 – 50 – 20) 930 Barrels	12,22,200
Stock of 180 (930 – 750) barrels $\dfrac{12{,}22{,}200 \times 180}{930} =$	2,36,555

Illustration 6 (Loss of goods in transit .and at Consignee's place)

Ahmcd Mills of Ahmedabad consigned 500 tins of 20 Kg each of coconut oil to S.K. Distributors of Delhi (@ Rs. 40 per Kg. and incurred following expenses

	Rs.
Freight and Insurance in transit	5,000
Loading Charges	1,000

During transit 10 tins were accidentally destroyed, The consignee took the delivery and accepted a bill of Rs. 3,50,000 drawn by Ahmed Mills at three months duration S.K. Distributors sold 400 tins @ Rs. 55 per Kg. and reported to Ahmcd Mills a further loss of 15 tins due to fire at go-down. The consignee incurred following expenses:

	Rs.
Clearing charges	9,800
Godown rent	6,000
Selling and Distribution expenses	3,500

S.K. Distributors arc entitled a commission of 5% plus 1% Del credere. Insurance Company admitted a claim of Rs. 5,000. You arc required to prepare necessary ledger accounts in the books of Ahmed Mills.

Solution : **In the Books of Ahmcd Mills**

CONSIGNMENT ACCOUNT

		Rs.		Rs.
To Goods Sent on Consignment		4,00,000	By S.K. Distributors (Sales)	4,40,000
To Bank (Expenses)			(400 × 20 × 55)	
Freight and Insurance	5,000		By Abnormal Loss A/c$^{(1)}$	8,120
Loading Charges	1,000	6,000	(Loss in Transit)	
To S.K. Distributors (Exp.)			By Abnormla Loss A/c$^{(2)}$	12,480
Claring Charges	9,800		(Loss by fire at go down)	
Go down Rent	6,000		By Stock on Consignment$^{(3)}$	62,400
Sellingand Distribution Exp.	3,500	19,300		
To S.K. distributors (Commission)				
Ord. Commission @ 5%	22,000			
Del. Credere @ 1%	4,400	26,400		
To Profit on Consignment Transferred to P & L A/c		71,300		
		5,23,000		5,23,000

S.K. DISTRIBUTORS A/c

	Rs.		Rs.
To Consignment A/c (Sales)	4,40,000	By Consignment A/c (Expenses)	19,300
		By Bills Receivable	3,50,000
		By Consignment A/c (Commission)	26,400
		By Balance c/d	44,300
	4,40,000		4,40,000

GOODS SENT ON CONSIGNMENT A/c

	Rs.		Rs.
To Trading A/c	4,40,000	By Consignment A/c	4,40,000
	4,40,000		4,40,000

(1) ABNORMAL LOSS ACCOUNT

	Rs.		Rs.
To Consignment A/c (Loss in Transist)	8,150	By Insurance Claims	5,000
To Consignment A/c (Loss by fire)	12,480	By Profit and Loss A/c (Bal figure)	15,630
	20,630		20,630

Working notes : Rs.

(1) **Loss in Transit :**

Cost of Oil destroyed

(10 tins of 20 each) 200 kg @ 40 per kg. — 8,000

Add Direct Proportionate Expenses of Consignor

Freight and Insurance in transit Rs. 5,000

Loading Chages Rs. 1000 = $\frac{6{,}000 \times 10 \text{ Tins}}{500 \text{ Tins}}$ — 120

8,120

(2) **Loss by fire at godown :**

15 Tins of 20 kg each @ Rs. 40 per kg — 12,000

Add Direct proportionate Expenses of Consignor $\left(\frac{6{,}000 \times 15 \text{ Tins}}{500 \text{ Tins}}\right)$ — 180

Add Direct proportionate Expenses of Consignee

Clearing Charges Rs. $\frac{9{,}800 \times 15 \text{ Tins}}{490 \text{ Tins}}$ — 300

12,480

(500 Tins – 10 destroyed in transit)

(3) **Stock on Consignment :**

75 Tins of 20 kg each @ Rs. 40 per kg — 60,000

Add Direct proportionate expenses of consignor $\left(\frac{6{,}000 \times 75}{500}\right)$ — 900

Add Direct proportionate Expenses of Consignee $\left(\frac{9{,}800 \times 75}{490}\right)$ — 1,500

62,400

SHORTAGE OF GOODS (STOCK)

Sometime a shortage or deficiency may arise in stock at Consignee's godown at the time of stock taking. Such shortage or deficiency is valued on the same basis as the value of unsold stock. Usually such loss is borne by the Consignor who records the following entries

(i) Stock Deficiency Account Dr.
To Consignment Account

(ii) Profit and Loss A/c Dr.
To Stock Deficiency A/c

However, in case if it is agreed that such deficiency is to be made good by the Consignee, then the following entry will be recorded,

(i) Consignee's A/c Dr.
To Consignment A/c

Alternatively, the entries can be recorded.

Stock Deficiency Account Dr.
To Consignment A/c

(ii) Consignee's Account Dr.
To Stock Deficiency A/c

Illustration 7 (Stock Deficiency)

X Consigned 1,000 shirts @ Rs. 100 each and paid the following expenses:

Freight	2,000
Insurance	1,000

Y took the delivery and incurred Rs. 2,000 as clearing charges and Rs. 3,500 as rent of the godown. Y accepted a 3 months bill drawn by X for Rs. 40,000. An account sale was received from Consignee who reported sale of 820 shirts @ Rs. 200»each and deficiency of 10 shirts disclosed by actual physical stocktaking. The Consignee was entitled to a commission @ 5% on gross sale proceeds.

You are required to prepare necessary ledger accounts in the books of X.

Solution : **In the books of X**

ONSIGNMENT ACCOUNTS

		Rs.		Rs.
To Goods sent on Consignment		1,00,000	By Y (Sale)	
To Cash (Expenses) :			820 @ Rs. 200 each	1,64,000
Freight	2,000		By Stock Deficiency A/c (1)	1,050
Insurance	1,000	3,000	By Stock on Consignment A/c (2)	17,850
To Y (Expenses)				
Clearing Charges	2,000			
Go-down Rent	3,500	5,500		
To Y (commission) @ 5%		8,200		
To Profit transferred to P & L A/c		66,200		
		1,82,900		1,82,900

Y (CONSIGNEE'S) ACCOUNT

	Rs.		Rs.
To Consignment A/c (Sales)	1,64,000	By Bill Receivable	40,000
		By Consignment A/c (Expenses)	5,500
		By Consignment A/c (Commission)	8,200
		By Balance c/d	1,10,300
	1,64,000		1,64,000

Working notes :

		Rs.
(1)	Calculation of Stock Deficiency	
	Cost of 10shirts @ Rs. 100	1,000
	Add Direct proportionate Expenses of Consignor	
	Freight and Insurance $\left(\frac{3,000}{1,000}\times 10\right)$	30
	Add Direct proportionate Expenses of Consignee	
	Clearing charges $\left(\frac{2,000}{1,000}\times 10\right)$	20
		1,050
(2)	Value of Closing Stock	
	170 Shirts @ Rs. 100 each	17,000
	Add Direct proportionate expenses of Consignor. $\left(\frac{3,000}{1,000}\times 170\right)$	510
	Add Direct proportionate expenses of Consignee $\left(\frac{2,000}{1,000}\times 170\right)$	340
		17,850

Illustration 8 (Commission and bonus to Consignee)

A of Allahabad consigned 1,000 bags of rice to D of Delhi. The cost price was Rs. 600 per bag but the consignment invoice was out to show a gross profit of 20% on invoice price. D reported that he had sold 3/4th of the consignment at a profit of 25% on sales and he had incurred Rs. 16,250 as freight and landing charges and Rs. 3,750 by way of go-down rent. Consignor spent Rs. 3.000 earlier as expenses in dispatching the goods D was entitled to a commission of 5% on sales and 10% of the net proceeds as bonus after charging both commission and bonus. The consignee sent the balance due to A by a demand draft.

Show the necessary ledger accounts in the books of A.

Solution : **In the Books of 'A'**

CONSIGNMENT ACCOUNT

	Rs.		Rs.
To Goods sent on consignment	7,50,000	By D (Sales)	6,00,000
(1,000 @ Rs. 750*)		750 bags @ 800** each	
To Cash : Dispatch expenses	3,000	By Goods Sent on Consignment	1,50,000
To D : Freight and landing charges	16,250	(loading) (1,000 @ Rs. 150)	
Go-down rent	3,750	By Stock on Consignment[(2)]	1,92,313
Commission	30,000		
Bonus[(1)]	50,000		
To Stock Reserve (250 × 150)	37,500		
To Profit transferred to P & L A/c	51,813		
	9,42,313		9,42,313

D'S ACCOUNT

	Rs.		Rs.
To Consignment A/c	6,00,000	By Consignment A/c (Expenses)	20,000
		By Consignment A/c	80,000
		(Commission and Bonus)	
		By Bank Draft	5,00,000
	6,00,000		6,00,000

GOODS SENT ON CONSIGNMENT ACCOUNT

	Rs.		Rs.
To Consignment A/c	1,50,000	By Consignment Account	7,50,000
To Purchases transferred to Trading A/c	6,00,000		
	7,50,000		7,50,000

Working notes : * Calculation of Invoice Price

	Rs.
Let the invoice price be	100
Profit	20
Cost price	80
Rate of Profit on Cost	20/80/or 1/4
Cost price of a bag of rice	Rs. 600
Add Profit (@ 1/4 on cost)	Rs. 150
Invoice price per bag	Rs. 750

**** Calculation of Selling price**		Rs.
Let the sale price be		100
Profit		25
Cost price		75
Rate of profit on Cost		25/75 or 1/3
Cost price of a bag of rice		600
Add profit (1/3 on cost)		200
Sale price per bag		800
(1) Calculation of bonus		Rs.
Sale proceeds (Gross)		6,00,000
3/4th of $1,000 \times 800$		
Less Commission @ 5%	30,000	
Expenses of Consignee	20,000	50,000
Proceeds before bonus		5,50,000
@ 10% of net proceeds after charging such bonus $\frac{5,50,000}{110} \times 10 =$		50,000
(2) Stock on Consignment		Rs.
Invoice price of 1/4th of Consignment 250 bags @ 750		187,500
Add Direct proportionate Expenses of Consignor		
Dispatch expenses $\left(3,000 \frac{1}{4}\right)$		750
Add Direct proportionate expenses of consignee		
Freight and landing charges (Rs. $16,250 \times 1/4$)		4,063
		192,313

Illustration 9 (Stock taken over by consignee)

M of Madurai consigned 2,500 Calculators costing Rs. 60 each to B of Bhopal. M drew on B a bill for Rs. 1,12,500 at 3 months duration which was duly accepted by B. The Consignee reported sale of 1,000 calculators @ Rs. 80 each for cash and another 1,000 @ Rs. 82 per calculator on credit basis. M paid freight and insurance of Rs. 1,250 and other forwarding expenses-of Rs. 500. B incurred Rs. 750 as Octroi and carriage. B was entitled to a commission @ 5% and 2% as del-credere on total gross sale proceeds. B sent an account sales showing as a deduction the commission due and expenses incurred by him. The calculators remaining unsold were taken over by B @ Rs. 82 per calculator as his own stock. The amount due to M was sent by a demand draft.

You are required to prepare necessary ledger accounts in the books of M and B. A customer to whom 5 calculators were sold on credit basis became insolvent and nothing could be recovered from him.

Solution :

In the Books of M

CONSIGNMENT ACCOUNT

	Rs.		Rs.
To Goods sent on Consignment	1,50,000	By B (Sales Proceeds)	
To Bank (Expenses)		Cash : 1,000 @ Rs. 80	80,000
Freight and Insurance	1,250	Credit : 1,000 @ Rs. 82	82,000
Forwading Expenses	500	By B (Stock taken over)	
To B (Octroi and Carriage)	750	500 @ Rs. 82	41,000
To B (Commission including Dcl-Credere)*	14,210		
To Profit transferred to P & L A/c	36,290		
	2,03,000		2,03,000

* Gross sale proceeds includes goods taken over by consignee at an agreed price. Hence commission @ 7% (5% + 2%) has been calculated on Rs. 2,03,000 (*i.e.* Rs. 80,000 + 82,000 + 41,000).

GOODS SENT ON CONSIGNMENT A/c

	Rs.		Rs.
To Purchases transferred to Trading A/c	1,50,000	By Consignment A/c	1,50,000
	1,50,000		1,50,000

B'S ACCOUNT

	Rs.		Rs.
To Consignment A/c (Sales)	1,62,000	By Bill Receivable	1,12,500
To Consignment A/c (Goods taken by B)	41,000	By Consignment A/c (Expenses)	750
		By Consignment A/c (Commission)	14,210
		By Bank (D.D.)	75,540
	2,03,000		2,03,000

In the Books of B

M's ACCOUNT

	Rs.		Rs.
To Cash (Expenses)	750	By Cash	80,000
To Commission	14,210	By Debtors (Consignment)	82,000
To Bills Payable	1,12,500	By Purchases	41,000
To Bank	75,540		
	2,03,000		2,03,000

CONSIGNMENT DEBTORS A/c

	Rs.		Rs.
To M's A/c	82,000	By Cash	81,590
		By Bad debts	410
	82,000		82,000

BAD DEBTS ACCOUNT

	Rs.		Rs.
To Consignment Debtors	410	By Commission A/c	410
	410		410

COMMISSION ACCOUNT

	Rs.		Rs.
To Bad debts	410	By M's A/c	14,210
To P & L A/c	13,800		
	14,210		14,210

GRADED ILLUSTRATIONS

Illustration 1 (Loss in Transit & Insurance Claims)

X Consigned 1,000 fancy ceiling fans costing Rs. 1,000 each to his agent Y and spent Rs. 750 for carriage, Rs. 8,000 for freight and Rs. 3,250 on insurance-in-transit. Y received the delivery of 950 fancy ceiling fans. Account sales showed that 750 fans were sold for Rs. 9,80,000 and Y incurred Rs. 3,500 on carriage and Rs. 6,000 for customs duty at the time of taking delivery. Y was entitled to commission @ 6% on sales effected by him. He incurred expenses amounting to Rs. 2,000 for repairing damaged fans remaining in the stock. X lodged a claim with the insurance company, which was admitted at Rs. 32,500. Show the Consignment Account and the Account of Y in the books of X.

[C.A. (Entrance) May 1980. Adapted]

Solution : **In the hooks of X**

CONSIGNMENT ACCOUNT

		Rs.		Rs.
To Goods sent on Consignment		10,00,000	By Y (Sales)	9,80,000
To Cash (Expenses)			By Insurance Company (Claims)	32,500
Carriage	750		By Profit & Loss A/c (1)	18,100
Freight	8,000		(Loss)	
Insurance	3,250	12,000	By Stock on consignment (2)	2,04,400
To Y				
Carriage	3,500			
Customs duty	6,000			
Comission @ 6%	58,800			
Repair	2,000	70,300		
To Profit transferred to				
Profit & Loss A/c		152,700		
		12,35,000		12,35,000

Y'S ACCOUNT

	Rs.			Rs.
To Consignment A/c (Sales)	9,80,000	By Consignmen A/c (Exp)		
		Carriage	3,500	
		Customs duty	6,000	
		Repairs	2,000	
		Commission	58,800	70,300
		By Balance c/d		9,09,700
	9,80,000			9,80,000

Working notes :

		Rs.
(1)	Calculation of abnormal loss (Damages in transit)	50,000
	Cost of 50 fancy ceiling fans @ Rs. 1,000	
	Add Direct proportionate expenses of the Consignor $\left(12{,}000 \frac{50}{1{,}000}\right)$	600
		50,600
	Loss = Value of good damaged less insurance Claims	
	Rs. 50,600 – 32,500	18,100
(2)	Stock on Consignment	
	Cost of unsold fans	
	200 fans @ 1,000	2,00,000
	Add Direct proportionate Expenses of Consignor $\left(\frac{12{,}000 \times 200}{1{,}000}\right)$	2,400
	Add Direct proportionate expenses of Consignee	
	(Carriage and Customs duty) $\left(\frac{9{,}500 \times 200}{950}\right)$	2,000
		2,04,400

Illustration 2 (Goods in Transit)

Shri Mehta of Mumbai consigns 1,000 cases of goods costing Rs. 100 each to Sri Sundram of Chennai. Shri Mehta pays the following expenses in connection with the consignment:

	Rs.
Carriage	1,000
Freight	3,000
Loading Charges	1,000

Shri Sundram sells 700 cases at Rs. 140 each and incurs the following expenses:

	Rs.
Clearing Charges	850
Warehousing Charges	1,700
Packing and Selling Expenses	600

It is found that 50 cases have been lost in transit and 100 cases arc still in transit. Shri Sundram is entitled to a commission of 10% on gross sales. Draw up consignment Account and Sundram's Account in the books of Shri Mehta

[CA (Inter) May1981]

Solution :

In the Books of Shri. Mehta

CONSIGNMENT ACCOUNT

		Rs.		Rs.
To Goods sent on Consignment		1,00,000	By Sundram (Sales)	98,000
To Cash (Expenses)			700 cases @ Rs. 140 each	
Carriage	1,000		By Profit & Loss A/c (1)	
Freight	3,000		(Abnormal)	5,250
Loading	1,000	5,000	By Stock on Consignment (2)	15,900
To Sundram (Exp. And Comm.)			(with Consignee)	
Clearing Charges	850		– In transit	10,500
Warehousing charges	1,700			
Packing and Selling Exp.	600			
Commission	9,800	12,950		
To Profit transferred to P & L A/c		11,700		
		129,650		129,650

SUNDRAM'S ACCOUNT

	Rs.			Rs.
To Consignment A/c (Sales)	98,000	By Consignment A/c		
		Claring Charges	850	
		Warehousing Charges	1,700	
		Packing and Selling Exp.	600	
		Commission	9,800	12,950
		By Balance c/d		85,050
	98,000			98,000

Working Notes :

		Rs.
(1)	Loss in Transist	5,000
	Cost of Cases lost in transit @ Rs. 100 each	
	Add Direct proportionate Expenses of Consignor $\left(\frac{5,000 \times 50}{1,000}\right)$	250
		5,250
(2)	Stock on Consignment (Withthe Consignee)	
	Cost of 150 Cases @ Rs. 100 each	15,000
	Add Direct proportionate Expenses of Consignor $\left(\frac{5,000 \times 150}{1,000}\right)$	750
	Add Direct proportionate Expenses of Consignee $\left(\frac{850 \times 150}{850}\right)$	150
	(Clearing Charges only) (1,000 Less lost 50 Less in transit 100)	15,900

(3) Stock-in-Transit

	Rs.
Cost of 100 Cases in-transit @ Rs. 100 each	10,000
Add Direct proporationate expenses of Consignor $\left(\frac{5{,}000 \times 100}{1{,}000}\right)$	500
	10,500

Illustration 3 (Invoice Price)

A consigned goods B costing Rs. 1,00,000. The Proforma Invoice price was made to show a profit of 25% on cost. A paid freight and insurance Rs. 2,000. B sold part of Consignment for Rs.88,000 at uniform price of 10 percent over invoice and spent Rs. 3,000 as **ware-housing** charges, Rs.1,000 as selling expenses. B is entitled to commission of 5 per cent on sales and 20% of the net profit after charging such commission on sales. B paid amount due by Bank draft. Draw up Consignment Account and B's Account in the bo6ks of A. **[C.A. (Inter) May 1982]**

Solution :

In the Books of A

CONSIGNMENT ACCOUNT

		Rs.		**Rs.**
To Goods sent on consignment		125,000	By B (Sales)	88,000
To Cash (Expenses)			By Goods sent on	
(Freight and Insurance)		2,000	Consignment	25,000
To B (Expenses)			(Loading)	
Ware Housing Chages	3,000		By Stock on Consignment (1)	45,720
Selling Expenses	1,000	4,000		
To B (Commission)				
On Sales @ 5% 88,000	4,400			
@ 20% on Rs. 14,320 (on Profit)	2,864(2)	7,264		
To Stock Reserve (Loading)*		9,000		
Profit transferred to P & L A/c		11,456		
		158,720		158,720

* (45,000 × 25/125)

B'S ACCOUNT

	Rs.			**Rs.**
To Consignment A/c (Sales)	88,000	By Consignment A/c (Expesnes)		
		Warehousing Exp.		3,000
		Selling Exp.		1,000
		By Consignment A/c		
		Commission on Sale	4,400	
		Commission on Profit	2,864	7,264
		By Bank (Draft)		76,736
	88,000			88,000

Working notes :

			Rs.
(1)	Stock on Consignment		
	Cost of goods sent on Consignment		1,00,000
	Add Loading (25% on cost)		25,000
	Invoice price of goods sent on consignment		1,25,000
	Less Invoice price of goods sold		
	Sale price		
	Less Excess of Sales price overinvoice price	88,000	
	10% on invoice price		
	or 1/11 on sale price	8,000	80,000
			45,000
	Add Direct proportionate Expenses of Consignor at cost		
	$\left(\frac{2,000 \times 36,000}{1,00,000}\right)$ Or at I.P. $\left(\frac{2,000 \times 45,000}{1,25,000}\right)$		720
			45,720
(2)	Profit before commission on Profit but after cmmission on sale		14,320
	20% of 14,320		2,864

Illustration 4 (Defectives Returned to Consignor)

Meena and Co. of Calcutta who sent 100 sewing machines on consignment to Najma of Patna and spent Rs. 2,500 on packing. The cost of each machine was 1,120 but it was invoiced at 25% above cost.

One case containing 5 machines was lost in transit. Najma was asked to pay Rs. 4,750 as freight of the remaining machines. She had .to spend Rs. 950 as cartage and octroi duty and Rs. 1.900 as godown rent. She sold 75 machines @ Rs. 1,900. She found 10 machines defective therefore returned them to Calcutta at a cost of Rs. 500. Najma is entitled to a commission of 5% on invoice price plus 20% of any excess realised on the invoice price and 1% del credere commission. Najma could not realise sale proceeds of 5 machines.

Prepare Consignment Account, Consignee's Account. Consignment Stock Account and Consignment Stock Reserve Account in the Books of Meena and Co. **[B.Com (Pass) D.U. 1983-Modified]**

Solution :

In the Books of Meena and Co.

CONSIGNMENT ACCOUNT

		Rs.		Rs.
To Goods Sent on consignment[(1)]		140,000	By Najma (Sales)	142,500
To Cash (Packing Exp.)		2,500	By Goods sent on Consignment (Returns)	11,200
To Najma (Expenses)				
Freight	4,750		By Goods sent on Consignment[(2)] (Loading)	28,000
Cartage and octroi duty	950			
Go down rent	1,900		By Loss in transit[(3)]	5,725
Expenses on machines returned	500	8,100	(Abnormal Loss)	
To Najma (Commission)[(2)]		14,175	By Stock on Consignment[(4)]	14,850
To Reserve on Stock on Consignment		2,800		
To Profit transferred to P & L A/c		34,700		
		202,275		202,275

* 10 machines @ Rs. 1,120

NAJMA'S ACCOUNT

	Rs.			Rs.
To Consignment (Sales)	1,42,500	By Consignment A/c (Expenses)		
		Freight	4,750	
		Cartage and OCtroi duly	950	
		Go downRent	1,900	
		Exp. on goods Returned	500	8,100
		By Consignment A/c (Commission)		14,175
		By Balance c/d		1,20,225
	1,42,500			1,42,500

STOCK ON CONSIGNMENT A/c

	Rs.		Rs.
To Consignment A/c	14,850	By Balance c/d	14,850
	14,850		14,850

RESERVE ON STOCK ON CONSIGNMENT A/c

	Rs.		Rs.
To Balance c/d	2,800	By Consignment A/c	2,800
	2,800		2,800

Working notes :

		Rs.
(1)	Invoice price of goods sent on Consignment	
	Cost of one machine	1,120
	Add 25% of Cost	280
	Invoice price of one machine	1,400
	Invoice price of 100 machines (100 x 1,400)	1,40,000
(2)	Loading on Goods sent on Consignment (100 × 280)	28,000
(3)	Loss in Transit	
	Cost 5 Machines @ Rs. 1,120	5,600
	Add Direct proportionate Expenses of Consignor $\left(2,500 \times \frac{5}{100}\right)$	125
		5,725
(4)	Value of Stock on Consignment	
	Invoice price of stock on Consignment 10 machines @ Rs. 1,400	14,000
	Add Direct proportionate Expenses of Consignor $\frac{2,500 \times 10}{100}$	250
	Add Direct proportionate Expenses of Consignee	
	(Freight + Cartage and Octroi) $\frac{5,700 \times 10}{95}$	600
		14,850

(5) Commission :

	Rs.
5% Commission on Invoice price of machines sold	
75 @ 1,400 each = $\left(\dfrac{1,05,000 \times 5}{100}\right)$	5,250
20% on Excess of Sale price over Invoice price	
75 (1,900 – 1,400) = $\left(\dfrac{37,500 \times 20}{100}\right)$	7,500
1% on Total (Credit) Sales $75 \times 1,900 = \left(\dfrac{1,42,500 \times 1}{100}\right)$	1,425
	14,175

Illustration 5 (Commission on Sale and Profit)

On 1.9.2007 goods costing Rs. 66,000 were consigned by X to his agent Y at a proforma invoice price which was 20% above Cost. X paid insurance and freight charges amounting to Rs. 2,500. Y was allowed Rs. 6,000 per annum towards establishment cost, 5% commission on gross sales and 3% del credere commission. He was also allowed 5% extra Commission on the profit on such consignment sales after charging such commission. Y incurred an expense of Rs. 510 as landing charges. Three fourth of goods were sold at $33\frac{1}{3}\%$ profit on cost, half of which were on credit. Half of the balance of goods was damaged and a claim on insurance company was made for Rs. 8,800 which was settled at a discount of 10 per cent.

You are required to prepare a consignment account and Abnormal loss Account in the books of X for the year ended 31st December 2007. **[C.A. (Inter) May, 1984-Modified]**

Solution :

In the Books of X

CONSIGNMENT ACCOUNT

		Rs.			Rs.
To Goods Sent on Consignment		79,200	By Y (Sales)		
To Cash (Expenses)			Cash	33,000	
Insurance and Freight		2,500	Credit	33,000	66,000
To Y (Expenses)			By Goods Sent on Consignment		13,200
Establishment Charges	2,000		(Loading)		
Landing Charges	510	2,510	By Abnormal Loss A/c		8,626
To Y (Commission)			By Stock on Consignment		10,276
On Sale	5,280				
On profit	332	5,612			
To Stock Reserve		1,650			
To Profit transferred to P & L A/c		6,630			
		98,102			98,102

ABNORMAL LOSS ACCOUNT

	Rs.		Rs.
To Consignment	8,626	By Insurance Claims	7,920
		By Profit and Loss A/c	706
	8,626		8,626

Working notes :

(1) Establishment charges have been taken in to account on the basis of period covered in consignment i.e. 4 months (1.9.2007 to 31.12.2007)

(2) Commission " is worked out as under

	Rs.
5% on Total sales (Rs. 66,000)	3,300
3% on Credit Sales (Del Credere)	1,980
5% on Profit after charging such commission $\left(\frac{6,962 \times 5}{105}\right)$	332
	5,612

(3) Abnormal loss:

Cost of goods damaged	
Goods sold	3/4
Unsold	1/4
Half of which damaged i.e. 1/2 of 1/4 =1/8	
	Rs.
1/8 of Goods (Cost) sent on consignment	8,250.00
Add Direct proportionate Expenses of Consignor 1/8 of 2.500	312.50
Add 1/8 of (Direct prop. Exp. of Consignee) 510	63.75
	8,626.25

(4)

Stock on consignment (at Invoice Price) l/8lh of 79,200	9,900.00
Add Direct proportional Expenses of Consignor 1/8 * 2,500	312.50
Add Direct proportionate Expenses of Consignee 1/8 of 510	63.75
	10,276.25
	Rs. 10276

(5) Loading has been worked out as follows:

Let Cost price be	100
Profit	20
Invoice price	120
Loading	20/120/ or 1/6 on invoice price

Illustration 6 (Commission on sales & on profit)

Zuben Consigns 2000 cassettes to Suzie costing Rs. 15 each. The Proforma invoice is made out to him a figure to show a gross profit of 20% on sales, below which the consignee is not allowed to sell. The consignee sells half the consignment at a profit of 25% on sales. The expenses arc Freight and Insurance Rs. 1,500 paid by consignor, Landing charges and import duty etc. Rs. 1,000 paid by consignee. The Consignee is entitled to a commission of 5%, on sales and l/6th of profits after charging both commission and share of profits. Suzie remits a sight draft for the balance to settle the account Show the necessary accounts in the books of consignor. **[ICWA (Inter) Dec. 1984- Modified]**

Solution :

In the Books of Zuben

CONSIGNMENT ACCOUNT

	Rs.		Rs.
To Goods Sent on Consignment (1)	37,500	By Suize (Sale) (2)	20,000
To Cash (Feight and Insurance)	1,500	By Goods Sent on	
To Suzie (Landing charges and I. duty)	1,000	Consignment (Loading) (1)	7,500
To Suzie (Commission) (4)	1,393	By Stock on Consignment (3)	20,000
To Stock Reserve (1,000 × 3.75)	3,750		
(Loading on Stock on Consignment)			
To Profit transferred to P & L A/c	2,357		
	47,500		47,500

GOODS SENT ON CONSIGNMENT ACCOUNT

	Rs.		Rs.
To Consignment A/c (Loading)	7,500	By Consignment A/c	37,500
To Trading Account	30,000		
	37,500		37,500

SUZIE'S ACCOUNT

	Rs.		Rs.
To Consignment A/c (Sales)	20,000	By Consignment A/c	
		(Landingcharges and Important duty)	1,000
		By Consignment A/c (Commission)	1,393
		By Bank (draft)	17,607
	20,000		20,000

Working notes :

Let Invoice price be	100	(1)	Invoice price of Cassette	Rs.
Profit	20		Cost of one Cassette	15.00
Cost	80	*Add*	Profit 20% on Sale means	
Profit in relation, to Cost	20/80		25% on Cost	3.75
or 1/4 = 25%			Invoice price of a Cassette	18.75
Invoice price of goods sent on Consignment 2,000 @ 18.75				37,500
Actual Cost (2,000 x 15)				30,000
Loading				7,500

(2) Sales

Let Sale price be	100		Cost of Cassettes sold	
Profit	25		1,000 Cassettes @ Rs. 15 each	15,000
Cost	75			
Profit in relation to cost	25/75	*Add*	Profit 25% on Sales means 1/4 on	
or	1/3		Sales or 1/3 on Cost	5,000
				20,000

(3) Stock on Consignment at invoice price	
Invoice price of 1,000 Cassettes (Unsold) 1,000 x 18.75	18,750
Add Direct proportionate expenses of Consignor 1/2 of Rs. 1,500 (Freight and Insurance)	750
Add Direct proportionate expenses of Consignee 1/2 of Rs. 1,000 (Landing Charges and Import duty)	500
	20,000
(4) Commission	Rs.
Commission on Sale @ 5% on Rs. 20,000	1,000
Commission on Profit	
l/6lh on profit before charging such commission on profit	
i.e. l/7th on profit after charging such commission on profit	
Profit before charging 2,750	
Commission after charging = 1/7 of 2,750	393
	1,393

Illustration 7 (Commission on excess of selling price and Trading Account)

V.K. Traders of Delhi purchased 10,000 pieces of sarees @ Rs. 100 each out, of these 6,000 sarees were sent to Jaipur on Consignment at the selling price of Rs. 120 per saree. The Consignor paid Rs. 3,000 for packaging and freight. The Consignee sold 5,000 sarees @ Rs. 125 per saree and incurred Rs. 1,000 for selling expenses and remitted Rs. 5,00,000 to Delhi on account. The Consignee is entitled to a Commission of 5% on total sales plus a further 20% Commission on any surplus price realised over Rs. 120 per saree. 3,000 sarees were sold at Rs. 110 per saree Owing to slowdown in the market the selling price (Rs. 120) of sarees has come down by 10%.

Prepare Consignment Account and Trading Account in the books of V.K. Traders of Delhi and their account in the books of Consignee at Jaipur. **[C.A. (Entrance) June,1984 - Modified]**

Solution : **In the books V.K. Traders**

CONSIGNMENT ACCOUNT

	Rs.		Rs.
To Goods Sent on Consignment	7,20,000	By Consignee's A/c (Sales)	6,25,000
To Cash (Expenses) (Packing and Freight)	3,000	By Goods Sent on Consignment (Loading)$^{(3)}$	1,20,000
To Consignee's A/c (Selling Expenses)	1,000	By Stock on Consignment$^{(1)}$	1,00,500
To Consignee's A/c (Commission)$^{(2)}$	36,250		
To Profit transferred to Trading and Profit & Loss A/c	85,250		
	8,45,500		8,45,500

TRADING AND PROFIT & LOSS A/c

		Rs.		Rs.
To Purchases	10,00,000		By Sales 3,000 Sarees @ Rs. 110	3,30,000
Less Goods Sent on			By Closing Stock	1,00,000
Consignmen to			By Profit on Consignment to Jaipur	85,250
Jaipur	6,00,000	4,00,000		
To Gross Profit c/d		1,15,250		
		5,15,250		5,15,250

In the Books of Consignee
V.K. TRADERS ACCOUNT

	Rs.		Rs.
To Cash (Selling Expenses)	1,000	By Bank/Debtors (Sales)	6,25,000
To Commision	36,250		
To Bank (Remittance)	5,00,000		
To Balance c/d	87,750		
	6,25,000		6,25,000

Working notes :

(1) Stock on Consignment (at Cost) — Rs.

1.000 sarees @ Rs. 100 — 1,00,000

Add ' Direct proportionate expenses of Consignor $\frac{3{,}000 \times 1{,}000}{6{,}000}$ — 500

1,00,500

or Stock on Consignment at (market price) Net realisable value

1,000 sarees @ Rs. 108 (120 Less 10%) — 1,08,000

Less Commission on sales @ 5% — 5,400

1,02,600

Value of Stock = Cost price or market price (Net realisable value) which ever is less

Hence Cost price is less

Thus Stock on Consignment is = 1,00,500

(2) Commission

Commission on Sale @ 5% on Rs. 6,25,000 — 31,250

Plus 20% on Sale price in excess of Rs. 120 per saree

$(6{,}25{,}000 - 6{,}00{,}000) = \frac{25{,}000 \times 20}{100}$ — 5,000

36,250

(3) Loading

6,000 Sarees @ Rs. 20 per Saree — 1,20,000

Illustration 8 (Goods despatched back by consignee)

Ali of Calcutta sent a consignment of cotton goods to Osman of Delhi invoiced at Rs.1,00,000. The invoice price was made by adding 25% to the Cost. The expenses incurred by Ali were: Packing Rs. 2,400, Carriage etc. Rs. 1,600, Insurance Rs. 1,200 and other expenses Rs. 2,600.

After three months he received an Account Sales intimating that half the consignment was sold at Rs. 60,000. The expenses incurred by the consignee Rs. 3,000 as freight, Fire insurance Premium Rs. 1.800 and other expenses Rs. 1,000. His Commission was 6% on Sales and del –credere Commission $1\frac{1}{2}$%.

But no sale could be made of the remainder, so it was brought back after another nine months at a further cost of Rs. 6,000. The goods were damaged and valued at 20% below cost. Give ledger Accounts in the books of both the parties. **[B. Com (P) D.U. 1986 - Adapted]**

Solution : **In the Books of**

ALI CONSIGNMENT ACCOUNT

		Rs.		**Rs.**
To Goods Sent on Consignment		100,000	By Osman (Sales)	60,000
To Cash (Expenses)			By Goods Sent on Consignment	20,000
Packing	2,400		(Loading)	
Carriage	1,600		By Stock on Consignment (1)	32,000
Insurance	1,200		By Loss transferred to P & L A/c	12,100
Other Exp.	2,600	7,800		
To Expenses				
Freight	3,000			
Fire Insurance Premium	1,800			
Other Expenses	1,000	5,800		
To Osman (Commission)	3,600			
Del. Credere	900	4,500		
To Osman (Expenses on goods returned)		6,000*		
		1,24,100		1,24,100

OSMAN'S ACCOUNT

	Rs.		**Rs.**
To Consignment A/c (Sales)	60,000	By Consignment A/c (Exp.)	5,800
		By Consignment A/c (Comm.)	4,500
		By Consignment A/c (Exp.)	6,000
		By Balance c/d	43,700
	60,000		60,000

In the books of Osman
ALI'S ACCOUNT

	Rs.		Rs.
To Cash (Exp.)	5,800	By Sales	60,000
To Commission	4,500		
To Cash (Exp.)	6,000		
To Balance c/d	43,700		
	60,000		60,000

Working Notes :

		Rs.
(1)	Stock on Consignment	
	Invoice price of goods sent on consignment	1,00,000
	Less Profit included in the invoice price	
	25% profit included in the invoice price	
	25% profit on cost means 20% on Invoice price	20,000
	Cost of goods sent on Consignment	80,000
	Less Goods sold (at cost)	
	Half of the Consignment	40,000
	Balance left unsold	40,000
	Less 20% (due to damaged goods)	8,000
	Stock on Consignment	32,000

*(2) Expenses on return are assumed to be incurred by Osman (Consignee)

*(3) Since goods are damaged the direct proportionate expenses have been ignored for the purpose of valuation of closing stock on consignment.

Illustration 9 (Opening Stock and Insolvency)

Star Mills Ltd. Surat sends regular consignment of yarn to X who is selling agent of the Mill and is entitled to a commission 10 paisa per Kg. of yarn sold. This included del-credere commission. Following further information is furnished to you:

On 1.7.2007, stock of yarn with the agent 20,000 Kg. costing Rs. 50,000. During the year ended 30th June 2008: the total quantity of yarn consigned 1,60,000 Kg. at-Rs. 3 per Kg. The total quantity of yarn sold 1,50,000 Kg at Rs. 3.75 per Kg, these included the opening stock of 20.000 Kg. Total remittances by the agent Rs. 5,10,000. Railway freight paid by agent Rs. 40,000. Of the sales made X could not collect Rs. 11,000 due to insolvency of the customer. 5,000 Kg. of yarn were damaged in transit by Railway for which the agent recovered Rs. 6,000. The damaged goods were sold at the rate of Rs. 1.50 per Kg.

Show the following ledger accounts in the books of Star Mills Ltd. for the year ended 30th June 2008.

(i) Consignment Account (ii) X's Account (iii) Goods Damaged in Transit A/c.

[ICWA (Inter) Dec. 1986-Mollified]

Solution : **In the Books of Star Mills Ltd.**

CONSIGNMENT ACCOUNT

	Rs.		Rs.
To Stock on Consignment (20,000 kg)	50,000	By X (Sales) 1,50,000 kg @ 3.75	5,62,500
To Goods on Consignment (1,60,000 kg)	4,80,000	By Goods Damaged in Transit A/c[(1)]	16,250
To X (Railway Freight)	40,000	By Stock on Consignment A/c[(2)]	81,250
To X (Commission)	15,000		
To Profit transferred to P & L A/c	75,000		
	6,60,000		6,60,000

GOODS DAMAGED IN TRANSIT A/C

	Rs.		Rs.
To Consignment Account	16,250	By X (Insurnace Claims)	6,000
		By X (Sales) @ Rs. 1.5 per kg	7,500
		By P & L A/c (B.F.)	
		(Abnormal loss)	2,750
	16,250		16,250

X'S ACCOUNT

	Rs.		Rs.
To Consignment Account (Sales)	5,62,500	By Consignment A/c (Freight)	40,000
To Goods damaged A/c	6,000	By Consignment A/c (Commission)	15,000
(Insurance Claims)		By Bank (Remittances)	5,10,000
To Goods damaged A/c (Sales)	7,500	By Balance c/d	11,000
	5,76,000		5,76,000

Working notes :

(1) Value of goods damaged in Transit — Rs.

	Rs.
Cost of 5,000 Kg of yarn damaged in transit @ Rs. 3 per Kg	1,5000
Add Direct proportionate Expenses of Consignor	——
Add Direct proportionate Expenses of Consignee	
Railway Freight $\frac{40{,}000 \times 5{,}000}{160{,}000}$	1,250
	16,250

(2) Value of Closing Stock

	Rs.
25,000 kg of yarn @ Rs. 3 per kg	75,000
Add Direct proportionate expenses of Consignor	
Add Direct proportionate expenses of Consignee $\frac{40{,}000 \times 25{,}000}{1{,}60{,}000}$	6,250
	81,250

(3) Since consignee is entitled to del-credere commission, the loss due to insolvency of a customer will be borne by consignee and hence ignored in the consignment account.

(4) Damaged goods have also been sold by consignee. It is presumed that there is no Commission on Sale of damaged goods.

Illustration 10 (Goods destroyed twice by fire)

On 1.7.2006 M of Chennai consigned goods of the value of Rs. 1.00.000 to P of Patna. This was made by adding 25% on Cost. M paid there-on Rs. 5,000 for freight and Rs. 3,000 for insurance. During transit one-tenth of the goods were totally damaged by fire and a sum of Rs.4.800 was realised from the insurance Company.

On arrival of goods P paid Rs. 3.600 as carriage to go-down. During the year ended 30th June 2007 P paid Rs. 7,200 for go-down rent and Rs. 3,800 as selling expenses. One-ninth of the remaining goods were again destroyed by fire in go-down and nothing was recovered from the Insurance company.

On 1. 6. 2007 P sold half the original goods for Rs. 60,000 and charged commission of 5% on sales. On 30th June 2007 P sent a bank draft to M for the amount so far due from him.

You are required to prepare the following ledger Accounts in the Books of M of Chennai for the year ended 30th June, 2007.

(i) Consignment to Patna Account

(ii) Goods destroyed by fire Account and

(iii) Personal Account of P (Consignee) **[ICWA (Inter) Dec.1987-Adapted]**

Solution : **CONSIGNMENT TO PATNA A/C**

		Rs.		Rs.
To Goods Sent on Consignment		100,000	By P (Sale)	60,000
To Cash (Expenses)			By Goods Destroyed by fire (1)	10,800
Freight	5,000		By Goods Destroyed by fire (2)	11,200
Insurance	3,000	8,000	By Goods Sent on Consignment (Loading)	20,000
To P (Expenses) Carriage	3,600			
Go down Rent	7,200		By Stock on Consignment (3)	33,600
Selling Exp.	3,800	14,600		
To P (Commission)		3,000		
To Stock Reserve		6,000		
To Profit transferred to P & L A/c		4,000		
		1,35,600		1,35,600

GOODS DESTROYED BY FIRE A/C

	Rs.		Rs.
To Consignment to Patna A/c	10,800	By Insurance Claims	4,800
To Consignment to Patna A/c	11,200	By Abnormal loss transfered to P & L A/c	17,200
	22,000		22,000

P (CONSIGNEE'S) A/C

	Rs.			Rs.
To Consignment to Patna (Sales)	60,000	By Consignment to Patna A/c (Exp.)		
		– Carriage	3,600	
		– Rent of go down	7,200	
		– Selling Expenses	3,800	14,600
		By Consignment to Patna A/c (Commission)		3,000
		By Bank (draft)		42,400
	60,000			60,000

Working notes :

		Rs.
(1)	Goods destroyed by fire (First)	
	1/10th of goods (1/10 x 1,00,000)	10,000
	Add Direct proportionate Expenses of Consignor 8,000 × 1/10	800
		10,800
(2)	Goods destroyed by fire (Second) 1/9 of 90,000 (Remaining goods)	10,000
	Add Direct proportionate Expenses of Consignor $8{,}000 \times \frac{10{,}000}{1{,}00{,}000} =$	800
	Add Direct proportionate Expenses of Consignee (Carriage) 3,600 × 1/9	400
		11,200
(3)	Stock on Consignment:	
	Cost of goods (remaining unsold)	30,000
	Add Direct proportionate expenses of Consignor $\left(8000 \times \frac{30{,}000}{100{,}000}\right)$	2,400
	Add Direct Proportionate expenses of Consignee $\left(3{,}600 \times \frac{30{,}000}{90{,}000}\right)$	1,200
		33,600

Illustration 11 (Cash & credit sales)

On 1.9.2007 goods of the value of Rs. 2,64,000 were consigned by S of Bangalore to his agent M of Cochin at Proforma invoice price of 20% profit on cost. S paid insurance and other forwarding charges on consignment amounting to Rs. 10,000. M was allowed Rs. 2,000 being establishment cost. He was entitled to 5% commission on gross sales and an additional 3% Del. Credere Commission on credit sales only. M made an expense of Rs. 2,040 as landing charges.

Three fourth of the goods were sold at $33\frac{1}{3}\%$ profit on cost, half of which were credit sales. One half of the balance of goods was destroyed by fire and a claim lodged for Rs. 28,000 was settled at a discount of 10%. The balance of goods were in Stock. Show the Consignment Account and Stock Loss on Consignment Account as on 31st December 2007 in the Books of S.

[C.A. (Entrance) Nov. 1.987- Modified]

Solution :

In the Books of S

CONSIGNMENT ACCOUNT

		Rs.			Rs.
To Goods Sent on Consignment[(1)]		3,16,800	By M:[(2)]		
To Cash (Exp.)		10,000	Cash Sales	1,32,000	
(Insurance and forwardingcharges)			Credit Sales	1,32,000	2,64,000
To M (Exp.)			By Goods Sent on Consignment		52,800
Establishment charges	2,000		(Loading)		
Landing charges	2,040	4,040	By Stock lost on Consignment[(4)]		34,505
To M (Commission)[(3)]		17,160	By Stock on Consignment[(5)]		41,105
To Stock Reserve *		6,600			
To Profit transferred to P & L A/c		37,810			
		3,92,410			3,92,410

* Loading $\left(\frac{20}{120} \times 39{,}600\right)$

STOCK LOST ON CONSIGNMENT A/C

	Rs.		Rs.
To Consignment A/c	34,505	By Insurance Claims	25,200
		By Abnormal loss ransferred to P & L A/c	9,305
	34,505		34,505

Working notes :

(1) Invoice price of goods sent on Consignment

	Rs.
Cost of goods sent on Consignment	2,64,000
Add Profit ® 20% on Cost	52,800
	3,16,800

(2) Sales

Cost of 3/4th of goods sent on Consignment $\left(2{,}64{,}000 \times \frac{3}{4}\right)$	1,98,000
Add Profit on Sale @ 33 1/3 % on Cost	66,000
Total Sales	2,64,000
Credit Sales (1/2)	1,32,000
Cash Sales (1/2)	1,32,000

(3) Commission

5% on gross (Total) sales $\left(\frac{5}{100} \times 2{,}64{,}000\right)$	13,200
3% del credere on Credit Sales $\left(\frac{3}{100} \times 1{,}32{,}000\right)$	3,960
	17,160

(4)	Stock Lost on Consignment: 1/8 of 2,64,000	33,000
	Add Direct proportionate Expenses of Consignor (10,000 × 1/8)	1,250
	Add Direct Proportionate expenses of Consignee landing Charges. (2040 × 1/8)	255
		34,505
(5)	Stock on Consignment	
	Cost of goods (1/8 of Invoice price) 3,16,800	39,600
	Add Direct proportionate expenses of Consignor (1/8 of 10,000)	1,250
	Add Direct proportionate expenses of Consignee (1/8 of 2,040)	255
		41,105

Illustration 12 (Sales by inference based on commission)

Shri K. Murthy requests you to prepare a Consignment A/c for the year ended 31st March 2007 and for this purpose gives you the following information to ascertain the Profit on Consignment:

	Rs.
(i) Agent's Commission @ 5% on gross Sales	20,000
(ii) Cost of goods fully damaged in transit	20,000
(Insurance claims recovered Rs. 18,000)	
(iii) Expenses incurred by the Agent:	
Godown Rent	400
Landing and Clearing Charges	1,000
Advertisement	200
Transport Charges	900
Selling Expenses	1,000
(iv) Freight expenses incurred by Shri K. Murthy	2,000
(v) Cost of unsold stock lying with the Agent at the end of the year.	60,000

All sales were effected by the agent at a profit of 25% on Cost.

[ICWA (Inter) Dec. 1998 Modified]

Solution : **CONSIGNMENT ACCOUNT**

		Rs.		Rs.
To Goods Sent on Consignment(2)		3,80,000	By Consignee's A/c (Sales)(1)	4,00,000
To Cash (Freight)		2,000	By Goods damaged in Transit (Abnormal Loss)	2,000
To Consignee (Expenses)			By Insurance Company	18,000
Go-down Rent	400		By Stock on Consignment*	60,300
*Landing and Clearing Charges	1,000			
Advertisement	200			
*Transport Charges	900			
Selling Expenses	1,000	3,500		
To Consignee (Commission)		20,000		
To Profit transferred to P & L A/c		74,800		
		4,80,300		4,80,300

$$* \ 60{,}000 + \left(\frac{60{,}000 \times 1{,}900}{3{,}80{,}000}\right)$$

Working notes : Rs.

(1) Sales = Commission is 5% on Sales which is Rs. 20,000

$$\text{Sales} = 20{,}000 \times \frac{100}{5} \qquad \text{Rs. } 4{,}00{,}000$$

(2) Goods Sent on Consignment:

	Rs.
Sales (Calculated as above)	4,00,000
Less Profit @ 25% on Cost which is equal to 20% on Sales	80,000
	3,20,000
Add Cost of goods remaining unsold	60,000
	3,80,000

(3) Since the cost of goods damaged and Stock on Consignment has been given, the direct proportionate expenses of the consignee have been taken in to account for valuation of stock only. Damaged goods have been valued at cost as there are no direct expenses of consignor.

Illustration 13 (Valuation of stock & commission on cash collected)

Rama Consigned goods to Raveena her agent at Delhi at Cost price of Rs. 50,000. Rama's Accountant at the end of year drew up the Agent's account as under :

RAVEENA'S ACCOUNT

	Rs.		Rs.
To Goods	50,000	By Cash	30,000
To Profits & Loss A/c	4,125	By Balance c/d	24,125
	54,125		54,125

Raveena sold the goods for Rs. 56,250, which exceeded by Rs. 11,250 of their invoice price. She collected Rs. 47,500 after allowing discount of Rs. 2,500 to customers. Bad debts came to Rs. 1,250 and her expenses amounted Rs. 1,000. Raveena was entitled to a 5% Commission on Cash Collected. Balance of Stock is to be valued at invoice price.

From the above information, draw the accounts of Raveena, Consignment and Consignment Debtors in the books of Rama. **[C.A. (Inter) May 198' Adapted]**

Solution :

In the Books of Rama

CONSIGNMENT ACCOUNT

		Rs.		Rs.
To Goods Sent on Consignment		50,000	By Consignment Debtors (Credit Sales)	56,250
To Consignment Debtors:			By Stock on Consignment$^{(1)}$	5,000
Discount	2,500			
Bad Debts	1,250	3,750		
To Raveena (Exp.)		1,000		
To Raveena (Commission)		2,375		
To Profit transferred to P & L A/c		4,125		
		61,250		61,250

CONSIGNMENT DEBTORS ACCOUNTS

	Rs.			Rs.
To Consignment A/c (Sales)	56,250	By Raveena (Cash Collected)		47,500
		By Consignment A/c		
		Discount	2,500	
		Bad debts	1,250	3,750
		By Balance c/d		5,000
	56,250			56,250

The total amount due from Raveena and Consignment debtors is Rs. 19,125 i.e. (14,125 + 5,000). This can be verified by preparing Raveena's as a Consignee Account.

	Rs.
(1) Sales price of goods	56,250
Less Excess of S.P. over I. Price	11,250
Invoice Price of Goods Sold	45,000
Invoice Price (which is cost) of goods sent	50,000
Value of Closing Stock	5,000

RAVEENA (CONSIGNEE'S) A/C

	Rs.		Rs.
To Consignment A/c (Sales)	56,250	By Consignment A/c (Expenses)	1,000
		By Consignment A/c (Commission)	2,375
		By Consignment A/c (Discount)	2,500
		By Consignment A/c (Bad debts)	1,250
		By Cash (Sent)	30,000
		By Balance c/d (B.F.)	19,125
	56,250		56,250

Illustration 14 (Commission & Allowance)

Goods are invoiced by 'A', Consignor to his Agent 'B' at selling price. The agent reports sales made and collection of book debts by him by monthly advice. He received 5% Commission on Cash Collected plus an allowance of expenses at the rate of Rs. 400 per month.

During the half-year ended 30th September 2008 goods were invoiced to the Agent at a value of Rs. 80,600. Such goods cost A Rs. 59,000 plus freight and packing charges there on Rs. 3.740. During the same period, sales were made by the Agent amounted to Rs. 68,400. Debts collected were Rs., 57,600 and discounts were allowed amounting to Rs. 400. The agent remitted to A Rs. 56,000.

Some of the goods Consigned to B were, damaged in transit and claim on the insurance company was settled for Rs. 1,240. On 30th Sept. 2008 the stock in the hands of agent and unsold represented a cost to A Rs. 8,200.

Prepare the Consignment Account and account of B in the books of A for the half-year ended 30th September 2008. **[C.A. (Entrance) Nov. 1990 Modified]**

Solution :

CONSIGNMENT ACCOUNT

	Rs.		Rs.
To Goods Sent on Consignment	80,600	By B (Sales)	68,400
To Cash (Freight and Packing Charges)	3,740	By Goods Sent on Consignment (Loading) (80,600 – 59,000)	21,600
To B (Expenses allowed) @ 400 p.m. for 6 months	2,400	By Loss in Transit (1)	776
To B (Discount)	400	By Stock on Consignment (2)	8,720
To B (Commission) (@ 5% on Rs. 57,600)	2,880		
To Profit-transferred to P & L A/c	9,476		
	99,496		99,496

B'S ACCOUNT

	Rs.		Rs.
To Consignment A/c (Sales)	68,400	By Consignment A/c:	
		Discount	400
		Expenses Allowed	2,400
		Commission	2,880
		By Bank A/c	56,000
		By Balance c/d	6,720
	68,400		68,400

Working notes :

(1) Loss in Transit

	Rs.
Cost of goods sent on Consignment	59,000
Less Cost of goods sold $= \left(\frac{59{,}000 \times 68{,}400}{80{,}600}\right)$	50,070
Cost of goods remaining unsold	8,930
Stock with Consignee (as given)	8,200
Loss of goods at cost	730
Add Direct proportionate Expenses $\left(\frac{3740 \times 730}{59{,}000}\right)$	46
	776

(2) Value of Stock on Consignment

Cost of Stock on Consignment	8,200
Add Direct proportionate Expenses of Consignor $\left(\frac{3{,}740 \times 8{,}200}{59000}\right)$	520
	8,720

Illustration 15 (Bad debts & no del credere)

2000 Shirts were consigned by B and Co. of Delhi to S and Co. of Tokyo at a cost of Rs.150 each. B and Co. paid freight of Rs. 20,000 and insurance Rs. 3.000.

During the transit 200 Shirts were totally damaged by fire and S and Co. took delivery' of the remaining Shirts and paid Rs. 28,800 as custom duty.

S and Co. has sent a bank draft to B and Co. for Rs. 1,00,000 as advance payment 1,600 shirts were sold by him at Rs. 200 each. Expenses incurred by S and Co. on go-down rent and advertisement etc amounted to Rs. 4,000. He is entitled to a commission of 5 per cent.

One of the customers whom the goods were sold on credit could not pay the cost of 10 Shirts.

Prepare Consignment Account and account of S and Co. in the books of B and Co. The consignee settled it's account immediately. Nothing was recovered from the insurers for the damaged goods.

[C.A. (Entrance) Nov. 1991 Modified]

Solution :

In the Books of B and Co.

CONSIGNMENT ACCOUNT

		Rs.		Rs.
To Goods Sent on Consignment		3,00,000	By S and Co. (Sales)	3,20,000
To Cash (Exp.)			By Loss in Transit (I)	32,300
Freight	20,000		By Stock on Consignment (2)	35,500
Insurance	3,000	23,000		
To S. and Co. (Exp.)				
Custom duty	28,800			
Go down Rent and Adv.	4,000	32,800		
To S. and Co. (Commission)				
@ 5% on 3,20,000	16,000			
Bad debts	2,000	18,000		
To Profit transferred P & L A/c		14,000		
		3,87,800		3,87,800

S AND CO. ACCOUNT

	Rs.		Rs.
To Consignment A/c (Sales)	3,20,000	By Bank (Advance)	1,00,000
		By Consignment A/c:	
		Custom duty	28,800
		Rent and Advertising	4,000
		By Consignment A/c (Commission)	16,000
		By Consignment A/c (Bad debts)	2,000
		By Bank (Final settlement)	1,69,200
	3,20,000		3,20,000

Working notes :

(1) Loss in Transit

	Rs.
200 Shirts @ Rs. 150 (Cost) each	30,000
Add Direct proportionate expenses of consignor	
Freight and Insurance $\frac{23{,}000 \times 200}{2{,}000}$	2,300
	32,300

(2) Stock on Consignment

Cost of 200 Shirts @ 150 each	30,000
Add Direct proportional expenses of Consignor $23{,}000 \times \frac{200}{2{,}000}$	2,300
Add Direct proportionate expenses of Consignee	
Custom duty $28{,}800 \times \frac{200}{1{,}800}$	3,200
	35,500

Illustration 16 (Calculation of Goods Sent on Consignment)

The Account sales received from an agent disclosed the total sales effected by him amounted to Rs. 4,50,000. This included Rs. 3,12,500 for sales made at invoice price , which is cost, plus 25% and the balance at 10% above the invoice price. He incurred expenses to the value of Rs. 5,000 out of which a sum of Rs. 1,800 is of recurring nature. Forwarding expenses of the consignor totalled Rs. 2,400. The Agent had remitted the balance due from him through a Bank draft deducting the expenses, 5% commission on gross sales, Bad debts Rs. 850 and a Bills payable accepted by him for Rs. 10,000.

The value of unsold stock at original cost lying with the agent amounted to Rs. 50,000. You arc required to prepare the consignment Account and the Agent Account in the books of Consignor.

[ICWA (Inter) June 1990 Modified]

Solution :

In the Books of Consignor

CONSIGNMENT ACCOUNT

		Rs.		Rs.
To Goods Sent on Consignment(1)		5,00,000	By Consignee (Sales)	4,50,000
To Cash (Forwarding exp.)		2,400	By Stock on Consignment(2)	50,700
To Consignee (Exp.)			By Goods Sent on Consignment	1,00,000
Recurring Exp.	1,800		(Loading)	
Non-Recurring	3,200	5,000		
To Consignee (Commission)		22,500		
To Consignee (Bad debts)		850		
To Profit transferred to P & L A/c		69,950		
		6,00,700		6,00,700

CONSIGNEE'S ACCOUNT

	Rs.		Rs.
To Consignment A/c (Sales)	4,50,000	By Consignment A/c (Exp.) (Recurring and Non- recurring)	5,000
		By Consignment A/c (Commission)	22,500
		By Consignment A/c (Bad debts)	850
		By Bills Receivable	10,000
		By Bank (draft)	4,11,650
	4,50,000		4,50,000

Working notes :

	Rs.
(1) Goods Sent on Consignment Sales:	
Sales as per Account Sales	4,50,000
Sales at Invoice price or Sales at a profit of 25% on Cost (Given)	3,12,500
Sales at profit of 10% Invoice price (2)	1,37,500
Goods sold at 25% profit on Cost	3,12,500
Less Profit 20% on Sales price	62,500
Cost of goods sold at 25% on cost	2,50,000
**Add* Cost of goods sold at 10% profit on Invoice price	
Cost price is 100	
Invoice price is 125	
Sales price 10% above Invoice $=137.5=\left(1{,}37{,}500\times\frac{100}{137.5}\right)$	1,00,000
(i.e., 125 + 12.5)	
*Total Cost of Goods sold	3,50,000
Add Cost of goods remaining unsold (Stock)	50,000
Cost of Goods sent on Consignment	4,00,000
Add 25% Profit on Cost	1,00,000
Invoice price of Goods sent on Consignment	5,00,000
(2) Stock on consignment	50,000
Cost of (goods) Stock on Consignment	
Add Direct proportionate Expenses of Consignor $\left(2{,}400\times\frac{50{,}000}{4{,}00{,}000}\right)$	300
Add Direct proportionate Expenses of Consignee $\left(3{,}200\times\frac{50{,}000}{4{,}00{,}000}\right)$	400
	50,700

Illustration 17 (Calculation of selling price)

A Co. Ltd. manufactures and deals in edible oil consigned to their Banglore agent. 1,000 crates of oil (each crate containing 12 one-kilo sachets) in March 2008. The consignment was sent at 20% over the cost price of Rs. 30 per Kg. A Bill was drawn on the agent for 80% of the value of the consignment, which was met on presentation. Expenses incurred by company by way of freight, and insurance came to Rs. 12.000. The agent received the consignment by lorry and sold in March 2008, 900 crates at a profit margin of 25% on his cost (excluding Consignor's expenses) He found that 500 sachets had got damaged in transit The manufacturer accepted this as abnormal loss and these were sold to consumers at Rs. 20 per sachet. The insurance company settled the loss claim for Rs. 2,500. Agent incurred expenses of Rs. 5,000 on his own account (unconnected with the liability under the agreement and Rs. 3,000 on consignor's account. He is entitled to a commission of 5% on sales effected. By 15th April 2008, the agent remitted the balance due by him to company. Draw the accounts in the books of A Co. Ltd. to record the above transactions. **[C A (I). Nov. 1991 Modified]**

Solution : **In the Books of A Co. Ltd.**

CONSIGNMENT ACCOUNT

	Rs.		Rs.
To Good Sent on Consignment[(1)]	4,32,000	By Consignee's A/c (Sales)(2)	4,86,000
To Cash (Expenses) :		By Goods Sent on Consignment	72,000
Freight an Insurance	12,000	(Loading)	
To Consignee's A/c (Expenses)*	3,000	By Loss in Transit (4)	15,500
To Consignee's A/c (Commission) (3)	24,800	By Stock on Consignment (5)	25,900
To Stock Reserve	4,200		
To Profit transferred to P & L A/c	1,23,400		
	5,99,400		5,99,400

* Expenses incurred by consignee on his own account have ignored because the same are not covered by agreement.

LOSS IN TRANSIT A/C

	Rs.		Rs.
To Consignment A/c	15,500	By Consignee	10,000
		(Sale of damaged Sachets)	
		By Insurance Claims	2,500
		By Profit & Loss A/c	3,000
	15,500		15,500

CONSIGNEE'S ACCOUNT

	Rs.		Rs.
To Consignment A/c (Sales)	4,86,000	By Bank	3,45,600
To Loss in Transit A/c	10,000	By Consignment A/c (Expenses)	3,000
(Sale of damaged Sachets)		By Consignment A/c (Commission)	24,800
		By Bank	1,22,600
	4,96,000		4,96,000

Working notes :

	Rs.
(1) Goods Sent on Consignment at Invoice Price	
1,000 crates, each containing 12 One-kg. Sachets @ Rs. 30 per kg.	
i.e., 12,000 kg, @ Rs. 30 per kg	3,60,000
Add Profit @ 20% on Cost	72,000

	4,32,000
(2) Sales 900 crates × 12 kg. 10,800 kg @ Rs. 45 per kg*	4,86,000

*Cost to Consignee means invoice price which is Rs. 36, i.e., (30 + 20% thereon)

i.e. Rs. 36 per kg. 36

Add 25% there on 9 = 45 per kg.

(3) Commission	
@ 5% on Sales (Rs. 4,86,000)	24,300
@ 5% on Rs. 10,000 (500 Sachets @ Rs. 20)	500
	24,800
(4) Loss in Transit	
Cost of 500 Sachets or kg. @ Rs. 30 per kg.	15,000
Add Direct proportionate expenses of Consignor	
Freight and insurance Rs. $\left(12{,}000 \times \frac{500}{12{,}000}\right)$	500
	15,500
(5) Stock on consignment (at invoice price)	
700 kg, the invoice price of Rs. 36 per kg.	25,200
Add Direct proportionate Expenses of Consignor $\left(\frac{700}{12{,}000} \times 12{,}000\right)$	700
	25,900

Illustration 18 (Calculation of Invoice Price by Inference)

Rahim of Mumbai Consigned to Raju of Chennai goods to be sold at invoice price which represents 125% of cost. Raju is entitled to a commission of 10% on sales at invoice price and 25% of any excess realised over invoice price. The expenses on freight and insurance incurred by Rahim were Rs. 10,000. The account sales received by Rahim shows that Raju effected sales aggregating to Rs. 100,000 in respect of 75% of the consignment. His selling expenses to be reimbursed were Rs. 5,500. 10% of the consignment goods of the invoice value of Rs. 12,500 were destroyed in fire at Chennai godown and the Insurance Company paid Rs. 11,000 net of salvage. Raju remitted the balance in favour of Rahim.

Prepare Consignment Account and the Account of Mr. Raju in the books of Mr. Rahim along with necessary workings. **[C.A. (Foundation) June 1994 - Modified]**

Solution :

In the Books of Rahim

CONSIGNMENT ACCOUNT

	Rs.		Rs.
To Goods Sent on Consignment (1)	1,25,000	By Raju (Sales)	1,00,000
To Cash (Freight and Insurance)	10,000	By Loss by fire (3)	11,000
To Raju (Selling Expenses)	5,500	(Abnormal loss)	
To Raju (Commission) (2)	10,938	By Goods Sent on Consignment	25,000
To Stock Reserve	3,750	(Loading)	
To Profit transferred to P & L A/c	1,062	By Stock on Consignment (4)	20,250
	1,56,250		1,56,250

Abnormal Loss A/c

	Rs.		Rs.
To Consignment	11,000	By Insurance Claims	11,000
	11,000		11,000

RAJU (CONSIGNEE'S) ACCOUNT

	Rs.		Rs.
To Consignment A/c (Sales)	1,00,000	By Consignment A/c (Selling Expenses)	5,500
		By Consignment A/c (Commission)	10,938
		By Bank	83,562
	1,00,000		1,00,000

	Rs.
(1) **Goods Sent on Consignment at Invoice Price**	
Loss by fire at Invoice price	12,500
Which is 10% of the total value of Consignment	
Thus total value (Invoice price) of Consignment $12{,}500 \times \frac{100}{10} =$	1,25,000
(2) **Commission**	
Total amount of Sale proceeds	1,00,000
(representing 75% of Consignment)	
75% of Consignment at Invoice price	
(75% of 1,25,000)	93,750
Sale in excess of Invoice price	6,250
Commission @, 10% on 93,750 (Invoice price)	9,375
Commission @ 25% on 6,250 (Excess of Sale price over Invoice price)	1,562.50
	10,937.50
	10,938
(3) **Loss by fire** (at invoice price)	12,500
Cost of goods destroyed by fire $\left(\frac{12{,}500 \times 100}{125}\right) =$	10,000
Add Direct proportionate Expenses of Consignor	
10% of (Freight and Insurance Rs. 10,000)	1,000
Add Direct Proportionate Expenses of Consignee	Nil
	11,000
(4) **Stock on Consignment :**	
75% of Consignment is sold, 10% is destroyed by fire =	85%
Thus, 15% is Unsold Stock on Consignment	

(15% of Rs. 1,25,000) Invoice price of goods unsold	18,750
Add Direct proportionate Expenses of Consignor	
15% of (Freight and Insurance Rs.1 0,000)	1,500
Add Direct proportionate Expenses of Consignee	Nil
	20,250

Stock Reserve (25% on cost or 20% on Invoice price $18{,}750 \times \frac{20}{100} =$ 3,750

Illustration 19 (Consignment Account at Cost & at Invoice Price and Trading A/c)

M/S Shri Ram Saree Centre Delhi purchased 25,000 sarees @ Rs.250 each. Of these 15,000 sarees were sent on Consignment to M/s. Sita Saree Stores, Kanpur at a selling price of Rs.300 per saree. The Consignors paid Rs. 15,000 for packing, freight and insurance.

The Consignee sold 12,000 sarees @ Rs. 320 per Saree and incurred Rs. 5.000 towards selling expenses and remitted Rs. 25,00,000 to Delhi on account. The Consignees are entitled to a commission of 5% on total sales plus a further commission @ 35% on any surplus price realised over invoice price. 7,500 sarees were sold @ Rs. 280 per saree by the consignor. Owing to fall the market price, the value of stock of sarees in hand is to be reduced by 10%. You are required

(i) To prepare Consignment account at invoice price and the account of M/s. Sita Sarees stores in the books of Consignor.

(ii) To prepare the consignment Account by Cost price method and Trading Account in the Books of Consignor. **[C.A. (Foundation) May 1996 Adapted]**

Solution : **In the Books of M/s Shri Rum Saree Centre**

(I) CONSIGNMENT ACCOUNT (AT INVOICE PRICE)

	Rs.		Rs.
To Goods Sent on Consignment	45,00,000	By M/s Sita Saree Stores (Sales)	38,40,000
15,000 Sarees @ Rs. 300		12,000 Sarees @ Rs. 320	
To Bank (Expenses) Packing,		By Goods Sent on Consignment	7,50,000
Freight and Insurance	15,000	(Loading)	
To M/s Sita Saree Stores:-		(15,000 Sarees @ Rs. 50)	
Selling Expenses	5,000	By Stock on Consignment (2)	903,000
Commission (1)	276,000		
To Stock Reserve	150,000		
(3,000 @ 50)			
To Profit transferred to P & L A/c	547,000		
	54,93,000		54,93,000

SITA SAREE CENTRE A/C

	Rs.		Rs.
To Consignment A/c (Sales)	38,40,000	By Consignment A/c	
		Selling Expenses	5,000
		Commission	2,76,000
		By Bank (remittance)	25,00,000
		By Balance c/d	10,59,000
	38,40,000		38,40,000

Working notes : Rs.

(1) Commission on Rs. 38,40,000 @ 5% 1,92,000

Commission on Excess of Sales proceeds over invoice price (38,40,000 – 36,00,000) @ 35% on 2,40,000 84,000

2,76,000

(2) Stock on Consignment (at Invoice price) 3,000 Sarees @ Rs. 300 per Saree 9,00,000

Add Direct proportionate Expenses of Consignor $\left(15{,}000 \times \frac{3{,}000}{15{,}000}\right)$ 3,000

9,03,000

(3) As per the instruction in the question the value of closing stock in hand has been valued at cost less 10% whereas value of stock on consignment remaining unchanged.

(II) CONSIGNMENT ACCOUNT (AT COST)

	Rs.		Rs.
To Goods Sent on Consignment		By M/s Sita Saree Stores	
15,000 Sarees @ Rs. 250	37,50,000	(12,000 Sarees @ Rs. 320)	38,40,000
To Bank (Packing, Freight and Insurance)	15,000	By Stock on Consignment (1)	7,53,000
To M/s Sita Saree Stores:			
Selling Expenses	5,000		
Commission	2,76,000		
To Profit transferred to			
Trading and (P & L A/c)	5,47,000		
	45,93,000		45,93,000

TRADING ACCOUNT

For the year ended

	Rs.		Rs.
To Purchases		By Sales (7,500 Sarees @ 280)	21,00,000
25,000 Sarees @ Rs. 250	62,50,000	By Goods Sent on Consignment (15,000 Sarees)	37,50,000

To Gross Profit transferred to P & L A/c	7,09,500	By Consignment A/c (Profit)	5,47,000
		By Closing Stock 2,500 Sarees @ Rs. 225 (250 Less 10%)	5,62,500
	69,59,500		69,59,500

Working notes :

(1) Stock on Consignment 3,000 Sarees @ Rs. 250 — 7,50,000

Add Direct proportionate Expenses of Consignor $\left(15{,}000 \times \frac{3{,}000}{15{,}000}\right)$ — 3,000

7,53,000

Illustration 20 (Calculation of Commission)

X of Kolkata on 15th January, 2007 sent to Y of Mumbai a consignment of 250 CTVs costing Rs. 10,000 each. Expenses of Rs. 7,000 were met by Consignor. Y of Mumbai spent Rs. 4,500 for clearance on 30th January 2007 and selling expenses were Rs. 500 per CTV as and when the sale was made by Y. Y sold, on 4th March 2007, 150 CTVs at Rs. 14,000 per CTV again on 10th April, 75 CTVs at Rs. 14,400 per TV.

Y was entitled to a commission of Rs. 500 per TV sold plus one-fourth of the amount by which the gross sale proceeds less total commission there on exceeded a sum calculated at the rate of Rs. 12,500 per TV sold. Y sent the account sales and the amount due to X on 30th April 2007 by bank draft.

You are required to show the Consignment Account and Y's Account in the books of X

[C.A. (Foundation). May 1997- Modified]

Solution : **CONSIGNMENT ACCOUNT**

	Rs.		Rs.
To Goods Sent on Consignment	25,00,000	By Y (Sales)	
To Cash (Expenses)	7,000	150 @ Rs. 14,000	21,00,000
To Y (Clearing charges)	4,500	By Y (Sales)	
To Y (Selling expenses)	1,12,500	75 TVs @ Rs. 14,400	10,80,000
225 TVs @ Rs. 500		By Stock on Consignment (1)	2,51,150
To Y (Commission) (2)	1,63,500		
To Profit transferred to P & L A/c	6,43,650		
	34,31,150		34,31,150

Y (CONSIGNEE'S) ACCOUNT

	Rs.		Rs.
To Consignment A/c (Sales)	21,00,000	By Consignment A/c (Clearing Charges)	4,500
To Consignment A/c (Sales)	10,80,000	By Consignment A/c (Selling Exp.)	1,12,500
		By Consignment A/c	1,63,500
		(Commission)	28,99,500
	31,80,000		31,80,000

Working notes :

(1) **Stock on Consignment**

	Rs.
25 CTVs Rs. 10,000	2.50.000
Add Direct proportionate Expenses of Consignor $\left(7{,}000 \times \frac{25}{250}\right)$	700
Add Direct proportionate Expenses of Consignee $\left(4{,}500 \times \frac{25}{250}\right)$	450
	2,51,150

(2) **Commission**

Commission @ Rs. 500 per CTV sold

(Fixed) 225x500 1,12,500

Add 25% of Excess of Sale proceeds over (Rs. 28,12,500 + Commission)

[Rs. 28,12,500 (225 @ Rs. 12,500) and Total Commission]

x = 1/4 of (Rs. 21,00,000 + Rs. 10,80,000 – 28,12,500 – 1,12,500 – x

i.e., commission on Excess sale proceeds]

x = 1/4 of (31,80,000 – 29,25,000 – x)

x = 1/4 of (2,55,000 – x)

or 5x = 2,55,000

x = 51,000

Total Commission = Rs. 1,12,500 + Rs. 51,000 = **Rs. 1,63,500**.

Illustration 21 (Commission)

On 1.1.2007 D of Delhi consigned 500 bicycles to K of Kanpur costing Rs. 1,000 each and paid Rs. 5,400 as freight and Rs. 1,600 as insurance-in-transit. The Consignee, K took the delivery and paid Rs. 3,000 on account of clearing charges. K reported to D that 350 bicycles were sold @ Rs. 1,600 and 100 bicycles @ Rs. 1,750 per bicycle and incurred Rs. 15 per bicycle as selling and distribution expenses. K is entitled to a commission of Rs. 100 per bicycle sold plus 50% of the amount by which the gross sale proceeds less total commission there on, exceeded a sum calculated at the rate of Rs. 1,500 per bicycle sold. K sent the amount due to D on 31.3.2007.

You are required to prepare Consignment Account and K's A/c the books of D.

[C.A. (Inter) Adapted]

Solution :

In the Books of D

CONSIGNMENT ACCOUNT

		Rs.		Rs.
To Goods Sent on Consignment		5,00,000	By K (Sales)	
To Bank (Expenses)			350 bicycles (a). Rs. 1, 600 each	5,60,000
Freight	5,400		100 bicycles (fit, Rs. 1,750 each	1,75,000
Insurance-in-transit	1,600	7,000	By Stock on Consignment (2)	51,000

To K (Expenses)			
Clearing Charges	3,000		
Selling and Distribution expenses	6,750		
(450 × 15)			
To K (Commission)[1]	50,000		
To profit-transferred to P & L A/c	2,19,250		
	7,86,000		7,86,000

(1) Calculation of Commission payable to K

Total Commission = no. of bicycles sold x 100 + 50% of (Sale proceeds-No. of bicycles. X 1,500– Total Commission.)

Let Total Commission be x

X = 450 x 100 + 50% of (7,35,000 – 450 x 1,500 – x)

X = 45,000 + 1/2 (7,35,000 – 6,75,000 – x)

X = 45,000 + (30,000 – x/2)

2x = 90,000 + 60.000 – x

3x = 1,50,000

X = Rs. 50,000

(2) Stock on Consignment

		Rs.
Cost of 50 bicycles @ Rs. 1,000 each		50,000
Add Direct proportionate expenses of Consignor		
Freight	Rs. 5,400	
Insurance-in transit	Rs. 1,600 $\left(\dfrac{7{,}000 \times 50}{500}\right)$	700
Add Direct proportionate expenses of Consignee		
Clearing Charges $\left(\dfrac{3{,}000 \times 50}{500}\right)$		300
		51,000

K (CONSIGNEE'S) ACCOUNT

	Rs.		Rs.
To Consignment Account (Sales)		By Consignment Account:	
350 bicycles @ Rs. 1,600 each	5,60,000	(Clearing Charges)	3,000
100 bicycles @ Rs. 1,750 each	1,75,000	(Selling and Distribution Expenses)	6,750
		By Consignment A/c (Commission)	50,000
		By Bank	6,75,250
	7,35,000		7,35,000

Illustration 22 (Commission on the basis of Excess of S.P. over I.P.)

B of Bangalore sent on consignment 250 sewing machines to C of Chennai at the invoice price of Rs. 1,500 each. C was to receive a commission of 10% on sales including 2% del-credere and 10% of any profit that may remain on the basis of invoice price. C was to bear all expenses after the machines reach to his godown. The Cost of each machine was Rs. 1,200. B incurred Rs. 4,500 as freight and forwarding expenses including insurance-in-transit of Rs. 1,000.

10 machines were damaged during transit. -The insurer admitted a claim of Rs. 10,000 only. C took the delivery of the consignment and paid on Rs. 4,800 as Octroi, Cartage and loading and unloading charges. C sold 200 machines @ Rs. 1,800, half of which were sold on credit basis. C failed to recover sales proceeds from a customer to whom 2 machines were sold on credit basis. C remitted the amount due to B. The selling and distribution expenses incurred by C amounted to Rs. 2,500.

Prepare Consignment Account, Abnormal Loss A/c and C's Account in the books of B and B's Account in the books of C.

Solution : **CONSIGNMENT ACCOUNT**

	Rs.		Rs.
To Goods Sent on Consignment	3,75,000	By C (Sales)	
To Bank (Freight, Forwarding		200 machines (a) Rs. 1,800	3,60,000
and Insurance)	4,500	By Goods Sent on Consignment	
To C (Octroi, Cartage, Loading		(Loading) (250 × 300)	75,000
and Unloading)	4,800	By Abnormal Loss A/c (1)	12,180
To C (Commission) (3)	37,640	By Stock on Consignment (2)	61,520
To Consignment Stock Reserve A/c	12,000		
To Profit transferred to P/am) L A/c	74,760		
	5,08,700		5,08,700

ABNORMAL LOSS A/C

	Rs.		Rs.
To Consignment A/c	12,180	By Insurance Claims	10,000
		By Profit and Loss A/c	2,180
	12,180		12,180

C'S ACCOUNT

	Rs.		Rs.
To Consignment A/c (Sales)	3,60,000	By Consignment A/c (Expenses)	4,800
		By Consignment A/c (Commission)	37,640
		By Bank	3,17,560
	3,60,000		3,60,000

Working notes :

(1) Calculation of Abnormal loss

	Rs.
Cost of 10 machines damaged during transit (1 0 @ 1,200)	12,000
Direct proportionate Expenses of Consignor $\left(4{,}500 \times \frac{10}{250}\right)$	180
	12,180

(2) Valuation of Closing Stock (at Invoice Price)

Invoice price of 40 machines (4 0 x 1,500)	60,000

Add Direct proportionate expenses of Consignor $\left(4{,}500 \times \frac{40}{250}\right)$	720
Add Direct proportionate Expenses of Consignee $\left(4{,}800 \times \frac{40}{240}\right)$	800
	61,520

(3) Commission payable to 'C'

8% Normal Commission Rs. $\left(3{,}60{,}000 \times \frac{8}{100}\right)$	28,800
2% Del-Credere on Rs. 3,60,000	7,200
	36,000
plus 10% profit that may remain on the basis of Invoice Price (The invoice price is presumed to be the cost price)	1,640
	37,640
Sales (Actual)	3,60,000
Abnormal Loss at Invoice price (Invoice price plus direct proportionate expenses)	15,180*
Stock on Consignment at Invoice price	61,520*
	4,36,700

Less Invoice price of goods sent	3,75,000	
Consignor's Expenses	4,500	
Consignee's Expenses	4,800	
Consignee's Commission	36,000	
(before profit)		4,20,300
Excess of SP – IP before commission		16,400
Commission Rs. $\left(16{,}400 \times \frac{10}{100}\right)$		1,640
(10% of Profit)	Total Commission (36,000 + 1,640)	37,640

(4) Stock Reserve

40 machines @ Rs. 300 12.000

(5) Expenses incurred by the Consignee after the goods reached to his godown have not been debited to consignment Account as the same has to be borne by the consignee.

QUESTIONS

1. Differentiate between consignment and sale.
2. What is an Account Sale? How will you distinguish it from an Invoice?
3. How will you ascertain the value of :
   Abnormal loss in Transit and
   Abnormal loss at Consignee's place

4. What is the accounting treatment of bad debts in the books of Consignor and Consignee?
5. How will you deal with the recurring and non-recurring expenses while valuing closing stock on Consignment?
6. How will you treat the normal and abnormal losses in the Consignment Account.
7. Write Short notes on :
   - Shortage of Stock
   - Stock taken over by consignee
   - Del-credere and Over-riding commission.

PROBLEMS

1. X Sent 100 CTVs to Y on consignment. The cost of each TV was Rs. 12.000 but was invoiced to Y at 25% profit on cost. The expenses incurred by X were as under:

	Rs.
Freight	7,000
Insurance	3,000

During transit one CTV was destroyed and the Insurance Company paid Rs. 9,000 towards the claim. Y sold 70 CTVs at Rs. 15,000 each and he paid for storage and insurance Rs. 3.400. Y accepted a bill of exchange for Rs. 5,00,000 at three months drawn by X who discounted immediately with his banker at 6% p.a. It was agreed that Y is to gel 5% commission.

You are required to prepare necessary ledger accounts in the books of X. **[C.A. (E) Adapted]**

Ans. Profit Rs. 1,99,600

Abnormal loss Rs. 3,100

Stock on Consignment at Invoice, Price Rs. 4,37.900.

2. B Consigned to A 1,000 calculators. Cost of each calculator was Rs. 190. B incurred expenses of Rs. 5,000 on dispatch of these goods. A informed B that he had sold 680 calculators @ Rs. 280 each and 110 calculators @ Rs. 270 each and had spent Rs.15.200 on behalf of the consignor. 10 calculators were found defective and were sold for Rs. 500 according to the instructions of consignor. A was entitled to a commission of 6% on gross sales and included del-credere commission. A could recover only rs. 2,500 from a customer to whom 10 calculators were sold on credit basis for Rs. 2,800. All other sales were made on cash basis. Prepare necessary ledger Accounts in the books of both the parties. **[C.S. (Foundation) June 1999 Adapted]**

3. A Company sent 450 bales of cotton to it's consignee at profit of 20% on sale. The cost price of each bale was Rs. 600. The following were the expenses incurred in connection with this consignment.
   (i) Rs. 1,350 paid by the company for dispatching goods,
   (ii) Rs. 3,000-paid by the consignee by way of freight, duty and landing charges.
   (iii) Rs. 1,500 paid by the consignee by way of godown rent, salaries of salesmen. His commission was 4% on turnover.

   The Consignee sold 2/3rd of the consignment at invoice price. You are required to calculate:
   - Value of stock at invoice price and
   - profit earned **[C.A. (E) Adapted]**

   Ans. Stock Rs. 1,13,950; Profit Rs. 30,150

4. On 15th January 2008 X of Kolkata sent a consignment of 750 Calculators costing Rs.100 each. Expenses of Rs 1,050 met by consignor Y of Mumbai spent Rs. 2,250 for clearance and selling expenses were Rs. 10 per calculator.

   Y sold 450 calculators @ Rs. 160 and 225 calculators @ Rs. 172;Y was entitled to a commission of Rs. 25 per calculator sold plus one-forth of the amount by which the gross sale proceeds less total commission there on exceeded a sum calculated at the rate of Rs. 125 per calculator sold. Y Sent the amount due to X on 30th June 1998.

   You are required to show the consignment Account and Y's Account in the books of X.

   [C.A. (E) Adapted]

   Ans. Profit Rs. 14,715

   Commission Rs. 18,765

5. X Consigned goods on 1st March, 2007 of the value of Rs. 1,00,000 to Y and incurred freight and insurance of Rs. 6,000. X's accounting year was ending on 31st December 2007 and Y was entitled to 5% on gross sales. Y sent an account sales for the period ended 30th June. 2007 which showed the following.

   (i) 60% of goods were sold for Rs. 80,000 out of which Rs. 65,000 were actually received.

   (ii) Y had incurred expenses of Rs. 3,000 for goods consigned and Rs. 2.000 for goods sold.

   On 1.7.2007 X incurred bank charges of Rs. 100 for cashing the draft which Y had sent along with the above statement of account. Y sent in further statement of account for the following 6 months which disclosed that:

   (i) The remaining goods were sold for Rs. 55,000 and had incurred Rs. 1,500.

   (ii) Y had realised cash for all sales except for Rs. 1,000, which were irrecoverable. On 5.1.2008 X incurred bank charges of Rs. 80 for collecting draft received from Y for the balance.

   Prepare necessary ledger accounts in the books of X **[C.A. (E) Adapted]**

   Ans. Profit on consignment Rs. 6,230 Stock Rs. 43,600.

6. N consigns 1,000 bats costing Rs. 500 each to S for sales and incurs Rs. 4.000 towards freight and Rs. 1,000 for insurance S was able to take delivery of 900 bats only and 100 bats were destroyed in transit. Insurance company admitted the claim and paid the same. S will be entitled to a commission of 5% on sales, 2% del-credere commission on credit sales only. He will be entitled for additional commission of 25% of the excess if the sale price exceeds the cost price by more than 20%. S has spent Rs. 2,000 towards sales expenses. The account sale is as under: 500 bats at Rs. 600 per bat for cash and 200 bats at Rs. 700 per bat for credit. Consignment debtors paid their dues except one customer to whom 4 bats sold for Rs. 2.800. could pay only Rs. 800.

   Show consignment account, consignment debtors account S's Account and commission calculation.

   [C.A. (Entrance) Dec. 1985 - Modified]

   Ans. Profit on Consignment Rs. 54,700 Commission Rs. 29,800

7. On 1.1.2007, Lila and Co. of Kolkata Consigned 100 cases of milk powder to Sheila and Co. of Mumbai. The goods were charged at a proforma invoice value of Rs. 10,000 including a profit of 25% on invoice price. On the same date consignors paid Rs. 600 for freight and insurance. On 1.7.2007 the consignee paid import duly Rs. 1.000 dock dues Rs.200 and sent to the consignor a bank draft of Rs. 4,000 as advance. On 1st August the consignee sold 80 cases for Rs. 10.500 and sent a remittance for the balance due to the consignors after deducting Commission at the rate of 5% on gross sale proceeds. Show the consignment Account and Sheila and Co. Account in the books of Lila and Co. **[C.A. (Entrance) Nov. 1988 - Modified]**

   Ans. Profit Rs. 2,535; Stock Rs. 2,360.

8. On 1.1.2007 Das of Kolkata consigned 1,000 electronic watches costing Rs. 100 each. Freight and insurance amounted to Rs. 6.300. The Consignee was entitled to a commission of 10%. on gross sales. On 1.3.2001 the consignee returned 100 defective watches and incurred Rs. 750 on freight and insurance.

An Account Sales was received from consignee showing sale of 800 watches for Rs.1,50,000. go-down rent Rs. 2,500 Carriage outward Rs. 200, advertisement Rs. 1.800. The consignee sent a demand draft for the balance due on 30th June 2001 when Das closes his books of accounts.

The Consignee sold the remaining watches for Rs. 35.000 incurring expenses of Rs. 1.000 and sent a second Account sales on 31st August, 2007 accompanied by demand draft for the amount due.

You are required to prepare Consignment Account and Consignee's Account in the books of Das.

Ans. Stock on Consignment on 30.6.2007 Rs. 10,700

Profit up to 30.6.2007 Rs. 44,150

Profit on Sale of Stock Rs. 19,800

9. B of Mumbai sent on Consignment 5,000 T-Shirts costing Rs. 120 each to C of Kolkata. The consignee sold 40% of T-Shirts @ Rs. 160 per T-Shirt for cash and other 40% @ Rs. 165 per T-Shirt on credit and took over the balance to his own stock at Rs. 160 each. B paid freight and insurance Rs. 5,000 and other expenses Rs. 2,000. C incurred Rs. 500 as carriage. Rs.400 on octroi and Rs. 1,050 as selling expenses. C was entitled to a commission @ 5% and 2% as Del-credere commission on total gross sale proceeds. A customer to whom goods on credit basis were sold for Rs. 2,000 became insolvent and nothing could be recovered from him. Show the relevant accounts in the books of Consignor.

Ans. Profit on Consignment Rs. 1,43,300

10. Adnan Enterprises of Delhi consigned 500 bales of wool to Cyma Corporation of Kanpur. The cost of each bale was Rs. 750 but the consignment invoice price was fixed to yield a gross profit of 20% on cost price. The consignee reported that 75% of the consignment was sold at profit of 25% on sales. The consignee incurred Rs. 3,750 as freight and landing charges, Rs. 2,250 as go-down rent. Earlier consignor has spent Rs. 1,800 as forwarding expenses. Cyma was entitled to a commission of 5% on sales and 20% on the net proceeds as bonus after charging both bonus and commission.

Prepare necessary ledger accounts.

Ans. Profit Rs. 10,212 Stock Rs. 95,137 (at Cost) Commission; 18,750 Bonus Rs. 58.375.

11. On 1,4.2007 Z consigned 2000 Sarees to A costing Rs. 300 each at the proforma. Invoice price to cover a profit of 20% on soles. The consignee was allowed to sell below invoice price On 30th April. 2007, the consignee sold half of the consignment at a profit of 25% on sales. The expenses incurred by the consignor as freight and insurance amounted to Rs.12.500 where as consignee paid Rs. 7,500 as landing and custom charges. A is entitled to a commission of 5% on sale and 1/6 of the profit after charging up both commission and share of profits A sent the demand draft for the balance due to Z. **[I.C.W.A. -Adapted]**

Ans. Stock on Consignment at invoice price Rs. 3,85,000 Commission Rs. 30,000 Profit Rs.60,000.

12. Premier watch Co. of Kolkata sent 500 wrist watches costing Rs. 360 each at the proforma Invoice price of Rs. 450 each to D of Delhi. The following expenses were paid by the company.

Freight Rs. 9,000 Cartage Rs. 600, Insurance Rs. 2,400. The consignee was entitled to a commission of 3% plus 2% del-credere on gross sale proceeds. D accepted a bill of Rs. 60,000 drawn by the consignor as an advance.

25 watches were stolen-in-transit. to Delhi and an insurance claim of Rs. 8,400 was received in final settlement. The consignee sent the following Account sales.

		Rs.
Sale proceeds of 400 watches		1.92.000
Less Clearing Charges	Rs. 2,280	
Storage	Rs. 3,720	
Commission	Rs. 9,600	
	Net Proceeds	1,76,400

You arc required preparing necessary ledger accounts in the books of both the parties.

[K.Com (H) Kolkata Univ-Adapted]

Ans. Profit on Consignment Rs. 23,160

Abnormal loss (In transit) Rs. 9,600 (at Cost)

Stock on Consignment Rs. 29,160 (at Cost)

13. Yogi of Delhi sent on consignment of goods costing Rs. 1,80.000 to Gheethandhari of Chennai at invoice price showing a profit of 331/3% on cost. Yogi paid Rs. 1,200 as carriage and Rs. 4,800 as freight and insurance. Goods costing Rs. 18,000 were destroyed while in -transit and the Insurance Company admitted the full claim.

Gheethandhari paid Rs. 960 as carriagc inward and Rs. 2,400 as godown rent. Two-thirds of the goods received by consignor were sold, and a demand draft for the sale proceeds after deducting the expenses and commission due, was sent to Yogi. The terms of agreement provided 5% ordinary commission and 2½ %/del-credere.

Show the relevant account in the books of both the parties.

Ans. Profit on Consignment Rs. 21,260

Abnormal loss Rs. 24,600 at invoice price

Stock on consignment Rs. 74,120 at invoice price.

❑❑❑

10

JOINT VENTURE ACCOUNTS

MEANING OF JOINT VENTURE

Joint Venture is that business preposition where two or more persons undertake to complete a specific business preposition and share profits or losses arising there from as per terms and conditions of agreement. It is in fact, a temporary partnership without firm's name with a limited liability. It ceases to exist or wound up as soon as the "specific venture" is completed. The persons entering in to joint venture agreement are known as co – ventures. Usually, the joint ventures are undertaken in respect of construction or contract business, purchase and sale of properties, underwriting of shares or debentures, film production and joint venture consignment etc. According to J.R. Batliboi", a joint venture is practically a partnership between two or more persons confined to a particular venture or piece of business. The venture may take the shape of a joint consignments of goods, a speculation in shares, (undertaking, underwriting/guaranteeing) or any other similar form of enterprise."

Salient features :

1. Joint venture is an agreement between two or more persons for the completion of a specific business preposition.
2. Joint Venture is a temporary partnership without name.
3. The parties to the joint venture agreement are known as co-venturers who contribute capital (Cash or kind or both) and share profits/losses as per agreement. In the absence of an agreement they share profits or losses equally.
4. The Joint Venture comes to an end on the completion of business preposition undertaken.
5. The liability of all Co – Venturers is limited to the specific venture alone when agreement stands terminated.

Distinction between Joint Venture and Partnership

		Joint Venture	**Partnership**
1.	Name	Usually, it is without any trade name	The partnership firms always have specific trade name.

2.	Members	Members of joint venture are Known as Co – Venturers. The minimum number of members is two and there in no limit for maximum.	Members of the firm are known as partners. The minimum number of members is two and maximum 20 but in case of banking business it is 10.
3.	Nature	It is purely temporary in nature. It comes to an end after the completion of specific job or particular business activity.	It is not restricted to a particular business activity. It is a continuous business operation.
4.	Ascertainment of Profit & Loss	Profits or losses are ascertained for each venture on it's completion. Accounting period concept is not followed.	There is regular annual ascertainment of profits or losses under accounting period concept
5.	Registration of agreement	There is no registration of agreement to make it enforceable against the third parties.	The agreement has to be registered to make it enforceable against the third parties.
6.	Implied authority	Co-venturers have no implied authority.	Partners have implied authority.
7.	Liability	The liability of members is limited and ceases on the completion of specific job. There is no joint and several liabilities.	The liability of all partners is unlimited along with the joint and several liabilities.
8.	Members' others business	Co – Venturers may have their own independent business of similar nature.	The partners cannot have or run their own independent business of similar nature.
9.	Act	The joint venture is not governed by any special Act. The provisions of Partnership Act apply.	The partnership is governed by Indian Partnership Act of 1932.
10.	Books of Accounts	It is not necessary to prepare and maintain separate permanent record of accounts	The firms are required to maintain a separate set of books of accounts on permanent basis.

Distinction between Joint Venture and Consignment

		Joint Venture	Consignment
1.	Nature of Business	Joint Venture is carried on for a specific business preposition/ period or for limited purpose by Co-Venturers who are the owners. It is purely temporary in nature.	The business activity is undertaken by the Consignee who is not the owner of business. It is not for specific period or business activity preposition.
2.	Parties under agreement	The persons/ parties entering into Joint Venture are known as Co-Venturers.	The parties/persons to consignment are called consignor and consignee.
3.	Mutual Relationship	Relationship among the Co-Venturers is that of a principal as well as that of agent. A Co-Venturer acts on his own behalf as well as on behalf of all other Co-Venturers	The relationship between Consignor and Consignee is that of principal and agent. The Consignee acts on behalf of consignor.
4.	Provisions of Act.	The provisions of Partnership Act cover Joint Venture.	Provisions of Contract Act relating to agency apply.
5.	Authority	All the Co-Venturers may have implied authority to buy and sell goods and receive and make payments.	A consignee does not have any implied authority but has to act as per the instructions of the Consignor.

6.	Risk	All Co-Venturers bear the risk as per agreement.	Consignee does not bear any risk except that of bad debts and that too against the del-credere commission.
7.	Sharing of profits & losses	The profits or losses are shared by the Co-Venturers as per agreement. In the absence of an agreement the profits and losses are shared equally.	The consignee does not share profits or losses but he is entitled commission as agreed upon. The profit or loss belongs to Consignor only.

Accounting for the Joint Venture Transactions

There are three methods of recording transactions of a Joint Venture business.

(i) When separate set of books of accounts is maintained.

(ii) When no separate set of books of accounts is maintained. but all transactions are recorded in the books of one or each venturer .

(iii) When all venturers maintain accounts. Under this method each Co-Venturer records his own transactions. It is known as Memorandum Joint Venture Account.

(1) When separate set of books is maintained

This method is applied when the size of venture undertaken is larger and period of it's completion longer. Under this system following accounts are maintained.

(a) Joint Bank Account

(b) Joint Venture Account

(c) Co-Venturers' Personal Accounts

(a) Joint Bank Account records all actual receipts and actual payments whether these are of capital nature. It is opened with the co-venturers' initial contribution and closed by making them final payments It is debited with the amount received from sale of goods (in case of trading venture) or money received from contractor (Contract Venture), sale of shares (in case of speculation & under-writing business) or from distributors (in case of film production). Whereas Joint Bank Account is credited with the payments made to suppliers (creditors for goods) for purchase of materials required for construction, purchase of plant, payment of wages, fees or any other remuneration to workers, depending upon the nature of business. It is to be noted that all such cash transactions are processed through joint Bank Account. However, if any co-venturer makes any payments for any expenses out of his own personal funds, such an amount will not be recorded in the Joint Bank Account but will be credited to concerned co-venturer's account. It is like a Cash Book.

(b) Joint Venture Account is prepared to ascertain the profits or losses arising from the joint venture completed. It is a nominal account by nature, which is debited with all expenses incurred on venture, goods/materials supplied by the co-venturers and with the amount of goods/materials purchased for the joint venture undertaken. It is credited with the amount of sales (Trading venture), contract price (contract venture) commission received (underwriting of shares) and goods/materials taken by the co-venturers. The residual figure profit or loss is transferred to co-venturers' accounts in the agreed ratio. It is simply a substitute of Trading and Profit & Loss Account.

(c) Co-Venturers' Personal Accounts are like the Capital Accounts of a partnership firm. These accounts are credited with the amount of initial contribution (cash or kind), amount of expenses paid for joint venture out of personal fund, goods/materials supplied to joint venture business at any stage of completion, and with the amount of profit made. These accounts are debited with the share of loss, materials, goods and plant etc. taken by venturers. The balancing figure is settled through Joint Bank Account.

Under this method following Journal entries are recorded

1. When initial cash contribution is made by the co-venturers.

   Joint Bank A/c Dr. with the total amount

   To Co-Venturers' A/c with individuals' contribution

   (Being initial cash contributed)

2. When goods/materials or any other item contributed by any co-venturer.

   Joint Venture A/c Dr

   To Co-Venturere's A/c

   (Being contribution made in kind)

3. When goods are purchased:

   (a) For Cash

   Joint Venture A/c Dr

   To Joint Bank A/c

   (Being goods purchased for cash)

   (b) On Credit

   Joint Venture A/c Dr

   To Suppliers (creditors) A/c

   (Being goods purchased on credit)

4. When expenses are paid out of Joint Bank Account

   Joint Venture A/c Dr

   To Joint Bank A/c

   (Being expenses paid)

5. When expenses are paid by any Co-Venturer.

   Joint Venture A/c Dr

   To Co-Venturer's A/c

   (Being expenses paid by Co-Venturer)

6. When goods are sold/contract price is received/commission is received for Cash

   Joint Bank A/c Dr

   To Joint Venture A/c

   (Being goods sold*/contract* price received/commission* received for Cash)

   *Whichever is applicable?

7. When sale proceeds received by any venturer retained by him

   Co-Venturer's A/c Dr

   To Joint Venture A/c

   (Being sale proceeds retained by the venturer)

8. When goods are sold on Credit
   Debtors A/c Dr
   To Joint Venture A/c
   (Being goods sold on credit)
9. When cash is collected fort debtors (credit customers)
   Joint Bank A/c Dr
   To Debtors' A/c
   (Being cash received from debtors)
10. When goods/materials or any other item (plant etc.) is taken over by any co-venturer
   Co-Venturer A/c Dr
   To Joint Venture A/c
   (Being goods*/Materials*/other item taken over by Co-Venturer)
   *Whichever is applicable?
11. When payment is made to Creditors
   Creditors A/c Dr
   To Joint Bank A/c
   (Being payment made to Creditors)
12. When goods are returned by Debtors/or there are bad debts/or discount is allowed to debtors.
   Joint Venture A/c Dr
   To Debtors A/c
   (Being goods returned*/Bad debts*/discount allowed* to debtors)
   *Which ever is applicable?
13. When any Co-Venturer entitled to any commission or salary.
   Joint Venture A./c Dr
   To Co-Venturer's A/c
   (Being commission/salary payable to co-venturer)
14. When there is profit*
   Joint Venture A/c Dr (Total amount of profit)
   To Individual Co-Venturers' A/c (with co-venturer's respective share)
   *A reverse entry will be recorded for loss.
15. When final settlement is made
   (a) If there is debit balance of any Venturer
   Joint Bank A/c Dr
   To Co-Venturer's A/c
   (Being cash brought in by the Co-Venturer)
   (b) For credit Balance
   Co-Venturer's A/c Dr (with individual amount)
   To Joint Bank A/c (with total)
   (Being final payment made to Co-Venturers)

* The required ledger accounts can be prepared on the basis of journal entries.

Ledger Accounts (Formats)

JOINT VENTURE A/C

To Joint Bank A/c (goods purchased for cash)	x x x	By Joint Bank A/c (sale proceeds/contract price)	x x x
To Co-Venturer's A/c (goods/material supplied by Venturer)	x x x	By Debtors A/c (goods sold on credit)	x x x
To Creditors A/c (goods/materials purchased on credit)	x x x	By Co-Venturer's A/c (sale proceed retained)	x x x
To Joint Bank A/c (expenses paid)	x x x	By Co-Venturer's A/c (unsold stock taken over)	x x x
To Co-Venturer's A/c (Commission) (or expenses paid by co-venturer)	x x x		
To Debtors A/c (Bank debts/discount (allowed or returns by debtors)	x x x		
To Profit transferred to Co-Venturers' A/cs*	x x x	By Loss transferred to Co-Venturers' A/cs*	x x x
	x x x		x x x

CO VENTURERS' ACCOUNTS

To Joint Venture A/c (Sale proceeds retained)	x x x	x x x	By Joint Bank A/c (initial Cash contribution)	x x x	x x x
To Joint Venture A/c (Goods/Material etc taken over)	x x x	x x x	By Joint Venture A/c (goods etc contributed)	x x x	x x x
To Joint Venture A/c (Loss)*	x x x	x x x	By Joint Venture A/c (Expenses etc/commission)	x x x	x x x
To Joint Bank A/c (Final settlement)	x x x		By Joint Venture A/c (Profit)*	x x x	x x x
	x x x	x x x		x x x	x x x

* Only one entry for profit or loss as the case may be.

JOINT BANK ACCOUNT

To Co-Venturer's A/c (Initial contribution (say) X	......	By Joint Venture a/c (Cash Purchases)	
Y	......	By Joint Venture a/c (Expenses)	
To Joint Venture A/c (Sale Proceeds)	......	By Creditors (Cash Paid)	
To Debtors (Cash collected)	......	By Co-venturer's A/c X	......
		(Final settlement) Y	......
	......		......

Illustration 1 (Construction Contract)

A, B, and C undertake to construct a housing complex for X Ltd. The contract price is agreed at Rs. 75,00,000 to be paid in cash Rs, 66,00,000 by four installments and the balance amount in 8% Debentures of the company. A Joint Bank Account was opened with the initial contribution made by co-ventures as given below.

A : Rs. 900,000; B : Rs. 11,25,000 ; C : Rs. 6,00,000

A got building plan prepared and paid Rs. 75,000 as architect's fees.

B brought a plant (Mixer) and other implement worth Rs. 2,40,000.

C brought a Motor lorry, which was valued at Rs. 2,25,000.

Following payment were made from Joint Bank Account.

	Rs.
Materials	36,90,000
Wages	22,50,000
Sundry Expenses	60,000
Plant	1,80,000

On the completion of work Mixing Plant is sold for Rs.1,50,000 and other plant and implements for Rs.30,000.

C takes back the Motor Lorry at Rs.1,20,000. A takes over the 8% Debentures at a valuation of Rs.8,40,000

Prepare necessary ledger accounts to close the books of joint venture.

Solution : **JOINT VENTURE ACCOUNT**

	Rs.		Rs.
To Joint Bank A/c		By Joint Bank A/c	66,00,000
Materials	36,90,000	By 8% Debentures	9,00,000
Wages	22,50,000	By Joint Bank A/c	
Sundry Expenses	60,000	Sale of Mixing Plant	1,50,000
Plant	1,80,000	Sale of other Plant	30,000
To A (Architect's Fees)	75,000	By C (Motor Lorry)	1,20,000
To B (Mixing Plant)	2,40,000		
To C (Motor Lorry)	2,25,000		
To Loss on transfer of 8% Debentures	60,000		
To Profit transferred to			
A 3,40,000			
B 3,40,000			
C 3,40,000	10,20,000		
	78,00,000		78,00,000

CO-VENTURERS' ACCOUNTS

	A Rs.	B Rs.	C Rs.		A Rs.	B Rs.	C Rs.
To Joint Venture A/c				By Joint Bank A/c	9,00,000	11,25,000	6,00,000
(Debentures)	8,40,000			By Joint Venture A/c	75,000		
To Joint Venture A/c			1,20,000	(Architect's Fees)			
(Motor Lorry)				By Joint Venture A/c		2,40,000	
To Joint Bank A/c	4,75,000	17,05,000	10,45,000	(Mixing Plant)			
(Final settlement)				By Joint Venture A/c			2,25,000
				(Motor Lorry)			
				By Joint Venture A/c	3,40,000	3,40,000	3,40,000
				(Profit)			
	13,15,000	17,05,000	11,65,000		13,15,000	17,05,000	11,65,000

JOINT BANK ACCOUNT

	Rs.		Rs.
To A	9,00,000	By Joint Venture A/c :	
B	11,25,000	Materials	36,90,000
C	6,00,000	Wages	22,50,000
To Joint Venture A/c		S. Expenses	60,000
(Part of contract price)	66,00,000	Plant	1,80,000
To Joint Venture A/c		By A	4,75,000
(Sale of plants)	1,80,000	B	17,05,000
(1,50,000 + 30,000)		C	10,45,000
	94,05,000		94,05,000

Illustration 2 (Engineering Contract)

X and Y, engineering contractors, undertook jointly to build and install a new machinery for A Ltd. at a contract price of Rs. 6,70,000. As per the terms of contract Rs.4,25,000 was payable in cash in five equal installments and balance in fully shares in A Ltd. A joint bank account was opened with the deposits from X Rs. 2,25,000 and Y Rs,. 1,00,000. They agreed to share profits and losses in the ratio of 60% and 40%

Following transactions were reported.

	Rs.
Amount advanced to suppliers for supply of materials	2,60,000
Value of materials supplied by the suppliers	4,45,000
Balance amount paid to suppliers in full and final settlement	1,77,500
Paid Wages	1,80,000
Materials purchased for cash	12,500
Materials supplied by X	46,250
Consultation Fees paid	16,250

The contract was completed and the price was duly received
X took all the shares at an agreed value of Rs. 2,35,000 and
Y took the stock of materials worth Rs.17,000 at Rs.13,750.
Prepare Joint Venture A/c., Co-Venturers Accounts and Joint Bank A/c

Solution :

JOINT VENTURE A/C

	Rs.		Rs.
To Suppliers A/c (Materials)	4,45,000	By Joint Bank A/c	
To Joint Bank A/c		(Contract price in cash)	425,000
Wages	1,80,000	By Shares in A Ltd.	
Materials	12,500	(Balance of contract price	245,000
To X (Materials)	46,250	By Y (Materials taken)	13,750
To Loss on Shares (2)	10,000	By Discount from	
To Joint Bank A/c	16,250	Suppliers (1)	7,500
(Consultation Fees)		By Loss transferred to	
		X	11,250
		Y	7,500
	7,10,000		710,000

CO-VENTURERS' ACCOUNTS

	X Rs.	Y Rs.		X Rs.	Y Rs.
To Joint Venture A/c (material)		13,750	By Joint Bank A/c	2,25,000	1,00,000
To Joint Venture A/c			By Joint Venture A/c	46,250	
(Loss)	11,250	7,500			
To Shares in A Ltd.	235,000				
To Joint Bank A/c	25,000	78,750			
	2.71,250	1,00,000		2,71,250	1,00,000

JOINT BANK A/C

	Rs.		Rs.
To X	225,000	By Suppliers A/c (Advance)	260,000
Y	100,000	By Suppliers A/c (Final settlement)	177,500
To Joint Venture A/c		By Joint Venture A/c (wages)	180,000
(Contract price in cash)	425,000	By Joint Venture A/c (Materials)	12,500
		By Joint Venture A/c (Consultation Fees)	16,250
		By X	25,000
		By Y	78,750
	750,000		750,000

Working Notes :

(1) Discount from suppliers is a profit has been credited to Joint Venture Account. It is calculated as under:

		Rs.
Value of Materials Supplied		4,45,000
Less Advance	2,60,000	
Final Balance	1,77,500	(4,37,500)
(in full settlement)		
Discount Availed		7,500

(2) Loss on transfer of shares has been debited to joint venture A/c.

	Rs.
Value of shares received from A Ltd.	
Rs. (6,70,000 – 4,25,000)	2,45,000
(contract price less cash received)	
Less Agreed Value of Shares taken by X	(2,35,000)
Loss	10,000

Illustration 3 (Trading Venture)

X and Y entered in to a joint venture to purchase and sell second hand cars and agreed to share profits and losses in the ratio of 3:2. They opened a Joint Bank Account by making initial deposits of Rs. 1,50,000 and Rs. 1,00,000 respectively. They purchased 3 Maruti Cars for Rs. 1,20,000 and spend Rs. 25,000 on the repairs and replacement of tyres. X paid Rs. 2,500 for advertisement to sell the cars Z a friend of theirs purchased one Maruti Car at price a of Rs. 75,000. Another Car was sold for Rs. 80,000. The Co-Venturers also purchased an old model of Ford for Rs.25,000 and an Ambassador for Rs, 17,500. The expenses of repairs and reconditioning for these cars amounted to Rs. 10,000 and Rs. 12,500 respectively. Another dealer of Car helped X and Y to sell one Maruti and an Ambassador Car for Rs. 85,000 and Rs. 55,000. He was paid a commission @ 5% on sale proceeds. The Ford was retained by X at an agreed value of Rs. 40,000. Y paid rent of the shop Rs. 5,500.

Prepare Joint Venture Account, Joint Bank Account and Accounts of X & Y sharing final settlements.

Solution :

JOINT VENTURE ACCOUNT

	Rs.			Rs.
To Joint Bank A/c	1,20,000	By Joint Bank A/c		
(Purchase of 3 Maruti Cars)		(Sale Proceeds)		
To Joint Bank A/c		1 Maruti	75,000	
Repairs etc	25,000	1 Maruti	80,000	1,55,000
To X (Advertisement)	2,500	By Joint Bank A/c		
To Joint Bank A/c		Maruti	85,000	
(Ford & Ambassador) (25,000 + 17,500)	42,500	Ambassador	55,000	1,40,000
To Joint Bank A/c		By X (Ford)		40,000

	Rs.		Rs.
(Repairs & Reconditioning) (10,000 + 12,500)	22,500		
To Joint Bank A/c			
(Commission @ 5% on 1,40,000)	7,000		
To Y (Rent)	5,500		
To Profit Transferred to			
X 66,000			
Y 44,000	1,10,000		
	3,35,000		3,35,000

CO-VENTURERS' ACCOUNTS

	X Rs.	Y Rs.		X Rs.	Y Rs.
To Joint Venture (Ford)	40,000	- - -	By Joint Bank A/c	1,50,000	1,00,000
To Joint Bank A/c (Final Settlement)	1,78,500	1,49,500	By Joint Venture A/c (Advertisement)	2,500	
			By Joint Venture A/c (Rent)	- - -	5,500
			By Joint Venture A/c (Profits)	66,000	44,000
	2,18500	1,49500		2,18500	1,49500

JOINT BANK ACCOUNT

	Rs.		Rs.
To X (Contribution)	1,50,000	By Joint Venture A/c (Proceeds of Cars)	1,20,000
To Y (Contribution)	1,00,000	By Joint Venture A/c (Repairs etc)	25,000
To Joint Venture A/c (Sale proceeds)	1,55,000	By Joint Venture A/c (Purchase of Cars)	42,500
To Joint Venture A/c (Sale proceeds)	1,40,000	By Joint Venture A/c (Repairs etc)	22,500
		By Joint Venture A/c (Commission)	7,000
		By X	1,78,500
		By Y	1,49,500
	5,45,000		5,45,000

Illustration 4 (Underwriting of Shares)

On 1.1.2008 A and B entered into a Joint Venture agreement to underwriting the subscriptions of 80,000 shares of Rs. 20 each issued by Z Ltd. at a premium of Rs. 5 per share. The underwriting commission is agreed at 4%

Public subscribed for 70,000 shares and the remaining were taken up by the underwriters as per agreement. A & B contributed Rs. 1,50,000 and Rs. 1,30,000 respectively which was deposited in a Joint Bank Account. They incurred Rs. 6,000 as dealing and miscellaneous expenses. On 31st March 2008, they received a draft for underwriting commission.

On 1.4.2008, of the shares purchased from the company 80% were sold in the open market at the ruling price of Rs. 30 per share and the reaming were taken up by them in the profit sharing ratio which was 3 : 2 .

Show the necessary Ledger Accounts.

Solution :

JOINT VENTURE ACCOUNT

	Rs.		Rs.
To Joint Bank A/c (10,000 shares @ Rs. 25 per share)	2,50,000	By Joint A/c (Commission) $\left(80{,}000 \times 25 \times \frac{4}{100}\right)$	80,000
To Joint Bank A/c (Expenses)	6,000	By Joint Bank A/c (Salc proceeds of shares)	2,40,000
To Profits transferred to		By A (Shares taken up)	30,000
A 68,400			
B 45,600	1,14,000	By B (Shares taken up)	20,000
	3,70,000		3,70,000

CO-VENTURES'

	A Rs.	B Rs.		A Rs.	B Rs.
To Joint Venture A/c (Shares taken up)	30,000	20,000	By Joint Bank A/c	1,50,000	1,30,000
			By Joint Venture A/c	68,400	45,600
To Joint Bank A/c To (Final Settlement)	1,88,400	1,55,600			
	2,18,400	1,75,600		2,18,400	1,75,600

JOINT BANK ACCOUNT

	Rs.		Rs.
To A (contribution)	1,50,000	By Joint Venture A/c (Purchase of shares)	2,50,000
To B (contribution)	1,30,000		
To Joint Venture A/c (Commission)	80,000	By Joint Venture A/c (Exp.)	6,000
To Joint Venture A/c		By A (Final payment)	1,88,400
(Sale proceeds of shares)	2,40,000	By B (Final payment)	1,55,600
	6,00,000		6,00,000

Illustration 5 (Film/Documentary Production)

Rohit and Rohan entered into joint venture to prepare documentary film to create awareness about the AIDS among the masses. Delhi Door Darshan agreed to pay Rs. 25,00,000. It was agreed that each co-venturer to contribute Rs.2,50,000each and share profits & losses equally. The initial contributions of the co-venturers were deposited in a Joint Bank Account. They incurred the following expenses.

	Rs.
Purchase of Camera and other equipments	175,000
Film Materials	265,000
Purchase of Van	500,000
Fees of Casts and film shooting expenses	580,000
Salaries & wages of unit workers	790,000
Office Expenses including license Fees	68,000
Hire Charges for other equipments	135,500
Tour and Travel expenses	45,000

On completion of the firm, some objections were raised by the inspecting panel of D.D. some scenes has to be changed which cost Rohit & Rohan Rs. 54,500.

The amount of Rs.25,00,000 was released by government in five equal instalments. Due to delay in second instalment a loan of Rs. 2,00,000 @ 12% interest p.a. has to be arranged. The amount was repaid after one quarter through Joint Bank Account.

Camera was taken over by Rohit at an agreed price of Rs. 25,000. Van was taken over by Rohan after charging depreciation of 25%. Other equipments were found useless and sold as scrap for Rs. 5000 only

Prepare necessary Ledger Accounts.

Solution :

JOINT VENTURE ACCOUNT

		Rs.		Rs.
To Joint Bank A/c :			By Joint Bank A/c	25,00,000
Camera & other Equipments		1,75,000	By Rohit (Camera)	25,000
Film Materials		2,65,000	By Rohan (Van)	
Van		5,00,000	(5,00,000 Less 25%)	3,75,000
Fees & Shooting Expenses		5,80,000	By Joint Bank A/c	
Salaries & Wages		7,90,000	(Sale of other Equipments)	5,000
Office Expenses & License Fees		68,000		
Hire Charges		1,35,500		
Tour & Travel Expenses		45,000		
To Joint Bank A/c (Editing Cost)		54,500		
To Joint Bank A/c (Interest)		6,000		
To Profit transferred to				
Rohit	1,43,000			
Rohan	1,43,000	2,86,000		
		29,05,000		29,05,000

CO-VENTURER'S ACCOUNTS

	Rohit Rs.	Rohan Rs.		Rohit Rs.	Rohan Rs.
To Joint Venture A/c	25,000	3,75,000	By Joint Bank A/c	2,50,000	2,50,000
To Joint Bank A/c			By Joint Venture A/c		
(Final Settlement)	3,68,000	1,8,000	(Profit)	1,43,000	1,43,000
	3,93,000	3,93,000		3,93,000	3,93,000

JOINT BANK ACCOUNT

	Rs.		Rs.
To Rohit (Deposit)	2,50,000	By Joint Venture A/c :	
To Rohan (Deposit)	2,50,000	Camera & other Equipments	1,75,000
To Bank Loan A/c	2,00,000	film Materials	2,65,000
To Joint Venture A/c	25,00,000	Van	5,00,000
To Joint Venture A/c		Fees & Shooting Expenses	5,80,000
(Scrap)	5,000	Salaries Wages	7,90,000
		Office Expenses etc.	68,000
		Hire Charges	1,35,500
		Tour & Travel Expenses	45,000
		By Joint Venture A/c (Editing Cost)	54,500
		By Joint Venture A/c (Interest)	6,000
		By Bank Loan A/c	2,00,000
		By Rohit	3,68,000
		By Rohan	18,000
	32,05,000		32,05,000

II. Recording of all transactions in the Books of one/each Co-Venturer

Under this method one of the co-venturers is entrusted with the task of recording all joint venture transactions to ascertain the profits and losses made including final settlements of venturers. He may be allowed some extra remuneration for rendering such services. Usually, following accounts are prepared.

1. Joint Venture Account
2. Other Co-Venturers' personal Accounts

Sometime each Co-Venturer maintains record of all joint venture transactions. It happens when each party informs other co-venturers regarding transactions made by him at regular intervals.

Joint Venture Account is prepared to find out profit or loss arising from joint venture. The venturer maintaining the accounting records transfers his share to Profit & Loss and share of other-venturers to their respective personal accounts.

The Personal Accounts of other co-venturers are prepared as discussed under first method

Journal Entries

(1) When Co-Venturers make initial contribution to joint venture business.

Cash or Bank A/c Dr
To Co-Venturers A/c
(Being amount contributed by co-venturers)

(2) When goods are purchased for Cash

Joint Venture A/c Dr
To Cash/Bank
(Being Cash purchases made)

(3) When goods are purchased or credit

Venture A/c Dr
To Creditors/suppliers A/c
(Being goods purchased on credit)

(4) When goods are supplied by other Co-Venturer

Venture A/c Dr
To Co-Venturer's A/c
(Being goods brought in by other venturers)

(5) When goods are supplied by the Co-Venturer recording transactions.

Joint Venture A/c Dr.
To Purchases A/c
(Being goods supplied for joint venture out of stock)

(6) When expenses are paid

Joint Venture A/c Dr.
To Cash/Bank A/c
(Being expense paid on Joint Venture)

(7) When expenses are paid by other co-venturer

Joint Venture A/c Dr.
To Co-Venturer's A/c
(Being expenses of joint venture paid by ——- name of co-venturer)

(8) When goods are sold for Cash

Cash/Bank A/c Dr.
To Joint Venture A/c
(Being goods sold for Cash)

(9) When goods are sold on Credit.

Debtors A/c Dr.
To Joint Venture A/c
(Being sold on Credit)

(10) When goods are sold by other Co-Venturer

Co-Venturer A/c Dr.
To Joint Venture A/c
(Being goods sold by ———name of the venturer)

(11) When Cash is received from debtors

Cash/Bank A/c Dr.

To Debtors' A/c

(Being Cash received from debtors)

(12) When Cash is received from other Co-Venturer who sold the goods.

Cash/Bank Dr.

To Co-Venturer A/c

(Being Cash received from ————)

(13) When Bills Receivable are received from Debtors/Co-Venturer

Bills Receivable A/c Dr.

To Debtrors/Co-Venturer's A/c

(Being Bills received from ———)

(14) On discounting the Bills

Bank A/c Dr.

Discount A/c Dr.

To Bills Receivable

(Being bills discounted)

(15) On Transferring the discount to Joint Venture A/c

Joint Venture A/c Dr.

To Discount A/c*

(Being discount charged to Joint Venture A/c)

* Discount is not a charge on Joint Venture. It is debited to Joint Venture A/c when all the Venturers agree. In the absence of any specific instructions, students should make a foot note regarding its treatment.

(16) When there are bad debts/discount is allowed to Debtors.

Joint Venture A/c Dr.

To Debtors A/c

(Being bad debts/discount allowed charged to Joint Venture A/c)

(17) When goods (remaining Sock/any other item) are taken over by other Venturer

Co-Venturer's A/c Dr.

To Joint Venture A/c

(Being goods/name of other item (Plant etc) taken over by ————)

(18) When goods/materials are taken over by the venturer recording transactions.

Purchase A/c Dr. (For Business)

Drawings A/c Dr. (For self Consumption)

To Joint Venture A/c

(Being goods/materials taken-over for ———)

(19) When there are profits

Joint Venture A/c Dr

To Profit & Loss A/c -(own share)

To Co-Venturers' A/c -(other co-venturers' share)

(Being profits distributed)

(20) If there is a loss, a reverse entry will be recorded.

(21) When payment is made to Creditors/Suppliers:

Creditors/Suppliers A/c Dr

To Cash/ Bank A/c

(Being Cash/Bank paid to Creditors)

(22) When the amount is received from other Co-Venturer at the time of Final settlement.

Cash/Bank A/c Dr.

To Co-Venturer A/c

(Being balance received from———-on final settlement)

(23) When the amount is paid to other Co-Venturers at the time of final settlement.

Co-Ventuirers' A/c Dr.

To Cash/Bank

(Being Cash paid to ——- on final settlement)

Illustration 6 [Trading]

Dennis and Dinesh entered into a Joint Venture to & sell scrap and agreed to share profits & losses equally.

On 1.1. 2008 Dinesh purchased scrap costing Rs.72,000. He paid Rs.2,500 as freight, loading and unloading charges. He sent the scrap costing Rs. 48,000 to Dennis out of this lot.

Dennis sent Rs.36,000 to Dinesh and purchased in auction scrap worth Rs.60,000 half of which was sent to Dinesh. Carriage Charges of Rs.1,200 were also paid by Dennis.

On 25.2.2008 Dinesh sold most of goods for Rs.66,000 and the goods costing Rs. 4,000 were taken over at an agreed price of Rs. 5,000.

On 31.3.2008 Dennis sold the entire stock of scrap for Rs. 20,000 Scrap worth Rs. 3,000 was found unsaleable. It was agreed to write it off. Selling expenses incurred by Dennis amounted to Rs. 2,700.

On 1.4.2008 the account were settled between them.

Show Joint Venture Account and Dennis Account in the books of Dinesh.

Solution : **In the Books of Dinesh**

JOINT VENTURE ACCOUNT

	Rs.		Rs.
To Cash (Purchases)	72,000	By Dennis (Goods sent)	48,000
To Cash (Expenses)	2,500	By Dennis (Goods retained)	30,000
To Dennis A/c (Purchases)	60,000	By Dennis (Sale)	20,000
To Dennis A/c (Expenses)	1,200	By Cash (Sale)	66,000
To Dennis A/c (Selling Expenses)	2,700	By Goods (Scrap) taken over	5,000
To Dennis A/c (Profit)	15,300		
To Profit & Loss A/c	15,300		
	1,69,000		1,69,000

DENNIS ACCOUNT

	Rs.		Rs.
To Joint Venture A/c	48,000	By Cash	36,000
To Joint Venture A/c	30,000	By Joint Venture A/c	60,000
To Joint Venture A/c	20,000	By Joint Venture A/c	1,200
To Cash (Final settlement)	17,200	By Joint Venture A/c	2,700
		By Joint Venture A/c	15,300
	1,15,200		1,15,200

Illustration 7 (Underwriting)

P and Q entered into a Joint Venture of underwriting and guaranteeing the subscription of newly formed joint stock company. The company issued 25,000 shares of Rs.10 each at Rs.11 per share. The expenses of issue up to allotment were to be paid by P & Q who shared profits and losses in the ratio of 3:2. The consideration for guarantee being 2,500 other shares of 10 each fully paid.

P paid for registration, advertising and printing and stationery Rs.3000., Rs.2,700 and Rs.1,200 respectively.

Q paid for office rent Rs.2,000, legal charges Rs.2,500 and salaries Rs.1,800.

The issue was made public and shares subscribed fell short of the full issue by 2,000 shares. P took over on joint account and paid for the same in full. Company paid underwriting commission in fully paid shares. P and Q sold 2,000 shares each @ Rs.12.5 per share and remaining were taken up by them in the profit sharing ratio at an agreed value of Rs. 12 per share. Prepare Joint Venture Account and Q's Account in the books of P.

II How the joint venture A/c and other co-venturer A/c will appear if the same are prepared in the books of Q.

Solution :

Books of P

JOINT VENTURE ACCOUNT

		Rs.		Rs.
To Cash A/c	Rs.		By Cash (2,000 @ Rs.12.5)	25,000
Registration Fees	3,000		(Sale Proceeds of Shares)	
Advertising	2,700		By Q (2,000 @ Rs.12.5)	25,000
Printing & Stationery	1,200	6,900	(Sale Proceeds of Shares)	
To Q			By Shares in New Company	3,600
Rent	2,000		(300 shares @ Rs.12)	2,400
Legal Charges	2,500		By Q (200 shares @ Rs. 12)	
Salaries	1,800	6,300		
To Cash (2,000 @ Rs.11)		22,000		
(Unsubscribed shares taken-up)				
To Q (Profit)	8,320			
To Profit & Loss A/c	12,480	20,800		
		56,000		56,000

Q'S ACCOUNT

	Rs.		Rs.
To Joint Venture A/c (sale proceeds)	25,000	By Joint Venture A/c (Expenses)	6,300
		By Joint Venture A/c (Profit)	8,320
To Joint Venture A/c (Shares taken-up)	2,400	By Cash (Cash received against final settlement)	12,780
	27,400		27,400

Books of Q
JOINT VENTURE ACCOUNT

		Rs		Rs
To Cash	Rs.		By Cash Sale Proceeds) 2,000 shares @ Rs. 12.5	25,000
Rent	2,000			
Legal Charges	2,500		By P Sale (Proceeds)	
Salaries	1,800	6,300	2,000 shares @ Rs. 12.5	25,000
To P			By Shares in New Co.	
Registration Fees	3,000		(200 Shares @ 12)	2,400
Advertising	2,700		By P (Shares taken up)	
Stationery	1,200	6,900	(300 shares @ Rs. 12)	3,600
To P (shares taken up & final for) 2,000 shares @ Rs. 11		22,000		
To P	12,480			
To Profit & Loss A/c	8,320	20,800		
		56,000		56,000

P'S ACCOUNT

	Rs.		Rs.
To Joint Venture A/c (Sale proceeds)	25,000	By Joint Venture A/c (Expenses)	6,900
To Joint Venture A/c (300 Shares taken up)	3,600	By Joint Venture A/c (Shares Subscribed)	22,000
		By Joint Venture A/c	12,480
To Cash A/c (cash paid) (Final settlement)	12,780		
	41,380		41,380

Illustration 8 (Simple)

A and B agreed to enter into a joint venture to by and sell second hand vehicles and to share profits and losses in the ratio of 5:3 respectively. It was agreed that A would record all details of the venture in his books of accounts.

On 1st April 2008, B purchased two vehicles and paid cash Rs. 50,000 on 15th April. He spent Rs. 6,000 on repairs, Rs, 700 on insurance and Rs. 1000 as driver's wages. He sold the vehicles a week later for Rs. 70,000 subject to cash discount of 2% if paid within seven days. He paid the proceeds of sale into his bank account five days later.

On 1st May A purchased five vehicles for Rs. 1,25,000 of which he managed to sell three vehicles for Rs.90,000 for Cash on the same day without incurring any expenses. The fourth vehicle was sold for Rs.33,750 and on 15th May, he received a Bill Receivable to be presented for payment in three months time.

On 30th June, the fifth vehicle was still unsold and it was agreed that B should take over the vehicle at a valuation of Rs. 18,750. On the same date the parties made a settlement between each other, A agreeing to take the bill receivable at a value of Rs. 32,950.

You are required to prepare:

Joint Venture Account and 'B's Account in the books of A. **[C.A. (E) Modified]**

Solution : **In the books of A**

JOINT VENTURE ACCOUNT

	Rs.		Rs.
To B		By B (Sales)	70,000
Purchases	50,000	By Bank	90,000
Repairs	6,000	By Bills Receivable A/c (Sales)	33,750
Insurance	700	By B (Vehicle taken over)	18,750
Driver's Wages	1,000		
*Discount (2% on Rs. 70,000)	1,400		
To Bank			
(Purchases)	1,25,000		
To Bill Receivable A/c			
(Loss on taking over)	800		
To Profit transferred to			
P & L A/c 17,250			
B 10,350	27,600		
	212,500		212,500

B'S ACCOUNT

	Rs.		Rs.
To Joint Venture A/c		By Joint Venture A/c (Purchases)	50,000
(Sales)	70,000	By Joint Venture A/c (Expenses)	7,700
To Joint Venture A/c		By Joint Venture A/c (Discount)	1,400
(Vehicle taken over)	18,750	By Joint Venture A/c (Share of Profit)	10,350
		By Bank A/c (Final settlement)	19,300
	88,750		88,750

* Discount and loss on taking over of a B/R is treated as a joint venture loss.

Illustration 9 (Valuation of goods taken over by co-venturer)

Paul and Lal entered into a joint venture for buying and selling condemned railway materials. The profit or loss was to be shared in the proportion of 2:3.

In an railway auction, material worth Rs. 75,000 was purchased by Paul who also paid Rs.5,000 for freight and unloading expenses. Paul drew a bill on Lal at a two months demand for Rs. 50,000. The bill was discounted for Rs. 49,750.

Other transactions relating to Joint Venture were as follows:

- Purchase of material costing Rs.35,000 by Lal
- Paul paid Rs.750 for carriage outward Rs.1,250 as commission and Rs.500 as traveling expenses.
- Lal paid rent of the godown Rs.4,500 and other sundry expenses Rs.675.
- Sales effected by Paul amounted to Rs.87,750, whereas Lal sold goods for Rs.58,500.

Goods costing Rs.1,000 Rs,1,500 were retained by Paul and Lal respectively and these were charged to them at a price so as to show the same rate of gross profit as is made on the sales. Paul was credited with a sum of Rs.1,500 to cover the cost of warehousing and insurance. The discount on bill is to be treated a charge on Joint Venture.

Prepare Joint Venture A/c and Paul's A/c in the books of Lal showing final settlement.

Solution : **Books of Lal**

JOINT VENTURE ACCOUNT

	Rs.		Rs.
To Paul A/c		By Paul A/c (Sale proceeds)	87,750
Purchases	75,000	By Bank A/c (Sale Proceeds)	58,500
Freight	5,000	By Paul A/c (goods taken over)1	1,300
Discount	250	(1000 + 300) (Cost + 30%)	
Carriage outward	750	By Goods (stock) taken over 2	1,950
Commission	1,250	(Cost + 30%)	
Travelling Expenses	500	(Rs.1,500 + 450)	
Warehousing & Insurance	1,500		

To Bank A/c			
Purchases	35,000		
Rent	4,500		
Sundry Expenses	675		
To Paul's A/c (Profit)	10,030		
To Profit & Loss A/c	15,045		
	149,500		149,500

PAUL'S ACCOUNT

	Rs.		Rs.
To Joint Venture A/c (Sale Proceeds)	87,750	By Joint Venture A/c (Purchases)	75,000
To Bills Payable A/c	50,000	By Joint Venture A/c (Expenses)	9,250
To Joint Venture A/c (Goods taken over)	1,300	By Joint Venture A/c (Profit)	10,030
		By Bank A/c (Final Settlement)	44,770
	139,050		139,050

Working note :

Unsold stock has been taken over on the basis of gross profit rate

Gross Profit = Sales less cost of Goods sold

Total sales = Rs. 87,750 + 58,500 = Rs. 1,46,250

Cost of Goods sold* = Rs. 1,12,500

Gross Profit = 33,750

$$\text{Rate of Gross profit} = \frac{33{,}750 \times 100}{1{,}12{,}500} = 30\% \text{ on cost}$$

*COGS = Opening Stock + Purchases + Freight – Closing Stock

= Nil + 75,000 + 35,000 + 5,000 – 2,500

= Rs. 1,12,500

Illustration 10 (Construction Contract)

Amar and Akbar enter into Joint Venture to take a building contract for Rs.36,00,000. they provide the following information regarding the expenditure incurred by them.

	Amar Rs.	Akbar Rs.
Bricks and Sand	3,20,000	55,000
Cement	5,00,000	1,75,000
Wood	2,00,000	3,25,000
Steel	1,95,000	4,50,000
Wages	—	4,05,000
Architect's Fees	1,50,000	—
License Fees	—	75,000
Plant	—	3,00,000

Unused material worth Rs. 80,000 was taken over by Amar.

Plant was valued at Rs. 1,50,000 at the end of contract which was taken over by Akbar. The contract amount was received in three equal installments on the basis of works certified and completed. The contract money was received by Amar.

You are required to prepare.

(1) Joint Venture Account and Akbar's Account in the books of Amar and

(2) Joint Venture Account and Amar's Account in the books of Akbar.

Solution :

JOINT VENTURE ACCOUNT

		Rs.		Rs.
To Bank : (Materials)			By Bank	36,00,000
Bricks & Sand	3,20,000		(Contract money)	
Cement	5,00,000		By Akbar (Plant)	1,50,000
Wood	2,00,000		By Materials (Takeover)	80,000
Steel	1,95,000	12,15,000		
To Akbar (Materials)				
Bricks & Sand	55,000			
Cement	1,75,000			
Wood	3,25,000			
Steel	4,50,000	10,05,000		
To Bank (Architects Fees)		1,50,000		
Akbar (Wages)		4,05,000		
Akbar (License Fees)		75,000		
Akbar (Plant)		3,00,000		
Akbar (Profit)	3,40,000			
Profit & Loss A/c	3,40,000	6,80,000		
		38,30,000		38,30,000

AKBAR'S ACCOUNT

	Rs.		Rs.
To Joint Venture (Plant)	1,50,000	By Joint Venture (Materials)	10,05,000
To Bank (Final settlement)	19,75,000	By Joint Venture (Wages)	4,05,000
		By Joint Venture (License Fees)	75,000
		By Joint Venture (Plant)	3,00,000
		By Joint Venture (Profit)	3,40,000
	21,25,000		21,25,000

Books of Akbar

JOINT VENTURE ACCOUNT

		Rs.		Rs.
To Bank : (Materials)			By Amar	36,00,000
Bricks & Sand	55,000		(Contract price)	
Cement	1,75,000		(Material takenover)	80,000
Wood	3,25,000		By (Plant) taken over	1,50,000
Steel	4,50,000	10,05,000		
To Bank (Wages)		4,05,000		
To Amar (Materials)				
Bricks & Sand	3,20,000			
Cement	5,00,000			
Wood	2,00,000			
Steel	1,95,000	12,15,000		
To Amar (Architect's Fees)		1,50,000		
To Bank (License Fees)		75,000		
To Bank (Plant)		3,00,000		
To Amar (Profit	3,40,000			
To Profit & Loss A/c	3,40,000	6,80,000		
		38,30,000		38,30,000

AMAR'S ACCOUNT

	Rs.		Rs.
To Joint Venture	36,00,000	By Joint Venture (Materials)	12,15,000
(Contract Price)		By Joint Venture (Architecture Fees)	1,50,000
To Joint Venture	80,000	By Joint Venture (Profit)	3,40,000
(Materials Taken over)		By Bank (Final settlement)	19,75,000
	36,80,000		36,80,000

III. Memorandum Joint Venture Account Method

Under this method each co-venturer keeps a record of his own transactions relating to joint venture in his own ledger. He does not record the transactions of other coventurer. The recording procedure may be summed up as follows.

1. Each co-venturer opens a "Joint Venture with ———— (name of other co-venturer) Account. It is not a nominal account like a Joint Venture A/c (already discussed under first two methods) but a personal account by nature. It does not disclose profit or loss arising from joint venture. Each co-venturer debits the Account with the amount paid and credits the Account with every receipt.

2. In order to ascertain profit or loss on Joint Venture, a Memorandum Joint Venture Account is prepared. This account can be prepared only when all co-venturers produce a copy of transactions recorded by each of them in their respective ledgers. In fact all transactions affecting profit or loss are recorded in the Memorandum Joint Venture Account. Debit items of "Joint Venture with ...... Account" are recorded to the debit also side and credit items to the credit side of Memorandum Joint Venture Account. It should be noted that items not affecting profit or loss are not considered in the Memorandum Joint Venture Account. For example Cash sent or Cash received by one venturer to other will not enter in this Account.

Illustration 11

L and M entered into Joint Venture to buy and sell defense disposal goods. L purchased goods worth Rs.1,40,000 and dispatched ¾ th goods to M incurring Rs.4,000 as freight and insurance charges. Goods worth Rs.7,000 were damaged in transit. Insurance company paid Rs. 2,000 in full settlement of the claim. L sold the entire lot in his possession for Rs.45,000. He received Rs.60,000 from M through Bank Draft.

M took the delivery of the goods sent by L and incurred the following expenses:

Clearing Charges	700
Carriage	1,200
Rent	2,500
He reported the sale as follows:	
2/3 rd of the goods sent by L for	1,05,200
Damaged Goods for	6,800
Remaining stock at	32,000

It is agreed that they are entitled to commission @10% on the respective sales effected by them and profits and losses to be shared by L & M in the ratio of 2:1

M remits to L the balance amount due on 31st March 2008. You are required to show the books of L and M. Also prepare Joint Venture Memorandum Account.

Solution :

In the Books of L

JOINT VENTURE WITH M ACCOUNT

	Rs.		Rs.
To Bank (Purchase of goods)	1,40,000	By Bank (Insurance Claims)	2,000
To Bank (Freight & Insurance)	4,000	By Bank (Sales)	45,000
To Commission (1)	4,500	By Bank (Remittance from M)	60,000
To Profit & Loss A/c (Share of profit)	15,800	By Bank (Final settlement)	57,300
	1,64,300		1,64,300

In the books of M

JOINT VENTURE WITH L ACCOUNT

	Rs.		Rs
To Bank (Expenses)		By Bank (sales)	
Clearing Charges	700	- 2/3rd of Goods sent	1,05,200
Carriage	1,200	- Damaged goods	6,800
Rent	2,500	- Remaining Stock	32,000
To Bank (Remittance to L)	60,000		
To Commission (2)	14,400		
To Profit & Loss A/c			
(Share of profit)	7,900		
To Bank (Remittance to A)			
Final settlement)	57,300		
	1,44,000		1,44,000

(1) Commission to L has been calculated @ 10% on Sales of Rs.45,000.

(2) Commission to M is worked out @ 10% on total sales of Rs. 1,44,000.

MEMORANDUM – JOINT VENTURE ACCOUNT

	Rs.		Rs.
To L:		By L:	
Purchases	1,40,000	Insurance Claims	2,000
Freight and Insurance	4,000	Sales	45,000
Commission	4,500	By M:	
To M:		Sales (total)	1,44,000
Clearing Charges	700		
Carriage	1,200		
Rent	2,500		
Commission	14,400		
To Profit on Joint Venture			
L 15,800			
M 7,900	23,700		
	1,91,000		1,91,000

Illustration 12 (Calculation of Insurance Claim)

A and B entered into Joint Venture to buy and sell second – hand air conditioners. A purchased for cash 50 air conditioners including 10 split AC's at an average price of Rs.8,000 during the quarter ending 31st March 2008.

B spent the following amounts:

	Rs.
Spare Parts	36,000
Labour Charges	48,000
Testing Charges	4,000
Painting, Polishing and Insurance.	52,000
New compressors for 10 split AC's	60,000

Split Air-conditioners having new compressors were sold for Rs.25, 000 each. The air conditioers were sold as follows:

- 17 AC's @ Rs.12,500 each and 5 split AC's by A
- 18 AC's @ Rs.12,000 each and 4 split AC's by B

Due to short circuit one split AC got totally damaged and the Insurance Company paid the actual cost of AC to B

Prepare Joint Venture Memorandum Account & Joint Venture with Co-Venturer's Account to find out profit & balance due to and due from.

Solution : MEMORANDUM - JOINT VENTURE ACCOUNT

	Rs.		Rs.
To A (Purchases)	4,00,000	By A (Sales)	
50 AC's @ Rs. 8,000		17 AC's @ Rs. 12,500	
To B (Expenses)		5 split AC's @ Rs. 25,000	3,37,500
- Spare Parts	36,000	By B (Sales)	
- Labour Charges	48,000	18 AC's @ Rs.12,000	
- Testing Charges	4,000	4 split AC's @ Rs.25,000	3,16,000
- Painting & Insurance etc.	52,000	By B (Insurance Claims) (1)	16,800
- Compressors	60,000		
To A (profit)	35,150		
To B (profit)	35,150		
	6,70,300		6,70,300

In the books of A : JOINT VENTURE WITH B ACCOUNT

	Rs.		Rs.
To Bank (Purchases)	4,00,000	By Bank (Sales)	3,37,500
To Profit & Loss A/c (Profit)	35,150	By Balance c/d	97,650
	4,35,150		4,35,150

In the books of B : JOINT VENTURE WITH A ACCOUNT

	Rs.		Rs.
To Bank (Expenses)		By Bank (Sales)	3,16,000
- Spare parts	36,000	By Bank (Insurance Claims)	16,800
- Labour Charges	48,000		
- Testing Charges	4,000		
- Painting & Insurance	52,000		
- Compressors	60,000		
To Profit & Loss Account	35,150		
To Balance c/d	97,650		
	3,32,800		3,32,800

Working Note :

(1) Calculation of Insurance claimed by Insurance Company.

			Rs.
Purchase price of 50 Air Conditioners @ Rs.8,000			400,000
Add Expenses incurred on reconditioning & Repairs			
Spare parts used		36,000	
Labour Charges		48,000	
Testing Charges		4,000	
Painting & Insurance etc.		52,000	1,40,000
Cost of 50 AC's	=		5,40,000
Cost of 1 AC	=		10,800
Cost of split AC with new Compressor			
Cost of 10 Compressors 60,000			
Cost of one Compressor			6,000
Cost of split AC with New Compressor			16,800

Since cost of buying, repairs & reconditioning of ordinary AC's and Split AC's is not given separately, the total amount spent has been averaged. Since all split AC's were fitted with new compressors, the cost of new compressor has been added to average cost to get the actual cost of split AC.

MISCELLANEOUS ILLUSTRATIONS

Illustration 12 (Joint Venture, Consignment and Unsold Stock)

On 1.4.2008 Brown and White entered in to Joint Venture to Consign goods to Yellow, and agreed to share profits & losses equally. Brown purchased goods costing Rs.90,000 and consigned to Yellow. He paid Rs.7,500 as freight and transit insurance.

White also purchased goods worth Rs.55,000 which were consigned to Yellow after incurring Rs.4,500 as forwarding expenses.

Yellow reported that 3/4 th of the goods received were sold for Rs.2,20,000. The sale proceeds was remitted to Brown after deducting 5% commission on sales. Brown and White decided to close their books of accounts on 30th September 2008, and to make interim settlement.

During October half of the remaining goods were spoiled, due to moisture. These were sold at 60% of the actual cost. Remaining goods were sold at 20% profit on cost. The proceeds was sent to White after deducting 5% commission on sales. On 31st October the accounts of Joint Venturers were settled.

Prepare Memorandum Joint Venture Account and Joint Venture account with other co-venturer.

Solution : **MEMORANDUM JOINT VENTURE ACCOUNT**

	Rs.		Rs.
To Brown		By Yellow (Sales)	2,20,000
Goods sent (Purchases)	90,000	By Stock (1)	39,250
Freight & Insurance	7,500		
To White			
Goods Sent (Purchases)	55,000		
Forwarding Expenses	4,500		
To Yellow (Commission) (2)	11,000		
To Profit transferred to			
Brown 45,625			
White 45,625	91,250		
	2,59,250		2,59,250
To Stock b/d	39,250	By Yellow (Sale of damaged Goods)(3)	11,775
To Yellow (Commission)*	1,765	By Yellow (Sale of remaining goods)(4)	23,550
		By Loss : Brown	2,845
		White	2,845
	41,015		41,015

* 5% of (11,775 + 23,550)

In the Books of Brown

JOINT VENTURE WITH WHITE ACCOUNT

2008		Rs.	2008		Rs.
1.4.	To Bank:			By Bank (Sales-Commission)	2,09,000
	(Goods Purchased & Consigned)	90,000		(Received from Yellow)	
	Freight & Insurance	7,500		By Stock c/d	
	To Profit & Loss A/c (Profit)	45,625	30.9	(1/2 of the Stock)	19,625
	To Bank				
	(Remittance)	85,500			
		2,28,625			2,28,625
1.10	To Stock b/d	19,625	1.10	By Profit & Loss A/c	
				(Loss)	2,845

			31.10	By Bank (Remittance) (Final settlement)	16,780
		19,625			19,625

In the books of White

JOINT VENTURE WITH BROWN ACCOUNT

	Rs.		Rs.
To Bank		By Bank (Received for Brown)	85,500
(Goods Purchased & Consigned)	55,000	By Stock (1/2 of Stock) c/d	19,625
Forwarding Expenses	4,500		
To Profit & Loss A/c			
(Share of profit)	45,625		
	1,05,125		1,05,125
To Balance (Stock) b/d	19,625	By Bank (Sales - Commission)	33,560
To Bank (Remittance)		By Profit & Loss A/c	2,845
(Final settlement)	16,780		
	36,405		36,405

Working Notes :

	Rs.
(1) Value of Closing Stock	
Cost of goods purchased and consigned by Brown	90,000
Add Expenses (Freight and Insurance)	7,500
Cost of goods purchased and consigned by White	55,000
Add Expenses (Forwarding Expenses)	4,500
	1,57,000
Less Cost of goods sold (3/4)	1,17,750
Cost of goods unsold on 30.9.2008	39,250
(2) Commission up to 30.9.2008	11,000
5% on Rs.2,20,000	
(3) Sale proceeds of damaged goods	
Cost of damaged goods (1/2 of Stock)	19,625
Sale proceeds = 60% of cost	11,775
(4) Sale of remaining Stock (1/2 of 39,250)	19,625
Add 20%	3,925
	23,550

Illustration 14 (Joint Venture with interest on Capital)

A and B entered into Joint Venture for purchase and sale of jute. They agreed to share profits and losses in proportion of two-third and one-third and also to be entitled to an interest @6% per annum on monthly basis on capital employed by each of them. The following transactions took place between themselves.

(i) On 1.10.2008, A purchased 700 bales of Jute @ Rs. 275 each, the brokerage being Rs.5 per bale.

(ii) On 1st November, B purchased 600 bales of Jute @ Rs.310 per bale the brokerage being Rs.5 per bale.

(iii) On 1st December, B sold 350 bales of Jute @ Rs.345 per bale the brokerage being Rs.5 per bale and he retained the proceeds.

(iv) On 31st December, A sold 800 bales of Jute @ Rs.330 per bale the brokerage being Rs.5 per bale and he also retained the sale proceeds.

It was also agreed that each of the partners will at first, sell from his own purchases and then, if required, from the stock purchased by other one. The balance of stock was to be divided between the partners in the profit sharing ratio. The stock being valued at cost to the partner concerned on 31st December, the partners settled their accounts. Prepare necessary ledger accounts.

[C.A. (I) (Adapted)]

Solution : **JOINT VENTURE ACCOUNT**

			Rs.				Rs.
To	A			By	B (Sales)	1,20,750	
	Purchases	1,92,500			*Less* Brokerage	1,750	1,19,000
	Brokerage	3,500	1,96,000	By	A (Sales)	2,64,000	
To	B				*Less* Brokerage	4,000	2,60,000
	Purchases	1,86,000		By	A (Stock taken over)		31,500
	Brokerage	3,000	1,89,000	By	B (Stock taken over)		15,750
To	A (Interest) (1)		2,940				
To	B (Interest) (2)		1,295				
To	Profit transferred to						
	A		24,677				
	B		12,338				
			4,26,250				4,26,250

CO-VENTURERS' ACCOUNTS

		A Rs.	B Rs.			A Rs.	B Rs.
To	Joint Venture A/c	2,60,000	1,19,000	By	Joint Venture A/c	1,96,000	1,89,000
	(Sales)			By	Joint Venture A/c	2,940	1,295
To	Joint Venture A/c	31,500	15,750		(Interest)		
	(Stock)			By	Joint Venture A/c	24,677	12,338
To	A (Final settlement)		67,883	By	B (Final settlement)	67,883	
		2,91,500	2,02,633			2,91,500	2,02,633

Working notes :

(1) Interest allowed to A on Rs.1,96,000 @6% p.a. for 3 months i.e. from 1st October to 31st December

$$\left(\text{Rs.}1{,}96{,}000 \times \frac{6}{100} \times \frac{3}{12}\right) = 2{,}940$$

(2) Interest allowed to B on Rs.1,89,000 @6% p.a. for one month	Rs. 945
and on Rs.70,000 (Rs. 1,89,000 – 1,19,000 sale proceeds) for one month	Rs. 350
	1,295

Illustration 15 (Development of sites)

A and B enter into a Joint Venture to develop some sites and sell them on the understanding that the result of the venture would be shared of 2:3. It is also agreed that cash investment from Co-Venturers would be entitled to interest at 10% p.a.

A plot measuring five acres of agricultural land was purchased for Rs.4,80,000 and for this purpose loan from Bank was arranged to the extent of 80% of cost of land @ 16% p.a. interest. On 1.7.2005 the registration formalities were completed and the vendors were paid off the balance of purchase price by A. The expenses of registration amounted to Rs.37,900 were also met by A.

B incurred the following cost in connection with preparation of the lay out & advertisement etc.

1.08.2008	–	Leveling and engineering cost paid to architects and Town Planners @ Rs.2,000 per ground
1.09.2008	–	Municipal Fees @ Rs. 3,200 per ground
1.10.2008	–	Advertisement Expenses Rs. 1,40,000
31.12.2008	–	Entertainment Expenses Rs. 8,960

Plots were advertised and entire area was dealt with as under.

(a) 15% of the total area was to be left for roads, market place, park and school.

(b) 10 plots each of 3, 2 ½, and 1½ grounds were made

(c) The remaining area was taken equally by A & B at cost.

(d) 1½ grounds plots carried a premium of 50%, 2 ½ grounds plots a premium of 40% and 3 grounds plots a premium of 25% on cost.

(e) B to receive 8% of the sale proceeds as management fee for his efforts. All transactions were processed through Joint Bank. The transactions were completed by 31st December. Prepare necessary ledger accounts.

Note : 1 Acre is equal to 18 grounds of 2,400 sq. feet. **[C.A. (Inter) Adapted]**

Solution : **JOINT VENTURE ACCOUNT**

	Rs.		Rs.
To Joint Bank A/c	3,84,000	By Joint Bank A/c (8)	12,92,000
(80% cost of land)		(Sale proceeds of plots)	
To A (20% of Cost of land		By A (Plots taken over)	44,200
and registration charges) (1)	1,33,900	By B (Plots taken over)	44,200

		Rs.		Rs.
To	Joint Bank A/c (Interest) (2)	30,720		
To	B			
	Leveling & Engineering Cost (3)	1,80,000		
	Municipal Fees	2,88,000		
	Advertisement	1,40,000		
	Entertainment Expenses	8,960		
To	A (Interest) (5)	6,695		
To	B (Interest) (6)	20,600		
To	B (Management fees) (7)	1,03,360		
To	Profit transferred fees)			
	A 33,666			
	B 50,499	84,165		
		13,80,400		13,80,400

CO-VENTURERS' ACCOUNTS

	A Rs.	B Rs.		A Rs.	B Rs.
To Joint Venture A/c (Plots taken over)	44,200	44,200	By Joint Venture A/c (Cash payments for expenses)	1,33,900	6,16,960
To Joint Bank A/c (Final settlement)	1,30,061	7,47,219	By Joint Venture A/c (Interest)	6,695	20,600
			By Joint Venture A/c (profit)	33,666	50,499
			By Joint Venture A/c (Fees)	—	1,03,360
	1,74,261	7,91,419		1,74,261	7,91,419

JOINT BANK ACCOUNT

	Rs.		Rs.
To Bank Loan	3,84,000	By Joint Venture A/c	3,84,000
To Joint Venture A/c	12,92,000	By (80% of cost of land)	
(Sale proceeds of plots)		By Bank loan (Paid off)	3,84,000
		By Joint Venture A/c	
		(Interest on Loan)	30,720
		By A	1,30,061
		By B	7,47,219
	16,76,000		16,76,000

Working notes :

			Rs.
(1) Amount Paid by 'A'			
Registration Charges			37,900
20% of cost of land			96,000
			1,33,900
(2) Interest on Loan of Rs. 3,84,000 @ 16% p.a. for 6 months (From 1.7.2008 to 31.12.2008)			30,720
(3) Levelling Charges & Engineering Cost			
1 Acre =	18 grounds		
5 Acre (Total Area purchased) =	90 grounds		
Less Area left for Road, market etc.	13,5 grounds		
(15% of 90 grounds)	76.5 grounds		
10 (Ten) plots of 3 grounds = 30			
10 plots of 2 ½ grounds = 25			
10 plots of 1 ½ grounds = 15	70.0 grounds		
Available for A & B	6.5 grounds		
Levelling Charges @ Rs.2,000 per ground			Rs.
For 90 grounds =			1,80,000
(4) Municipal Fees for 90 grounds @ Rs. 3,200 =			2,88,000
(5) Interest on Cash investment @ 10% p.a. for 6 months A paid for balance of cost of land and registration charges. $\left(1{,}33{,}900 \times \frac{10}{100} \times \frac{6}{12}\right)$			6,695
(6) Interest paid to B on Rs. 6,16,960			
On Rs.1,80,000 for 5 months (1.8 to 31.12)		7,500	
On Rs.2,88,000 for 4 months (1.9 to 31.12)		9,600	
On Rs.1,40,000 for 3 months (1.10 to 31.12)		3,500	
On Rs. 8,960 Nil (Expenses incurred on 31.12)		-------	20,600
(7) Management Fees @ 8% on Sales (Rs.12,92,000)			1,03,360

(8) Sale proceeds of plots

Since plots have been sold at different rate of premium on Cost, it is necessary to work out the actual cost of plots after taking into account the expenditure incurred on acquisition, leveling and development of site.

Cost of land	4,80,000
Add Registration fee	37,900
Levelling & Engineering Cost	1,80,000
Municipal Fees	2,88,000
Interest on Bank Loan	30,720

Interest on Cash investments of	
A	6,695
B*	17,100
(*excluding interest on advertisement and Entertainment Expenses)	10,40,415

(20,600 – 3,500)

$$\frac{\text{Total cost Rs. } 10,40,415}{76.5 \text{ grounds}} = 13,600 \text{ per ground App.}$$

(Although the cost per ground works out to be Rs.13,600.196 but for the sake of convenience only Rs. 13,600 have been taken into account)

	Rs.
Thus 1½ ground = 15 plots @ Rs.13,600 + 50%	20,400
2½ ground = 25 plots @ Rs.13,600 + 40%	19,040
3 ground = 30 plots @ Rs.13,600 + 25%	17,000

		Rs.
Sale proceeds	15 x 20,400	3,06,000
	25 x 19,040	4,76,000
	30 x 17,000	5,10,000
		12,92,000

Illustration 16 (Consignment and Joint Venture)

On 1st January 2008 'A' manufacturer of sports materials at Ludhiana sent a consignment of 1000 cricket bats to D of Delhi to be sold on consignment basis at a commission of 20%. Such commission to cover the consignee's expenses but not the freight charges of the goods to Delhi. The cost of each bat is Rs.150 but is invoiced at Rs.200 each.

A case containing 20 bats was lost in transit. The Insurer paid Rs. 2,000 only in full settlement of claim. The consignee paid Rs.2,500 as freight charges and further spent Rs. 1,500 as selling expenses. Consignor's expenses amounted to Rs.7,500. The consignee accepted a bill of exchange drawn by consignor for three months for Rs.80,000 which was discounted at 6% per annum with the bankers. D sold 75% of the bats consigned at the rate of Rs.250 per bat. The balance was remitted on 31st March 2008.

On 1.4.2008, the parties decided to convert their relationship to that of a Joint Venturer, on the terms that the cost of each bat would be taken at Rs.200. A to get an interest of 8% p.a. on this investment and D to get commission of 10% on sales. Profits & Losses are to be shared equally. Prepare necessary accounts in the books of A and record the adjusting entry required on conversion of the terms of dispatch. The working should form the part of your answer. **[C.A. (Inter) – Adapted]**

Solution : **CONSIGNMENT ACCOUNT**

	Rs.		Rs.
To Goods sent on consignment	2,00,000	By D (Sales) (750 @ Rs.250)	1,87,500
To Bank (Expenses)	7,500	By Goods sent on Consignment (Loading)	50,000
To D (Freight)	2,500		
To D (Commission) (20% on Rs.1,87,500)	37,500	By Bank (Insurance Claim)	2,000
To Stock Reserve	11,500	By Abnormal Loss (1)	1,200
To Profit on Consignment transferred to P&L A/c	30,000	By Stock Consignment (2)	48,300
	2,89,000		2,89,000

D'S ACCOUNT

	Rs.		Rs.
To Consignment A/c	1,87,500	By Bills Receivable A/c	80,000
		By Consignment A/c (Exp.)	2,500
		By Consignment A/c (Commission)	37,500
		By Bank (Final settlement)	67,500
	1,87,500		1,87,500

MEMORANDUM JOINT VENTURE ACCOUNT

	Rs.		Rs.
To Goods sent on Joint Venture	200,000	By Sales (D)	187,500
To Expenses – A	7,500	By Insurance Claims	2,000
– D	2,500	By Closing Stock	48,300
To Commission (D)	18,750		
To Interest (3)	4,000		
To Discount on bill (4)	1,200		
To Profit on Joint Venture			
A	1,925		
D	1,925		
	237,800		237,800

Working notes :

(1) Abnormal Loss :

		Rs.
Cost of 20 bats @ Rs. 150		3,000
Add Direct proportionate expenses (in Transit)		
Consignor	7,500	
Consignee (Freight)*	2,500	
$\left(\frac{10,000 \times 20}{1,000}\right)$		200
		3,200
Less Insurance Claims		2,000
		1,200

* Since consignee paid freight, which is paid on the basis of goods consigned (1,000 bats), and not on the basis of goods received it has been included, for the purpose of valuing the cost of bats lost in transit. Usually the consignee's expenses are not included for the purpose of valuing loss in transit, because consignee incurs expenses on or after goods, are received.

(2) Stock on Consignment

	Rs.
Invoice price of stock of bats	
230 bat @ Rs.200	46,000
Add Direct Proportionate Expenses of Consignor $\left(\frac{7,500}{1,000} \times 230\right)$	1,725
Add Direct Proportionate Expenses of Consignee (Freight) $\left(\frac{2,500 \times 230}{1,000}\right)$	575
	48,300

(3) Interest on Investment

On Rs. 2,00,000 @ 8% p.a. for 3 months $= \left(2,00,000 \times \frac{8}{100} \times \frac{3}{12}\right)$

= Rs. 4,000

(4) Discounting charges are purely financial charges, which are not charged to consignment account but considered under Joint Venture.

$$\left(\text{Rs. } 80,000 \times \frac{6}{100} \times \frac{3}{12}\right) = \text{Rs. } 1,200$$

(5) Adjustment on conversion of consignment in to Joint Venture :
Under consignment 'D' has received Rs. 37,500 as commission whereas he is entitled to receive Rs. 18,750 as commission and Rs. 1,925 as share of profit under joint venture. Hence A is to recover Rs. 16,825 from D (37,500 – 1,925).

Illustration 17 (Changing profit sharing ratio)

X and Y enter into a Joint Venture to build a multistoried building. They agreed to share the Profits & Losses equally upto Rs. 60,000 of the profits or Losses and thereafter shared in the proportion of 3:2.

X contributes plant worth Rs. 48,000 and pays registration expenses of Rs. 12,000 Y Contributes plot of land on which building is to be built. The land is valued at Rs.1,20,000. The details of other expenses incurred are as under:

	Rs.
Materials	1,92,000
Labour Charges	90,000
Electricity installation charges	28,000
Plumbering works	26,000

All these expenses were paid out of Joint Bank Account At the end of venture X agreed to take back the plant at Rs. 12,000 Y sold off the multistoried building for a total of Rs. 6,48,000. Y kept one flat valued at Rs.2,16,000 for himself in lieu of his expected share of profits. The Venturers who had agreed to maintain their venture accounts in separate sets of books, ask you to prepare the Joint Venture Account, Joint Bank Account and Venturers Capital Account. **[I.C.W.A. (Inter) Adapted]**

Solution : In the books of X

JOINT VENTURE ACCOUNT

	Rs.		Rs.
To Plant	48,000	By Joint Bank A/c	6,48,000
To Cash (Registration)	12,000	(Sale of building)	
To Y (Plot)	1,20,000	By Y (Flat)	2,16,000
To Joint Bank A/c		By X (Plant)	12,000
Materials	1,92,000		
Labour	90,000		
Electricity Charges	28,000		
Plumbering	26,000		
To Profit - X 2,10,000			
- Y 1,50,000	3,60,000		
	8,76,000		8,76,000

JOINT BANK ACCOUNT

	Rs.		Rs.
To Joint Venture A/c		By Joint Venture A/c	
(Sale proceeds)	6,48,000	Materials	1,92,000
		Labour	90,000
		Electricity Installation	28,000
		Plumbering works	26,000
		By X	2,58,000
		By Y	54,000
	6,48,000		6,48,000

Y'S ACCOUNT

	Rs.		Rs.
To Joint Venture A/c (Flat)	2,16,000	By Joint Venture A/c (Plot)	1,20,000
To Joint Bank A/c		By Joint Venture A/c (Profit)	1,50,000
(Final settlement)	54,000		
	2,70,000		2,70,000

In the Books of Y

X ACCOUNT

	Rs.		Rs.
To Joint Venture A/c (Plant)	12,000	By Joint Venture A/c (Plant)	48,000
To Joint Bank A/c	2,58,000	By Joint Venture A/c (Registration)	12,000
(Final settlement)		By Joint Venture A/c (Profit)	2,10,000
	2,70,000		2,70,000

Working note :

Profits have been divided between X and Y as follows

	X	Y
Profit up to Rs.60,000 equally	30,000	30,000
Balance (360,000 – 60,000) in 3:2 ratio	1,80,000	1,20,000
	2,10,000	1,50,000

Illustration 18

A of Chennai and B of Delhi entered into Joint Venture on 1.4.2008 for the purpose of buying second hand cars, recondition and sell them as diesel air conditioned car. A has agreed to buy second hand cars and recondition them and fit diesel engines. B has agreed to fix air conditioners and sell them at Delhi. They have agreed to share profits and losses equally and settle their accounts at the end of each year.

The following are the details of purchases, sales and expenses incurred by A and B.

		A	B
		Rs.	Rs.
Cost of 10 Cars		5,00,000	——
Reconditioning expenditure		45,000	——
Cost of 10 diesel engines		30,000	——
Labour Charges		18,000	32,000
Purchase of 8 air conditioners		——	4,00,000
Buying commission @ 5%		25,000	——
Selling Commission @ 5%		——	60,000
Sale value realised on sale of 8 Cars		——	12,00,000
Freight	- Local	10,000	8,000
	- Delhi	30,000	——
Rent	- Office	9,000	10,000
	- Garage	13,500	20,000
Insurance		18,000	20,000
Miscellaneous expenses		6,300	10,000

B sent a cheque for Rs. 6,00,000 to A on 1.10.2008. Of the balance of 2 Cars, one car met with an accident on the way to garage before reconditioning and the Insurance Company settled the claim at Rs. 30,000 at a total loss. The old petrol engines were sold @ Rs.500 per engine and one diesel engine was sold at Rs.3,000 by A. All of them were sold before 1.10.2008. A retained the balance one car as non-air-conditioned diesel car for his personal use which was priced at average cost.

A and B settled their accounts through crossed cheque you are required to prepare.

(i) Memorandum Joint Venture Account.

(ii) Joint Venture Account with B in the books of A.

(iii) Joint Venture Account with A in the books of B. **[C.A. (Foundation) see 1993-modified]**

Solution : MEMORANDUM JOINT VENTURE ACCOUNT

	Rs.		Rs.
To A:		By A (Sales):	
Cost of Cars	5,00,000	- Petrol Engines 9 @ Rs.500	4,500
Reconditioning Expenses	45,000	- Diesel Engines	3,000
Cost of diesel engines	30,000	By A - Insurance Claims	30,000
Labour Charges	18,000	- Cost of Car taken	68,700
Commission on purchase	25,000	By B (Sales)	12,00,000
Freight	40,000		
Rent	22,500		
Insurance	18,000		
Miscellaneous expenses	6,300		
To B:			
Purchases (A.C)	4,00,000		
Labour Charges	32,000		
Commission on sales	60,000		
Freight	8,000		
Rent	30,000		
Insurance	20,000		
Miscellaneous expenses	10,000		
To Profit transferred to : -			
A 20,700			
B 20,700	41,400		
	13,06,200		13,06,200

In the books of A

JOINT VENTURE WITH B ACCOUNT

	Rs.		Rs.
To Bank		By Bank: (Advance from B)	6,00,000
Cost of Cars	5,00,000	- Sales of petrol Engines	4,500
Reconditioning Expenses	45,000	- Sales of Diesel Engines	3,000
Cost of diesel Engines	30,000	- Insurance Claims	30,000
Labour Charges	18,000	By Motor Car taken over	68,700
Commission on purchases	25,000	By Bank (Final settlement)	19,300
Freight	40,000		
Rent	22,500		
Insurance	18,000		
Miscellaneous Expenses	6,300		
To Profit & Loss A/c (Profit)	20,700		
	7,25,500		7,25,500

In the Books of B

JOINT VENTURE WITH A ACCOUNT

		Rs.			Rs.
To	Bank (Advance sent)	6,00,000	By	Bank (Sale proceeds)	12,00,000
	Labour Charges	32,000			
	Cost of air conditioners	4,00,000			
	Selling Commission	60,000			
	Freight	8,000			
	Rent	30,000			
	Insurance	20,000			
	Miscellaneous Expenses	10,000			
	Profit & Loss A/c (Profit)	20,700			
	Bank (Final settlement)	19,300			
		12,00,000			12,00,000

Working notes :

The Cost of Car taken by A has been worked out as under:

	Rs.
Cost of Car (5,00,000 ÷ 10)	50,000
Cost of diesel Engine (30,000 ÷ 10)	3,000
Freight (Local) (10,000 ÷ 10)	1,000
Buying Commission (25,000 ÷ 10)	2,500
* Reconditioning Expenditure (4,5000 ÷ 9)	5,000
* Labour Charges (18,000 ÷ 9)	2,000
* Office Rent & Garage Rent (22,500 ÷ 9)	2,500
* Insurance Charges (18,000 ÷ 9)	2,000
* Miscellaneous Exp. (6,300 ÷ 9)	700
	68,700

Since one Car met with an accident before reconditioning hence expenses on reconditioning, labour charges office rent & Garage rent, insurance and miscellaneous expenses relate to 9 Cars only.

Illustration 19

A and B enter into Joint Venture as dealers in land with effect from 1.7.2008. On the same day A advanced Rs. 8,10,000 and plot of land measuring 9,000 sq. meters, was purchased with this money. It was decided to sell the land in smaller plots and plan was prepared at the cost of Rs. 9,000 paid by B. In the said plan 1/3rd of the total area of the land was left over for the public roads and the remaining land was divided into 6 plots of equal size. On 1.11.2008 two of the plots were sold @ Rs. 270 per sq. meter the buyer deducting Rs. 9,000 per plot for stamp duty, and registration expenses agreed to be borne by the sellers. The remaining plots were sold at net price of 225 per sq. meters on 31.12.2008. The sale proceeds of all the plots were received by A. After charging interest @ 6% per annum on the investments of A (allowing for money received by him) and allowing 1% on the net sale proceeds of plots as commission to B, the net profit of Joint Venture is to be shared in the proportion of ¾ to A and ¼ to B.

Draw up the Memorandum Joint Venture and personal accounts in the books of A and B, showing the balance payable by one to the other. Assume that Joint Venture was completed on 31st December 2008. **[B. Com (D U) Adapted]**

Solution : **MEMORANDUM JOINT VENTURE ACCOUNT**

	Rs.		Rs.
To A: Purchases	8,10,000	By A : (Sale proceeds) (2)	14,22,000
(Cost of land)		A : Interest (3)	5,220
: Interest (1)	24,300		
To B:			
Expenses	9,000		
Commission	14,220		
To Profit : A	4,27,275		
: B	1,42,425		
	14,27,220		14,27,220

In the books of A

JOINT VENTURE WITH B ACCOUNT

	Rs.		Rs.
To Bank	8,10,000	By Bank (Sales proceeds)	14,22,000
To Interest	24,300	By Interest	5,220
To Profit & Loss A/c (Profit)	4,27,275		
To Bank (Balance paid on final settlement)	1,65,645		
	14,27,220		14,27,220

In the Books of B

JOINT VENTURE WITH 'A' ACCOUNT

	Rs.		Rs.
To Cash (Expenses)	9,000	By Bank	
To Commission	14,220	(Balance received on final settlement)	1,65,645
To Profit & Loss A/c (Profit)	1,42,425		
	1,65,645		1,65,645

Working notes :

(1) Interest payable to A:

On Rs. 8,10,000 @ 6% p.a. for 6 months (From 1.7.2008 to 31.12.2008)

$$\left(8{,}10{,}000 \times \frac{6}{100} \times \frac{6}{12}\right) \quad \text{Rs. } 24{,}300$$

(2) Sale Proceeds

Area of land purchased	9,000	Sq. mtr.
Less Area for Roads (1/3)	3,000	Sq. mtr.
	6,000	Sq. mtr.
Area of one plot (6,000 ÷ 6)	1,000	Sq. mtr.

	Rs.
Sale of 2 plots i.e. 2000 Sq. mtr. @ Rs.270 p.m.	5,40,000
Less stamp duty @ Rs.9,000 per plot	18,000
	5,22,000
Sale proceeds of remaining 4 plot. i.e. 4,000 Sq. mtr. @ Rs. 225 per Sq. mtr.	9,00,000
Total sale proceeds	14,22,000

(3) Interest to be charged to 'A'

On Rs. 5,22,000 @ 6% p.a. for 2 months (From 1.11.2008 to 31.12.2008)

$$\left(5{,}22{,}000 \times \frac{6}{100} \times \frac{2}{12}\right) \quad \text{Rs. } 5{,}220$$

Illustration 20

A of Delhi and B of Banglore entered into a Joint Venture for purchase and sale of one lot of Mopeds. The cost of each Moped was Rs.3,600 and the fixed retail selling price Rs.4,500. The following were the recorded transactions.

2008

Jan. 1 'A' purchased 100 Mopeds paying Rs.72,000 in cash on account.

'A' raised a loan from Canara Bank for Rs.50,000 @ 10% p.a. interest, repayable with interest on 1.3.2008

'A' forwarded 80 Mopeds to B incurring Rs. 2,880 as forwarding and insurance charges

Jan.7 'B' received the consignment and paid Rs.720 as clearing charges.

Feb. 1 'A' sold 5 Mopeds for cash

'B' sold 20 Mopeds for cash

'B' raised a loan of Rs. 1,50,000 from Bank repayable with interest at 18% p.a. on 1.3.2008

'B' telegraphically transferred Rs.1,50,000 to A incurring charges of Rs.50. A paid balance due for the Mopeds.

Feb. 26. 'A' sold the balance Mopeds for cash

'B' sold the balance Mopeds for Cash

'A' paid selling expenses Rs. 5,000

'B' paid selling expenses Rs. 20,000

On 1.3.2008, Accounts were settled between the veturers and loans repaid; profit being appropriated equally. You are required to prepare, Memorandum Joint Venture Account, Joint Venture with B Account in A's books, Joint Venture with A Account B's Books.

[C.A. (Entrance) June 1981, Modified]

Solution : **MEMORANDUM JOINT VENTURE ACCOUNT**

	Rs.		Rs.
To A:		By A (Sales)	
Purchases (100 Mopeds)	3,60,000	5 Mopeds @ Rs. 4,500	22,500
Forwarding and Insurance	2,880	15 Mopeds @ Rs. 4,500	67,500
Interest on Loan (1)	1,500	By B (Sales)	
Selling Expenses	5,000	80 Mopeds @ Rs. 4,500	3,60,000
To B:			
Clearing Charges	720		
Interest on Loan (2)	2,250		
T.T. Charges	50		
Selling Expenses	20,000		
To Profit:			
A 28,800			
B 28,800	57,600		
	4,50,000		4,50,000

In the Books of 'A'

JOINT VENTURE WITH B ACCOUNT

	Rs.		Rs.
To Bank : Cost of Purchases		By Bank (Sale proceeds)	
(Paid on Account)	72,000	5 Mopeds @ Rs.4,500	22,500
- Forwarding Charges	2,880	By Bank (Remittance from B)	1,50,000
- Selling Expenses	5,000	By Bank (Sale Proceeds)	
- Interest on Loan	1,500	15 Mopeds @ Rs. 4,500	67,500
- Cost of Purchases		By Bank (Received in final settlement)	1,58,180
(Balance)	2,88,000		
To Profit & Loss Account			
(Share of Profit)	28,800		
	3,98,180		3,98,180

In the Book of 'B'

JOINT VENTURE WITH 'A' ACCOUNT

	Rs.		Rs.
To Bank : Clearing Charges	720	By Bank (Sales)	90,000
- Remittances	1,50,000	20 Mopeds @ Rs. 4,500	2,70,000
- Bank Charges	50	60 Mopeds @ Rs. 4,500	
- Selling Expenses	20,000		
- Interest on Loan	2,250		
- Profit & Loss A/c (Profit)	28,800		
To Bank (Final settlement)	1,58,180		
	3,60,000		3,60,000

Working note :

(1) Interest on Loan paid by 'A'
On Rs. 50,000 @ 18% p.a. for 2 months = Rs.1,500

(2) Interest on Loan paid by 'B'
On Rs. 1,50,000 @ 18% p.a. for one months = Rs. 2,250

Illustration 21

M and N entered into Joint Venture for the purchase and sale of second hand motor cars and to share profits and losses in the ratio of 3:2. On 1st January 2005 M bought 5 Cars for Rs. 43,000 and paid Rs. 1,600 as Tax and insurance. On 31st January 2005, he sold these cars for Rs. 58,000 out of which he remitted Rs.11,000 to N paying balance in to his own bank account.

On January 5,2005 N bought 3 cars for Rs. 36,000 and paid Tax and insurance amounting to Rs. 1,400 and repair charges Rs. 2,000. He sold one car on 1st February for Rs.14,000 which he paid into his own bank account.. M then took over other cars at valuation of Rs.26,000 and the venture was closed on 5th February 2005.

Prepare the Memorandum Joint Venture Account and the Joint Venture account with N in the books of M and Joint Venture A/c with M in the books of N. **[C.A. (Entrance) May 1988 – Modified]**

Solution : MEMORANDUM JOINT VENTURE ACCOUNT

	Rs.		Rs.
To M : - Cost of 5 Cars	43,000	By M (Sales)	58,000
- Tax & Insurance	1,600	By N (Sales)	14,000
To N : - Cost of 3 Cars	36,000	By M (Cars taken over)	26,000
- Tax & Insurance	1,400		
- Repair Charges	2,000		
To Profit : M	8,400		
N	5,600		
	98,000		98,000

In the books of M

JOINT VENTURE WITH N ACCOUNT

	Rs.		Rs.
To Bank - (Cost of Cars)	43,000	By Bank (Sales)	58,000
- Tax & Insurance	1,600	By Cars taken over	26,000
To Bank - (Remitted to N)	11,000		
To P & L A/c (Profit)	8,400		
To Bank (Final settlement)	20,000		
	84,000		84,000

In the Books of N

JOINT VENTURE WITH M ACCOUNT

	Rs.		Rs.
To Bank - Cost of Cars	36,000	By Bank (Received from M)	11,000
- Tax & Insurance	1,400	By Bank (Sales)	14,000
- Repairs Charges	2,000	By Bank (Final Settlement)	20,000
To P & L A/c (Profit)	5,600		
	45,000		45,000

Illustration 22

Bhim and Arjun entered into Joint Venture for buying and selling plastic goods and agreed to share profits and losses in the ratio of 3:2.

On 1.10.2007, Bhim purchased goods at a cost of Rs.60,000 and half of the goods were handed over to Arjun. On 15.10.2007 he again purchased goods worth Rs. 20,000. He incurred expenses of Rs. 2,000.

On 16.10.2007, Arjun also made a purchase of Rs. 37,500 and on the same day he sent to Bhim goods worth Rs. 15,000. He incurred Rs. 900 on certain expenses. On October 20, Bhim, in order to help Arjun, sent Rs. 16,000 to him. Both the parties sold goods a profit of 25% on sale.

On 31st March 2008, Bhim had unsold stock of Rs. 12,500. Of these goods costing Rs.5,000 were taken away by him and the reminder sold for Rs. 8,000. Arjun was able to sell away compete goods except the goods costing Rs. 2,500 which were badly damaged and were treated as unsale able. Rs. 3,000 owing to Bhim was unrecoverable and treated as joint loss. On 31st March 2008, parties decided to close the books.

You are required to prepare (a) Joint Venture Account as it would appear in the books of Bhim recording his own transactions and (b) Memorandum Joint Venture Account showing the profit or loss of the venture. **[ICWA (I) Dec. 1989 Modified]**

Solution : **MEMORANDUM JOINT VENTURE ACCOUNT**

	Rs.		Rs.
To Bhim:		By Bhim:	
Purchases	60,000	Sales (1)	70,000
Purchases	20,000	Stock takenover	5,000
Expenses	2,000	Sales	8,000
Bad debts	3,000	By Arjun:	
To Arjun:		Sales (2)	66,667
Purchases	37,500		
Expenses	900		
To Profit			
Bhim:	15,760		
Arjun:	10,507		
	1,49,667		1,49,667

In the Books of Bhim

JOINT VENTURE WITH ARJUN ACCOUNT

	Rs.		Rs.
To Bank (Purchases)	60,000	By Bank (Sales less bad debts) (70,000 - 3,000)	67,000
To Bank (Expenses)	2,000		
To Bank (Purchases)	20,000	By Stock taken over	5,000
To Bank (remitted to Arjun)	16,000	By Bank (Sales)	8,000
To Profit & Loss A/c (Profit)	15,760	By Bank (Final settlement)	33,760
	113,760		113,760

Working notes :

(1) Sales effected by Bhim and Arjun

	(1) Bhim	(2) Arjun
Purchases	60,000	37,500
Purchases	20,000	
	80,000	37,500
Less Sent to other party	30,000	15,000
	50,000	22,500
Add Received from other party	15,000	30,000
	65,000	52,500
Less Unsold	12,500	2,500
Cost of goods sold	52,500	50,000
Add Profit (25% on Sales) or 33?% on cost	17,500	16,667
	70,000	66,667

QUESTIONS

1. What do you understand by Joint Venture? How it is different from Partnership and Consignment?
2. Explain briefly various methods of Joint Venture Accounting.
3. What is Memorandum Joint Venture Account? Is it different from Joint Venture with Co-Venture Account? Explain.

PROBLEMS

1. A and B entered into Joint Venture sharing profits & losses in the ratio of 3:2. They opened a Joint Bank Account. A and B paid into Joint Bank Account Rs. 75,000 and 60,000 respectively as capital. A purchased goods for Rs. 45,000 and paid Rs. 7,500 freight, brokerage & other expenses out of Joint Bank Account. He also supplied materials out of his own stock worth Rs. 4,500. He sold the entire stock of goods for Rs. 75,000 which was deposited to Joint Bank Account.
   B purchased goods for Rs. 37,500 and incurred Rs. 4,500 on various expenses out of Joint Bank Account. He sold all the goods for Rs. 66,000 except goods worth Rs. 3,000, which were taken by him form personal use. The sale proceeds was deposited to Joint Bank Account.
   Prepare necessary ledger accounts showing the final settlement between the venturers.
   Ans.

	Rs.
Profit on Joint Venture	45,000
Amount paid to A	1,06,500
Amount paid to B	75,000

2. Ram Rahim and Robert enter into Joint Venture to buy and sell woolen garments. They agreed to share profits & losses in the ratio of 2:2:1.
   Ram purchased garments worth Rs. 30,000 and paid Rs. 7,500 on various expenses.
   Rahim supplied woolen garments for Rs. 15,000 and incurred Rs. 5,000 as expenses and brokerage.
   Robert incurred Rs. 2,500 as selling expenses.
   Rahim and Robert sold the garments for Rs. 75,000. The sales effected by Rahim was double of that Robert's sales. The sale proceeds was retained by them in the proportion of sales effected by them. The remaining stock worth 6,250 was taken up by Rahim and Robert in 4:1 ratio. Final settlement was made on the closing date.
   Ans. Profit Rs. 21,250, Sales by Rahim 50,000 & Robert Rs. 25,000
   Amount paid by Rahim Rs. 26,500, Cash paid by Robert Rs. 19,500
   Amount Received by Ram Rs. 46,000.

3. M of Mumbai and K of Kolkata enter into joint venture to consign scrap to A of Agra.. They shared profits & losses equally. A is entitled to a commission of 10% of the net proceeds after charging such commission. M sent 50 tonnes of scrap costing Rs. 4,300 per tonne and paid freight and other expenses which amounted to Rs. 30,000 K sent 70 tonnes of scrap @ Rs. 5,000 per tonne and paid freight and forwarding expenses of Rs. 40,000. All the scrap was sold @ Rs. 10,000 per tonne by A who incurred Rs. 12,000 as selling expenses. He remitted Rs. 5,00,000 to M and balance of the net proceeds to K by bank drafts.
   You are required to show the necessary ledger accounts in the books of M & K to record own transactions and to prepare Memorandum Joint Venture Account. **[ICWA (I) June 1987 – Modified]**
   Ans. Profit Rs. 4,45,000; Commission Rs. 1,08,000.

4. A and B jointly underwrite and place on the market 50,000 shares of B.M. Ltd. of Rs. 10 each. It was agreed with company that they would be allotted 2,000 shares as fully paid towards their remuneration. Their profit sharing ratio is 3:2.

Applications are received for 45,000 shares A paid Rs. 4,000 for postage and advertisement, in addition to 60% of the amount required to take up short subscription. B financed the balance amount. These are accounted for through Joint Bank Account. All the shares including those allotted for remuneration were sold. A sold 3,000 shares for Rs. 35,000 and B sold the balance shares for Rs. 48,000. B incurred Rs. 2,000 as expenses. Sale proceeds were retained individually.

Show necessary accounts in the books of the venturers, which were separately started for this purpose. Account was settled through Bank Account.

Ans. Profit Rs. 27,000 **[C.A. (Inter) Modified]**

5. X and Y entered into joint venture for purchase and sale of second hand machineries and to share profits and losses in the ratio of 3:2 On 1.1.2005 X purchased 10 machineries for Rs.1,29,000 and paid Rs. 4,800 on freight and insurance. On 15th January he sold these machineries for Rs. 1,74,000 out of which he remitted Rs. 33,000 to Y and paying the balance into his own bank account. On 31st January Y bought 6 machineries for Rs. 1,08,000 and incurred Rs. 4,200 on freight and insurance, Rs. 6,000 on repairs. He sold 2 machineries for Rs. 42,000 which he paid into his own bank account. X took over other machineries at a valuation of Rs 78,000. The Venture was closed on 31st March 2006. Prepare Memorandum Joint Venture Account and the Account of Joint Venture with Y in the books of X.

Ans. Profit Rs. 42,000 Payment to y Rs. 60,000. **[C.A. (Entrance) – Adapted]**

6. Khan and Khanna jointly take up the work of constructing a building at a agreed price of Rs. 14,00,000 payable in cash Rs. 9,60,000 and in fully paid shares of a company for the balance of contract price. A joint Bank Account was opened with the initial contribution of Rs. 3,00,000 and Rs. 2,00,000 by Khan & Khanna respectively.

The contract price was realised and following costs were incurred.

	Rs.
Materials purchased out of Joint Bank Account.	8,40,000
Wages paid out of Joint Bank Account	2,60,000
Architect's Fees out of Joint Bank Account	24,000

Khan took all the shares of the company at an agreed valuation of Rs. 3,51,000 treating loss on shares as joint venture loss. Khanna took the remaining stock of materials at Rs. 36,000.

You are required to prepare Joint Venture Account, Joint Bank Account and Co-Venturers' Account. Khan & Khanna agreed to share profits and losses in the ratio of 3:2. **[C.A. (Entrance) Adapted]**

Ans. Profit Rs. 1,15,000

7. A and B decided to work a Joint Venture for the sale of electric motors. On 1.4.2005, A purchased 200 electic motors @ Rs. 1,750 each and dispatched 150 electric motors to B incurring Rs. 10,000 as freight, insurance and other forwarding charges. 10 motors were damaged in transit on 1.5.2005. Rs. 5,000 was received by A from Insurance Company in full settlement of claim. On 15.5. 2005 A sold 50 electric motors @ Rs. 2,250 each. He received Rs. 1,50,000 from b on 1.6.2005.

On 15th May 2001, B took delivery of electric motors and incurred the following expenses.

	Rs.
Clearing Charges	1,250
Repaires Charges on motors damaged in transit	3,000
Go-down rent	6,000

B reported sale of motors as follows.

10 electric motors (damaged)	@	1,700	each
40 electric motors	@	2,200	each
20 electric motors	@	3,150	each
80 electric motors	@	2,500	each

It is agreed that the venturers are entitled to commission at 10% on the respective sales effected by them and to share profits & losses in the ratio of 2:1.

Accounts are settled on 30th June 2005. You are required to prepare.

- Joint Venture Account in the books of A and
- Memorandum Joint Venture Account. **[C.A. (Foundation Nov. 97, - Modified]**

Ans. Profit : Rs. 59,550 ; Amount paid by B to A Rs. 14,3450 (Final settlement)

8. T of Tata Nagar and N of Nagpur entered into a Joint Venture to trade together in buying and selling of small equipments. Profits to be shared in the ratio of 2:3 T under took to make purchases and N to effect sales N remitted Rs. 75,000 to T towards the joint venture. T purchased equipments worth Rs. 60,000 and paid Rs. 28,000 on repairs, 2.5% as buying commission and Rs. 2,700 for sundry expenses. These equipments were sent to N at Nagpur.

N took the delivery and incurred Rs. 4,500 towards Railway Freight, Rs. 2,100 towards Octroi. He sold equipments for Rs. 1,05,000 and kept the remaining for himself at an agreed value of Rs. 22,500. N incurred the following expenses:

Go-down rent Rs. 1,350, Insurance Rs. 1,680, Brokerage Rs. 2,400 and Miscellaneou Expenses Rs. 1,920. Both parties decided to close the venture. You are required to prepare (1) Memorandum Joint Venture Account and Co- Venturer's Account in the books of each Co-Venturer showing the amount due to and due from. **[I.C.W.A – (Inter) Modified]**

Ans.	Profit on Joint Venture	Rs. 21,350
	Balance due to T	Rs. 25,740

9. P and Q enter into an agreement for the purpose of purchasing land and converting it into plots. The purchase price of Rs.12,80,000 and legal expenses of Rs. 88,800 are paid by P who borrowed money from Bank.

Q provided materials costing Rs.4,64,000 for the leveling of land and the development of plots. 10 plots of 200 sq. mts. Each and 5 plots of 400 sq. mts. each are sold @ Rs.600 per square meters and @ Rs.560 per square meter respectively. The sale proceeds of 5 plots of 200 sq. mtrs each are received by Q The balance is received by P who paid Rs. 1,20,000 for sales expenses. P repaid the loan and interest there on amounted to Rs. 76,800.

The agreement provides that after crediting P with the interest charged on the borrowed money and allowing P 15% on the cost of leveling to cover overhead expenses, P is to receive two-third of the profit and Q one-third. Each party's ledger contains records of his own receipts and payments on the Joint Account. You are required to prepare (i) a statement showing the result of the Venture and (ii) the account of the Venturer in each party's ledger as it will finally appear. **[C A (Entrance) - Adapted]**

Ans. Profit on Joint Venture Rs. 2,20,800

Amount paid by P to Q Rs. 7,200

10. A and B entered into a Joint Venture to purchase and sell crackers during Deepawali season. Profits & Losses were to be shared equally by them A was to purchase crackers from Delhi to be sent to B at Mumbai for sale. On 1.8.2005 A purchased crackers worth Rs. 1,00,000 and incurred the following expenses in sending it to B.

	Rs.
Forwarding Charges	6,000
Insurance Charges	2,000

He immediately drew upon B a bill of Rs. 1,00,000 for three months. The acceptance was discounted at 18% p.a. B incurred the following expenses.

	Rs.
Cartage	3,000
Commission	5,000
Rental Charges	4,000

The entire stock of crackers was sold for Rs. 2,00,000 B forwarded a cheque to A for the amount due on 31st October 2005.

You are required to prepare

(1) Memorandum Joint Venture Account

(2) Joint Venture with B Account in the books of A

(3) Joint Venture with A Account in the books of B **[C A (Foundation) Nov. 1996 – Modified]**

Ans. Profit on Joint Venture Rs. 75,500

Amount paid by A to B Rs. 50,250

11. X and Y enter into a Joint Venture to build a multi – storied building. They agree to share profits & losses equally up to Rs.50,000 from the venture, there after the profits& losses are to be shared in the following proportion.

X = 3/5

Y = 2/5

X contributes plant and machinery worth Rs. 40,000 and meets registration expenses of Rs.10,000. Y contributed the plot on which the building is to be built, valued at Rs. 1,00,000.

Other expenses incurred are:

	Rs.
Fuel and Electricity	40,000
Building Materials	1,60,000
Labour Charges	75,000
Advertisement Expenses	5,000

All the expenses were met from the Bank Account opened for Joint Venture. At the end of the Venture X Agreed to take the Plant & Machinery valued at Rs. 10,000.

Y sold off the multi storied building for a total of Rs. 7,20,000 and collected all dues from the buyers except for one flat, valued at Rs. 1,80,000 which he kept for himself in lieu of his expected share of profit.

The Venture who have agreed to maintain Venture Account in separate set of books, ask you to prepare the Joint Venture Account and Venturers' Capital Accounts. **[I C W A (Inter) June 1988]**

Ans. Profit Rs. 4,80,000

Amount paid to X Rs. 3,23,000

12. X and Y entered into Joint Venture of underwriting the subscription at par of the entire share Capital of Rama Ltd. consisting of 10,000 shares of Rs, 10 each and to pay all expenses up to allotment. They were to share the profits in the ratio of 3:2 respectively. The consideration in return for the guarantee was 1,200 other shares of Rs. 10 each fully paid to be issued to them.

X provided the fund for registration fees Rs. 1,200 advertising Rs. 1,100, printing and stationery Rs. 950. Y contributed towards payment of office rent Rs. 300, legal charge Rs. 1,550 and staff salaries Rs. 900.

The prospectus was issued and the applications fell short of the full issue by 1,500 shares. X took over on Joint Account and paid for the same in full. They received 1,200 shares fully paid as under - writing – commission. They sold all their shares at Rs. 12 per share. The proceeds were shared by X for 1,500 shares and by Y for balance.

Write up Joint Venture Account and Co-Venture's A/c in the books of both parties.

[B. Com. (Pass), D. U., 1998]

Ans. Profit Rs. 11,400, Y pays Rs. 7,090 to X.

13. A , B and C jointly undertake to construct a Public School building at a price of Rs.25,00,000 to be paid as follows :

Rs. 20,00,000 in 4 equal installments of Rs. 5,00,000 each and balance in Debentures of a Ltd. company. They agreed to share profits and losses in the proportion of 2:2:1 end contributed Rs.3,00,000 Rs. 3,75,000 and 2,00,000 respectively, which were deposited in Joint Bank Account.

A got the plans prepared by an architect and paid his fees of Rs. 35,000 B brought into venture a concrete mixer of the value of Rs. 1,25,000 while C has brought for the Venture a truck of the Value of Rs. 1,00,000. The Venturers paid following amounts out of Joint Bank Account.

	Rs.
Plant	1,20,000
Materials	12,00,000
Wages	9,75,000

On completion of contract A took the unused materials worth Rs. 70,000. The concrete mixer was taken back by B at a valuation of Rs. 60,000 while C took back truck after charging depreciation @ 40%. The plant was sold for Rs. 30,000. The contract price was received in full. A took debentures at an agreed value of Rs. 3,50,000. Show Joint Venture Account, Joint Bank Account and Co-Venturer's Account.

Ans. Profit Rs. 15,000

14. A and B enter into Joint Venture to purchase and develop certain land as Residential Estate. For this purpose a Joint Bank Account was opened where in A deposited Rs. 3,00,000 and B deposited Rs. 2,00,000. A piece of land measuring 1800 sq meters was purchased @ Rs. 150 per sq. mtrs. The following expenses were paid from the Joint Bank Account.

	Rs.
Cost of leveling	70,000
Compensation to hutment dwellers	25,000
Cost of fencing	15,000
Municipal Taxes	10,000
Architect's Fees	5,000
Solicitor's Fees	18,000
Miscellaneous Expenses	10,000

It was decided to sell land in smaller plots of 50 sq. mtrs. each. One – sixth of the area was left over for public roads. 10 plots were sold at Rs. 600 per sq. mtr. through brokers who were paid brokerage @ 2% on sale price of land. A retained one plot of land for his personal use at an agreed value of Rs. 25,000. The remaining plots were sold at a consolidated price of Rs. 3,81,000 directly. A and B shared profits & losses in the proportion of the amount invested by them. All transactions have been effected through Bank Account. Income from sale of timber amounted to Rs. 10,000.

Prepare necessary Ledger. Accounts

Ans. Profit Rs. 2,75,000 Amount paid to A Rs. 4,40,000

Amount paid to B Rs. 3,10,000

15. R and S entered into a Joint Venture to buy and sell CTV sets. On 1.7.2005 R sent a draft for Rs. 10,00,000 in favour of S who purchased 200 sets at the rate of Rs. 8,000 each. The sets were sent to R by lorry under freight "to pay" for Rs. 8,000 and were cleared by R.

On 15.7.2005. R effected the sales as under:

16th July	20 sets @	Rs. 12,000 at 10% discount on sale price
31st July	100 sets @	Rs. 11,200
15th August	80 sets @	Rs. 10,800 at 5% discount on sale price

On 25th Aught 2005, R settled the account by sending draft in favour of S, profits being shared equally. Prepare Memorandum Joint Venture Account and Joint Venture with S Account in the books of R.

[C A (I) Modified]

Ans. Profit Rs. 5,48,800

R pays S Rs. 8,74,400

❑❑❑

Unit-V

11

ACCOUNTING FOR THE HIRE PURCHASE SYSTEM

MEANING

It is a system of selling goods whereby risk involved in "transaction" is kept to the minimum. It has the advantage of credit sale and ensures regular and periodical recovery of money through instalments while keeping the title of goods safe. According to Pickles, "Hire purchase is the system under which the property is acquired by payments made in instalments, during the period of which the title in the property remains with the Hire Vendor. The payments prior to the final instalment are regarded as being purely in respect of hire, and title of the property does not pass to the hire purchaser until such final payment or some other condition provided for in the contract has been fulfilled. Hire Purchase Act 1972 section 2 (c) states :

"Hire Purchase agreement means an agreement under which goods are let on hire, and the hirer has an option to purchase them in accordance with the terms of agreement." It includes an agreement under which :

(1) Possession of goods is given by the owner to a person on a condition that such person will pay the agreed amount in periodical instalments,

(2) The property in the goods is to pass such person on the payment of the last of such instalments and

(3) Such person has the right to terminate the agreement at any time before the property in goods so passes.

Section 4 of Hire Purchase Act 1972 states that Hire Purchase Agreement contains :

(i) The hire-purchase-price of goods to which agreement relates,

(ii) The Cash Price of goods.

(iii) The date on which the agreement shall be deemed to have commenced,

(iv) Number of instalments by which the hire purchase price is to be paid, the amount of each of these instalments, and the date, upon which it is payable and the person to whom and the place where it is payable,

(v) The goods to which agreement relates,

(vi) Where any part of hire purchase price is to be paid otherwise than by cash or cheque, the hire purchase agreement shall contain a description of that part of price.

Thus Hire purchase transaction involves an agreement between Hire Vendor and Hire purchaser whereby hire vendor gives the delivery of goods to the Hire purchaser on signing of an agreement and after down payment, if any. The hire purchaser undertakes to pay the cash price/balance in agreed number of instalments together with interest. The property in goods shall be transferred from Hire Vendor to Hire purchaser only when the last installment is paid. This is due to the fact that every installment is treated as hire and consequently, Hire Vendor has a right to repossess the goods on the failure of Hire purchaser to pay any installment.

Installment Purchase System

A hire purchase agreement is distinct and different from installment system. In the former "property in goods" (ownership) does not pass until the final installment has been paid whereas under installment system "property" in goods (ownership) is transferred immediately on delivery of goods and on signing of agreement, just as in case of credit sale.

Distinction between Hire Purchase, Installment Payment and Credit Sale

Hire Purchase	Installment System	Credit Sales
1. It is an agreement of hire.	1. It is an agreement of sale.	1. It is also an agreement of sale.
2. Property in goods (ownership) is transferred from Hire - Vendor to Hire purchaser only when the last installment is paid.	2. Ownership is transferred immediately on signing of agreement.	2. Ownership is transferred at the time of sale.
3. Price is paid by Hire purchaser through installment which is treated as hire.	3. Every installment is treated as part of price.	3. Payment is made subsequently in lump sum or according to terms of sale.
4. The Hire Vendor has a right to repossess goods in case of default.	4. The seller has no right to repossess. He can sue only for the amount due.	4. On default, the seller cannot repossess goods but has right to recover the amount due.
5. The Hire purchaser cannot transfer or tamper the goods until he pays final installment.	5. The buyer has right to sell, transfer or dispose off the goods at any time.	5. The buyer has right to sell the goods immediately on or after delivery.
6. The Hire purchaser has the right to terminate the agreement if he does not want to pay rest of the instalments.	6. The buyer has no right to terminate the agreement and return the goods.	6. The buyer has no right to return goods except when these are defective or substandard as compared to specification.

EXPLANATION OF CERTAIN IMPORTANT TERMS

1. Cash Price : It is the actual price of goods charged under normal cash sale or the amount paid for outright purchase.

2. Hire Purchase Price : The total amount payable under the terms of hire-purchase agreement in the form of down payment and instalments. It consists of cash price plus interest.3. Down payment:

It is the amount paid by Hire Purchaser to Hire Vendor at the time of signing of agreement or at the time of delivery of goods.

4. Hire Purchaser : Also known as Hirer, the one who purchases goods under hire-purchase agreement.

5. Hire Vendor : The person who sells goods under hire-purchase agreement. It is also known as hire purchase company.

6. Hire : Each installment paid by Hire-purchaser is treated as 'hire'. It includes part of cash price (principal) and interest' due.

7. Hire Purchase Charges : The difference between Hire Purchase price and Cash price.

8. Net Hire Purchase Charges : It is the difference between net hire purchase price and cash price.

9. Net Cash Price : It is the total cash price less deposit, if any.

10. Net Hire Purchase Price : The total amount of hire purchase price as reduced by:

(i) delivery expenses

(ii) insurance charges, if any, and

(iii) registration fees of agreement etc.

Statutory Limit on Hire Purchase Charges

The difference between Hire Purchase price and the Cash price represents Hire Purchase Charges. It is, in fact, the total amount of interest to be paid by Hire purchaser to Hire Vendor over the period of payment of instalments. To avoid higher rate of interest charged by Hire Vendor section 7 puts the maximum limit of 30% of such installment or the charges as may be ascertained with the help of following formula :

$$SC = \frac{CI \times R \times T}{100}$$

where

SC = Stands for statutory charges

CI = the amount of cash price installment

R = Rate as determined by Central Govt. in consultation with Reserve Bank of India

T = Time, expressed in years and fraction thereof that elapses between date of agreement and the date on which the hire-purchase installment, corresponding to the cash price installment, is payable under agreement.

Right of Hire-Purchaser to Purchase Goods taken on Hire

In case a hire-purchaser intends to make outright purchase of the goods taken on hire after the agreement has been signed and delivery taken he can do so by giving 14 days notice to the Hire Vendor as required under the Hire Purchase Act u/s 7. He shall be required to pay the amount due to hire vendor after deducting the rebate allowed under the Act. The rebate can be worked out as under :

$$\text{Rebate} = \frac{2}{3}\left(\frac{\text{Hire Purchase Charges} \times \text{No. of Installments due}}{\text{Total No. of installments}}\right)$$

e.g. X Purchases a machine under hire purchase agreement. The cash price being Rs. 60,000. He pays Rs. 2,000 down and is required to pay the balance in 14 instalments of Rs. 5,000 each. Xgives 14 days notice to hire vendor expressing his willingness to buy the machine after seven instalments have been paid. Find out amount of rebate and the amount, which A would be required to pay under Section 7

	Rs.
Cash price of the Machine	60,000
Hire Purchase Price = (Down payment + Amount to be paid by way of instalments)	
= 2,000 + (5,000 × 14)	72,000
Hire Purchase Charges	12,000

$$\text{Rebate} = \frac{2}{3}\left(\frac{\text{Hire Purchase Charges} \times \text{No. of Installments due}}{\text{Total No. of installments}}\right)$$

$$\text{Rebate} = \frac{2}{3}\left(\frac{1{,}2000 \times 7}{14}\right) = \text{Rs. } 4{,}000$$

$$\text{Amount Payable} = \text{Instalments due} - \text{Rebate}$$
$$= 5{,}000 \times 7 - 4{,}000 = \text{Rs. } 31{,}000$$

TERMINATION OF AGREEMENT

The Hire Purchase Act gives the hire purchaser the right to terminate agreement at any time by giving 14 days notice to the hire vendor. However he shall be required to pay a sum as stipulated in the agreement or as per the provisions of the Act, whichever is less. The Hire Purchase Act provides that :

(1) Where total sum **paid** and **due** in respect of hire-purchase price immediately before termination exceeds one-half (1/2) of the **hire purchase** price the hire purchaser is **not required** to pay any amount on termination.

(2) Where total sum paid and due in respect of hire-purchase price immediately before termination does not exceed half of the hire-purchase price, the hire purchaser shall be liable to pay the **difference**- between half (1/2) of the hire purchase price and amount already paid or the amount so stipulated in the agreement whichever is less.

Example : X purchased a computer under hire purchase agreement. The cash price of the computer is Rs. 1,00,000. He is required to pay Rs. 20,000 as down payment and 10 instalments of Rs. 10,000 each. The Hire purchase agreement provided that the hire purchaser will be required to pay Rs. 15,000 if he terminates agreement. Find out the amount payable by X if he terminates agreements after paying :

(a) 6 installments (b) 3 installments (c) 2 installments

Solution : Hire purchaser price = Down payment + amount of each installment × No. of instalments

$$\text{HPP} = \text{Rs. } (20{,}000 + 10{,}000 \times 10) = 1{,}20{,}000$$

(a) Amount paid by Hire purchaser

	Rs.
Down payment	20,000
6 instalments of Rs. 10,000 each	60,000
Hire purchase price (due and paid)	80,000

Since this amount exceeds half (1/2) of Hire purchase price (1,20,000) i.e. Rs. 60,000, he is not required to pay any amount to Hire Vendor.

(b) Amount paid is Rs. 20,000 Down plus 3 instalments of Rs. 10,000 each = Rs. 50,000. This amount does not exceed half (1/2 of 1,20,000). He is required to pay Rs. 10,000 (being lower of Rs. 15,000 as stipulated in the Agreement) i.e. difference between half of the hire-purchase price and amount due and paid.

(c) Amount paid is Rs. 20,000 + 2 instalments of Rs. 10,000 each.
i.e.Rs. 40,000 Amount payable = (1/2 of HPP - Amount paid) = (60,000 - 40,000)
i.e.Rs. 20,000 or Rs. 15,000 whichever is less. Therefore he will pay Rs. 15,000 only.

ACCOUNTING FOR HIRE PURCHASE TRANSACTIONS

(In the Books of Hire Purchaser)

There are various methods of recording hire-purchaser transactions such as :

- A
  - 1. Cash Price Method
    - I Full Cash Price
    - II Down Payment/ Accrual Method
  - 2. Interest Suspense Account Method
- B
  - 3. Debtors System
  - 4. Stock & Debtors System

The first two methods of recording hire purchase transactions are adopted when goods are in the nature of capital assets of substantial value, such as machinery, car, computer, truck or motor bus etc.

The third and fourth method is applied when there are number of items involved in one hire purchase transaction. These items are relatively of small value.

For the purpose of recording hire purchase transactions of high value items, only cash price method has been adopted. Usually the Interest Suspense Account Method is adopted under Installment Purchase System. For the sake of understanding it has been explained through journal entries only.

1. Cash Price Method

Under this method the asset is recorded at its full cash price and presumed to be the property of the business. The following entries are recorded in the books of Hire Purchaser and Hire Vendor.

In the books of Hire Purchaser

Journal Entries

Al Total Cash Price Method I

First Year			
1. On signing of Hire Purchase agreement and taking delivery of asset	Asset A/c To Hire Vendor A/c	Dr	with Total Cash Price
2. On making down payment	Hire Vendor's A/c To Bank A/c	Dr	Down payment

3. When interest becomes due at the time of paying installment	Interest A/c To Hire Vendor's A/c	Dr	Interest amount
4. When installment is paid	Hire Vendor's A/c To Bank A/c	Dr	with the amount of Instalment
5. When depreciation is charged on closing of books of accounts	Depreciation A/c To Asset A/c	Dr	
6. On closing the interest and depreciation accounts by transferring to Profit and Loss Account.	Profit & Loss A/c To Interest A/c To Depreciation A/c	Dr	

Second and subsequent years

Entries no. 3,4, 5 & 6 will be repeated with their respective amount of interest and depreciation provided.

Note : The other methods of recording hire-purchase-transactions have been explained to develop understanding of various methods adopted by different hire-purchasers. But for the sake of uniformity, the most common and popular method of Total Cash Price Method, as explained above, has been adopted throughout this chapter.

	Accrual Method II		
1. On signing of Contract and taking delivery	No entry		
2. On making down payment	Asset A/c To Bank A/c	Dr	with down payment
3. When first installment falls due	Asset A/c Interest A/c To Hire Vendor's A/c	Dr Dr	with the amount of part of Cash Price with the amount of interest with total
4. When the first installment-is paid	Hire Vendor's A/c To Bank A/c	Dr	with the amount of installment
5. When depreciation is charged on closing the books of Accounts	Depreciation A/c To Asset A/c	Dr	with the amount of Depreciation
6. On transferring the interest and depreciation to Profit & Loss Account	Profit & Loss Account A/c To Interest A/c To Depreciation A/c	Dr	

Entries no. 3, 4, 5 and 6 will be repeated in the subsequent years with their respective amount of interest and depreciation.

Treatment of Depreciation

There is some controversy over the charging of depreciation by hire purchaser. Some authorities are of the view that depreciation should not be charged by hire purchaser who is not the legal owner of the asset acquired under hire purchase agreement. Hence charging of any depreciation will be treated as an error of principle.

The other view supports the charging of depreciation for various reasons. Firstly the hire purchaser has acquired the asset for the purpose of use in his own business with an intention to become the owner of the asset and not for resale. Secondly, if depreciation is not charged, it will inflate the profits of years during which it is used. And thirdly, when he becomes the owner (after last installment is paid) the written down value will be much less as compared to original cash price due to usage and wear and tear.

Hence it is advisable to charge depreciation since the date of it's acquisition under hire-purchase agreement.

A 2 Interest Suspense Method

Under this method Asset account is recorded at cash price but the Hire Vendor is given credit for hire purchase price. The difference between the hire purchase price and cash price, being hire purchase charges, debited to Interest Suspense Account. This Interest Suspense Account is credited by the amount of interest actually accrued at the time of paying installment. Hence this account is totally wiped out at the end of last installment. Following entries are recorded in the books of Hire purchaser.

First Year			
1. On signing of contract and taking the delivery of Asset	Assets A/c Interest Suspense A/c To Hire Vendor's A/c	Dr Dr	with cash price with hire purchase charges with Hire Purchase Price
2. On making down payment	Hire Vendor's A/c To Bank A/c	Dr	the amount of down payment
3. When First installment falls due	Interest A/c To Interest Suspense A/c	Dr	with the amount of Interest due
4. When first installment is paid	Hire Vendor's A/c To Bank A/c	Dr	with the amount of installment paid
5. On Charging Depreciation	Depreciation A/c To Asset A/c	Dr	with the amount of depreciation
6. On closing the interest and depreciation Account by transfer to Profit & Loss Account	Profit & Loss A/c To Interest A/c To Depreciation A/c	Dr	

Only Entries no. 3, 4, 5 & 6 will be recorded in subsequent years.

Journal Entries in the Books of Hire Vendor

There are two methods of recording hire-purchase transactions which are adopted by Hire Vendor :

1. Sales Method 2. Interest Suspense Account

1. Sales Method

1. On signing of contract and giving delivery	Hire Purchaser's A/c To Hire - Purchase Sales A/c	Dr	with the Total Cash price
2. On receiving down payment	Bank A/c To Hire Purchaser's	Dr	with the amount of cash down

3.	When installment becomes due	Hire Purchaser's A/c To Interest A/c	Dr	with the amount of interest due
4.	When installment is received	Bank A/c To Hire Purchaser's A/c	Dr	with amount of instalment
5.	On transferring the interest of Profit & Loss A/c	Interest A/c To Profit & Loss A/c	Dr	with the amount of interest

Note : Entries 3, 4 & 5 will be repeated in the subsequent years till the final installment is received. The second method is being explained hereunder to develop understanding among students about the other method used by Hire Vendor. However, for all practical purposes the first method based on total cash price, which is sale price, has been adopted.

2. Interest Suspense Account Method

1.	On signing of Contract and giving delivery	Hire Purchaser's A/c To Hire Purchase-Sale A/c To Interest Suspense A/c	Dr	with the total amount with cash price Total interest amount
2.	On receiving down payment	Bank A/c To Hire Purchaser's A/c	Dr	down payment. amount
3.	When installment falls due	Interest Suspense A/c To Interest A/c	Dr	the amount of interest due
4.	On receiving first installment	Bank A/c To Hire Purchaser's A/c	Dr	the amount of instalment
5.	On transferring the interest to Profit & Loss A/c	Profit and Loss A/c To Interest A/c	Dr	

Note : Entries no. 3, 4 & 5 will be repeated during the subsequent years with their respective amount of interest and installment amount.

Calculation of Missing figure

Beside other information a Hire purchase agreement must contain the Hire purchase price and cash price, number and amount of each installment. It does not specify the hire purchase charges or interest, which is represented by the difference between hire-purchase price and cash price. But problem is to calculate periodical interest. And again, for examination purposes, different types of problems are being given for the purpose of developing proper understanding of the subject matter. There may be different types of situations namely,

1. When amount of yearly, half yearly, quarterly or monthly (i.e. installment-wise) interest is not given.
2. When Rate of interest is not given.
3. When Cash price is not given : (a) Simple Method, (b) Annuity Method.
4. When amount of instalments is not given.
5. When Cash price and Rate of interest are not given.
6. Miscellaneous-Problem of two yearly instalments.

I. Calculation of Interest

Illustration 1

On 1-1-2005 X purchased a computer from M/s. Software Ltd. on hire purchase basis. The cash price of the computer is Rs. 65,000 payable Rs. 5,000 as cash down and three instalments of .Rs. 23,000, Rs. 22,000 and Rs. 21,000 at the end of 2005, 2006 and 2007 respectively. Interest is charged @ 5% p.a. Record (i) Journal entries and prepare necessary ledger accounts in the books of X, who closes his books of accounts on 31st December each year and charges Depreciation @ 20% on Straight line basis and (ii) Journal entries and Ledger Accounts in the books of M/s. Software Ltd.

Solution : **TABLE SHOWING CALCULATION OF INTEREST**

Date/Installment No.	Cash Price/ Amount due Rs.	Down Payment/ Amount of Instalment Rs.	Interest due	Part of Cash Price (Installment- Interest) Rs.
1-1-2005	65,000			
Down payment	5,000	5,000	–	5,000
1-1-2005	60,000			
Interest @ 5%	3,000			
31-12-2005	63,000			
Ist Installment	23,000	23,000	3,000	20,000
1-1-2006	40,000			
Interest @ 5%	2,000			
31-12-2006	42,000			
IInd Installment	22,000	22,000	2,000	20,000
1-1-2007	20,000			
Interest @ 5%	1,000			
31-12-2007	21,000	21,000	1,000	20,000
IIIrd Instalment	21,000			

JOURNAL ENTRIES IN THE BOOKS OF X

			Rs.	Rs.
2005	Computer A/c Dr		65,000	
Jan 1	To M/s Softwares Ltd. A/c			65,000
	(Being Computer acquired under hire purchase agreement)			
	M/s Softwares Ltd. A/c Dr		5,000	
	To Bank A/c			5,000
	(Being down payment made)			
Dec. 31	Interest A/c Dr		3,000	
	To M/s Softwares Ltd. A/c			3,000
	(Being interest & installment become due)			

	M/s Softwares Ltd. A/c	Dr		23,000	
	To Bank A/c				23,000
	(Being first installment paid)				
	Depreciation A/c	Dr		13,000	
	To Computer A/c				13,000
	(Being depreciation charged)				
Dec. 31	Profit and Loss A/c	Dr		16,000	
	To Interest A/c				3,000
	To Depreciation A/c				13,000
	(Being interest and depreciation transferred to Profit & Loss A/c)				
2006	Interest A/c	Dr		2,000	
Dec. 31	To M/s Softwares Ltd.				2,000
	(Being interest and installment become due)				
	M/s Softwares Ltd. A/c	Dr		22,000	
	To Bank A/c				22,000
	(Being second installment paid)				
	Depreciation A/c	Dr		13,000	
	To Computer				13,000
	(Being depreciation charged)				
	Profit & Loss A/c	Dr		15,000	
	To Interest A/c				2,000
	To Depreciation A/c				13,000
	(Being interest and depreciation transferred to Profit & Loss A/c)				
2007	Interest A/c	Dr		1,000	
Dec. 31	To M/s Softwares Ltd.				1,000
	(Being interest & installment become due)				
	M/s Softwares Ltd. A/c	Dr		21,000	
	To Bank A/c				21,000
	(Being third & final installment paid)				
	Depreciation A/c	Dr		13,000	
	To Computer A/c				13,000
	(Being depreciation charged)				
	Profit & Loss A/c	Dr		14,000	
	To Interest A/c				1,000
	To Depreciation A/c				13,000
	(Being interest and depreciation transferred to Profit & Loss A/c)				

M/S SOFTWARES LTD (HIRE VENDOR'S) A/C

Date		Rs.	Date		Rs.
2005			2005		
Jan. 1	To Bank A/c (Down Payment)	5,000	Jan. 1	By Computer A/c	65,000
			Dec. 31	By Interest @ 5% on 60,000	3,000
Dec. 31	To Bank A/c (First Installment)	23,000			
	To Balance c/d	40,000			
		68,000			68,000
2006			2006		
Dec. 31	To Bank A/c (Second Installment)	22,000	Jan. 1	By Balance b/d	40,000
			Dec. 31	By Interest @ 5%	2,000
	To Balance c/d	20,000			
		42,000			42,000
2007			2007		
Dec. 31	To Bank A/c (Third A/c)	21,000	Jan. 1	By Balance b/d	20,000
			Dec. 31	By Interest @ 5%	1,000
		21,000			21,000

COMPUTER ACCOUNT

Date		Rs.	Date		Rs.
2005			2005		
Jan. 1	To M/s Softwares Ltd. A/c	65,000	Dec. 31	By Depreciation A/c	13,000
				By Balance c/d	52,000
		65,000			65,000
2006			2006		
Jan. 1	To Balance b/d	52,000	Dec. 31	By Depreciation A/c	13,000
				By Balance c/d	39,000
		52,000			52,000
2007			2007		
Jan. 1	To Balance b/d	39,000	Dec. 31	By Depreciation A/c	13,000
				By Balance c/d	26,000
		39,000			39,000
2008					
Jan. 1	To Balance b/d	26,000			

INTEREST A/C

Date		Rs.	Date		Rs.
2005			2005		
Dec. 31	To M/s Softwares Ltd. A/c	3,000	Dec. 31	By Profit & Loss A/c	3,000
2006			2006		
Dec. 31	To M/s Softwares Ltd. A/c	2,000	Dec. 31	By Profit & Loss A/c	2,000
2007			2007		
Dec. 31	To M/s Software Ltd. A/c	1,000	Dec. 31	By Profit & Loss A/c	1,000

In the Books of M/s Softwares Ltd. (Hire Vendor)
Journal Entries

				Rs.	Rs.
2005 Jan. 1	X's A/c	Dr		65,000	
	To Hire Purchase Sales A/c				65,000
	(Being computer sold to X on hire purchases basis)				
	Bank A/c	Dr		5,000	
	To X A/c				5,000
	(Being amount received on signing of contract)				
Dec. 31	X's A/c	Dr		3,000	
	To Interest A/c				3,000
	(Being interest & installment become due)				
	Bank A/c	Dr		23,000	
	To X A/c				23,000
	(Being amount of installment received)				
	Interest A/c	Dr		3,000	
	To Profit & Loss A/c				3,000
	(Being interest transferred to Profit & Loss Account				
2006 Dec. 31	X's A/c	Dr		2,000	
	To Interest A/c				2,000
	(Being interest and installment become due)				
	Bank A/c	Dr		22,000	
	To X				22,000
	(Being second installment received)				
	Interest A/c	Dr		2,000	
	To Profit & Loss A/c				2,000
	(Being interest transferred to Profit & Loss A/c)				

2007				
Dec. 31	X's A/c Dr		1,000	
	To Interest A/c			1,000
	(Being interest and installment become due)			
	Bank A/c Dr		21,000	
	To X A/c			21,000
	(Being installment amount received)			
	Interest A/c Dr		1,000	
	To Profit & Loss A/c			1,000
	(Being interest transferred to Profit & Loss Account)			

X (HIRE PURCHASER'S) A/C

Date		Rs.	Date		Rs.
2005			2005		
Jan. 1	To Higher Purchase Sales	65,000	Jan. 1	By Bank A/c	5,000
Dec. 31	To Interest A/c @ 5% on 60,000	3,000	Dc. 31	By Bank A/c	23,000
				By Balance c/d	40,000
		68,000			68,000
2006			2006		
Jan. 1	To Balance b/d	40,000	Dec. 31	By Bank A/c	22,000
Dec. 31	To Interest A/c @ 5%	2,000		By Balance c/d	20,000
		42,000			42,000
2007			2007		
Jan. 1	By Balance b/d	20,000	Dec. 31	By Bank A/c	21,000
Dec. 31	To Interest A/c @ 5%	1,000			
		21,000			21,000

INTEREST A/C

Date		Rs.	Date		Rs.
2005			2005		
Dec. 31	To Profit & Loss A/c	3,000	Dec. 31	By X A/c	3,000
2006			2006		
Dec. 31	To Profit & Loss A/c	2,000	Dec. 31	By X A/c	2,000
2007			2007		
Dec. 31	To Profit & Loss A/c	1,000	Dec. 31	By X A/c	1,000

II. When Rate of Interest is not given

Illustration 2

On 1-1-2005 Arun purchased a machine on hire purchase basis. The cash price of the machine was Rs. 45,000. The terms of payment being Rs. 5,000 down and balance in 3 equal installments of Rs. 15,000 each, payable on 31st December every year.

Prepare Machinery Account and Hire Vendor's Account in the Books of Arun who closes his books of Accounts on 31st December each year. Depreciation is charged @ 20% p.a. on Diminishing balance.

Solution :

Hire Purchase Price – Cash Price = Interest

Hire Purchase Price = Down Payment + Total amount of installments

= Rs. 5,000 + (Rs. 15,000 × 3) = Rs. 50,000

Interest = Rs. 50,000 – Rs. 45,000 = Rs. 5,000

When rate of interest is not given, the amount of interest is apportioned in the ratio of amount outstanding by the end of each year. This has been shown as under:

Year	Amount Outstanding at the end of year Rs.	Rate of Amount outstanding	Interest apportioned	Amount of Interest Rs.
2005	50,000 – 5,000 = 45,000	3	3/6 × 5,000	2,500
2006	45,000 – 15,000 = 30,000	2	2/6 × 5,000	1,667
2007	30,000 – 15,000 = 15,000	1	1/6 × 5,000	833
		6		5,000

In the books of Arun (Hire Purchaser)
MACHINERY ACCOUNT

Date		Rs.	Date		Rs.
2005			2005		
Jan. 1	To hire Vendor A/c	45,000	Dec. 31	By Depreciation A/c @ 20%	9,000
				By Balance c/d	36,000
		45,000			45,000
2006			2006		
Jan. 1	To Balance b/d	36,000	Dec. 31	By Depreciation A/c @ 20%	7,200
				By Balance c/d	28,800
		36,000			36,000
2007			2007		
Jan. 1	To Balance b/d	28,800	Dec. 31	By Depreciation A/c @ 20%	5,760
				By Balance c/d	23,040
		28,800			28,800
2008					
Jan. 1	To Balance b/d	23,040			

HIRE VENDOR'S A/C

Date		Rs.	Date		Rs.
2005			2005		
Jan. 1	To Bank (Down Payment)	5,000	Jan. 1	By Machinery A/c	45,000
Dec. 31	To Bank (First Installment)	15,000	Dec. 31	By Interest A/c	2,500
	To Balance c/d	27,000			
		47,500			47,500
2006			2006		
Dec. 31	To Bank (Second Installment)	15,000	Dec. 31	By Balance b/d	27,500
	To Balance c/d	14,167		By Interest A/c	1,667
		29,167			29,167
2007			2007		
Dec. 31	To Bank A/c	15,000	Jan. 1	By Balance b/d	14,167
	(Final Installment)		Dec. 31	By Interest A/c	833
		15,000			15,000

III. When Cash Price is not given (Simple Method)

In some cases the cash price of the asset purchased under hire purchase agreement is not given. It is necessary to work out the cash price from the down payment and installments given. It should be remembered that asset is debited with the actual cash price. In order to calculate cash price, interest should be separated from the amount of various installments payable by the hire purchaser. The amount so arrived at plus cash down, if any, give you cash price of the asset. But to begin with one should start calculation from the last installment. If for example there are 4 yearly installments and the rate of interest being 10% then interest for the last year will be:

$$\text{Amount of last Installment} \times \frac{\text{Rate}}{100 + \text{Rate}} \text{ i.e., } \frac{10}{110} \text{ or } \frac{1}{11}$$

Thus, $\frac{1}{11}$ of last installment will give you amount of interest and amount of last installment less interest will be the part of principal (cash price) paid with the fourth (last) installment. Thereafter

- The interest included in third installment shall be calculated on the basis of amount due by the end of third year i.e. $\frac{1}{11}$ of (Amount of third installment + Part of Cash Price of fourth installment).
- The interest so calculated will be deducted out of the amount of third installment to get part of principal (Cash price) included there in.
- Similarly the interest included in the second 1/11 installment will be worked out taking 1/11 of amount due by the end of second year i.e. 1/11 of (Amount of second installment + part of cash price of fourth and third installments) then part of cash price = Installment less interest.
- Likewise interest included in First installment will be = 1/11 of (Amount of first installment + part of cash price of fourth, third and second installments) and to get part of cash price included in first installment, interest will be subtracted from the amount of first installment.

Since down payment does not include any interest the cash price will be equal to cash down + part of cash price paid with various installments.

Illustration 3

On 1-1-2004 Mr. Aman purchased a Computer from M/s Satyam Computers on hire-purchase basis. The terms of payment being Rs. 8,000 down, Rs. 13,600 at the end of 2004, Rs. 9,000 at the end of the year 2005, Rs. 4,600 by the end of the year 2006 and Rs. 8,400 at the end of 2007. Interest is charged @ 5% p.a. Aman charges depreciation @ 20% on written down basis. Books are closed 31st December every year. Aman paid all the installments as and when these fell due. Prepare Computer A/c and M/s Satyam Computers Account in the books of Aman.

Solution : **In the books of Aman (Hire Purchaser)**

CALCULATION OF CASH PRICE

Year	Installment Amount Rs.	Amount Outstanding Rs.	Interest Rs.	Cash Price (Instalment – Interest) Rs.
At the end of year 2007	8,400	8,400	$8{,}000 \times \frac{5}{105}$ Rs. 400	8,400 – 400 = 8,000
At the end of year 2006	4,600	8,000 + 4,600 = 12,600	$12{,}600 \times \frac{5}{105}$ Rs. 600	4,600 – 600 = 4,000
At the end of year 2005	9,000	8,000 + 4,000 + 9,000 = 21,000	$21{,}000 \times \frac{5}{105}$ Rs. 1,000	9,000 – 1,000 = 8,000
At the end of year 2004	13,600	8,000 + 4,000 + 8,000 + 13,600 = 33,600	$33{,}600 \times \frac{5}{105}$ Rs. 1,600	13,600–1600 = 12,000
1-1-2004 Down Payment	8,000	40,000	—	8,000 = 8,000
	Hire Purchase Price Rs. 43,600	—	Total Interest Rs. 3,600	Total Cash Price = Rs. 40,000

COMPUTER ACCOUNT

Date		Rs.	Date		Rs.
2004			2004		
Jan. 1	To M/s Satyam Computers A/c	40,000	Dec. 31	By Depreciation A/c @ 20%	8,000
				By Balance c/d	32,000
		40,000			40,000

2005			2005		
Jan. 1	To Balance b/d	32,000	Deec. 31	By Depreciation A/c	6,400
				By Balance c/d	25,600
		32,000			32,000
2006			2006		
Jan. 1	To Balance b/d	25,600	Dec. 31	By Depreciation A/c	5,120
				By Balance c/d	20,480
		25,600			26,500
2007			2007		
Jan. 1	To Balance b/d	20,480	Dec. 31	By Depreciation A/c	4,096
				By Balance c/d	16,384
		20,480			20,480
2008					
Jan. 1	To Balance b/d	16,384			

M/S SATYAM COMPUTERS (HIRE VENDOR'S) A/C

Date		Rs.	Date		Rs.
2004			2004		
Jan. 1	To Bank A/c (Down payment)	8,000	Jan. 1	By Computer A/c	40,000
Dec. 31	To Bank A/c (First Installment)	13,600	Dec. 31	By Interest A/c @ 5%	1,600
	To Balance c/d	20,000		on Rs. 32,000	
		41,600			41,600
2005			2005		
Dec. 31	To Bank A/c	9,000	Jan. 1	By Balance b/d	20,000
	To Balance c/d	12,000	Dec. 31	By Interest A/c @ 5%	1,000
		21,000			21,000
2006			2006		
Dec. 31	To Bank A/c	4,600	Jan. 1	By Balance b/d	12,000
	To Balance c/d	8,000	Dec. 31	By Interest A/c @ 5%	600
		12,600			12,600
2007			2007		
Dec. 31	To Bank A/c	8,400	Jan. 1	By Balance b/d	8,000
			Dec. 31	By Interest A/c @ 5%	400
		8,400			8,400

IV. Calculation of Cash Price by Annuity Method

The cash price of asset is can also be calculated with reference to Annuity Table which shows the present cash value of future payment. In other words, if we multiply the annuity figures by the amount of installment the result will be the cash value (price) of the installment. It is worked out on the basis of specific rate of interest for a specific period. This is also known as 'Present Value Method'. There may be two possibilities when :

(a) The reference to Annuity Table shows that present value of one rupee for one, two and three years at 5% interest is :

0.9529,

0.9070,0.8639 respectively

Calculate the cash price of asset if the hire purchaser pays Rs. 11,650 as down payment and three yearly installments of Rs. 15,000 each at the end of 1st, IInd & IIIrd year.

Cash Price = Down payment + (First installment x Reference to annuity table) + (Second installment x Reference to Annuity table) + (Third installment x Reference to Annuity table)

= Rs. 11,650 + (15,000 × 0.9529) +(15,000 + 0.9070) + (15,000 x 0.8639)

= Rs. 11,650 + (14,286) + (13,605) +(12,959)

= Rs. 52,500

(b) Alternatively, sometime annuity table shows present value of annuity of Re. 1 @ 5% p.a. interest for three years is Rs. 2.7233. The method is applied if amount of installment is equal. In the above example this formula can be applied. The cash price will be as under :

Cash Price = Down payment + (yearly installment x reference to Annuity Table)

Cash Price = Rs. 11,650 + (15,000 × 2.7233)

= Rs. 11,650 + 40,850

= Rs. 52,500

Note : The annuity value of rupee one for three years is 2.7233, which can be worked out as under:

0.9524

+ 0.9070

+ 0.8639

= 2.7233

However, students should remember that the second approach can be applied only if the amount of each installment is equal. In case of uneven or unequal amount of installment the first method should be applied i.e. by multiplying the yearly installment with reference to annuity table of each year. Students themselves can derive the present value of annuity by applying following formula :

$$\text{Cash Price} = \text{DP} + \frac{1}{(1+r)^1} + \frac{1}{(1+r)^2} + \frac{1}{(1+r)^3} + \frac{1}{(1+r)^4} \text{ and so on.}$$

If rate of interest is 10% then the present value of annuity of one rupee will be:

$$= \frac{1}{(1+0.1)^1} + \frac{1}{(1+0.1)^2} + \frac{1}{(1+0.1)^3} + \frac{1}{(1+0.1)^4} \text{ and so on}$$

$$= \frac{1}{(1.1)} + \frac{1}{(1.1\times1.1)} + \frac{1}{(1.1\times1.1\times1.1)} + \frac{1}{(1.1\times1.1\times1.1\times1.1)}$$

$$= 0.909 + 0.826 + 0.751 + 0.683$$

The installment amount of first year, second year, third and fourth year will be multiplied by their respective value so derived above. The total will be increased by the down payment, if any, to get the cash price. In case of equal installments the sum of annuity reference will be multiplied by single installment i.e., Amount of one Installment x (0.909 + 0.826 + 0.751 + 0.683) or Amount of one installment x 3.169.

However, in case of unequal intervals of time between various equal or unequal installments, first method i.e. individual installment and individual annuity reference method should be adopted.

V. When Amount of Installment is not given

Under this method the cash price and rate of interest are given. After down payment the balance of cash price is paid in equal installments together with interest accrued till date.

Illustration 4

On 1-4-2005 X Ltd. purchased a machine costing Rs. 80,000 from Y Ltd. on hire purchase basis. The terms of payment being Rs. 5,000 down and balance in three annual equal installments together with interest @ 6% p.a. X Ltd. charges depreciation @ 20% on written down value basis and closes its Books of Accounts 31st December every year.

Show the Machinery and Hire Vendor's Account in the books of X Ltd., presuming that all the installments have been paid as and when these fell due.

Solution : Calculation of interest and installment amount

Cash price Rs. 80,000
Less Down payment Rs. 5,000
Balance Rs. 75,000 in 3 equal installments (Rs. 25,000 each instalment)
Rs. 25,000 plus interest @ 6% p.a. on Rs. 75,000 = 4,500
Interest for the Second year @ 6% on Rs. 50,000 = 3,000
Interest for the Third year @ 6% on Rs. 25,000 = 1,500
Thus First installment will be of Rs. 29,500 i.e. (25,000 + 4,500)
Second installment of Rs. 28,000 i.e. (25,000 + 3,000) and
Third installment of Rs. 26,500 i.e. (25,000 + 1,500)

In the Books of X Ltd.

MACHINERY ACCOUNT

Date		Rs.	Date		Rs.
2005			2005		
April 1	To Y Ltd.	80,000	Dec. 31	By Depreciation @ 20% for 9 months	12,000
				By Balance c/d	68,000
		80,000			80,000
2006			2006		
Jan. 1	To Balance b/d	68,000	Dec. 31	By Depreciation @ 20%	13,600
			Dec. 31	By Balance c/d	54,400
		68,000			68,000
2007			2007		
Jan. 1	To Balance b/d	54,400	Dec. 31	By Depreciation	10,880
			Dec. 31	By Balance c/d	43,520
		54,400			54,400
2008	To Balance b/d	43,520			

Y LTD. (HIRE VENDOR'S) A/C

Date		Rs.	Date		Rs.
2005			2005		
April	To Bank (Down Payment)	5,000	April 1	By Machinery A/c	80,000
2006					
March 31	To Bank (Ist Installment)	29,500	2006	By Interest @ 6% on Rs. 75,000	4,500
March 31	To Balance c/d	50,000	March 31		
		84,500			84,500
2007			2006		
March 31	To Bank (IInd Installment)	28,000	April 1	By Balance b/d	50,000
March 31	To Balance c/d	25,000	2007		
			March 31	By Interest @ 6%	3,000
		53,000			53,000
2008			2007		
March 31	To Bank	26,500	April 1	By Balance b/d	25,000
			2008		
			March 31	By Interest @ 6%	1,500
		26,500			26,500

VI. When Cash Price and Rate of Interest are not given

Under such a situation an assumption has to be made that Cash price included in each installment is equal. There are two methods of calculation of cash price and interest.

(a) Least Difference Method (b) Algebric Equation Method

(a) Least Difference Method

Under Least difference method the difference between the two installments (i.e. Last and Last but one) is taken as the basis of interest, which is apportioned for the last year. The interest for earlier year is given weight-age in the reverse order 1, 2, 3, 4 & so on. For example if there are four annual installments, the difference between third & fourth will be taken as basis, and given weight age of 1, 2, 3.,& 4 for fourth, third, second & first year's interest respectively.

Illustration 5

P purchased an Air conditioner from Q on hire purchase basis, the terms of payment being Rs.2,600 as down payment, Rs. 6,720 on First installment, Rs. 6,440 on Second installment. Rs.6,160 on Third installment & Rs. 5,880 on last installment Calculate the Cash price of air conditioner.

Solution : The difference between Third and Fourth installment is Rs. 280 (6,160 – 5,880) which represents last year's (4th year) interest, to be given weight age in the reverse order of 1, 2, 3 & 4.

		Rs.
Thus Fourth year's interest is	Rs. 280 × 1	280
Third year's interest	Rs. 280 × 2	560
Second year's interest	Rs. 280 × 3	840
First year's interest	Rs. 280 × 4	1,120

The Cash Price		**Rs.**
	Down Payment	2,600
+	First Installment less interest (6,720 – 1,120)	5,600
+	Second Installment less interest (6,440 – 840)	5,600
+	Third Installment less interest (6,160 – 560)	5,600
+	Fourth Installment (5,880 – 280)	5,600
	Cash Price	25,000

(b) Algebric Equation Method

It is based on the same presumption of equal amount of cash price included in each installment Taking last installment as basis which includes part of cash price C and interest 1 an algebric equation can be derived there from :

$$C + 1 = \text{Amount of last installment}$$

Taking same illustration of least difference method the equation for various years can be derived While doing so one thing is to be remembered that 'C' (part of Cash price with each year's installment) is constant and it is 'i' (interest) which varies and declines year after year due to decrease in the outstanding balance. Since payment toward cash price is an even (equal) amount the reduction in the interest charges be uniform i.e. 7, 6, 5, 4, 3, 2, 1 etc. depending upon the number oF installments.

Therefore - (taking last illustration as the basis)

Fourth year's equation $= C + I = 5{,}880$ ...(1)

Third year's equation $= C + 2i = 6{,}160$ ...(2)

Second year's equation $= C + 3i = 6{,}440$ ...(3)

First year's equation $= C + 4i = 6{,}720$ ...(4)

Now simplifying the equations

Fourth & Third taken together $= 2C + 3i = 12{,}040$ ...(1)

Second & First taken together $= 2C + 7i = 13{,}160$ ...(2)

$$\begin{array}{r} - \quad - \quad - \\ \hline -4i = -1{,}120 \end{array}$$

Interest $i = 280$

Substituting the value of :

$$2C + 3i = 12{,}040$$

$$2C + 3 \times 280 = 12{,}040 \text{ or } 2C = 12{,}040 - 840$$

$$2C = 11{,}200$$

$$C = 5{,}600$$

Thus in each installment part of cash price is Rs. 5,600, hence in four installments it will be Rs. 22,400 and if down payment is added, we will get Total Cash Price :

which is 22,400 + 2,600 = Rs. 25,000.

The interest will be Rs. 280, 560, 840 and Rs. 1,120 respectively for fourth, third, second and first installment respectively.

VII. Miscellaneous

(i) When installments are paid after every two years

When an hire-purchase agreement provides for payment of installments after every two years then the payment of interest may be either at yearly rest or at two yearly rest. Yearly rest refers to compound rate of interest and two yearly rest refers to Simple interest. For example if an hire-purchase agreement provides for charging of interest @ 10% p.a. at yearly rest for installments payable after every two years then the effective rate will be 21%.

Rs. 100 @ 10% in the first year earns Rs. 10 and becomes	Rs. 110
And in the second year earns Rs. 11 (i.e. 10% on Rs. 110)	Rs. 11
Thus it becomes	Rs. 121

Therefore effective rate is 21%

But where interest is calculated at two yearly rest it becomes only 20% i.e. 10% + 10%

Illustration 6

M purchased a machinery on hire-purchase basis and pays Rs. 5,000 down and Rs. 8,150 at the end of two years from the date of signing of agreement, Rs. 7,100 at the end of four years from the date of signing of agreement and Rs. 6,050 at the end of six years from the date of signing of agreement. Hire vendor charges interest at 10% per annum at yearly rest. Calculate cash price and interest paid with each installment.

Solution : **CALCULATION OF INTEREST & CASH PRICE**

Year	Amount of Installment Rs.	Amount of outstanding Rs.	Interest Rs.	Cash Price Rs.
At the end of Sixth year	6,050	6,050	$6{,}050 \times \frac{21^*}{121} = 1{,}050$	6,050 – 1,050 = 5,000
At the end of Fourth year	7,100	5,000 + 7,100 = 12,100	$12{,}100 \times \frac{21^*}{121} = 2{,}100$	7,100 – 2,100 = 5,000
At the end of the Second year	8150	5,000 + 5,000 + 8,150 = 18,150	$18{,}150 \times \frac{21^*}{121} = 3{,}150$	8,150 – 3,150 = 5,000
Down Payment	5,000	—	—	= 5,000 Total Cash Price Rs. 20,000

* Since it is a case of two yearly instalments and interest is charged @ 10% p.a. at yearly rest, the effective rate becomes 21% as explained (10% for First year + 11% for Second year on Compound interest basis).

Note : Students should read the language of the question very carefully and note as to whether interest is charged at yearly rest or two yearly rest in case of instalments payable at two years' interval.

(ii) When instalments are paid at six months' interval

Where hire purchase agreement provides for payment of instalments after every six months, then point worth noting will be the rate of interest. In case the question mentions interest rate with "per annum" (p.a.), every instalment will include the interest for 6 months only. Thus reducing the interest by half e.g. if interest is payable @ 10% p.a. on the outstanding amount of Rs. 20,000, then interest will be Rs. 1,000 for 6 months' period and thus reducing the rate at 5% on Rs. 20,000.

However, where the words "per annum" (p.a.) are not given - then for interest calculation period will be ignored. If it is 10% on Rs. 20,000, the interest would be Rs. 2,000 irrespective of the period or interval of installment. But in both the cases depreciation will be charged on the date of closing of books of accounts keeping in mind the rate of depreciation with or without "per annum" in the first year of agreement.

Illustration 7 (Half yearly Installments)

Yogesh purchased a Motor Car from India Motor Ltd. on 1-1-2005 on hire purchase basis. The cash price of the car was Rs. 2,50,000. He agreed to pay Rs. 50,000 down and balance in four half-yearly installments together with interest @ 6% p.a.

Yogesh prepares his accounts annually on 31st December and writes off depreciation @ 20% p.a. under written down method.

You are required to show India Motor Ltd. Account and Motor Car Account in the books of Yogesh for the year ended 31st December 2005 and 2006.

Solution :

Cash Price	2,50,000
Less Down payment	50,000
	2,00,000

Cash price included in each installment 2,00,000 ÷ 4 = 50,000

Amount of Installment = (Cash Price Rs. 50,000 plus interest due)

INDIA MOTOR LTD. ACCOUNT

Date		Rs.	Date		Rs.
2005			2005		
Jan. 1	To Bank (Down Payment)	50,000	Jan. 1	By Motor Car	2,50,000
June 30	To Bank (1st Installment)	56,000	June 30	By Interest @ 6% p.a. on 2,00,000 for 6 months	6,000
Dec. 31	To Bank (IInd Inst.)	54,500	Dec. 31	By Interest @ 6% p.a. on 1,50,000 for 6 months	4,500
Dec. 31	To Balance c/d	1,00,000			
		2,60,500			2,60,500
2006			2006		
June 30	To Bank (IIIrd Inst.)	53,000	Jan 1	By Balance b/d	1,00,000
Dec. 31	To Bank (IVth Inst.)	51,500	June 30	By Interest @ 6% p.a. for 6 months	3,000
			Dec. 31	By Interest @ 6% p.a. for 6 months	1,500
		1,04,500			1,04,500

MOTOR CAR A/C

Date		Rs.	Date		Rs.
2005			2005		
Jan. 1	To India Motor Ltd.	2,50,000	Dec. 31	By Depreciation @ 20%	50,000
			Dec. 31	By Balance c/d	2,00,000
		2,50,000			2,50,000
2006			2006		
Jan. 1	To Balance b/d	2,00,000	Dec. 31	By Depreciation	40,000
			Dec. 31	By Balance c/d	1,60,000
		2,00,000			2,00,000
2007	To Balance b/d	1,60,000			

DEFAULT & REPOSSESSION

When a hire purchaser fails to pay any instalment and makes a default, the hire vendor has every right to re-possess goods as per the Hire Purchase Agreement. Under such a situation the hire vendor forfeits the amount of installments already received, thus treating the amount of installments paid as hire charges. At this stage hire vendor has two options :

(i) Full Repossession or Complete repossession where all goods sold on hire purchase basis are repossessed.

(ii) Partial Repossession.

Under this, part of total goods sold on hire purchase are repossessed and balance of goods are retained by the hire-purchaser.

ACCOUNTING TREATMENT IN CASE OF FULL REPOSSESSION

Books of Hire Purchaser

The Hire-purchaser records usual entries to the date of default. But when on the date of default the goods are seized by the Hire Vendor, he closes both the accounts, viz. Hire Vendor's and Asset Account by recording the following entries :

(i)	Hire Vendor'sA/c	Dr	with the amount outstanding
	To Asset A/c		

This entry shows the transfer of asset to Hire Vendor's account against the amount (balance) standing to his credit. This way, the account of hire vendor is closed.

(ii) (a) Profit and Loss A/c	Dr	with the balancing figure
To Asset A/c		(if there is loss)
(b) Asset A/c	Dr	with the balancing figure
To Profit & Loss A/c		(if there is profit)

The hire purchaser will record either of two entries. If the debit side of asset account exceeds its credit side (after transferring the balance of Hire Vendor's A/c) the account will be closed by transferring the excess (Loss) to Profit & Loss A/c.

Whereas the asset account shows the excess of credit side over debit side, such difference (Profit) will again be transferred to Profit & Loss A/c.

This way, Asset Account is also closed.

Books of Hire Vendor

The Hire Vendor also records all the entries up to the date of default as usual except for the default. On the date of default the Hire-purchaser's Account is closed by transferring the balance (which represents amount due) to the Goods Repossessed Account which is opened only when goods are seized from the Hire Purchaser. The Hire Vendor records the following entry:

Goods Re-possessed A/c	Dr	With the amount standing to the
To Hire Purchaser's A/c		debit of Hire Purchaser's A/c

The Goods Repossessed Account is further debited with the expenses incurred in connection with repair or conditioning of the goods so repossessed and credited with the amount of actual sale price. The difference, if any, is transferred to Profit & Loss Account which represents either profit or loss on resale. Following entries are recorded:

Goods Repossessed A/c	Dr	With the amount of expenses
To Cash		
Cash or Bank A/c (Debtors) A/c	Dr	With the amount of sale price
To Goods Repossessed A/c		
Goods Repossessed A/c	Dr	with the difference if there is profit
To Profit & Loss A/c		
OR		
Profit & Loss A/c	Dr	if there is loss
To Goods Repossessed A/c		

Illustration 9

Modern Printers purchased a printing machine from Machine Tools. Ltd. on hire-purchase basis on 1-1-2005. The Cash price of the machine was Rs. 2,50,000 which was payable as under. 20% of the cash price to be paid at the time of taking delivery and balance in Four equal installments together with interest @ 6% p.a. payable annually by the end of each year. Modern Printers writes off depreciation @ 20% on Diminishing balance. Modern Printers failed to pay the installment due on 31st December 2006. Machine Tools. Ltd. took possession of the machine and incurred Rs. 10,000 on its reconditioning and sold the same for Rs. 1,80,000.

Show the necessary ledger accounts in the books of both the parties presuming that Books are closed 31st December each year.

Solution : **In the Books of Modern Printers (Hire Purchaser)**

MACHINERY ACCOUNT

Date		Rs.	Date		Rs.
2005			2005		
Jan. 1	To I.M. T. Ltd.	2,50,000	Dec. 31	By Depreciation @ 20%	50,000
			Dec. 31	By Balance c/d	2,00,000
		2,50,000			2,50,000
2006			2006		
Jan. 1	To Balance b/d	2,00,000	Dec. 31	By Depreciation	40,000
			Dec. 31	By Machine Tools Ltd.	1,59,000
			Dec. 31	By Profit & Loss A/c	1,000
		2,00,000			2,00,000

MACHINE TOOLS LTD. A/C

Date		Rs.	Date		Rs.
2005			2005		
Jan. 1	To Bank (down Payment)	50,000	Jan. 1	By Machinery A/c	2,50,000
Dec. 31	To Bank (1st Installment)	62,000	Dec. 31	By Interest @ 6% on Rs. 2,00,000	12,000
Dec. 31	To Balance c/d	1,50,000			
		2,62,000			2,62,000
2006			2006		
Dec. 31	To Machinery A/c	1,59,000	Jan. 1	By Balance b/d	1,50,000
			Dec. 31	By Interest @ 6%	9,000
		1,59,000			1,59,000

Working Note :

Amount of installments has been calculated as under :

	Rs.
Cash price of machinery	2,50,000
Less 20% being down payment	50,000
To be paid in Four equal installments	2,00,000

Amount of Installment = 2,00,000 + 4 = 50,000 plus Interest accrued.

Books of Hire Vendors (Machine Tools Ltd.)

MODERN PRINTERS ACCOUNT

Date		Rs.	Date		Rs.
2005			2005		
Jan. 1	To Hire Purchase Sales	2,50,000	Jan. 1	By Bank (D.P.)	50,000
Dec. 31	To Interest @ 6% on 2,00,000	12,000	Dec. 31	By Bank (1st Inst.)	62,000
			Dec. 31	By Balance c/d	1,50,000
		2,62,000			2,62,000

2006			2006		
Jan. 1	To Balance b/d	1,50,000	Dec. 31	By Goods	
Dec. 31	To Interest @ 6%	9,000		Repossessed A/c	1,59,000
		1,59,000			1,59000

GOODS REPOSSESSED A/C

Date		Rs.	Date		Rs.
2006			2006		
Dec. 31	To Modern Printers A/c	1,59,000	Dec. 31	By Bank (Resale)	1,80,000
	To Cash (Expenses)	10,000			
	To Profit & Loss A/c (Profit)	11,000			
		1,80,000			1,80,000

PARTIAL REPOSSESSION

When, in case of default by hire-purchaser, the Hire Vendor does not seize or repossess the entire lot of goods sold under hire-purchase system but a part thereof and thus leaving the balance with the hire purchaser, this situation is treated as that of partial repossession. However, this is possible only when there is a mutual agreement between the Hire purchaser and Hire Vendor regarding the basis of :

(i) Valuation of assets/goods being repossessed

(ii) Payment of future installments including interest (if there is a change in the old agreement).

Accounting Treatment

There is as such, no difference between Full Repossession and Partial Repossession, as far as accounting treatment is concerned. Whatever entries are recorded in case of "Full Repossession" same entries shall be recorded under 'Partial Repossession'. The only difference is the basis of valuation of the goods repossessed. As stated above it is the result of mutual agreement and goods are repossessed at "Agreed Value". However there may be many possibilities under "Partial Repossession" :

(i) The Repossessed goods may be valued on the basis of enhanced rate of depreciation. It means "agreed value" at which goods/Assets are repossessed is calculated after charging depreciation at a rate which is higher than the rate of depreciation applied by hire-purchaser. For example, Hire purchaser charges depreciation @ 15% p.a. on Straight Line / or written down value method, the Hire Vendor may repossess goods at a depreciation of 20%, 25% or 30% as the case may be, depending upon the mutual agreement.

(ii) The "Agreed Value" for the purpose of repossession may also be based upon "certain percentage of the amount paid". For example repossessed goods may be valued at amount paid (excluding interest) less 10%, 20% or 40% (or any other percentage) against these repossessed goods. For example, out of the 5 machines purchased on hire-purchase, 3 machines are being repossessed at 20% less of the amount paid against these repossessed machines. If the amount paid towards the cash price of these 3 machines amount to Rs. 60,000, then these three (3) machines will be valued at Rs. 48,000 i.e. Rs. 60,000 less 20% (i.e. Rs. 12,000).

(iii) The goods/assets may also be repossessed on the basis of certain percentage of amount outstanding against these goods/assets. If for example a hire purchaser acquires 4 cars on hire purchase basis @ Rs. 2,00,000 each and pays Rs. 2,80,000 in all i.e. Rs. 70,000 per car till the date of default. The hire vendor repossesses 3 cars, leaving one with the hire purchaser, on the basis of 60% of the amount remaining outstanding. In this case the "agreed value" of these three repossessed car will be 60% of {(2,00,000 - 70,000) x 3} i.e. Rs. 2,34,000.

(iv) Any lump sum amount, as determined under mutual agreement, having no relation with cash price, written down value, depreciation rate, amount outstanding or amount paid, may be taken as Agreed Value of goods repossessed.

(v) "Agreed Value" may also be given as certain percentage of cash price or hire purchase price of the goods/assets repossessed.

It is to noted that "Goods" are meant for hire vendor and "assets" for the hire-purchaser.

Illustration 10 (Valuation at higher rate of depreciation)

City Transport Ltd. purchased 5 Motor Lorries from Bharat Motors Ltd. on 1-1-2005. The Cash price of motor lorry was Rs. 5,00,000 each. Payment was to be made Rs. 2,50,000 down and balance was payable in 5 equal installments together with interest @ 6% p.a. at the end of each year. City Transport Ltd. writes off depreciation @ 20% p.a. on written down value basis. City Transport paid two installments but could not pay the third. Bharat Motors Ltd. repossessed the 3 Motor lorries and City Transport Ltd. was allowed to retain two Motor lorries on the condition that the value of other three Motor lorries would be adjusted against the amount due. These three Motor lorries were valued on the basis of 30% depreciation annually on written down value method.

Show Motor lorries Account and Bharat Motors Ltd. Account in the books of City Transport Ltd. for three years.

Solution : **In the Books of City Transport Ltd.**

MOTOR LORRIES ACCOUNT

Date		Rs.	Date		Rs.
2005			2005		
Jan. 1	To Bharat Motors Ltd.	25,00,000	Dec. 31	By Depreciation	5,00,000
				By Balance c/d	20,00,000
		25,00,000			25,00,000
2006			2006		
Jan 1	To Balance b/d	20,00,000	Dec. 31	By Depreciation	4,00,000
				By Balance c/d	16,00,000
		20,00,000			20,00,000
2007			2007		
Jan. 1	To Balance b/d	16,00,000	Dec. 31	By Depreciation	3,20,000
				By Bharat Motors Ltd.(1)	5,14,500
				By Profit & Loss A/c (Balancing figure)	2,53,500
				By Balance c/d	5,12,000
		16,00,000			16,00,000

BHARAT MOTORS LTD. ACCOUNT

Date		Rs.	Date		Rs.
2005			2005		
Jan. 1	To Bank (Down Payment)	2,50,000	Jan. 1	By Motor Lorries A/c	25,00,000
Dec. 31	To Bank (1st Installment)	5,85,000	Dec. 31	By Interest @ 6% on	
	To Balance c/d	18,00,000		22,50,000	1,35,000
		26,35,000			26,35,000
2006			2006		
Dec. 31	To Bank (IInd Installment)	5,58,000	Jan. 1	By Balance b/d	18,00,000
	To Balance c/d	13,50,000	Dec. 31	By Interest @ 6%	1,08,000
		19,08,000			19,08,000
2007			2007		
Dec. 31	To Motor Lorries A/c	5,14,500	Jan. 1	By Balance b/d	13,50,000
	To Balance c/d	9,16,500	Dec. 31	By interest @ 6%	81,000
		14,31,000			14,31,000
			2008		
			Jan. 1	By Balance b/d	9,16,500

Working Note :

(1) The "Agreed Value" at which 3 Motor Lorries have been repossessed is worked out as under :

3 Lorries Repossessed	Rs.	W.D.V. of 2 Lorries Retained	Rs.
Cash Price of M. Lorries	15,00,000	Cash Price of 2 Lorries	10,00,000
Less Depreciation @ 30% for 2005	(4,50,000)	Less Depreciation @ 20% for 2005	(2,00,000)
W.D.V. on 1-1-2006	10,50,000	W.D.V. on 1-1-2006	8,00,000
Less Depreciation @ 30% for 2006	(3,15,000)	Less Depreciation @ 20% for 2006	(1,60,000)
	7,35,000	W.D.V. on 1-1-2007	6,40,000
Less Depreciation @ 30% for 2007	(2,20,500)	Less Depreciation @ 20% for 2007	(1,28,000)
Agreed value of Lorries Repossessed	5,14,500	W.D.V. as on 1-1-2008	5,12,000

Illustration 11 (Valuation at cash price less discount)

H-Tech Computer Center acquired 3 computers from Delhi Software Agencies on hire-purchase basis on 1-1-2006. The cash price of each computer was Rs. 60,000. The terms of payments were as under :

20% of cash price at the time of signing on contract which was immediately followed by delivery, 30% of cash price plus interest accrued @ 8% p.a. at the end of first year and the remainder in Two equal installments together with interest @ 8% p.a.

H-Tech Computer Center paid the first installment but could not pay the next. It was agreed that Hire Vendor would repossess two computers and one would be retained by the Hire purchaser. Delhi Software Agencies agreed to allow H-Tech Computer Center a credit for the amount paid against these two computers less 20%. H-Tech charges depreciation @ 20% p.a on written down value basis and closes its books of accounts 31st December each year.

Delhi Softwares Ltd. spent Rs. 5,650 on updating the computers and sold them for cash @ Rs. 35,000 each.

Show the necessary Ledger Accounts in the books of both the parties.

Solution : **In the Books of H-Tech Computer Center**

COMPUTERS ACCOUNT

Date		Rs.	Date		Rs
2006			2006		
Jan. 1	To Delhi Softwares. Ltd.	1,80,000	Jan. 1	By Depreciation® 20%	36,000
			Dec. 31	By Balance b/d	1,44,000
		1,80,000			1,80,000
2007			2007		
Jan. 1	To Balance b/d	1,44,000	Dec. 31	By Depreciation	28,800
				By Delhi Softwares Ltd. (1)	48,000
				By Profit & Loss A/c(B.F.) (Loss on Repossession)	28,800
				By Balance c/d	38,400
		1,44,000			1,44,000
2008					
Jan. 1	To Balance b/d	38,400			

DELHI SOFTWARES LTD.

Date		Rs.	Date		Rs.
2006			2006		
Jan. 1	To Bank (Down Payment)	36,000	Jan. 1	By Computers A/c	1,80,000
Dec. 31	To Bank (1st Installment)	65,520	Dec. 31	By Interest @ 8% on Rs. 1,44,000	11,520
	To Balance c/d	90,000			
		1,91,520			1,91,520
2007			2007		
Dec. 31	To Computers A/c	48,000	Jan. 1	By Balance b/d	90,000
	To Balance c/d	49,200	Dec. 31	By Interest @ 8%	7,200
		97,200			97,200
			2008		
			Jan. 1	By Balance b/d	49,200

Working Note :

(1) Agreed value of computer repossessed has been calculated as under :

	Rs.
Cash paid against these two computers. Down payment @ 20% of Cash price	24,000
Cash paid on 1st installment being 30% of Cash price	36,000
Total cash price paid	60,000
Less 20% as per Agreement	12,000
Agreed Value of two computers seized	48,000

In the Books of Delhi Software Agencies

H-TECH COMPUTER CENTRE A/C

Date		Rs.	Date.		Rs.
2006			2006		
Jan. 1	To Higher Purchas sales	1,80,000	Jan. 1	By Bank (Down Payment)	36,000
Dec. 31	To Interest @ 8% on Rs. 1,44,000	11,520	Dec. 31	By Bank (1st Installment)	65,520
				By Balance c/d	90,000
		1,91,520			1,91,520
2007			2007		
Jan. 1	To Balance b/d	90,000	Dec. 31	By Goods Respossessed A/c	48,000
Dec. 31	To Inerest @ 8%	7,200		By Balance c/d	49,200
		97,200			97,200
2008					
Jan. 1	To Balance b/d	49,200			

GOODS RESPOSSESSED A/C

Date		Rs.	Date		Rs.
2007			2007		
Dec. 31	To H-Tech Computer	48,000	Dec. 31	By Bank (Resale)	70,000
	To Bank (Expenses)	5,650			
	To Profit & Loss A/c (Profit on resale)	16,350			
		70,000			70,000

Important Note : Students must differentiate between 'Full Repossession' and 'Partial Repossession' as far as the value of goods repossessed is concerned. In case of 'Full Repossession' the **'Balance due'**, on the date of default, is taken as the 'Value of goods' repossessed whereas 'Agreed Value' (Value arrived at with mutual agreement by any of the methods explained earlier) is taken as the 'value' of goods repossessed in case of Partial Repossession.

Illustration 12 (Valuation based on cash price)

On 1-1-2005 Metro Tourist Services acquired 4 Taxi Cars from Padmini Motors under Hire purchase agreement. The cash price of each Car was Rs. 2,25,000, which was payable Rs. 1,00,000 as cash down and the balance in 4 annual installments together with interest @ 9% p.a. at the end of each year. Metro Tourists Services charges depreciation @ 15% per annum on straight line method. It paid first two instalments but could not pay the third and as a consequence Padmini Motors took repossession of 3 Taxi; Cars which were considered worth 40% of Cash price. Fourth taxi was left with Metro Tourists Services on the condition that interest due till date is paid immediately which was duly complied with by the hire purchaser. Hire Vendor spent Rs. 25,000 on the repair & conditioning of Taxies which were sold for Rs. 3,25,000.

Show the Ledger Accounts in the books of both the parties for the year 2005, 2,006 and 2007.

Solution : **In the Books of Metro Tourist Services**

PADMINI MOTORS ACCOUNT

Date		Rs.	Date		Rs.
2005			2005		
Jan. 1	To Bank (Down Payment)	1,00,000	Jan. 1	By Taxi Cars A/c	9,00,000
Dec. 31	To Bank (Ist Installment)	2,72,000	Dec. 31	By Interest @ 9%	72,000
	To Balance c/d	6,00,000		(on Rs. 8,00,000)	
		9,72,000			9,72,000
2006			2006		
Dec. 31	To Bank (IInd Installment)	2,54,000	Jan. 1	By Balance b/d	6,00,000
	To Balance c/d	4,00,000	Dec. 31	By Interest @ 9%	54,000
		6,54,000			6,54,000
2007			2007		
Dec. 31	To Bank (Interest)	36,000	Jan. 1	By Balance b/d	4,00,000
	To Taxi Cars A/c (2)	2,70,000	Dec. 31	By Interest @ 9%	36,000
	To Balance c/d	1,30,000			
		4,36,000			4,36,000

TAXI ACCOUNT

Date		Rs.	Date		Rs.
2005			2005		
Jan. 1	To Padmini Motors	9,00,000	Dec. 31	By Depression @ 15%	1,35,000
				By Balance c/d	7,65,000
		9,00,000			9,00,000
2006			2006		
Jan. 1	To Balance b/d	7,65,000	Dec. 31	By Depreciation	1,35,000
				By Balance c/d	6,30,000
		7,65,000			7,65,000

2007			2007		
Jan. 1	To Balance b/d	6,30,000	Dec. 31	By Depreciation	1,35,000
				By Padmini Motor (2)	2,70,000
				By Profit & Loss A/c (BF)	1,01,250
				(Loss on Surrender)	1,23,750
				By Balance c/d	
		6,30,000			6,30,000

In the Books of Padmini Motors

METRO TOURISTS SERVICES ACCOUNT

Date		Rs.	Date		Rs.
2005			2005		
Jan. 1	To Hire Purchase Sales	9,00,000	Jan. 1	By Bank (Down Payment)	1,00,000
Dec. 31	To Interest @ 9% on Rs. 8,00,000	72,000	Dec. 31	By Bank (Ist Instalment)	2,72,000
				By Balance c/d	6,00,000
		9,72,000			9,72,000
2006			2006		
Jan. 1	To Balance b/d	6,00,000	Dec. 31	By Bank (IInd Instalment)	2,54,000
Dec. 31	To Interest @ 9%	54,000		By Balance c/d	4,00,000
		6,54,000			6,54,000
2007			2007		
Jan. 1	To Balance b/d	4,00,000	Dec. 31	By Bank (Interest)	36,000
Dec. 31	To Interest @ 9%	36,000		By Goods Repossessed A/c	2,70,000
				By Balance c/d	1,30,000
		4,36,000			4,36,000
2008					
Jan. 1	To Balance b/d	1,30,000			

GODS REPOSSESSED ACCOUNT

Date		Rs.	Date		Rs.
2007			2007		
Dec. 31	To Metro Tourists Services	2,70,000	Dec. 31	By Bank (resale)	3,25,000
	To Bank (Expenses)	25,000			
	To Profit & Loss A/c (Profit)	30,000			
		3,25,000			3,25,000

Working Notes :

(1) Interest outstanding for the year 2007 has been paid by the hire purchaser as per agreement with Hire Vendor.

(2) Agreed Value of goods repossessed :

	Rs.
Cash price of 3 cars repossessed (2,25,000 * 3)	6,75,000
40% thereof	2,70,000

GRADED ILLUSTRATIONS

Illustration 1 (Cash Price is not given)

On 1-1-2005 A Taxi Service Centre acquired 3 Taxies on hire-purchase basis from a Automobile company. The payment was to be made as under :

	Rs.
On signing of agreement	10,350
At the end of First year	19,965
At the end of Second year	19,965
At the end of Third year	19,965
Total Hire Purchase Price	70,245

Nothing more was payable after 3rd installment. All the installments are duly paid by the Taxi Service Centre. Interest was reckoned @ 10% p.a. Depreciation was charged @ 20% p.a. on diminishing balance. Taxi Service Centre closes its books of accounts on 31st December every year. Prepare : (1) Automobile Co. Account, (2) Taxi Account and (3) Interest Account.

[ICWA (Inter), Dec. 1984-Modified]

Solution : **CALCULATION OF CASH PRICE**

Instalment	Amount of Instalment Rs.	Interest Rs.	Cash Price Rs.
Third Instalment	19,965	$\left(19{,}965 \times \frac{10}{110}\right) = 1{,}815$	$19{,}965 - 1{,}815 = 18{,}150$
Second Instalment	19,965	$\left(19{,}965 + 18{,}150 \times \frac{10}{110}\right) = 3{,}465$	$19{,}965 - 3{,}465 = 16{,}500$
First Instalment	19,965	$\left(19{,}965 + 18{,}150 + 16{,}500 \times \frac{10}{110}\right) = 4{,}965$	$19{,}965 - 4{,}965 = 15{,}000$
Down Payment	10,350	—	10,350
			Total Cash Price 60,000

AUTOMOBILE COMPANY A/C

Date		Rs.	Date		Rs.
2005			2005		
Jan. 1	To Bank (Down Payment)	10,350	Jan. 1	By Taxi A/c	60,000
Dec. 31	To Bank (Ist Instalment)	19,965	Dec. 31	By Interest @ 10% on 49,650 (60,000 – 10,350)	4,965
	To Balance c/d	34,650			
		65,965			64,965
2006			2006		
Dec. 31	To Bank (IInd Instalment)	19,965	Jan. 1	By Balance b/d	34,650
	To Balance c/d	18,150	Dec. 31	By Interest @ 10%	3,465
		38,115			38,115
2007			2007		
Dec. 31	To Bank (IIIrd Instalment)	19,965	Dec. 31	By Balance b/d	18,150
				By Interest	1,815
		19,965			19,965

TAXI ACCOUNT

Date		Rs.	Date		Rs.
2005			2005		
Jan. 1	To Automobil Co.	60,000	Dec. 31	By Depreciation	12,000
				By Balance c/d	48,000
		60,000			60,000
2006			2006		
Jan. 1	To Balance b/d	48,000	Dec. 31	By Depreciation	9,600
				By Balance c/d	38,400
		48,000			48,000
2007			2007		
Jan. 1	To Balance b/d	38,400	Dec. 31	By Depreciation	7,680
				By Balance c/d	30,720
		38,400			38,400
2008					
Jan. 1	To Balance	30,720			

INTEREST ACCOUNT

Date		Rs.	Date		Rs.
2005			2005		
Dec. 31	To Automobile Co.	4,965	Dec. 31	By Profit @ Loss A/c	4,965
2006			2006		
Dec. 31	To automobile Co.	3,465	Dec. 31	By Profit & Loss A/c	3,465
2007			2007		
Dec. 31	To Automobile Co.	1,815	Dec. 31	By Profit & Loss A/c	1,815

Illustration 2 (Rate of Interest not given)

X purchases a T.V. set on hire purchase basis for Rs. 5,000 and makes the payment in the following order :

	Rs.
Down payment	1,000
1st Installment after one year of the agreement	2,000
2nd Installment after two years of the agreement	1,000
3rd Installment after three years of the agreement	1,000
The Cash price of the T.V. set	4,300

Prepare necessary Ledger Accounts in the books of Hire Vendor. **[B.Com. (H), DU, 1990]**

Solution :

Hire Purchase Price – Cash Price = Interest

Rs. 5,000 – Rs. 4300 = Rs. 700

Hence in the absence of rate of interest, it will be apportioned in the ratio of amount outstanding at the end of each year.

	Rs.	Ratio	
Amount outstanding by the end of first year	4,000	4	(5,000 – 1,000)
Amount outstanding by the end of Second year	2,000	2	(4,000 – 2,000)
Amount outstanding by the end of Third year	1,000	1	(2,000 – 1,000)

Hence interest is to be apportioned in the ratio of 4 : 2 : 1

$$\text{First year's interest} = \left(700 \frac{4}{7}\right) = \text{Rs. } 400$$

$$\text{Second year's interest} = \left(700 \frac{2}{7}\right) = \text{Rs. } 200$$

$$\text{Third year's interest} = \left(700 \frac{1}{7}\right) = \text{Rs. } 100$$

In the Books of Hire Vendor

X (HIRE PURCHASER'S) ACCOUNT

		Rs.			Rs.
First Year			First Year		
First day	To Hire Purchase Sales	4,300	First day	By Cash (Down Payment)	1,000
Last day	To Interest	400	Last day	By Cash (1st Installment)	2,000
			Last day	By Balance c/d	1,700
		4,700			4,700

Second year			Second year		
First day	To Balance b/d	1,700	Last day	By Cash (IInd Installment)	1,000
Last day	To Interest	200	Last day	By Balance c/d	900
		1,900			1,900
Third year					
First day	To Balance b/d	900	Third year	By Cash (IIIrd Instalment)	1,000
Last day	To Interest	100	Last day		
		1,000			1,000

Illustration 3 (General)

On 1-1-2005, Global Press purchased a printing machinery on hire purchase system from Modern Machinery Company. The payment was to be made as Rs. 30,000 down and balance in three installments of Rs. 20,000 each payable on 31st December. The Vendor Company charged interest @ 8% p.a. Global Press provided depreciation @ 10% p.a. on diminishing balance and paid all installments. It closes its books on 31st December every year. The Cash down value of the machine was Rs. 81,543. Show the (a) Modern Machinery Company's Account and (b) Printing Machine Account in the books of Global Press for 3 years.

[ICWA (Inter), Dec. 1986-Modifi]

Solution :

In the Books of Global Press

MODERN MACHINERY COMPANY A/C

Date		Rs.	Date		Rs.
2005			2005		
Jan. 1	To Bank (Down Payment)	30,000	Jan. 1	By Printing Machine	81,543
Dec. 31	To Bank (Ist Installment)	20,000	Dec. 31	By Interest @ 8% on Rs. 51,543	4,123
Dec. 31	To Balance c/d	35,666			
		85,666			85,666
2006			2006		
Dec. 31	To Bank (IInd Instalment)	20,000	Jan. 1	By Balance b/d	35,666
Dec. 31	To Balance c/d	18,519	Dec. 31	By Interest & 8%	2,853
		38,519			38,519
2007			2007		
Dec. 31	To Bank (IIIrd Inst.)	20,000	Jan. 1	By Balance b/d	18,519
			Dec. 31	By Interest @ 8%	1,481
		20,000			20,000

PRINTING MACHINE A/C

Date		Rs.	Date		Rs.
2005			2005		
Jan. 1	To Modern Machinery Co.	81,543	Dec. 31	By Depreciation @ 10%	8,154
			Dec. 31	By Balance c/d	73,389
		81,543			81,543

2006 Jan. 1	To Balance b/d	73,389	2006 Dec. 31	By Depreciation	7,339
				By Balance c/d	66,050
		73,389			73,389
2007 Jan. 1	To Balance b/d	66,050	2007 Dec. 31	By Depreciation	6,605
				By Balance c/d	59,445
		66,050			66,050
2008 Jan. 1	To Balance b/d	59,445			

Illustration 4 (Last Installment not given)

On 1-1-2005, X purchased Machinery from Y on hire purchase system. The terms of payment being Rs. 5,000 on delivery and the balance by following installments on 31st December each year :

2005	Rs. 10,000
2006	Rs. 10,000
2007	Balance amount

Y charged interest at 10% on the yearly balances. The cash value of the machinery on delivery was Rs. 30,000. Depreciation @ 20% p.a. on diminishing balances was written off in each year

X paid all the installments on the due date. Show the Machinery Account and Y's Account in the books of X for three years to 31st December 2007. **[ICWA (Inter), Dec. 1987-Modified]**

Solution : **In the Books of X (Hire Purchaser)**

MACHINERY ACCOUNT

Date		Rs.	Date		Rs.
2005 Jan. 1	To Y (Hire Vendor)	30,000	2005 Dec. 31	By Depreciation @ 20%	6,000
				By Balance c/d	24,000
		30,000			30,000
2006 Jan. 1	To Balance b/d	24,000	2006 Dec. 31	By Depreciation	4,800
				By Balance c/d	19,200
		24,000			24,000
2007 Jan. 1	To Balance b/d	19,200	2007 Dec. 31	By Depreciation	3,840
				By Balance c/d	15,360
		19,200			19,200

Y (HIRE VENDOR'S) A/C

Date		Rs.	Date		Rs.
2005			2005		
Jan. 1	To Bank (Down Payment)	5,000	Jan. 1	By Machinery	30,000
Dec. 31	To Bank (Ist Instalment)	10,000	Dec. 31	By Interest @ 10% on Rs. 25,000	2,500
Dec. 31	To Balance c/d	17,500			
		32,500			32,500
2006			2006		
Dec. 31	To Bank (IInd Installment)	10,000	Jan. 1	By Balance b/d	17,500
Dec. 31	To Balance c/d	9,250	Dec. 31	By Interest @ 10%	1,750
		19,250			19,250
2007			2007		
Dec. 31	To Bank (Final Installment)	10,175	Jan. 1	By Balance b/d	9,250
			Dec. 31	By Interest @ 10%	925
		10,175			10,175

Illustration 5 (Calculation of Cash Price)

A machinery is sold on hire purchase. The terms of payment are four annual installments of Rs. 6,000 at the end of each year commencing from the date of agreement. Interest is charged at 20% and is included in the annual payment of Rs. 6,000. Show Machinery Account and Hire Vendor Account in the books of the Hire purchaser who defaulted in the payment of the third yearly installment whereupon the Hire Vendor repossessed the machinery. The Hire purchaser provides depreciation @ 10% p.a. on written down value. All working should form part of your answer.

[C.A. (Inter), Nov. 1988-Modified & B.Com. (H), DU, 1995)]

Solution : **CALCULATION OF CASH PRICE**

		Interest Rs.	Cash Price Rs.
IV th Installment	$6{,}000 \times \frac{20}{120} =$	1,000	5,000
IIIrd Instalment	$(5{,}000 + 6{,}000) \times \frac{20}{120} =$	1,833	4,167
IInd Installment	$(5{,}000 + 4{,}167 + 6{,}000) \times \frac{20}{120} =$	2,528	3,472
Ist Installment	$(5{,}000 + 4{,}167 + 3{,}472 + 6{,}000) \times \frac{20}{120} =$	3,106	2,894
	Total Cash Price		15,533

In the books of Hire Purchaser

MACHINER'S ACCOUNT

		Rs.			Rs.
Ist year	To Hire Vendor	15,533	Ist year	By Depreciation	1,553
				By Balance c/d	13,980
		15,533			15,533
IInd year	To Balance b/d	13,980	IInd year	By Depreciaton	1,398
				By Balance c/d	12,582
		13,980			13,980
IIIrd year	To Balance b/d	12,582	IIInd year	By Depreciation	1,258
				By Hire Vendor's A/c	11,000
				By Profit & Loss A/c (BF) (Loss on Repossession)	324
		12,582			12,582

HIRE VENDOR'S ACCOUNT

		Rs.			Rs.
1st year	To Bank (Ist Installment)	6,000	Ist year	By Machinery A/c	15,533
	To Balance c/d	12,639		By Interest @ 20%	3,106
		18,639			18,639
IInd year	To Bank (IInd Insallment)	6,000	IInd year	By Balance b/d	12,639
	To Balance c/d	9,167		By Interest @ 20%	2,528
		15,167			15,167
IIIrd year	To Machinery A/c	11,000	IIIrd year	By Balance b/d	9,167
				By Interest @ 20%	1,833
		11,000			11,000

Illustration 6 (Equal Installments of Cash Price)

On 1-1-2004 X Ltd. purchased a Motor Car from Y Ltd. on hire purchase basis. The cash price of which was payable as Rs. 12,000 down and the balance in three equal annual installments together with interest at 10% p.a. The amount of last installment including interest was Rs.17,600. Depreciation was to be provided at 20% p.a. on reducing balance. At the end of three years of service, the Motor Car was sold for Rs. 30,000 cash. Show (a) Motor Car Account and (b) Hire Vendor's Account in the books of hire purchaser for three years. **[ICWA (Inter), June 1984-Modified]**

Solution : **CALCULATION OF CASH PRICE**

Amount payable on last installment	Rs. 17,600 (Cash Price + Interest)
This includes interest @ 10% p.a.	
i.e., $\frac{10}{110} \times 17{,}600$	Rs. 1,600
Cash price included in Third installment	Rs. 16,000

	Rs
Cash price included in all the three installments 16,000 × 3 =	48,000
(Since all the installments in respect of Cash price are equal and interest is paid on accrual basis the cash price of last installment has been multiplied by the total number of installments payable)	
Add Down Payment	12,000
Total Cash Price	60,000

In the Books of Hire Purchaser

MOTOR CAR ACCOUNT

		Rs.			Rs.
2004			2004		
Jan. 1	To Y Ltd. (Hire Vendor)	60,000	Dec. 31	By Depreciation @ 20%	12,000
				By Balance c/d	48,000
		60,000			60,000
2005			2005		
Jan. 1	To Balance b/d	48,000	Dec. 31	By Depreciation	9,600
				By Balance c/d	38,400
		48,000			48,000
2006			2006		
Jan. 1	To Balance b/d	38,400	Dec. 31	By Depreciation	7,680
				By Cash	30,000
				By Profit & Loss A/c (Loss on Sale)	720
		38,400			38,400

Y LTD (HIRE VENDOR'S) ACCOUNT

		Rs.			Rs.
2004			2004		
Jan. 1	To Bank (down Payment)	12,000	Jan. 1	By Motor Car	60,000
Dec. 31	To Bank (First Installment)	20,800	Dec. 31	By Interest @ 10% on Rs. 48,000	4,800
	To Balance c/d	32,000			
		64,800			64,800
2005			2005		
Dec. 31	To Bank (IInd Installment)	19,200	Jan. 1	By Balance b/d	32,000
	To Balance c/d	16,000	Dec. 31	By Interest @ 10%	3,200
		35,200			35,200
2006			2006		
Dec. 31	To Bank	17,600	Jan. 1	By Balance b/d	16,000
				By Interest @ 10%	1,600
		17,600			17,600

Illustration 7 (Half-yearly Installments and Cash Price)

On 1-7-2006 Eastern Printers purchased a printing machine on hire purchase basis, payments to be made Rs. 10,000 on the said date and the balance in three half-yearly installments of Rs. 8,200, Rs. 7,440 and Rs. 6,300 commencing from 31st December 2006. The Hire Vendor charged interest @ 10% per annum calculated at half-yearly rests.

Eastern Printers closed their books annually on 31st December and provide depreciation at 10% p.a. on diminishing balance in each year.

Determine the cash price of the machine and show the necessary ledger accounts in the books of Eastern Printers. **[C.A. New Scheme, May 1978-Adapted]**

Solution : **DETERMINATION OF CASH PRICE**

Since interest is being charged after every six months, the effective rate for interest calculation purposes becomes 10 x 6/12 = 5%.

Installment	Amount of Installment Rs.	Interest calculation Rs.	Cash Price = Installment – Interest Rs.
Third & Final Installment	6,300	$6{,}300 \times \frac{5}{105} = \text{Rs. } 300$	$6{,}000 = (6{,}300 - 300)$
Second Installment	7,440	$(6{,}000 + 7{,}440)\frac{5}{105} = \text{Rs. } 640$	$6{,}800 = (7{,}440 - 640)$
First Installment	8,200	$(6{,}000 + 6{,}800 + 8{,}200) \times \frac{5}{105}$ $= \text{Rs. } 1{,}000$	$7{,}200 = (8{,}200 - 1{,}000)$
Down Payment	10,000	—	10,000 = (10,000 – Nil)
Total Cash Price			30,000

In the Books of Eastern Printers

PRINTING MACHINE A/C

		Rs			Rs
2006			2006		
July 1	To Hire Vendor's A/c	30,000	Dec. 31	By Depreciation @ 10% for 6 months	1,500
				By Balance c/d	28,500
		30,000			30,000
2007			2007		
Jan. 1	To Balance b/d	28,500	Dec. 31	By Depreciation	2,850
		28,500			2,850
2008					
Jan. 1	To Balance b/d	22,650			

HIRE VENDOR'S ACCOUNT

		Rs.			Rs
2006			2006		
Jule 1	To Bank (Down Payment)	10,000	July 1	By Printing Machine	30,000
Dec. 31	To Bank (Ist Installment)	8,200	Dec. 31	By Interest @ 10% p.a. for 6 months on Rs. 20,000	1,000
	To Balance c/d	12,800			
		31,000			31,000
2007			2007		
July 1	To Bank (IInd Installment)	7,440	Jan. 1	By Balance b/d	12,800
Dec. 31	To Bank (Final Instalment)	6,300	Dec. 31	By Interest @ 10% 0.a. for 6 months	640
				By Interest @ 10% p.a. for 6 months on Rs. 6,000	300
		13,740			13,740

Illustration 8 (Down Payment & Cash Price)

Dobson Ltd. had purchased a machinery on hire purchase system from Hind Machinery Ltd The terms are that they would pay Rs. 20,000 down on 1-1-2003 and 5 annual installments of Rs. 11,000 each commencing from 1-1-2004. They charged depreciation on machinery at the rate of 15% p.a. under diminishing balance system.

Hind Machinery Ltd. had charged interest at the rate of 10% p.a. Show Machinery Account and Hind Machinery Ltd. Account to record the above transactions in the books oi Dobson's Ltd. till the installments are paid off. Dobson's Accounting year ends on 31st December each year.

[C.A. (Inter), N.S., May 1980-Modifted]

Solution :

CALCULATION OF CASH PRICE

Installment	Amount of Installment Rs.	Interest included in Installment Rs.	Cash Price = Installment – Interest Rs.
5th Installment	11,000	$11{,}000 \times \frac{10}{100}$ Rs. 1,000	1,000 = (11,000 – 1,000)
4th Installment	11,000	$(10{,}000 + 11{,}000) \times \frac{10}{110} = \text{Rs.}\,1{,}909$	9,091 = (11,000 – 1,909)
3rd Installment	11,000	$(10{,}000 + 9{,}091 + 11{,}000) \times \frac{10}{110} = 2{,}725$	8,265 = (11,000 – 2,735)
2nd Installment	11,000	$(10{,}000 + 9{,}091 + 8{,}265 + 11{,}000) \times \frac{10}{110} = 3{,}847$	7,513 = (11,000 – 3,487)
1st Installment	11,000	$(10{,}000 + 9{,}091 + 8{,}265 + 7{,}513 + 11{,}000) \times \frac{10}{110} = 4{,}170$	6,830 = (11,000 – 4,170)
Downpayment	20,000	—	20,000 = (20,000 – Nil)
		Total Cash Price	61,700

In the Books of Dobson's Ltd.

MACHINERY ACCOUNT

		Rs.			Rs.
2003			2003		
Jan. 1	To Hind Machinery Ltd.	61,700	Dec. 31	By Depreciation @ 15%	9,255
				By Balance c/d	52,445
		61,700			61,700
2004			2004		
Jan. 1	To Balance b/d	52,445	Dec. 31	By Depreciation	7,867
				By Balance c/d	44,578
		52,445			52,445
2005			2005		
Jan. 1	To Balance b/d	44,578	Dec. 31	By Depreciation	6,687
				By Balance c/d	37,891
		44,578			44,578
2006			2006	By Depreciation	
Jan. 1	To Balance b/d	37,891	Dec. 31	By Balance c/d	5,684
					32,207
		37,891			37,891
2007			2007		
Jan. 1	To Balance b/d	32,207	Dec. 31	By Depreciation	4,831
				By Balance c/d	27,376
		32,207			32,207

HIND MACHINERY ACCOUNT

		Rs.			Rs.
2003			2003		
Jan. 1	To Bank (Down Payment)	20,000	Jan. 1	By Machinery A/c	61,700
Dec. 31	To Balance c/d	45,870	Dec. 31	By Interest @ 10% p.a. on Rs. 41.700	4,170
		65,870			65,870
2004			2004		
Jan. 1	To Bank (First Installment)	11,000	Jan. 1	By Balance b/d	45,870
Dec. 31	To Balance c/d	38,357	Dec. 31	By Interest @ 10% p.a. on Rs. 34,870	3,487
		49,357			49,357

2005			2005		
Jan. 1	To Bank (IInd Installment)	11,000	Jan. 1	By Balance b/d	38,357
Dec. 31	To Balance c/d	30,092	Dec. 31	By Interest @ 10% 0.a. on Rs. 27,357	2,735
		41,092			41,092
2006			2006		
Jan. 1	To Bank (IIIrd Installment)	11,000	Jan. 1	By Balance b/d	30,092
Dec. 31	To Balance c/d	21,001	Dec. 31	By Interest @ 10% p.a. on Rs. 19,092	1,909
		32,001			32,001
2007			2007		
Jan. 1	To Bank (IIIrd Installment)	11,000	Jan. 1	By Balance b/d	21,001
Dec. 31	To Balance c/d	11,001	Dec. 31	By Interest @ 10% p.a. on Rs. 10,001	1,000
		22,001			22,001
2008			2008		
Jan. 1	To Bank	11,000	Jan. 1	By Balance b/d	11,001*

*Due to fractions.

Illustration 9 (Partial Repossession)

Transport Ltd. purchased 2 Trucks costing Rs. 80,000 each from Auto Ltd. on 1-1-2005 on the hire purchase system. The terms were: Payment on delivery Rs. 20,000 for each Truck. Remainder in 3 equal installments together with interest at 10% p.a. to be paid at the end of each year.

Transport Ltd. writes off 25% depreciation each year on the diminishing balance method. Transport Ltd. paid the installments due on 31st December 2005 and on 31st December 2006 but could not pay the Final installment. Auto Ltd. repossessed one Truck adjusting its value against the amount due. The repossession was done on the basis of 30% depreciation on the diminishing balance method. Write up the ledger account in the books of Transport Ltd. **[C.A. (Inter), May 1975-Modified]**

Solution : **In the Book of Transport Ltd.**

TRUCKS ACCOUNT

		Rs.			Rs.
2005			2005		
Jan. 1	To Auto Ltd	1,60,000	Dec. 31	By Depreciation @ 25%	40,000
				By Balance c/d	1,20,000
		1,60,000			1,60,000
2006			2006		
Jan. 1	To Balance b/d	1,20,000	Dec. 31	By Depreciation @ 25%	30,000
				By Balance c/d	90,000
		1,20,000			1,20,000

2007			2007		
Jan. 1	To Balance b/d	90,000	Dec. 31	By Depreciation @ 25%	22,500
				By Auto Ltd.*	27,440
				By Profit & Loss A/c (BF)	6,310
				By Balance c/d"	33,750
		90,000			90,000

AUTO LTD. ACCOUNT

		Rs.			Rs.
2005			2005		
Jan. 1	To Bank (Down Payment)	40,000	Jan. 1	By Truck Account	1,60,000
Dec. 31	To Bank (Ist Installment)	52,000	Dec. 31	By Interest @ 10% on	12,000
	To Balance c/d	80,000		Rs. 1,20,000	
		1,72,000			1,72,000
2006			2006		
Dec. 31	To Bank (IInd Installment)	48,000	Jan. 1	By Balance b/d	80,000
	To Balance c/d	40,000	Dec. 31	By Interest @ 10%	8,000
		88,000			88,000
2007			2007		
Dec. 31	To Truck A/c	27,440	Jan. 1	By Balance b/d	40,000
	To Balance c/d	16,560	Dec. 31	By Interest @ 10%	4,000
		44,000			44,000
			2008		
			Jan. 1	By Balance b/d	16,560

Working Notes :

*The value of Truck Repossessed and value of Truck retained has been worked out as under :

Truck Repossessed	Rs.	Truck Retained	Rs.
Cash Price	80,000	Cash Price	80,000
Depreciation @ 30% for 2005	24,000	Depreciation @ 25% for 2005	20,000
	56,000	W.D.V. as on 1-1-2006	60,000
Depreciation @ 30% for 2006	16,800	Depreciation @ 25% for 2006	15,000
	39,200	W.D.V. as on 1-1-2007	45,000
Depreciation @ 30% for 2007	11,760	Depreciation @ 25% for 2007	11,250
	27,440	W.D.V. as on 1-1-2008	33,750

Illustration 10 (Goods Repossessed valued at higher rate of depreciation)

Bombay Roadways Ltd. purchased three trucks costing Rs. 1,00,000 each from Hindustan Auto Ltd. on 1st January 2003 under hire purchase system. The terms were : payment on delivery Rs. 25,000 for each truck and balance of the principal amount by 3 equal installments plus interest a 15% p.a. to be paid at the end of each year.

Bombay Roadways Ltd. writes off 25% depreciation yearly on the diminishing balance method Bombay Roadways Ltd. paid the installments due on 31st December 2003 and 31st December 2004 but could not pay the final installment.

Hindustan Auto Ltd. repossessed two trucks adjusting its values against the amount due. The repossession was done on 1st January 2006 on the basis of 40% depreciation on diminishing balance method.

(a) Write up the ledger accounts in the Books of Bombay Roadways Ltd. showing the above transactions up to 1-1-2006.

(b) Show the disclosure of balances arising from the above in the Balance Sheet of Bombay Roadways Ltd. as on 31-12-2005. **[C.A. (Inter), May 1982-Modified]**

Solution : **In the Books of Bombay Roadways Ltd.**

TRUCKS ACCOUNT

		Rs.			Rs.
2003			2003		
Jan. 1	To Hindustan Auto Ltd.	3,00,000	Dec. 31	By Depreciation @ 25%	75,000
			Dec. 31	By Balance c/d	2,25,000
		3,00,000			3,00,000
2004			2004		
Jan. 1	To Balance b/d	2,25,000	Dec. 31	By Depreciation @ 25%	56,250
			Dec. 31	By Balance c/d	1,68,750
		2,25,000			2,25,000
2005			2005		
Jan. 1	To Balance b/d	1,68,750	Dec. 31	By Depreciation @ 25%	42,188
			Dec. 31	By Balance c/d	1,26,562
		1,68,750			1,68,750
2006			2006		
Jan. 1	To Balance b/d	1,26,562	Jan. 1	By Hindustan Auto Ltd.	43,200
				By Profit & Loss A/c	41,175
				By Balance c/d	42,187
		1,26,562			1,26,562

HINDUSTAN AUTO LTD, ACCOUNT

		Rs.			Rs.
2003			2003		
Jan. 1	To Bank (Down Payment)	75,000	Jan. 1	By Trucks Account	3,00,000
Dec. 31	To Bank (Ist Installment)	1,08,750	Dec. 31	By Interest @ 15% on	33,750
	(75,000 + 33,750)			Rs. 2,25,000	
	To Balance c/d	1,50,000			
		3,33,750			3,33,750

2004			2004		
Dec. 31	To Bank (IInd Installment)	97,500	Jan. 1	By Balance b/d	1,50,000
	(75,000 + 22,500)			By Interest @ 15%	22,500
	To Balance c/d	75,000			
		1,72,500			1,72,500
2005			2005		
Dec. 31	To Balance c/d	86,250	Jan. 1	By Balance b/d	75,000
			Dec. 31	By Interest @ 15%	11,250
		86,250			86,250
2006			2006		
Jan. 1	To Trucks Account*	43,200	Jan. 1	By Balance b/d	86,250
	To Balance c/d	43,050			
		86,250			86,250
				By Balance b/d	43,050

Value of Trucks Repossessed	Rs.	Value of Truck Retained	Rs.
Cash Price of 2 Trucks	2,00,000	Cash Price of Truck	1,00,000
Less Depreciation @ 40% for 2003	80,000	*Less* Depreciation @ 25% for 2003	25,000
	1,20,000		75,000
Less Depreciation @ 40% for 2004	48,000	*Less* Depreciation @ 25% for 2004	18,750
	72,000		56,250
Less Depreciation @ 40% for 2005	28,800	*Less* Depreciation @ 25% for 2005	14,063
	43,200	W.D.V. as on 1-1-2006	42,187

Amount of Installments is calculated as under :

	Rs.
Cash Price of 3 Trucks	3,00,000 less 75,000
Less Down Payment Balance	2,25,000 to be paid in 3 equal Installment plus interest
Cash price of each Installment	75,000

BALANCE SHEET OF BOMBAY ROADWAYS (SKELETON)

As on 31st December 2003

Liabilities	Rs.	Assets		Rs.
Hindustan Auto Ltd.	1,50,000	Trucks	3,00,000	2,25,000
		Less Depreciation	75,000	

As on 31st December 2004

Liabilities	Rs.	Assets		Rs.
Hindustan Auto Ltd.	75,000	Trucks	2,25,000	1,68,750
		Less Depreciation	56,250	

As on 31st December 2005

Liabilities	Rs.	Assets		Rs.
Hindustan Auto Ltd.	43,050	Trucks	1,68,750	
		Less Depreciation	42,188	
			1,26,562	
		Less W.D.V. of Two		
		Trucks Repossessed	84,375*	42,187
		Profit & Loss Account		41,175

* Repossessed Value 43,200, Loss on Repossession 41, 175.

Illustration 11 (Valuation at a percentage of Cash Price paid)

A Ltd. sold 3 cars for a total cash sale price of Rs. 6,00,000 on hire purchase basis to B on 1-1-2003. The terms of agreement provided for Rs. 1,20,000 as down payment and the balance of cash price in three equal installments together with interest at 12% p.a. calculated at yearly rest. The installments were payable on the following dates :

First installment	on 31 -12-2004
Second installment	on 31-12-2005
Third installment	on 31 -12-2006

B paid the two installments in time but could not pay the third installment on due date. As a consequence, the hire vendor repossessed the two cars and valued them at 60% of the cash price paid. B charges depreciation at 15% p.a. on diminishing balance method.

Prepare necessary ledger accounts in the books of B.

[B.Com. (Hon.), DU, 1995 (Old Course)-Modified]

Solution : **In the Books of B (Hire Purchaser)**

CARS ACCOUNT

		Rs.			Rs.
2003			2003		
Jan. 1	To A Ltd.	6,00,000	Dec. 31	By Depreciation @ 15%	90,000
				By Balance c/d	5,10,000
		6,00,000			6,00,000
2004			2004		
Jan. 1	To Balance b/d	5,10,000	Dec. 31	By Depreciation	76,500
				By Balance c/d	4,33,500
		5,10,000			5,10,000
2005			2005		
Jan. 1	To Balance b/d	4,33,500	Dec. 31	By Depreciation	65,025
				By Balance c/d	3,68,475
		4,33,500			4,33,500

2006 Jan. 1	To Balance b/d	3,68,475	2006 Dec. 31	By Depreciation	55,271
				By A Ltd.	1,76,000
				By Profit & Loss A/c (BF)	32,802
				By Balane c/d	1,04,402
		3,68,475			3,68,475

A LTD. ACCOUNT

		Rs.			Rs.
2003			2003		
Jan. 1	To Bank (Down Payment)	1,20,000	Jan. 1	By Cars A/c	6,00,000
Dec. 31	To Balance c/d	5,37,600	Dec. 31	By Interest @ 12% p.a. on 4,80,000	57,600
		6,57,600			6,57,600
2004			2004		
Jan. 1	To Bank (Ist nstalment)*	2,82,112[(1)]	Jan. 1	By Balance b/d	5,37,600
Dec. 31	To Balance c/d	3,20,000	Dec. 31	By Interest @ 12% p.a.	64,512
		6,02,112			6,02,112
2005			2005		
Dec. 31	To Bank (IInd Installment)	1,98,400	Jan. 1	By Balance b/d	3,20,000
	To Balance c/d	1,60,000	Dec. 31	By Interest @ 12% p.a.	38,400
		3,58,400			3,58,400
2006			2006		
Dec. 31	To Cars Account (2)	1,76,000	Jan. 1	By Balance b/d	1,60,000
	To Balance c/d	3,200	Dec. 31	By Interest 12% p.a.	19,200
		1,79,200			1,79,200

(1) Cash price of 3 cars Rs. 6,00,000 less down payment Rs. 1,20,000 = 4,80,000 ÷ 3 = Rs. 1,60,000

* First Installment = Rs. 1,60,000 + Interest (for 2003) Rs. 57,600 + Interest (for 2004) Rs. 64,512 = Rs. 2,82,112

(2) Value of Cars Repossessed: 60% of cash price paid = 60% of 2/3 (1,20,000 + 1,60,000 + 1,60,000) = Rs. 1,76,000.

Illustration 12 (Partial Repossession & subsequent installments)

X Transport Ltd. purchased from Delhi Motors three tempos costing Rs. 50,000 each on the hire-purchase system on 1-1-2006. The payment was to be made Rs. 30,000 down and the remainder in three equal annual installments payable on 31st December together with interest @ 9%. X Transport Ltd. writes off depreciation @ 20% on diminishing balance. It paid the installment due at the end of first year i.e. 31st December 2006 but could not pay the next on 31st December 2007. Delhi Motors agreed to leave one tempo with the purchaser adjusting the value of the other two tempos against the amount due on 1-1-2008. The tempos were valued on the basis on 30% depreciation annually. Show the necessary accounts in the books of X Transport Ltd. for the years 2006, 2007 and 2008.

[C.A. (Inter), May 1990-Modified]

Solution : **In the Books of X Transport Ltd.**

DELHI MOTORS ACCOUNT

		Rs.			Rs.
2006			2006		
Jan. 1	To Bank (Down Payment)	30,000	Jan. 1	By Tempo A/c	1,50,000
Dec. 31	To Bank (Ist Instalment)	50,800	Dec. 31	By Interest @ 9% on 1,20,000	10,800
	To Balance c/d	80,000			
		1,60,800			1,60,800
2007			2007		
Dec. 31	To Tempos A/c	49,000	Jan. 1	By Balance b/d	80,000
	To Balance c/d	38,200	Dec. 31	By Interest @ 9%	7,200
		87,200			87,200
2008			2008		
Dec. 31	To Bank	41,638	Jan. 1	By Balance b/d	38,200
			Dec. 31	By Interest @ 9%	3,438
		41,638			41,638

TEMPOS ACCOUNT

		Rs.			Rs.
2006			2006		
Jan. 1	To X Transport Ltd.	1,50,000	Dec. 31	By Depreciation @ 20%	30,000
				By Balance c/d	1,20,000
		1,50,000			1,50,000
2007			2007		
Jan. 1	To Balance b/d	1,20,000	Dec. 31	By Depreciation	24,000
				By X Transport Ltd (1)	49,000
				By P & L A/c (BF)	15,000
				By Balance c/d (2)	32,000
		1,20,000			1,20,000
2008			2008		
Jan. 1	To Balance b/d	32,000	Dec. 31	By Depreciation @ 10%	6,400
				By Balance c/d	25,600
		32,000			32,000
2009					
Jan. 1	To Balance b/d	25,600			

Working Notes :

Value of Tempos repossessed and written down value of Tempo retained has been worked out as under :

(1) Value of 2 Tempos Repossessed	Rs.	(2) Value of 1 Tempo retained	Rs.
Cash price of 2 Tempos	1,00,000	Cash price of 1 Tempo	50,000
Depreciation® 30%	30,000	Depreciation @ 20% (for 2006)	10,000
As per agreement (for the year 2006)	70,000		40,000
W.D.V.as on 1-1-2007		Depreciation @ 20% for 2007	8,000
Depreciation @ 30% for the year 2007	21,000	W.D.V. as on 1.1.2008	32,000
	49,000		

Illustration 13 (Repossessed price is given)

Rajesh purchased seven Trucks on hire-purchase on 1-7-2004. The cash price of each Truck was Rs. 50,000. He was to pay 20% of the cash price at the time of delivery and the balance in five half-yearly installments starting from 31-12-2004 with interest @ 5% p.a.

On Rajesh's failure to pay the installment due on 30-6-2005 it was agreed that Rajesh would return 'Three trucks' to Hire Vendor and remaining 'four' could be retained by him. The returning price of 'Three Trucks' was Rs. 40,500. Rajesh charges depreciation @ 20% p.a.

Hire Vendor after spending Rs. 1,000 on repairs sold away all the three trucks for Rs.40,000. Show Trucks Account and Hire Vendor's Account in the Books of Rajesh and Rajesh's Account and Goods Repossessed Account in the books of the Hire Vendor assuming that their books are closed on 30th June every year. **[B.Com. (H), DU, 1991-Modified]**

Solution :

In the Books of Rajesh

TRUCKS ACCOUNT

		Rs.			Rs.
2004			2004		
July 1	To Hire Vendor A/c	3,50,000	June 30	By Depreciation @ 20%	70,000
				By Hire Vendor's Account	40,500
				By Profit & Loss A/c* (BF)	79,500
				By Balance c/d	1,60,000
		3,50,000			3,50,000
2005					
July 1	To Balance b/d	1,60,000			

HIRE VENDOR'S ACCOUNT

		Rs.			Rs.
2004			2004		
Jan. 1	To Bank (Down Payment)	70,000	July 1	By Trucks	3,50,000
Dec. 31	To Bank (Ist Installment)	63,000	Dec. 31	By Interest @ 5% p.a. for 6 months on Rs. 2,80,000	7,000
2005			2005		
June 30	To Truck A/c	40,500	June 30	By Interest @ 5% p.a. on Rs. 2,24,000 for 6 months	5,600
	To Balance c/d	1,89,100			
		3,62,600			3,62,600

Loss on Repossession can also be worked out as under :

	Rs.
Written down value of Three Trucks repossessed as on the date of default (i.e. cost less Depreciation) (1,50,000 Less Dep. @ 20%)	1,20,000
Less "Agreed Value" as given in the question	40,500
Loss on repossession	79,500

In the Books of Hire Vendors

RAJESH ACCOUNT

		Rs.			Rs.
2004			2004		
July 1	To Hire-Purchase Sales	3,50,000	July 1	By Bank (Down Payment)	70,000
Dec. 31	To Interest @ 5% p.a. on Rs. 2,80,000 for 6 months	7,000	Dec. 31	By Bank (1st Installment)	63,000
2005			2005		
June 30	To Interest @ 5% p.a. on Rs. 2,24,000 for 6 months	5,600	June 30	By Goods Repossessed	40,500
				By Balance c/d	1,89,100
		3,62,600			3,62,600
2006					
July 1	To Balance b/d	1,89,100			

GOODS REPOSSESSED A/C

		Rs.			Rs.
2005			2005		
June 30	To Rajesh Account	40,500	June 30	By Bank (Resale)	40,000
	To Cash (Expenses)	1,000		By Profit & Loss A/c (Loss)	1,500
		41,500			41,500

Illustration 14

B Company purchased on 1st October, 2007 from D Company five trucks costing 5,00,000 each on hire-purchase system. Payment was to be made as follows :

10% of cash price down and four instalments of 25% of cash price at the end of each subsequent half-year.

Payment due on 30th September, 2008 could not be made. After negotiation, the hire purchaser was allowed to keep three trucks on the condition that the value of the other two trucks would be adjusted against the amount due, the trucks being valued at cost less 25% depreciation.

B co. closes its books on 31st March each year and depreciation is charged at 15% p.a. on trucks on the original cost.

Prepare : Trucks Account, D Company Account, B Company Account.

[B. Com (P) D.U., 1999, Modified]

Solution :

	Rs.
Cash price of 5 trucks @ Rs. 5,00,000 each	25,00,000
Cash down payment (10% of Cash Price)	2,50,000
Instalment (25% of Cash Price)	6,25,000
Total interest (i.e., 10% of cash price)	2,50,000

Since the rate of interest has not been given the amount of interest included in each instalment will be ascertained by dividing the total interest in the ratio of hire-purchase price outstanding in the beginning of each period. The ratio comes to 4 : 3 : 2 : 1.

Instalment		Interest
1	2,50,000 × 4/10	1,00,000
2	2,50,000 × 3 /10	75,000
3	2,50,000 × 2/10	50,000
4	2,50,000 × 1/10	25,000

The ledger account can now be prepared as follows :

Books of B (Hire Purchaser)

TRUCKS ACCOUNT

		Rs.			Rs.
2007 Oct. 1	To D Co. A/c (hire Vendor)	25,00,000	2008 March 31	By Depreciation A/c	1,87,500
				By Balance c/d	23,12,500
		25,00,000			25,00,000
2008 Apr. 1	To Balance b/d	23,12,500	2008 Sept. 30	By Depreciation A/c	1,87,500
				By D Co. (Hire Vendor)	7,50,000
				By Profit & Loss A/c (Loss on seizure of trucks)	1,00,000
				By Balance c/d	12,75,000
		23,12,500			23,12,500

D COMPANY ACCOUNT (HIRE VENDOR)

		Rs.			Rs.
2007 Oct. 1	To Bank (Cash Down)	2,50,000	2007 Oct. 1	By Truck Account	25,00,000
2008	To Bank	6,25,000	2008		
Mar. 31	To balance c/d	17,25,000	Mar. 31	By Interest	1,00,000
		26,00,000			26,00,000
2008 Sep. 30	To Trucks A/c	7,50,000	2008 1 Apr.	By Balance b/d	17,25,000
Sep. 30	To Balance c/d	10,50,000		By Interest	75,000
		18,00,000			18,00,000

Loss on truck seized

	Rs.
Book value of trucks as per B's Company Books	
(Rs. 10,00,000 less Depreciation @ 15% on Original cost Rs. 1,50,000) =	8,50,000
Less : Value at which truck have ben taken by the vendor	7,50,000
(10,00,000 less Depreciation @ 25% Rs. 2,50,000)	
Loss on seizure	1,00,000

Books of Hire Vendor (D. Company)

B COMPANY ACCOUNT

		Rs.			Rs.
2007			2007		
Oct. 1	To H.P. Sales A/c	25,00,000	Oct. 1	By Cash	2,50,000
2008			2008		
March 31	To Interest	1,00,000	March 31	By Cash	6,25,000
				By Balance b/d	17,25,000
		26,00,000			26,00,000
2008			2008		
Apr 1	To Balance c/d	17,25,000	Sept. 30	By Goods Repossessed A/c	7,50,000
2008			2008		
Sept 30	To Interest	75,000	Sept. 30	By Balance c/d	10,50,000
		18,00,000			18,00,000

Illustration 15

On 1st April, 2005, Rahul purchased five machines on hire purchase system from Varun Ltd. The cash price of each machine was Rs. 30,000, the terms of payment were :

(a) Down Payment Rs. 30,000.

(b) Six half yearly instalments of Rs. 23,500 each payable on September 30 and March 31 every year.

Rahul wrote off depreciation @ 10% p.a. on diminishing balance method.

Rahul paid installment due upto March 31, 2007 but due to financial crisis could not pay the installmen due on September 30, 2007. After negotiations, it was agreed that the vendor would repossess two machines for which Rahul would get credit for the amount paid towards thecost of two machines less 25% thereof.

Varun Ltd. sold both the machines for Rs. 23,800 after incurring Rs. 700 on repairs.

You are aksed to give

(i) Varun Ltd. A/c, Machines A/c in the books of Rahul and

(ii) Rahul A/c and Goods Repossessed A/c in the books of Varun Ltd.

[B. Com (P), D.U. 2005 (b)]

Solution :

In the books of Rahul

MACHINES ACCOUNT

		Rs.			Rs.
2005			2006		
April 1	To Varun Ltd.	1,50,000	March 31	By Depreciation	15,000
				By Balance c/d	1,35,000
		1,50,000			1,50,000
2006			2007		
April 1	To Balance b/d	1,35,000	March 31	By Depreciation A/c	13,500
				By Hire Vendor A/c (4)	31,800
				By P & L A/c (Loss)	16,800
				By Balance c/d (5)	72,900
		1,35,000			1,35,000

VARUN'S ACCOUNT

		Rs.			Rs.
01.04.05	To Bank A/c	30,000	01.04.05	By Machines A/c	1,50,000
30.09.05	To Bank A/c	23,500	30.09.05	By Interest A/c	6,000
31.03.05	To Bank A/c	23,500	31.03.06	By Interest A/c	5,000
31.03.05	To Balance c/d	84,000			
		1,61,000			1,61,000
30.09.06	To Bank A/c	23,500	01.04.05	By Balance b/d	84,000
31.03.07	To Bank A/c	23,500	30.09.06	By Interest A/c	4,000
31.03.07	By Balance c/d	44,000	31.03.07	By Interest A/c	3,000
		91,000			91,000
30.09.07	To Machines A/c	31,800	01.04.07	By Balance b/d	44,000
	To Balance c/d	14,200	30.09.07	By Interest A/c	2,000
		46,000			46,000

In The Books of Varun Ltd.

RAHUL'S ACCOUNT

		Rs.			Rs.
01.04.05	To Hire Purchase Sales	1,50,000	01.04.05	By Bank A/c	30,000
30.09.05	To Interest A/c	6,000	30.09.05	By Bank A/c	23,500
31.03.06	To Interest A/c	5,000	31.03.06	By Bank A/c	23,500
			31.03.06	By Balance c/d	84,000
		1,61,000			1,61,000

01.04.06	To Balance b/d	84,000	30.09.06	By Bank A/c	23,500
30.09.06	To Interest A/c	4,000	31.03.07	By Bank A/c	23,500
31.03.07	To Interest A/c	3,000	31.03.07	By Balance c/d	44,000
		91,000			91,000
01.04.07	To Balance b/d	44,000	30.09.07	By Goods Repossessed A/c	31,800 *
30.09.07	To Interest A/c	2,000	30.09.07	By Balance c/d	14,200
		46,000			46,000

GOODS REPOSSESSED A/C

		Rs.			Rs.
30.09.07	To Rahul A/c	31,800	30.09.07	By Cash (Sale)	23,800
	To Cash (Expenses)	700		By P & L A/c (Loss)	8,700
		32,500			32,500

* Value of repossessed goods :	Rs.
Down payment	30,000
Four Instalments of Rs.23,500 each	94,000
Total amount paid	1,24,000
Less Interest paid with instalments (6000+5000+4000+3000)	(18,000)
Cash price paid on 5 machines	1,06,000
Cash price paid on 2 machines	42,400
Less 25%	10,600
	31,800

Working Note :

Interest = Hire-Purchase Less Cash Price

HPP = DP + 23,500 × 6

$= 30{,}000 + 1{,}41{,}000 \quad = 1{,}71{,}000$

Cash Price (30,000 × 5) = 1,50,000

Interest = 21,000

Apportioned in the 6 : 5 : 4 : 3 : 2 : 1 ratio.

QUESTIONS

1. Distinguish between Hire-purchase system, Installment sale and credit sale.
2. Explain the provisions of Hire- purchase agreement under Hire Purchase Act. 1972.
3. Is there any statutory limit on hire-purchase charges? Explain.
4. Write short notes on :

   (i) Default and repossession

(ii) Cash price and Hire purchase price

5. Distinguish between Hire Purchase System and Installment Purchase System.

[B.Com. (H), DU, 1996, 1997 and 1998]

PROBLEMS

1. A purchased a motor car on 1st January 2003 from Hindustan Motors Ltd., on Hire Purchase basis. He agreed to pay Rs. 34,500 on taking delivery of the motor car and pay three annual installments of Rs. 66,550 each. The Vendors charged interest @ 10% p.a. A wrote off depreciation @ 20% p.a. on the straight line basis. Pass Journal Entries in the Books of A.

   Ans. Cash Value : Rs. 2,00,000, Interest : Rs. 16,550; Rs.-11,550; Rs. 6,050.

2. Mr. X bought a machine on 1 January 2003 on Hire Purchase basis of payment which were as follows :

	Rs.
On signing the agreement	17,500
At the end of First year	21,000
At the end of Second year	12,250
At the end of Third year	7,700
	58,450

   Interest included in Rs. 58,450 was charged on the cash price @ 10% p.a. You are asked to ascertain the cash price of the machine and write up the necessary ledger accounts in the books of Mr. X.

   Ans. Cash Value : Rs. 52,500; Interest : Rs. 3,500, Rs. 1,750, Rs. 700.

3. Mr. Y acquired on 1 January 2003 a machine under Hire Purchase agreement which provides for 5 half-yearly installments of Rs. 15,000 each, the first installment being due on 1st July 2003 assuming that the applicable rate of interest is 10% p.a. Calculate the Cash value of the machine. **[C.A. (Final), Adapted]**

   Ans. Cash Value : Rs. 64,940; Interest : Rs. 3,248, Rs. 2,660, Rs. 2,043, Rs. 1,395, Rs. 715.

4. ABC Ltd. sells Machine on the Hire Purchase System. The terms of payment for the sale of a Machine are : Rs. 25,000 on delivery, Rs. 26,000 at the end of the first year, Rs. 24,000 at the end of the second year, and Rs. 22,000 at the end of the third year, inclusive of financial charges.

   Find out the Cash Price of the Machine. **[CA. (Final), Adapted]**

   Ans. Cash Price : Rs. 85,000; Interest : Rs. 6,000, Rs. 4,000, Rs. 2,000.

5. XYZ Co. Ltd. purchased a computer on Hire Purchase System on 1 January 2000 from ABC . ,td. and agreed to pay the price in five installments as stated below and also agreed to pay 10% interest on unpaid balance of Cash Price. XYZ Co. Ltd. decided to depreciate the computer by 10% on Reducing Balance Method. Ascertain the Cash Price and prepare the Computer account for Five years in the Books of XYZ Co. Ltd.

   1st Installment of Rs. 19,500 paid on 31-12-2000
   2nd Installment of Rs. 18,200 paid on 31-12-2001
   3rd Installment of Rs. 16,900 paid on 31-12-2002
   4th Installment of Rs. 15,600 paid on 31-12-2003
   5th Installment of Rs. 14,300 paid on 31-12-2004

   Ans. Cash Price : Rs. 65,000; Interest : Rs. 6,500, Rs. 5,200, Rs. 3,900, Rs. 2,600 & Rs. 1,300.

6.

On 1st July 2003, XY Ltd. purchased an Air-conditioner on Hire purchase basis, payments to be made Rs. 14,000 on the said date and the balance in three half-yearly installments of Rs. 11,480, Rs. Rs.10,416 and Rs. 8,820 commencing from 31st December 2003. The Vendor charged interest @ 10% p.a.

XY Ltd. closes their books annually on 31st December and provides depreciation @ 10% p.a. on Diminishing Balance in each year.

Determine the Cash Price of the Air conditioner and show the necessary ledger accounts in the books of XY Ltd. **[C.A. (Inter), Adapted]**

Ans. Cash Price : Rs. 42,000; Interest : Rs. 1,400 + Rs. 896 + Rs. 420.

7. S J Ltd. purchased a scooter on Hire Purchase System on 1st July 2003. The Hire Purchase Price of Rs. 30,000 is payable by bi-annual installments of Rs. 6,000 each. The Seller charges interest on unpaid Cash Price @ 6% p.a.

Calculate the Cash Price and prepare necessary accounts in the books of seller assuming that the payment is made on 1st January and 1st July and the accounts are closed on 31st December every year.

Ans. Cash Price : Rs. 27,478, Interest : Rs. 824 + Rs. 669 + Rs. 509 + Rs. 344 + Rs. 175.

8. ABC Ltd. had purchased a Computer under Hire Purchase System from XYZ Ltd. The terms of payment being Rs. 50,000 down on 1st January 2000 and 5 annual installments of Rs.27,500 each on 31st December. They charged depreciation on Computer @ 15% under diminishing balance system.

XYZ Ltd. had charged interest @ 10% p.a. Show the computer A/c and XYZ account to record the above transactions in the books of ABC Ltd. till the installments are paid off. ABC Ltd. has accounting year ending on 31st December each year. **[C.A. (Inter), Adapted]**

Ans. Cash Price : Rs. 1,54,245; Interest : Rs. 10,425, Rs. 8,718, Rs. 6,840, Rs. 4,773 and Rs.2,500.

9. A colour TV is sold on hire purchase for Rs. 7,995. An amount of Rs. 615 is payable on delivery and the balance in 12 quarterly installments of Rs. 615 each. The cash price is Rs. 6,825. Determine the amount of interest included in the hire purchase price which should be credited to the profit and loss account of the hire vendor. **[C.A. (Inter), Adapted]**

Ans. First year Rs. 630; Second year Rs. 390; Third year Rs. 150.

Hint. Apportion interest on the basis of total numbers of months falling between installments in each Year

Hence,	First year	—	12, 11, 10, 9 which is = 42
	Second year	—	8, 7, 6, 5 which is = 26
	Third year	—	4, 3, 2, 1 which is = 10
			i.e., in 21: 13: 5 ratio

10. On 1st January 2001, M/s XYZ & Co. took delivery from ABC Ltd. of one Machine on Hire Purchase System, Rs. 10,000 being paid on delivery and the balance in five installments of Rs.15,000 each payable annually on 31st December. The Vendor Co. charges interest @ 5% p.a. on yearly balance. The Cash down value of the Machinery was Rs. 75,000.

Show the Vendors A/c, Interest A/c, Machinery A/c in the books M/s XYZ & Co. for five years. Provide depreciation @ 20% on Diminishing Balance Method. **[B.Com., DU, Modified]**

Ans. Interest : Rs. 3,250; Rs. 2,665; Rs. 2,045; Rs. 1,400; and Rs. 640.

11. Mr. A purchased an A.C. on 1st January 1999 under Hire Purchase System. The Cash Price of the A.C. was Rs. 37,250. The terms of the agreement provided at the end of every six months, for the payments of Rs. 10,000 over two years.

The first payment was to be made on 30th June 1999. The rate of interest was 6% p.a. Mr. A writes off 10% depreciation on the reducing balance system and closes his books on the 30th June every year.

Mr. A could not pay the installment due on 30th June 2000 and as a result, the hire vendor took back the possession of the A.C.

Give the A.C. A/c and Vendor's A/c in the Books of Mr. A and show the loss suffered by him.

[B.Com., DU, Modified]

Ans. Interest : Rs. 1,118; Rs. 850; Rs. 578; Rs. 205. Loss on repossession Rs. 12,053

12. Mr. X purchased a Computer from CAB Co. for Rs. 70,000, payment to be made Rs. 18,750 down and three installments of Rs. 18,750 each at the end of each year. Mr. X depreciates assets @ 10% p.a. on Written Down Value Method.

Because of the financial difficulties, Mr. X after having paid down payment and first installment at the end of the first year could not pay second installment and the seller took possession of the Computer.

Prepare Computer Account and Hire Vendor's Account in the books of Mr. X. Also give Hire Purchaser Account in the books of CAB Co.

Ans. Interest : Rs. 2,500; Rs. 1,667; and Rs. 833. Loss on repossession: Rs. 23,633.

13. On 1st January 2003, P purchased furniture from Q on Hire Purchase basis. Cash price of the furniture was Rs. 30,000. Rs. 7,740 to be paid on the date of purchase and five annual installments of Rs. 5,000 payable on 31st December every year. Q charged interest @ 4% p.a., on the yearly Balances. P failed to pay the installment due on 31st December 2004. Thereupon Q took possession of the furniture and value the same in his books after charging 20% depreciation on Diminishing balance Method annually. In January 2005, he incurred Rs. 1,250 as reconditioning and repairing expenses and resold the furniture for Rs. 22,500. Show P's A/c and Repossessed Furniture A/c in the Books of Q. **[B.Com., DU, Modified]**

Ans. Interest : Rs. 890 and Rs. 726. Value of Repossessed Furniture : Rs. 19,200. Profit on Re-sale : Rs. 2,050.

14. ABC Traders Purchased two Scooters costing Rs. 48,000 each from HCL Motors on 1 st January 2002 under Hire Purchase System. The terms were: Payment on delivery Rs. 12,000 for each scooter and balance in three equal installments together with interest at 10% p.a. to be paid at the end of each year.

ABC Traders writes off 25% depreciation on the Diminishing Balance Method.

ABC Traders paid the instilments due on 31st December 2002 and on 31st December 2003 but could not pay the final installment.

HCL Motors repossessed one Scooter adjusting its value against the amount due. The repossession was done on the basis of 30% Depreciation on Diminishing Balance Method.

Write up the ledger accounts in the books of HCL Motors showing the above transactions.

[C. A.-Adapted]

Ans. Value of Scooter repossessed : Rs. 16,464, Value of Machine Retained : Rs. 20,250.

15. B purchased seven Cars on Hire Purchase System on 1-7-2003. The Cash Price of each car was Rs. 95,000. He was to pay 20% of the cash Purchase Price at the time of delivery and the balance in five half-yearly installments starting from 31-12-2003 with interest @ 5%.

On B's failure to pay the installment due on 30-06-2004, it was agreed that B would return 3 cars to the Vendor and remaining 4 would be retained by him. The vendor agreed to allow him a credit for the amount paid against these 3 cars less 25%.

Show the relevant A/cs in the Books of B assuming that his books are closed on 30th in June every year and depreciation @ 20% is charged on Cars.

Show also B's a/c in the books of Vendor. **[B.Com., DU, Modified]**

Ans. Value of Seized Cars : Rs. 76,950, Value of Retained Cars : Rs. 3,04,000.

16. On 1st January 2000, five Computers were purchased by X under Hire Purchase System. The Cash Price of each Computer is Rs. 82,500. The payment was to be made as follows :

10% cash down.

25% of cash price at the end of each of the subsequent half-years.

The payment due on 31st December 2000 could not be made and hence Computers were seized by the vendor but after negotiations, X was allowed to keep three Computers on the condition that the value of the other two Computers would be adjusted against the amount due, the Computers being valued at cost less 25% depreciation. X's books were closed on 30th June each year and he charged 15% depreciation on Computers on the original cost.

The Vendor spent Rs. 9,000 on getting the Computer reconditioned and sold them for Rs.1,42,500. Show the various accounts in the books of both parties. **[B.Com., DU, Adapted]**

Ans. Loss on Default to buyer : Rs. 16,500, Profit to Vendor : Rs. 9,750.

17. PQ Vehicles Ltd. purchased 2 Cars, each costing Rs. 2,00,000 from Auto Ltd. on 1st January 1999 on Hire Purchase System. The terms were :

Payment on Delivery Rs. 50,000 for each Car.

Remainder in 3 equal installments altogether with interest @ 10% p.a. to be paid at the end of each year.

PQ Vehicles Ltd. writes off 25% depreciation each year on Diminishing Balance Method. It paid the installments due on 31st December 1999 and 31st December 2000 but could not pay the final installment. Auto Ltd. repossessed one car adjusting its value against the amount due. The repossession was done on the basis of 30% depreciation on the diminishing balance method. The vendor spent Rs. 21,400 for the Repairs and Overhauling of the car and sold it for Rs. 1,00,000.

Write up the ledger accounts in the books of both parties. **[CA & ICWA (Inter), Adapted]**

Ans. Loss on default – Rs. 15,775

Profit on Resale – Rs. 10,000

18. X Transport Ltd. Purchased from Mahindra Motors 3 tempos costing Rs. 1,00,000 each on hire purchase basis on 1-1-2005 20% of the cost was to be paid down and the balance in 3 equal annual installments together with interest @ 9% at the end of each year. X Transport Ltd. paid the installments due on 31st December, 2005 but could not pay thereafter. Mahindra Motors agreed to leave one tempo with the purchaser on 1-1-2006 adjusting the value of the other two tempos against the amount due on that date. The tempos recovered were valued on the basis of 30% depreciation annually. X transport Ltd. Charges depreciation on tempos @ 20% on diminishing balance method.

M/s. Mahindra Motors incurred Rs. 10,000 on repairs of tempos and resold them at profit of 5% on total cost. Write up necessary ledger accounts in the books of both parties giving effect to the above transactions.

[B.Com (P), D.U, 1997]

Ans. Balance to the Tempo A/c Rs. 64,000

Balance to The Mahindra Motors A/c Rs. 34,400

Loss on Repossession Rs. 20,000

19. X purchased 5 trucks on hire-purchase basis on October1, 2006. The cash price of each truck was Rs. 5,50,000. X was to pay 20% of the cash price at the time of delivery and 25% of the cash price at the end of each of the four subsequent half-years beginning from March 31, 2007.

On X's failure to pay the installment due on September 30, 2007, it was agreed that X could keep three trucks on the condition that the value of the two trucks would be adjusted against the amount due, the trucks being valued at cost less 25% depreciation.

Show the relevant accounts in the books of X, assuming that the books of account are closed every year on March 31, and depreciation @ 15% is charged on the original cost of the trucks.

[C.S. Foundation, Dec-1997]

Ans.	Loss on Repossession	Rs. 1,10,000
	Balance of Trucks A/c	Rs. 15,26,250
	Balance of Hire Vendor A/c	Rs. 10,72,500

20. On 1-1-2007 X, a television dealer bought 5 television sets from Dolphia Television Co. on hire-purchase basis. The cash price of each set was Rs. 20,000. it was agreed that Rs. 25,000 should be paid immediately and the balance in three installments of Rs. 30,000 each at the end of the each year. The television Co. charges interest @ 10% p.a. The buyer depreciates television sets at 20% p.a. on the diminishing balance method.

X paid cash down and two installments but failed to pay the last installment. Consequently, the Television Co. repossessed three sets leaving two sets with the buyer and adjusting the value of 3 sets against the amount due. The sets repossessed were valued on the basis of 30% depreciation p.a. on the written down value. The sets repossessed were sold by the Television Co. for Rs. 30,000 after necessary repairs amounting to Rs. 5,000. Open the necessary ledger accounts in the book of both the parties.

[Delhi, B.Com (P), D.U, 1996 (Modified)]

Ans.	Loss on repossession	Rs. 10,140
	Balance of T.V sets A/c	Rs. 20,480
	Balance of Hire vendor A/c	Rs. 9,420

❑❑❑

Unit-VI

12 BRANCH ACCOUNTING

The new, growing or expanding organisations have various options to exercise for the purpose of selling and distribution of their products. Such organisations aim to cover wide range of area to reach maximum number of customers thereby increasing the volume of turnover. Usually, in order to eliminate middlemen (Wholesalers & Retailers), to retain control over distribution, to keep the business secrets intact, and to avoid the chances of duplicate or similar products being mixed with the genuine ones so as to make customers quality conscious, most organisations rely upon branches. These branches are spread over a big area. These may be located in the same city, or different cities within the country or even outside country. The main establishments are known as Head Office and its subsidiary units within a city, country or outside country are known as branches. In India the well-known branches all over the country are that of Bata Shoe Co., Mafat Lal Group, Binny's Show-rooms, & DCM Ltd. From the accounting point of view these branches can be divided in the three categories :

1. Dependent Branches
2. Independent or Autonomous Branches
3. Foreign Branches.

1. ACCOUNTING FOR THE DEPENDENT BRANCHES

Dependent Branches, as the name itself suggests are wholly and mainly dependent on Head office for all their requirements. These branches get all instructions from the head office in connection with its operation or activities. Such branches are just the Sales Depots or outlets of main establishment (Head office), which perform all functions of sending goods for the branch, meeting expenses thereof, and maintaining accounting records. Dependent branches perform only sales functions and send information relating to sales, Cash or Credit, stock unsold and expenses (petty) incurred if any. The salient features of dependent branches are as follows :

1. Branches get all their supplies (goods) from the Head office. Outside purchase is not allowed except under certain circumstances and with the prior permission from the head office.
2. Goods are sold by Branches at a price fixed by the Head office which sends goods either at cost or cost plus profit or at selling price.

3. Branches are allowed to sell goods in cash, on credit or for both as per the instructions of Head Office.
4. All expenses of Branch are paid by Head Office.
5. Branch, however, may be allowed to maintain petty Cash balance.
6. Branches are required to deposit all cash received from Customers in the Head Office Account of a Bank.
7. Branches do not perform accounting function but send all information to Head Office for accounting purposes. However, the branches are required to maintain :
   (i) A Stock register to record movement of goods to and fro Head Office.
   (ii) A Cash Book to record cash received from customers, remitted to H.O., received from H.O. and to ascertain balance due from customers or due to H.O.
   (iii) A Petty Cash Book showing details of petty expenses and the balance, if any.
   (iv) Debtors Ledger—to record credit sale.

ACCOUNTING TREATMENT IN THE BOOKS OF HEAD OFFICE

A Head Office may adopt any one of the following methods of accounting to ascertain the result of Branch operations :

(a) Debtors System (b) Stock and Debtors System
(c) Wholesale Branch System (d) Final Accounts System.

(a) Debtors System

Under this method, Head Office opens Branch Account, which is in the nature of Debtors Account. It debits the Branch Account with the goods sent and cash sent for expenses whereas credits the Branch Account with the amount of Cash received from branch, goods returned by branch and balances of various assets with the branch if any. That is why this system of accounting is known as Debtors System. However the Branch Account so prepared by Head Office is nominal by nature. The excess of credits over debits represents profits and excess of debits over credits shows loss incurred by the branch concerned.

JOURNAL ENTRIES IN THE BOOKS OF HEAD OFFICE

1. (a) When goods are sent to Branch at Cost

Branch Account	Dr	With the actual Cost
To Goods Sent to Branch Account		

(b) (i) When goods are sent to Branch at Invoice Price or Selling Price

Branch Account	Dr	With the amount of invoice
To Goods Sent to Branch Account		

(ii) Goods Sent to Branch Account	Dr	With the amount of profit element (Loading) included in invoice price.
To Branch Account		

2. When goods are returned by Branch to Head Office

(a) If goods were sent by H.O. at Cost :

Goods Sent to Branch Account	Dr	With the actual cost of goods
To Branch Account		returned

(b) If goods were sent by H.O. at Invoice or selling price

(i) Goods Sent to Branch Account	Dr	With the invoice price of goods
To Branch Account		returned
(ii) Branch Account	Dr	With the amount of profit (loading)
To Goods Sent to Branch Account		included in the goods returned

3. Transfer the Goods Sent to Branch Account to Trading Account

Goods Sent to Branch A/c	Dr	With actual cost of goods sent to
To Trading A/c		branch after adjusting the returns

4. When Cash/Cheque is sent for Branch expenses or Branch expenses are reimbursed by Head Office

Branch Account	Dr	With the actual account
To Cash/Bank Account		

5. When goods are sold by Branch either for Cash or on Credit

NO ENTRY

6. When Cash is remitted by Branch to H.O.

Cash/Bank A/c	Dr	With the amount actually received
To Branch Account		

7. When unsold stock is left with the Branch

(a) If goods were sent at cost

Closing Stock A/c	Dr	With the actual Cost
To Branch Account		

(b) If goods were sent at Invoice or selling price

(1) Closing Stock A/c	Dr	With the Invoice price of unsold
To Branch Account		stock
(2) Branch Account	Dr	With the profit (loading) element
To Stock Reserve		included in the closing stock

8. When there are other closing balances such as debtors, petty cash, prepaid expenses if any

Debtors Account	Dr	With the amount of debtors at the end
Petty Cash Account	Dr	With the balance of petty cash
Prepaid Expenses A/c	Dr	With the amount of prepaid expenses.
Furniture/Computer (Any other Asset) A/c	Dr	With the W.D.V. of the asset
To Branch Account		With the Total

9. On Closing the Branch Account

(i) If Credit side exceeds the debit side, there is profit : the entry will be :

Branch Account	Dr	With the amount of Profit
To General Profit & Loss A/c		

(ii) If debit side exceeds the credit side, there is loss and the entry will be :

General Profit and Loss A/c Dr With the amount of loss

To Branch Account

10. The closing balances of one year become the opening balances of next year and the following entry shall be recorded in the beginning of next year :

Branch Account Dr

To Petty Cash at Branch

To Branch Debtors

To Branch Stock

To Prepaid Expenses or

To Any other asset with the branch *

*It may be furniture, a typewriter or a computer etc.

Note : Branch Account does not show the depreciation on fixed, if any, but the written down value of the various fixed assets (Furniture, Typewriter, Computer etc.) is shown to the credit side of the Branch Account (i.e. opening value less depreciation).

11. Closing Balance of any liability (O/s expenses if any)

Branch Account Dr

To O/s Expenses Account

And a reverse entry shall be record in the beginning of next year

In the books of Head Officc
BRANCH ACCOUNT (AT COST) (A Format)

	Rs.		Rs.
To Balance b/d	------	By Balance b/d (liability)	------
Petty Cash	------	Outstanding Rent/Salaries	------
Debtors	------	By Cash/Bank A/c (Remittances) :	------
Prepaid Expenses	------	Cash Sales	------
Stock at Cost	------	Cash Collected from Debtors	------
Furniture/Computer (Any other Asset)	------	By Goods Sent to Branch	------
To Goods Sent to Branch (at Cost)	------	(Returns by branch at Cost)	------
To Cash/Bank	------	By Balance c/d	
Salaries	------	Petty Cash	------
Rent	------	Debtors	------
Advertisement or Other Expenses	------	Prepaid Expenses	------
To Balance c/d (liabilities)		Stock at Cost	------
O/s Expenses	------	Furniture/Computer (Any other Asset) after Depreciation	------
To Profit*- transferred to General		By Loss*- transferred to General	------
P& L A/c (B.F.)	------	P & L A/c (B.F.)	------
	------		------

*Balancing figure is either profit or loss.

Illustration 1 (General)

From the following information, prepare Branch Account in the Books of Head Office for the year ended 31st December 2008.

	1-1-2008	31-12-2008
	Rs.	Rs.
Stock with the Branch	48,000	72,000
Debtors	32,000	48,000
Petty Cash	130	30

During the year following transactions were recorded	Rs.
Goods sent to branch during the year	2,60,000
Cash Sales during the year	1,20,000
Credit Sales	1,44,000
Goods returned by Branch	4,800
Cash received from Credit Customers	1,28,000
Cash sent to Branch for :	
Rent	2,400
Salary	4,800

Solution : **In the books of Head Office**

BRANCH ACCOUNT

	Rs.			Rs.
To Balance b/d		By Bank (Remittances):		
Petty Cash	130	Cash Sales	1,20,000	
Debtors	32,000	Collected from Customers	1,28,000	248,000
Stock	48,000	By Goods Sent to Branch (Returns)		4,800
To Goods Sent to Branch	2,60,000	By Balance c/d		
To Cash (Expenses):		Petty Cash		30
Salaries	4,800	Debtors		48,000
Rent	2,400	Stock		72,000
To Profit-transferred to General Profit & Loss A/c	25,500			
	3,72,830			3,72,830

SOME IMPORTANT ADJUSTMENTS

1. Petty Cash—Simple Vs. Imprest

Petty Cash is maintained by Branch under two ways :

1. Simple 2. Imprest

Under simple method of petty cash there is no minimum balance, which is desired to be maintained. The branch manager is given cash for petty expenses when the present balance is fully exhausted. For example if in the beginning the petty Cash balance appear at Rs. 500 and out of it petty expenses paid by branch manager amount to Rs. 280, then the closing balance Rs 220 will be shown to the credit side of Branch Account as closing balance. When the entire of amount of remaining Rs. 220 are spent, then the Head Office will further advance any sum, not necessarily equal to initial balance of Rs. 500, to the branch manager to meet petty expenses. Hence under simple system of petty cash the opening and closing balances are need not to be equal.

However, under "Imprest System" of petty cash, the branch manager is reimbursed an amount equal to the actual expenses incurred by him during the year. Hence, a minimum balance of petty cash is always maintained under "imp-rest system" of petty cash and thus opening and closing balances of petty cash will always be equal.

There will be no Journal Entry when expenses are incurred and paid by branch manager under Simple System. The difference between the opening and closing balances, will automatically, set off and adjust the expenses in the Branch Account.

BRANCH ACCOUNT (Extract)

To Petty Cash Balance (Op.)	500		
		By Petty Cash Balance (Closing)	220

This shows that branch manager has paid Rs. 280 as petty expenses which stand debited to Branch Account.

However Under "Imprest system" of petty cash the following entry shall be recorded.

Branch Account	Dr	280	
To Cash			280

(Being petty Cash expenses reimbursed to branch manager)

BRANCH ACCOUNT (Extract)

To Petty Cash balance (Op.)	500*		
To Cash (P. Expenses)	280	By Petty Cash (closing) balance	500*

*No Change

2. Expenses paid by Branch Manager

When expenses relating to a branch are paid by the branch manager, then no entry is recorded in the Branch Account whereas this amount so incurred is deducted from the amount to be remitted to Head Office. **[Remittance is equal is Cash Sales and Cash Collected from credit customers.]**

3. Depreciation

In case there are certain fixed assets for branch use and it is desired to charge depreciation thereon, even then no entry for depreciation shall be recorded in the Branch Account. Only the opening value of asset and closing value (opening value less depreciation) of asset will be shown to the debit and credit side respectively and this process itself adjusts the depreciation for accounting purposes.

4. Purchase of Fixed Assets

In case any asset is acquired by the Branch Manager with the prior approval of Head Office, remittances made to Head Office will be reduced by the amount paid for acquiring the new asset. If it is purchased on credit basis, the same shall be shown as a liability at the end. However, in both the cases the assets so acquired is to be shown with closing balances of other assets.

5. Sale of Fixed Assets

A sale of any fixed asset (existing) increases the amount of remittances and in turn reduces the value of branch assets at the end. In case the fixed asset has been sold on credit basis, it will have no effect on remittances and branch assets at the end. Only the nature of fixed asset will be changed into current asset. Profit or Loss on sale of fixed asset is not shown at all in Branch Account.

6. Items Relating to Credit Sales

The items relating to Branch Debtors, except cash received from credit customers, are not shown to Branch Account. These being bad debts, returns inwards, discount allowed and allowances to debtors etc. are not shown in the Branch Account at all. These are taken to the credit side of Branch Debtors Account.

Illustration 2 (Simple Petty Cash)

Delhi Head Office sends goods to it's Kanpur Branch at cost. From the following particulars relating to Kanpur Branch for the year ended 31st December 2007, prepare Branch Account.

		Rs.
Stock at Kanpur Branch on	1st January	12,800
Debtors at Kanpur Branch on	1st January	11,200
Petty Cash at Kanpur Branch on	1st January	1,600
Goods sent to Branch		64,000
Cash Sales		24,000
Cash received from Credit Customers		48,000
Goods returned by Branch		3,200
Expenses paid by Head office :		
Salaries		12,800
Rent		1,600
Petty Expenses		1,920
Bad debts		800
Good returned by credit customers		6,400
Discount allowed		2,400
Debtors as on 31st December		16,000
Stock as on 31st December		19,200
Petty cash as on 31st December		1,280

Solution :

In the Books of Delhi Head Office

KANPUR BRANCH ACCOUNT

	Rs.			Rs.
To Balance b/d		By Bank (Remittances):		
Stock	12,800	Cash Sales	24,000	
Debtors	11,200	Cash received from credit		
Petty Cash	1,600	Customers	48,000	72,000

To Goods Sent to Branch	64,000	By Goods Sent to Branch (Returns)	3,200
To Cash (Expenses):		By Balance c/d	
Salaries	12,800	Stock	19,200
Rent	1,600	Debtors	16,000
Petty Expenses	1,920	Petty Cash	1,280
To Profit-transferred to General			
P&LA/c	5,760		
	1,11,680		1,11,680

"CALCULATION OF MISSING FIGURE"

Sometime the opening or closing balances of some of the assets or cash received from debtors are not given in the question, and in the absence of such information the Branch Account cannot be prepared and as such profit or loss cannot be ascertained. In order to locate the missing figure respective assets accounts are prepared. Take for example the closing balance of debtors is not given. Then a Branch Debtors Account will be prepared. It starts with an opening balance, if any, and debited with the credit sales or items which increase the amount of debtors. It is credited with the items reducing the amount of debtors such as cash received from debtors, B/R, bad debts, returns inwards etc. The balancing figure is the closing balance of debtors. Similarly other assets accounts such as Petty Cash, Stock or Furniture Account may be opened to trace the missing figure. The format of Debtors Account is as follows :

SUNDRY DEBTORS ACCOUNT (Format)

	Rs.		Rs.
To Balance b/d (Opening)	------	By Cash Received from debtors	------
To Credit Sales	------	By Bills Receivables	------
To Bills Receivable Dishonored	------	By Returns Inwards	------
		By Discount Allowed	------
		By Bad debts	------
		By Allowances	------
		By Balance c/d (Closing)	------
	------		------

Illustration 3

All Goods are sent by Delhi Head Office to its branches. The Branches are supposed to deposit cash daily to the Head Office Account in the Bank. From the following particulars prepare Branch Account :

	Rs.
Stock (1st January)	2,64,000
Debtors (1st January)	40,800
Petty Cash (1st January)	2,400
Goods sent to Branch	4,80,000
Cash received from credit customers	5,04,000

Cash sales	63,600
Goods returned to Head Office	9,600
Cheques sent to branch for : Rent	14,400
Salaries	24,800
Other Expenses	1,600
Returns Inward	12,000
Bad debts	7,200
Credit sales	5,36,400
Allowances to Customers	6,000
Stock (31st December)	3,13,000
Petty Cash	2,000

In the Books of Delhi Head Office

BRANCH ACCOUNT

	Rs.			Rs.
To Balance b/d		By Bank (Remittances) :		
Stock	2,64,000	Cash Sales	63,600	
Debtors	40,800	Cash Received from		
Petty Cash	2,400	Credit Customers	5,04,000	5,67,600
To Goods Sent to Branch	4,80,000	By Goods Sent to Branch (Returns)		9,600
To Cash (Expenses):		By Balance c/d		
Salaries	14,400	Stock		3,13,000
Rent	24,800	Debtors		48,000
Other Expenses	1,600	Petty Cash		2,000
To Profit-transferred to				
General P & L A/c	1,12,200			
	9,40,200			9,40,200

BRANCH DEBTORS A/C

	Rs.		Rs.
To Balance b/d	40,800	By Cash	5,04,000
To Credit Sales	5,36,400	By Returns Inwards	12,000
		By Allowances	6,000
		By Bad debts	7,200
		By Balance c/d (B.F.)	48,000
	5,77,200		5,77,200

Illustration 4 (Petty Cash on Imp-rest System)

Kanpur Branch receives all goods from its Allahabad Head Office who pays all branch expenses except petty expenses, which are met by Branch Manager who maintains petty cash on imp rest basis.

All cash received is deposited in Head Office Bank Account the same day. From the following particulars, you are required to ascertain profit or loss made by Branch under Debtors system.

2007	Rs.		Rs.
Jan. 1 Petty Cash	2,500	Goods returned by Customers	3,500
Debtors	28,500	Cash sent for :	
Stock	37,500	Salaries	30,000
Transactions during the year:		Rent	20,000
Goods sent to Branch	2,56,000	2007	
Allowance to Customers	500	Dec. 31	
Goods returned by Branch	16,000	Stock	50,800
Cash Sales	87,000	Debtors	35,000
Credit Sales	2,45,000	Petty Cash	?
Discount Allowed	2,500		

Bad debts	1,500
Petty Expenses paid by Branch	1,200
Furniture purchased by Branch with the prior Permission of Head Office	15,000

It is decided to charge depreciation @ 10% on Furniture

Solution : **In the Books of Head Office**

KANPUR BRANCH ACCOUNT

	Rs.			Rs.
To Balance b/d		By Bank (Remittances)		
Stock	37,500	Cash Sales	87,000	
Debtors	28,500	*Collected from Debtors	2,30,500	
Petty Cash	2,500	*Less* Furniture Purchased	(15,000)	3,02,500
To Goods Sent to Branch	2,56,000	By Goods Sent to Branch (Returns)		15,000
To Cash (Expenses):		By Balance c/d		
Salaries	30,000	Stock		50,800
Rent	20,000	Debtors		35,000
Petty Expenses	1,200	Petty Cash		2,500
To Profit-transferred to		Furniture (15,000 - 1,500)		13,500
General P & L A/c	43,600			
	4,19,300			4,19,300

PETTY CASH A/C

	Rs.		Rs.
To Balance b/d	2,500	By Expenses	1,200
To Cash (Reimbursement)	1,200	By Balance c/d	2,500
	3,700		3,700

BRANCH DEBTORS A/C

	Rs.		Rs.
To Balance b/d	28,500	By Cash (Balancing figure)	2,30,500
To Credit Sales	2,45,000	By Returns Inwards	3,500
		By Allowances	500
		By Bad debts	1,500
		By Discount Allowed	2,500
		By Balance c/d	35,000
	2,73,500		2,73,500

Note : Under Imp-rest System of Petty cash, the Head office reimburses the Branch to the extent of actual petty expenses paid by Branch.

I. WHEN GOODS ARE SENT TO BRANCH AT INVOICE PRICE

In order to maintain business secrets and to conceal margin of profits from Branch Manager, the Head Office usually sends goods to its branch at invoice or selling price, which is made of cost plus profit margin. Under this situation Branch Manager does not know the actual cost of goods sent by Head Office and the profit earned thereon. However, while preparing Branch Account, the Head Office makes necessary adjustment entries for the purpose of setting off the profit element (margin or loading) included in the various items to ascertain the actual profits earned by Branch. The accounts, which include profit margin, are :

1. Goods sent to Branch
2. Goods returned by Branch
3. Opening Stock with Branch
4. Closing Stock with Branch

Following adjustment entries are recorded :

1. For Goods sent to Branch at invoice price

   Goods Sent to Branch A/c Dr with the amount of loading

   To Branch Account

   (Being loading on GSTB adjusted or credited to Branch A/c)

2. For Goods returned by Branch

   Branch Account Dr with the amount of loading

   To Goods Sent to Branch A/c

   (Being loading on Goods returned adjusted)

Alternatively only one entry for Goods sent less Return may be recorded for adjusting the loading.

3. Adjustment entry for Opening stock

   Stock Reserve A/c Dr with the amount of loading

   To Branch Account

4. Adjustment entry for closing stock

   Branch Account Dr with the amount of loading

   To Stock Reserve Account

There is no difference between the formats of Branch Account at cost and Branch Account at invoice price. The format of Branch Account (at cost) has already been given when the goods are sent at cost. But when the goods are sent at invoice or selling price the above additional entries are also recorded to set off the inflated figures of above aforesaid accounts which may be shown as on next page :

BRANCH ACCOUNT AT INVOICE PRICE (Only additional & inflated items)

	Rs.		Rs.
To Balance b/d		By ------	------
Stock (1)	at Invoice Price	------	------
------		By Stock Reserve (1)	Profit element
------		(Loading on Op. Stock)	
------		By Goods Sent to Branch (3)	at Invoice Price
To Goods Sent to branch (2)	at Invoice Price	(Goods Returned)	
To Goods to Branch (3)	at profit	By Goods Sent to Branch (2)	Profit
(Loading on goods returned)	Element	(Loading on Goods sent)	Element
To Stock Reserve (4)	"	By Balance c/d	
(Loading on Closing Stock)		Stock (4)	at Invoice
------		------	Price
------		------	
------		------	

CALCULATION OF LOADING OR PROFIT ELEMENT

While calculating the loading or profit element which is included in the various accounts, as explained above, the care must be taken to find out actual amount of loading. The main point to note is the expression of profit i.e. whether profits are being expressed in relation to cost price or Invoice/ Selling price. In case profits are expressed in relation to cost, then cost should be taken 100 and if the profits are given in relation to Invoice price or selling price then Invoice price or selling price should be presumed to be 100. Take for example if goods are sent at cost plus 25%, then rate of profit in terms of cost is 25% or $\frac{1}{4}$ and in term of invoice price it is $\frac{25}{125}$ i.e., $-\frac{1}{5}$ or 20% This is worked out as under.

Cost price = 100 (because profits are expressed in terms of cost)

Profit = 25

Invoice Price = 125 (cost + profit)

And similarly if goods are sent at a profit of 25% of 25% on invoice or selling price, the rate of profit in relation to "Invoice Price" is 25% or $\frac{1}{4}$ and in terms of "Cost Price" it is $\frac{1}{3}$ or $33\frac{1}{3}$ % It is arrived at as under :

Ler Invoice Price be 100

Profit = 25

Cost price = (100 – 25) 75 (Invoice price less profit)

Rate of profit to the cost is $\frac{25}{75}$ i.e., $\frac{1}{3}$ or $33\frac{1}{3}$ %

There can be innumerable examples of fractions as well (as shown under) :

1. Profit rate in relation to Cost	=	Profit in relation to Invoice Price
If it is $\frac{1}{5}$	=	$\frac{1}{6}$ i.e., $\frac{1}{(5+1)}$
$\frac{2}{7}$	=	$\frac{2}{9}$ i.e., $\frac{2}{(7+2)}$
$\frac{3}{7}$	=	$\frac{3}{10}$ i.e., $\frac{3}{(7+3)}$
$\frac{4}{15}$	=	$\frac{4}{19}$ i.e., $\frac{4}{(15+4)}$
$\frac{6}{19}$	=	$\frac{6}{25}$ i.e., $\frac{6}{(19+6)}$ and so on

II. WHEN PROFITS ARE EXPRESSED IN RELATION TO INVOICE PRICE

1. Profit rate in relation to Invoice Price	=	Profit in relation to relation to Cost
If it is $\frac{1}{7}$	=	$\frac{1}{6}$ i.e., $\frac{1}{(7-1)}$
$\frac{2}{9}$	=	$\frac{2}{7}$ i.e., $\frac{2}{(9-2)}$
$\frac{3}{10}$	=	$\frac{3}{7}$ i.e., $\frac{3}{(10-3)}$
$\frac{4}{15}$	=	$\frac{4}{11}$ i.e., $\frac{4}{(15-4)}$ and so on

Illustration 5 (Branch Account at Invoice Price)

The Chennai Head Office sends goods to its branches at cost plus 25%. There is a standing instruction for branches to send all cash daily to Head Office. All expenses of branch are paid by Kolkata Head Office except petty cash expenses, which are met by Branch itself which is allowed to maintain petty cash balance of Rs. 2,000 on imprest system.

	Rs.
Stock at Branch on 1st January at In voice Price	25,600
Debtors at Branch on 1st January	12,800
Petty Cash balance on 1st January	2,000
Branch Prepaid Rent on 1st January	500
Branch Furniture on 1st January	19,200
Goods sent to Branch at Invoice Price	95,000
Goods returned by Branch at Invoice Price	5,000
Cash sent to Branch for Expenses :	
Salaries @ Rs. 2,000 p.m.	24,000
Rent paid @ Rs. 1,500 p.m.	18,000

Petty Expenses	900
Cash Sales at Branch	45,000
Cash collected from credit customers of Branch	75,000
Credit sales made at Branch	85,000
Bad debts	500
Discount allowed to credit customers	800
Stock at Branch on 31st December	35,000

Depreciate furniture @ 10%

You are required to prepare Branch Account in the H.O. Books

Solution : **In the Books of Head Office**

BRANCH ACCOUNT

	Rs.			Rs.
To Balance b/d		By Bank (Remittances)		
Stock	25,600	Cash Sales	45,000	
Debtors	12,800	Collected from Debtors	75,000	120,000
Petty Cash	2,000	By Stock Reserve (Loading*)		5,120
Prepaid Rent	500	By Goods Sent to Branch (Loading*)		19,000
Furniture	19,200	By Goods Sent to Branch (Returns)		5,000
To Goods Sent to Branch	95,000	By Balance c/d		
To Goods Sent to Branch		Stock		35,000
(Loading on returns)	1,000	Debtors(1)		21,500
To Cash (Expenses) :		Petty Cash		2,000
Salaries	24,000	Prepaid Rent		500
Rent	18,000	Furniture (19,200-1,920)		17,280
Petty Expenses	900			
To Stock Reserve				
(Loading on Cl. Stock*)	7,000			
To Profit transferred to P & L A/c	19,400			
	225,400			225,400

* $\left(\text{Loading is } \frac{1}{5} \text{ or } \frac{25}{125}\right)$ i.e., Cost Price $= 100$

Profit $= 25$

Invoice Price $= 125$

Rate $\frac{25}{125}$ or $\frac{1}{5}$th on Invoice Price.

(1) DEBTORS ACCOUNT

	Rs.		Rs.
To Balance b/d	12,800	By Cash	75,000
To Credit Sales	85,000	By Discount Allowed	800
		By Bad debts	500
		By Balance c/d	21,500
	97,800		97,800

Illustration 6 (Purchases by Branch)

M/s Soha Ltd. Mumbai is having a branch at Delhi. Goods are sent by Head Office to its Delhi Branch at 33-1/3% profit on invoice price. Branch is instructed to deposit cash daily in the Head Office account in the Bank. All expenses are paid by Head Office except petty expenses which are paid by Branch Manager who is allowed to maintain a minimum balance of petty cash of Rs. 2,500 on Imprest System. From the following particulars prepare Branch Account for year ended 31st December 2007.

	Rs.
Jan. 1 Balances :	
Stock at Branch at Invoice Price	36,000
Debtors at Branch	7,200
Creditors at Branch	2,160
Rent prepaid up to 31st March 2007	540
Petty Cash -	2,500
Computer at Branch	14,400
Transactions during the year :	
Goods sent to Branch less Returns (at Invoice Price)	1,87,200
Cash Sales	1,44,000
Credit Sales	91,000
Cash collected from Credit customers	92,000
Discount Allowed	900
Bad debts	360
Cash purchases by branch after permission from H.O.	18,900
Paid to creditors	14,000
Expenses paid by Head office for Branch :	
Salaries paid	25,000
Rent paid for one year on 1-4-2007	18,000
Fire insurance premium paid up to 31-3-2008 (one years' premium)	1,000
Petty Expenses paid by Branch Manager "	1,200
Dec. 31 Stock at Branch at Invoice price	54,000
Debtors/Creditors	?/5,400
Petty Cash	?
Computer	After 10% Depreciation

Solution :

In the Books of Head Office

BRANCH ACCOUNT

		Rs.		Rs.
To Balance b/d			By Balance b/d	
Stock		36,000	Creditors	2,160
Debtors		7,200	By Bank (Remittances)(3)	2,03,100
Petty Cash		2,500	(see Cash Account)	
Prepaid Rent		540	By Stock Reserve*	12,000
Computer		14,400	(Loading 1/3 of 36,000)	
To Goods sent to Branch		1,87,200	By Goods sent to Branch*	62,400
To Bank (Expenses):			(Loading 1/3 on 1,87,200)	
Salaries	25,000		By Balance c/d	
Rent	18,000		Stock	54,000
Fire Insurance Premium	1,000	44,000	Debtors (1)	4,940
To Stock Reserve*		18,000	Petty Cash (4)	2,500
(Loading 1/3 on 54,000)			Prepaid Rent (5)	4,500
To Cash (Petty Cash) Expenses		1,200	Prepaid Insurance (6)	250
To Balance c/d (Creditors)		5,400	Computer (14,400 – 1,440)	12,960
To Profit transferred to P & L A/c		42,370		
		3,58,810		3,58,810

(1) DEBTORS ACCOUNT

	Rs.		Rs.
To Balance b/d	7,200	By Cash	92,000
To Credit Sales	91,000	By Discount allowed	900
		By Bad debts	360
		By Balance c/d	4,940
	98,200		98,200

(2) CREDITORS ACCOUNT

	Rs.		Rs.
To Cash	14,000	By Balance b/d	2,160
To Balance c/d	5,400	By Purchase (B.F.)	17,240
	19,400		19,400

(3) CASH ACCOUNT

	Rs.		Rs.
To Balance b/d	—	By Purchases	18,900
To Cash Sales	1,44,000	By Creditors	14,000
To Debtors	92,000	By Remittances	2,03,100
	2,36,000		2,36,000

(4) PETTY CASH ACCOUNT

	Rs.		Rs.
To Balance c/d	2,500	By Expenses	1,200
To Cash	1,200	By Balance c/d	2,500
	3,700		3,700

Profit @ *$33\frac{1}{3}$% on Invoice price means $\frac{1}{3}$ on Invoice price or $\frac{1}{2}$ on Cost price

(5) Prepared Rent for 3 months $= 18{,}000 \times \frac{3}{12} =$ Rs. 4,500

(6) Prepaid Fire Insurance Premium for 3 months $= 1{,}000 \times \frac{3}{12} =$ Rs. 250 **(Jan., Feb. & March)**

(b) Stock and Debtors System

Under this system following accounts are prepared in the Books of Head Office to ascertain profits or loss made by branch :

1. Branch Stock Account
2. Branch Debtors Account
3. Branch Expenses Account
4. Branch Adjustment Account
5. Branch Profit & Loss Account

1. Branch Stock Account

This account is maintained to exercise control over movement of stock of goods so as to find out any shortage or surplus arising there from. It shows the value of opening or closing stock at "Invoice Price". The salient feature of Branch Stock Account is to record all transactions pertaining to movement of goods at "Invoice Price". Even the sales (Cash or Credit), losses (Normal or abnormal), pilferage or wastage, accidental or transit losses are all shown at "invoice price". If a sale is made for more than or less than the invoice price, due adjustment is made for the excess or shortfall. For example, if goods costing Rs. 60,000 have been sold for Rs. 85,000 whereas goods are invoiced at cost plus 33-1/3% then the excess of sales price over invoice price Rs. 5,000 (85,000-80,000) will be transferred to Branch Adjustment Account. If this is not done the Branch Stock Account will not reveal the actual shortage or surplus at invoice price. Similarly if "loss by fire" which is a abnormal loss by nature, is given at cost, it will also be converted into invoice price.

2. Branch Debtors Account

This account is already explained under Debtors System.

3. Branch Expenses Account

This account shows the details of various expenses incurred at Branch by Head Office. Salaries, wages, freight, Discount, Commission, Bad debts, Carriage, rent, allowance, depreciation etc. are debited to Branch Expenses account and total thereof is transferred to Branch Profit & Loss Account.

4. Branch Adjustment Account

This account deals with the profit element (loading) included in the various items of Branch Stock Account except sales. The loading represents excess of "invoice price" over "cost price". The loading of Opening Stock and Goods sent to branch is credited to Branch Adjustment Account whereas loading or profit element included in the closing stock, Shortage, Abnormal losses is debited to Branch Adjustment Account. However, surplus represents the whole profit element and hence the entire amount is credited to Branch Adjustment Account. Similarly, normal loss like leakage, loss of weight or shrinkage etc. is wholly debited to Branch Adjustment Account. The balancing figure shows gross profit or gross loss which is transferred to Branch Profit & Loss A/c.

5. Branch Profit & Loss Account

Branch Profit and Loss Account shows the net profit earned or net loss made by the branch after making due adjustments for the various losses at cost and for all expenses (as shown in the Branch Expenses Account) out of Gross Profit/Loss transferred from Branch Adjustment Account.

RECORDING OF JOURNAL ENTRIES UNDER STOCK AND DEBTORS SYSTEM

1. When goods are sent to branch at "Invoice price"

   Branch Stock Account Dr — With the invoice price of goods sent

   To Goods Sent to Branch Account

2. When Goods are returned by Branch

   Goods Sent to Branch Account Dr — At invoice price

   To Branch Stock Account

3. When goods are sold for cash

   Cash Account Dr

   To Branch Stock Account

4. When goods are sold on credit

   Branch Debtors Account Dr

   To Branch Stock Account

5. When goods are returned by debtors to Branch

   Branch Stock Account Dr

   To Branch Debtors Account

6. When goods are returned by debtors (branch Customers) direct to Head Office

   Branch Stock Account Dr

   To Branch Debtors Account and

   Goods Sent to Branch Account Dr — and

   To Branch Stock Account — or

   Goods Sent to Branch Account Dr

   To Branch Debtors Account

7. When Cash is received by Branch from its debtors
   Branch Cash Account Dr
   To Branch Debtors Account
8. When expenses of Branch are paid by Head Office
   Branch Expenses Account Dr
   To Cash/Bank Account
9. When branch expenses are paid by the Branch
   Branch Expenses Account Dr
   To Branch Cash Account
10. When there are Bad debts, discount or allowances to debtors
   Branch Expenses Account Dr
   To Branch Debtors Account
11. When the depreciation is to be provided Branch
   Branch Expenses Account Dr
   To Branch Fixed Assets Account
12. When there is a Normal Loss of goods
   Branch Adjustment Account Dr With the amount of loss at Invoice Price
   To Branch Stock Account
13. When there is Abnormal loss
   Branch Adjustment Account Dr With the profit element
   Branch Profit & Loss Account Dr With Cost
   To Branch Stock Account With Invoice Price

   or

   (i) Abnormal Loss A/c (Shortage, loss in Transits, loss by fire etc.) Dr with Invoice Price
   To Branch Stock Account
   (ii) Branch Adjustment Account Dr With Profit element
   Branch Profit & Loss Account Dr With cost
   To Abnormal Loss Account With Invoice Price

*14. When there is "Surplus" in the Branch Stock
   Branch Stock Account Dr
   To Branch Adjustment Account

***Note :** Same entry will be recorded when goods are sold at higher than the invoice price with amount of difference (Excess of Sale Price over I.P.). A Reverse entry will be recorded with the difference if goods are sold at less than the "Invoice Price".

15. For loading on Opening Stock
   Stock Reserve Account Dr
   To Branch Adjustment Account
16. For loading on Closing Stock or Goods in Transit
   Branch Adjustment Account Dr
   To Stock Reserve Account
17. For Loading on Goods sent to Branch
   Goods Sent to Branch Account Dr
   To Branch Adjustment Account

Note : A reverse entry shall be recorded for "goods returned by Branch" and "Goods transferred by Branch to other branch ".

18. When the profit is earned by the Branch

Branch Adjustment Account Dr
To General Profit & Loss Account

Note : A reverse entry will be recorded if there is loss

19. For recording transfer entry of "goods sent to branch"

Goods Sent to Branch Account Dr at Cost
To Purchases or Trading A/c

However a "Proforma" of various accounts to be prepared under Stock and Debtors System will enable the students to understand the process of preparation of these accounts.

PROFORMA BRANCH STOCK ACCOUNT
(Always at Invoice Price)

	Rs.		Rs.
To Balance b/d	------	By Branch Cash (Cash Sales)	------
(Opening Stock with Branch)	------	By Branch Debtors (Credit Sales)	------
To Goods Sent to Branch	------	By Goods Sent to Branch (Returns to H.O.)	------
To Branch Debtors	------	By Branch Adjustment A/c (Being reduction in	
(Return Inwards)		Invoice Price)	
To Surplus (i) transferred to Branch		(Excess of Invoice Price over Selling Price)	
Adjustment A/c	------	By Normal Loss transferred to Branch	------
(Excess of Branch Stock credit side		Adjustment A/c	
over debit side)		By Abnormal Loss transferred to Branch	
To Surplus (ii) transferred to Branch		Adjustment A/c with loading and	
Adjustment A/c	------	Branch Profit & Loss A/c with cost	------
(Excess of Sale Price over Invoice Price)		By Balance c/d	
		Goods in Transit	------
		Closing Stock	------

BRANCH DEBTORS ACCOUNTS

	Rs.		Rs.
To Balance b/d	------	By Branch Cash (Collection from	
To Branch Stock (Credit Sales)	------	credit Customers/Debtors	------
To Bill Receivables Dishonoured	------	By Cash (Collected by H.O. from	
		Credit customers of Branch)	------
		By Bills Receivables	------
		By Branch Stock (Returns Inwards)	------

		By Bad debts By Discount allowed By Allowances } transferred to Branch Expenses A / c or P &L A / c	------ ------
		By Balance c/d	------

*Normal loss such as shrinkage, leakage, loss of weight due to evaporation.

**Abnormal loss includes shortage, pilferage, theft or loss by accident or fire etc.

BRANCH EXPENSES ACCOUNT

	Rs.		Rs.
To Branch Cash (expenses paid by Branch)	------	By Balance transferred to	
To Cash/Bank (expenses paid by H.O.)		Branch P & L A/c	
To Branch Debtors:			
Discount allowed			
Allowances			
Bad debts			
To Fixed Assets (Depreciation)	------		------

BRANCH ADJUSTMENT ACCOUNT (Only with loading)

	Rs.		Rs.
To Stock Reserve (Loading on Closing Stock)	------	By Stock Reserve (Loading on Opening Stock)	------
To Branch Stock (Excess of I.P. over S.P.)	------	By Goods Sent to Branch (Loading on goods sent)	------
To Goods Sent to Branch (Loading on Goods returned by Branch or returned by customers direct to H.O.	------ ------	By Surplus (i) Excess of credit side of Branch Stock over debit side	------
To Branch Stock A/c (Normal loss)		By Surplus (ii) Excess of Sale price over Invoice price	------
To Branch Stock A/c (Abnormal loss or shortage with loading)		By Gross Loss-transferred to P & L A/c	------
To Gross Profit transferred to Branch P &L A/c	------ ------		
	------		------

BRANCH PROFIT AND LOSS ACCOUNT

	Rs.		Rs.
To Branch Stock (Abnormal Loss or Shortage at Cost)	------	By Gross Profit transferred from Branch Adjustment A/c	------
To Branch Expenses*	------	By Insurance claims receivable (if any)	------
To Net Profit transferred to General P & L A/c	or ------	By Net Loss-transferred to General P & L A/c	------
	------		------

* **Note :** Students should remember that under "Debtors System" the Cash sent by H.O. for expenses is shown to the debit of Branch Account whereas "Expenses actually incurred" are charged to Branch Profit & Loss A/c.

Illustration 7 (Shortage & Loss by Fire)

Goods are invoiced to Branch at cost plus 25%. From the following particulars relating to Jaipur Branch for the year ended 31st March 2007, prepare necessary ledger accounts to ascertain profit or loss under Stock and Debtors system.

	Rs.
Stock at Branch on 1-4-2006 at invoice price	25,000
Goods sent to Branch during the year at Invoice Price	1,60,000
Goods received by Branch till 31-3-2007 at I.P.	1,42,000
Cash Sales at Branch	35,000
Credit Sales at Branch	90,000
Loss by Fire at Cost	2,000
Stock at Branch at Cost on 31-3-2007	30,000
Debtors on 1-4-2006	10,000
Discount allowed to Debtors	500
Bad debts	750
Rent of Branch	5,000
Salaries & Commission paid to Salesmen	7,000
Debtors on 31-3-2007	12,500

Solution : **In the Books of Head Office**

BRANCH STOCK ACCOUNT (AT INVOICE PRICE)

	Rs.			Rs.
To Balance b/d	25,000	By Sales :		
To Goods Sent to Branch	1,60,000	Branch Cash (Cash Sales)	35,000	
		Branch Debtors (Credit Sales)	90,000	1,25,000
		By Abnormal Loss (loss by fire) (1)		2,500
		By Shortage (Balancing figure)		2,000
		By Balance c/d		
		In Transit* (2)		18,000
		In Hand		37,500
	1,85,000			1,85,000

BRANCH DEBTORS ACCOUNT

	Rs.		Rs.
To Balance b/d	10,000	By Branch Cash (B.F.)	86,250
To Credit Sales	90,000	(Collected from Debtors)	
		By Discount allowed	500
		By Bad debts	750
		By Balance c/d	12,500
	1,00,000		1,00,000

BRANCH EXPENSES ACCOUNT

	Rs.		Rs.
To Cash :		By Balance transferred to	
Rent	5,000	Branch P & L A/c	13,250
Salaries & Commission	7,000		
To Branch Debtors:			
Bad debts	750		
Discount allowed	500		
	13,250		13,250

BRANCH ADJUSTMENT ACCOUNT

	Rs.		Rs.
To Branch Stock A/c :		By Stock Reserve (on Op. Stock)	5,000
Loading on loss by fire	500	By Branch Stock-Loading on	32,000
Loading on Shortage	400	Goods Sent to Branch	
To Stock Reserve:			
Loading on Closing Stock	7,500		
Loading on Goods in Transit	3,600		
To Gross Profit transferred to			
Branch P & L A/c	25,000		
	37,000		37,000

BRANCH PROFIT & LOSS ACCOUNT

	Rs.		Rs.
To Branch Stock A/c		By Gross Profit b/d	25,000
Abnormal Loss at cost	2,000		
Shortage at Cost	1,600		
To Branch Expenses A/c	13,250		
To Net Profit transferred to			
General P & L A/c	8,150		
	25,000		25,000

Working Notes :

(1) Loss by fire at Invoice Price

Since Profit in relation to Cost is 25% Cost is 100 Profit is 25 and Invoice Price 125

Invoice Price = Cost + 25% thereof i.e. 2,000 + 25% or 500 = 2,500

Thus rate of profit on Invoice price = $\frac{25}{125}$ or $\frac{1}{5}$. Therefore loading has been calculated on Various items at $\frac{1}{5}$ of invoice price.

(2) Goods in Transit is equal to Goods sent Less Goods Received i.e. Rs.18,000 (1,60,000-1,42,000).

Illustration 8 (Goods Sent to Branch Account)

X Ltd. has a branch at Delhi. Goods are sent at invoice price, which is 33-1/3% above cost. During first quarter of the year goods costing Rs. 4,12,500 were sent to Delhi Branch. At the end of quarter the Branch Manager reported a sale of Rs. 3,75,000. Goods invoiced at Rs. 7,500 to Delhi Branch were returned to Head office, and goods costing Rs. 1,23,750 were lying unsold with the Branch. Expenses at Branch amounted to Rs. 16,875.

You are required to prepare :

1. Delhi Branch Stock Account
2. Goods Sent to Branch Account
3. Branch Adjustment Account
4. Branch Profit & Loss Account

Solution : **In the Books of H.O.**

DELHI BRANCH STOCK ACCOUNT (AT I.P.)

	Rs.		Rs.
To Goods Sent to Branch (4,12,500 + 33-1/3%) (4,12,500 +1,37,500)	5,50,000	By Branch Cash (Cash Sales)	3,75,000
		By Goods Sent to Branch (Returns by Branch to H.O.)	7,500
		By Shortage-transferred to Branch Adjustment & P & L A/c (B.F.)	2,500
		By Balance c/d (1,23,750 + 41,250)	1,65,000
	5,50,000		5,50,000

GOODS SENT TO DELHI BRANCH ACCOUNT

	Rs.		Rs.
To Delhi Branch Stock A/c (Returns)	7,500	By Delhi Branch Stock A/c	5,50,000
To Purchases (B.F) or 3/4 of 5,42,500	4,06,875		
To Branch Adjustment A/c (Loading on net goods sent) 1/4 of (5,50,000 -7,500)	1,35,625		
	5,50,000		5,50,000

BRANCH ADJUSTMENT AND PROFIT & LOSS A/C

	Rs.		Rs.
To Branch Stock A/c (Loading on Shortage) (1/4 of 2,500)	625	By Goods Sent to Branch (Net) (Loading)	1,35,625
To Stock Reserve (1/4 × 1,65,000) (Loading on 'Closing Stock)	41,250		
To Gross Profit transferred to P & L Account	93,750		
	1,35,625		1,35,625

To Branch Stock A/c (Shortage at cost) (2,500 – 625)	1,875	By Gross Profit b/d	93,750
To Branch Expenses A/c	16,875		
To Net Profit transferred to General P & L A/c	75,000		
	93,750		93,750

Illustration 9 (Normal & Abnormal Losses)

Mumbai Head Office invoices goods to its Pune Branch at a gross profit of 25% on selling price. Branch Manager is instructed to deposit cash every week in the Head Office Account after deducting 1% commission on gross sales-both cash and credit. From the following particulars ascertain profit or loss made by Branch under Stock and Debtors system for quarter ending on 31st March 2006.

	Rs.
Stock at Branch at Invoice price on 1-1-2006	97,500
Goods Sent to Branch at Cost	6,00,000
Expenses incurred at Branch	35,000
Goods returned by Branch to H.O. at Invoice price	20,000
Cash sales as reported by Branch Manager	5,00,000
Credit Sales at Branch	2,50,000
Loss of weight valued at cost price	4,500
Pilferage at invoice price	6,500
Stock at Branch on 31-3-2006 at cost	83,250
Goods still in transit as reported by Manager at I.P.	25,000

Solution : **In the Books of Mumbai Head Office**

BRANCH STOCK ACCOUNT AT (I.P.)

	Rs.		Rs.
To Balance b/d	97,500	By Branch Cash (Cash Sales)	5,00,000
To Goods Sent to Branch (6,00,000 + 2,00,000)	8,00,000	By Branch Debtors (Credit Sales)	2,50,000
		By Goods Sent to Branch (Returns)	20,000
To Surplus (Balancing figure)	21,000	By Normal Loss (Loss of weight) transferred to Br. Adjustment A/c (4,500+1,500)	6,000
		By Pilferage-Abnormal loss transferred to Branch Adjustment and P & L A/c	6,500
		By Balance c/d	
		In Transit	25,000
		At Branch (83,250 + 27,750)	1,11,000
	9,18,500		9,18,500

GOODS SENT TO BRANCH ACCOUNT

	Rs.		Rs.
To Branch Stock A/c (Returns)	20,000	By Branch Stock Account	8,00,000
To Branch Adjustment A/c	1,95,000		
(Loading on 7,80,000 @ 25%)			
To Purchases (Balancing figure)	5,85,000		
or (75% of 7,80,000)			
	8,00,000		8,00,000

BRANCH ADJUSTMENT ACCOUNT

	Rs.		Rs.
To Branch Stock A/c		By Stock Reserve	24,375
Loading on Pilferage	1,625	(Loading on Op. Stock)	
Normal Loss	6,000	By Goods Sent to Branch	195,000
To Stock Reserve:		By Branch Stock A/c (Surplus)	21,000
Loading on Closing Stock	27,750		
Loading on Goods in Transit	6,250		
To Gross Profit c/d	198,750		
	240,375		240,375
To Branch Stock A/c	4,875	By Gross Profit b/d	1,98,750
(Pilferage at Cost) (6,500-1,625)			
To Branch Expenses	42,500		
(35,000 + Commission @ 1% on Sales 7,500)			
To Net Profit transferred			
to General P & L A/c	1,51,375		
	198,750		198,750

Illustration 10 (Goods Sent to Branch not given)

Aligarh Branch receives all its supplies from Delhi Head Office who invoices goods at 20% profit on invoice price. From the following particulars relating to Aligarh Branch prepare necessary ledger accounts to ascertain profit or loss under Stock & Debtors System.

	Rs.
Goods sold by Branch during the year (at cost)	9,35,000
Cash Sales	2,55,000
Credit Sales	?
Branch Expenses paid by Head Office :	
Salaries	51,000
Rent	20,400
Other Expenses	13,600

Normal Loss (Shrinkage) at cost	10,000
Stock at Branch at Cost (on 1st January)	85,000
Debtors at Branch (on 1st January)	1,19,000
Stock at Branch at cost (on 31st December)	1,27,500
Debtors at Branch (on 31st December)	1,61,500
Bad debt	3,750

Solution : **In the Books of Delhi Head Office**

ALIGARH BRANCH STOCK ACCOUNT (AT INVOICE PRICE)

	Rs.		Rs.
To Balance b/d	1,06,250	By Branch Cash (Cash sales)	2,55,000
(85,000 + 21,250)		By Branch Debtors (Credit sales) (1)	9,13,750
To Goods Sent to Branch	12,34,375	By Normal Loss transferred to	
(Balancing figure)		Branch Adjustment A/c	12,500
		By Balance c/d (1,27,500 + 31,875)	1,59,375
	13,40,625		13,40,625

(1)		
	Cost of goods sold	9,35,000
	Add Profit @ 25% on cost	2,33,750
	Total Sales	11,68,750
	Less Cash Sales	2,55,000
	Credit Sales	9,13,750

BRANCH DEBTORS ACCOUNT

	Rs.		Rs.
To Balance b/d	1,19,000	By Cash (Bal. Figure)	8,67,500
To Credit Sales	9,13,750	By Bad debts	3,750
		By Balance c/d	1,61,500
	10,32,750		10,32,750

GOODS SENT TO BRANCH ACCOUNT

	Rs.		Rs.
To Branch Adjustment A/c	2,46,875	By Branch Stock Account	12,34,375
(20% of 12,34,375)			
To Purchases (Bal. Figure)	9,87,500		
	12,34,375		12,34,375

BRANCH ADJUSTMENT ACCOUNT

	Rs.		Rs.
To Branch Stock (Normal Loss)	12,500	By Stock Reserve	
To Stock Reserve	31,875	(Loading on Op. Stock)	21,250
(Loading on C.I. Stock)		By Goods Sent to Branch	
To Gross Profit c/d	2,23,750	(Loading) (20% of 12,34,375)	2,46,875
	2,68,125		2,68,125
To Branch Expenses A/c*	88,750	By Gross Profit b/d	2,23,750
To Net Profit transferred to General			
P&LA/c	1,35,000		
	2,23,750		2,23,750

BRANCH EXPENSES ACCOUNT

	Rs.		Rs.
To Cash-Salaries	51,000	By Balance transferred to	
Rent	20,400	Branch Adjustment A/c	88,750
Other Expenses	13,600		
To Branch Debtors (Bad debts)	3,750		
	88,750		88,750

Illustration 11 (Sale of Goods at a price higher than the Invoice Price)

Delhi Head Office invoices goods to its Ludhiana Branch at 20% less than the catalogue price which is "cost plus 50%. Cash sales" were to be made at invoice price and credit sales at catalogue price. From the following particulars prepare necessary ledger accounts to ascertain profit or loss made by branch under Stock and Debtors System.

	Rs.
Stock at Branch in the beginning at Invoice Price	9,600
Stock at Branch at the end at Invoice Price	12,600
Debtors in the beginning	8,000
Debtors at the end	19,000
Goods sent to Branch at Invoice Price	1,05,600
Cash sales at Branch	36,800
Credit sales at Branch	80,000
Cash collected from credit customers	68,640
Expenses at Branch including bad debts	3,360
Bad debts	360

Solution :

Let cost price be	100
Catalogue Price (Cost + 50%)	150
Invoice Price (20% less) (150- 30)	120

BRANCH STOCK ACCOUNT

	Rs.		Rs.
To Balance b/d	9,600	By Branch Cash (Cash Sales)	36,800
To Goods sent to Branch A/c	1,05,600	By Branch Debtors (Credit Sales)	80,000
To Branch Adjustment A/c	16,000	By Shortage-transferred to	
(Excess of catalogue price over Invoice price)		Branch Adjustment A/c	1,800
		By Balance c/d	12,600
	1,31,200		1,31,200

BRANCH DEBTORS ACCOUNT

	Rs.		Rs.
To Balance b/d	8,000	By Cash	68,640
To Credit Sales	80,000	By Bad debts	360
		By Balance c/d	19,000
	88,000		88,000

BRANCH EXPENSES A/C

	Rs.		Rs.
To Cash (Expenses)	3,000	By Balance transferred to	3,360
To Branch Debtors (B/Debts)	360	Branch P & L A/c	
	3,360		3,360

GOODS SENT TO BRANCH ACCOUNT

	Rs.		Rs.
To Branch Adjustment A/c (1/6)	17,600	By Branch Stock	1,05,600
To Purchases (B.F.) (5/6)	88,000		
	1,05,600		1,05,600

BRANCH ADJUSTMENT ACCOUNT

	Rs.		Rs.
To Branch Stock Shortage	300	By Stock Reserve	1,600
(Loading)		(Loading on Op. Stock @ 1/6)	
To Stock Reserve	2,100	By Goods Sent to Branch A/c (Loading)	17,600
(Loading on C.I. Stock @ 1/6)		By Branch Stock (Excess of catalogue	16,000
To Gross Profit c/d	32,800	Price over Invoice Price)	
	35,200		35,200
To Shortage at Cost	1,500	By Gross Profit b/d	32,800
To Branch Expenses A/c	3,360		
To Net Profit transferred to	27,940		
General P & L A/c			
	32,800		32,800

GRADED ILLUSTRATIONS

Illustration 1

Tip Top Co., Delhi has a branch in Calcutta. It invoices goods to the branch at selling price which is cost plus 25 %from the following particulars prepare Branch Account. Branch Debtors Account and Goods sent to the branch Account in the books of Tip Top Co., Delhi :

		Rs.
Stock at Branch as on 1-1-2008 (at invoice price)		15,400
Debtors at Branch as on 1-1-2008		8,250
Petty cash as on 1-1-2008		250
Goods supplied to the Branch (at invoice price)		75,600
Remittance from the Branch		
Cash sales	5,250	
Realisation of debts	78,870	84,120
Amount sent to branch :		
Salary	3,720	
Rent etc.	1,200	
Petty Cash	1,500	6,420
Stock at Branch as on 31-12-2008 (at Invoice Price)		11,575
Sundry Debtors at the Branch as on 31-12-2008		25,230
Petty Cash as on 31-12-2008		375

From the above show the Branch Account in the Head Office books.

[B.Com (P), D.U, 1998, Adapted]

Solution : **Delhi Head Office Books**

CALCUTTA BRANCH ACCOUNT

		Rs.			Rs.
To Balance b/d			By Stock Reserve A/c		
Stock	15,400		(Loading on opening Stock)		3,080
Debtors	8,250		(15,400 × 25/125)		
Petty Cash	250	23,900	By Remittances :		
To Goods sent to Branch A/c		75,600	Cash Sales	5,250	
To Cash – Expenses			Collected from Debtors	78,870	84,120
Salary	3,720		By Goods sent to Branch A/c-		
Rent etc.	1,200		Loading		
Petty Cash	1,500	6,420	(75,600 × 25/125)		15,120
To Stock Reserve A/c			By Balance c/d		
Loading on Closing stock (11,575 × 25/125)		2,315	Stock	11,575	
			Debtors	25,230	
To Net profit Tr. to Profit & Loss A/c		31,265	Petty cash	375	37,180
		1,39,500			1,39,500

BRANCH DEBTORS ACCOUNT

	Rs.		Rs.
To Balance b/d	8,250	By Cash	78,870
To Sales – Credit (bal. fig)	95,850	By Balance c/d	25,230
	1,04,100		1,04,100

Illustration 2

From the details given below relating to Patna Branch for the year ending March 31, 2008 prepare Patna Branch account and Branch Debtors account in the books of Head Office show your working clearly. Goods are invoiced to give a profit of 20% of selling price.

	Rs.
Stock on 1st April 2007	5,000
Debtors on 1st April 2007	2,000
Furniture on 1st April 2007	1,000
Petty Cash on 1st April 2007	200
Insurance prepaid on 1st April 2007	50
Salaries due on 1st April 2007	1,000
Goods sent to branch	40,000
Cash Sales	55,000
Total Sales	70,000
Cash received from debtors	16,000
Goods returned by the branch	500
Goods returned by the Debtors	200
Cash sent to the branch for :	
Rent	3,600
Salaries	10,200
Petty Cash	600
Insurance (Upto June 2008)	400
Petty cash expenses incurred by the branch	500
Stock on 31.03.2008	3,000
Depreciate Furniture by 20%	

[B.Com (P), D.U, 1999, Modified]

Solution : **In the Books of Head Office**

PATNA BRANCH ACCOUNT

		Rs.		Rs.
To Balance b/d			By Balance b/d	
Stock	5,000		Salaries Outstanding	1,000
Debtors	2,000		By Goods Returned to H.O	500
Furniture	1,000		By Remittances [55,000+16,000]	71,000
Petty Cash	200		By Goods Sent to Branch less Return	
Insurance Prepaid	50	8,250	(loading)	
			[39,500 x 20/100]	7,900
To Goods sent to Branch		40,000		
To Bank A/c :			By Stock Reserve	1,000
Rent	3,600		By Balance c/d	
Salaries	10,200		Stock	3,000
Petty cash	600		Petty cash [200 + 600 – 500]	300
Insurance	400	14,800	Prepaid Insurance	100
To stock reserve			[400 × 1/4]	
[3,000 × 20/100]		600	Furniture [1,000 – 200]	800
To Net Profit Transferred to			Debtors	800
General profit and loss A/c		22,750		
		86,400		86,400

BRANCH DEBTORS ACCOUNT

	Rs.		Rs.
To Balance b/d	2,000	By Cash A/c	16,000
To Credit Sales	15,000	By Sales Return	200
[70,000 – 55,000]		By Balance c/d	800
	17,000		17,000

Illustration 3 (Closing Stock not given)

(1) From the following particulars, prepare Branch Account, showing the profit or loss of the branch for the year ended 31st March 2006 :

	Rs.
Stock at Branch on 1-4-2005	30,000
Goods sent to branch during the year	90,000
Cash sales	1,20,000
Expenses of Branch paid by Head Office :	
Salaries	10,000
Other Expenses	2,000

Closing Stock could not be ascertained, but it is known that the branch usually sells goods at Cost plus 20%. The branch manager is entitled commission of 5% on the profit of the branch before charging such commission. **[C.A. Ent., Nov. 1978-Modified]**

Solution :

CALCULATION OF CLOSING STOCK

BRANCH STOCK (AT COST)

	Rs.		Rs.
To Balance b/d	30,000	By Cost of Goods Sold	
To Goods Sent to Branch	90,000	(Sales-Profit) 1,20,000-20,000(1)	1,00,000
		By Balance c/d (B.F.)	20,000
	1,20,000		1,20,000

BRANCH ACCOUNT

	Rs.		Rs.
To Balance b/d		By Bank (Remittances):	
Opening Stock	30,000	Cash Sales	120,000
To Goods Sent to Branch	90,000	By Balance c/d	
To Bank (Expenses):		Closing Stock	20,000
Salaries	10,000		
Other Expenses	2,000		
To Manager's Commission O/s (2)	400		
To Net Profit transferred to			
General P& L A/c	7,600		
	140,000		140,000

Working Notes :

(1) Calculation of Cost of goods sold

Since profits are expressed in relations to Cost Price

Thus Cost price is	100
Profit is	20
Selling Price is	120

Rate of Profit on selling price $\frac{20}{120}$ or $\frac{1}{6}$

Sale : is Rs. 1,20,000 less 1/6 thereof (Profit) = Cost of goods sold = Rs. 1,00,000

(2) Manager is entitled 5% commission on profit 'before' charging such commission Profit before Commission is 8,000 - thus 5% thereof i.e. Rs. 400.

Illustration 4 (Insurance Claims)

From the following particulars relating to Delhi Branch for the year ended 31st March 2009, prepare Branch Account in the Books of Head Office. Show your working clearly.

	Rs.
Stock at Branch on 1-4-2008	25,000
Debtors at Branch on 1-4-2008	10,000
Furniture at Branch on 1-4-2008	6,000

Petty Cash at Branch on 1-4-2008	1,000
Insurance prepaid at Branch on 1-4-2008	300
Salaries O/s at Branch on 1-4-2008	4,000
Goods sent to Branch during the year	2,00,000
Cash Sales during the year	2,70,000
Total Sales	3,50,000
Cash received from Debtors	65,000
Cash paid by Debtors direct to Head Office	5,000
Goods returned by Branch	2,000
Goods returned by Debtors	1,000
Cash sent to Branch for Expenses :	
Rent @ Rs. 800 p.m.	9,600
Salary @ Rs. 4,000 p.m.	48,000
Petty Cash	2,000
Insurance paid up to 30th June 2009	1,200
Petty Cash expenses	2,200
Discount allowed to Debtors	500
Stock at Branch on 31-3-2009	15,000
Depreciation on Furniture @ 10% p.a.	

Goods costing Rs. 2,500 were damaged in transit and a sum of Rs. 2,000 was recovered from Insurance Company in full settlement of claim. **[B.Com. (H), DU, 1988-Modified]**

Solution :

In the Books of Head Office

DELHI BRANCH ACCOUNT

	Rs.			Rs.
To Balance b/d		By Balance b/d (Salaries O/s)		4,000
Stock	25,000	By Bank (Remittances):		
Debtors	10,000	Cash Sales	270,000	
Furniture	6,000	Collected from Debtors	70,000	
Petty Cash	1,000	(65,000 + 5,000)		
Prepaid Insurance	300		340,000	
To Goods Sent to Branch Less Returns	1,98,000	Insurance Claims received	2,000	3,42,000
To Bank (Expenses)		By Balance c/d		
Rent	9,600	Stock		15,000
Salaries	48,000	Debtors (1)		18,500
Petty Cash	2,000	Furniture(2)		5,400
Insurance	1,200	Petty Cash(3)		800
To Balance c/d (Salaries O/s)	4,000	Insurance prepaid (4)		300
To Net Profit-transferred to				
General P & L A/c	80,900			
	3,86,000			3,86,000

(1) BRANCH DEBTORS ACCOUNT

	Rs.		Rs.
To Balance b/d	10,000	By Cash (65,000 + 5,000)	70,000
To Credit Sales		By Returns Inwards	1,000
(Total Sales - Cash Sales)		By Discount allowed	500
(3,50,000 - 2,70,000)	80,000	By Balance c/d	18,500
	90,000		90,000

(2) Furniture in the beginning Rs. 6,000
Less Depreciation @ 10% p.a. Rs. 600
Furniture at the end Rs. 5,400

(3) PETTY CASH ACCOUNT

	Rs.		Rs.
To Balance b/d	1,000	By Petty Expenses	2,200
To Bank	2,000	By Balance c/d	800
	3,000		3,000

(4) Insurance paid up to June 2009 Rs. 1,200

Prepaid for (April to June 3 months) $1{,}200 \times \frac{3}{12} = \text{Rs. } 300.$

Illustration 5 (Goods-in-Transit)

A Trader has a branch at Kolkata to which goods are invoiced at cost plus 20%. From the following particulars you are required to prepare 'Branch Account' for the year ending 31st December 2007.

	Rs.
Stock at Branch on 1st January	24,000
Stock at Branch on 31st December	18,000
Goods Received from Head office	30,000
Cash sales at Branch	17,500
Credit sales at Branch	41,000
Collection from Debtors	37,900
Branch Expenses paid by Head office	3,000
Branch expenses paid by Branch	6,000
Expenses unpaid	1,400
Closing Debtors on 31st December	9,160
Goods in Transit	3,600

[B.Com. (Hons.), DU, 1997-Modified]

Solution :

In the Books of Head office

KOLKATA BRANCH ACCOUNT

	Rs.		**Rs.**
To Balance b/d		By Bank (Remittances) (2)	49,400
Stock	24,000	By Stock Reserve (3)	4,000
Debtors	6,060	By Goods Sent to Branch (Loading)(4)	5,600
To Goods Sent to Branch*	33,600	By Balance c/d	
(Including in transit)		Stock	18,000
To Bank (Expenses)	3,000	Goods in transit	3,600
To Stock Reserve (1)	3,600	Debtors (5)	9,160
To Balance c/d (Expenses O/s)	1,400		
To Net Profit-transferred to			
General P & L A/c	18,100		
	89,760		89,760

* Goods Sent to Branch = Goods Received from H.O. + Goods-in-Transit.

Working Notes :

(1) Stock Reserve on closing stock :

Cost price	100
Profit	20
Invoice Price	120

Thus rate of profit on Invoice price is 20/120 or 1/6

Reserve on : Closing Stock = 18,000x1/6 = Rs. 3,000

Goods in Transit = 3,600x1/6 = Rs. 600 = 3,600

(2) Remittances :

	Rs.
Cash Sales	17,500
Cash received from Debtors	37,900
	55,400
Less Expenses paid by Branch	6,000
	49,400

(3) Stock Reserve on Opening Stock

1/6 of Rs. 24,000 = Rs. 4,000

(4) Loading on Goods Sent

30,000 + 3,600 = 33,600 x 1/6 = Rs. 5,600

(Goods Received + In-transit)

(5) BRANCH DEBTORS ACCOUNT

	Rs.		Rs.
To Balance b/d (B.F.)	6,060	By Cash	37,900
To Credit Sales	41,000	By Balance c/d	9,160
	47,060		47,060

Illustration 6 (Different Selling Prices)

Delhi Head office invoices goods to its Noida Branch at 20% less than the list price which is cost plus 100 per cent with instructions that cash sales were to be made at invoice price and credit sales at list price. From the following particulars available from Noida Branch, prepare :

(a) Branch Stock Account

(b) Branch Debtors Account

(c) Noida Branch Account to reveal the profit for the year ending on 31st March 2009.

		Rs.
Stock on in the beginning at Invoice price		18,000
Debtors in the beginning		10,000
Personal Computer at Branch		50,000
Goods received from Head office at Invoice price		1,80,000
Cash Sales		82,000
Credit Sales		1,20,000
Goods in transit at the end	10,000	
Cash sent to Branch for expenses		32,000
Actual expenses of Branch		30,000
Stock at the end at Invoice Price		16,000
Bad debts written off		400
Goods returned by customers direct to Head office at list price		1,500
Debtors at the end		8,100
Depreciate personal Computer by		20%

[B.Com. (H), DU, 1993-Modifled]

Solution : **In the Books of Head Office**

NOIDA BRANCH STOCK ACCOUNT (AT INVOICE PRICE)

	Rs.			Rs.
To Balance b/d	18,000	By Branch Sales :		
To Goods Sent to Branch	1,90,000	Cash	82,000	
(Including in transit)		Credit less Returns	1,18,500	2,00,500
To Excess of list price (1)		By Goods Sent to Branch (Returns)		1,200
Over invoice price		By Shortage (Balancing figure)		4,000
(20% of 1,18,500)	23,700	By Balance c/d		
		Stock at Branch		16,000
		Stock in Transit		10,000
	2,31,700			2,31,700

BRANCH DEBTORS ACCOUNT

	Rs.		Rs.
To Balance b/d	10,000	By Cash (Balancing figure)	1,20,000
To Credit Sales	1,20,000	By Bad debts	400
		By Return Inwards	1,500
		By Balance c/d	8,100
	1,30,000		1,30,000

Working Note :

(1) Cost price is 100

List price is (100+100) 200

Invoice price is 20% less i.e. (200 – 40) 160

Hence for the credit sales which is at list price 20% is shown as excess or extra profit to calculate the shortage, if any.

NOIDA BRANCH ACCOUNT

	Rs.		Rs.
To Balance b/d		By Bank (Remittances) :	
Stock	18,000	Cash Sales 82,000	
Debtors	10,000	Collection from Debtors 1,20,000	202000
Personal Computer	50,000	By Stock Reserve*	6750
To Goods Sent to Branch		By Goods Sent to Branch (Returns)	1500
including in transit	1,90,000	By Goods Sent to Branch* (Loading)	71250
To Bank (Expenses)	32,000	By Balance c/d	
To Goods Sent to Branch**	750	Stock	16000
(Loading on Returns)		Goods in transit	10000
To Stock Reserve (including in transit)*	9,750	Debtors	8100
To Profit-transferred to General P & L A/c	47,100	Personal Computer less Depreciation	40,000
		Cash (32,000 – 30,000)	2,000
	3,57,600		3,57,600

* Loading on Opening stock, Closing stock including goods in transit, Goods Sent to Branch and goods returned by Branch has been worked out by 60/160 rate.

** Since goods have been returned by customers direct to H.O., the profit element @ 100/200 has been adjusted.

Illustration 7 (Invoice Price of Goods sent not given)

On 1st January 2006, goods costing Rs. 1,32,000 were invoiced by Chennai Head office to its branch at Delhi and charged a selling price to produce a gross profit of 25 per cent on the selling price. At the end of month, the return from Delhi Branch showed that the sales were Rs. 1,50,000. Goods invoiced at Rs. 1,200 to Delhi Branch have been returned to Chennai Head office. The closing stock at Delhi

Branch was Rs. 24,000 at selling price. Record the above transactions in Branch Stock Account, Branch Adjustment Account, Goods Sent to Branch Account in the Head office Books and close the said accounts on 31st January 2006. **[C.A. (Inter), 1981-Modified]**

Solution : **In the Books of Head Office**

BRANCH STOCK ACCOUNT (AT INVOICE PRICE)

	Rs.		Rs.
To Goods Sent to Branch*	1,76,000	By Branch Cash (Cash Sales)	1,50,000
(1,32,000 + Loading 1/3 thereof		By Goods Sent to Branch (Returned)	1,200
Rs. 44,000)		By Shortage transferred to Branch Adjustment A/c and Branch P & L A/c (B.F.)	800
		By Balance c/d	24,000
	1,76,000		1,76,000

GOODS SENT TO BRANCH ACCOUNT

	Rs.		Rs.
To Branch Stock Account (Returned)	1,200	By Branch Stock Account	1,76,000
To Branch Adjustment A/c	43,700		
To Purchases (Bal. figure)	1,31,100		
	1,76,000		1,76,000

BRANCH ADJUSTMENT ACCOUNT

	Rs.		Rs.
To Stock Reserve		By Goods Sent to Branch A/c	43,700
(Loading on Closing Stock 1/4 of 24,000)	6,000	(Loading)	
To Branch Stock-Shortage (1/4 of 800)	200		
To Gross Profit c/d	37,500		
	43,700		43,700

BRANCH PROFIT & LOSS ACCOUNT

	Rs.		Rs.
To Shortage at Cost	600	By Gross Profit b/d	37,500
To Net Profit-transferred to G. P & L A/c	36,900		
	37,500		37,500

Illustration 8 (Normal Loss & Surplus)

Limelight Ltd. with a head office in Kolkata, opened a branch at Kanpur on 1-1-2005. All sales were to be made on credit basis. All goods required by the Branch were supplied by the company from Kolkata and were invoiced to the branch at 20 per cent above cost. During the year ended 31st December 2005, the following transactions took place :

	Rs.
Goods sent to Kanpur Branch (at Cost to H.O.)	22,000
Returns to Kolkata Head Office (at Cost to H.O.)	840
Sales as shown by Kanpur Branch report	19,670
Cash received from debtors and remitted to Kolkata	15,190
Debtors balance at Branch written off as bad	640

Loss of goods at branch through pilferage is estimated at 1 per cent of goods received. The stock of goods held by the Branch on 31st December 2005 amounted to Rs. 5,820 at invoice price.

You are required to record the entries in the appropriate accounts in the Head office Ledgers showing the balances as on 31st December 2005 and the Branch Gross Profit for the year ended on that date. **[ICWA (Inter), June 1981-Modified]**

Solution : **In the Books of Head Office**

BRANCH STOCK ACCOUNT (AT INVOICE PRICE)

	Rs.		Rs.
To Goods Sent to Branch		By Branch Debtors (Credit sales)	19,670
(Cost+Loading 20%) (22,000+4,400)	26,400	By Goods Sent to Branch (Returns)	1,008
To Surplus - transferred to		(840 + 168)	
Branch Adjustment A/c	362	By Pilferage (Normal loss 1%	
		transferred to Br. Adjustment A/c)	264
		By Balance c/d	5,820
	26,762		26,762

GOODS SENT TO BRANCH ACCOUNT

	Rs.		Rs.
To Branch Stock A/c	1,008	By Branch Stock Account	26,400
To Branch Adjustment Account	4,232		
To Purchases (Bal. figure)	21,160		
	26,400		26,400

BRANCH DEBTORS ACCOUNT

	Rs.		Rs.
To Credit Sales	19,670	By Branch Cash	15,190
		By Bad debts	640
		By Balance c/d	3,840
	19,670		19,670

BRANCH ADJUSTMENT ACCOUNT

	Rs.		Rs.
To Stock Reserve (Loading on Closing Stock) 1/6 of 5,820	970	By Goods Sent to Branch A/c (Loading)	4,232
To Branch Stock Account (Normal loss) (Pilferage) (1/6 of 264)	264	By Balance Stock A/c (surplus)	362
To Gross Profit c/d	3,360		
	4,594		4,594

BRANCH PROFIT & LOSS ACCOUNT

	Rs.		Rs.
To Branch Debtors (Bad debts)	640	By Gross Profit b/d	3,360
To Net Profit transferred to General P & L A/c	2,720		
	3,360		3,360

Working Notes :

(1) Cost Price is 100
Profit is 20
Invoice Price is 120
Therefore Loading on invoice price is 20/120 or 1/6.

(2) Pilferage is treated as (Normal) being 1% of goods received i.e. Rs. 264 at invoice price the entire amount has been taken to Branch Adjustment A/c rather than splitting in loading and in cost.

Illustration 9 (Calculation of Goods-in-Transit)

Ronald Ltd. Kanpur started a Branch at Mumbai on 1-4-2008 to which goods were sent at 20% above cost. The Branch makes both cash and credit sales. Branch expenses are met from branch Cash and balance is remitted to head office. The Branch does not maintain double entry books of accounts and necessary accounts relating to branch are maintained in H.O. books.

Following details are given for the year ended 31st March 2009 :

	Rs.
Cost of goods sent to Branch	50,000
Goods received by Branch till 31st March 2009 at Invoice Price	54,000
Credit sales for the year	58,000
Bad debts and Discount written off	200
Cash remitted to Head office	43,000
Expenses incurred at Branch	12,000
Debtors on at the end	20,800

Cash in hand on at the end	2,000
Cash remitted by Head Office to Branch for expenses	3,000
Closing Stock at Branch at Invoice price	6,000

Show the Ledger Accounts according to Stock & Debtors system in the Books of Head Office and determine the profit or loss of the Branch for the year ended on 31st March 2009.

[C.A. (Inter), Nov. 1984-Modified]

Solution : **In the Books of Head Office**

BRANCH STOCK ACCOUNT (AT INVOICE PRICE)

	Rs.		Rs.
To Goods Sent to Branch	60,000	By Branch Cash (Cash Sales)	17,000
(50,000 + 20% thereof)		By Branch Debtors (Credit Sales)	58,000
To Surplus transferred to Branch		By Balance c/d	
Adjustment A/c	27,000	Stock in Transit (1)	6,000
		Stock in hand	6,000
	87,000		87,000

GOODS SENT TO BRANCH ACCOUNT

	Rs.		Rs.
To Branch Adjustment A/c (Loading)	10,000	By Branch Stock A/c	60,000
To Purchases (Bal. figure)	50,000		
	60,000		60,000

BRANCH DEBTORS ACCOUNT

	Rs.		Rs.
To Credit Sales	58,000	By Branch Cash (Bal. Figure)	37,000
		By Bad debts	200
		By Balance c/d	20,800
	58,000		58,000

BRANCH CASH ACCOUNT

	Rs.		Rs.
To Bank (for Expenses)	3,000	By Branch Expenses	12,000
To Branch Debtors	37,000	By Bank — Remittance to H.O.	43,000
To Br. Cash Sales (Balancing Figure)	17,000	By Balance c/d	2,000
	57,000		57,000

BRANCH ADJUSTMENT ACCOUNT

	Rs.		Rs.
To Stock Reserve*	2,000	By Goods Sent to Branch (Loading)	10,000
(including in transit)		By Branch Stock A/c — Surplus	27,000
To Gross Profit c/d	35,000		
	37,000		37,000

BRANCH PROFIT & LOSS ACCOUNT

	Rs.		Rs.
To Branch Debtors — Bad debts	200	By Gross Profit b/d	35,000
To Branch Expenses	12,000		
To Net-Profit-transferred to	22,800		
G. P & L A/c	35,000		35,000

* Loading on Stock is 1/6

i.e. Cost Price is	100
Profit is	20
Invoice Price is	120

Rate of loading on I.P. 20/120 or 1/6

Working Note :

	Rs.
(1) Goods Sent to Branch at Invoice Price	60,000
(Cost + Profit) (50,000 + 10,000)	
Less Invoice Price of Goods Received	54,000
Good-in -Transit at Invoice Price	6,000

Illustration 10 (Selling at more than the Invoice Price)

R. K. Industries, Mumbai has a Branch at Banglore and goods are invoiced at Cost plus 25%. The Branch makes sales both for Cash and on credit. Branch expenses are paid direct from H.O. and the Branch has to remit all cash received in the Head Office Bank Account. From the following particulars relating to calendar year 2009, prepare Ledger accounts in the Books of H.O. and ascertain Branch profits. Branch does not maintain any books of accounts, but sends weekly returns to Head Office.

		Rs.
Goods received from Head Office at Invoice Price		60,000
Returns to Head Office at invoice price		1,200
Stock at Branch on 1st January		6,000
Sales :	Cash	20,000
	Credit	36,000
Sundry Debtors at Branch on 1st January		7,200

Cash received from Debtors	32,000
Discount allowed to Debtors	600
Bad debts	400
Sales returns at Branch	800
Rent, Rates and Taxes at Branch	1,800
Salaries, Wages and Bonus at Branch	6,000
Office expenses	600
Stock at Branch on 31st December	12,000

[C.A. (I), 1093-Modified]

Solution :

Let Cost price be	100
Profit	25
Invoice Price	125

Rate of Loading on Invoice price 25/125 or 1/5

BRANCH STOCK ACCOUNT (AT INVOICE PRICE)

	Rs.		Rs.
To Balance b/d	6,000	By Branch Cash (Cash Sales)	20,000
To Goods Sent to Branch	60,000	By Branch Debtors (Credit Sales Less Return)	35,200
To Surplus transferred to Branch Adjustment A/c	2,400	By Goods Sent to Branch (Return)	1,200
		By Balance c/d	12,000
	68,400		68,400

GOODS SENT TO BRANCH ACCOUNT

	Rs.		Rs.
To Branch Stock A/c (Return)	1,200	By Branch Stock A/c	60,000
To Branch Adjustment A/c (Loading 1/5 of 58,800)	11,760		
To Purchase transfer (Bal. figure)	47,040		
	60,000		60,000

BRANCH DEBTORS ACCOUNT

	Rs.		Rs.
To Balance b/d	7,200	By Cash	32,000
To Credit Sales	36,000	By Discount allowed	600
		By Bad debts	400
		By Return Inwards	800
		By Balance c/d	9,400
	43,200		43,200

BRANCH ADJUSTMENT ACCOUNT

	Rs.		Rs.
To Stock Reserve	2,400	By Stock Reserve A/c	1,200
(Loading on Closing Stock)		(Loading on Op. Stockl/5*6,000)	
To Gross Profit c/d	12,960	By Goods Sent to Branch (Loading)	11,760
		By Branch Stock - Excess of sales price over invoice price	2,400
	15,360		15,360

BRANCH PROFIT & LOSS ACCOUNT

	Rs.		Rs.
To Branch Expenses (Rates, Salaries Office Exp.) (1,800 + 6,000 + 600)	8,400	By Gross Profit b/d	12,960
To Branch Debtors			
Discount Allowed	600		
Bad debts	400		
To Net-Profit-transferred to P & L A/c	3,560		
	12,960		12,960

Illustration 11 (Loss-in-Transit & Insurance Claims)

A company sends goods to its branch at cost plus 25%. The following particulars are available in respect of a Branch for the year ended 31st March 2009 :

	Rs.
Opening Stock at Cost to the Branch	80,000
Goods sent to the Branch at Invoice price	12,00,000
Loss in Transit at Invoice price	15,000
Sales : Cash	10,00,000
Credit	2,19,000
Pilferage at Invoice price	6,000
Expenses incurred in cash by the Branch	60,000
Closing Stock at Branch at Cost to the Head Office	32,000
Recovery-from the Insurance Company against loss in transit	10,000
Depreciation on Branch Fixed assets	17,000

Prepare :

(1) Branch Stock Account

(2) Goods Sent to Branch Account

(3) Branch Adjustment Account &

(4) Branch Profit & Loss Account in the books of Head Office.

[C.A. (Inter), Nov. 1988 (Modified)]

Solution : BRANCH STOCK ACCOUNT (AT INVOICE PRICE)

	Rs.		Rs.
To Balance b/d*	80,000	By Branch Cash (Cash Sales)	10,00,000
To Goods Sent to Branch	12,00,000	By Branch Debtors (Credit Sales)	2,19,000
		By Pilferage (Abnormal loss transferred to Br. Adjustment & Br. P & L A/c)	6,000
		By Loss in Transit - (Abnormal Loss) transferred to Br. Adjustment & Br. P & L A/c	15,000
		By Balance c/d (32,000 + 8,000) (Cost + Loading)	40,000
	12,80,000		12,80,000

GOODS SENT TO BRANCH ACCOUNT

	Rs.		Rs.
To Branch Adjustment A/c (Loading 1/5 of 12,00,000)	2,40,000	By Branch Stock A/c	12,00,000
To Purchases-(4/5 of 12,00,000)	9,60,000		
	12,00,000		12,00,000

*Goods at cost to the Branch means goods sent by H.O. at invoice price.

BRANCH ADJUSTMENT ACCOUNT

	Rs.		Rs.
To Stock Reserve (Loading on Closing Stock @1/5)	8,000	By Stock Reserve (Loading on Op. Stock @1/5)	16,000
To Branch Stock A/c		By Goods Sent to Branch (Loading @ 1/5 on 12,00,000)	2,40,000
Pilferage -(1/5 of 6,000)	1,200		
Loss in Transit (1/5 of 15,000)	3,000		
To Gross Profit c/d	2,43,800		
	2,56,000		2,56,000

BRANCH P & L ACCOUNT

	Rs.		Rs.
To Branch Stock		By Gross Profit b/d	2,43,800
Pilferage at Cost (6,000 – 1,200)	4,800	By Insurance Claims	10,000
Loss in Transit (15,000 – 3,000)	12,000		
To Branch Expenses A/c			
Cash Expenses	60,000		
Depreciation	17,000		
To Net Profit transferred to General Profit & Loss A/c	1,60,000		
	2,53,800		2,53,800

Illustration 12 (Selling at less than the Invoice Price)

Delhi Head Office supplies goods to its Branch at Kanpur at invoice price which is Cost plus 50%. All cash received by the Branch is remitted to Delhi and all Branch expenses are paid by the H.O. From the following particulars related to Kanpur Branch for the year 2009, prepare (i) Branch Account and (ii) Branch Stock Account, Branch Debtors Account, and Branch Adjustment Account in the Books of Head Office so as to find out the gross profit and net profit made by branch :

			Rs.
Stock at Branch on 1st January at Invoice price			60,000
Branch Debtors on 1st January			12,000
Petty Cash on 1st January			100
Goods received from Head Office at Invoice Price			1,86,000
Goods Returned to Head Office			3,000
Credit Sales less returns			84,000
Allowance to Customers off selling price already adjusted while invoicing			2,000
Cash received from Debtors			90,000
Discount allowed to Debtors			2,400
Expenses paid by Head Office :	Rent	2,400	
	Salaries	24,000	
	Petty Cash	1,000	27,400
Cash Sales			1,04,000
Stock at Branch on 31st December at Invoice Price			54,000
Petty Cash Balance on 31st December			100

[B. Com. (H) DU, 1989-Modified]

Solution :

(I) BRANCH ACCOUNT

		Rs.			Rs.
To Balance b/d			By Bank (Remittances)		
Petty Cash		100	Cash Sales	1,04,000	
Debtors		12,000	Cash from Debtors	90,000	194,000
Stock		60,000	By Goods Sent to Branch (Returns)		3,000
To Good Sent to Branch		1,86,000	By Goods Sent to Branch (Loading)		62,000
To Bank (Expenses)			(1/3 of 1,86,000)		
Rent	2,400		By Stock Reserve (Loading on		20,000
Salaries	24,000		Opening Stock)		
Petty Cash	1,000	27,400	By Balance c/d		
To Goods Sent to Branch			Petty Cash		100
(Loading on Returns)		1,000	Debtors* (see Debtors A/c)		3,600
To Stock Reserve		18,000	Stock		54,000
(Loading on Closing Stock-1/3 of 54,000)					
To Net-Profit -transferred to					
General P & L A/c		32,200			
		3,36,700			3,36,700

(II) BRANCH STOCK ACCOUNT (AT INVOICE PRICE)

	Rs.		Rs.
To Balance b/d	60,000	By Branch Cash (Cash sales)	1,04,000
To Goods Sent to Branch	1,86,000	By Branch Debtors (Credit sales)	84,000
To Surplus - Transferred to		By Branch Adjustment A/c (Allowance)*	2,000
Branch Adjustment A/c	1,000	By Goods Sent to Branch	3,000
		By Balance b/d	54,000
	2,47,000		2,47,000

BRANCH DEBTORS ACCOUNT

	Rs.		Rs.
To Balance b/d	12,000	By Branch Cash	90,000
To Credit Sales	84,000	By Branch Expenses (Discount)	2,400
		By Balance c/d (Bal. Figure)	3,600
	96,000		96,000

BRANCH EXPENSES ACCOUNT

	Rs.		Rs.
To Cash (Exp.): Rent	2,400	By Balance transferred to	
Salaries	24,000	Branch P & L A/c	29,800
Petty Exp.	1,000		
To Branch Debtors (Discount)	2,400		
	29,800		29,800

BRANCH ADJUSTMENT ACCOUNT

	Rs.		Rs.
To Stock Reserve	18,000	By Stock Reserve	20,000
(Loading on Closing Stock)		(Loading on op. stock)	
To Goods Sent to Branch	1,000	By Goods Sent to Branch	62,000
(Loading on Returns)		(Loading on goods sent)	
To Branch Stock (Allowance)*	2,000	By Branch Stock-Surplus	1,000
To Gross Profit c/d	62,000		
	83,000		83,000

BRANCH PROFIT & LOSS A/C

	Rs.		Rs.
To Branch Expenses A/c	29,800	By Gross Profit b/d	62,000
To Net Profit-transferred to General	32,200		
Profit & Loss Account			
	62,000		62,000

***Working Note :** Since Branch Stock A/c is prepared at Invoice price, "any allowance", which makes the sale less than the invoice price, will be credited to Branch Stock A/c and debited to Branch Adjustment Account.

Illustration 13 (New Branch & Direct Expenses)

M/s A One Traders, opened a Branch at Delhi on 1-7-2008. The goods were sent by the Head Office to Branch and invoiced at Selling price to the Branch, which was 125% of the Cost price of the Head Office. The following are the particulars relating to the transactions of Delhi Branch :

			Rs.
Goods sent to Branch (at Cost to Head Office)			2,80,800
Sales :	Cash		1,25,000
	Credit		1,75,000
Cash collected from Debtors,			1,56,000
Discount allowed			4,000
Returns from Debtors			5,000
Cash sent to Branch for :			
	Wages	3,000	
	Freight	11,000	
	Other Expenses	6,000	20,000
Spoiled cloth in bales written off at invoice price			500
Stock on 30th June 2009 at invoice price			55,500

Ascertain the profit or loss for Delhi Branch for the year ended 30th June 2006 after preparing Branch Stock Account and Branch Debtors Account. **[B.Com. (H), DU, 1991-Modified]**

Solution : **In the Books of Head Office**

BRANCH STOCK ACCOUNT (AT INVOICE PRICE)

	Rs.		Rs.
To Goods Sent to Branch	3,51,000	By Branch Cash (Cash sales)	1,25,000
(2,80,800 × 125/100)		By Branch Debtors (Credit Sales)	1,75,000
To Branch Debtors (Returns inward)	5,000	By Spoilage transferred to	
		Branch Adjustment A/c (Loading)	100
		Branch P & L A/c (Cost)	400
		By Balance c/d	55,500
	3,56,000		3,56,000

BRANCH DEBTORS ACCOUNT

	Rs.		Rs.
To Credit Sales	1,75,000	By Cash	1,56,000
		By Discount Allowed	4,000
		By Returns Inwards	5,000
		By Balance c/d	10,000
	1,75,000		1,75,000

GOODS SENT TO BRANCH ACCOUNT

	Rs.		Rs.
To Branch Adjustment A/c	70,200	By Branch Stock A/c	3,51,000
To Purchases	2,80,800		
	3,51,000		3,51,000

BRANCH ADJUSTMENT ACCOUNT

	Rs.		Rs.
To Branch Stock:		By Goods Sent to Branch A/c	70,200
Spoilage (Loading)	100	(Loading)	
To Stock Reserve	11,100		
(Loading on Closing Stock)			
To Direct Expenses (wages & freight)	14,000		
To Gross Profit c/d	45,000		
	70,200		70,200

BRANCH PROFIT & LOSS ACCOUNT

		Rs.		Rs.
To Spoilage at Cost		400	By Gross Profit b/d	45,000
To Branch Expenses (indirect):				
Other Expenses	6,000			
Discount	4,000	10,000		
To Net Profit-transferred				
to Gen. P & L A/c		34,600		
		45,000		45,000

Illustration 14 (Authorised Reduction in Selling Price)

Cyma Stores of Delhi operates a retail branch at Chennai. The Head Office makes all purchases and the Branch is charged cost plus 50%. All cash received by Chennai Branch is remitted to Delhi. Branch expenses are paid by the Branch out of an imp-rest account which is reimbursed by Delhi Head Office.The Branch keeps a sales ledger and certain essential subsidiary books, but otherwise all branch transactions are recorded at Delhi. On 1st January 2008 stock in trade at the branch at selling price amounted to Rs. 6,000 and debtors balances were Rs. 4,000.

During the year ended 31st December 2008 the following branch transactions were made :

	Rs.
Goods received from Delhi at selling price	15,000
Cash Sales	6,900
Goods returned to Delhi at selling price	300

Credit Sales less returns	6,300
Authorised reductions in selling price of goods sold	150
Cash received from Debtors	4,800
Debtors written off as irrecoverable	200
Cash discount allowed to Debtors	150

A consignment of goods despatched to the branch on 28th December with a selling price of Rs. 180 was not received until 5th January and has not been included in stock figure, which at selling price was Rs. 7,290. The expenses relating to the branch for the year ended 31 st December amounted to Rs. 1,800.

You are required (a) to write up the Branch Stock account and Branch Debtors account maintained at Delhi with a view to control stock and debtors and (b) prepare Trading and Profit & Loss Account of the branch for the year ended 31st December 2008.

Note : Any stock unaccounted for is to be regarded as normal wastage and pilferage.

[B.Com. (H), DU, 1992-Modified]

Solution : **In the Books of Head Office**

BRANCH STOCK ACCOUNT

	Rs.		Rs.
To Balance b/d	6,000	By Branch Cash (Cash Sales)	6,900
To Goods Sent to Branch	15,180	By Branch Debtors (Credit Sales)	6,300
(including in transit)		By Branch Adjustment A/c	150
		(being reduction in price)	
		By Goods sent to Branch (Returns)	300
		By Shortage-Branch Adjustment A/c (B.F)	60
		By Balance c/d	
		Stock in Transit	180
		Stock in Hand	7,290
	21,180		21,180

GOODS SENT TO BRANCH ACCOUNT

	Rs.		Rs.
To Branch Stock A/c (Returns)	300	By Branch Stock Account	15,180
To Branch Adjustment A/c (Loading)	4,960		
To Purchases (Cost)	9,920		
	15,180		15,180

BRANCH DEBTORS ACCOUNT

	Rs.		Rs.
To Balance b/d	4,000	By Cash	4,800
To Credit Sales	6,300	By Bad debts	200
		By Discounts	150
		By Balance c/d	5,150
	10,300		10,300

BRANCH ADJUSTMENT ACCOUNT

	Rs.		Rs.
To Stock Reserve*	2,490	By Stock Reserve*	2,000
(Loading on Cosing Stock & Goods in transit)		(Loading on Opening Stock)	
To Branch Stock:		By Goods Sent to Branch*	4,960
Shortage (Normal)	60	(Loading)	
Reduction in Selling Price	150		
To Gross Profit c/d	4,260		
	6,960		6,960

BRANCH PROFIT & LOSS ACCOUNT

		Rs.		Rs.
To Branch Debtors A/c			By Gross Profit b/d	4,260
Bad debts	200			
Discount allowed	150	350		
To Branch Expenses		1,800		
To Net Profit-transferred to				
Gen. P & L A/c		2,110		
		4,260		4,260

BRANCH TRADING AND PROFIT & LOSS ACCOUNT
For the year ended 31st December 2008

	Rs.		Rs.
To Opening Stock (at cost)	4,000	By Sales:	
To Goods Sent to Branch	9,920	Cash	6,900
To Gross Profit c/d	4,260	Credit	6,300
		By Closing Stock (at cost)	4,980
		(Including in transit)	
	18,180		18,180
To Sundry Expenses	1800	By Gross Profit b/d	4,260
To Bad debts	200		
To Discount allowed	150		
To Net Profit-transferred to			
Gen. P & L A/c	2,110		
	4,260		4,260

*Rate of loading on invoice price is 1/3 which is calculated as under :

Cost Price	100
Profit	50
Invoice Price	150

Loading on I.P. 50/150 or 1/3

Illustration 15 (Calculation of Closing Stock)

Maria Ltd. has a Branch at Lucknow. Goods are invoiced from Head Office at cost price 50% Branch remits all cash received to Head Office and all expenses are met by Head Office.

Prepare necessary accounts in the books of Maria Ltd. under stock and debtors system to show profit earned at branch from the following :

		Rs.
Stock on 1st Jan (at invoice price)		15,600
Debtors on 1st Jan		8,700
Goods invoice at cost during the year ended 31st December		36,000
Sales at branch :	Cash	35,000
	Credit Sales	30,100
Cash collected from debtors		29,800
Goods returned by debtors		1,500
Surplus in Stock (at invoice price)		300
Discount allowed to Debtors		350
Expenses at Branch		6,700

Solution : In the Books of Head Office

BRANCH STOCK ACCOUNT (AT INVOICE PRICE)

	Rs.		Rs.
To Balance b/d	15,600	By Branch Cash (Cash Sales)	35,000
To Goods Sent to Branch	54,000	By Branch Debtors (Credit Sales)	30,100
(36,000 + 18,000)		By Balance c/d (Bal. Figure)	6,300
To Branch Debtors (Sales return)	1,500	(Closing Stock)	
To Surplus-transferred to			
Branch Adjustment A/c	300		
	71,400		71,400

GOODS SENT TO BRANCH ACCOUNT

	Rs.		Rs.
To Branch Adjustment A/c (Loading)	18,000	By Branch Stock Account	54,000
To Purchases	36,000		
	54,000		54,000

BRANCH DEBTORS ACCOUNT

	Rs.		Rs.
To Balance b/d	8,700	By Cash	29,800
To Credit Sales	30,100	By Returns Inwards	1,500
		By Discount allowed	350
		By Balance c/d (Balancing figure)	7,150
	38,800		38,800

BRANCH ADJUSTMENT ACCOUNT

	Rs.		Rs.
To Stock Reserve (1/3 x 6,300)	2,100	By Stock Reserve (1/3 × 15,600)	5,200
(Loading on Closing Stock)		(Loading on Opening Stock)	
To Gross Profit c/d	21,400	By Branch Stock A/c-Surplus	300
		By Goods Sent to Branch (Loading)	18,000
	23,500		23,500

BRANCH PROFIT & LOSS ACCOUNT

	Rs.		Rs.
To Branch Expenses A/c	6,700	By Gross Profit b/d	21,400
To Branch Debtors-(Discount)	350		
To Net Profit transferred to			
Gen. P & L A/c	14,350		
	21,400		21,400

*Loading at Invoice Price is 1/3

Cost Price	100	
Profit	50	
Invoice price	150	Rate 50/150 or 1/3

Illustration 16 (Opening Balance of Branch Adjustment A/c)

X Ltd. has its Branch at Delhi, Goods are invoiced to the branch at cost plus 33-1/3%. On 1st January, the following balances appeared in the Head Office ledger :

	Rs.
Branch Debtors Account	15,000
Branch Stock Account at Selling price	6,000
Branch Adjustment Account (Cr)	1,500

The following were the transactions of the branch during the year :

Cash Sales	7,500
Credit Sales	1,50,000
Goods from Head Office at Selling price	1,80,000
Cash received from Branch Debtors	1,44,000
Discount allowed to Branch Debtors	3,690
Branch Expenses paid by Head Office	37,500
Stock at branch at 31st Dec.	24,000

Prepare necessary accounts in the Books of Head Office according to Stock and Debtors system.

[B.Com. (H), DU, 1991 (Suppl.)-Modified]

Solution : **BRANCH STOCK ACCOUNT (AT INVOICE PRICE)**

	Rs.		Rs.
To Balance b/d	6,000	By Branch. Cash (Cash Sales)	7,500
To Goods Sent to Branch	1,80,000	By Branch Debtors (Credit Sales)	1,50,000
		By Abnormal Loss-Shortage transferred to Branch Adjustment and Branch P&LA/c (B.F.)	4,500
		By Balance c/d	24,000
	1,86,000		1,86,000

BRANCH DEBTORS ACCOUNT

	Rs.		Rs.
To Balance b/d	15,000	By Cash	1,44,000
To Credit Sales	1,50,000	By Discount allowed	3,690
		By Balance c/d	17,310
	1,65,000		1,65,000

GOODS SENT TO BRANCH ACCOUNT

	Rs.		Rs.
To Branch Adjustment A/c (Loading)	45,000	By Branch Stock	1,80,000
To Purchases (Cost)	1,35,000		
	1,80,000		1,80,000

BRANCH EXPENSES ACCOUNT

	Rs.		Rs.
To Cash (Br. Exp.)	37,500	By Balance transferred to Branch P & L A/c	41,190
To Br. Debtors (Discount)	3,690		
	41,190		41,190

BRANCH ADJUSTMENT ACCOUNT

	Rs.		Rs.
To Branch Stock-Shortage (Loading)*	1,125	By Balance b/d* (or Loading on Opening Stock)	1,500
To Stock Reserve (Balance c/d)* (Loading on Closing Stock)	6,000	By Goods Sent to Branch*	45,000
To Gross Profit c/d	39,375		
	46,500		46,500
To Shortage at Cost (Br. Stock)	3,375	By Gross Profit b/d	39,375
To Branch Expenses A/c	41,190	By Net Loss transferred to Gen. P & L A/c	5,190
	44,565		44,565

*Loading is $\dfrac{33\frac{1}{3}}{133\frac{1}{3}}$ or $\dfrac{1}{4}$

Illustration 17 (Accounting for more than one Branch)

Punjab Soap Mills Ltd. has two Branches, Ambala and at Ludhiana. Goods are invoiced to branch at Cost plus 50%. Branches remit-all cash received to the Head Office and all expenses are met by Head Office. From the following particulars prepare necessary accounts under stock and debtors system to show the profit

	Ambala Rs.	Ludhiana Rs.
Stock on 1st January at Invoice Price	9,300	15,600
Debtors on 1st January	6,800	8,700
Goods invoiced to Branches at Cost	34,000	36,000
Sales at Branches : Cash	25,010	35,000
Credit	31,000	30,100
Cash collected from Debtors	30,400	29,800
Goods returned by Debtors	1,200	1,500
Goods transferred from Ludhiana to Ambala	2,100	2,100
Surplus in Stock	—	300
Shortage in Stock	450	—
Discount allowed to Debtors	200	350
Expenses	5,400	6,700

[B.Com. (Madurai), 1993-Modified]

Solution : In the Books of Head Office

BRANCH STOCK ACCOUNT (AT INVOICE PRICE)

	Ambala Rs.	Ludhiana Rs.		Ambala Rs.	Ludhiana Rs.
To Balance b/d	9,300	15,600	By Branch Cash (Cash sales)	25,010	35,000
To Goods Sent to Branch (Cost + Loading)	51,000	54,000	By Branch Debtors (Credit sales)	31,000	30,100
To Branch Debtors (sales return)	1,200	1,500	By Goods Sent to Branch (Transfer to other Br.)	—	2,100
To Goods sent to Branch (Transfer from other Branch)	2,100	—	By Shortage-transferred to Br. Adjustment A/c	450	—
To Surplus-Br. Adjustment A/c	—	300	By Balance c/d (B.F.)	7,140	4,200
	63,600	71,400		63,600	71,400

GOODS SENT TO BRANCH ACCOUNT

	Ambala Rs.	Ludhiana Rs.		Ambala Rs.	Ludhiana Rs.
To Branch Stock A/c	—	2,100	By Branch Stock Account	51,000	54,000
To Branch Adjustment A/c (17,000 + 700) 1/3(54,000 – 2,100)*	17,700	17,300*	By Branch Stock A/c	2,100	
To Purchases	35,400	34,600			
	53,100	54,000		53,100	54,000

BRANCH DEBTORS ACCOUNT

	Ambala Rs.	Ludhiana Rs.		Ambala Rs.	Ludhiana Rs.
To Balance b/d	6,800	8,700	By Branch Cash	30,400	29,800
To Credit Sales	31,000	30,100	By Sales Returns	1,200	1,500
			By Discount allowed	200	350
			By Balance c/d	6,000	7,150
	37,800	38,800		37,800	38,800

BRANCH ADJUSTMENT ACCOUNT

	Ambala Rs.	Ludhiana Rs.		Ambala Rs.	Ludhiana Rs.
To Stock Reserve (Loading Cl. Stock)	2,380	1,400	By Stock Reserve (Loading on Op. Stock)	3,100	5,200
To Shortage (Loading) (Branch Stock A/c)	150	—	By Goods Sent to Branch	17,700	17,300
			By Surplus-Branch Stock A/c		300
To Gross Profit c/d	18,270	21,400			
	20,800	22,800		20,800	22,800
To Shortage at Cost	300	—	By Gross Profit b/d	18,270	21,400
To Branch Expenses	5,400	6,700			
To Branch Debtors (Discount)	200	350			
To Net Profit-transferred to Gen. P & L A/c	12,370	14,350			
	18,270	21,400		18,270	21,400

Illustration 18 (Cheques Dishonoured)

Soha and company with its Head Office at Kolkata has a branch at Delhi. Goods are invoiced to the Branch at Cost plus 33-1/3% which is the selling price. The following information is given in respect of the Branch for the year ended 31st March 2008 :

	Rs.
Goods sent to Branch at Invoice Price	4,80,000
Stock at Branch on 1-4-2007 at Invoice Price	24,000
Cash Sales	1,80,000
Returns from Customers	6,000
Branch Expenses paid by Head Office	53,500
Branch Debtors on 1-4-2007	30,000
Discount allowed	1,000
Bad debts	1,500
Stock at Branch on 31-3-2008 at Invoice Price	48,000
Branch Debtors on 31-3-2008	36,500
Collections from Debtors	2,70,000
Branch Debtors cheques returned dishonoured	5,000

You are required to prepare Branch Stock Account Branch Debtors Account and Branch Adjustment Account to reveal the profit of the Branch for the year.

[I.C.W.A. (I), 1988-Modified)

Solution : **In the Books of Head Office**

BRANCH STOCK ACCOUNT

	Rs.		Rs.
To Balance b/d	24,000	By Branch Cash (Cash Sales)	1,80,000
To Goods Sent to Branch	4,80,000	By Branch Debtors (Credit Sales)	2,80,000
To Branch Debtors (Sales Returns)	6,000	By Shortage-transferred to Branch Adjustment & Br. P & L A/c (B.F.)	2,000
		By Balance c/d	48,000
	5,10,000		5,10,000

BRANCH DEBTORS ACCOUNT

	Rs.		Rs.
To Balance b/d	30,000	By Cash	2,70,000
To Credit Sales (Bal. Figure)	2,80,000	By Discount allowed	1,000
To Cheques Dishonoured	5,000	By Bad debts	1,500
		By Returns Inwards	6,000
		By Balance c/d	36,500
	3,15,000		3,15,000

BRANCH ADJUSTMENT ACCOUNT

	Rs.		Rs.
To Stock Reserve (1/4 of 48,000)	12,000	By Stock Reserve (1/4 of 24,000)	6,000
To Branch Stock-Shortage (1/4 of 2,000)	500	By Goods Sent to Branch (1/4 of 4,80,000)	1,20,000
To Gross Profit c/d	1,13,500		
	1,26,000		1,26,000
To Shortage at Cost (Br. Stock)	1,500	By Gross Profit b/d	1,13,500
To Branch Expenses	53,500		
To Branch Debtors (Discount & B. Debts)	2,500		
To Net Profit transferred to General P&LA/c	56,000		
	1,13,500		1,13,500

* Cost is 100; Profit $33\frac{1}{3}$%; Invoice Price = $133\frac{1}{3}$; Rate of loading on Invoice Price = $33\frac{1}{3} / 133\frac{1}{3}$ = 1/4.

Illustration 19 (Surplus from Branch Stock)

Delhi Head Office supplied goods to its Kanpur Branch at invoice price which is cost plus 50%. All cash received by the branch is remitted to Delhi and all Branch Expenses are paid by the Head Office. From the following particulars relating to Kanpur Branch for the year 2007, prepare :

(1) Branch Stock Account
(2) Branch Debtors Account
(3) Branch Expenses Account &
(4) Branch Adjustment Account, in the books of Head Office so as to ascertain the gross profit and net profit made by the Branch.

	Rs.
Cash Sales	1,04,000
Stock with Branch at Invoice price on 1st January	60,000
Branch Debtors on 1st January	12,000
Petty Cash Balance on 1st January	100
Goods received from Head Office at Invoice price	1,86,000
Goods returned to Head Office	13,000
Credit Sales less returns	86,000
Cash received from Debtors	90,000
Discount allowed to Debtors	2,400
Expenses paid by Head Office :	
Rent	2,400
Salaries	24,000
Petty Cash	1,000
Stock with Branch at invoice price on 31st December	54,000
Petty Cash balance on 31st December	100

[B.Com. (H), DU, 1997-Modified]

Solution : **BRANCH STOCK ACCOUNT (AT INVOICE PRICE)**

	Rs.		Rs.
To Balance b/d	60,000	By Branch Cash (Cash Sales)	1,04,000
To Goods Sent to Branch	1,86,000	By Branch Debtors (Credit Sales)	86,000
To Surplus-transferred to	11,000	By Goods Sent to Branch A/c (Returns)	13,000
Branch Adjustment A/c (B.F.)		By Balance c/d	54,000
	2,57,000		2,57,000

BRANCH DEBTORS ACCOUNT

	Rs.		Rs.
To Balance b/d	12,000	By Cash	90,000
To Credit Sales	86,000	By Discount Allowed	2,400
		By Balance c/d	5,600
	98,000		98,000

BRANCH EXPENSES ACCOUNT

	Rs.		Rs.
To Rent	2,400	By Balance transferred to	
To Salaries	24,000	Branch P & L A/c	29,800
To Petty Expenses	1,000		
To Br. Debtors (Discount)	2,400		
	29,800		29,800

BRANCH ADJUSTMENT ACCOUNT

	Rs.		Rs.
To Stock Reserve (1/3 of 54,000)*	18,000	By Stock Reserve (1/3 of 60,000)*	20,000
To Goods Sent to Branch (Returns)* (1/3 of 13,000)	4,333	By Goods sent to Branch* (1/3 of 1,86,000)	62,000
To Gross Profit c/d	70,667	By Branch Stock A/c (Surplus)	11,000
	93,000		93,000
To Branch Expenses	29,800	By Gross Profit b/d	70,667
To Net Profit transferred to General P & L A/c	40,867		
	70,667		70,667

*Loading on invoice price is 50/150 or 1/3

i.e. Cost price	100
Profit	50
Invoice price	150

Rate of loading on invoice price 50/150 or 1/3

Illustration 20 (Normal and Abnormal Losses)

Soha Electrical has its branches at Chandigarh and Gwalior to whom goods are invoiced at cost plus 25%. Following information is available of the transactions at Chandigarh Branch for the year ending 31 st March 2009 :

	Rs.
Balances on 1 st April 2008	
Stock at Invoice price	40,000
Debtors	12,000
Petty Cash	150
Transactions during the year :	
Goods sent to Branch at Invoice price	4,20,000
Goods returned to Head Office at Invoice price	15,000
Cash Sales	1,05,000
Credit Sales	1,80,000

Normal Loss at Invoice price	350
Goods pilfered at Invoice price	3,000
Goods lost in fire at Invoice price	4,000
Insurance Company paid to Head Office for loss by fire	3,000
Cash sent for petty Expenses	32,000
Bad debts	400
Goods transferred to Gwalior Branch under instructions from H.O.	12,000
Insurance charges paid by Head Office	200
Goods returned by Debtors	500
Balance on 31st March :	
Petty Cash	250
Debtors	11,000
Stock	?

Note : Goods transferred to Gwalior Branch (given above) were in transit on 31st March.

Prepare : (i) Branch Stock Account (ii) Branch Adjustment Account (iii) Branch Profit & Loss A/c (iv) Stock Reserve A/c. **[B.Com. (H), DU, 1994-Modified]**

Solution : **In the Books of Head Office**

BRANCH STOCK ACCOUNT

	Rs.		Rs.
To Balance b/d	40,000	By Branch Cash (Cash Sales)	105,000
To Goods Sent to Branch	420,000	By Branch Debtors (Credit Sales)	180,000
To Branch Debtors (Sales Returns)	500	By Normal Loss-transferred to Branch Adjustment A/c	350
		By Abnormal Loss (transferred to Branch Adjustment A/c & P & L A/c)	
		Pilferage	3,000
		Loss by Fire	4,000
		By Goods Sent to Branch (Returns)	15,000
		By Goods Sent to Branch (Transfer)	12,000
		By Balance c/d (Bal. Figure)	1,41,150
	4,60,500		4,60,500

GOODS SENT TO BRANCH ACCOUNT

	Rs.		Rs.
To Branch Stock (Returns)	15,000	By Branch Stock A/c	4,20,000
To Branch Stock (Transfer)	12,000		
To Branch Adjustment A/c (Loading)	78,600		
To Purchases (Cost) (Bal. figure)	3,14,400		
	4,20,000		4,20,000

BRANCH ADJUSTMENT ACCOUNT

	Rs.		Rs.
To Stock Reserve (25/125 × 1,41,250)	28,230	By Stock Reserve (1/5 × 40,000)	8,000
(Loading on Closing stock)		(Loading on Op. stock)	
To Branch Stock A/c		By Goods Sent to Branch (Loading)	78,600
Normal Loss	350		
Abnormal Loss-Pilferage (1/5)	600		
Loss by Fire (1/5)	800		
To Gross Profit c/d	56,620		
	86,600		86,600

BRANCH PROFIT & LOSS ACCOUNT

	Rs.		Rs.
To Branch Stock: (Ab. Loss)		By Gross Profit b/d	56,620
Shortage at cost	2,400	By Insurance Claims	3,000
Loss by fire at cost	3,200		
To Branch Expenses (150 + 32,000 – 250)	31,900		
To Branch Debtors (Bad debts)	400		
To Cash (Insurance Charges)	200		
To Net Profit-transferred to General			
P & L A/c	21,520		
	59,620		59,620

Illustration 21 (Loss of Goods & Insurance Claims)

Inter City Traders have Head Office at Mumbai and a Branch at Kalyan. The goods are dispatched from Mumbai to Kalyan at cost plus 25%. The information pertaining to year 1st April 2007 to 31 st March 2008 is as under :

(i) The stock increased from Rs. 60,000 to Rs. 90,500 during the year,

(ii) The debtors increased from Rs. 20,000 to Rs. 32,000.

(iii) The goods received from Mumbai were invoiced at Rs. 6,50,000. Of these goods of Rs. 30,000 were sent to Shahpur Branch. Goods for Rs. 20,000 were returned to Mumbai since these were received in damaged condition,

(iv) Goods for Rs. 10,000 (invoice price) were lost at Branch. Insurance claim of Rs. 6,000 was received at Mumbai.

(v) Total sales were Rs. 5,60,000. Of these 40% were for cash and remaining on credit. One customer to whom goods worth Rs. 2,500 were sold, returned 20% of goods. He is not likely to pay Rs. 500 which is balance due from him.

(vi) Branch paid for the following expenses :
Salary Rs. 36,000, Rent Rs. 6,000, Printing & Stationery, Rs. 6,000 Freight outwards and Delivery charges Rs. 9,000, General expenses, Rs. 17,640. The cash balance increased from Rs. 100 to Rs. 460.

(vii) Mumbai office paid insurance premium on behalf of the Branch Rs. 1,000. It also charged Rs. 5,000 as depreciation on assets at Branch.

You are required to prepare necessary accounts in the Books of Mumbai Office under Stock & Debtors System. **[B.Com. (Mumbai), 1997 (Modified)]**

Solution : **In the Books of Head Office**

BRANCH STOCK ACCOUNT (AT INVOICE PRICE)

	Rs.		Rs.
To Balance b/d	60,000	By Branch Cash (Cash sales)	2,24,000
To Goods Sent to Branch A/c	6,50,000	By Branch Debtors (Credit sales)	3,36,000
To Branch Debtors (Sales Returns)	500	By Goods Sent to Branch (Transfer)	30,000
		By Goods Sent to Branch (Returns)	20,000
		By Abnormal Loss (Goods lost) Transferred to Branch Adjustment and Branch P & L A/c	10,000
		By Balance c/d	90,500
	7,10,500		7,10,500

GOODS SENT TO BRANCH ACCOUNT

	Rs.		Rs.
To Branch Stock A/c (Tr.)	30,000	By Branch Stock Account	6,50,000
To Branch Stock A/c (Return)	20,000		
To Branch Adjustment A/c (Loading)	1,20,000		
To Purchases (Cost)	4,80,000		
	6,50,000		6,50,000

BRANCH DEBTORS ACCOUNT

	Rs.		Rs.
To Balance b/d	20,000	By Cash (Bal. Figure)	3,23,000
To Credit Sales (Br. Stock A/c)	3,36,000	By Bad debts	500
		By Sales Returns	500
		By Balance c/d	32,000
	3,56,000		3,56,000

BRANCH EXPENSES ACCOUNT

	Rs.		Rs.
To Salary	36,000	By Balance transferred to Branch P & L A/c	74,640
To Rent	6,000		
To Printing & Stationery	6,000		
To Freight Outwards	9,000		
To General Exp.	17,640		
	74,640		74,640

BRANCH ADJUSTMENT ACCOUNT

	Rs.		Rs.
To Stock Reserve (Loading on Closing Stock) $\left(\frac{1}{5} \times 90{,}500\right)$	18,100	By Stock Reserve Loading on opening Stock) (60,000 × 1/5)	12,000
To Branch Stock- Abnormal Loss (Loading 1/5of 10,000)	2,000	By Goods Sent to Branch A/c	1,20,000
To Gross Profit c/d	1,11,900		
	1,32,000		1,32,000

BRANCH PROFIT & LOSS ACCOUNT

	Rs.		Rs.
To Abnormal Loss at cost	8,000	By Gross Profit b/d	1,11,900
To Branch Expenses	74,640	By Insurance Claims	6,000
To Branch Debtors (Bad debts)	500		
To Cash (Insurance Premium)	1,000		
To Depreciation (Br. Assets)	5,000		
To Net Profit transferred to General P & L A/c	28,760		
	1,17,900		1,17,900

Illustration 22 (Provision for Discount)

Bengal Trading Co. with its Head Office in Kolkata invoiced goods to its Branch at Mumbai at 20% less than catalogue price which is cost plus 50% with instruction that cash sales be made at 'invoice price' and credit sales at catalogue price less discount at 15% on prompt payment.

From the following particulars available from the branch, prepare Branch Trading and Profit & Loss Account and necessary accounts as per Stock and Debtors System for the year ended 31st March 2008 in Head Office Books :

	Rs.
Stock on 1-4-2007	12,000
Debtors on 1-4-2007	10,000
Goods received from Head Office	1,32,000
Cash Sales	46,000
Credit Sales	1,00,000
Discount allowed to Debtors	13,365
Cash realised from Debtors	85,635
Expenses at Branch	6,000
Remittances to Head Office	1,20,000
Debtors on 31 st March, 2008	11,000
Cash in hand on 31 st March, 2008	5,635
Stock on 31st March, 2008	15,000

It was further reported that a part of stock at branch was lost by fire (not covered by insurance) during the year whose value is to be ascertained and a provision of Rs. 1,337 should be made for discount allowed to debtors.

[C.A. (Inter), 1992 & B.Com. (H), DU, 1996-Modified]

Solution :

In the Books of Head Office

BRANCH STOCK ACCOUNT (AT INVOICE PRICE)

	Rs.		Rs.
To Balance b/d	12,000	By Branch Cash (Cash Sales)	46,000
To Goods Sent to Branch	1,32,000	By Branch Debtors (Credit Sales)	1,00,000
To Branch Adjustment A/c (Excess of Catalogue price over Invoice price)	20,000	By Abnormal Loss A/c (Loss by fire transferred to Branch Adjustment and P & L A/c)	3,000
		By Balance c/d	15,000
	1,64,000		1,64,000

BRANCH DEBTORS ACCOUNT

	Rs.		Rs.
To Balance b/d	10,000	By Cash	85,635
To Credit Sales	1,00,000	By Discount Allowed	13,365
		By Balance c/d	11,000
	1,10,000		1,10,000

BRANCH EXPENSES ACCOUNT

	Rs.		Rs.
To Branch Cash	6,000	By Balance transferred to Branch P & L A/c	19,365
To Branch Debtors (Discount)	13,365		
	19,365		19,365

BRANCH ADJUSTMENT ACCOUNT

	Rs.		Rs.
To Stock Reserve* (Loading on Closing Stock $\frac{1}{6} \times 15{,}000$)	2,500	By Stock Reserve* (Loading on Op. Stock $\frac{1}{6} \times 12{,}000$)	2,000
To Abnormal Loss A/c $\left(\frac{1}{6} \text{ of, } 3{,}000\right)$	500	By Branch Stock-Excess of Catalogue Price over Invoice price	20,000
		By Goods Sent to Branch (Loading)	22,000
To Gross Profit c/d	41,000		
	44,000		44,000

BRANCH PROFIT & LOSS ACCOUNT

	Rs.		Rs.
To Abnormal Loss (Br. Stock) at cost	2,500	By Gross Profit b/d	41,000
To Branch Expenses A/c	19,365		
To Provision for Discount	1,337		
To Net Profit transferred to General P & L A/c	17,798		
	41,000		41,000

"Loading has been calculated as under :

Let Cost price be 100

Catalogue Price 150

Invoice price 20% Less than Catalogue Price (150-30) 120

BRANCH TRADING AND PROFIT & LOSS ACCOUNT

For the year end 31st March 2006

	Rs.			Rs.
To Opening Stock (at cost)	10,000	By Sales :		
To Goods Received from H.O.	1,10,000	Cash	46,000	
(1,32,000 – 22,000)		Credit	1,00,000	1,46,000
To Gross Profit c/d	41,000	By Abnormal Loss		2,500
		(Loss by fire at cost) (3,000 – 500)		
		By Closing Stock (15,000-2,500)		12,500
	1,61,000			1,61,000
To Abnormal Loss	2,500	By Gross Profit b/d		41,000
To Expenses	6,000			
To Discount allowed	13,365			
To Provision for Discount	1,337			
To Net Profit transferred to Gen. P & L A/c	17,798			
	41,000			41,000

QUESTIONS

1. What is a "Branch". Explain briefly the various types of branches from accounting point of view.
2. Distinguish between "Debtors System" and "Stock & Debtors" system of branch accounting.
3. How will you deal with the following items under "Debtors System" and "Stock & Debtors System" :
   — Normal loss — Abnormal loss — Goods-in-Transit
4. Differentiate between "cash sent by head office to branch for expenses" and "expenses incurred by branch". Where these two are shown?
5. Write note on "imprest system" of petty cash.

PROBLEMS

1. A company with its Head Office at Mumbai has a branch at Kolkata. The Branch receives all goods from Head Office who also remits cash for all expenses. Sales are made by the branch on credit as well as for cash. Total sales by the branch for the year ended 31st March 2006 amounted to Rs 5,60,000 out of which 20% is cash sales. The following further information is relevant.

	01-04-05	31-03-06
	Rs.	Rs.
Stock in Trade	25,000	36,000
Debtors	60,000	48,000
Petty cash	120	180

Expenses actually incurred by branch during the year were:

	Rs.
Salaries	36,000
Rent	12,000
Petty Expenses	5,600

All sales are made by the branch at cost plus 25%.

You are required to prepare the Kolkata Branch Account in the books of Head Office for the year ended 31st March,2007.

Ans. Profit - Rs. 58,400.

2. A Head office in Delhi sends goods to its branch in Mumbai marked 20% above cost. From the following particulars show how the Branch Account will appear in the Head Office books. Also give the Journal Entries necessary for the Head Office to adjust the Branch Account for arriving at the profit or loss made by the Branch.

		Rs.			**Rs.**
Stock in the begining at the branch		27,000	Cheques Sent to branch:		
Debtors in the begining at the branch		45,000	Salary	13,500	
Petty Cash in the begining at the branch		450	Rent & Taxes	2,250	
Goods supplied to the branch		4,50,000	Petty Cash	1,650	17,400
Remittance from the branch:			Stock at branch at the end		45,000
Cash Sales	90,000		Debtors at branch at the end		72,000
Cash Received from			Petty Cash at branch at the end		300
Debtors	3,15,000	4,05,000			

Ans. Profit Rs. 54,450.

3. A Company of Delhi has a branch at Mumbai. Goods are sent by the Head Office at Invoice price which is at the profit of 20% on Cost price. All expenses of the branch are paid by the Head Office From the following particulars, prepare Branch A/c in the Head Office Books: (a) When goods are shown at Cost Price and (b) When goods are shown at Invoice Price :

	Rs.
Opening balance:	
Stock at Invoice price	1,32,000
Debtors	20,400
Petty Cash	1,200
Goods sent to branch at Invoice price	2,40,000
Expenses paid by Head Office:	
Rent	7,200
Wages	2,400
Salary	10,800
Remittances made to Head Office:	
Cash Sales	31,800
Cash Collected from Debtors	2,52,000
Goods Returned by Branch at Invoice price	4,800
Balances at the End:	
Stock at Invoice price	1,56,000
Debtors at the End	24,000
Petty Cash	300

Ans. Profit – Rs. 90,100.

4. The Delhi Stores invoices goods to their various branches at cost, and the branch sells the goods not only for cash but on credit also. Expenses of branches are paid by the Head Office. From the following particulars relating to Chennai Branch, prepare Branch Account in the books of Head Office.

		Rs.
Stock at Branch on 1st Jan 2006.		20,000
Debtors at Branch on 1st Jan. 2006		10,000
Petty Cash at Branch on 1st Jan. 2006		1,250
Furniture at Branch on 1st Jan. 2006		15,000
Goods sent by Branch during the year		55,000
Goods Returned by Branch		2,000
Cheques sent to Branch during the year for:		
Salaries	5,000	
Rent	2,500	
Petty Cash	750	8,250
Cash Remitted by Branch during the year:		
Cash Sales	25,000	
Cash from Debtors	22,500	47,500
Credit Sales during the year		62,500
Goods Returned by Debtors during the year		1,000
Discount allowed to Debtors		1,250
Bad Debts		250
Stock at Branch on 31st Dec. 2006		25,000
Petty Cash at Branch on 31st Dec. 2006		500
Write off depreciation on furniture @ 10%		

Ans. Profit: Rs. 26,500; Closing Debtors: Rs. 47,500.

5. ABC Ltd. has a Branch at New Delhi and the transactions of the Branch for the year ended 31st December 2006 were :

	Rs.	
Stock of Goods at Branch at 1-1-2006	32,200	(Invoice Price)
Goods Sent to Branch	2,39,400	(Invoice Price)
Salaries & Wages	13,020	
Gross Cash Sales by Branch	2,39,925	
Rates, Taxes & Insurance	3,080	
Rent	5,075	
Sundry Expenses	1,365	
Stock of goods on 31 st Dec. 2006	31,325	(Invoice Price)

The Branch Sales are exclusively cash and the goods sent to branch have been invoiced at 33-1 3% on cost. You are required to prepare the Branch Account, assuming that all cash sales proceeds are remitted to Head Office and all Expenses of the Branch are remitted from Head Office. **[ICWA, Adapted],**

Ans. Profit Rs. 37,179; Shortage at Invoice Price. Rs. 350.

6. Lal & Co. of Hyderabad have a branch at Delhi. All purchases are made by the head office and goods sent to branch are invoiced at selling price which is 20% above cost. All sales by the branch are on credit terms. Branch expenses are paid by the H.O and all cash received by the branch is remitted to the H.O. All branch transactions are recorded in the H.O. books. The balances relating to the branch in the H.O ledger on 1-1-2008 were as follows :

	Rs.
Branch Stock Account (Invoice price,)	26,000
Branch Debtors Account	25,750
Transactions during the year were :	
Goods sent to branch at invoice price	3,24,600
Returns from branch to H.O at invoice price	6,240
Cash received from Debtors	3,10,000
Discount allowed to Debtors	5,750
Branch expenses paid by H.O	30,000
Branch Stock Account (Invoice price) 31st December	48,180
Branch Debtors 31st December	10,000

Prepare in the H.O. books (a) Branch Stock Account, (b) Branch Debtors Account, (c) Branch Expenses Account, and (d) Branch Adjustment Account and P & L A/c. **[B.Com. (P) DU-Adapted]**

Ans.

	Rs.
Creditors	3,00,000
Gross Profit	50,000
Net Profit	9,250
Shortage	6,000 (at I.P.)

7. Zed Textiles opened a branch on 1st January 2008. Goods are invoiced at selling price which was fixed by adding 25% to the cost. From the following particulars relating to 2008. ascertain the profit or loss made at the branch under the Stock and Debtors Systems

	Rs.
Goods sent to Branch (invoice price)	1,40,000
Cash Sales	50,000
Credit Sales	70,000
Cash received from Debtors	62,400
Discount allowed to customers	1,600
Goods, returned by customers	2,000
Cash Remitted to Branch for:	
Rent	1,200
Salaries	6,000
Sundry Expenses	800
Defective Cloth found in the bales written off	200

[B.Com (Pass), D.U, Adapted]

Ans.

	Rs.
Gross Profit	23,600
Net Profit	13,840
Shortage	200 at I.P.

8. A Company with Head Office at Delhi has two retail shops at Cannaught Place and Noida, each with a separate manager. The ratio of gross profit to selling price is constant at each shop at 25% throughout the year. Each branch manager is entitled to a commission of 10% of the net profit earned by his branch, calculated before charging his commission, but subject to a deduction from such commission equal to 25% of any ascertained deficiency of branch stock. All goods were supplied to branches by H.O.

From the under mentioned figures, calculate the commission due to each manager for the year ended 31-12-2007.

	Connaught Place Branch Rs.	Noida Branch Rs.
Stock at 1st Jan. 2007, at cost	28,026	18,726
Goods to branches, at cost	1,08,630	65,220
Sales	1,35,480	87,840
Manager's Commission paid on account	900	600
Chargeable Expenses	18,420	13,530
Stock at 31-12-2007 at S.P.	46,248	32,928

[B.Com. (H), K.U., Adapted]

Ans. Commission due: Cannaught Place Manager: Rs. 519; Noida Manager: Rs. 201.

9. Everest Ltd. has a branch at Gurgaon. All purchases are made by the Head Office in Delhi and goods for the branch are delivered direct and charged out at selling price being cost plus 50%. All cash is received by the branch out of an imp rest account which is reimbursed by the Gurgaon office monthly. The Branch keeps a sales ledger and the necessary subsidiary books; otherwise all branch transactions are recorded in the books of Head Office. On April 2006, stock at the Branch at selling price amounted to Rs. 1,19,250 and Debtors Rs. 17,460. During the year ended 31-03-2007, the following transactions took place at the Branch:

	Rs.
Authorised Reduction in selling price	3,150
Discount allowed to Debtors	3,480
Cash Received from Debtors	1,14,780
Cash Sales	1,30,200
Credit sales less returns	1,21,260
Debtors written off	1,290
Goods received by branch at selling price	3,08,700
Goods returned to Head Office at selling price	5,040

A consignment of goods dispatched to the Branch in March 2007, with a selling price of Rs.4,620 was not received by the Branch until 10th April 2007, has not been included in the figures.

On 31-3-2007, stock at the Branch at selling price was Rs. 1,60,800.

You are required to write up the Branch Stock A/c, Branch Debtors A/c and Branch Adjustment Account in the Head Office books.

Ans. Profit Rs. 71,950.

10. National Ltd., Delhi has its branches at Mumbai and Chandigarh. It charges goods to its branches at cost plus 25%. Following information is available of the transactions of Mumbai branch for the year ended on 31-3-2008:

	Rs.
Balances on 1 -4-2007:	
Stock	75,000
Debtors	20,000
Petty Cash	175
Transactions during 2007-08 (Mumbai Branch):	
Goods sent to Branch at invoice price	8,12,500
Goods returned to Head Office at invoice price	25,000
Cash sales	2,50,000
Credit sales	4,37,500
Goods Pilfered (invoice price)	5,000
Goods lost in fire (invoice price)	12,500
Insurance Co. paid to H.O. for loss by fire at Mumbai	7,500
Cash sent for Petty Expenses	85,000
Bad Debts at Branch	1,250
Goods transferred to Chandigarh Branch under H.O. advice	37,500
Insurance charges paid by H.O.	1,250
Goods Returned by Debtors	1,250
Balances on 31-3-2008:	
Petty Cash	625
Debtors	30,000

Goods worth Rs. 37,500 (included above) sent by Mumbai Branch to Chandigarh Branch were in transit on 31-3-2008.

Show the following accounts in the books of National Ltd.:

(a) Mumbai Branch Stock A/c (b) Mumbai Branch Debtors A/c

(c) Mumbai Branch Adjustments A/c (d) Mumbai Branch Profit & Loss A/c

(e) Stock Reserve A/c (f) Goods Sent to Mumbai Branch A/c

[ICWA (Inter), Adapted]

Ans. Gross Profit Rs. 1,37,250; Net Profit Rs. 43,700.

11. The following information relates to XYZ Ltd. who operates a number of retail branches. Goods supplied to the branches are charged out at cost plus 33-1/3%.

Each branch maintains a Debtors ledger.

The following information relates to the Branch at Chennai for the year ended on 31-12-2005:

		Rs.
Credit Sales		1,22,750
Cash from Debtors		1,19,540
Cash Remitted to H.O.		2,35,060
Goods sent to Branch	2,46,200	
Stock at 1-1-2001		7,000
Cash discount allowed to Debtors		3,105
Expenses of Branch (paid by H.O.)		14,525
Stock at 31-12-2001		9,500
Goods Returned by branch		2,000
Authorised reduction in selling prices		360
Branch Debtor on 1-1-2001		17,010
Bad Debts written off		735

A consignment of goods sent by H.O. on 30-12-2005 amounting to Rs. 2,500 was not received until 4-1-2006 and therefore was not included in stock.

You are required to prepare a Trading and Profit & Loss A/c for the year ended 31-12-2005. Assume any difference in the Stock Account as normal loss.

Ans. Gross Profit: Rs. 58,870; Net Profit: Rs. 40,505; Normal loss: Rs. 570.

12. The following information and particulars relate to Delhi Branch for the year 2005-06:

	31-3-2005	31-3-2006
	Rs.	Rs.
Stock	50,000	75,000
Debtors	70,000	95,000
Petty Cash	250	120

Goods costing Rs. 5,50,000 were sold by the Branch at 25% profit on cost. Cash sales amounted to Rs. 1,50,000 and the rest credit sales. Branch spent Rs. 30,000 as salaries, Rs. 12,000 as rent and Rs. 8,000 as petty expenses. All expenses were remitted by Head Office. Branch receives all goods from Head Office.

You are required to prepare Branch Account in the books of Head Office and verify your answer by preparing Branch Trading and Profit and Loss Account. **[ICWA (I), Modified]**

Ans. Gross Profit Rs. 1,37,500; Net Profit Rs. 87,500; Goods Sent to Branch Rs. 5,75,000.

13. New Delhi Head Office of X Ltd. sends goods to its Amritsar Branch at 20% profit on invoice price. Cash sales are made at invoice price and credit sales at 20% above invoice price. From the following particulars you are required to prepare:

(a) Branch Account under Debtors System,
(b) Branch Stock Account, Branch Adjustment Account and Branch Debtors under Stock and Debtors System and
(c) Branch Trading and Profit & Loss Account under Final Accounts System.

	Rs.
Stock in the beginning	18,000
Stock at the end	45,000
Debtors in the beginning	45,000
Debtors at the end	67,500
Goods sent to Branch	1,80,000
Goods returned by Branch	6,750
Cash Sales	90,000
Credit Sales	67,500
Normal Loss	4,500
Discount Allowed	2,250
Purchases by Branch	6,750

Goods purchased by branch remained unsold and were included in the Closing Stock.

Ans. Net Profit Rs. 32,850.

Hint. Deduct purchases out of closing stock while calculating stock reserve.

14. During February 2008, goods costing Rs. 1,65,000 were invoiced by Delhi Head Office to its Branch at Mumbai and charged up at a selling price designed to produce a gross profit of 25% on the selling price. At the end of the month, the return from Mumbai Branch showed that the sales were Rs. 1,50,000. Goods invoiced at Rs. 3,000 to Mumbai Branch had been returned to Delhi Head Office. The closing stock at Mumbai Branch was Rs. 61,500 at selling price.

Record the above transaction in Mumbai Branch Stock A/c, Mumbai Branch Adjustment A/c & Goods sent to Mumbai Branch A/c in the H.O. Ledger & Balance the said account on February 28, 2002.

[C.A. (Inter), Adapted]

Ans. Gross Profit: Rs. 37,500; Net Profit: Rs. 33,375; Shortage Rs. 5,500.

15. AEC Ltd, sent goods to Sonipat Branch at cost plus 25%. You are given the following particulars:

	Rs.
Opening Stock at Branch at its cost	30,000
Goods sent to Branch at Invoice price	1,20,000
Loss of Transit at invoice price	15,000
* Theft at invoice price	6,000
Loss of weight (Normal) at invoice price	3,000
Sales	1,53,000
Expenses	48,000
Closing stock at branch at cost to branch	36,000
Claim received from the Insurance Co. for loss in transit	12,000

You are required to prepare in the Head Office Books:

(a) Branch Stock A/c (b) Branch Adjustment A/c (c) Branch Profit & Loss A/c

Also show your workings. **[C.A. (Inter), Adapted]**

Ans. Gross Profit: Rs. 78,600; Net Profit: Rs. 25,800.

Hint. Cost to Branch = Invoice Price.

16. On January 1, 2005, the goods invoiced by Delhi Head Office of a trader to its Lucknow Branch were Rs. 3,60,000 at selling price, being 33-1/3% on Cost price. For six months ended June 30, 2005, the branch return showed that the sales were Rs. 2,17,500. The goods invoiced at Rs. 15,000 were returned by the Branch to the Head Office. The closing stock at Lucknow Branch on June 30, 2005, was Rs. 1,26,000 at selling price.

Record the above transactions showing Lucknow Branch Stock A/c, Lucknow Branch Adjustment A/c and Goods Sent to Branch A/c in Delhi Head Office Books and Balance them at June 30, 2005.

[C.A. (Inter), Adapted]

Ans. Gross Profit: Rs. 54,375; Net Profit: Rs. 53,250.

17. Evergreen Ltd. with Head Office in Delhi, opened on January 1, 2005, a branch at Haryana where all sales were to be made on credit basis.

All goods required by the branch were supplied by the Company from Delhi and were invoiced to the branch at 20% above cost.

During the year ended 31 December 2005 the following transactions took place:

	Rs.
Goods sent to Haryana (at cost to H.O.)	1,87,000
Returns to Delhi office (at cost to H.O.)	7,140
Sales as shown by Haryana Branch Report	1,67,195
Cash Received from Debtors and remitted to Delhi	1,29,115
Debtors balances at Branch written off as Bad	5,440

Loss of goods at Branch through pilferage is estimated at 1% of goods received.

The stock of goods held by the Branch on 31st December 2005 amounted to Rs. 49,470 at Invoice Price.

You are required to record the entries in appropriate accounts in the H.O. Ledger showing the balances as on 31-12-2005 and Branch Gross Profit for the year ended on that date. **[ICWA (Inter), Adapted]**

Ans. Gross Profit: Rs. 30,430; Net Profit: Rs. 23,120.

18. Asian Traders, Mumbai, have opened branch at Udaipur on 1-7-2005. The goods were sent by H.O. to the Branch and invoiced at selling price of the branch, which was 125% of the cost price of the H.O.

The following are the particulars relating to the transactions of Udaipur branch:

		Rs.
Goods sent to Branch (at Cost of H.O.)		5,04,000
Sales: Cash		2,25,000
Credit		3,15,000
Cash collected from Debtors		2,80,800
Discount allowed		7,200
Cash sent to Branch for:		
Wages	5,400	
Freight	19,800	
Other Expenses including Godown Rent	10,800	36,000
Spoiled clothes in bales written off at Invoice Price		900
Stock on 30th June, 2006 at Invoice Price		99,900

Ascertain the profit or loss for the Udaipur Branch for the year ended on 30-6-2006 after preparing Branch Stock A/c and Branch Debtors A/c. **[B.Com. (Hons.), Delhi, 1991-Adapted]**

Ans. Gross Profit: Rs. 1,06,200; Net Profit: Rs. 62,280 Returns by Debtors: Rs. 9,000.

19. X Ltd. of Kolkata operates a branch at Chennai Goods are sent to the branch at selling price, which is cost plus 50%. Branch expenses are paid out of an imperest account which is reimbursed by H.O. On January 1, 2007 Stock in trade at Chennai at selling price, amounted to Rs. 27,690 and debtors to Rs. 5,480.

During the year 2007, the following transaction took place at the branch:

	Rs.
Goods received from Kolkata at Selling Price	93,720
Cash Sales	52,100
Credit Sales	43,190
Goods returned to H.O. at Selling price	1,440
Cash received from Debtors	39,860
Discount allowed to debtors	970
Bad debts	480
Expenses	14,380

On 31st December 2007 Stock at Chennai at Selling Price amounted to Rs. 24,570. Prepare necessary ledger account under Stock & Debtors System. **[B.Com (P), D.U, 2005]**

20. Lokesh Ltd sent goods to its Ratlam Branch at cost plus 25%. From the following particulars, prepare Branch Stock Account, Branch Adjustment and Branch Profit and Loss Account:

	Rs.
Opening stock at branch at I.P.	5,000
Goods sent to branch	20,000
Loss in transit at invoice price	2,500
Theft at invoice price	1,000
Loss in Weight (normal)	500
Sales	25,500
Expenses	8,000
Closing stock at branch at cost to branch	6,000
Claim received from insurance company for loss in transit by H.O.	2,000

[B.Com (P), 2004 (B)], 2006 (Modified), D.U]

Ans. Gross profit – Rs. 14,300, Net Profit- Rs. 5,500

21. Agra head office supplies goods to its branch at Alwar at invoice price, which is cost plus 50%. All cash received by the branch is remitted to Agra and all branch expenses are paid by the head office. From the following particulars related to Alwar Branch for the year 2007, prepare Branch debtors account Branch Stock Account and Branch Adjustment Account in the books of head office so as to find out the gross profit and net profit made by the branch.

		Rs.
Stock with Branch on 1-1-2007 (at invoice price)		66,000
Branch Debtors on 1-1-2007		22,000
Petty cash balance on 1-1-2007		500
Goods received from head office (at invoice price)	2,04,000	
Goods returned to head office		6,000
Credit Sales		87,000
Sales Returns		3,000

	Rs.	
Allowance to customers on selling price (already adjusted while invoicing)		2,000
Cash received from debtors		93,000
Discount allowed to debtors		2,400
Expenses (Cash paid by Head Office)		
Rent	2,400	
Salaries	24,000	
Petty Cash	2,000	28400
Cash Sales		1,06,000
Stock with Branch on 31-12-2007 (at invoice price)		69,000
Petty Cash Balance on 31-12-2007		100

[B.Com (P), D.U, 2001]

Ans. Net Profit – Rs. 28,800.

❑❑❑

Unit-VII

13 ACCOUNTING FOR THE DISSOLUTION OF PARTNERSHIP FIRMS

U/s 39 of the Partnership Act 1932, "The dissolution of partnership between all partners of a firm is called Dissolution of the Firm." It involves closing down of business so that it ceases to exist. However, there is a difference between "dissolution of firm" and "dissolution of partnership".

Dissolution of Firm

It means complete breakdown of the relation of partnership among all partners. In other words when all the partners resolve to dissolve the partnership and the organisation (firm) ceases to exist, business activities are discontinued and firm is wound up totally, it is regarded as "dissolution of firm".

Dissolution of Partnership

It involves only a change in the relation of the partners. It does not dissolve the firm but simply severs the partnership relation between the partners. Retirement, death, insolvency of one of the partners, brings the partnership to an end. The remaining partners continue to carry on the business under reconstituted firm. It means the dissolution of partnership severs or affects the partnership relation between outgoing partner and continuing partners. However, insolvency of all partners leads to dissolution of partnership and dissolution of firm as well.

Thus it is clear that dissolution of partnership does not necessarily mean dissolution of firm, but dissolution of firm necessarily means dissolution of partnership.

CIRCUMSTANCES WHICH CAUSE THE "DISSOLUTION OF FIRM"

A partnership firm can be dissolved in any one of the following cases:

1. Dissolution by Agreement

A firm may be dissolved with the consent of all partners or in accordance with the terms of "Partnership Deed". If the contract specifically provides that the firm would be dissolved after the expiry of specific period or after completion of a particular venture, then the firm would be dissolved as per the agreement.

2. Compulsory Dissolution

A firm is dissolved if all the partners are declared insolvent, even when all, except one of the partners are declared insolvent, the firm would be dissolved, because one person cannot constitute partnership firm, or if the business becomes unlawful, the firm is compulsorily dissolved.

3. Contingent Dissolution or Dissolution on the Happening of Certain Events

Subject to any agreement, a firm is dissolved on the happening of any of the following contingencies:

(a) Insolvency of a partner

(b) Death of a partner

(c) The expiry of the term for which firm was constituted

(d) Attainment of any objectives for which it was formed

4. Dissolution by Notice

Where the partnership is at will, the firm may be dissolved by any partner giving notice in writing to all other partners of his intention to dissolve the firm.

5. Dissolution under Court Order

The Court is empowered to order the dissolution of a firm consequent on a suit by a partner in the following cases:

(i) When a partner becomes insane or of unsound mind.

(ii) When a partner becomes incapable of performing his duties as partner.

(iii) When a partner is proved guilty of misconduct, which is likely to affect adversely the interest of business.

The following cases have been held to be sufficient grounds for "misconduct".

(a) Gambling by a partner on stock exchange whether connected with business or not.

(b) Fraudulent breach of trust by a partner.

(c) Persistent refusal or neglect by a partner to attend to the business.

(d) Taking away of partnership books by a partner.

6. Persistent Breach of Agreement

If a partner wilfully and persistently commits breach of agreement relating to the management of affairs of the firm or the conduct of its business and it is not reasonably practicable for the other partners to carry on the business of the firm with him. Thus if one of the partners keeps erroneous accounts and omits to enter the receipts or where mutual confidence is badly shaken, the court may order dissolution.

7. Transfer of Interest

If a partner has transferred the whole of his interest to other or has allowed his share to be sold for recovery of any arrears of land revenue due from him or attached under a decree.

8. Business Running at a Loss

If the business of the firm has been running into losses for a long time, the court may order for dissolution of the firm at the suit of a partner.

9. Any Other Ground

The court may dissolve a firm on any ground, which renders it just and equitable that the firm should be dissolved.

The court generally intervenes and decides about dissolution of any firm only when any one of the partners files a suit for winding up by citing any of the reasonable grounds stated above. The partner who is applying to the court for the dissolution of firm should himself be of sound mind, should not have committed any breach of agreement or guilty of misconduct.

LIABILITY OF A PARTNER ON DISSOLUTION

Liability for Acts of Partners done after Dissolution

When a firm is dissolved a public notice must be given of the dissolution. If this is not done, the partners continue to be liable as such to third parties for any act done by any of them after the dissolution, because in such a case the act of a partner done after the dissolution is deemed to be an act done before dissolution.

However, following are not liable for the acts done after dissolution of the firm and no notice of dissolution need be given

(a) The estate of deceased partner

(b) Insolvent partner

(c) The sleeping or dormant partner who retires

Settlement of Accounts

The mode of settlement of accounts among partners after the dissolution of a firm is determined by partnership agreement. In the absence of any partnership deed or specific agreement between them in this regard provisions of Sections 48, 49 and 55 of Indian Partnership Act 1932 shall apply.

Dissolution of a firm implies that the business assets belonging to the firm should be disposed of and out of money thus realised, the liabilities of the firm should be met. If realised value of the assets is insufficient to meet the liabilities, the deficiency should be recovered proportionately from the personal properties of solvent partners. If the assets of the firm are adequate to meet it's liabilities, then the surplus may be applied to settle partners' dues and capitals.The Provisions of sections 48, 49 and 55 are as under:

1. Treatment of Goodwill : In settling the accounts of a firm after dissolution, the goodwill is included in the assets and it may be sold either separately or along with other assets of the firm. [Section 55(i)], its valuation will depend upon the facts and circumstances of each case. It was stated in Page v. Ratliff (1896) 75 L.T. 371 that its value may be taken to be equal to three years' net profits. It is open to any of the partners to purchase the goodwill and carry on the business under the firm name.

2. Sharing of losses including deficiency : Where the firm has suffered losses or where the capital has dwindled, in such case if assets are insufficient to discharge the debts and liabilities of the firm, the partners shall bear the deficiency in the proportion in which they shared profits and losses. These losses including deficiencies of capital shall be paid or made good:

(a) First out of profits (i.e. undistributed profits in whatever form these may be such as Reserves etc.)

(b) Next out of capital, and

(c) Lastly, if need be, out of personal contributions of the partners in their profit sharing ratio [Section 48(a)].

3. Application of assets : The assets of the firm, including any sums contributed by the partners to make up the capital deficiencies should be applied for setting off the debts of the firm in the following manner:

(i) First, in paying off the debts due to third parties i.e. discharging external liabilities of the firm. Such as Creditors, Bills Payable, Bank Loan or other outstanding dues,

(ii) Then, in paying to any partner any advances or loans given by him in addition to or apart from his capital contribution i.e. meeting internal liabilities.

(iii) If any surplus is available after discharging the above liabilities, the capital contributed by the partners may be returned, if possible, in full or otherwise rateably.

(iv) The surplus if any, shall be divided amongst the partners in their profit sharing ratios.

Payment of Firm's Debts and Private Debts (Sec. 49)

Difficulty, some time, arises when the assets of the firm are insufficient to pay the firm's debts or where the partners themselves have become insolvent or are not otherwise able to pay their private or individual creditor. The Act lays down that:

(i) Partnership Creditors should be first paid out of the partnership assets i.e. business liabilities to be met out of business assets and surplus if any, each partner's share is applied in meeting, his personal debts.

(ii) Private Creditors (partners' personal liabilities) should be paid out of private assets (partner's own private estate) and if there is surplus it should be utilised to pay off firm's debts.

It should be noted that all partners are jointly and severally liable for the acts of the firm and it is, therefore, open to a creditor of the firm to proceed against the firm (all the partners) or against any one or more of them.

Example 1.

X, Y and Z are partners sharing profits and losses in the proportion of 3: 2: 1. Their position as on the date of dissolution was as under:

Firm's Assets	Rs.	Firm's Liabilities	Rs.
(Realisable value)	2,75,000		2,45,000
Partners' Private Estate		Partners' Private Liabilities	
X	25,000	X	40,000
Y	Nil	Y	10,000
Z	5,000	Z	Nil

In this case the surplus assets of the firm Rs. 30,000 (Rs. 2,75,000 - Rs. 2,45,000) will be shared by X, Y and Z in 3 : 2 : 1 ratio i.e. Rs. 15,000, Rs. 10,000 and Rs. 5,000 respectively which will be utilised to pay off balance of X's private debt (Rs. 40,000 - Rs. 25,000) Rs. 15,000, Rs.10,000 to meet Y's private liabilities and Rs. 5,000 paid to Z as he does not have any private debt.

Example 2.

The position of partners X, Y and Z who shared profits and losses equally stood as follows on the date of dissolution.

Firm's Assets		Firm's Liabilities	
Rs. 1,80,000 (Realisable value Rs. 1,20,000) Rs.		1,50,000	
Partners' Private Estate (Rs.)		Partners' Private Liabilities	
			Rs.
X	25,000 (Realisable Value)	X	12,000
Y	20,000 (" ")	Y	5,000
Z	15,000 (" ")	Z	2,000

In this case all partners are solvent and thus will contribute Rs. 30,000 (being loss on realisation) in their profit sharing ratio i.e. Rs. 10,000 each. In case the loss exceeds Rs. 30,000, the same can be recovered from the partners to the extent of surplus out of private estate.

Example 3.

On the date of dissolution the partners' position was as follows:

Partners' Private Estate		Partners' Private Debts	
	Rs.		Rs.
X	60,000 (Realisable Value Rs. 50,000)	X	30,000
Y	45,000 (Realisable Value Rs. 60,000)	Y	60,000
Z	30,000 (Realisable Value Rs. 18,000)	Z	15,000

In this case X can contribute Rs. 20,000 towards firm's debts if need be, whereas Y cannot contribute anything towards firm's losses as there is no surplus. However Z can contribute Rs.3,000 (Rs. 18,000 - Rs. 15,000) towards the firm's debts if need be. That is, partners can contribute out of their private estate i.e. surplus (after meeting their private liabilities, if any).

SIMPLE DISSOLUTION (ACCOUNTING PROCEDURE)

As soon as the firm is dissolved, under any of the circumstances cited above, it ceases to transact normal business but proceeds:

(i) to realise all assets, and

(ii) pay off all the liabilities out of the sums so realised, and

(iii) distribute the remaining sum amongst partners as per the provisions of the Act. To close the books of the firm various ledger accounts such as:
Realisation Account,
Partners' Capital Accounts
and Cash or Bank A/c are prepared.

I. JOURNAL ENTRIES TO CLOSE THE BOOKS OF THE FIRM

1. Opening Realisation Account

Dissolution refers to realisation (sale/disposal/transfer) of assets and payment/discharge of liabilities. The following steps are taken:

(i) On Transfer of all assets to be realised*

Realisation Account Dr With the total book values of assets

To Sundry Assets A/c

[Being transfer of individual assets (except fictitious assets) to Realisation A/c at their respective book values]

*Cash or Bank Balance is not transferred because it does not require realisation as it is already in liquid form.

*Debtors are to be transferred at gross value and provision for doubtful debts to be transferred separately.

*Fictitious assets such as Debit balance of Profit and Loss A/c, Advertisement Suspense A/c and other form of accumulated losses are not transferred to Realisation A/c.

(ii) Transfer of Liabilities* (external only*)

Sundry Liabilities A/c Dr With the book value

To Realisation A/c

(Being transfer of various liabilities to Realisation Account at book-value)

*Except Loan from a partner, credit balance of Profit & Loss Account, Reserves Accounts etc.

(iii) Sale/Disposal of Assets

Cash or Bank A/c Dr With the amount actually realised

To Realisation A/c

(Being individual assets realised for cash)

(iv) Asset taken over by any partner

Partner's Capital A/c Dr With an agreed value of asset taken over

To Realisation A/c

[Being asset (say furniture, stock or debtors) taken over by... (Name of the partner)]

(v) Settlement of liabilities

Realisation A/c Dr With the amount actually paid

To Cash/Bank A/c

(Being liabilities paid off)

(vi) Payment of Realisation Expenses

Realisation A/c Dr With Actual amount of expenses

To Cash/Bank A/c

(Being realisation expenses paid)

(vii) Expenses of Realisation paid by partner

Realisation A/c Dr

To Partner's Capital A/c

(viii) Certain liabilities assumed by any partner

Realisation A/c Dr With the amount of liability

To Partner's Capital A/c

(Being liability (Name) transferred to Partner's Capital A/c)

(ix) Profit on Realisation (when credit side exceeds the debit side)

Realisation A/c Dr

To Individual Partners' Capital A/cs

(Being profit on realisation transferred toPartners' Capital Accounts in the profit sharing ratio)

(x) Loss on Realisation (if debit side exceeds credit side of the Realisation A/c)

Individual Partner's Capital A/c Dr

To Realisation A/c

(Being loss on realisation transferred to Partners' Capital A/c)

2. Settlement of Partners' claims

(i) When there is any partner's loan or advance

(a) Partner's Loan/Advance A/c Dr With the amount Partners' loan

To Bank/Cash A/c

(Being loan of partner (Name) paid off)

or

(b) *Partner's Loan A/c Dr With the amount of Partner's loan

To Partner's Capital A/cs

(Being loan of the partner transferred to his Capital A/c)

*It is better to pay the loan directly through Cash or Bank A/c. under simple dissolution.

(ii) Transfer of any reserve or undistributed profits

Profit & Loss A/c Dr or any other form of undistributed profits

Reserves A/c Dr

To Partners' Capital A/cs

(Being Reserve or undistributed profits transferred to Partners' Capital Accounts in the profit sharing ratio)

(iii) Transfer of fictitious assets such as debit balance of P & L A/c, Advertisement Suspense A/c etc

Partners' Capital Accounts Dr With the book value

To Fictitious Assets (Names)

(Being accumulated losses or other fictitious assets transferred to partners' Capital Accounts)

(iv) Charging of Drawings Dr With the amount of drawings

Partners' Capital A/cs

To Drawings A/c

(Being drawings of various partners charged to their Capital Accounts)

(v) Final Payment or closing of Partners' Capital A/cs

(a) Partners' Capital A/cs Dr With the amount actually

To Bank/Cash A/c paid to partners

(Being final payment was made to partners)

(vi) In case the debit side of any partners' Capital A/c exceeds the credit side.

(b) Cash or Bank A/c Dr With the amount actually

To Partner's Capital A/c brought in by the partner

[Being amount of shortfall brought in by the partner (Name)]

II. LEDGER ACCOUNTS

In the Books of the firm

Realisation Account (a format)*

Particulars	Rs.	Particulars	Rs.
To Sundry Assets: Land & Building Plant & Machinery Computers Furniture & Fixtures Investments Stock Debtors (Gross) Bills Receivables	At their respective Book Values	By Sundry Liabilities: Sundry Creditors Bills Payable Bank Loans Provision for B. Debts	at their respective book value
		By Cash/Bank (Assets realised)	Amount Realised
		By Partner's Capital A/c (Asset taken over by partner)	Agreed value of the asset taken over
To Cash/Bank A/c (Liabilities discharged)	Amount Paid	By Cash/Bank (Unrecorded asset)	Realisable value
To Partner's Capital A/c (Liability assumed)	Amount of liability	By Partner's Capital A/c (Unrecorded asset taken over by partner)	
To Cash/Bank A/c (Expenses on realisation)	Expenses Paid		
To Partner's Capital A/c (Expenses)	Expenses paid by Partner		
To Cash/Bank A/c	Unrecorded liability paid off		
To Profit on Realisation Transferred to Partners' Capital A/cs in their profit sharing ratio		By Loss on Realisation Transferred to Partners' Capital A/cs in their profit sharing ratio	

* Likewise the Partners' Capital Accounts and Cash Bank A/c shall be drawn on the basis of journal entries recorded.

Note : If there are Current Accounts appearing in the Balance Sheet, all adjustments with regard to Asset taken over by partner or liability assumed, expenses of realisation paid by partner, profit or loss of Realisation A/c, transfer of Reserves or any other accumulated profits or charging of loss or fictitious assets, may be made in the Current Accounts of the partners which, in turn, shall be transferred to respective Capital Accounts of partners.

(a) In case any partner has credit balance of Current A/c

Partner's Current A/c Dr

To Partner's Capital A/c

(Being balance of Current A/c transferred to Capital A/c)

(b) If any partner has debit balance of current A/c

Partner's Capital A/c Dr

To Partner's Current A/c

(Being Current A/c balance transferred to Partners' Capital A/c)

Illustration 1

A, B and C are three partners sharing profits and losses in the ratio of 5: 3: 2. They decided to dissolve on 31st March 2008 when their Balance Sheet was as under:

Liabilities	Rs.	Assets	Rs.
Capital Accounts		Goodwill	6,000
A	20,000	Leasehold building	25,000
B	9,000	Machinery (Office)	5,000
C	18,000	Investments	7,000
Sundry Creditors	8,000	Stock	8,500
Bills Payable	2,000	Debtors	3,500
		Cash at Bank	2,000
	57,000		57,000

A agreed to take over the leasehold building for Rs. 40,000. B took over goodwill at book value Investments were taken over by C at 150%. The other assets realised as under:

	Rs.
Machinery at	80% of book value
Stock	7,000
Debtors	3,000

The creditors were discharged at Rs. 7,500 and Bills payable after availing a discount of Rs. 200 Expenses of dissolution amounted to Rs. 1,200.

Record Journal Entries and Prepare necessary Ledger Accounts.

Solution : **JOURNAL ENTRIES**

Date	Particulars		LF	Rs.	Rs.
2008	Realisation A/c	Dr.		55,000	
Mar. 31	To Goodwill				6,000
	To Leasehold Building				25,000
	To Machinery (Office)				5,000
	To Investments				7,000
	To Stock				8,500
	To Debtors				3,500
	(Being assets transferred to Realisation A/c)				
	Sundry Creditors A/c	Dr		8,000	
	Bills Payable A/c	Dr		2,000	
	To Realisation A/c				10,000
	(Being liabilities transfered to Realisation A/c)*				
	Bank A/c	Dr		14,000	
	To Realisation A/c				14,000
	(Being assets realised)				
	Machinery	4,000			
	Stock	7,000			
	Debtors	3,000			

	Particulars		L.F.	Dr.	Cr.
	Realisatio A/c	Dr		9,300	
	To Bank A/c				9,300
	(Being liabilities paid off)				
	Realisation A/c	Dr		1,200	
	To Bank A/c				1,200
	(Being expenses on dissolution paid)				
	A's Capital A/c	Dr		30,000	
	To Realisation A/c				30,000
	(Being building taken over by A)				
	B's Capital A/c	Dr		6,000	
	To Realisation A/c				6,000
	(Being good willwill taken over by A)				
	C's Capital A/c	Dr		10,500	
	To Realisation A/c				10,500
	(Being Investment taken over by A)				
	Realisation A/c	Dr		15,000	
	To A's Capital A/c				7,500
	To B's Capital A/c				4,500
	To C's Capital a/c				3,000
	(Being profit on Realisation transferred to Partners' A/c)				
	Bank A/c	Dr		12,500	
	To A's Capital A/c				12,500
	(Being Cash brought in by A)				
	B's Capital A/c	Dr		7,500	
	C's Capital A/c	Dr		10,500	
	To Bank A/c				18,000
	(Being Cash paid to B & C in final settlement of their account)				

REALISATION ACCOUNT

Particulars		Rs.	Particulars		Rs.
To Goodwill		6,000	By Sundry Creditors		8,000
To Leasehold Building		25,000	By Bills Payable		2,000
To Machinery (Office)		5,000	By Bank A/c		
To Investments		7,000	Machinery	4,000	
To Stock		8,500	Stock	7,000	
To Debtors		3,500	Debtors	3,000	14,000
To Bank A/c:			By A's Capital A/c		40,000
Sundry Creditors	7,500		(Leasehold Building)		

Bills Payable	1,800	9,300	By B's Capital A/c	6,000
To Bank (Expenses)		1,200	(Goodwill)	
To Profit transferred to			By C's Capital A/c	10,500
A's Capital A/c	7,500		(Investments)	
B's Capital A/c	4,500			
C's Capital A/c	3,000	15,000		
		80,500		80,500

PARTNERS' CAPITAL ACCOUNTS

Amount in Rs.

Particulars	A	B	C	Particulars	A	B	C
To Realisation A/c	40,000	6,000	10,500	By Balance b/d	20,000	9,000	18,000
(Asset taken)				By Realisation A/c	7,500	4,500	3,000
To Bank A/c	—	7,500	10,500	By Bank A/c	12,500	—	—
	40,000	13,500	21,000		40,000	13,500	21,000

BANK ACCOUNT

Particulars	Rs.	Particulars	Rs.
To Balance b/d	2,000	By Realisation A/c (Exp.)	1,200
To Realisation A/c	14,000	By Realisation A/c (Liab.)	9,300
To A's Capital A/c	12,500	By B's Capital A/c	7,500
		By C's Capital A/c	10,500
	28,500		28,500

UNRECORDED ASSETS AND UNRECORDED LIABILITY

Sometime on firms dissolution certain assets, which were either written off completely or were not recorded at all are found having some value. Such assets are treated as unrecorded assets and are credited to Realisation account with its realisable value e.g. an old typewriter which was written off completely was sold for Rs. 1,000. This will be recorded as under:

Cash/Bank A/c (amount realised)	Dr	1,000	
To Realisation A/c			1,000

(Being unrecorded asset (old Typewriter) sold for Rs. 1,000)

Similarly, a liability for which no provision was made, had to be paid on dissolution is known as: unrecorded liability. The amount paid is debited to Realisation. The following entry shall be recorded

Realisation A/c	Dr	With the actual
To Cash/Bank A/c		amount paid

(Being unrecorded liability paid off)

- In case an Unrecorded asset is taken over by any of the partners—then Partner's Capital A/c will be debited and Realisation A/c credited at an agreed value.
- If the same (Unrecorded asset) is taken over by creditors—then the agreed value of the unrecorded asset is deducted out of the amount due to creditors before making payment to creditors

e.g. An unrecorded asset worth Rs. 2,000 taken over by a creditor for Rs. 1,500. Then out of the total amount due to creditors a sum of Rs. 1,500 will be deducted and balance paid.

- In case, if any partner undertakes to discharge an unrecorded liability then the same shall be credited to Partner's Capital A/c. Following entry shall be recorded:

Realisation A/c	Dr	With the amount of unrecorded liability
To Partner's Capital A/c		

Illustration 2 (Unrecorded asset & Unrecorded liability)

A, B and C were partners sharing profits and losses in the ratio of 2 : 2 : 1. They agreed to dissolve the firm on 31st March 2009 when their Balance Sheet was as under:

Liabilities	Rs.	Assets		Rs.
Capital Accounts:		Plant & Machinery		19,200
A	32,000	Furniture		12,800
B	16,000	Investments		16,000
C	16,000	Stock		16,000
Current Accounts:		Sundry Debtors	20,800	
A	8,000	*Less* Provision	1,600	19,200
C	4,800	Cash at Bank		14,400
General Reserve	16,000	C's Current A/c		3,200
Sundry Creditors	8,000			
	1,00,800			1,00,800

The assets were realised as follows:	Rs.
Plant and Machinery	24,000
Furniture	16,000
Debtors	at 100%
Stock	12,800

Investments were taken over by C at book value. Creditors were paid at a discount of 10%. Expenses of realisation amounted to Rs. 320. There was an unrecorded asset of Rs. 1,600 which was taken over by A at Rs. 1,280 and there was an unrecorded liability amounted to Rs. 160. Record Journal Entries and show the necessary Ledger Accounts to close the books of the firm.

Solution : **JOURNAL ENTRIES**

		LF	Rs.	Rs.
2009	Realisation A/c Dr		84,800	
Mar. 31	To Plant & Machinery			19,200
	To Furniture			12,800
	To Investments			16,000
	To Stock			16,000
	To Debtors			20,800
	(Being asset transferred to Realisation A/c)			
	Sundry Creditors A/c Dr		8,000	
	Provision for D. Debts Dr		1,600	
	To Realisation A/c			9,600
	(Being liabilities transferred to Realisation A/c)			
	Bank A/c Dr		73,600	
	To Realisation A/c			73,600
	(Being assets realised)			
	C's Capital A/c Dr		16,000	
	To Realisation A/c			16,000
	(Being investment taken over by C)			
	Realisation A/c Dr		7,200	
	To Bank A/c			7,200
	(Being creditors paid at 10% discount)			
	Realisation A/c Dr		320	
	To Bank A/c			320
	(Being Realisation expenses paid)			
	A's Capital A/c Dr		1,280	
	To Realisation A/c			1,280
	(Being unrecorded asset taken over by A)			
	Realisation A/c Dr		160	
	To Bank A/c			160
	(Being unrecorded liability paid)			
	Realisation A/c Dr		8,000	
	To A's Capital A/c			3,200
	To B's Capital A/c			3,200
	To C's Capital a/c			1,600
	(Being profit on realisation transferred to partners' capital accounts)			

	General Reserve A/c Dr		16,000	
	To A's Capital A/c			6,400
	To B's Capital A/c			6,400
	To C's Capital A/c			3,200
	(Being general reserve transferred to partners' capital accounts in the profit sharing ratio)			
	A's Capital A/c Dr		48,320	
	B's Capital A/c Dr		30,400	
	C's Capital A/c Dr		1,600	
	To Bank A/c			80,320
	(Being final payment made to partners)			

REALISATION ACCOUNT

		Rs.		Rs.
To Plant & Machinery		19,200	By Sundry Creditors	8,000
To Furniture		12,800	By Provision for D. Debts	1,600
To Investments		16,000	By Bank:	
To Stock		16,000	Plant & Machinery	24,000
To Debtors		20,800	Furniture	16,000
To Bank (Creditors)		7,200	Stock	12,800
To Bank (Expenses)		320	Debtors	20,800
To Bank (Unrecorded liab.)		160	By C's Capital A/c (Investment)	16,000
To Profit transferred to:			By A's Capital A/c	1,280
A's Capital A/c	3,200		(Unrecorded Asset)	
B's Capital A/c	3,200			
C's Capital A/c	1,600	8,000		
		100,480		100,480

PARTNERS' CAPITAL ACCOUNTS

Particulars	A Rs.	B Rs.	C Rs.	Particualrs	A Rs.	B Rs.	C Rs.
To Current A/c	—	—	3,200	By Balance b/d	32,000	16,000	16,000
To Realisation A/c	1,280	—	16,000	By G. Reserve	6,400	6,400	3,200
(Assests Take over)				By Realisation A/c	3,200	3,200	1,600
To Bank A/c	48,320	30,400	1,600	By Current A/c	8,000	4,800	—
(Final Settlement)							
	49,600	30,400	20,800		49,600	30,400	20,800

BANK ACCOUNT

	Rs.		Rs.
To Balance b/d	14,400	By Realisation A/c	7,200
To Realisation A/c	73,600	(Creditors)	
(Assets Realised)		By Realisation A/c (Exp.)	320
		By Realisation A/c	160
		(Unrecorded Liability)	
		By A's Capital A/c	48,320
		By B's Capital A/c	30,400
		By C's Capital A/c	1,600
	88,000		88,000

RETURN OF PREMIUM (GOODWILL) ON PREMATURE DISSOLUTION

Where a new partner has paid any premium (goodwill) under the terms of admission or entering into partnership for a stipulated period of time, and if the firm is dissolved before the expiry of the stipulated period (Fixed term), then he (partner who paid premium) shall be entitled to refund of premium proportionate to unexpired period. The following adjustment entry shall be recorded.

Partner's Capital A/c (who received premium) Dr

To Partner's Capital A/c (who paid premium)

For example : A & B sharing profits and losses in the ratio of 3 : 2 admitted C who paid premium of Rs. 30,000 on 1-1-1990. Their new profit sharing ratio to be 3 : 2 : 1. As per the terms the firm was to be dissolved on 1-1-2005, but firm had to be dissolved on 1-1-2000. C demands the refund of his premium. In this case the amount of refund shall be calculated as under

$$\text{Amount of Premium Paid} \times \frac{\text{Unexpired Period}}{\text{Stipulated Period of partnership}}$$

$$\text{Rs.}\,30{,}000 \times \frac{5}{15} = \text{Rs.}\,10{,}000$$

The adjustment entry will be:

A's Capital A/c	6,000	
B's Capital A/c	4,000	
To C's Capital A/c		10,000

(Being refund of premium to C adjusted in the A & B's Capital Accounts in the profit sharing ratio)

Exceptions :

In the following cases, the premium will not be paid.

(a) If a firm is dissolved on account of the death of a partner or

(b) If the firm is dissolved due to misconduct of the partner claiming the refund or

(c) When there is specific provision denying refund of such premium.

It means if the firm is dissolved other than the above cited reasons, the claim for the refund of premium will be entertained.

PREPARATION OF PRE-DISSOLUTION BALANCE SHEET

Sometimes only the realised value of-assets is given in the question. In order to ascertain the profit or loss on realisation it is necessary to calculate the book value of assets. For this purpose, necessary adjustments have to be made in the Capital accounts of the partners with regard to interest on capital, drawings and interest there-on, if any, profit of the current year to ascertain the Capitals of partners on the date of dissolution. These capital balances so arrived at and liabilities standing on that date are put to liabilities side of Balance Sheet. If there are fictitious assets, the same should be put to the assets side of Balance Sheet. The balancing figure will give you the book value of the assets. This can be summarised into following steps:

1. Preparation of profit and loss adjustment account to carry necessary adjustments required to make capital balances up to date.
2. Incorporate these adjustments in the capital accounts of partners.
3. Locate the items of liabilities such as creditors, bills payable, loans or other outstanding dues, if any.
5. Accumulated profits such as reserves etc. and accumulated losses (being debit balance of Profit & Loss Account) and other fictitious assets (such as advertisement suspense account etc.) should also be pin pointed.
6. Arrange the above figures (information) in an orderly manner in a Balance Sheet.

The balancing figure is the book value of the assets. Alternatively, we can find out the assets (book value) through equation.

Capital + Liabilities = Total Assets*

Total Assets = Fixed Assets + Current Assets + Fictitious Assets Note: For the purpose of transferring the assets to the realisation account, cash and fictitious assets should be adjusted as follows:

Total Assets (as per equation) less Cash and Fictitious assets = Assets (Book value) to be transferred to Realisation A/c.

Illustration 3

A, B and C commenced business on 1st January 2007 and agreed to share profits and losses in the ratio of 2 : 2 : 1 and contributed Rs. 75,000, Rs. 56,250 and 37,500 respectively. The partnership deed provided for interest on Capital at 6% per annum. During the year the firm earned a profit of Rs. 50,125 before providing for interest on Capital @ 6% p.a. Drawings of the partners during the' year 2,007 were as under:

A	Rs.	17,500
B	Rs.	15,625
C	Rs.	10,000

Due to strained relations of partners the firm was dissolved on 31st December 2007. The assets realised Rs. 1,87,500. The creditors amounted to Rs. 30,000, were paid off at 5% discount. Realisation expenses of 1,750 were also paid by the firm.

You are required to prepare necessary Ledger Accounts to close the Books of the firm.

Solution :

PROFIT & LOSS ADJUSTMENT A/C

Particulars	Rs.	Particulars	Rs.
To Interest on Capital		By Net Profit	50,125
A	4,500		
B	3,375		
C	2,250		
To Profit transferred to Capital A/c's			
A	16,000		
B	16,000		
C	8,000		
	50,125		50,125

PARTNERS' CAPITAL ACCOUNTS

Particulars	A Rs.	B Rs.	C Rs.	Particulars	A Rs.	B Rs.	C Rs.
To Drawings	17,500	15,625	10,000	By Balance b/d	75,000	56,250	37,500
To Balance c/d	78,000	60,000	37,750	By Interest	4,500	3,375	2,250
				By P & L Adj. A/c (Net Profit)	16,000	16,000	8,000
	95,500	75,625	47,750		95,500	75,625	47,750

BALANCE SHEET
As on 31st December 2007
(Before dissolution)

Liabilities	Rs.	Assets	Rs.
Capital		Sundry Assets	2,05,750
A	78,000	(Balancing Figure)	
B	60,000		
C	37,750		
Sundry Creditors	30,000		
	2,05,750		2,05,750

REALISATION ACCOUNT

Particulars	Rs.	Particulars		Rs.
To Sundry Assets	2,05,750	By Sundry Creditors		30,000
To Cash A/c (Creditors)	28,500	By Cash A/c (Assets)		1,87,500
To Cash A/c (Expenses)	1,750	By Loss transferred to Capital Accounts		
		A	7,400	
		B	7,400	
		C	3,700	18,500
	2,36,000			2,36,000

PARTNERS' CAPITAL ACCOUNTS

Particulars	A Rs.	B Rs.	C Rs.	Particulars	A Rs.	B Rs.	C Rs.
To Realisation A/c	7,400	7,400	3,700	By Balance b/d	78,000	60,000	37,750
To Cash A/c	70,600	52,600	34,050				
	78,000	60,000	37,750		78,000	60,000	37,750

CASH ACCOUNT

Particulars	Rs.	Particulars	Rs.
To Realisation A/c (Sundry Assets)	1,87,500	By Realisation A/c (Creditors)	28,500
		By Realisation A/c (Expenses)	1,750
		By A's Capital	70,600
		By B's Capital	52,600
		By C's Capital	34,050
	1,87,500		1,87,500

Note : Since book value of assets was not given in the question, it was necessary to prepare Balance Sheet just before or on the date of dissolution. For this purpose interest profits & drawings have been adjusted in Capital Accounts. Thereafter, Balance Sheet has been drawn.

TREATMENT OF JOINT LIFE POLICY

1. When Joint Life Policy appears on the assets side of Balance Sheet, it is transferred to the debit side of Realisation Account and the amount so received from Insurance Company is credited to Realisation Account.
2. When Joint Life Policy and Joint Life Policy Reserve Fund appear on the asset side and liability side of Balance Sheet.

   Under this situation Joint Life Policy Account is transferred to the debit side of Realisation Account and Joint Life Policy Reserve Account to the credit side of Realisation Account. The amount so received from Insurance Company is credited to Realisation Account.
3. When only Joint Life Policy Reserve/Fund Account appears in the Balance Sheet.

   Under this case Joint Life Policy Reserve Fund should be distributed among partners in the profit sharing ratio.

   In case policy amount is already received, then no other entry shall be recorded.

And if, policy amount not received, then the entry for the receipt of amount from Insurance Company should be credited to Realisation Account.

Illustration 4

A, B and C sharing profits and losses in the ratio of 3 : 2 : 1 decided to dissolve the partnership as on 31st December 2007 when their Balance Sheet was as follows:

Liabilities	Rs.	Assets		Rs.
Capital Accounts:		Computers & Printers		72,900
A	72,000	Investments		37,500
B	36,000	Joint Life Policy		25,000
Joint Life Policy Fund	25,000	Stock		13,590
Investment Fluctuation Fund	11,000	Debtors	16,740	
Mrs A's Loan	18,000	*Less* Provision	1,080	15,660
Creditors	33,300	Cash at Bank		9,950
		C's Capital		20,700
	1,95,300			1,95,300

The Life policy was surrendered for Rs. 21,600. The Investments were taken over by A for Rs. 31,500. A agreed to discharge his wife's loan. B took over all the stocks at Rs. 12,600, Debtors of the value of Rs. 9,000 at Rs. 7,200. Computers & Printers were sold for Rs. 99,000. Remaining debtors realised at 50% less than the Book value. The expenses of realisation amounted Rs. 1,120. It was found that investments worth Rs. 5,400 were not recorded in the books and the same were taken over by one of the creditors at Rs. 5,000.

Prepare necessary Ledger Accounts to close the books of the firm

Solution : **REALISATION ACCOUNT**

Particulars		Rs.	Particulars		Rs.
To Computers & Printers		72,900	By Mrs. A's Loan		18,000
To Investments		37,500	By Sundry Creditors		33,300
To Joint Life Policy		25,000	By Provision for D. Debts		1,080
To Stock		13,590	By Joint Life policy Fund		25,000
To Debtors		16,740	By Investment Fluctuation Fund		11,000
To Cash A/c (Creditors)		28,300	By Cash A/c:		
(33,300 – 5,000)			Joint Life Policy	21,600	
To A's Capital A/c (Mrs A's loan)		18,000	Computers & Printers	99,000	
To Cash (Expenses)		1,120	Debtors	3,870	
To Profit trans. to Capital Accounts:			By A's Capital A/c (Invest)		124,470
A	25,500		By B's Capital A/c:		31,500
B	17,000		Stock	12,600	
C	8,500	51,000	Debtors	7,200	19,800
		264,150			264,150

PARTNERS' CAPITAL ACCOUNTS

Particulars	A Rs.	B Rs.	C Rs.	Particulars	A Rs.	B Rs.	C Rs.
To Balance b/d	—	—	20,700	By Balance b/d	72,000	36,000	—
To Realisation A/c (Assets taken over)	31,500	19,800	—	By Realisation A/c (Profit)	25,500	17,000	8,500
To Cash A/c	84,000	33,200	—	By Realisation A/c (Wife's loan)	18,000	—	—
				To Cash A/c	—	—	12,200
	1,15,500	53,000	20,700		1,15,500	53,000	20,700

CASH ACCOUNT

Particulars	Rs.	Particulars	Rs.
To Balance b/d	9,950	By Realisation A/c (Exp.)	1,120
To Realisation A/c (Assets taken over)	1,24,470	By Realisation A/c (Creditors)	28,300
To C's Capital A/c	12,200	By A's Capital A/c	84,000
		By B's Capital A/c	33,200
	1,46,620		1,46,620

GRADED ILLUSTRATIONS

Illustration 1 (Simple Dissolution)

A, B and C carrying on business sharing profits and losses equally, agreed to dissolve the partnership on 31st December, 2007.

BALANCE SHEET OF A, B & C
As on 31st December, 2007

Liabilities	Rs.	Assets	Rs.
Capital Accounts :		Land and Building	50,000
A	40,000	Plant and Machinery	40,000
B	10,000	Furniture	10,000
C	50,000	Stock	35,000
Loan from X	30,000	Sundry Debtors	25,000
Sundry Creditors	45,000	Cash in hand	15,000
	1,75,000		1,75,000

X agreed to take the entire stock in full settlement of his loan. Sundry debtors were realised at Rs. 20,000 and creditors were settled at Rs. 34,000. It was decided that A and B would take over the following assets at the following sums :

	Rs.
Land and Building	60,000
Plant and Machinery	30,000
Furniture	6,000

A and B decided to form a partnership firm sharing profits and losses in the ratio of 3 : 1. It was agreed that the firm would require a total capital of Rs. 1,00,000 and A & B would bring their capitals in proportion to their profit sharing ratio. Draw up the relevant accounts to close the books of A, B and C and prepare the Opening Balance Sheet of A and B. **[ICWA, Dec. 1979-Modified]**

Solution :

REALISATION ACCOUNT

Particulars	Rs.	Particulars		Rs.
To Land & Building	50,000	By Sundry Creditors		45,000
To Plant & Machinery	40,000	By Loan from X*		30,000
To Furniture & Fittings	10,000	By A & B:		
To Stock*	35,000	Land & Building	60,000	
To Sundry Debtors	25,000	Plant & Machinery	30,000	
To Cash (Creditors)	34,000	Furniture	6,000	96,000
		By Cash (Debtors)		20,000
		By Loss transferred to:		
		A's Capital A/c	1,000	
		B's Capital A/c	1,000	
		C's Capital A/c	1,000	3,000
	1,94,000			1,94,000

PARTNERS' CAPITAL ACCOUNTS

Particulars	A Rs.	B Rs.	C Rs.	Particulars	A Rs.	B Rs.	C Rs.
To Realisation A/c (Loss)	1,000	1,000	1,000	By Balance b/d	40,000	10,000	50,000
To A & B A/c	75,000	25,000	—	By Cash (B.F.)	36,000	16,000	—
To Cash A/c	—	—	49,000				
	76,000	26,000	50,000		76,000	26,000	50,000

CASH ACCOUNT

Particulars	Rs.	Particulars	Rs.
To Balance b/d	15,000	By Realisation A/c (Creditors)	34,000
To Realisation A/c (Debtors)	20,000	By C's Capital A/c	49,000
To A's Capital A/c	36,000	By A & B A/c	4,000
To B's Capital A/c	16,000		
	87,000		87,000

BALANCE SHEET OF A & B
As on 1st January 2008

Liabilities	Rs.	Assets	Rs.
A's Capital	75,000	Land and Building	60,000
B's Capital	25,000	Plant and Machinery	30,000
		Furniture	6,000
		Cash*	4,000
	1,00,000		1,00,000

A & B A/c

Particulars	Rs.	Particulars	Rs.
To Realisation A/c	96,000	By A's Capital A/c	75,000
(Assets taken over)		By B's Capital A/c	25,000
To Cash A/c**	4,000		
	1,00,000		1,00,000

Working Notes :

* Since 'stock' has been taken over by X against his loan no entry has been recorded in the Realisation A/c for the realisation of stock and payment of loan from X. Mere transfer of these items to Realisation Account makes necessary adjustments.

** As the total Capital of A & B is to be Rs. 1,00,000 the value of assets taken over is Rs.96,000 the balance of Rs. 4,000 being Cash taken to the Balance Sheet.

Illustration 2 (Dissolution & re-commencement)

X, Y and Z carrying on business since 1981 decided to dissolve their partnership on 30th June 2006 when their Balance Sheet was as under:

Liabilities	Rs.	Assets	Rs.
Capital Accounts:		Freehold Building	1,00,000
X	1,20,000	Machinery	60,000
Y	90,000	Motor Cars	12,000
Z	60,000	Tools	8,000
Sundry Creditors	34,000	Stock	37,000
		Debtors	62,000
		Cash	25,000
	3,04,000		3,04,000

Y and Z agreed to form a new partnership to carry on the business and it is agreed that they shall acquire from the old partnership firm the following assets at amounts shown hereunder:

	Rs.		Rs.
Stock	40,000	Motor Cars	25,000
Tools	5,000	Machinery	78,000
Freehold Building	84,000	Goodwill	60,000

The partnership agreement of X, Y and Z provided that trading profits and losses shall be divided in the ratio of 3 : 2 : 1 and Capital profits and losses shall be divided in proportion of their capital. Debtors realise Rs. 59,000 and discount amounts to Rs. 720 is secured on payments due to creditors.

Prepare the necessary accounts of X, Y and Z giving effect to these transactions and prepare the opening Balance Sheet of Y and Z who bring the necessary cash in the ratio of 3 : 2.

[C.A. (Inter), Nov. 1989-Modified]

Solution :

REALISATION ACCOUNT

Particulars		Rs.	Particulars		Rs.
To Freehold Building		1,00,000	By Sundry Creditors		34,000
To Machinery		60,000	By Y& Z:		
To Motor Cars		12,000	Freehold Building	84,000	
To Tools		8,000	Goodwill	60,000	
To Stock		37,000	Machinery	78,000	
To Debtors		62,000	Motor Cars	25,000	
To Cash (Sundry Creditors)		33,280	Tools	5,000	
To Profit transferred to:			Stock	40,000	2,92,000
X's Capital A/c	32,320		By Cash (Debtors)		59,000
Y's Capital A/c	24,240				
Z's Capital A/c	16,160	72,720			
		3,85,000			3,85,000

PARTNERS' CAPITAL ACCOUNTS

Particulars	X Rs.	Y Rs.	Z Rs.	Particulars	X Rs.	Y Rs.	Z Rs.
To Cash A/c	1,52,320	—	—	By Balance b/d	1,20,000	90,000	60,000
To Balance c/d*	—	1,75,200	1,16,800	By Realisation A/c	32,320	24,240	16,160
(Y & Z A/c)				By Cash (B.F.)	—	60,960	40,640
	1,52,320	1,75,200	1,16,800		1,52,320	1,75,200	1,16,800

CASH ACCOUNT

Particulars	Rs.	Particulars	Rs.
To Balance b/d	25,000	By Realisation A/c (S. Creditors)	33,280
To Realisation A/c (Debtors)	59,000	By X's Capital A/c	1,52,320
To Y's Capital A/c	60,960		
To Z's Capital A/c	40,640		
	1,85,600		1,85,600

Y & Z ACCOUNT

Particulars	Rs.	Particulars	Rs.
To Realisation A/c	2,92,000	By Y's Capital A/c	1,75,200
(Assets taken over)		By Z's Capital A/c	1,16,800
	2,92,000		2,92,000

BALANCE SHEET OF Y & Z
As on 1st July 2006

Liabilities	Rs.	Assets	Rs.
Y's Capital	1,75,200	Goodwill	60,000
Z's Capital	1,16,800	Freehold Building	84,000
		Machinery	78,000
		Motor Cars	25,000
		Tools	5,000
		Stock	40,000
	2,92,000		2,92,000

* Total value of assets taken over Rs. 2,92,000 to be total Capital of Y and Z in proportion of their profit sharing ratio i.e. 3:2

Illustration 3 (Unrecorded Asset)

Strong and Weak were partners in a firm sharing profits and losses in the ratio of 4 : 1. They decided to dissolve the partnership on 31st March 2007 on which date their Balance Sheet stood as follows:

Liabilities	Rs.	Assets		Rs.
Strong's Capital	80,000	Plant		60,000
Weak's Capital	30,000	Furniture		2,000
Bank Loan	10,000	Debtor	45,000	
Sundry Creditors	40,000	Less Provision for		
		Doubtful debts	2,000	43,000
		Trade marks		6,000
		Stock		30,000
		Cash		14,000
		Advertisement Expenses		5,000
	1,60,000			1,60,000

The realisation showed the following results:

(a) Debtors realised 90% of the book value.
(b) Trade marks Rs. 4,000. Furniture—Nil
(c) Goodwill was sold for Rs. 5,000.
(d) Plant and Stock was taken over by Strong for Rs. 72,000 and Rs. 18,000 respectively.
(e) An unrecorded asset estimated at Rs. 3,000 was sold for Rs. 1,000.

Discounts amounting to Rs. 400 were allowed by creditors while paying their claims. The expenses on realisation amounted to Rs. 2,000.

You are required to prepare the Realisation Account, Cash Book and Partners' Capital Accounts assuming that the settlement was made on 1st April 2007. **[I.C.W.A. (Inter), June 1986-Modified]**

Solution :

REALISATION ACCOUNT

Particulars	Rs.	Particulars		Rs.
To Plant	60,000	By Sundry Creditors		40,000
To Furniture	2,000	By Bank Loan		10,000
To Trademarks	45,000	By Provision for Doubtful debts		2,000
To Debtors	6,000	By Cash:		
To Stock	30,000	Debtors	40,500	
To Cash (Creditors)	39,600	Trademarks	4,000	
To Cash (Bank loan)	10,000	Goodwill	5,000	
To Cash (Expenses)	2,000	Unrecorded Asset	1,000	50,500
		By Strong's Capital A/c:		
		Plant	72,000	
		Stock	18,000	90,000
		By Loss transferred to:		
		Strong's Capital A/c	1,680	
		Weak's Capital A/c	420	2,100
	1,94,600			1,94,600

PARTNERS' CAPITAL ACCOUNTS

Particulars	Strong Rs.	Weak Rs.	Particulars	Strong Rs.	Weak Rs.
To Realisation A/c (Loss)	1,680	420	By Balance b/d	80,000	30,000
To Realisation A/c (Plant & Stock)	90,000	—	By Cash A/c	15,680	—
To Advertisement Expenses	4,000	1,000			
To Cash A/c	—	28,580			
	95,680	30,000		95,680	30,000

CASH ACCOUNT

Particulars	Rs.	Particulars	Rs.
To Balance b/d	14,000	By Realisation A/c (Creditors)	39,600
To Realisation A/c (Assets)	50,500	By Realisation A/c (Bank Loan)	10,000
		By Realisation A/c (Expenses)	2,000
To Strong's Capital A/c	15,680	By Weak's Capital A/c	28,580
	80,180		80,180

Illustration 4 (Debtors & Debt Collecting Agency)

Amar, Abhishek and Anurag sharing profits in the ratio of 3: 1: 1 agree upon dissolution and they would takeover certain assets and liabilities and carry on the business separately. The Balance Sheet as on 30th November 2007 was as follows:

Liabilities	Rs.	Assets		Rs.
Sundry Creditors	6,000	Cash		3,200
Loans	1,500	Debtors	24,200	
Capital Accounts		*Less* Provision	1,200	23,000
Amar	27,000	Stock		7,800
Abhishek	10,500	Furniture & Fixtures		1,000
Anurag	7,000	Sundry Assets		17,000
	52,000			52,000

(i) Goodwill is to be ignored,

(ii) Amar is to take over all Furniture and Fixtures at Rs. 800, debtors amounting to Rs.20,000 at Rs. 17,200. The Creditors of Rs. 6,000 is to be assumed by Amar at that figure,

(iii) Abhishek is to take over all the stock at Rs. 7,000 and certain sundry assets at Rs. 7,200 (being book value less 10%).

(iv) Anurag is to take over remaining sundry assets at 90% of the book value less Rs. 100 allowance and assume responsibility for the discharge of loan together with interest of Rs. 30 (accruing) which has not been recorded in the books of the firm.

(v) The expenses of dissolution were Rs. 270. The remaining debtors were sold to debt collecting agency for 50% of the book value. Prepare necessary ledger accounts in the books of the firm.

[I.C.W.A. (Inter), Dec. 1984-Modified]

Solution :

REALISATION ACCOUNT

Particulars	Rs.	Particulars		Rs.
To Debtors	24,200	By Provision for Bad debts		1,200
To Stock	7,800	By Sundry Creditors		6,000
To Furniture & Fixtures	1,000	By Loans		1,500
To Sundry Assets	17,000	By Amar's Capital A/c:		
To Amar's Capital A/c (Crs)	6,000	Furniture & Fixtures	800	
To Anurag's Capital A/c (Loans)	1,530	Debtors	17,200	18,000
To Cash (Expenses)	270	By Abhishek's Capital A/c:		
		Stock	7,000	
		Sundry Assets	7,200	14,200
		By Anurag's Capital A/c:		8,000
		Sundry Assets (1)		
		By Cash (Debtors to Debt		2,100
		Collecting agency) (2)		
		By Loss transferred to:		
		Amar's Capital A/c	4,080	
		Abhishek's Capital A/c	1,360	
		Anurag's Capital A/c	1,360	6,800
	57,800			57,800

PARTNERS' CAPITAL ACCOUNT

Particulars	Amar Rs.	Abhishek Rs.	Anurag Rs.	Particulars	Amar Rs.	Abhishek Rs.	Anurag Rs.
To Realisation A/c (Loss)	4,080	1,360	1,360	By Balance b/d	27,000	10,500	7,000
To Realisation A/c (Assets taken over)	18,000	14,200	8,000	By Realisation A/c (Creditors)	6,000	—	—
To Cash A/c	10,920	—	—	By Realisation A/c (Loans)	—	—	1,530
				By Cash A/c	—	5,060	830
	33,000	15,560	9,360		33,000	15,560	9,360

CASH ACCOUNT

Particulars	Rs.	Particulars	Rs.
To Balance b/d	3,200	By Realisation A/c (Expenses)	270
To Realisation A/c (Debtors)	2,100	By Amar's Capital A/c	10,920
To Abhishek's Capital A/c	5,060		
To Anurag's Capital A/c	830		
	11,190		11,190

Working Notes :

(1) Value of sundry assets taken over by Anurag has been workedout as under :

	Rs.
Total book value of Sundry Assets as per Balance Sheet	17,000
Less Book value of S. Assets taken overby $\left(7{,}200 \times \frac{100}{90}\right)$ Abhishek	8,000
	9,000
Less 10% as per agreement	900
	8100
Less Rs. 100 allowance as provided	100
	8000

(2) Value of Debtors takenover by Debts collecting agency.

Gross Book value of Debtors as per Balance Sheet	24,200
Less Book Value of debtors taken over by Amar	20,000
	4,200
Agreed value of debtors taken over by debt collecting agency (being 50%)	2,100

Illustration 5

A, B & C were partners sharing profits and losses in the proportion of 4:3:2. Their Balance Sheet as on 31st December 2007 was as under:

Liabilities	Rs.	Assets	Rs.
Capital Accounts :		Land & Building	55,000
A	40,000	Motor Car	15,000
B	20,000	Stock in Trade	20,000
C	10,000	Debtors	18,000
Sundry Creditors	40,000	Cash	2,000
	1,10,000		1,10,000

They agreed to dissolve the partnership on that date. A agreed to take over Stock and Debtors at a discount of 10%. B took over the Motor Car for Rs. 16,000. Land and Building was sold for Rs.75,000 and expenses of sale amounted to Rs. 1,600. Creditors were settled at a discount of 1.5%.

Show the relevant Ledger Accounts. **[I.C.W.A. (Inter), June 1987-Modified]**

Solution :

REALISATION ACCOUNT

Particulars		Rs.	Particulars	Rs.
To Land & Building		55,000	By Sundry Creditors	40,000
To Motor Car		15,000	By A's Capital A/c	34,200
To Stock in Trade		20,000	(Stock & Debtors at 10% less)	
To Debtors		18,000	By B's Capital A/c	16,000
To Cash (Creditors)		39,400	(Motor Car)	
To Cash (Expenses)		1,600	By Cash	75,000
To Profit transferred			(Land & Building)	
A's Capital A/c	7,200			
B's Capital A/c	5,400			
C's Capital A/c	3,600	16,200		
		1,65,200		1,65,200

PARTNERS' CAPITAL ACCOUNTS

Particulars	A Rs.	B Rs.	C Rs.	Particulars	A Rs.	B Rs.	C Rs.
To Realisation A/c	34,200	16,000	—	By Balance b/d	40,000	20,000	10,000
(Assets taken over)				By Realisation A/c	7,200	5,400	3,600
To Cash	13,000	9,400	13,600	(Profit)			
	47,200	25,400	13,600		47,200	25,400	13,600

CASH ACCOUNT

Particulars	Rs.	Particulars	Rs.
To Balance b/d	2,000	By Realisation A/c (Creditors.)	39,400
To Realisation A/c	75,000	By Realisation A/c (Expenses.)	1,600
(Land & Building)		By A's Capital A/c	13,000
		By B's Capital A/c	9,400
		By C's Capital A/c	13,600
	77,000		77,000

Problem 6 (Current Accounts)

C, S and R were partners in a firm sharing profits and losses in the ratio of 5 : 3 : 2. Due to difference in opinion they decided to dissolve the partnership with effect from 1st April 2008 on which date the firm's position was as under:

Liabilities	Rs.	Assets	Rs.
Capital Accounts :		Plant & Machinery	80,000
C	60,000	Furniture & Fixtures	45,000
S	40,000	Motor Car	25,000
R	30,000	Stock in Trade	30,000
Current Accounts :		Sundry Debtors	71,000
C	8,000	Cash at Bank	14,000
S	10,000	R's Current Account	3,000
S Creditors	1,20,000		
	2,68,000		2,68,000

The following information is given :

(i) Plant costing Rs. 40,000 was taken over by C at an agreed valuation of Rs. 45,000 and the remaining machineries realised Rs. 50,000.

(ii) Furniture and Fixtures realised Rs. 40,000.

(iii) Motor Car was taken over by S for Rs. 30,000

(iv) Sundry Debtors included a bad debt for Rs. 1,200 and the rest realised at a cash discount of 10%.

(v) Stock worth Rs. 5,000 was taken over by R for Rs. 5,200 and rest realised at 20% above the book value.

(vi) A creditor of Rs. 2,000 was untraceable and the other creditors accepted payments allowing 15% discount. Realisation expenses amounted to Rs. 5,000.

You are required to show the Realisation Account and the Capital Accounts of the partners on dissolution showing the payments to them. **[I.C.W.A. (Inter), Dec. 1989-Modified]**

Solution :

REALISATION ACCOUNT

Particulars		Rs.	Particulars		Rs.
To Plant & Machinery		80,000	By Sundry Creditors		1,20,000
To Furniture and Fixtures		45,000	By C's Capital A/c (Plant)		45,000
To Motor Car		25,000	By S's Capital A/c (Car)		30,000
To Stock in Trade		30,000	By R's Capital A/c (Stock)		5,200
To Sundry Debtors		71,000	By Bank:		
To Bank (Creditors) (1)		1,00,300	Machineries	50,000	
To Bank (Expenses)		5,000	Furniture & Fixtures	40,000	
To Profit transferred. To Capital Accounts:			Debtors (2)	62,820	
C	13,360		Stock (3)	30,000	1,82,820
S	8,016				
R	5,344	26,720			
		3,83,020			3,83,020

PARTNERS' CAPITAL ACCOUNT

Particulars	C Rs.	S Rs.	R Rs.	Particulars	C Rs.	S Rs.	R Rs.
To Current A/c	—	—	3,000	By Balance b/d	60,000	40,000	30,000
To Realisation A/c	45,000	30,000	5,200	By Current A/c	8,000	10,000	—
(Assets taken over)				By Realisation A/c	13,360	8,016	5,344
To Bank	36,360	28,016	27,144	(Profit)			
	81,360	58,016	35,344		81,360	58,016	35,344

BANK ACCOUNT

Particulars	Rs.	Particulars	Rs.
To Balance b/d	14,000	By Realisation A/c (Expenses)	5,000
To Realisation A/c	1,82,820	By Realisation A/c (Creditors)	1,00,300
(Assets realised)		By C's Capital Account	36,360
		By S's Capital A/c	28,016
		By R's Capital A/c	27,144
	1,96,820		1,96,820

Working Notes :

		Rs.
(1)	Creditors were paid Rs. (1,20,000 less 2,000 untraceable)	1,18,000
	Less 15%	17,700
		1,00,300

(2)	Debtors as per Balance Sheet	71,000
	Less Bad debts	1,200
		69,800
	Less 10%	6,980
	Debtors realised	62,820
(3)	Stock as per Balance Sheet	30,000
	Book Value of Stock taken over by R	5,000
		25,000
	Realisable Value 20% more (above book value)	5,000
	Stock realised	30,000

Illustration 7 (Joint Life Policy)

A, B and C are partners in a firm sharing profits and losses in the ratio 5:3:2. They agreed to dissolve the firm on 31st March 2007 on which date their Balance Sheet was as under:

Liabilities	Rs.	Assets	Rs.
A's Capital	10,000	Goodwill	3,000
C's Capital	70,000	Furniture	10,000
Reserve Fund	10,000	Joint Life Policy (Surrender Value)	20,000
Joint Life Policy Fund	20,000	Sundry Debtors	40,000
Sundry Creditors	18,000	Stock	22,000
Outstanding Rent	2,000	Cash at Bank	30,000
		B's Current A/c	5,000
	1,30,000		1,30,000

Furniture and Stock were taken over by A at an agreed valuation of Rs. 12,000 and Rs.15,000 respectively. Joint Life policy was surrendered and sundry debtors were realised in full after allowing a discount of 20%, Sundry Creditors were taken over by B who agreed to settle account with them at Rs. 17,000. The realisation expenses amounted to Rs. 1,000.

You are required to prepare ledger Accounts in the books of the firm.

[I.C.W.A. (Inter), Dec. 1990-Modified]

Solution :

REALISATION ACCOUNT

Particulars	Rs.	Particulars	Rs.
To Goodwill	3,000	By Sundry Creditors	18,000
To Furniture	10,000	By Outstanding Rent	2,000
To Joint Life Policy	20,000	By Joint Life Policy Fund	20,000
To Sundry Debtors	40,000	By A's Capital A/c	27,000
To Stock	22,000	(Furniture and Stock)	

		Rs.			Rs.
To B's Capital A/c (Sundry Crs.)		17,000	By Bank		
To Bank (o/s Rent)		2,000	J.L. Policy	20,000	
To Bank (Expenses)		1,000	Sundry Debtors	32,000	52,000
To Profit transferred to					
A's Capital A/c	2,000				
B's Capital A/c	1,200				
C's Capital A/c	800	4,000			
		1,19,000			1,19,000

PARTNERS' CAPITAL ACCOUNTS

Particulars	A Rs.	B Rs.	C Rs.	Particulars	A Rs.	B Rs.	C Rs.
To Current A/c	—	5,000	—	By Balance b/d	10,000	—	70,000
To Realisation A/c	27,000	—	—	By Reserve Fund	5,000	3,000	2,000
(Assets taken over)				By Realisation A/c	2,000	1,200	800
To Bank	—	16,200	72,800	(Profit)			
				By Realisation A/c	—	17,000	—
				(S. Creditors)			
				By Bank	10,000	—	—
	27,000	21,200	72,800		27,000	21,200	72,800

BANK ACCOUNT

Particulars	Rs.	Particulars	Rs.
To Balance b/d	30,000	By Realisation A/c (Expenses)	1,000
To Realisation A/c	52,000	By Realisation A/c (o/s Rent)	2,000
(J.L.P. & Debtors.)		By B's Capital A/c	16,200
To A's Capital A/c	10,000	By C's Capital A/c	72,800
	92,000		92,000

Illustration 8 (Unrecorded asset & Unrecorded liability)

A, B and C sharing profits in the ratio of 2: 2: 1 agreed upon dissolution of their partnership on 31st March 2007 on which date their Balance Sheet was under:

Liabilities		Rs.	Assets		Rs.
Capital Accounts :			Fixed Assets	200,000	
A		40,000	*Less* Provision for dep.	150,000	50,000
B		30,000	Joint Life Policy (Surrender Value)		10,000
Reserve Funds		10,000	Stock		8,000
Profit & Loss A/c		10,000	Investments	9,000	
Sundry Creditors	19,000		*Less* Fluctuation Fund	1,500	7,500

Less Provision for discount	500	18,500	Sundry Debtors	10,000	
Salaries O/s		7,000	*Less* Prov. for Bad Debts	500	9,500
			Cash at Bank		28,500
			C's Capital		2,000
		1,15,500			1,15,500

Investments were taken over by A at Rs. 6,000. Sundry Creditors of Rs. 10,000 were taken over by B who has agreed to settle account with them at Rs. 9,900, and remaining creditors were paid Rs. 7,500. Joint Life policy was surrendered and fixed assets realised Rs. 70,000. Stock and Sundry Debtors realised Rs. 7,000 and Rs. 9,000 respectively. One customer whose account was written off as bad, now paid Rs. 800 which is not included in Rs. 9,000 above. There was an unrecorded asset estimated at Rs. 3,000, half of which handed over to an unrecorded liability of Rs. 5,000 in settlement of claim of Rs. 2,500 and remaining half was sold in the market which realised Rs. 200 less.

B took over the responsibility of completing dissolution, he is granted a salary of Rs. 400 per month and he is to bear realisation expenses. Actual realisation expenses amounted to Rs. 1,100. Dissolution was completed and final payments were made on 31st July 2007. You are required to prepare Ledger Accounts in the books of the firm. **[B.Com. (H), DU, 1995-Modified]**

Solution : **REALISATION ACCOUNT**

Particulars		Rs.	Particulars		Rs.
To Fixed Assets		2,00,000	By Sundry Creditors		19,000
To Investments		9,000	By Salaries O/s		7,000
To Joint Life Policy		10,000	By Provision for Depreciation		1,50,000
To Stock		8,000	By Investment Fluctuation Fund		1,500
To Sundry Debtors		10,000	By Provision for Bad debts		500
To Provision for Discount		500	By Bank		
To Bank			Fixed Assets	70,000	
Sundry Creditors	7,500		Joint Life Policy	10,000	
Salaries O/s	7,000		Stock	7,000	
Unrecorded Liab. (2)	2,500	17,000	Debtors	9,000	
To B's Capital (Sundry Crs.)		9,900	Bad debts recovered	800	
To B's Capital (Salary) (3)		1,600	Unrecorded Asset (1)	1,300	98,100
To Profit transferred to Capital Account			By A's Capital (Investments)		6,000
A	6,440				
B	6,440				
C	3,220	16,100			
		2,82,100			2,82,100

PARTNERS'CAPITAL ACCOUNTS

Particulars	A Rs.	B Rs.	C Rs.	Particulars	A Rs.	B Rs.	C Rs.
To Balance	—	—	2,000	By Balance b/d	40,000	30,000	—
To Realisation A/c (Investment)	6,000	—	—	By Reserve Fund	4,000	4,000	2,000
				By Profit & Loss A/c	4,000	4,000	2,000
To Bank	48,440	55,940	5,220	By Realisation A/c (Profit)	6,440	6,440	3,220
				By Realisation A/c (Creditors)	—	9,900	—
				By Realisation A/c (salary)	—	1,600	—
	54,440	55,940	7,220		54,440	55,940	7,220

BANK ACCOUNT

Particulars	Rs.	Particulars	Rs.
To Balance b/d	28,500	By Realisation A/c (Creditors)	7,500
To Realisation A/c (Sundry Assets)	98,100	By Realisation A/c (Salaries O/s)	7,000
		By Realisation A/c (Unrecorded Liab.)	2,500
		By A's Capital	48,440
		By B's Capital	55,940
		By C's Capital	5,220
	1,26,600		1,26,600

Working Notes :

	Rs.
(1) Value of Unrecorded asset	3,000
Less Half handed over to unrecorded liability*	1,500
	1,500
Loss on disposal	200
Amount realised	1,300
(2) Unrecorded liability as given	5,000
Less settled against the unrecorded Asset*	2,500
Amount paid for	2,500

(3) Realisation expenses met by 'B' out of his personal funds are to be ignored. However, salary to B @ Rs. 400 p.m. for 4 months Rs. 1,600 will be debited to Realisation A/c (April, May, June and July) and credited to B's Capital A/c.

INSOLVENCY OF A PARTNER

The liability of all partners in a partnership firm is unlimited. They have to bear and meet business losses not only out of their business capital but out of their private property as well. When a partner is unable to make his business losses and deficiency good even out of his private assets, he is declared insolvent. Now question arises that how to set off losses and deficiency of an insolvent partner. Obviously, this deficiency has to be borne by solvent partners. But again problem arises that in what ratio should the deficiency of the insolvent partner be shared by the solvent partners?

Legal Position : The Indian Partnership Act does not specifically deal with the treatment of deficiency of a partner arising out of his insolvency as to the manner in which it should be met by solvent partners. There is no legal provision, which can be followed in such a situation. Therefore, such a case should be dealt with in the light of Partnership Deed. If there is an agreement among partners that loss arising on account of insolvency of either of the partners shall be shared by solvent partners in the profit sharing ratio, capital ratio or any other ratio, the agreed basis should be followed. However, Section 48(b) (ii) of Indian Partnership Act states, if a partner becomes insolvent or otherwise incapable of paying his share of the contribution, the solvent partners must share 'rateably' the available assets (including their own contribution to the capital deficiency).

Garner Vs. Murray Case

This relates to a historic judgement pronounced by Justice Joyce in 1903 in the Great Britain in a popular case filed by Murray. Prior to this case, no distinction was made between business loss and loss arising out of the insolvency of any partner. Both such losses were to be borne by partners in the profit sharing ratio. Murray, who had less than proportionate share of capital from his partner Garner in the firm, contended that loss on account of insolvency of a partner is a capital loss and not a business loss and hence such a loss should be borne by solvent partners in the capital ratio and not in the profit sharing ratio. Upholding the contention of Murray, Mr Justice Joyce gave the following verdict:

"The solvent partners are only liable to make good their share of deficiency, and that the remaining assets should be divided among them in proportion of their capitals."

This judgment can be interpreted as under:

1. That loss arising due to insolvency of a partner is a capital loss distinct from trading/business loss.
2. That such a capital loss (due to insolvency) is to be shared by solvent partners in the their capital ratio* standing on that date.
3. That solvent partners are required to bring cash equivalent to loss on realisation, if capitals are fluctuating.

* If the partners' capitals are fixed then the deficiency of insolvent partner is to be adjusted in the capital accounts of solvent partners in the fixed Capital ratio. It means all adjustments and transfers relating to .... Profit & Loss Account (Debit or credit balance), Reserves or other accumulated profits or loses including the loss on Realisation account shall be transferred to partners' respective Current Accounts. The final balance of current account (Debit or credit) will be transferred to respective capital account for final settlement.

However, if capitals are fluctuating, then the deficiency of insolvent partner shall be shared by solvent partners in the Capital ratio standing just before dissolution (or capital on that date after making pre-dissolution adjustments relating to accumulated losses or profits, drawings, interest on capital, salary, bonus, commission or other claims of partners, but before transferring any loss on account of realisation or giving any effect of realisation to Capital Accounts, such as taking over of any asset or liability etc.).It should be noted that if a solvent partner has debit balance of Capital he will not be required to bear deficiency of insolvent partner. It means only solvent partners with credit balance (after necessary adjustments but before making adjustments of realisation account) will bear the loss on account of deficiency of insolvent partners in the capital ratio.

APPLICATION IN INDIA

The Garner vs. Murray case does not contravene the provisions of section 48 of the Indian Partnership Act 1932 (as given earlier). No court in India has raised any objection against the implementation of verdict given by Mr. Justice Joyce in Garner vs. Murray case. Further no partner of any partnership firm has ever challenged this decision or filed a writ petition against its implementation. Thus this decision is also applicable in India provided there is no specific agreement among the partners relating to sharing of deficiency of a insolvent partner by the solvent partners. That is partnership deed is silent on this issue. If there is provision in the partnership deed as to the ratio in which capital deficiency of an insolvent partner shall be borne by solvent partners then the same ratio shall be applicable for this purpose.

However, this decision has been criticised on two grounds:

(i) That a solvent partner, however financially well off he may be, does not bear the loss or deficiency of insolvent partner if he does not have any credit balance of the Capital. This is against the very spirit of principle of equity and justice, because it does not take into account over all financial strength of solvent partners.

(ii) Secondly, when the final settlement of all partners has to be made immediately, it is unreasonable to ask from solvent partners to bring cash equivalent to loss on realisation.

Despite these shortcomings, this rule is widely applicable in India. As regards cash to be brought in by solvent partners, there is a practice to make only a notional entry, actually no cash is brought in.

The main point of this historic decision is to transfer deficiency of insolvent partner to the capital accounts of solvent partners in the Capital Ratio.

Therefore, while implementing the rule in Garner vs. Murray case following steps should be taken:

(1) Preparation of Realisation Account and transferring the balance (Profit or loss) to Capital Accounts of partners. (If capitals are fixed then to Current Accounts)

(2) Prepare Capital Accounts of all partners. Record entry of the cash brought in by solvent partners equivalent to loss of realisation.

(3) Transfer all accumulated losses and profits to partners Capital Accounts. (To current accounts if Capitals are fixed)

(4) Credit the Capital Account of the insolvent partner with the cash brought in by him.

(5) Ascertain the deficiency of insolvent partner.

(6) Ascertain the Capital balance of solvent partners to determine the ratio for the purpose of allocating deficiency of insolvent partners.

(7) Allocate the deficiency of insolvent partner among solvent partners in the capital (as calculated above) ratio i.e. Debit solvent partners' capitals in the capital ratio and credit insolvent partner's Capital with the amount of deficiency.

(8) The balancing figure of solvent partners is settled through cash. Solvent partners may bring in deficiency/shortage in cash if any, or withdraw the cash as the case may be.

Illustration 9

Following is the Balance Sheet of a firm of A,B,C & D as on 31st March 2008.

Liabilities	Rs.	Assets.	Rs.
Creditors	20,000	Sundry Assets	30,000
B's Loan	5,000	Cash at Bank	1, 000
Capitals		P & L A/c	15,000
A's	10,000	Drawings	
B's	6,000	B	2,000
C's	6,000	C	2,000
D's	3,000		
	50,000		50,000

They Shared profits and losses in the ratio of 2:3:3:2 respectively. The position of partners on the date of dissolution was as follows:

	Private Estate	Private Liabilities
A	10,000	15,000
B	20,000	6,000
C	5,000	4,000
D	8,000	9,000

The assets realized Rs. 26,000 and expenses of dissolution came to Rs. 1,000. Prepare ledger accounts giving effect to the dissolution. **[B.Com (P), D.U, 2005 (B)]**

Solution : **REALIZATION ACCOUNT**

	Rs.			Rs.
To Sundry Assets A/c	30,000	By Creditors A/c		20,000
To Bank (expenses) A/c	1,000	By Bank A/c		26,000
To Bank A/c (Creditors)	20,000	By Loss on realization transferred to		
		A's Capital	1,000	
		B's Capital	1,500	
		C's Capital	1,500	
		D's Capital	1,000	5,000
	51,000			51,000

PARTNERS' CAPITAL ACCOUNTS

Particulars	A Rs.	B Rs.	C Rs.	D Rs.	Particulars	A Rs.	B Rs.	C Rs.	D Rs.
To Drawings	—	2,000	2,000	—	By Balance b/d	10,000	6,000	6,000	3,000
To P & L A/c	3,000	4,500	4,500	3,000	By Bank A/c	—	2,000	1,000	—
To Realization (Loss)	1,000	1,500	1,500	1,000	By A's Capital A/c	—	—	1,000	1,000
To C's Capital A/c	1,000	—	—	—					
To D's Capital A/c	1,000								
To Bank A/c	4,000								
	10,000	8,000	8,000	4,000		10,000	8,000	8,000	4,000

BANK ACCOUNT

	Rs.		Rs.
To Balance b/d	1,000	By Realization A/c (Expenses)	1,000
To Realization A/c	26,000	By Realization A/c (Creditors)	20,000
To B's Capital A/c	2,000	By A's Loan A/c	5,000
To C's Capital A/c	1,000	By A's Capital A/c	4,000
	30,000		30,000

Illustration 10

A, B and C are partners sharing profits in the ratio of 2:2:1, their Balance Sheet as on 31st March 2007, the date of dissolution, was as follows.

Liabilities		Rs.	Assets	Rs.
Capital Accounts :	A	7,000	Fixed Assets A/c	21,000
	B	3,000	Current Assets A/c	2,000
	C	1,000	C's Current Account	3,000
Current Accounts :				
A		2,000		
B		1,000		
General Reserve		2,000		
Creditors		10,000		
		26,000		26,000

All Assets, leaving Rs. 500 out of current assets which constituted bank balance, realized Rs.8,000. C is unable to bring anything and is declared insolvent. On the date of dissolution, it was found that a contingent liability in respect of a bill discounted Rs. 800 has matured and the firm recovered only Rs. 200 from the acceptor of the bill. This is not included in Rs. 8,000 above. Realization expenses amounted to Rs. 100. Prepare ledger accounts to close the books of the firm according to Garner vs. Murray rule.

[B.Com (P), D.U, 2004 (B)]

Solution :

REALISATION ACCOUNT

		Rs.			Rs.
To Sundry Assets :			By Creditors		10,000
Fixed		21,000	By Bank :		
Current		1,500	Assets Realized	8,000	
To Bank :			Received from acceptor	200	8,200
Creditors	10,000		By Loss Transferred to :		
Expenses	100		A's Current A/c	6,080	
Contingent Liabilities	800	10,900	B's Current A/c	6,080	
			C's Current A/c	3,040	15,200
		33,400			33,400

C'S CURRENT ACCOUNT

	Rs		Rs.
To Balance b/d	3,000	By General Reserve	400
To Realization A/c-Loss	3,040	By Capital A/c (Transfer)	5,640
		(Balance Figure)	
	6,040		6,040

C'S CAPITAL ACCOUNT

	Rs.		Rs.
To Current A/c (Transfer)	5,640	By Balance b/d	1,000
		By A's Capital A/c	3,248
		By B's Capital A/c	1,392
		(Deficiency divided in 7 : 3)	
	5,640		5,640

PARTNERS' CURRENT ACCOUNTS

	A Rs.	B Rs.		A Rs.	B Rs.
To Realization A/c (Loss)	6,080	6,080	By Balance b/d	2,000	1,000
To Capital A/c (Transfer)	2,800	1,800	By General Reserve	800	800
(Bal. Fig.)			By Bank	6,080	6,080
	8,880	6,880		8,880	7,880

PARTNERS' CAPITAL ACCOUNTS

	A Rs.	B Rs.		A Rs.	B Rs.
To C's Capital A/c	3,248	1,392	By Balance b/d	7,000	3,000
To Bank (Bal. Fig.)	6,552	3,408	By Current A/c	2,800	1,800
	9,800	4,800		9,800	4,800

BANK ACCOUNT

	Rs.		Rs.
To Balance b/d	500	By Realization A/c (Liabilities Expenses)	10,900
To Realization A/c	8,200	By A's Capital A/c	6,552
To A's Capital A/c	6,080	By B's Capital A/c	3,408
To B's Capital A/c	6,080		
	20,860		20,860

Illustration 11

The following is the Balance Sheet of A, B, C as on 31st March 2007:

	Rs.		Rs.
Sundry Creditors	20,000	Cash	6,000
General Reserve	15,000	Stock	20,000
Capital Accounts :		Plant and Machinery	20,000
A	25,000	Sundry Debtors	10,000
B	15,000	Furniture	10,000
		C's Capital Account (overdrawn)	9,000
	75,000		75,000

On that date all the partners decided to dissolve the firm. The following arrangements were made for the dissolution:

C is declared insolvent but his estate could pay only Rs. 2,000. it is decided to auction the assets, which were auctioned as follows:

Furniture Rs. 7,000, Stock Rs. 16,000 and Plant Machinery Rs. 14,000. the Sundry Debtors were realized for Rs. 7,500. Sundry Creditors were paid off.

The cost of winding up came to Rs. 2,500. give necessary ledger accounts to close the books of the firm as per the decision of Garner Vs. Murray case. **[B.Com (P), D.U, 2006 Cat. 'B' Modified]**

Solution :

REALISATION ACCOUNT

	Rs.			Rs.
To Stock	20,000	By Sundry Creditors		20,000
To Plant & Machinery	20,000	By Cash (Assets realized)		44,500
To Sundry Debtors	10,000	By Capital A/cs : (Loss)		
To Furntiure	10,000	A	6,000	
To Cash (Creditors)	20,000	B	6,000	
To Cash (Expenses)	2,500	C	6,000	18,000
	82,500			82,500

PARTNERS' CAPITAL ACCOUNTS

	A Rs.	B Rs.	C Rs.		A Rs.	B Rs.	C Rs.
To Balance b/d	—	—	9,000	By Balance b/d	25,000	15,000	—
To Realization	6,000	6,000	6,000	By General Reserve	5,000	5,000	5,000
To C's Capital A/c	4,800	3,200	—	By Cash	6,000	6,000	2,000
To Cash	25,200	16,800	—	By A's Capital A/c	—	—	4,800
				By B's Capital A/c	—	—	3,200
	36,000	26,000	15,000		36,000	26,000	15,000

CASH ACCOUNT

	Rs.		Rs.
To Balance b/d	6,000	By Realization A/c	22,500
To Realization A/c	44,500	(Creditors & Expenses)	
To A's Capital A/c	6,000	By A's Capital A/c	25,200
To B's Capital A/c	6,000	By B's Capital A/c	16,800
To C's Capital A/c	2,000		
	64,500		64,500

Illustration 12 (Pre-dissolution Adjustments)

A, B and C were partners sharing profits and losses in the ratio of 2 : 2 : 1 respectively. The Balance Sheet of the firm as on 31st March 2007 was as follows:

Liabilities	Rs.	Assets		Rs.
A's Capital	1,46,000	Fixed Assets		2,00,000
B's Capital	54,000	Current Assets:		
C's" Capital	50,000	Stock	1,25,000	
C's Loan Account	25,000	Debtors	1,25,000	
Mrs. A's Loan	50,000	Cash	5,000	2,55,000
Sundry Creditors	1,25,000	Advance to B		20,000
Provision for Bad debts	25,000			
	4,75,000			4,75,000

The firm was dissolved on the date of Balance Sheet due to continued losses. After preparing the Balance Sheet as on 31st March 2007, it was discovered that purchases amounting to Rs. 20,000 in March 2007 were not recorded in the books, though the goods were received during March 2007.

Fixed assets realised Rs. 1,00,000, Stock Rs. 1,05,000 and debtors Rs. 1,02,500. Creditors were paid after deduction of discount @ 2%. The realisation expenses amounted to Rs. 5,400. A agreed to take over the loan of Mrs. A. B is insolvent and his estate is unable to contribute any thing. Prepare relevant accounts to close the books of the firm applying the decision in Garner vs. Murray.

[C.A. (Inter), Nov. 1993-Modified]

Solution :

REALISATION ACCOUNT

Particulars	Rs.	Particulars		Rs.
To Fixed Assets	2,00,000	By S. Creditors (1,25,000 + 20,000)		1,45,000
To Stock	1,25,000	By Mrs. A's Loan		50,000
To Debtors	1,25,000	By Provision for Bad debts		25,000
To Cash (Creditors)	1,42,100	By Cash:		
To Cash (Expenses)	5,400	Fixed Assets	1,00,000	
To A's Capital A/c	50,000	Stock	1,05,000	
(Mrs. A's loan)		Debtors	1,02,500	3,07,500
		By Loss transferred to:		
		A's Capital A/c	48,000	
		B's Capital A/c	48,000	
		C's Capital A/c	24,000	1,20,000
	6,47,500			6,47,500

PARTNERS' CAPITAL ACCOUNT

Particulars	A Rs.	B Rs.	C Rs.	Particulars	A Rs.	B Rs.	C Rs.
To P & L Adj. A/c	8,000	8,000	4,000	By Balance b/d	1,46,000	54,000	50,000
To Balance c/d	1,38,000	46,000	46,000				
	1,46,000	54,000	50,000		1,46,000	54,000	50,000
To Realisation A/c	48,000	48,000	24,000	By Balance b/d	1,38,000	46,000	46,000
(Loss)				By Cash A/c	48,000	—	24,000
To Advance to B	—	20,000	—	By Realisation A/c	50,000	—	—
To B's Capital A/c	16,500	—	5,500	(Mrs. A's Loan)			
To Cash A/c	1,71,500	—	40,500	By A's Capital A/c	—	16,500	—
				By C's Capital A/c	—	5,500	—
	2,36,000	68,000	70,000		2,36,000	68,000	70,000

CASH ACCOUNT

Particulars	Rs.	Particulars	Rs.
To Balance b/d	5,000	By Realisation A/c	1,42,100
To Realisation A/c	3,07,500	(Sundry Creditors)	
(Assets)		By Realisation A/c	5,400
To A's Capital A/c	48,000	(Expenses)	
To C's Capital A/c	24,000	By C's Loan A/c	25,000
		By A's Capital A/c	1,71,500
		By C's Capital A/c	40.500
	3,84,500		3,84,500

Working Notes :

(1) The omission to record purchases has resulted in an increase of profits and consequent increase in capital balance of partners. To rectify this error following entries have been recorded.

(a) Profit & Loss Adjustment A/c	Dr	20,000	
To Sundry Creditors			20,000
(b) A's Capital A/c	Dr	8,000	
B's Capital A/c	Dr	8,000	
C's Capital A/c	Dr	4,000	
To Profit & Loss Adjustment A/c			20,000

(2) The deficiency of B (insolvent partner) has been borne by solvent partners (A & C) in the Capital ratio after above adjustment which is 1,38,000 : 46,000 (3 : 1).

(3) The solvent partners have brought in cash equivalent to the loss on realisation

Illustration 13 (Mortgaged Loan & Secured overdraft)

A, B and C sharing profits and losses in the ratio of 4 : 3 : 2. Their Balance Sheet as on 31st Dec. 2007 was as follows:

Liabilities	Rs.	Assets		Rs.
A's Capital	20,000	Machinery		40,000
B's Capital	10,000	Stock		25,000
C's Capital	3,000	Debtors	18,000	
Loan (against the mortgage	25,000	*Less* Provision		
Of Machinery)		for Doubtful debts	1,000	17,000
Bank Overdraf	15,000	Cash		2,000
(Secured against stock)		Profit & Loss A/c		9,000
Sundry Creditors	20,000			
	93,000			93,000

The firm was dissolved on that date. Stock was taken over by the banker and it realised Rs.20,000. Bank paid back Rs. 4,000 after recovering its overdraft and interest there on. Machinery was disposed off for Rs. 24,000 and debtors realised Rs. 14,000 only. Loan was fully paid off along with interest due Rs. 1,000. Creditors were discharged at 10% discount. Expenses amounted to Rs.300 which were paid by A. C became insolvent and only Rs. 950 could be recovered from his private estate.

Prepare necessary ledger accounts to close the books of the firm. Apply Garner vs. Murray.

[B.Com. (H), DU, 1989-Modified]

Solution :

REALISATION ACCOUNT

Particulars		Rs.	Particulars		Rs.
To Machinery		40,000	By Loan		25,000
To Stock		25,000	By Sundry Creditors		20,000
To Debtors		18,000	By Bank Overdraft		15,000
To Cash:			By Provision for Doubtful- debts		1,000
Loan with interest	26,000		By Cash:		
Creditors	18,000	44,000	Machinery	24,000	
To A's Capital A/c (Expenses)		300	Debtors	14,000	
			Stock	4,000	42,000
			(after adjustment of Bank overdraft)		
			By Loss transferred to Capital Accounts		
			A	10,800	
			B	8,100	
			C	5,400	24,300
		1,27,300			1,27,300

PARTNERS' CAPITAL ACCOUNT

Particulars	A Rs.	B Rs.	C Rs.	Particulars	A Rs.	B Rs.	C Rs.
To Profit & Loss A/c	4,000	3,000	2,000	By Balance b/d	20,000	10,000	3,000
To Realisation A/c (Loss)	10,800	8,100	5,400	By Cash A/c (Realisation loss)	10,800	8,100	—
To C's Capital A/c (Deficiency)	2,400	1,050	—	By Realisation (Exp.)	300	—	—
				By Cash A/c	—	—	950
To Cash A/c	13,900	5,950	—	By A's Capital A/c	—	—	2,400
				By B's Capital A/c	—	—	1,050
	31,100	18,100	7,400		31,100	18,100	7,400

CASH ACCOUNT

	Rs.		Rs.
To Balance b/d	2,000	By Realisation A/c	44,000
To Realisation A/c	42,000	By A's Capital A/c	13,900
(Assets)		By B's Capital A/c	5,950
To A's Capital A/c	10,800		
To B's Capital A/c	8,100		
To C's Capital A/c	950		
	63,850		63,850

Working Note :

As per Garner vs. Murray Case, the solvent partners have brought in cash equivalent to loss on realisation. The Deficiency arising out of insolvency of C has been borne by A & B

(Solvent partners) in the ratio of their capitals standing on that date (but before realisation loss) i.e.16: 7.

[A = 20,000 Capital – 4,000 P & L A/c (Dr)]
[B = 10,000 Capital – 3,000 P & L A/c (Dr)]

Illustration 14 (Realisation Expenses and Commission to Partner)

K, L, M and N are partners in a firm sharing profits and losses in the ratio 4:1:2:3. Their Balance Sheet as on 31st March 2007 was as follows:

Liabilities	Rs.	Assets		Rs.
K's Capital	70,000	Sundry Assets		51,000
N's Capital	30,000	Sundry Debtors	35,000	
Sundry Creditors	30,000	*Less* Provision for		
		Doubtful debts	5,000	30,000
		Cash in hand		14,000
		L's Capital		20,000
		M's Capital		15,000
	1,30,000			1,30,000

On 1-4-2007, the firm was dissolved. The partnership agreement provides that the deficiency of an insolvent partner will be borne by the solvent partners in the ratio of Capitals as they stand just before dissolution. They agreed upon the following arrangements:

(1) K is to take over 60% of the book debts at 70% and N is to take over the balance at 75%. Further they are allowed Rs. 2,100 and Rs. 1,100 respectively to cover future losses.

(2) N is to realise sundry assets and to pay off the creditors. He is to receive Rs. 2,200 commission and to bear the expenses of realisation. He reports the result of realisation as follows:

Sundry assets realised at a loss of 2% on net collection and paid off the creditors at a discount of 30%. There was an unrecorded asset, which realised Rs. 2,200. Realisation expenses amount to Rs. 3,000 but the same is paid by the firm.

L is declared insolvent and a sum of 20% in a rupee is realised from his estate.

Prepare Realisation Account, Capital Accounts and Cash Account.

[I.C.W.A. (Inter), June 1983-Modified]

Solution :

REALISATION ACCOUNT

Particulars	Rs.	Particulars		Rs.
To Sundry Assets	51,000	By Sundry Creditors		30,000
To Sundry Debtors	35,000	By Provision for Bad debts		5,000
To Cash (Creditors)	21,000	By Cash		
To N's Capital A/c (1)	2,200	Sundry Assets (2)	50,000	
(Commission)		Unrecorded Asset	2,200	52,200
		By K's Capital A/c(3)		12,600
		(Debtors)		
		By N's Capital A/c(4)		9,400
		(Debtors)		
	1,09,200			1,09,200

PARTNERS' CAPITAL ACCOUNTS

Particulars	K Rs.	L Rs.	M Rs.	N Rs.	Particulars	K Rs.	L Rs.	M Rs.	N Rs.
To Balance b/d	—	20,000	15,000	—	By Balance b/d	70,000	—	—	30,000
To Realisation A/c (Debtors)	12,600	—	—	9,400	By Realisation A/c (Comm)	—	—	—	2,200
To Cash (Expenses) (5)	—	—	—	3,000	By K's Capital A/c	—	11,200	—	—
To L's Capital A/c (Deficiency)	11,200	—	—	4,800	By N's Capital A/c	—	4,800	—	—
					By Cash A/c	—	4,000	15,000	—
To Cash A/c	46,200	—	—	15,000					
	70,000	20,000	15,000	32,200		70,000	20,000	15,000	32,200

CASH ACCOUNT

Particulars	Rs.	Particulars	Rs.
To Balance b/d	14,000	By Realisation A/c (Creditors)	21,000
To Realisation A/c (Assets)	52,200	By N's Capital A/c (Expenses)	3,000
To L's Capital A/c (6)	4,000	By K's Capital A/c	46,200
To M's Capital A/c	15,000	By N's Capital A/c	15,000
	85,200		85,200

Working Notes :

1. As per agreement N is entitled commission of Rs. 2,200 and to bear of actual expenses of realisation, that is why only commission of Rs. 2,200 has been debited to Realisation a/c. Because the same has been treated as business expense. However, if the partners decide not to teat 'Realisation Expenses/Commission as business expense then this will not be debted to Realisation A/c.
2. Sundry Assets realised at 2% loss on net collection Rs. 51,000 x 100/102 = 50,000.
3. Debtors taken over by K has been worked out as under:

	Rs.
$35{,}000 \times \frac{60}{100} = 21{,}000$ at 70%	14,700
Less further allowance	2,100
	12,600

4. Debtors taken over by N

35,000 – 21,000 = 14,000 at 75%	10,500
Less further allowance	1,100
	9,400

5. Since expenses of realisation were to be borne by N in lieu of commission but the firm has paid the same, hence debited to N's Account.
6. L has brought in 20% of his deficiency, which is Rs. 20,000, and the remaining Rs. 16,000 has been borne by K and N in the Capital ratio (7: 3).

Illustration 15 (Garner vs. Murray)

A, B & C were partners. Their profit sharing ratio was 3:2:3. They dissolved their business. The Balance Sheet was as follows:

Liabilities	Rs.	Assets	Rs.
A's Capital	26,000	Land & Building	15,000
C's Capital	15,500	Stock	23,100
S. Creditors	34,000	Debtors	30,000
		Cash	2,500
		B's Capital	4,900
	75,500		75,500

The assets realised Rs. 26,000. Creditors agreed to take 75 paise in the rupee in full satisfaction. Expenses of dissolution amounted to Rs. 1,000. B became insolvent and 50% received from his private estate. Prepare Ledger Accounts in accordance with the decision in Garner vs. Murray's Case.

[C.A. (Inter), May 1991-Modified]

Solution :

REALISATION ACCOUNT

Particulars	Rs.	Particulas		Rs.
To Land & Building	15,000	By Sundry Creditors		34,000
To Stock	23,100	By Cash (Assets)		26,000
To Debtors	30,000	By Loss transferred to:		
To Cash (Creditors)	25,500	A's Capital A/c	12,975	
To Cash (Expenses)	1,000	B's Capital A/c	8,650	
		C's Capital A/c	12,975	34,600
*---	94,600			94,600

PARTNERS' CAPITAL ACCOUNTS

Particulars	A Rs.	B Rs.	C Rs.	Particulars	A Rs.	B Rs.	C Rs.
To Balance b/d	—	4,900	—	By Balance b/d	26,000	—	15,500
To Realisation A/c (Loss)	12,975	8,650	12,975	By Cash A/c	12,975	—	12,975
To B's Capital A/c	4,245	—	2,530	By Cash A/c	—	6,775	—
To Cash A/c	21,755	—	12,970	By A's Capital A/c	—	4,245	—
				By C's Capital A/c	—	2,530	—
	38,975	13,550	28,475		38,975	13,550	28,475

CASH ACCOUNT

Particulars	Rs.	Particulars	Rs.
To Balance b/d	2,500	By Realisation A/c (Expenses)	1,000
To Realisation A/c (Assets)	26,000	By Realisation A/c (Creditors)	25,500
To A's Capital* A/c	12,975	By A's Capital A/c	21,755
To C's Capital* A/c	12,975	By C's Capital A/c	12,970
To B's Capital A/c	6,775		
	61,225		61,225

Working Notes :

(1) The deficiency of B (insolvent partner) has been borne by A & C (Solvent partners) in the Capital ratio (52 : 31).

(2) Solvent partners (A & C) have brought in Cash equivalent to loss on realisation in accordance with the Garner vs. Murray rules.

Illustration 16 (Assets & Liabilities taken over by Individual Partners)

A, B, C and D were partners in a firm sharing profits and losses in the ratio of 4 : 1 : 2 : 3. The following was their Balance Sheet as on 31st March 2006 :

Liabilities	Rs.	Assets		Rs.
A's Capital	7,00,000	Stock		2,00,000
D's Capital	3,00,000	Debtors	3,50,000	
Sundry Creditors	3,00,000	Less Provision	50,000	3,00,000
		Other Assets		3,10,000
		Cash in hand		1,40,000
		B's Capital		2,00,000
		C's Capital		1,50,000
	13,00,000			13,00,000

On 31st March 2006, the firm was dissolved and the following points are agreed upon;

A is to takeover sundry debtors at 80% of book value. D is to take over the stock at 95% of the book value; C is to discharge sundry creditors. Other assets realised Rs. 3,00,000 and the expenses of realisation came to Rs. 30,000. B is found insolvent and Rs. 21,900 was realised from his estate.

Prepare Realisation Account, Capital Accounts of the partners and Cash Account. The Loss arising out of Capital deficiency may be distributed following the decision in Garner vs. Murray. Ignore the entry for cash brought in by solvent partners equal to their share of realisation loss.

[C.A. (Inter), Nov. 1996-Modified]

Solution :

REALISATION ACCOUNT

Partculars	Rs.	Particulars		Rs.
To Stock	2,00,000	By Sundry Creditors		3,00,000
To Debtors	3,50,000	By Provision for D. Debts		50,000
To Other Assets	3,10,000	By A's Capital A/c (Debtors)		2,80,000
To C's Capital A/c (Creditors)	3,00,000	By D's Capital A/c (Stock)		1,90,000
To Cash (Expenses)	30,000	By Cash A/c (Other assets)		3,00,000
		By Loss transferred to:		
		A's Capital A/c	28,000	
		B's Capital A/c	7,000	
		C's Capital A/c	14,000	
		D's Capital A/c	21,000	70,000
	11,90,000			11,90,000

PARTNERS' CAPITAL ACCOUNTS

Particulars	A Rs.	B Rs.	C Rs.	D Rs.	Particulars	A Rs.	B Rs.	C Rs.	D Rs.
TC Balance b/d	—	2,00,000	1,50,000	—	By Balance b/d	7,00,000	—	—	3,00,000
To Realisation A/c (Assets taken)	2,80,000	—	—	1,90,000	By Realisation A/c (S. Creditors)	—	—	3,00,000	—
To Realisation A/c	28,000	7,000	14,000	21,000	By Cash A/c	—	21,900	—	—
To B's Capital	1,29,570	—	—	55,530	By A's Capital	—	1,29,570	—	—
To Cash A	2,62,430	—	1,36,000	33,470	By D's Capital	—	55,530	—	—
	7,00,000	2,07,000	3,00,000	3,00,000		7,00,000	2,07,000	3,00,000	3,00,000

CASH ACCOUNT

Particulars	Rs.	Particulars	Rs.
To Balance b/d	1,40,000	By Realisation A/c (Expenses)	30,000
To Realisation A/c	3,00,000	By A's Capital A/c	2,62,430
To B's Capital A/c	21,900	By C's Capital A/c	1,36,000
		By D's Capital A/c	33,470
	4,61,900		4,61,900

Working Note :

The deficiency of B (insolvent partner) has been borne by A & D (solvent partners with credit Capital Balance) in the Capital ratio, 7 : 3. C, who does not have credit balance of Capital Account, does not bear the loss on account of insolvency of B.

Illustration 17 (Gerner vs. Murray & Fixed Capitals)

The firm of Kapil and Dev has four partners and as on 31st March 2007, its Balance Sheet stood as follows:

Liabilities	Rs.	Assets	Rs.
Capital Accounts		Land	50,000
F. Kapil	2,00,000	Building	2,50,000
S. Kapil	2,00,000	Office Equipment	1,25,000
R. Dev	1,00,000	Computers	70,000
Current Accounts		Debtors	4,00,000
F. Kapil	50,000	Stock	3,00,000
S. Kapil	1,50,000	Cash at Bank	75,000
R. Dev	1,10,000	Other Current Assets	22,600
Loan from NBFC	5,00,000	B. Dev's Current Account	87,400
Current Liabilities	70,000		
	13,80,000		13,80,000

The partners have been sharing profits and losses in the ratio of 4 : 4 : 1 : 1. It has been agreed to dissolve the firm on 1-4-2007 on the basis of following understanding:

The following assets are to be adjusted to the extent indicated with respect to the book values:

(a) Land 200%, Building 120%, Computer 70%, Debtors 95% and Stock 90%.

(b) In the case of loan, the lenders are to be paid at their insistence a prepayment premium of 1%.

(c) B. Dev is insolvent and no amount is recoverable from him. His rather, R. Dev, however, agrees to bear 50% of his deficiency. The balance of the deficiency is agreed to be apportioned according to Law.

Assuming that the realisation of the assets and discharge of liabilities are carried out immediately. Show the Cash Account, Realisation A/c and Partners' Account. **[C.A. (Inter), May 1995-Modified]**

Solution :

REALISATION ACCOUNT

Particulars		Rs.	Particulars		Rs.
To Land		50,000	By Loan for NBFC		5,00,000
To Building		2,50,000	By Current Liabilities		70,000
To Office Equipments		1,25,000	By Bank:		
To Computers		70,000	Land	1,00,000	
To Debtors		4,00,000	Building	3,00,000	
To Stocks		3,00,000	Computers	49,000	
To Other Current Assets		22,600	Office Equipments	1,25,000	
To Bank			Debtors	3,80,000	
Loan	5,00,000		Stocks	2,70,000	
Add Premium @ 1%	5,000		Other Current Assets	22,600	12,46,600
Current Liab.	70,000	5,75,000			
To Profit transferred to Capital A/cs of:					
F. Kapil	9,600				
S. Kapil	9,600				
R. Dev	2,400				
B. Dev	2,400	24,000			
		18,16,600			18,16,600

PARTNER'S CAPITAL ACCOUNTS*

Particulars	F. Kapil Rs.	S. Kapil Rs.	R. Dev Rs.	B. Dev Rs.	Particulars	F. Kapil Rs.	S. Kapil Rs.	S. Dev Rs.	B. Dev Rs.
To Currents	—	—	—	87,400	By Balance b/d	2,00,000	2,00,000	1,00,000	—
To B. Dev's A/c (Transfer)	—	—	42,500	—	By Curent A/c	50,000	1,50,000	1,10,000	—
					By Realisation (Profit)	9,600	9,600	2,400	2,400
To B's Dev's A/c (Deficiency)	17,000	17,000	8,500	—	By R. Dev's A/c	—	—	—	42,500
					By F. Kapil's A/c	—	—	—	17,000
To Bank A/c	2,42,600	3,42,600	1,61,400	—	By S. Kapil's A/c	—	—	—	17,000
					By R. Dev's A/c	—	—	—	8,500
	2,59,600	3,59,600	2,12,400	87,400		2,59,600	3,59,600	2,12,400	87,400

CASH AND BANK ACCOUNT

	Rs.		Rs.
To Balance b/d	75,000	By Realisation A/c	5,75,000
To Realisation A/c	12,46,600	(Loan & Liabilities)	
(Sundry Assets)		By F. Kapil	2,42,600
		By S. Kapil	3,42,600
		By R. Dev	1,61,400
	13,21,600		13,21,600

Working Notes :

1. Alternatively Current Accounts would have been prepared and the balances thereof transferred to partners' respective Capital Accounts.
2. It is to be noted that solvent Partners are not required to bring Cash equivalent to loss on Realisation as the Capitals are fixed.

Illustration 18 (Commission on the Amount Payable to other Partners)

A, B, C and D were partners sharing profits and losses in the ratio of: 3: 2: 2 respectively. The following is the Balance Sheet as on 31st March 2006.

Liabilities	Rs.	Assets		Rs.
A's Capital	40,000	Furniture		8,000
B's Capital	30,000	Scooter		14,000
A's Loan	20,000	Stock		20,000
S. Creditors	31,000	Debtors	32,000	
		Less Provision	1,000	31,000
		Cash in hand		4,000
		C's Capital		12,000
		D's Capital		32,000
	1,21,000			1,21,000

It was decided to dissolve the firm with effect from 31st March 2006. B was appointed to liquidate the assets and pay the creditors. He was to bear the expenses of realisation which amounted to Rs. 500.

B was also entitled to receive 5% commission on the amounts payable to A including for his loan, but excluding the cash brought in by A towards his share of loss on realization, after charging such commission. A has agreed to bear this commission wholly himself. The assets were realised Rs. 54,000. Creditors were paid in full. In addition, a sum of Rs. 5,000 was also paid to staff on retrenchment in full settlement of their claims. D was insolvent and the partners accepted Rs. 7,400 from his estate in full settlement.

Applying the rule in Garner vs. Murray, prepare the necessary Ledger Accounts.

Solution :

REALISATION ACCOUNT

		Rs.			Rs.
To Stock		20,000	By Sundry Creditors		31,000
To Debtors		32,000	By Provision for D. Debts		1,000
To Furniture		8,000	By Cash (Sundry Assets)		54,000
To Scooter		14,000	By Loss transferred to:		
To Cash:			A's Capital A/c	7,200	
Sundry Creditors	31,000		B's Capital A/c	7,200	
Compensation	5,000	36,000	C's Capital A/c	4,800	
			D's Capital A/c	4,800	24,000
		1,10,000			1,10,000

PARTNERS' CAPITAL ACCOUNTS

Particulars	A Rs.	B Rs.	C Rs.	D Rs.	Particulars	A Rs.	B Rs.	C Rs	D Rs.
To Balance b/d	—	—	12,000	32,000	By Balance b/d	40,000	30,000	—	—
To Realisation A/c (Loss)	7,200	7,200	4,800	4,800	By A's Loan	20,000	—	—	—
					By Cash A/c	7,200	7,200	—	—
To D's Capital A/c (Deficiency)	16,800	12,600	—	—	By A's Capital A/c (Commission)	—	1,714	—	—
To B's Capital A/c (Commission)	1,714	—	—	—	By Cash A/c	—	—	16,800	7,400
					By A's Capital A/c	—	—	—	16,800
To Cash A/c	41,486	19,114	—	—	By B's Capital A/c	—	—	—	12,600
	67,200	38,914	16,800	36,800		67,200	38,914	16,800	36,800

CASH ACCOUNT

	Rs.		Rs.
To Balance b/d	4,000	By Realisation A/c (Sundry Creditors and Compensation)	36,000
To Realisation A/c (Sundry Assets)	54,000		
To A's Capital A/c	7,200	By A's Capital A/c	41,486
To B's Capital A/c	7,200	By B's Capital A/c	19,114
To C's Capital A/c	16,800		
To D's Capital A/c	7,400		
	96,600		96,600

Working Notes :

1. The deficiency arising out of the insolvency of D has been borne by A & B in the Capital ratio (4 : 3). C, though solvent, does not bear any deficiency as he has no capital balance to his credit. However, he brings realisation loss in cash as he is solvent.

2. B is entitled commission @ 5% on the amount finally paid to A (including loan but excluding cash brought in by him equivalent to loss on realisation) after charging his commission which has been worked out as under.

$$\text{Amount payable before commission} \times \frac{5}{105}$$

$$\text{i.e., } (40{,}000 + 20{,}000 - 7{,}200 - 16{,}800)\ 36{,}000 \times \frac{5}{105} = \text{Rs. } 1{,}714 \text{ app}$$

3. The expenses of realisation, which B agrees to bear himself, have been ignored. It is presumed that these have been paid privately.
4. The commission payable to B by A has been mutually adjusted as A has agreed to bear this commission wholly himself. Had it been treated as business expense then this commission would have been transferred to Realisation A/c.
5. Students should note that "Commission" payable to any partner in lies of "Realisation Expenses" will be charged to Realisation Account only if it is to be treated as business expense.

INSOLVENCY OF ALL PARTNERS

On dissolution when the liabilities of the firm cannot be discharged in full out of the business assets as well as partners private estates, all the partners are said to be insolvent.

Under such situation liabilities are classified in two categories:

1. Secured liabilities and
2. Unsecured liabilities

Secured liabilities are those liabilities which have lien or mortgage on any or some or whole of the assets of the firm. Such liabilities are paid out of the sum realised from such mortgaged asset/assets. These may be fully secured or partly secured. In case of fully secured liabilities, the surplus is available to unsecured liabilities. If there are more than one unsecured liabilities (such as creditors for goods and Bills payable) the payment is made on prorata basis. For example a firm takes a Loan of Rs. 90,000 from a Bank against the mortgage of Building which realises Rs. 1,00,000 on dissolution. This bank loan will be treated as fully secured liability and surplus of Rs. 10,000 will be available to unsecured creditors on prorata basis.

On the other hand, if loan from Bank amounts to Rs. 1,20,000 and the value of security (building as above) remains at Rs. 1,00,000, then Rs. 20,000 will be treated as unsecured creditors (liability) and paid on prorata basis with other unsecured creditors. Thus any liability which is fully secured or partly secured has to be paid out of the proceeds of assets/assets mortgaged.

A liability which is neither secured by specific charge nor by floating charge (charge against whole of the assets) is treated as unsecured liability, such as creditors and bills payable etc.

ACCOUNTING TREATMENT

The insolvency of the firm i.e. insolvency of all partners may have either of the two situations:

I. When total Cash available with the firm can be estimated. In other words, the total amount realised from sale of assets, surplus from secured creditors if any, and the amount contributed by partners is clearly given. The amount brought in by partners is given in absolute figure i.e. X, Y or Z brings Rs. 1,000; 2,000 or any other amount.

II. When available cash cannot be estimated or ascertained, because amount contributed by either of the partners is given in relative term e.g. X, Y or Z brings of the deficiency on his own account. It requires use of algebric equation.

I. Under first situation when cash available (total) can be ascertained, the unsecured liabilities should not be transferred to Realisation Account but should be paid through Cash or Bank Account. The difference between the book value of liabilities including unrecorded if any, and amount actually paid, be transferred to Deficiency Account. The steps to be taken under first method can be summarised as under:

1. Prepare Realisation Account without transferring the unsecured liabilities.
2. Prepare Cash or Bank Account showing the full and partial discharge of fully secured/partly secured creditors. Expenses of realisation, if any, should be paid first on priority basis even before fully secured creditors are paid.
3. Prepare Partners Capital Accounts. The surplus or deficiency of partners to be transferred to Deficiency Account.
4. Prepare unsecured creditors (liabilities) Account and after making partial payment, transfer the balance to Deficiency Account if e.g. total amount payable to unsecured creditors is Rs. 2,50,000 whereas amount available for them is Rs. 1,80,000 only then Rs. 70,000 will be transferred to Deficiency Account. Following entry shall be recorded.

Unsecured Liabilities (such as BP creditors etc.) A/c	Dr	2,50,000	
To Bank A/c			1,80,000
To Deficiency A/c			70,000

5. Prepare Deficiency Account and make sure that both sides of the account agree.

II. When total cash available cannot be ascertained Or (Use of algebric equation)

Second method involves following steps:

1. Prepare Cash Account, ignoring the cash to be brought in by the partner who brings cash in relative term say 1/2 or 1/3 or_of the deficiency on his own account.
2. Prepare Realisation Account (Memorandum) and transfer all liabilities and discharge the same to the extent the amount available as per cash or bank Account.
3. Prepare Capital Account of the partner who brings Cash in relative term (as per point 1) and ascertain the deficiency after transferring all items relating to his Capital Account.
4. Derive an algebric equation presuming that he brings X amount which is to be paid to unsecured creditors. Since payment made to creditors is debited to Realisation Account, it will increase the loss of realisation which in turn, increase the debit balance (deficiency) of the partner concerned.

Suppose, Loss on realisation before cash contribution of (say) C, a partner in firm of A, B & C with equal profit sharing ratio, is Rs. 30,000. If C brings X amount and loss on realisation will be Rs. 30,000 + x and share of C will be $= 10{,}000 + \frac{x}{3}$

Now suppose that C had a deficiency of Rs. 8,000 earlier now his deficiency will be 8,000 + X/3. If he brings half of his own deficiency, then following equation can be derived.

$$X = \frac{1}{2} of \left(8000 + \frac{x}{3}\right)$$

$$X = 4000 + \frac{x}{6}$$

$$6X - X = 24,000$$

$$5X = 24,000$$

$$X = 4,800$$

Therefore amount brought in by C will be Rs. 4,800. Once this amount is worked out, then the Realisation Account, Partners Capital Accounts and Cash or Bank Account will again be prepared to close the book of firm.

Alternatively, the amount contributed by C can be worked out as follows:

Cs Share of profit or loss is 1/3

He contributes half of his deficiency i.e. 1/2 of 1/3 = 1/6

Thus C contributes 1/6th

Therefore, remaining deficiency is 1 – 1/6 = 5/6

For 5/6 the contribution is Rs. 8,000 (being the deficiency of C).

For recovering full deficiency the contribution will be Rs. 9,600 i.e. (8,000 × 6/5)

But C contributes (Half) of the full deficiency i.e. Rs. 9,600 × 1/2 = Rs. 4,800.

Thus C brings Rs. 4,800 only.

Illustration 19 (Deficiency Account)

A, B and C are equal partners whose Balance Sheet on 31st December 2007 was as follows:

Liabilities	Rs.	Assets	Rs.
A's Capital	8,000	Land & Building	20,000
C's Capital	5,000	Furniture and Fittings	8,000
A's Loan	10,000	Plant & Machinery	20,000
Sundry Creditors	50,000	Stock	8,000
		Debtors	10,000
		Cash in hand	500
		B's Capital	6,500
	73,000		73,000

Due to lack of liquidity and weak financial position of the partners, the firm was dissolved. A & C were not able to contribute anything and a sum of Rs. 2,000 received from B. All of them were declared insolvent. The assets realised as under:

Stock Rs. 5,000, Plant & Machinery Rs. 10,000; Furniture and Fittings Rs. 2,000; Land & Building Rs. 8,000 and Debtors Rs. 5,500 only. Realisation expenses amounted to Rs. 500.

You are required to close the books of the firm. **[B.Com. (H), DU, 1982 & 2005-Adapted]**

Solution :

REALISATION ACCOUNT

	Rs.			Rs.
To Land & Building	20,000	By Cash		
To Plant & Machinery	20,000	Land & Building	8,000	
To Furniture & Fittings	8,000	Plant & Machinery	10,000	
To Stock	8,000	Furniture & Fittings	2,000	
To Debtors	10,000	Stock	5,000	30,500
To Cash (Expenses)	500	Debtors	5,500	
		By Loss Transferred to Capital Accounts :		
		A	12,000	
		B	12,000	
		C	12,000	36,000
	66,500			66,500

PARTNERS' CAPITAL ACCOUNTS

Particulars	A Rs.	B Rs.	C Rs.	Particulars	A Rs.	B Rs.	C Rs.
To Balance b/d	—	6,500	—	By Balance b/d	8,000	—	5,000
To Realisation A/c (Loss)	12,000	12,000	12,000	By A's Loan	10,000	—	—
				By Cash	—	2,000	—
To Deficiency	6,000	—	—	By Deficiency A/c	—	16,500	7,000
	18,000	18,500	12,000		18,000	18,500	12,000

CASH ACCOUNT

	Rs.		Rs.
To Balanc e b/d	500	By Realisation A/c (Expenses)	500
To B's Capital A/c	2,000	By Sundry Creditors (Balancing Figure)	32,500
To Realisation A/c	30,500		
	33,000		33,000

SUNDRY CREDITORS ACCOUNT

	Rs.		Rs.
To Cash	32,500	By Balance b/d	50,000
To Deficiency A/c	17,500		
	50,000		50,000

DEFICIENCY ACCOUNT

	Rs.		Rs.
To B's Capital A/c	16,500	By Sundry Creditors A/c	17,500
To C's Capital A/c	7,000	By A's Capital A/c	6,000
	23,500		23,500

Illustration 20

The Balance Sheet of A, B & C who were sharing profits and losses in the ratio of 2:2:1, was as follows on 31st March 2008, the date of dissolution.

Liabilities	Rs.	Assets	Rs.
Sundry Creditors	1,20,000	Cash	1,000
Bank Loan (with a Charge on stock)	50,000	Stock	60,000
A's Capital	30,000	Other Assets	1,09,000
B's Capital	20,000	Goodwill	30,000
		C's Capital	20,000
	2,20,000		2,20,000

Stock realised Rs. 52,000 and other assets were sold for Rs. 90,000. Expenses on realisation amounted to Rs. 3,000. Assuming all partners are insolvent, prepare necessary ledger accounts to close the books of the firm. **[B.Com. (H), DU, 1987-Modified]**

Solution :

REALISATION ACCOUNT

	Rs.		Rs.
To Goodwill	30,000	By Cash	
To Other Assets	1,09,000	Stock	52,000
To Stock	60,000	Other Assets	90,000
To Cash (Expenses)	3,000	By Loss transferred to :	
		A's Capital A/c	24,000
		B's Capital A/c	24,000
		C's Capital A/c	12,000
	2,02,000		2,02,000

PARTNERS' CAPITAL ACCOUNTS

Particulars	A Rs.	B Rs.	C Rs.	Particulars	A Rs.	B Rs.	C Rs.
To Balance b/d	—	—	20,000	By Balance b/d	30, 000	20,000	—
To Realisation A/c (Loss)	24,000	24,000	12,000	By A/c	—	4,000	32,000
To Deficiency A/c	6,000	—	—				
	30,000	24,000	32,000		30,000	24,000	32,000

CASH ACCOUNT

	Rs.		Rs.
To Balance b/d	1,000	By Realisation A/c (Expenses)	3,000
To Realisation A/c	1,42,000	By Bank Loan	50,000
(Stock + other assets)		By Sundry Creditors	90,000
		(Balancing figures)	
	1,43,000		1,43,000

SUNDRY CREDITORS ACCOUNT

	Rs.		Rs.
To Cash	90,000	By Balance c/d	1,20,000
To Deficiency A/c	30,000		
	1,20,000		1,20,000

DEFICIENCY ACCOUNT

	Rs.		Rs.
To B's Capital	4,000	By Sundry Creditors	30,000
To C's Capital	32,000	By A's Capital	6,000
	36,000		36,000

Illustration 21 (Private assets & Private liabilities)

X, Y and Z were partners in a business. Their Balance Sheet as on 31st March 1999 was as follows:

Liabilities	Rs.	Assets	Rs.
X's Capital	1,60,000	Properties	4,00,000
Y's Capital	1,00,000	Machinery	4,00,000
X's Loan	2,00,000	Fixtures	1,60,000
Payables (Creditors)	10,00,000	Stock	1,60,000
		Book Debts	2,00,000
		Cash	10,000
		Z's Capital (creditors)	1,30,000
	14,60,000		14,60,000

Due to bad financial position of the partners, the firm was dissolved and all partners were declared bankrupt. The assets were realised as follows: Book debts 45% Less, Properties Rs. 1,60,000; Stock Rs. 1,00,000; Machinery Rs. 2,00,000 and Fixtures Rs. 40,000. Realisation Expenses amounted Rs. 10,000. The private financial position of partners was as follows:

	Private Liabilities	Private Assets
	Rs.	Rs.
X	2,50,000	2,50,000
Y	2,00,000	1,80,000
Z	2,30,000	2,50,000

Prepare : Realisation Account, Bank Account, Payable (Creditors) Account, Deficiency Account and Partners Capital Accounts. **[B.Com. (H), DU, 1999]**

Solution :

REALISATION ACCOUNT

	Rs.			Rs.
To Properties	4,00,000	By Cash :		
To Machinery	4,00,000	Properties	1,60,000	
To Fixtures	1,60,000	Machinery	2,00,000	
To Stock	1,60,000	Fixtures	40,000	
To Book Debts	2,00,000	Stock	1,00,000	
To Cash (Expenses)	10,000	Book Debts	1,10,000	6,10,000
		By Loss transferred to :		
		X's Capital A/c	2,40,000	
		Y's Capital A/c	2,40,000	
		Z's Capital A/c	2,40,000	7,20,000
	13,30,000			13,30,000

CASH ACCOUNT

	Rs.		Rs.
To Balance b/d	10,000	By Realisation A/c (Exp.)	10,000
To Realisation A/c (Assets)	6,10,000	By Reaisation A/c (Payables) (Balancing figure)	6,30,000
To Y's Capital A/c	20,000		
	6,40,000		6,40,000

PARTNERS' CAPITAL ACCOUNT

Particulars	X Rs.	Y Rx.	Z Rs.	Particulars	X Rs.	Y Rs.	Z Rs.
To Balance b/d	—	—	1,30,000	By Balance b/d	1,60,000	1,00,000	—
To REalisation A/c (Loss)	2,40,000	2,40,000	2,40,000	By X's Loan	2,00,000	—	
				By Cash		20,000	—
To Deficiency A/c	1,20,000	—	—	By Deficiency A/c	—	1,20,000	3,70,000
	3,60,000	2,40,000	3,70,000		3,60,000	2,40,000	3,70,000

PAYABLES' (CREDITORS) ACCOUNT

	Rs.		Rs.
To Cash A/c	6,30,000	By Balance b/d	10,00,000
To Deficiency A/c	3,70,000		
	10,00,000		10,00,000

DEFICIENCY ACCOUNT

	Rs.		Rs.
To Y's Capital A/c	1,20,000	By Payables A/c	3,70,000
To Z's Capital A/c	3,70,000	By X's Capital A/c	1,20,000
	4,90,000		4,90,000

Illustration 22 (Secured and Unsecured Creditors)

Following is the Balance Sheet as on 31st March 2001 of a firm, having three partners Alfa, Beta and Gama sharing profits and losses equally.

Liabilities	Rs.	Assets.	Rs.
Sundry Creditors	20,000	Cash	3,120
Loan (Secured by Furniture)	10,000	Stock	15,630
Capital Accounts :		Debtors	4,720
Alfa	8,000	Furniture	9,530
Beta	6,000	Profit & Loss A/c	12,000
Gamma	1,000		
	45,000		45,000

The firm was dissolved due to insolvency of all partners. Stock was sold for Rs. 9,900 while furniture fetched Rs. 5,000. Rs. 4,100 were received from debtors. Realisation expenses totalled Rs. 220. Nothing could be recovered from Beta and Gama, but Rs. 600 could be collected from Alfas private estate. Close the books of the firm. **[C.S. (Foundation), Dec. 1994-Modified]**

Solution :

REALISATION ACCOUNT

	Rs.				Rs.
To Furniture	9,530	By Cash :		5,000	
To Stock	15,630	Furniture		9,900	
To Debtors	4,720	Stock		4,100	19,000
To Cash (Expenses)	220	Debtors			
		By Loss transferred to :			
		Alfa's Capital	3,700		
		Beta's Capital	3,700		
		Gamma's Capital	3,700		11,100
	30,100				30,100

PARTNERS' CAPITAL ACCOUNTS

Particulars	Alfa Rs.	Beta Rs.	Gamma Rs.	Particulars	Alfa Rs.	Beta Rs.	Gamma Rs.
To Profit & Loss A/c	4,000	4,000	4,000	By Balance b/d	8,000	6,000	1,000
To Realisation A/c (Loss)	3,700	3,700	3,700	By Cash A/c	600	—	—
To Deficiency A/c	900	—	—	By Deficiency A/c	—	1,700	6,700
	8,600	7,700	7,700		8,600	7,700	7,700

CASH ACCOUNT

	Rs.		Rs.
To Balance b/d	3,120	By Realisation A/c (Expenses)	220
To Realisation A/c (S. Assets)	19,000	By Loan A/c (5,000 + 3,500)	8,500
To Alfa's Capital	600	By Creditors A/c	14,000
	22,720		22,720

LOAN ACCOUNT

	Rs.		Rs.
To Cash (equivalent to Realisable value of furniture)	5,000	By Balance b/d	10,000
To Cash (Shared with creditors in 5,000 : 20,000 proportion) or 1 : 4	3,500		
To Deficiency A/c	1,500		
	10,000		10,000

SUNDRY CREDITORS ACCOUNT

	Rs.		Rs.
To Cash (Proportionately)	14,000	By Balance b/d	20,000
To Deficiency A/c	6,000		
	20,000		20,000

DEFICIENCY ACCOUNT

	Rs.		Rs.
To Beta's Capital A/c	1,700	By Loan A/c	1,500
To Gamma's Capital A/c	6,700	By Sundry Creditors A/c	6,000
		By Alfa's Capital A/c	900
	8,400		8,400

Illustration 23 (Use of Algebric equation & charge on specific asset)

A, B and C were in partnership sharing profit and losses in the ratio of 2:3:5. They prepared the following balance sheet on 31st December 2000, when they decided to dissolve:

Liabilities	Rs.	Assets	Rs.
A's Capital	60,000	Plant & Machinery	5,00,000
B's Capital	80,000	Stock	50,000
C's Capital	60,000	Debtors	50,000
Loan from Bank (against the security of Plant & Machinery)	3,00,000	Advance to A	40,000
		Cash	10,000

Loan from C	40,000	Profit & Loss A/c	1,50,000
Trade Creditors	2,50,000		
Bills Payable	10,000		
	8,00,000		8,00,000

Plant and Machinery realised Rs. 3,50,000, Debtors Rs. 30,000 and Stock Rs. 40,000. A has a private estate valued at Rs. 1,00,000 and his liabilities amounted to Rs. 40,000. The private estate realised Rs. 60,000 only. B is insolvent, C can pay only 50 paise in the rupee of what is payable on his own account to the firm.

Prepare Ledger Accounts, assuming that the loss on realisation is to be determined after considering the amount ultimately paid to creditors. **[B.Com. (H), DU, 1988-Modified]**

Solution :

REALISATION ACCOUNT

	Rs.			Rs.
To Plant & Machinery	5,00,000	By Loan from Bank		3,00,000
To Stock	50,000	By Sundry Creditors		2,50,000
To Debtors	50,000	By Bills Payable		10,000
To Cash (Bank Loan)	3,00,000	By Cash :		
To Cash (Creditors + BP)*	1,56,667	Plant & Machinery	3,50,000	
		Stock	40,000	
		Debtors	30,000	4,20,000
		By Loss transferred to:		
		A's Capital	15,333	
		B's Capital	23,000	
		C's Capital	38,334	76,667
	10,56,667			10,56,667

PARTNERS' CAPITAL ACCOUNTS

Particulars	A Rs.	B Rs.	C Rs.	Particulars	A Rs.	B Rs.	C Rs.
To Realisation A/c (Loss)	15,333	23,000	38,334	By Balance c/d	60,000	80,000	60,000
To Profit & Loss A/c	30,000	45,000	75,000	By C's Loan A/c	—	—	40,000
To Advance to A	40,000	—	—	By Cash	20,000	—	6,667*
To A's Capital A/c	—	5,333	—	By B's Capital A/c	5,333	—	6,667
To C's Capital A/c	—	6,667	—				
	85,333	80,000	1,13,334		53,333	80,000	1,13,334

CASH ACCOUNT

	Rs.		Rs.
To Balance b /d	10,000	By Realisation A/c	3,00,000
To Realisation A/c	4,20,000	(Bank Loan)	
(Assets)		By Realisation A/c	1,56,667
To A's Capital	20,000	(Creditors + BP)	
To C's Capital	6,667		
	4,56,667		4,56,667

*Please see the working note.

Working Note :

In this question, C brings 50% of his own deficiency which can be ascertained only after realisation loss which, in turn, can be determined only after the payment to creditors and Bills payable. Thus, we have to ascertain the amount of cash available after C brings required amount of cash, but this can be worked out only after realisation loss. For this purpose following memorandum accounts shall be prepared presuming that he brings X amount.

REALISATION ACCOUNT (Memorandum)

	Rs.			Rs.
To Plant and Machinery	5,00,000	By Loan from Bank		3,00,000
To Stock	50,000	By Trade Creditors		2,50,000
To Debtors	50,000	By Bills Payable		10,000
To Cash :		By Cash :		
Bank Loan	3,00,000	Plant & Machinery		3,50,000
To Creditors & Bills Payable*	1,50,000 + x	Debtors		30,000
		Stock		40,000
		By Loss transferred to :		
		A's Capital	14,000 + 3x/10	
		B's Capital	21,000 + 3x/10	
		C's Capital	35,000 + 5x/10	70,000 + x
	10,50,000 + x			10,50,000 + x

CS CAPITAL ACCOUNT (Memorandum)

	Rs.		Rs.
To Realisation A/c (Loss)	$35{,}000 + \frac{5x}{10}$	By Balance b/d	60,000
To Profit & Loss A/c	75,000	By C's Loan A/c	40,000
		By Proposed Deficiency before he brings any Cash	$10{,}000 + \frac{5x}{10}$
	$1{,}10{,}000 + \frac{5x}{10}$		$1{,}10{,}000 + \frac{5x}{10}$

***CASH ACCOUNT (Memorandum)**

	Rs.		Rs.
To Balance b/d	10,000	By Realisation A/c (Loan)	3,00,000
To REalisation A/c (Assets)	4,20,000	By Creditors & Bills Payable (Balancing figure)	1,50,000 + x
To A's Capital A/c	20,000		
To C's Capital A/c	x		
	4,50,000 + x		4,50,000 + x

Now Cs deficiency is Rs. 10,000 before he brings any cash. But he brings 50% of the deficiency arising on his own account. Any cash brought in by C will increase the cash paid to creditors and bills payable, which in turn, increase the loss on account of realisation. This loss, again, shall be debited to Partners Capital Accounts in the profit sharing ratio (as indicated by x in the memorandum Accounts). Thus the payment to creditors increases by x amount and so is the loss on realisation. But Cs share increases by x/2 i.e. 5/10 of x. This can be summed up as under:

C's deficiency: Rs. 10,000 (as per his Capital A/c before he brings any cash)

C's deficiency, Rs. (10,000 + x/2)after he brings cash which is paid to creditors

But he contributes 50% of total deficiency i.e.

$$x = 50\% \text{ of } (10{,}000 + x/2)$$
$$x = 1/2\,(10{,}000 + x/2)$$
$$x = 5{,}000 + x/4$$
$$4x = 20{,}000 + x$$
$$4x - x = 20{,}000$$
$$x = 6{,}667$$

Thus C will bring Rs. 6,667

Arithmetically : C's share is 1/2. He contributes 50% or 1/2 of his dificiency, i.e., 1/4. Thus, remaining deficiency is 1 – 1/4 = 3/4 for which he is required to contribute Rs. 10,000. For total dificiency contribution will be 10,000 × 4/3 = Rs. 13,333. But C contributes 50%, thus he brings 1/2 of 13,333, i.e., Rs. 6,667.

Hence total payment to be made to Creditors and Bills payable would be Rs. 1,56,667.

Illustration 24 (Use of equation & charge on all assets)

Rahim, Zaidi and Tahir shared profits and losses in the ratio of 5 : 3 : 2 respectively. On 31st December 2008 their Balance Sheet was as under:

Liabilities	Rs.	Assets	Rs.
Rahim's Capital	30,000	Furniture	11,000
Zaidi's Capital	20,000	Stock	48,000
Tahir's Capital	10,000	Cash	1,000
Bank Loan	10,000	Profit & Loss A/c	40,000
Trade Creditors	30,000		
	1,00,000		1,00,000

The Bank has a charge on all the assets. Furniture realised Rs. 3,000 while the entire stock was sold for Rs. 25,000. Zaidis, private estate realised Rs. 6,000, his private creditors were Rs. 5,000. Tahir was unable to contribute anything. Rahim paid one-third of what was finally due from him (taking the payment also into account) except on account of other partners.

Prepare Realisation Account, Cash Book and Partners Capital Accounts, passing all matters relating to realisation of assets and payment of liabilities through the Realisation Account. Clearly show your calculation regarding cash brought in by Rahim.

[B.Com. (H), DU, 1986, 1996-Modified, 1999 (Old Course)]

Solution :

REALISATION ACCOUNT

	Rs.			Rs.
To Furniture	11,000	By Bank Loan		10,000
To Stock	48,000	By Creditors		30,000
To Cash (Bank Loan)	10,000	By Cash :		
To Cash (Creditors)*	20,200	Furniture	3,000	
		Stock	25,000	28,000
		By Loss transferred to :		
		Rahim's Capital A/c	10,600	
		Zaidi's Capital A/c	6,360	
		Tahir's Capital A/c	4,240	21,200
	89,200			89,200

PARTNERS' CAPITAL ACCOUNTS

Particulars	Rahim Rs.	Zaidi Rs.	Tahir Rs.	Particulars	Rahim Rs.	Zaidi Rs.	Tahir Rs.
To Realisation A/c (Loss)	10,600	6,360	4,240	By Balance b/d	30,000	20,000	10,000
To Profit & Loss A/c	20,000	12,000	8,000	By Cash	200*	1,000	—
To Rahim's Cap. A/c	—	400	—	By Zaidi's Cap. A/c	400	—	2,240
To Tahir's Cap. A/c	—	2,240	—				
	30,600	21,000	12,240		30,600	21,000	12,240

CASH ACCOUNT

Particulars	Rs.	Particulars	Rs.
To Balance b/d	1,000	By Realisation A/c (Bank Loan)	10,000
To Realisation A/c (Assets)	28,000	By Realisation A/c (Creditors)	20,200
To Zaidi's Capital A/c	1,000		
To Rahim's Capital A/c	200		
	30,200		30,200

*see the working note.

Working Note :

Students should recall that use of x or algebric equation is done only when any partner brings cash on account of his own deficiency which can be ascertained after payment to unsecured creditors who cannot be paid in full for short of cash. In this question total cash available before Rahim brings any Cash is as follows:

	Rs.
Opening balance	1,000
Realisation from assets	28,000
Zaidi	1,000
	30,000

As against the liabilities of

Bank Loan (Which is secured against the charge of all assets)	10,000
Trade Creditors	30,000
	40,000

It means only Rs, 20,000 can be paid to creditors. In such a situation loss of Realisation will be Rs. 21,000 i.e. book value of assets (11,000 + 48,000) less realised value of assets (3000 + 25,000) = 31,000 less gain on payment to creditors (30,000 - 20,000) and Rahims share in the realisation loss Rs. 10,500. Thus determining the Rahims deficiency on his own account will be Rs. 500 i.e. Rs. 30,000 (Capital) less (Realisation loss 10,500 + P & L A/c (Dr) 20,000). But he brings one-third of what was finally due from him only. Thus let us suppose he brings x amount. Thus his total deficiency will be = 500 + x/2 (i.e. half of the additional realisation loss). Therefore he brings 1/3 of (500 + x/2)

$$x = 1/3\,(500 + x/2)$$
$$x = 500/3 + x/6$$
$$6x = 1{,}000 + x$$
$$6x - x = 1{,}000$$
$$x = 200$$

Thus he brings Rs. 200 only.

Illustration 25 (Use of equation & partly secured creditors)

A, B and C had the following Balance Sheet as on 31st December 2001:

Liabilities	Rs.	Assets.	Rs.
A's Capital	20,000	Fixed Assets	40,000
B's Capital	20,000	Stock	20,000
C's Capital	10,000	Sundry Debtors	24,000
Loan from A	10,000	Cash at Bank	1,000
Loan from Mrs. A (With a charge on stock)	15,000	Loss	30,000
Sundry Creditors	40,000		
	1,15,000		1,15,000

The firm was dissolved. Stock realised Rs. 10,000 and fixed assets and debtors realised Rs. 30,000 in all. The Private position of the partners was as under:

	Private Estate	Private Liabilities
	Rs.	Rs.
A	10,000	15,000

B 8,000 6,000

C was able to bring 50 paise in the rupee of what was payable on his own account to the partnership. The partners shared profits and losses in the ratio of 4 : 3 : 3 for A, B and C respectively.

The loss on realisation is to be determined after considering the amount finally paid to creditors.

You are required to close the books of the firm by preparing the necessary ledger accounts.

[B.Com. (H), DU, 1994-Modified]

Solution :

REALISATION ACCOUNT

	Rs.			Rs.
To Fixed Assets	40,000	By Loan from Mrs. A		15,000
To Stock	20,000	By Sundry Creditors		40,000
To Sundry Debtors	24,000	By Cash :		
To Cash (Mrs. As Loan) (1)	10,000	Stock	10,000	
To Cash (Sundry Creditors & Mrs. A's Loan)*	38,059	Fixed Assets & Debtors	30,000	40,000
		By Loss transferred to :		
		A's Capital A/c	14,823	
		B's Capital A/c	11,118	
		C's Capital A/c	11,118	37,059
	1,32,059			1,32,059

PARTNERS' CAPITAL ACCOUNTS

Particulars	A Rs.	B Rs.	C Rs.	Particulars	A Rs.	B Rs.	C Rs.
To Loss	12,000	9,000	9,000	By Balance b/d	20,000	20,000	10,000
To Realisation A/c (Loss)	14,823	11,118	11,118	By A's Loan	10,000	—	—
To C's Capital A/c	3,177	1,882	—	By Cash	—	2,000	5,059*
				By A's Capital	—	—	3,177
				By B's Capital	—	—	1,882
	30,000	22,000	20,118		30,000	22,000	20,118

CASH ACCOUNT

	Rs.		Rs.
To Balance b/d	1,000	By Realisation A/c (Mrs. A's Loan)	10,000
To Realisation A/c (Assets)	40,000		
To B's Capital	2,000	By Realisation A/c (S. Creditors & Mrs. A's Loan Paid proportionately)	38,059
To C's Capital	5,059*		
	48,059		48,059

*See the working note (2).

Working Notes :

(1) Mrs. As loan has been paid in the first instance to the extent of amount realised from sale of stock i.e. Rs. 10,000, as it was secured against the stock only. The balance of Rs. 5,000 is treated as unsecured and has been paid along with the creditors on prorata basis. Therefore the total cash available after partners have brought in whatever cash they could, has been paid to both_Mrs. A and Sundry Creditors.

(2) To calculate cash brought in by C take the following steps:

(a) Estimate the total cash available before C brings in cash.

(b) Prepare Realisation Account showing payment to creditors and Mrs. A Loan (of course with the available cash).

(c) Prepare Cs Capital account to determine deficiency of his account.

(d) Apply the formula of x as shown below:

		Rs.
(i)	Total Cash available	
	Balance as per B/s	1,000
	Realisation of Assets	40,000
	B brings in	2,000
	(Pvt. Estate Pvt. Liab.)	43,000

(ii)	Loss on Realisation:			Rs.
	Fixed Assets	40,000	Mrs. As Loan	15,000
	Stock	20,000	Sundry Creditors	40,000
	Debtors	24,000		55,000
		84,000		
	Amount Realised	40,000	*Less* Available Cash	43,000
	Loss on Sale of Assets	44,000	Gain on payment of Liabilities	12,000

Thus net loss 44,000 less 12,000 = 32,000 Cs share = 9,600

(iii) Cs Capitals deficiency

Cs Capital 10,000 less (Share in loss 9,000 + 9,600 R. Loss) = Rs. 8,600

This deficiency will increase, proportionate to his profit sharing ratio, by the amount he brings in cash. Suppose C brings x amount, his total deficiency will be as follow:

$$x = 8{,}600 + 3/10 \text{ of } x$$

but he brings 50% of his deficiency i.e. 1/2 of (8,600 + 3x/10) or x = 4,300 + 3x/20

i.e. $20x = 8{,}6000 + 3x$

$$20x - 3x = 86{,}000$$

$$17x = 86{,}000$$

$$x = 5{,}059 \text{ (app.)}$$

QUESTIONS

1. Distinguish between dissolution of partnership and dissolution of the firm.
2. Explain the circumstances which cause dissolution of firm.

3. Under what circumstances the court can order for dissolution of the firm.
4. Write a note on Garner vs. Murray rule and its applicability in India. **[B.Com. (H), DU, 1992, 1985]**
5. Write short notes on: Solvent Vs. Insolvent partner Secured Vs. Unsecured creditors Private Assets Vs. Business Assets Liability of a partner in a firm.

PROBLEMS

1. The following is the Balance Sheet of A and B as on 31-12-2005.

BALANCE SHEET As on 31-12-2005

Liabilities		Rs.	Assets		Rs.
Capital Accounts :			Furniture		11,200
A	28,000		Plant		78,400
B	22,400	50,400	Investments		28,000
Reserve Fund		14,000	Cash at Bank		32,200
Loan from W		28,000	Stock-in-trade		16,800
(Wife of A)			Sundry Debtors	56,000	
Loan from B		42,000	*Less* Provisions	2,800	53,200
Sundry Creditors		1,06,400	Profit & Loss A/c		21,000
		2,40,800			2,40,800

The firm was dissolved on 31-12-2005and the following was the result:

(1) B took over Investments at an agreed value of Rs. 22,400 and agreed to pay off the loan to W (Wife of A).

(2) The assets realised as under: Stock Rs. 14,000; Debtors Rs. 51,800; and Plant Rs. 70,000. Furniture Rs. 12,600. Expenses on Realisation amounted to Rs. 3,080.

(3) The Sundry Creditors were paid off less 2-1/2% discount. A and B shared profits & losses in the ratio of 3 : 2. Show Realisation a/c, Bank a/c and the Capital a/cs of the partners.

Ans. Loss on Realisation A : Rs. 10,332, B : Rs. 6,888
Final Payment A : Rs. 19,068 B : Rs. 54,712

2. A, B and C are partners, sharing profits & losses in the ratio 2:2: 1. They agreed to dissolve the firm on 31-12-2005 and on that date the Balance Sheet of the firm was as follows:

BALANCE SHEET
As on 31-12-2005

Liabilities		Rs.	Assets		Rs.
Capital Accounts :			Plant & Machinery		18,000
A	30,000		Furnture		12,000
B	15,000		Investments		15,000
C	15,000	6,000	Stock		15,000
General Reserve		15,000	Sundry Debtors	19,500	
Sundry Creditors		7,500	*Less* Provision for Bad Debts	1,500	18,000

Current Accounts :			Cash at Bank	13,500
A	7,500		Current A/c :	
B	4,500	12,000	C	3,000
		94,500		94,500

The assets were realised as under:

Plant and Machinery Rs. 22,500; Stock Rs. 12,000, Furniture Rs. 15,000, Debtors in full, Investments were taken over by C at Book value, Creditors were paid at a discount of 10%. Realisation Expenses amounted to Rs. 300. There was an unrecorded asset of Rs. 1,500, which was taken over by A at Rs. 1,200 and there was an unrecorded liability amounted to Rs. 150. Close the Books of the firm.

Ans.	Profit on Realisation :	A 3,000,	B 3,000,	C 1,500
	Final Payment to partners :	A 45,300,	B 28,500,	C 1,500

3. A, B and C are in partnership sharing profits & losses in the proportion of 1/2, 1/3 and 1/6 respectively. They decided not to continue the business and to dissolve partnership on 1-10-2006, on which date the Balance Sheet of the firm was as follows:

BALANCE SHEET
As on 1-10-2006

Liabilities		**Rs.**	**Assets**	**Rs.**
Capitals :			Premises	33,345
A	26,000		Machinery	14,040
B	15,600	41,600	Stock	10,946
Contingency Reserve		7,800	Sundry Debtors	20,579
Sundry Creditors		26,338	Bills Receivable	1,105
Bank Loan		6,656	C's Account	1,625
			Cash at Bank	754
		82,394		82,394

The assets realised the following amounts:

Premises Rs. 20,150; Machinery Rs. 10,400; Stock Rs. 12,090; Debtors Rs. 19,019; Bills Receivable Rs. 1,105; The Goodwill was sold for Rs. 3,250.

Discounts amounting to Rs. 416 were allowed by creditors on the payment of their claims.

The Expenses on Realisation amounted to Rs. 585. During the course of dissolution, a liability under an action for damages was settled at Rs. 15,600 against Rs. 13,000 provided in the books of the firm. Prepare the necessary accounts showing the net result of the realisation and the cash distribution amongst partners.

Ans.	Loss on Realisation	A : Rs. 8,385,	B : Rs. 5,590,	C : Rs. 2,795
	Payment	A : Rs. 21,515,	B : Rs. 12,610	
	Cash Brought in by	C : Rs. 3,120		

4. X, Y and Z sharing profits, in 3 : 1 : 1 agree upon dissolution. They each decide to take over certain assets & liabilities and continue business separately.

BALANCE SHEET
As on 31-12-2005

Liabilities		Rs.	Assets		Rs.
Capitals			Furniture		1,200
X	33,000		Stock		9,360
Y	12,000		Cash at Bank		3,840
Z	8,400	53,400	Sundry Assets		20,400
Loan		1,800	Debtors	29,040	
Creditors		7,200	*Less* : Bad Debts Provision	1,440	27,600
		62,400			62,400

It is agreed that:

(1) Goodwill is to be ignored.

(2) X is to take over all the fixtures at Rs. 960; Debtors amounting to Rs. 24,000 at Rs.20,640. The Creditors of Rs. 7,200 to be assumed by X at that figure.

(3) Y is to take over all the stocks at Rs. 8,400 and some of the sundry assets at Rs. 8,640 (being Book value less 10%).

(4) Z is to take over the remaining sundry assets at 90% of Book value less Rs. 120 allowances and assume responsibility for the discharge of the loan, together with accruing interest of Rs. 36 which has not been recorded in the books of the firm.

(5) The expenses of dissolution were Rs. 324. The remaining debtors were sold to a debt collecting agency for 50% of a Book value.

Prepare Realisation a/c; Partners' Capital a/cs & Bank a/c.

Ans. Loss on Realisation : X : Rs. 4,896, Y : Rs. 1,632, Z : Rs. 1,632

Final Payment : X : Rs. 13,704, Y : Rs. 6,672 (brought in), Z : Rs. 996 (brought in)

5. The following is the Balance Sheet as at 31st March 2001 of X,Y & Z carrying on business in partnership sharing profits and losses in ratio of 2 : 2 : 1.

BALANCE SHEET
As on 31-3-2006

Liabilities	Rs.	Assets	Rs.
Capitals :		Fixed Assets	1,75,000
X	1,00,000	Sundry Debtors	75,000
Y	62,500	Stock	25,000
Mortgage Loan	1,00,000	Cash at Bank :	12,500
Reserve	15,000		
Sundry Creditors	25,000	Z's Capital a/c	15,000
	3,02,500		3,02,500

They decided to dissolve the partnership and the following arrangements were agreed upon:

(1) Fixed Assets include :

(a) Motor Car Rs. 13,750 taken by Y at an agreed value of Rs. 22,500 after necessary repairing cost amounting to Rs. 5,000 borne by the firm.

(b) Land & Building Rs. 1,25,000 subject to mortgage loan, taken over by X at an agreed value of Rs. 1,50,000 subject to mortgage loan to be taken over at Rs. 1,00,000.

(2) Other Assets (excluding cash) and creditors are taken over by W Ltd. in consideration of issue of Rs. 12,500 Equity Shares of Rs. 10 each fully paid. These shares are taken over at total agreed value of Rs. 1,20,000 equally by X & Y.

(3) Creditors for Rs. 6,250 not provided for in the books had to be paid.

Prepare the following accounts assuming that the final settlement was made by the partners bringing in the amounts due from them.

(1) Realisation Account (2) Partners' Capital Accounts (3) Bank Account

Ans. Profit on Realisation X Rs. 12,500, Y Rs. 12,500, Z Rs. 6,260
Cash Payment : X Rs. 8,500
Cash Brought in: Y Rs. 1,500
Z Rs. 5,750

6. X and Y trading as partners sharing profits and losses as 2 : 1. The business is conducted from offices in Delhi & Mumbai. The partnership is dissolved w.e.f. 31-3-2006. X takes over the Delhi business and Y takes over the Mumbai business.

BALANCE SHEET
As on 31-3-2006

Liabilities		Rs.	Assets		Rs.
Capitals			Goodwill		24,000
X	1,20,000		Furniture & Fittings		21,600
Y	31,800	1,51,800	Sundry Debtors		
Z		25,800	Delhi	24,000	
Sundry Creditors			Mumbai	12,000	36,000
			Cash at Bank		96,000
		1,77,600			1,77,600

Goodwill and Furniture & Fittings were revalued as under:

	Goodwill	Furniture & Fittings
Delhi	Rs. 19,200	Rs. 10,200
Mumbai	Rs. 9,600	Rs. 8,640

Each partner took over the book debts of his connection at their book value less 5% by way of provision for Bad Debts. X undertook to pay the creditors of the firm.

The Expenses on dissolution were Rs. 3,000 which were paid by the firm and it was also agreed that Rs. 6,000 and Rs. 600 should be allowed to X & Y respectively towards the future cost of repairs to the premises previously occupied by the firm.

Prepare the necessary accounts to close the books of the firm.

Ans. Loss on Realisation : X Rs. 6,240, Y Rs. 3,120
Cash Payment X Rs.93,360
Cash Brought in Y Rs. 360

BALANCE SHEET
As on 30-06-2006

Liabilities		Rs.	Assets		Rs.
Sundry Creditors		38,750	Cash at Bank		5,000
A's Loan		25,000	Sundry Debtors	40,000	
Partners' Capitals			*Less* : Provision	1,250	38,750
A	50,000		Stock-in-Trade		25,000
B	37,500	87,500	Furniture & Fittings		10,000
			Trade Marks		17,500
			C's Drawings		40,000
			D's Drawings		15,000
		1,51,250			1,51,250

The firm was dissolved as on the above date, B being appointed to realise the assets and pay off the liabilities. He was entitled to receive 5% as his remuneration on the amounts finally paid to other partners towards their capital.

The expenses of realisation were to be defrayed by him. The assets realised as follows:

Sundry Debtors Rs. 27,500; Stock Rs. 20,000; Furniture Rs. 2,500 and Trade Marks Rs.10,000.

Sundry Creditors were paid off in full including a contingent liability of Rs. 6,250 in respect of bills discounted. Expenses of realisation amounting to Rs. 1,250 were paid by the firm. As C was insolvent, only Rs. 9,250 could be recovered from his private estate.

Close the books of the firm applying the rule in the leading case of Garner vs. Murray.

Ans. Loss on Realisation : A Rs. 11,250 B Rs. 11,250
C Rs. 7,500 D Rs. 7,500

Commission payable to B by A : Rs. 1,340

Final Payment : A Rs. 26,802.50; B : Rs. 21,197.50; C : deficiency Rs. 38,250

Hint. Payment to be made to A before charging Commission
= Rs. 28,142.5 i.e. (61,250 – 33,107.5).

Commission will be : Rs. 28,1425 × $\frac{5}{105}$ = Rs. 1,340.

7. Ram, Rahim and Antony were in partnership sharing profits and losses in the ratio of 1/2, 1/3 and 1/6. They decided to dissolve the partnership firm on 31st March 2002, when their Balance Sheet was as under:

Liabilities	Rs.	Assets	Rs.
Sundry Creditors	5,67,000	Goodwill	4,56,300
Bank Overdraft	6,06,450	Plant & Machinery	6,07,500
Joint Life Policy Reserve	2,65,500	Furniture	64,650
Loan from Mrs. Ram	1,50,000	Stock	2,36,700
Capital Accounts :		Sundry Debtors	5,34,00
Ram	4,20,000	Joint Life Policy	2,65,000
Rahim	2,25,000	Commission Receivable	1,40,550
Antony	1,20,00	Cash in Hand	48,750
	23,53,950		23,53,950

The following details are relevant for dissolution:

(i) The Joint life policy was surrendered for Rs. 2,32,500.

(ii) Ram took over goodwill and plant & machinery for Rs. 9,00,000.

(iii) Ram also agreed to discharge Bank overdraft and his wife's loan.

(iv) Furniture and stocks were divided equally between Ram and Rahim at an agreed valuation of Rs. 3,60,000.

(v) Sundry Debtors were assigned to firm's creditors in full satisfaction of their claims,

(vi) Commission receivable was received in toto in time.

(vii) A bill discounted was subsequently returned dishonoured and proved value less Rs.30,750 (including Rs. 500 noting charges).

(viii)Ram paid the expenses of dissolution amounting to Rs. 18,000. (ix) Antony agreed to receive Rs. 1,50,000 in full satisfaction of his rights, title and interest in the firm.

You are required to close the books of the firm. **[C.A. (Inter), Nov. 1998-Modified]**

Ans. Profit on Realisation A/c Rs. 1,11,600

Final Payments :	Ram	Rs. 1,63,410
	Rahim	Rs. 77,640
	Antony	Rs. 1,50,000 (as agreed)

Hint.

1. Antony has been paid Rs. 1,50,000 (as per agreement) as against his due amount of Rs. 1,38,600. The difference of Rs. 11,400 has been borne by Ram and Rahim in the profit sharing ratio.
2. No entry is required regarding assignment of debtors to creditors in full satisfaction of their claims. Mere transfer of debtors and creditors to Realisation Account will adjust the accounts.
3. Bills dishonoured have to be paid.

INSOLVENCY

8. A, B, C and D were partners sharing profit and losses in the ratio of 3 : 3 : 2 : 2. The following is their balance sheet as at 30th June 2001.

9. X, Y and Z are partners in a firm dealing in hardware and sharing profits & losses 4:3:3 respectively, decide to dissolve, and appoint Y to pay 5% of the amounts realised from stock and Debtors as his remuneration, and is to bear all the expenses of realisation. The following is the Balance Sheet as on Dec. 31, 2005, the date of dissolution.

BALANCE SHEET
As on 31-12-2005

Liabilities		Rs.	Assets		Rs.
Capitals :			Cash at Bank		22,500
X	4,50,000		Debtors	6,82,500	
Y	3,00,000	7,50,000	*Less* : Reserve for		
Creditors		8,85,000	Bad Debts	37,500	6,45,000
			Stock		9,00,000
			Capital A/c		
			Z (Over withdrawn)		67,500
		16,35,000			16,35,000

Y reports the realisation results follows:

Debtors realised Rs. 5,25,000; Stock realised Rs. 6,75,000; Goodwill was sold for Rs.30,000; Creditors were paid Rs. 8,62,500 in full settlement. Outstanding creditors Rs. 7,500 had also been paid.

The Expenses of realisation came to Rs. 9,000, which Y met personally.

X and Y agree to receive from Z Rs. 45,000 in full settlement of the firm's claim against him.

Show the necessary ledger accounts (assuming that Garner vs. Murray principle is applied).

Ans. Loss on Realisation : X : Rs. 1,44,000, Y : Rs. 1,08,000, Z : Rs. 1,08,000

Final (Amount) Payment : X : Rs. 3,71,700, Y : Rs. 3,07,800

10. L, M, H & S are partners in a firm, sharing profits & losses in the ration 4:1:2:3. The following is their Balance Sheet as at 31st March 2006.

BALANCE SHEET
As on 31-03-2006

Liabilities		Rs.	Assets		Rs.
Sundry Creditors			Cash at Bank		21,000
Capitals		45,000	Sundry Debtors	52,500	
L	1,05,000		*Less* : Provision	7,500	45,000
S	45,00		Other Assets		76,500
		1,50,000			
			M's Capital		30,000
			H's Capital		22,500
		1,95,000			1,95,000

On the 31st March 2006, the firm is dissolved. The partnership agreement provides that the deficiency of an insolvent partner will be borne by the solvent partners in the ratio of capitals as they stand just before dissolution. The following arrangements are agreed upon:

(1) L is to take over 60% of Book Debts at 70% and S is to take over the balance at 75%. Further, they are to be allowed Rs. 3,150 and Rs. 1,650 respectively to cover future losses.

(2) S is to realise other assets and to pay off the creditors. He is to receive 5% gross commission on the amounts finally payable to other partners but to bear expenses of realisation. He reports the results of realisation as follows: Other assets realise at loss of 2% on net collection and pay off the creditors at a discount of 30%. Realisation expenses amount to Rs.4,500. M is declared insolvent and a dividend of 20% in a rupee is realised from his estate.

Prepare Bank Account, Realisation Account, Capital Account and Deficiency Account.

Ans. Loss on Realisation : Nil

Hint. Commission payable to S :

Gross amount payable to L, Rs. 69,300

$$\text{Commission} = 69{,}300 \times \frac{5}{105} = \text{Rs. } 3{,}300$$

11. A, B and C were partners. After transferring $\frac{1}{10*}$ of the profit to Reserve, they were sharing profits and losses in the ratio of $\frac{5}{10}, \frac{2}{10}$ & $\frac{2}{10}$ respectively. On 31st December 2005, their Balance Sheet was a under :

BALANCE SHEET
As on 31-12-2005

Liabilities		Rs.	Assets		Rs.
Partners' Capital			Fixed Assets		30,000
A	18,000		Stock-in-Trade		45,000
B	24,000		Sundry Debtors	30,000	
C	12,000	54,000	*Less* : Provision	1,800	28,200
Reserve		5,400	Cash		1,200
Sundry Creditors		45,000			
		1,04,400			1,04,400

On 1st January 2005, the firm was dissolved. It was then discovered that:

(1) Goods purchased on credit for Rs. 3,000 on 26-12-2005 were included in stock but this purchase was not recorded in the books.

(2) Cheques received from debtors amounting to Rs. 3,000 had been omitted from the books of accounts and appropriated by C for his own use.

(3) Goods costing Rs. 4,500 were removed and sold by C for Rs. 3,000. All the partners agree that the goods should have realised Rs. 5,400.

A creditor took some items of stock (Book value Rs. 12,000) in full satisfaction of his claim for Rs. 9,000 only. Others were paid at a rebate of 10% after realisation of assets as detailed below: Fixed assets: Rs. 18,000; Sundry Debtors 10% less than the book value and stock (excluding those accepted by creditors) 50% of Book value. Expenses of dissolution were to be borne by B who was to receive as his commission @ 2% of realisation. C proved to be insolvent with no surplus from his private estate. Prepare necessary ledger accounts.

Ans. Loss on Realisation : A : Rs. 16,485, B : Rs. 6,595.50 C : Rs. 6,595.50

Final Payment : A : Rs. 21,750, B : Rs. 26,232

12. X, Y and Z are partners sharing profits & losses as 5 : 3 : 2. The business is dissolved on 31-12-2005, when the Balance Sheet stood as below:

BALANCE SHEET
As on 31-12-2005

Liabilities		Rs.	Assets	Rs.
Capitals :			Machinery	1,20,000
X	24,000		Car	24,000
Y	96,000		Stock	1,44,000
Z	48,000	1,68,000	Debtors	1,08,000
Creditors		2,40,000	Cash and Bank	12,000
		4,08,000		4,08,000

Machinery and Stock are sold for Rs. 60,000 and Rs. 43,200 respectively. Car is taken by Y for Rs. 28,800. Debtors realise Rs. 48,000.

Deficiency of any partner in Capital Account is to be met by other partners in profit sharing ratio. X is insolvent; Z can bring in Rs. 12,000 only.

Preparer necessary accounts in the books of the firm.

Ans. Loss on Realisation : X : Rs. 1,08,000; Y : Rs. 64,800; Z : Rs. 43,200

Hint. First the deficiency of X's Capital to be borne by Y and Z in 3 : 2, thereafter deficiency of Z's Capital of Rs. 16,800 to be borne by Y.

13. A, B & C are partners sharing profit & losses in the ratio 3:2:1. Their Balance Sheet as at 31-12-2005 stands under:

BALANCE SHEET
As on 31-12-2005

Liabilities		Rs.	Assets	Rs.
Sundry Creditors		1,25,000	Sundry Assets	2,40,000
Capital A/cs :				
A	1,00,000		C's Capital	10,000
B	25,000	1,25,000		
		2,50,000		2,50,000

The firm is dissolved as on 31st December 2005. Sundry Assets realised @ 50% of their Book value. B and C both are insolvent. B's private estate has got a surplus of Rs. 5,000 and that of C Rs. 12,500.
Close the books of the firm.

Ans. Loss on Realisation : A : Rs. 60,000; B : Rs. 40,000; C : Rs. 20,000
Final Payment : A : Rs. 5,000

Hint. The deficiency of both B's and C's Capital A/c are to borne by A alone of Rs. 27,500 (Rs. 10,000 + Rs. 17,500).

14. A, B, C are partners sharing profits & losses as 5 : 3 : 2. The business is dissolved on 31st Dec. 2001 when the Balance Sheet stands as below:

BALANCE SHEET
As on 31-12-2005

Liabilities		Rs.	Assets	Rs.
Capitals :			Machinery	80,000
A	16,000		Motor Car	16,000
B	64,000		Stock	96,000
C	32,000	1,12,000	Debtors	72,000
Creditors		1,60,000	Cash at Bank	8,000
		2,72,000		2,72,000

Machinery & Stock are sold for Rs. 40,000 and Rs. 28,800 respectively. Motor Car is taken by B for Rs. 19,200. Debtors realise Rs. 32,000.
According to Partnership deed, the deficiency of any partner in capital A/c is to be met by other partners in profit sharing ratio A is insolvent and C can bring in Rs. 8,000 only. Prepare the accounts in the books of the firm.

Ans. Loss on Realisation : A : Rs. 72,000; B : Rs. 43,200; C : Rs. 28,800

Hint. A is insolvent and nothing can be contributed. Thus A's deficiency of Rs. 56,000 has been debited to B and C in the ratio of 3 : 2. Again C could give only Rs. 8,000 and this results in deficiency of Rs. 11,200. This amount has again been debited to B's A/c.

15. A, B & C are partners sharing profits and losses in the ratio of 3: 2: 1. The firm was dissolved on 31st December 2005 when their financial position was as under:

BALANCE SHEET
As on 31-12-2005

Liabilities		Rs.	Assets	Rs.
Capitals :			Land & Building	15,000
A	30,000		Plant	14,000
B	15,000	45,000	Patents	5,000
Creditors		26,070	Furniture	1,600
			Stock	13,400
			Debtors	16,070
			Cash in hand	5,00
			C's Capital	1,000
		71,070		71,070

Realisations were as follows :	Rs.
Land and Buildings	12,300
Plant	10,000
Patents	Nil
Furniture	500
Stock	10,000
Debtors	13,600 and
Realisation Expenses amount to	310

There was a contingent liability for Rs. 1,000 not provided is now materialised. C is insolvent and is unable to bring anything to meet his deficiency. You are required to close the books of the firrr in accordance with decision in Garner vs. Murray.

Ans. Realisation Loss : A : Rs. 9,990; B : Rs. 6,660; C : Rs. 3,330

Deficiency of C i.e. Rs. 4,330 met in 2 : 1 ratio by

A : Rs. 2,887; B : Rs. 1,443

Final Settlement (Amount Paid)

A : Rs. 27,113; B : Rs. 13,557

16. X, Y & Z are partners in a firm sharing profits & losses in the ratio of 30%, 40% and 30% respectively. They decided to dissolve the firm and appointed X to realise the assets. X is to receive 5% remuneration on amount realised and is to bear all expenses of realisation. On dissolution of the firm on 31st December 2005, Balance Sheet was as under:

BALANCE SHEET
As on 31-12-2005

Liabilities		Rs.	Assets		Rs.
Creditors		60,000	Cash		1,800
Bills Payable		10,800	Debtors	55,200	
Capitals			*Less* : Provision	3,600	51,600
X	24,000		Stock		66,000
Y	36,000	60,000	Furniture		6,000
			Z's Capital Over withdrawn		5,400
		1,30,800			1,30,800

X reports the realisation result as follows:
Debtors Rs. (40,800), Stock Rs. 48,000, Furniture Rs. 2,400, Goodwill is sold for Rs. 2,400. Creditors were paid~Rs.58,200 and Bills Payable in full. Outstanding creditors of Rs. 600, which were not recorded in the books were also paid. Realisation Expenses amounted to Rs. 960 which were met by X personally. X and Y agree to receive from Z Rs. 3,600 in full settlement of the firm's claim against him. Garner vs. Murray Rule is applicable. Prepare necessary Accounts.

Ans. Realisation Loss : X : Rs. 8,640; Y : Rs. 11,520; Z : Rs. 8,640
Z's Capital Deficiency of Rs. 10,440 in 2 : 3 Capital Ratio by :
X : Rs. 4,176; Y : Rs. 6,264
Final Payment : X : Rs. 15,984; Y : Rs. 18,216

Hint. Commission is not to be treated as business expenses.

17. Partnership of A, B & C was dissolved on 1st November 2001, when their financial position was as under:

BALANCE SHEET
As on 1-11-2001

Liabilities		Rs.	Assets	Rs.
A's Loan A/c		9,250	Cash in hand	1,875
Bank Loan		4,750	Furniture	10,000
Creditors	12,500		Building	3,750
Less : Reserve	625	11,875	Plant & Machinery	15,000
Capitals			Goodwill	8,500
A	9,750		P & L A/c	10,000
B	3,250			
C	10,250	23,250		
		49,125		49,125

Furniture and Building realised for Rs. 15,000 Machinery taken over by C at an agreed value of Rs. 13,500. Goodwill proved value less.
Creditors accepted Rs. 14,000 in full satisfaction of debt. Other liabilities paid in full. Realisation Expenses amounted to Rs. 1,500 Partners share profit in the ratio of 1/10, 1/2 and 2/5. B declared as insolvent and firm recovered Rs. 188 from him. Show Ledger Accounts.

Ans. Loss on Realisation : A : Rs. 1,237.50; B : Rs. 6,187.50; C : Rs. 4,950
Deficiency of B borne by : A : Rs. 4,520; C : Rs. 3,230
Final Payment : A : Rs. 4,230; C : Rs. 10,480 (brought in).

18. P, Q, R & S were in partnership. Their position on 30th June 2002 was as follows:

BALANCE SHEET
As on 30-06-2002

Liabilities		Rs.	Assets		Rs.
Capitals			Sundry Assets		76,800
P	16,800		Loss to date		36,000
Q	19,200		Current A/cs :		
R	9,600		Q	9,600	
S	7,200	52,800	R	2,400	12,000
Sundry Creditors		72,000			
		1,24,800			1,24,800

They shared profits & losses 4:3:2:1. They decided to dissolve on this date. The assets realised Rs. 64,800. P & Q are both insolvent. Q's private assets amount to Rs. 24,000 and his private liabilities are Rs. 16,800. S's private assets are Rs. 16,800 and his private liabilities are Rs.14,400. Partnership deed provided interalia that the deficiency of an insolvent partner is to be borne by solvent partners in the profit sharing ratio.

Show the accounts concerned assuming that all transactions are put through on 30th September 2002 and Q's estate realised only Rs. 9,600 and S's estate realised Rs. 12,000.

Ans. Realisation Loss : P : Rs. 4,800; Q : Rs. 3,600; R : Rs. 2,400; S : Rs. 1,200
Deficiency of P and Q (i.e. Rs. 7,200) in 2 : 1 ratio borne by :
R : Rs. 4,800; S : Rs. 2,400 **[B. Com (H) DU.]**

19. A, B and C are three partners in a firm with profit sharing ratio of 5 : 3 : 2. The Balance Sheet of the firm was as under on 31st March 2000:

Liabilities	Rs.	Assets	Rs.
A's Capital A/c	60,000	Computers	80,000
B's Capital A/c	40,000	Furniture	10,000
C's Capital A/c	20,000	Investments	30,000
Bank Loan	20,000	Profit & Loss A/c	80,000
Bill Payable	20,000		
Sundry Creditors	40,000		
	2,00,000		2,00,000

The bank loan was secured by the charge on Investments. The assets realised as follows :

		Rs.
Computer	—	40,000
Furniture	—	4,000
Investments	—	14,000

B's private estate realised Rs. 12,000, his private liabilities amounted to Rs. 10,000, C was insolvent. A could contribute just 1/3rd of what was finally due from him on his own account.

Show necessary ledger Accounts.

❑❑❑